Your career journey
A guide to getting started on your career journey, including advice on choosing your ideal career and firm, an insight into the opportunities available across the legal profession, and guidance around boosting your employability.

Developing a growth mindset
An insight into the importance of developing a growth mindset, with a focus on effective personal branding, overcoming imposter syndrome, dealing with rejection and managing your wellbeing.

Practical networking and LinkedIn
An in-depth guide to networking, including practical tips for networking one-on-one and in a virtual setting, advice on how to use LinkedIn effectively, and personal insights and anecdotes to help you boost your confidence and shift your mindset.

CVs, cover letters and applications
A comprehensive guide to writing successful CVs, cover letters and applications, including in-depth advice on answering career and firm motivation questions, researching firms, and drawing skills and strengths from a broad range of experiences.

Psychometric tests
An in-depth look at Watson Glaser, verbal reasoning, logical reasoning and situational judgement tests, including full-length practice tests and practical tips on how to improve your technique.

Preparing for interviews and assessment centres
Practical advice and insider tips on how to effectively tackle assessment centres, including ice breakers, competency and motivation interviews, group and negotiation exercises, presentations, psychometric tests and virtual interviews.

Succeeding during internships
Guidance on how to convert internships into job offers, including insights into how firms expect you to behave, how to tackle the work, how to excel during team presentations and negotiation exercises, and how to prepare for final interviews.

Commercial awareness in context
This course explains the meaning of commercial awareness, how it comes up in interviews, how to develop it, what to consider when discussing current affairs, and how to structure your answers to commercial awareness questions.

Discussing current affairs and industry trends
This course offers in-depth advice on how to research into and confidently discuss current affairs, including how to select which news stories to focus on, what to consider when reading the news, and how to structure your discussions in interviews.

Mergers and acquisitions
This course offers a solid grounding in the legal, commercial and financial knowledge required for commercial law interviews and internships, including explanations of key M&A-related terminology and jargon.

Understanding training contracts
A comprehensive insight into training contracts, including practice area overviews, an explanation of common trainee tasks, an insight into the skills trainees need to demonstrate and an overview of typical training contract challenges.

A law firm's role on transactions
This course talks you through two case studies from real commercial law interviews, including discussion of the role of the firm's key practice areas and various legal and commercial terms and concepts.

Launching, running and growing a business
Insider insights into the processes and challenges involved in launching, running and growing a business, from developing, branding and marketing an idea, to raising funding, selling, collaborating, and keeping on top of legal and business admin.

Bootcamps & Masterclasses
Recordings from previous City Career Series bootcamps and masterclasses, including sessions covering applications, interviews, networking, assessment centres, commercial awareness, internships, training contracts, growth mindsets, Q&As and more.

www.commerciallaw.academy

Contents

| Introduction | 3 |

| Business Law | 5 |

Company Decision Making • Setting Up A Business • Directors • Shareholders • Joint Ventures • Allotting Shares • Debt and Equity Finance • Acquisitions • Drafting • Share Buybacks • Insolvency • Challenging Transactions

| Taxation & Accounts | 85 |

Business Taxation • Business Accounts • Solicitors' Accounts

| Property Law | 121 |

Introduction to Property Law • Title Investigation • Pre-contract Searches • Planning Law, Building Regulations and Environmental Law • Drafting and Exchanging the Contract for Sale • Completion • Drafting • Unregistered Land • Commercial Security of Tenure • Terms of a Lease • Alienation • Rent Review • Landlord's Remedies

| Civil Litigation | 167 |

Introduction to Civil Litigation • Commencement of a Claim • Reply and Defence • Allocation and Case Management • Disclosure and Inspection • Witnesses • Experts • Settlement and Part 36 Offers • Pre-trial, Trial and Costs, Interim Applications and Injunctions • Foreign Jurisdictions • Alternative Dispute Resolution • Enforcement • Appeals

| Criminal Litigation | 217 |

Police Powers • Advising a Client at the Police Station • Bail • Allocation • Evidence and Witnesses • Sentencing

| Wills & Administration of Estates | 241 |

The Succession Estate and the Will • Distribution under the Intestacy Rules • Inheritance Tax • Grant of Representation • Administering the Estate: Duties and Powers of Personal Representatives

| Professional Conduct & Regulation | 255 |

Solicitors' Regulation Authority Standards & Regulations (2019) • Money Laundering and Client Due Diligence • Financial Services and Markets Act 2000

| Professional Skills | 279 |

Legal Research • Professional Writing • Legal Drafting • Interviewing & Advising • Advocacy

There is a more detailed table of contents for each module at the start of each section of this handbook

Introduction

This is a Legal Practice Course Stage I revision guide. It covers the following core modules:

- Business Law
- Business Taxation and Business Accounts
- Solicitors' Accounts
- Property Law
- Civil Litigation
- Criminal Litigation
- Wills & Administration of Estates
- Professional Conduct & Regulation
- Professional Skills
- Drafting

What makes this revision guide unique?

Detail and coverage: this is the most detailed LPC revision guide available. It includes: a multitude of defined terms; comprehensive, yet easily digestible explanations of key concepts; a variety of procedure plans and flowcharts; and full statutory references throughout.

Full colour and format: this is the only full colour LPC revision guide on the market, which ensures that concepts can be introduced and explained as clearly and concisely as possible. The format has been developed over a number of years to facilitate readers' understanding and retention of information.

Illustrative examples: there are many practical, illustrative examples of exam questions and suggested answers throughout this guide, helping to clarify and contextualise the information contained in each topic.

How should you use this handbook to prepare?

This handbook has been designed for you to work through from start to finish. We define terms when they are first introduced, so if you start reading part way through the guide and come across terms that you do not understand, it is likely that they have been defined in an earlier section.

Please take this handbook as a supplemental tool to help you to clarify concepts and consolidate your understanding of topics when preparing for seminars and revising for exams. We have focused on providing content that we believe to be the most relevant and integral for the LPC, but LPC courses vary significantly and change regularly. For these reasons, **always use this handbook in conjunction with your course notes, lectures and seminars, as it is not intended as a replacement for your course materials.**

This handbook was written only by authors that secured top training contracts and achieved distinctions on the LPC. It was also edited and proofread by a wide range of contributors, from ex-City lawyers and careers advisors, to Maths graduates and Finance post-graduates. We believe that this has helped us to ensure that the content is as clear, concise, accurate and comprehensive as possible for the purposes that this handbook was designed to achieve.

However, this is not a comprehensive *textbook* and, like all the guides on the market, it does not cover every concept that comes up on the LPC in enough depth to give you a full understanding of all the materials included as part of your course. We encourage you to research into all the terms and concepts contained within in greater depth, as they are by no means definitive or guaranteed to be wholly or objectively accurate. For instance, terms have been defined throughout but many of these definitions are subjective, so check whether your module leaders/course materials favour particular definitions.

Take particular care to recognise elements of modules that you are expected to know for your course but are missing from this guide, and concepts included that you are not expected to know. In addition, remember that the law is constantly developing. Significant changes may occur part way through your course and these changes may or may not form part of the content that you are expected to know and apply in your exams. For this reason, you should always check whether the law has evolved since this guide was published and know which version of the law your module leaders wish you to focus on. We do however print our guides on multiple occasions throughout the year so as to ensure they remain as up-to-date as possible.

Tabbing

If you are able to take course materials into your exams, we recommend that you tab them carefully. A lot of the content that you are required to apply in your exams is contained in your statutory materials, so developing a good tabbing system can significantly reduce the amount of content that you have to memorise. You must however understand the content in order to apply it effectively.

If you start to tab your materials early on in the course (as lecturers tend to recommend that you do), be sure to note down your tabbing system so that you do not get confused when it comes to revising for exams. It is also probably worth holding off tabbing until you fully understand concepts, otherwise you will waste time later on having to remove/reapply tabs (and may end up ripping pages of your book doing so).

It took some of us days to properly tab our materials for our stage 1 exams, so we recommend that you do not leave yourself only a couple of hours the night before an exam to do it.

Colour coding throughout this handbook

Drafting suggestions/examples are highlighted in orange throughout.

Note that there is no dedicated "drafting" section within the handbook; instead we have included examples of how to tackle drafting questions in the relevant sections of each module so that each example can be understood in context.

Cases, legislation and other references are highlighted in yellow throughout.

> 📖 **Definitions are set out in boxes like this.**

Examples of procedure plans are indicated by orange headings.

> **Examples are set out in boxes like this.**

We hope that you have found this guide useful (if so, please tell everyone you know about it!). To reiterate, remember to always use this in conjunction with your course notes, lectures and seminars, as it is not intended as a replacement for your course materials.

Feedback

We hope that you find this guide useful (if you do, please tell everyone you know about it!). Any feedback would be greatly appreciated. Please let us know if you find any mistakes or if there is any information missing that you would have liked us to include. As an incentive, we will randomly select people that have provided useful feedback throughout the year to receive a refund of the purchase price of this handbook. You can contact us through information@citycareerseries.com and facebook.com/CityCareerSeries.

All there is left to say now is best of luck with your exam preparation and stage 2!

Business Law

Business Law

Company Decision Making — 7
Meetings • written resolution procedure • notice • resolutions • voting at general meetings

Setting Up A Business — 9
Incorporating a company • choosing a company name • constitutional documents • altering a company's Articles of Association • converting a shelf company • procedure plans for converting a shelf company • PSC Register

Directors — 19
Directors' duties • substantial property transactions • long-term service contracts • procedure plan for approving substantial property transactions and long-term service contracts • loans, quasi-loans and credit transactions

Shareholders — 27
Removal of a director • employment law • shareholder rights • minority shareholders

Joint Ventures — 33
Advantages and disadvantages • joint venture agreements • joint venture legal structures

Allotting Shares — 38
Key concepts • different types of shares • procedure plan for allotting shares • calculating voting rights

Debt and Equity Finance — 44
Debt vs. Equity • debt finance: overdrafts and term loans • security

Acquisitions — 49
Financial assistance • share sale vs. asset sale • due diligence • warranties • disclosure • indemnities • listed companies and acquisitions

Drafting — 57
Drafting key terms • compromises • limitation clauses • "boilerplate" clauses • conditions precedent • restrictive covenants • warranties and indemnities • termination • dealing with common issues • execution clauses

Share Buybacks — 68
Funding a share buyback • capital redemption reserve • calculating changes in voting rights • procedure plans for share buybacks

Insolvency — 76
When is a company insolvent? • directors' obligations • financial difficulties: procedures • priority

Challenging Transactions — 81
Voidable transactions • transactions at an undervalue • preferences • floating charges • transactions defrauding creditors • wrongful trading • fraudulent trading • misfeasance • director disqualification

Note that your Business Law exam may also include questions on professional conduct. These questions typically focus on the **Financial Services and Markets Act 2000**, although be sure to check the focus of your particular LPC course. The **Financial Services and Markets Act 2000** has been covered in the *Professional Conduct & Regulation* module in this handbook, rather than in the *Business Law* module.

Company Decision Making

Companies must make decisions all the time. Certain decisions must be approved (voted on) by a company's board of directors (the "Board") in board meetings and/or the company's shareholders in general meetings (GMs). Decisions in these meetings will only be valid and binding if the quorum is met. This section introduces key terminology relating to meetings, voting and resolutions used throughout this module. The key statutes for this section include:

Companies Act 2006 ("CA 06"): this is the main statute that you will use in Business Law. It sets out many of the procedures that must be followed by businesses and the rights and obligations of parties including directors and shareholders.

Companies Act 1985 ("CA 85"): this is the main statute that governed companies before the CA 06 came into force. Like the CA 06, it sets out many of the procedures that must be followed by businesses and the rights and obligations of parties including directors and shareholders.

Meetings

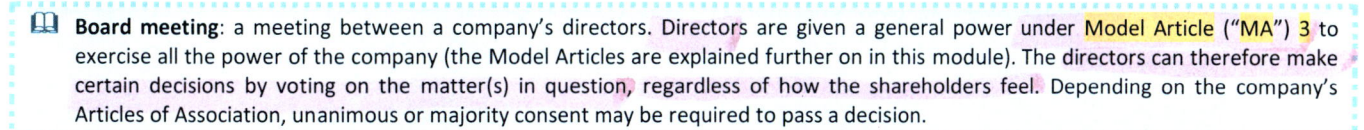

- **Board meeting**: a meeting between a company's directors. Directors are given a general power under Model Article ("MA") 3 to exercise all the power of the company (the Model Articles are explained further on in this module). The directors can therefore make certain decisions by voting on the matter(s) in question, regardless of how the shareholders feel. Depending on the company's Articles of Association, unanimous or majority consent may be required to pass a decision.

- **Shareholder meeting/general meeting**: a meeting between a company's shareholders. Some decisions (typically more transformative decisions such as changing the company name) must be approved by shareholders. "Shareholder meeting" and "general meeting" are synonymous.

Written resolution procedure

Shareholders can sometimes pass decisions without the need for a general meeting. It may sometimes be preferable for *private* companies to secure approval for proposed courses of action using the written resolution procedure under CA 06 s. 288, as this does not require the convening of a general meeting (and thus the attendance of shareholders or their proxies). To pass a written resolution, shareholders representing the required percentage of the total voting rights of eligible members must vote in favour CA 06 s. 296(4).

- **Written resolution procedure**: this procedure can be used to pass ordinary and special resolutions and involves the company sending out the written resolution document to shareholders and explaining the proposed course(s) of action. Shareholders can vote by sending to the company an authenticated document (e.g. the written resolution document) identifying the relevant resolution and indicating their agreement CA 06 s. 296(1). The procedure is not available for public limited companies and cannot be used by private limited companies to (for instance) remove directors or auditors. Private limited companies may use the procedure even if their Articles of Association prohibit its use CA 06 s. 300.

Notice

Parties that are entitled to attend meetings must be given notice. The amount of notice that must (legally) be given before a meeting can take place depends largely on the type of meeting taking place.

Board meeting

- A "reasonable" period must be given, which takes into account the number of directors entitled to attend and their respective locations etc. This is set out in the case of Browne v La Trinidad.

General meeting

- The default notice that must be given for a general meeting is 14 days CA 06 s. 307(1). However, CA 06 s. 360(1)+(2) clarifies that in this context, 14 days means 14 "clear" days, so you do not count the day on which notice is given and the day of the general meeting itself as part of the 14 days. Therefore the general meeting would take place on day 16, as the day the notice is sent out and the day the meeting is held do not count as part of the 14 days (board meeting 1 = day 1, days 2-15 are "clear days", so the general meeting cannot be held until day 16).

- A general meeting can be held earlier if enough shareholders consent to "short notice". Explain this in an exam, noting that if only a few shareholders exist, consent to short notice should be easy to secure.

- **Short notice**: provided consent is given by a majority (in number) of the shareholders that together hold at least 90% in nominal value of the shares giving the right to attend and vote at the general meeting, the general meeting can be held on "short notice" (e.g. the same day as board meeting 1) CA 06 s. 307(4)-(6). If the requisite number of shareholders have consented to short notice, then evidence of this consent must be sent to all shareholders along with the notice before the general meeting takes place. Note that the 90% threshold can be increased in a company's Articles of Association (therefore making it more difficult for the company to take advantage of the short notice procedure).

- The notice for a general meeting should include: (a) the time, date and location of the meeting CA 06 s. 311; (b) the precise wording of any special resolutions that will be voted on in the meeting CA 06 s. 283(6); and (c) a statement that a member may appoint a proxy CA 06 s. 325(1).

- It is also good practice (but not required) when preparing the notice to set out the precise wording of any ordinary resolution(s) to be proposed at the general meeting.

> **Member:** this is a term that can be used interchangeably with "shareholder".

Resolutions

Whether a decision can/must be made by directors at a board meeting or by shareholders at a general meeting is dictated by statute and the Model Articles (and will depend on the nature of the proposed decision). The same applies for the question of which voting threshold must be met to pass/approve a particular decision.

Board decisions

> **Board resolution**: directors in board meetings can pass board resolutions either by simple majority (more than 50% voting in favour) MA 7(1) or unanimous decision MA 8. The default position (in the Model Articles) is that a simple majority will carry the vote. Where there is a deadlock, the chairman has the casting vote MA 13. Votes are indicated by a show of hands.

Shareholder decisions

> **Ordinary resolution**: some decisions require approval by "ordinary resolution", meaning that more than 50% of those voting must approve the decision in accordance with CA 06 s. 282(1) (this is known as a "simple majority"). The statute governing a particular decision sets out the type of resolution required. For instance, unless a particular provision in the Companies Act specifies that a "special resolution" is required, the word "resolution" is taken to mean "ordinary resolution".

> **Special resolution**: decisions that require approval by "special resolution" must be approved by at least 75% of those attending (including by proxy) and entitled to vote at the meeting in which the resolution is voted on CA 06 s. 283(1).

Note that where the written resolution procedure is used to pass a particular decision, the nature of that decision will determine whether an ordinary resolution or a special resolution will be required to pass it. For instance, if the written resolution needs to be passed by ordinary resolution, it will require more than 50% of those voting using the written resolution procedure to vote in favour (e.g. by indicating their vote on the written resolution document, signing it, then returning it to the company).

Voting at general meetings

Shareholders vote in general meetings. However, individual shareholders can appoint proxies, whilst corporate shareholders (e.g. a parent company that owns the shares of its subsidiaries) can appoint corporate representatives to vote on the company's behalf. If a corporate representative is voting, it is good practice to show a board minute evidencing that the corporate shareholder gave authority to the person claiming to be its corporate representative.

> **Proxy:** someone nominated by a shareholder to participate/vote in a meeting on his or her behalf CA 06 s. 324.

> **Corporate representative**: an individual appointed by a company to attend meetings and vote on its behalf CA 06 s. 323.

> **Minutes:** companies must note down and keep a record of who is present and in attendance at meetings and what is discussed and decided. These notes are referred to as "minutes" (a "board minute" means a note taken in a board meeting).

Voting in a meeting by show of hands is the default voting method used by shareholders MA 42. However, shareholders can alternatively demand a poll vote (depending on the circumstances) or may instead have to vote on a decision using the written resolution procedure.

> **Show of hands**: this involves parties indicating their vote in person at a meeting. Each voting party is given *one* vote (regardless of the number of shares they hold) and the vote is passed if the required majority (in number) votes in favour.

> **Poll vote:** shareholders can demand a poll vote instead of a show of hands in accordance with MA 44. On a poll vote, each shareholder has one vote for *each* share held. Poll votes therefore give more influence to the shareholders that hold the greatest number of shares.

> **Written resolution vote**: as mentioned above, shareholders can vote by sending to the company an authenticated document (e.g. the written resolution document) identifying the relevant resolution and indicating their agreement CA 06 s. 296(1).

Setting Up A Business

There are various different forms that businesses can take. Each form has different advantages and disadvantages and will better suit different types of businesses. You may be required to compare and contrast these different forms in an exam.

	Limited Company	**Partnership**	**Limited Liability Partnership**
Relevant statute(s)	Companies must comply with a variety of statutes, regulations and codes. The most notable statute is the Companies Act 2006.	Partnership Act 1890	Limited Liability Partnerships Act 2000 Limited Liability Partnership Regulations 2001
Legal status of the business	Body corporate (separate legal personality).	Partnerships are not separate legal entities.	Body corporate (separate legal entity).
Documents	Incorporation documents, e.g. the Articles of Association.	It is not a legal obligation to have a Partnership Agreement in place, but it is highly recommended.	It is not a legal obligation to have an LLP Agreement in place, but it is highly recommended.
Investor liability	Limited to the amount not yet paid up on shares.	Partners are personally liable on for all contracts that bind the firm.	Partners are not personally liable for more than their capital share in the LLP.
People required to set up the business	A minimum of one shareholder is required to set up a business CA 06 s. 7(1). Shareholders are the owners of limited companies.	A minimum of 2 partners is required to commence a partnership. The partners own the business.	A minimum of 2 partners is required to commence a partnership. The partners own the business.
Reporting and disclosure	An annual Confirmation Statement must be filed with Companies House. Companies must also keep a register of persons with significant control. Annual accounts must be filed at Companies House. Notify Companies House when certain events occur (e.g. name/membership /office changes). Information on directors, secretaries, shareholders and share capital must be disclosed (including any changes), as well as certain shareholder resolutions that have been passed.	No requirement to prepare accounts (although there is an implication that partnerships should do so anyway).	An annual Confirmation Statement must be filed with Companies House. Limited Liability Partnerships must also keep a register of persons with significant control. Annual accounts must be filed at Companies House. Notify Companies House when certain events occur (e.g. name/membership /office changes).
Expenses	Registration fee and (if relevant) the cost of having solicitors draft the incorporation documents. Ongoing expenses relating to the above filing obligations and the cost of having accounts audited (note: small businesses are exempt from the requirement to have their accounts audited).	The cost of having solicitors draft the partnership agreement (if the partners decide to have one in place).	Registration fee and (if relevant) the cost of having solicitors draft the LLP Agreement. Ongoing expenses relating to the above filing obligations and the cost of having accounts audited (although small LLPs are exempt from the requirement to have their accounts audited).
Methods of financing	Limited companies can raise capital through issuing shares and through borrowing. Limited companies can offer floating charges (explained later) to lenders to incentivise them to lend.	Partnerships can raise capital through borrowing. They *cannot* issue shares or create floating charges.	LLPs can raise capital through borrowing (they *cannot* issue shares). LLPs can offer floating charges (explained later) to lenders to incentivise them to lend.
Tax	Companies pay corporation tax on their profits.	Partners are taxed individually on their received share of the partnership's profits.	Partners are taxed individually on their received share of the LLP's profits.

> **Persons with Significant Control Register ("PSC Register"):** this register is publicly available through Companies House. It publicly discloses the names of people (including legal entities) who can influence or control a company. This includes (a) persons who hold more than 25% of the company's shares; (b) persons who hold more than 25% of the company's voting rights; and (c) persons who hold the right to appoint or remove the majority of the Board. There is more detail on the PSC Register at the end of this chapter.

Incorporating a Company

A company has no legal personality and cannot trade before it has been incorporated CA 06 s. 16. Incorporation occurs when Companies House issues the company's Certificate of Incorporation. Incorporating a company involves a number of steps that must be followed in order to ensure compliance with the law. Your knowledge of these steps may be assessed on the LPC, so understanding the procedures involved is key. A company cannot ratify agreements made before it is incorporated, meaning that if an individual signs a contract on behalf of a company that has not yet been incorporated, the contract will take effect as one made by that individual in their personal capacity. That individual will therefore be personally liable for any breach of the contract CA 06 s. 51, although he/she could be indemnified by the organisation (e.g. parent company) on whose behalf they are acting.

- **Certificate of incorporation:** once a company has been validly incorporated (set up), a certificate of incorporation is the document issued as proof. Private companies can start trading at this stage, although public companies cannot commence trading until the Registrar issues a trading certificate.

- **Companies House/Registrar of Companies:** Companies House is an agency that is responsible for the incorporation, administration and dissolution of companies in the United Kingdom. It is sometimes referred to as the "Registrar of Companies".

- **Parent/holding company:** a company that owns (or partially owns) the shares in another company (its "subsidiary").

- **Subsidiary:** a subsidiary is a company, the shares of which are owned (or partially owned) by a parent/holding company.

Private Limited Companies vs. Public Limited Companies

Whether a company is a private limited company or public limited company will determine the laws by which it is governed, in addition to its rights and obligations. All companies are governed by the Companies Act 2006, their own constitutional documents and a wide variety of regulation and codes of conduct. However, public companies are subject to more onerous regulatory and disclosure requirements (and thus incur greater costs) than private companies, in part due to the larger scope of their operations (and thus the number of people that may be affected by their actions). Private companies cannot offer shares to the public (meaning they can only offer shares to select individuals/organisations), whilst public companies must issue at least £50,000 worth of shares.

	Private Company	**Public Company**
Name	Private Limited Company (Ltd) CA 06 s. 59(1).	Public Limited Company (Plc) CA 06 s. 58(1).
Minimum number of shareholders required?	One CA 06 s. 7.	One CA 06 s. 7.
Minimum number of directors required?	At least one CA 06 s. 154(1).	At least two CA 06 s.154(2).
Is a company secretary required?	No CA 06 s. 270(1).	Yes CA 06 s. 271.
Documents required before trading can commence?	Certificate of incorporation CA 06 s. 15. Can commence business as soon as it is incorporated.	Certificate of incorporation CA 06 s. 15. Trading certificate: issued by the Registrar and confirms that the company's allotted share capital is not less than the minimum (see below) CA 06 s. 761.
Minimum share capital that must be issued upon incorporation?	Must issue at least one share.	Must allot at least £50,000 worth of shares at the outset CA 06 s. 763(1).
Minimum amount that must be paid up on share capital?	No minimum (shares can be issued without being paid for immediately).	At least 25% of the nominal value of the shares must be paid up CA 06 s. 586(1). Payment must be in cash (unless the consideration has been independently valued CA 06 s. 593).
Can shares be offered "to the public"?	No CA 06 s. 755(1)(a).	Yes, this is not prohibited by CA 06, but there are considerable other restrictions imposed by the Financial Services and Markets Act 2000.

- **Nominal value:** the face value of a share without taking into account any premium charged by the issuer or any increase in market value since the share was issued.

- **Offer to the public:** for the purposes of the above table, offer "to the public" means an offer to any section of the public, however selected CA 06 s. 756(2), but not offers that are made only to specific people/institutions CA 06 s. 756(3).

- **Paid up share capital:** when a share is purchased, the purchaser may not have to pay all the money due for that share at the outset, instead paying some of the amount due at a later stage. The amount they do pay contributes towards the amount of "paid up" share capital. Whilst there are no restrictions on the amount that must be "paid up" for private companies, there are restrictions for public companies.

- **Share capital:** the funds that a company has raised by issuing shares.

Application to incorporate a private company limited by shares

To set-up a private limited company, you must submit an application to Companies House, including CA 06 s. 9:

- **Form IN01**: this will include the company's name and registered office; a statement that the company's liability is limited by shares; and a statement that the company is to be private.
- **Articles of Association**: Model Articles will automatically be adopted if tailored Articles of Association are not provided at this stage.
- **Memorandum of Association**.
- **Proposed officers**: details of the company's proposed officers (i.e. directors and, if applicable, secretaries).
- **Statement of Capital** CA 06 s. 10: this sets out (a) the total number of shares for which the subscribers are subscribing; (b) the aggregate nominal value of these shares; (c) details of the rights attached to each class of share; (d) the total number of shares in each class; (e) the aggregate nominal value of shares in each class; and (f) the aggregate amount (if any) to be unpaid on the shares. The Statement of Capital must also state the number, nominal value and class(es) of shares to be taken by each individual subscriber, in addition to the amount to be paid up and the amount (if any) to be unpaid on each share.
- **Statement of Compliance** CA 06 s. 13: a statement confirming compliance with the Companies Act 2006 registration requirements.

Note that the Articles of Association and Memorandum of Association are explained in more detail in the *Constitutional Documents* section below.

Choosing a Company Name

When deciding which name to use for a company, the following must be considered:

- The name cannot already have been registered CA 06 s. 66.
- The name cannot be too similar to an existing name CA 06 s. 67.
- The name cannot be misleading.
- The name cannot be offensive CA 06 s. 53.
- The name must comply with guidance on sensitive words and expressions CA 06 s. 55. For instance, some names must be approved by the Secretary of State (e.g. names including "University", "NHS", "Royal", "British" "Society", "Trust" etc.) and some names must be approved by *both* the Secretary of State *and* the relevant regulators (e.g. names including "Dentistry" and "Banking").

The name of a company can be changed in two ways: (1) by special resolution; or (2) by amending the Articles of Association to include a new name. The latter may be preferable where numerous changes need to be made, as one special resolution to approve the new Articles of Association will be more efficient than effecting individual resolutions to effect numerous changes.

Constitutional Documents

A company's constitutional documents set out what a company can and cannot do. They may for instance restrict a company from taking certain action, or from doing so without securing the required approval. The main constitutional document is the Articles of Association and many companies adopt the Model Articles of Association upon incorporation. Companies must also have a Memorandum of Association.

- **Articles of Association ("Articles")**: a constitutional document created when a company is incorporated. The Articles are essentially a contract between the company and its shareholders CA 06 s. 33 that sets out the rights and obligations of the respective parties, including restrictions on the actions a company can take without board or shareholder approval.

- **Model Articles of Association ("Model Articles")**: a standard form of Articles that a company can choose to adopt and if necessary, tailor to its specific needs. Adopting the Model Articles can be much quicker (and cheaper) than writing new Articles from scratch, so many companies either fully adopt them, or adopt a majority of them and make a few amendments/additions. The position set out in the Model Articles is provided throughout the *Business Law* chapter of this guide. In an exam, be sure to check whether the relevant company has adopted the Model Articles. If it has not, check the exam paper to see whether extracts are given of the company's bespoke Articles.

- **Memorandum of Association ("Memorandum")**: for companies incorporated under the Companies Act 2006, the Memorandum of Association states that the subscribers (i.e. shareholders): (a) wish to form a company under the Companies Act 2006; and (b) agree to take at least one share. The Memorandum must be in the prescribed form and authenticated by each subscriber CA 06 s. 8.

A company's Articles must comply with the law (which the Model Articles do). However, they must also be commercially viable. For instance, if the company has only one shareholder, the Articles would not be commercially viable if they state that decisions can only be taken if agreed to by two or more shareholders. On the next page, we have set out some of the key elements contained within a company's Articles, including: objects, spending limits and quorums.

Objects

"Objects" clauses set out the types of activities that companies are authorised/not authorised to undertake. For instance, the "objects" clause in the constitutional documents of a bakery could include baking and selling bread, whilst the "objects" clause in the constitutional documents of a car manufacturer could include manufacturing and selling cars, repairing cars, and selling spare car parts.

Companies Act 1985

Companies incorporated before the Companies Act 2006 came into force had to list out all the types of business that they could engage in. If a company engaged in business that was not provided for in the objects clause, it would be acting outside of its authority, which could give other parties the right to take action against it (or the employees responsible).

Companies Act 2006

However, the position has changed for companies incorporated under the Companies Act 2006. The default position for these companies is that their objects are *unrestricted* CA 06 s. 31. This means that they can engage in any type of business without acting outside of their authority. This freedom can be restricted by explicitly prohibiting certain actions in the Articles (i.e. amending the Model Articles so that the company's "objects" are not unrestricted). Note that CA 06 s. 28 states that companies incorporated before the Act came into force will retain their (restricted) objects clause. These companies can however amend their Articles to include an unrestricted objects clause (stating that CA 06 s. 28 does not apply).

If a company pursues a particular course of action in contravention of any restriction in its constitutional documents, the validity of this act cannot be called into question CA 06 s. 39. This essentially means that a third party will be protected if it enters into a transaction with a company that lacked the authorisation/capacity to transact (the onus is *not* on the third party to check whether the company has the authorisation/capacity to act). Instead, any parties adversely affected by the company exceeding its authority (e.g. shareholders) will have to take action against the company and/or employees responsible.

Spending limits

A company's Articles may restrict the amount of money that it may spend without securing shareholder approval. If the limits are set too low, this could adversely affect the company's ability to trade effectively and take advantage of opportunities that arise. A special resolution (passed in a general meeting) or a written resolution would be required to increase the spending limits by amending the Articles.

Instead of imposing spending limits in a company's Articles, the directors can simply agree between themselves to adhere to particular spending limits (giving effect to the agreement by board resolution). Amending these limits would subsequently only require an additional board resolution, making the process easier. Note that a board cannot alter spending limits that are *already* set out in a company's Articles without first securing shareholder approval, since an amendment to a Company's Articles can only be made following the passing of a shareholder resolution (see below).

Quorums

> **Quorum:** the number of qualifying parties (e.g. directors at a board meeting, shareholders at a general meeting) that must be present and eligible to vote at a meeting in order for decisions passed at that meeting to be valid and binding.

Board meeting

The default position in the Model Articles is that two or more serving directors must be present, unless the directors have agreed to a higher quorum (by board resolution) MA 11(2) or the company's Articles set a higher quorum. However, if the company has only one director (and the Articles do not require it to have more than one director), the quorum will be one director MA 7(2). Directors with a personal interest in the outcome of resolutions will not count towards the quorum when voting on those resolutions MA 14.

General meeting

Where a company has only one shareholder, the quorum will be one CA 06 s. 318(1). Where there is more than one shareholder, the default position is that the quorum is two CA 06 s. 318(2). However, a company's Articles may set a higher quorum (and this quorum can be changed by special resolution). For instance, if a company is set up by five friends who want to ensure that they will be involved in all the decisions, the quorum could be set at five. The Articles will not be valid however if the quorum is higher than the total number of shareholders.

Written resolutions

Note that there is no quorum for written resolutions. Written resolutions must be sent to all parties that are eligible to vote. Recipients that fail to submit a vote are taken to have abstained. So long as the required majority votes in favour, the decision will be approved. The company could therefore use the written resolution procedure as a more flexible alternative if, for instance, the quorum in the Articles requires *all* shareholders to attend a meeting to approve a particular decision (i.e. if the written resolution procedure is not used).

Altering a Company's Articles

A company's Articles can only be amended by special resolution CA 06 s. 21. Once Articles have been amended, a copy must be filed with Companies House within 15 days CA 06 s. 26. However, Articles can only be amended if the proposed amendments pass the legality test. Moreover, changes should only be made if they are commercially viable.

- **Legality test:** Articles must not conflict with legislation. For instance, the Articles cannot set out a quorum that is lower than the minimum quorum allowed by CA 06 s. 318, or allow directors to unilaterally alter the Articles (in conflict with the CA 06 s. 21(1) requirement that a special resolution is required to make such amendments). Where legislation is silent on a point, alterations relating to that point are permitted (e.g. you can amend MA 13 to remove the Chairman's casting vote, as there is no statutory requirement for a Chairman to be given a casting vote).
- **Commerciality test:** Articles should suit the size, nature and objectives of the company in question. For instance: low spending limits and a small quorum would probably not suit large companies that tend to make large purchases and have thousands of shareholders; and removing a Chairman's casting vote could result in deadlock if there are an even number of directors. However, restricting the ability of individual directors to spend large amounts of money without approval could help a board of directors to monitor/manage budgets more carefully and increase shareholder confidence in the company.

Converting a Shelf Company

Converting a shelf company involves a number of steps and procedures that must be followed in order to ensure compliance with the law. Your knowledge of these steps may be assessed on the LPC, so understanding the procedures involved is key.

> **Shelf company:** a company that has been incorporated (set up) to be used in the future by another party. Incorporating a company in advance means it will be quicker and easier in the future for a party to commence trading through that company. Law firms typically set up a number of generic 'shelf companies' for clients to use in the future.

Clients will however typically have to make certain changes to tailor the shelf company to suit their business/needs, for instance registering new parties as directors and changing the registered business address. The Model Articles and Companies Act 2006 set out the procedures that must be followed when converting a shelf company. The below table sets out the changes that typically need to be made to a shelf company before it can be used by another party. Note that the Model Articles are in the Butterworths Company Law Handbook.

Required action	Who effects the change	Authority	Resolution required	Meeting required
1. Change name of shelf company	Shareholders.	CA 06 s. 77(1)	Special resolution (unless an alternate method is set out in the Articles).	Shareholder meeting (unless the Articles provide otherwise).
2. Appoint new directors	Outgoing directors or the shareholders.	MA 17(1)	Board resolution.	Board meeting.
3. Existing directors resign	Outgoing directors (they submit their letters of resignation).	MA 18(f)	Board resolution.	Board meeting.
4. Appoint new chairman	Outgoing director who was Chairman would automatically cease being chairman on his resignation. New directors vote for new Chairman.	MA 12(1)	Board resolution.	Board meeting.
5. Appoint company secretary	Directors.	MA 3 CA 06 s. 270(1)	Not specified in CA 06 but generally will be appointed by Board Resolution.	Board meeting.
6. Transfer shares to new owner(s) using stock transfer form	Directors. If company will only have one member (shareholder) after the transfer, a statement must be made to this effect.	CA 06 s. 112(2) CA 06 s. 123(2)(a)	Board resolution.	Board meeting.
7. Change accounting reference date	Giving notice to registrar.	CA 06 s. 392(1)	Board resolution to instruct the company secretary to fill in required Companies House form (**form AA01**).	Board meeting.
8. Appoint auditors (name, contact details etc.)	Appointed by directors at any time before 1st period for appointing auditors. Shareholders can appoint at times specified in CA 06 s. 485.	CA 06 s. 485(3)	Board resolution.	Board meeting.
9. Change registered office	Giving notice to registrar.	CA 06 s. 87(1)	Board resolution to instruct secretary to fill in required Companies House form (**form AD01**).	Board meeting.

Procedure Plans

On the LPC, you may have to answer assessment questions that require you to set out, in detail, the procedures required to effect some of the changes to a shelf company detailed above. The procedure is likely to involve either: (a) shareholders voting on a decision in a general meeting; or (b) shareholders voting on a decision using the written resolution procedure. Plans for both methods of effecting company changes have been set out below.

Some of the information you include in each section will be generic, regardless of the particular change(s) you are effecting. Try to remember the following structure when setting out the requirements and content for meetings: **open/reconvene meeting → notice → quorum → agenda → voting → close/adjourn meeting** (the meaning of these elements is explained in the procedure plan below). However, the meeting agendas and resolutions required will need to reflect the legal requirements for each particular action, for instance the type of meeting or resolution required to approve a particular decision.

Your LPC institution may focus more on particular actions, or expect differing levels of detail (e.g. very specific statutory references). The number of marks allocated to a procedure plan in an exam may indicate the required level of detail (for instance, the inclusion of particular post-meeting matters). It is therefore important to use this section in tandem with the classes and materials delivered by your tutors. It can be useful to start by listing out the resolutions that will be required to effect certain changes, as this will determine the agendas of each meeting and the voting thresholds that you must acknowledge throughout.

General meeting procedure plan for converting a shelf company

The tasks set out in the *Converting a Shelf Company* table are dealt with in a variety of meetings, as illustrated in the below procedure plan. It is important that you know in which meeting each specific task is dealt with. You may be expected to give full authority for each task in your exam, which would involve giving references from the Companies Act and Model Articles. You may only be required to make one specific change (e.g. changing the company name), in which case, only include the relevant details from the below procedure plan.

Board Meeting 1

1. **Who calls the meeting?** *explain who can call the meeting*

   Any director can call the meeting MA 9(1).

2. **Notice** *set out the period of notice that must be given before the meeting can take place*

   Reasonable notice must be given Browne v La Trinidad.

3. **Quorum** *state the required quorum for the decision to validly pass*

   The default position is that two or more serving directors must be present, unless the directors have agreed to a higher quorum (by board resolution) MA 11(2) or the company's Articles set a higher quorum. However, if the company has only one director (and the Articles do not require it to have more than one director), the quorum will be one director MA 7(2). When answering an exam question, state who is present and who is in attendance, and then conclude on the facts whether the quorum has been met.

   📖 **Present**: in this context, those that are "present" are those that count towards the quorum, e.g. qualifying directors.

   📖 **In attendance**: in this context, those that are "in attendance" are those that are attending the meeting, but do not count towards the quorum, e.g. the directors' solicitors.

4. **Agenda** *set out the agenda in light of the action(s) that your client intends to take, using the statutory references listed above (in the Converting a Shelf Company section)*

   (a) Report on the formation of the company.

   (b) Undertake tasks specifically relating to converting a shelf company.

   - Appoint new directors MA 17(1)(b), company secretary MA 3 (note, only public companies are *required* to have secretaries CA 06 s. 271) and Chairman MA 12(1).
   - Existing directors MA 18(f), secretary (if relevant) and chairman to resign. Note that the director resignations must take place *after* the new directors have been appointed, as a company must have at least one director at all times CA 06 s. 154.
   - Approve transfers of shares to the new shareholder(s) and enter the new shareholder(s) into the Register of Members CA 06 s. 113. If the shelf company will only have one member (shareholder) post-transfer, a statement to this effect must be made CA 06 s. 123(2)(a).

   (c) Call a general meeting CA 06 s. 302. The directors must:

   - Approve form of notice of the general meeting. This notice should include:
     (i) The time, date and location of the meeting CA 06 s. 311
     (ii) The precise wording of any special resolutions that will be voted on in the general meeting CA 06 s. 283(6)
     (iii) A statement that a member may appoint a proxy CA 06 s. 325(1).
   - Direct company secretary to give notice of the general meeting in accordance with CA 06 s. 308. It should be given to shareholders CA 06 s. 310(1)(a), directors CA 06 s. 310(1)(b) and (if appointed) the company's auditors CA 06 s. 502(2).
   - It is also good practice to set out the precise wording of any ordinary resolution(s) to be proposed at the general meeting.

5. Voting *set out who votes and the resolution required*

The board must agree by board resolution (either unanimous decision or simple majority on a show of hands) on the issues set out in the agenda MA 7(1) + MA 8. If there is deadlock, the Chairman has the casting vote MA 13.

6. Adjourn or close board meeting

If the board meeting will reopen within 24 hours, it will "adjourn" at this stage. If the board meeting will not reopen for more than 24 hours (e.g. if the general meeting will not take place for a few days) then the meeting will "close" (rather than "adjourn") at this stage. Ensure you do not lose marks by getting this terminology incorrect in an exam.

Post Board Meeting 1 Matters

1. Make the relevant filings at Companies House

(a) File **form AP01** to notify Companies House of the director appointments within 14 days CA 06 s. 167(1).

(b) File **form TM01** to notify Companies House of the director resignations within 14 days CA 06 s. 167(1).

(c) File **form AP03** to notify Companies House of the secretary appointment within 14 days CA 06 s. 276(1)(a).

(d) File **form TM02** to notify Companies House of the secretary resignation within 14 days CA 06 s. 276(1)(a).

(e) File **forms PSC02 and PSC07** to notify Companies House of changes to the PSC register within 14 days of updating the PSC register CA 06 s. 790VA.

2. Amend company books

(a) Amend Register of Directors to reflect the changes to the board CA 06 s. 162(2).

(b) Amend Register of Secretaries to reflect the appointment of a new secretary CA 06 s. 275.

(c) Amend Register of Members to reflect the changes to the shareholders CA 06 s. 113. If the converted company is left with only one shareholder, this must also be stated in the Register of Members CA 06 s. 123.

(d) New share certificates must be issued within 2 months (and old share certificates cancelled) CA 06 s. 776.

> 📖 **Register of Members:** a list of a company's shareholders' names and addresses, and the dates on which they became shareholders. Remember, "members" is synonymous with "shareholders" in this context.

3. Draw up minutes

Draw up minutes from the board meeting and keep these for at least 10 years CA 06 s. 248(1).

Note that these matters can be dealt with after Board Meeting 2 if the general meeting is held on short notice (see below) as the 14-day time limit will not have passed by the time Board Meeting 2 takes place.

General Meeting

1. Open general meeting

2. Notice

The default notice that must be given for a general meeting is 14 days CA 06 s. 307(1). However, CA 06 s. 360(1)+(2) clarifies that in this context, 14 days means 14 "clear" days, so you do not count the day on which notice is given and the day of the general meeting itself as part of the 14 days.

However, if consent to hold the meeting on short notice is given, the general meeting can be held earlier CA 06 s. 307(5). Explain this in an exam, noting that if only a few shareholders exist, consent to short notice should be easy to secure.

3. Quorum

Where a company has only one shareholder, the quorum will be one CA 06 s. 318(1). Where there is more than one shareholder, the default position is that the quorum is two CA 06 s. 318(2). However, check the company's Articles in case a higher quorum has been set.

4. Agenda

Propose and (shareholders) vote on the resolutions required to convert the shelf company (see below).

5. Voting

Special resolution to change the name of the company CA 06 s. 77(1).

- This must be passed by at least 75% of those attending and entitled to vote CA 06 s. 283(1).
- Shareholders (including corporate representatives and proxies) can vote by a show of hands MA 42 unless a poll vote is demanded (in accordance with MA 44).

6. Close general meeting

You do not "adjourn" the meeting, as it will not be reopened.

Board Meeting 2

1. **Reconvene/open board meeting**

   If board meeting 1 was "adjourned", then "reconvene" the meeting. If it was "closed", then "open" the meeting.

2. **Who calls the meeting?**

   Any director can call the meeting MA 9(1).

3. **Notice**

   Reasonable notice must be given Browne v La Trinidad.

4. **Quorum**

   Same as for board meeting 1.

5. **Agenda**

   (a) Chairman report that the special resolution was passed at the general meeting.

   (b) Undertake tasks specifically relating to converting a shelf company.
   - Change the company's registered office CA 06 s. 87(1).
   - Change the company's Accounting Reference Date CA 06 s. 392(1). Note that the Accounting Reference Date cannot be changed to a date that is more than 18 months after the shelf company has been converted CA 06 s. 391(5).
   - Appoint company auditors CA 06 s. 485(3).

   (c) Direct the company secretary to deal with post meeting matters.

6. **Voting**

   The board must agree by board resolution (either unanimous decision or simple majority on a show of hands) on the issues set out in the agenda MA 7(1) + MA 8. If there is deadlock, the Chairman has the casting vote MA 13.

7. **Close board meeting**

Post Board Meeting 2 Matters

1. **Make the relevant filings at Companies House**

   (a) File a copy of the special resolution within 15 days and pay the fee CA 06 s. 30(1).

   (b) If the Articles have been amended, a copy of the new Articles must be filed within 15 days CA 06 s. 26(1).

   (c) File **form NM01** to notify Companies House of name change CA 06 s. 78(1). A Certificate of Incorporation will then be issued, referencing the new company name. The change of name takes effect from the date of issue CA 06 s. 81(1). The company must also comply with the CA 06 s. 82 requirement to disclose its name in specified locations.

   (d) File **form AD01** to notify Companies House of the change of registered office as soon as possible CA 06 s. 87.

   (e) File **form AA01** to notify Companies House of the change of Accounting Reference Date as soon as possible CA 06 s. 392.

2. **Draw up minutes**

   (a) Draw up minutes from the general meeting and keep these for at least 10 years CA 06 s. 355(1).

   (b) Draw up minutes from the board meeting and keep these for at least 10 years CA 06 s. 248(1).

Written resolution procedure plan for altering a company's Articles

In an exam, you may be required to write out a procedure plan for a certain course of action (e.g. changing a company's name, altering its Articles etc.) using the written resolution procedure under CA 06 s. 288. Remember that this procedure does not require a general meeting to be convened (and thus the physical attendance of shareholders or their proxies). Read the question carefully before you start, as there are quite a few stories of people writing pages setting out the "board meeting → general meeting → board meeting" structure before realising that the question focuses on the written resolution procedure. Some elements of the written resolution procedure mirror elements of the general meeting procedure plan (above), but familiarise yourself with the differences.

Board Meeting 1

1. **Who calls the meeting?**

   Any director can call the meeting MA 9(1).

2. **Notice**

   Reasonable notice must be given Browne v La Trinidad.

3. **Quorum**

   The default position is that two or more serving directors must be present, unless the directors have agreed to a higher quorum (by board resolution) MA 11(2) or the company's Articles set a higher quorum. However, if the company has only one director (and the Articles do not require it to have more than one director), the quorum will be one director MA 7(2). State who is present and who is in attendance, then conclude on the facts whether the quorum has been met.

4. Agenda

(a) Propose a written resolution.
- Directors can do this under CA 06 s. 288(3)(a) and must follow the procedure set out in CA 06 s. 291.

(b) Approve the form/content of the written resolution document (to be sent out to shareholders).
- Include instructions on how to vote CA 06 s. 291(4)(a).
- State the last date by which votes must be submitted (the lapse date) CA 06 s. 291(4)(b).
- The default time period before the opportunity to vote will lapse is 28 days from the *circulation date* (this is the date on which copies of the written resolution are sent to members CA 06 s. 290). However, check whether the company's Articles specify a different time period, as the time period specified in the Articles will override the default position CA 06 s. 297(1). Note that the time period is *not* 28 *clear* days, as CA 06 s. 297 is not listed under CA s. 360 (which sets out the provisions to which the "clear day" counting rule applies).

(c) Resolve to send the resolution to all eligible members CA 06 s. 291(2) and the company's auditors CA 06 s. 502(1).
- "Eligible members" means all shareholders who would be entitled to vote on the resolution(s) on the date on which the written resolution is circulated CA 06 s. 289.
- If all eligible members are present, the written resolution can be approved immediately.

5. Voting

The board must agree by board resolution (either unanimous decision or simple majority on a show of hands) on the issues set out in the agenda MA 7(1) + MA 8. If there is deadlock, the Chairman has the casting vote MA 13.

6. Adjourn or close board meeting

If the board meeting will reopen within 24 hours (e.g. if there are only two shareholders and both are ready to immediately vote on the written resolution), it will "adjourn" at this stage. If the board meeting will not reopen for more than 24 hours (e.g. if the written resolution will not lapse for 28 days and the company has to wait for a number of shareholders to return their votes during this period) then the meeting will "close" (rather than "adjourn") at this stage.

Between board meetings

Pass the written resolution

- To pass a written resolution, shareholders representing the required percentage of the total voting rights of eligible members must vote in favour CA 06 s. 296(4). Shareholders can vote by sending to the company an authenticated document (e.g. the written resolution document) identifying the relevant resolution and indicating their agreement (or disagreement) CA 06 s. 296(1).
- Amending the Articles requires a special resolution CA 06 s. 21, meaning that at least 75% must vote in favour CA 06 s. 283(2).
- Corporate representatives can indicate agreement on behalf of corporate shareholders CA 06 s. 323.

Board Meeting 2

1. Reconvene/open board meeting

If board meeting 1 was "adjourned", then "reconvene" the meeting. If it was "closed", then "open" the meeting.

2. Who calls the meeting?

Any director can call the meeting MA 9(1).

3. Notice

Reasonable notice must be given Browne v La Trinidad.

4. Quorum

Same as for board meeting 1.

5. Agenda

(a) Chairman report that the special resolution was passed by written resolution.

(b) Direct the company secretary to deal with post meeting matters.

6. Voting

There is nothing for the board to vote on in this meeting. You would only consider this if the scenario in an exam requires the board to take actions that require board resolutions (for instance, appointing a director as was the case in the above procedure plan).

7. Close board meeting

Post Board Meeting 2 Matters

1. Make the relevant filings at Companies House

(a) File a copy of the special resolution within 15 days. CA 06 s. 29(1)(a) states that CA s. 30(1) applies to written resolutions.

(b) A copy of the new Articles must be filed within 15 days CA 06 s. 26(1).

2. Draw up minutes

Draw up minutes from the board meeting and keep these for at least 10 years CA 06 s. 248(1).

3. Written resolution

Keep a record of the written resolution for at least 10 years CA 06 s. 355(1)(a).

PSC Register

Since April 2016, UK companies and LLPs are required to hold and maintain a register of people who have significant control over a company ("PSC Register"), which must be made available for public inspection and filed at Companies House. Listed companies that are subject to Chapter 5 of the Financial Conduct Authority's Disclosure and Transparency Rules are exempt from this requirement (e.g. companies listed on the London Stock Exchange Main Market or AIM), as are companies traded on an EEA regulated market or on specified markets in the United States, Israel, Japan and Switzerland CA 06 s. 790B. The Persons with Significant Control regime ("PSC Regime") is governed by CA 06 Part 21A.

> **Persons with Significant Control ("PSC"):** a Person with Significant Control is an *individual* who meets one or more of the following "specified conditions" in relation to a company (these conditions are set out in CA 06 Schedule 1A, Part 1):
>
> 1. Directly or indirectly holds more than 25% of the shares;
> 2. Directly or indirectly holds more than 25% of the voting rights;
> 3. Directly or indirectly holds the right to appoint or remove a majority of the directors;
> 4. Otherwise has the right to exercise, or actually exercises, significant influence or control over the company; and/or
> 5. Has the right to exercise, or actually exercises, significant influence or control over the activities of a trust or firm which itself satisfies one or more of the first four conditions (such trust or firm not being a legal person).

The PSC Register is therefore a register of *individuals* which states the *relevant particulars* (set out in CA 06 s. 790K) for each Person with Significant Control. These particulars include: names, addresses, countries of residence, nationalities, nature of interests (i.e. the specified condition(s) that those individuals fulfil), and the date on which each individual became registerable as a Person with Significant Control.

Although it is not possible for a company to be a Person with Significant Control, a company can be entered on the PSC Register if it is a "relevant legal entity". Under CA 06 s. 790C(6), a company is a relevant legal entity if:

- It would have come within the definition of "Person with Significant Control" had it been an individual; and
- It is subject to its own disclosure requirements (this is the case if: (a) the PSC Regime applies to it; or (b) it has voting shares admitted to trading on a regulated market which is situated in an EEA state CA 06 s. 790C(7)).

Obligations of a company to which the PSC Regime applies

A company must take reasonable steps to ascertain whether there is anyone who is a registerable person or a registerable relevant legal entity in relation to that company and, if so, to identify them CA 06 s. 790D(1). The company must give notice to anyone whom it knows or has reasonable cause to believe is a registerable person or a registerable relevant legal entity in relation to it CA 06 s. 790D(2). Such notice should require the addressee:

- (If addressed to an individual) to state whether or not he or she is a registerable person in relation to the company and, if so, to confirm or correct any particulars of his or hers that are included in the notice, and supply any particulars that are missing CA 06 s. 790D(3);
- (If addressed to a company) to state whether or not it is a relevant legal entity in relation to the company and, if so, to confirm or correct any of its particulars that are included in the notice, and supply any that are missing.

Obligations of a PSC/Relevant Legal Entity to which the PSC Regime applies

If a person knows or ought to have known that they are a registerable person (or a company knows or ought to have known that it is a registerable relevant legal entity) in relation to a company, they must notify the company of their status and provide the required details (i.e. the relevant particulars described above) CA 06 s. 790G(1) + (2).

Any person who receives a notice from the company (as describe above) must confirm or supply the information within one month CA 06 s. 790g(2) + (3).

Sanctions for non-compliance

Failure to comply with the above obligations is punishable by a fine and/or up to two years imprisonment CA 06 s. 790F.

Directors

Company directors are subject to a wide range of obligations and responsibilities. Some of these responsibilities are embodied in a series of duties in the Companies Act 2006, whilst others arise out of the company's Articles, various codes of conduct (for instance the Corporate Governance Code) and contractual agreements with third parties (e.g. shareholders). It is worth noting that before the Companies Act 2006 was introduced, directors were bound by common law duties and equitable principles. These are still relevant, although do not typically form an integral part of LPC courses. CA 06 s. 170(3) + (4) confirm that regard must be had to the corresponding common law duties and equitable principles when interpreting and applying the statutory duties listed above.

Directors' Duties

Consideration of directors' duties often comes up in LPC exam questions. The directors owe these duties to the *company*, which means only *the company* can enforce them. Directors' duties are overarching principles that always apply, so when answering exam questions that involve advising directors on how to act, try to keep these in the back of your mind and refer to them where necessary. The key duties are set out below.

Duty to act within their powers CA 06 s. 171

A company's Articles or the Companies Act 2006 may prohibit directors from entering into transactions of a certain value or type without shareholder consent. This provision places directors under a statutory duty not to permit such transactions without first following the required approval (e.g. an ordinary resolution in general meeting).

Duty to promote the success of the company CA 06 s. 172

Directors have an overarching duty to act in a way that they believe will benefit the company. This provision sets out a series of 'stakeholder factors' which directors should consider when making decisions. These include:

- The likely consequences of the decision in the long term.
- The interest of the company's employees.
- The need to foster the company's business relationships with customers, suppliers and others.
- The impact on the community and environment.
- The need to build and preserve the company's reputation for maintaining high standards of business conduct.

Duty to exercise independent judgment CA 06 s. 173

Directors must not compromise their own independence. This duty is not usually one of the main focuses of the LPC.

Duty to exercise reasonable care, skill and diligence CA 06 s. 174

The director must meet a certain objective standard, below which no director can fall CA 06 s. 174(2)(a). Directors are also expected to apply the general knowledge, skill and experience that they actually have CA 06 s. 174(2)(b), introducing a subjective test (which may be of a higher standard than the objective test).

Duty to avoid conflicts of interest CA 06 s. 175

Directors must avoid situations where a conflict between their personal interests and the interests of the company could arise (unless authorised by the other directors in accordance with this section). CA 06 s. 175 does *not* apply to transactions between a company and its directors (e.g. if the company is giving the director a loan). Such situations are instead covered by CA 06 s. 177 (see below).

Duty not to accept benefits from third parties CA 06 s. 176

Directors must not accept gifts or other benefits from third parties if received as a result of their position as director.

Duty to declare personal interests in transactions that the company is entering into CA 06 s. 177

For instance, if a director has an interest in the proposed substantial property transaction (explained later), he/she must declare the nature and extent of his/her interest to the other directors before the transaction is entered into. This duty includes indirect interests, for instance if a director of Company A is also a shareholder of Company B, and Company A and Company B are considering entering into a transaction. CA 06 s. 177(6)(b) provides an exception where the other directors are already aware (or ought reasonably to have been aware) of the personal interest, whilst CA 06 s. 177(6)(c) provides an exception where directors are seeking approval of their service contracts. However, interested parties should be advised to declare anyway to ensure the declaration is recorded in the board minutes (in case the transaction is later disputed).

Relationship between CA 06 s. 177 and Model Article 14

Note that this section only creates a duty to *disclose* an interest; it is MA 14 that restricts the ability of directors to *vote* when they have a personal interest in a transaction. MA 14 prohibits a director with an interest in a transaction from voting on whether the transaction can be approved. The interested director will also not count toward the quorum in the board meeting whilst the other directors are voting on whether to approve the transaction. Note that it is not generally considered to contravene MA 14 if the interested director votes on other resolutions in the same board meeting (e.g. the resolution to call a general meeting). In addition, there are certain exceptions that will allow an interested director to vote however, for instance if MA 14 has been disapplied by shareholders or if the director's interest cannot reasonably be regarded as likely to give rise to a conflict of interest MA 14(3)(b).

Breach of Directors' Duties

Consequences of a breach

The consequences of a breach of duty are the same as if the corresponding common law rule or equitable principle were breached CA 06 s. 178. To reiterate, directors owe their duty to the company, so the remedies below are for the benefit of the company. These include:

- Awarding damages (this is the *only* remedy available for breach of CA 06 s. 174, as this duty is not a *fiduciary* duty).
- Granting an injunction to prevent the proposed transaction from taking place (if it has not yet gone ahead).
- Voiding the transaction/requiring the director(s) to restore company property that was disposed of (if the transaction has already gone ahead).
- Requiring the director(s) to account for profit (if they have made a gain).
- Banning the director(s) from taking a directorship for up to 15 years.

Avoiding claims for breach of duty

There are various actions directors can take to avoid breaching their duties, including:

- Building the stakeholder factors into the company's Corporate Social Responsibility policies.
- Undertaking sufficient research, due diligence and financial projections before committing to courses of action.
- Ensuring detailed board minutes are drawn up evidencing that duties/stakeholder factors were considered in the context of particular decisions.
- Preparing subsequent reports to explain how their actions promoted the success of the company.

> **Due diligence:** refers to the process under which a potential buyer and its advisors carry out in-depth investigations into many aspects of a proposed target company, in order to gain a solid understanding of that company's business and/or market. Due diligence can help a potential buyer to decide whether to go ahead with the purchase and if so, at what price and on which terms.

Ratification

Where a breach of directors' duties has occurred, the action that resulted in that breach can in certain instances be ratified, absolving the director of liability. Negligence, default, breach of duty and breach of trust can be ratified CA 06 s. 239, although fraudulent and illegal actions cannot. To ratify an act, more than 50% of the shareholders must consent. The director in breach (if he/she is also a shareholder) and persons connected to them (see below) cannot vote on the relevant ordinary resolution to ratify CA 06 s. 239(4).

> **Ratification:** where decisions made by directors are retrospectively approved (or "ratified").

Persons connected with a director

> **Persons connected with a director:** a person is "connected" with a director when that person is: (a) a family member of the director CA 06 s. 252(2)(a), defined in CA 06 s. 253(2) as including spouses, civil partners, children and parents (but not siblings, uncles/aunts, nephews/nieces and grandparents CA 06 s. 253(3)); (b) a body corporate connected to the director CA 06 s. 253(2)(b), defined in CA 06 s. 254 as including any company in which the director and persons connected to him/her hold 20% or more of that company's share capital; (c) a business partner of the director CA 06 s. 252(2)(d).

Director indemnities

Directors can seek indemnities from the company to protect themselves from the potential consequences of certain future breaches (this is permitted under some circumstances by MA 52).

However, companies are prohibited from indemnifying directors against: claims for negligence, default, breach of duty and breach of trust CA 06 s. 232; the cost of defending civil proceedings brought by the company if judgement is given against them CA 06 s. 234(3)(b)(ii); or for failing to produce a Confirmation Statement (previously known as the Annual Return), as this is criminal in nature CA 06 s. 234(3)(a)(i) + (b)(i). Note that a company could pay the director's costs up front, but the director would have to reimburse the company for these costs if judgement goes against that director CA 06 s.205.

Directors will want these indemnities in their service contracts (Executive Directors) or agreed to in a Deed of Indemnity (for Non-Executive Directors) so that they can be personally enforced.

> **Director indemnity:** if Company A gives Director B an indemnity, then Company A is agreeing in advance to give pound for pound compensation to Director B if scenarios covered by the indemnity take place (for instance, Director B being ordered to pay damages for breach of duty).

Insurance

Directors (or the companies that employ them) can also purchase insurance to cover certain liabilities CA 06 s. 233(2)(a). However, this is subject to certain public policy constraints, for instance criminal wrongdoings cannot be insured against.

Substantial Property Transactions

CA 06 s. 190: a company must secure approval by ordinary resolution before entering into an arrangement to acquire (or sell) a substantial non-cash asset directly or indirectly from (or to) any of the following parties:

- Its directors CA 06 s. 190(1)(a).
- Directors of its holding company CA 06 s. 190(1)(a) (not directors of its subsidiaries however).
- A person *connected* to one of its directors ("connected" is defined in the above section) CA 06 s. 190(1)(a).

When answering this question, you must consider the following definitions:

> 📖 **"Substantial"**: an asset is "substantial" for these purposes if its value exceeds £100,000 CA 06 s. 191(2)(b) or if the value exceeds £5,000 but represents more than 10% of the company's asset value CA 06 s. 191(2)(a). "Asset value" in this context means a company's "net assets" CA 06 s. 191(3), so check the company's most recent statutory accounts for this figure.

> 📖 **"Non-cash asset"**: any property or interests in property other than cash CA 06 s. 1163.

> Taupo Ltd has a subsidiary, Sky Dive Ltd (Sky Dive Ltd is not a wholly owned subsidiary of Taupo Ltd). Mrs Gund is a director of Sky Dive, but not a director of Taupo Ltd. If Mrs Gund were to purchase a property from Taupo Ltd with a value of £150,000, would this require shareholder approval under CA 06 s. 190?
>
> Mrs Gund is purchasing a "substantial non-cash asset" for the purposes of CA 06 s. 190. However, Mrs Gund is not a director of Taupo Ltd (or Taupo Ltd's holding company if it has one). This transaction does not therefore fall within the provisions of CA 06 s. 190(1), so no shareholder approval is required.

Exceptions

Share buybacks do not constitute "substantial property transactions" for these purposes, as directors with an interest in shares being bought back would be acting in their capacity as *shareholders* (CA 06 s. 192(a) provides this exception). Moreover, if the company involved in the transaction is a wholly owned subsidiary of another company (i.e. it has a parent company), the shareholders of the *parent* company should approve the transaction instead CA 06 s. 190(4)(b).

Defences

A director will not be liable under CA 06 s. 190 for authorising the company to enter into a substantial property transaction, if any of the following circumstances apply:

1. The director concerned took all reasonable steps to ensure the company's compliance CA 06 s. 195(6).
2. The director concerned and any persons connected to them (if relevant) can show that they had no knowledge of the circumstances resulting in the contravention CA 06 s. 195(7).

Consequences of breach

If the company and/or interested director(s) fail to follow the correct procedure, the contract is not automatically void. The company (i.e. the shareholders) simply has the *right* to void it CA 06 s. 195 or to ratify (retrospectively approve) the transaction by ordinary (shareholder) resolution CA 06 s. 196.

Relevant directors' duties

Note that the approval of a substantial property transaction by ordinary resolution is a scenario to which CA 06 s. 177 (duty to declare a personal interest in a transaction), CA 06 s. 172 (duty to promote the success of the company) and MA 14 (voting where a conflict of interest exists) will apply.

Procedure for approval

General meeting procedure

Substantial property transactions can be approved using a similar procedure to that included in the *Converting a Shelf Company* section of this chapter, although there are a few differences that you must take into account.

- Any directors with an interest in the transaction should disclose their interests to the board in board meeting 1 to fulfil CA 06 s. 177. Even if the board is already aware of their interest (in which case the CA 06 s. 177(6)(b) exception could apply), they should disclose anyway so that their disclosure is recorded in a board minute.

- The contract must be approved by ordinary resolution in the general meeting (meaning more than 50% of those voting must approve the decision in accordance with CA 06 s. 282(1)).

- Directors with an interest in the transaction *can* vote in their capacity as shareholders (if they hold shares) in the general meeting. However, interested directors do not count in the quorum for, and cannot vote on, the board resolutions to approve the substantial property transaction in board meeting 2 (or sign the contract on the company's behalf) MA 14.

Written resolution procedure

Again, a written resolution procedure similar to that included in the *Converting a Shelf Company* section of this chapter can be used in this context. However, the lapse date (usually 28 days) means the procedure could take much longer than approving the proposed transaction using the general meeting procedure (unless there are a small number of shareholders and they are ready to complete the written resolution procedure quickly).

There is a full procedure plan for approving substantial property transactions after the next section (the procedure plan also covers approval of directors' service contracts).

Long-term Service Contracts

Where directors are to be offered contracts of employment ("service contracts"), shareholder approval may be required depending on the terms of that contract.

Is a director being offered a "long-term service contract"?

First, you must assess whether the guaranteed duration of employment that the director(s) will be offered exceeds two years. Under CA 06 s. 188, the contract must be approved by ordinary resolution of the shareholders if the term of employment set out in the contract *could* (at the director's discretion) or *does* exceed two years, and during that two-year period the company:

(a) Is unable to terminate the contract; or

(b) Can only terminate under limited circumstances that are outside the company's control (e.g. only if the director is guilty of gross misconduct).

If a company has the freedom to prevent the contract exceeding 2 years (i.e. through giving notice to the director) then this is not a "long-term service contract" for the purposes of CA 06 s. 188, even if the contract is for an indefinite term.

Procedure for approval

General meeting procedure

Long-term service contracts can be approved using a similar procedure to that included in the *Converting a Shelf Company* section of this chapter, although there are a few differences that you must take into account.

- The director to whom the long-term service contract is being offered is *not* legally obliged to declare his/her interest in the contract CA 06 s. 177(6)(c).

- The proposed long-term service contract must be put on display at the company's registered office (for shareholders to view) for at least 15 days before the general meeting takes place CA 06 s. 188(5)(b). This means that the shortest notice to which the shareholders can agree using the "short notice" procedure (explained in the *Converting a Shelf Company* section earlier in this module) is 15 days. This means short notice is of little benefit in this context.

- The contract must be approved by ordinary resolution in the general meeting (meaning more than 50% of those voting must approve the decision in accordance with CA 06 s. 282(1)).

- Interested directors *can* vote in their capacity as shareholders (if they hold shares) in the general meeting. However, they do not count towards the quorum for, and cannot vote on, the board resolution to enter into the long-term service contract (and cannot sign the long-term service contract on the company's behalf) MA 14.

Written resolution procedure

Again, a written resolution procedure similar to that earlier in the chapter for amending a company's Articles can be used in this context. The requirement to display the contract for 15 days does not exist when approving long-term service contracts by written resolution CA 06 s. 188(5)(a), although the lapse date (usually 28 days) means the procedure could take much longer than approving a contract using the general meeting procedure.

Failure to secure approval

If shareholder approval is not secured, only the provisions in the contract that fall under CA 06 s. 188 will be void. For instance, a provision allowing a director to extend their contract indefinitely at their own discretion would be void; instead, the contract would be deemed to contain a term entitling the company to terminate the contract at any time on reasonable notice CA 06 s. 189(b). However, other terms such as those relating to payment, working hours etc. would remain binding. Note that breaching CA 06 s. 188 is a civil (not criminal) offence CA 06 s. 189.

Business Law

Procedure Plan

General meeting procedure plan for approving substantial property transactions and long-term service contracts

This is a procedure plan for a company looking to take part in a substantial property transaction and approve a director's long-term service contract.

Board Meeting 1

1. **Who calls the meeting?**

   Any director can call the meeting MA 9(1).

   [handwritten: The board will discuss the proposed changes and will then resolve it.]

2. **Notice**

   Reasonable notice must be given Browne v La Trinidad.

   [handwritten: need to give notice to any other directors; Doesn't have to be in writing can be an orally]

3. **Quorum**

   The default position is that two or more serving directors must be present, unless the directors have agreed to a higher quorum (by board resolution) MA 11(2) or the company's Articles set a higher quorum. However, if the company has only one director (and the Articles do not require it to have more than one director), the quorum will be one director MA 7(2). State who is present and who is in attendance, then conclude on the facts whether the quorum has been met.

4. **Disclosures of interests**

   Any directors with an interest in the substantial property transaction should disclose their interests to the board to fulfil CA 06 s. 177. Even if the board is already aware of their interest (in which case the CA 06 s. 177(6)(b) exception could apply), they should disclose anyway so that their disclosure is recorded in a board minute.

   The director(s) to whom the long-term service contract is being offered are not legally obligated to declare their interest in the contract being approved CA 06 s. 177(6)(c). However, it is good practice to do so in board meeting 1 anyway.

5. **Agenda**

   Call a general meeting CA 06 s. 302. The directors must:

   - Approve form of notice of the general meeting. This notice should include:
     (i) The time, date and location of the meeting CA 06 s. 311.
     (ii) The precise wording of the required ordinary resolutions (this is not legally required, but is good practice).
     (iii) A statement that a member may appoint a proxy CA 06 s. 325(1).
   - Direct company secretary to give notice of the general meeting in accordance with CA 06 s. 308. It should be given to shareholders CA 06 s. 310(1)(a), directors CA 06 s. 310(1)(b) and (if already appointed) the company's auditors CA 06 s. 502(2).

6. **Voting**

   The board must agree by board resolution (either unanimous decision or simple majority on a show of hands) on the issues set out in the agenda MA 7(1) + MA 8. If there is deadlock, the Chairman has the casting vote MA 13.

7. **Close board meeting**

   The board meeting cannot reopen within 24 hours due to the 15 day inspection requirement for the long-term service contract (see below), so board meeting 1 should be "closed", not "adjourned".

Post Board Meeting 1 Matters

1. **Draw up minutes**

   Draw up minutes from the board meeting and keep these for at least 10 years CA 06 s. 248(1).

2. **Display proposed long-term service contract(s)**

   The proposed long-term service contract(s) must be put on display for shareholders to view at the company's registered office for at least 15 days before the general meeting takes place CA 06 s. 188(5)(b).

General Meeting

1. **Open general meeting**

2. **Notice**

   The shortest notice to which the shareholders can agree using the "short notice" procedure under CA 06 s. 307(4)-(6) is 15 days, as this is the minimum period for which the proposed contract must be displayed for shareholders to view CA 06 s. 188(5)(b). This means short notice is of little benefit in this context. Where short notice is not used, the default notice that must be given for a general meeting is 14 *clear* days CA 06 s. 307(1) + CA 06 s. 360(1)+(2).

3. Quorum

Where a company has only one shareholder, the quorum will be one CA 06 s. 318(1). Where there is more than one shareholder, the default position is that the quorum is two CA 06 s. 318(2). However, check the company's Articles in case a higher quorum has been set.

4. Agenda

Propose and (shareholders) vote on the resolutions required to continue with the share allotment.

5. Voting

(a) Ordinary resolution to enter into the contract relating to the substantial property transaction CA 06 s. 190(1).

(b) Ordinary resolution to approve the duration of the service contract(s) to be entered into CA 06 s. 188(2).

More than 50% of those voting must approve the decision in accordance with CA 06 s. 282(1). Shareholders (including corporate representatives and proxies) can vote by a show of hands MA 42 unless a poll vote is demanded (in accordance with MA 44).

6. Close general meeting

You do not "adjourn" the meeting, as it will not be reopened.

Board Meeting 2

1. Open board meeting

We do not "reconvene" the board meeting, as board meeting 1 was closed (not "adjourned").

2. Who calls the meeting?

Any director can call the meeting MA 9(1).

3. Notice

Reasonable notice must be given Browne v La Trinidad.

4. Quorum

Same as stated in board meeting 1. However, directors with a personal interest in the outcome of resolutions will not count towards the quorum when those resolutions are voted on MA 14. This means that the quorum must be met *without* counting the interested directors whilst the board is voting on whether to approve entry into (and approve a signatory for) the long-term service contract and the substantial property transaction.

5. Agenda

(a) Chairman report that the ordinary resolutions were passed at the general meeting.

(b) Propose board resolutions to:

- Approve entry into, and authorise a signatory for, the substantial property transaction.
- Approve entry into, and authorise a signatory for, the long-term service contract.
- Direct the company secretary to deal with post meeting matters.

6. Voting

The board must agree by board resolution (either unanimous decision or simple majority on a show of hands) on the issues set out in the agenda MA 7(1) + MA 8. If there is deadlock, the Chairman has the casting vote MA 13. Parties with an interest in the substantial property transaction and/or the long-term service contract(s) cannot vote on whether to enter into the respective contracts MA 14.

7. Close board meeting

Post Board Meeting 2 Matters

1. Draw up minutes

(a) Draw up minutes from the general meeting and keep these for at least 10 years CA 06 s. 355(1).

(b) Draw up minutes from the board meeting and keep these for at least 10 years CA 06 s. 248(1).

2. Other tasks

(a) Retain a copy of the long-term service contract at the company's registered office for inspection CA 06 s. 228(1)+(2) or such other place as has been notified to the registrar CA 06 s. 228(4).

(b) If the long-term service contract is for a *new* director, then you must file **form AP01** to notify Companies House of the director appointment within 14 days CA 06 s. 167(1).

Loans, Quasi-loans and Credit Transactions

There are prohibitions on a company entering into certain types of transactions with its directors, the directors of its holding company or persons connected to such directors. Note that there is a general exception to the below prohibitions. Under CA 06 s. 204, approval is not required if the company provides a director with funds for the following reasons:

- To meet expenditure incurred/to be incurred by the director for company purposes; or
- To enable a director to properly perform their duties as an officer of the company (or avoid incurring the expenditure required to do so).

Loans, guarantees and security

> **Loan:** involves one party lending an amount of money to another party, either in one bulk payment or in instalments. In return, the lender will typically charge interest on the amount lent.

> **Guarantee:** involves a guarantor (e.g. a parent company) making a legal promise to a lender that they will fulfil any outstanding financial obligations covered under the guarantee if the borrower (e.g. a subsidiary of the parent company) defaults on a loan.

> **Security:** taking security over a borrower's assets can increase a lender's chance of receiving back its money if the borrower defaults on the loan. There are many types of security, including mortgages, fixed and floating charges and guarantees. Some of these are considered in more detail further into this handbook.

Director of a company/holding company

CA 06 s. 197 prohibits all public and private limited companies from giving loans to their directors or the directors of their holding companies, or providing a guarantee or security in connection with a loan (e.g. from a bank) unless the transaction is approved by its shareholders.

However, this is subject to the following exceptions:

- A loan, a guarantee or security can be given to a director/the director of a holding company without shareholder approval if the company giving the loan is a *wholly-owned* subsidiary of another company CA 06 s. 197(5)(b). Approval is instead required from the holding (parent) company's shareholders CA 06 s. 197(2).
- A loan can be given to the director of a *subsidiary* without shareholder approval (as this scenario is not prohibited by CA 06 s. 197).
- Shareholder approval is not required if the loan is for less than £10,000 CA 06 s. 207(1).

Person connected to a director of a company/holding company

CA 06 s. 200 prohibits public companies, and private companies that are *connected* to public companies, from giving a loan to persons *connected* to their directors or the directors of their holding companies, or providing a guarantee or security in connection with a loan to such persons/holding companies, unless the transaction is approved by their shareholders (i.e. there is no prohibition for private companies with *no connection* to a public company, but there would be a prohibition for, for example, a private subsidiary of a public holding company).

However, this is subject to the following exceptions:

- A loan, a guarantee or security can be given without shareholder approval if the company giving the loan/security/guarantee is a *wholly-owned* subsidiary of another company CA 06 s. 200(6). Approval is instead required from the holding (parent) company's shareholders CA 06 s. 200(2).
- A loan can be given to the director of a *subsidiary* without shareholder approval (as this scenario is not prohibited by CA 06 s. 197).
- Shareholder approval is not required if the loan is for less than £10,000 CA 06 s. 207(1).

> **"Connected parties":** to reiterate, a person is "connected" with a director when that person is:
> (a) a family member of the director CA 06 s. 252(2)(a), defined in CA 06 s. 253(2) as including spouses, civil partners, children and parents (but not siblings, uncles/aunts, nephews/nieces and grandparents CA 06 s. 253(3));
> (b) a body corporate connected to the director CA 06 s. 253(2)(b), defined in CA 06 s. 254 as including any company in which the director and persons connected to him/her hold 20% or more of that company's share capital;
> (c) a business partner of the director CA 06 s. 252(2)(d).

Quasi-loans

📖 **Quasi-loan**: this involves a company repaying a loan given by a third party (e.g. a bank) to one of its directors or a director of its holding company (or a person connected to such a director) on the understanding that the director/connected person will reimburse the company for the money paid at a later stage CA 06 s. 199.

CA 06 s. 198 prohibits public companies, and private companies that are *connected* to public companies, from giving quasi-loans to their directors or the directors of their holding companies, unless the transaction is approved by their shareholders. The same applies to persons connected to such directors CA 06 s. 200. However, shareholder approval is not required if the loan is for less than £10,000 CA 06 s. 207(1).

Credit transactions

📖 **Credit transaction**: a transaction involving a company providing goods or services to one of its directors on a credit basis, meaning that the director will repay the company at a later date CA 06 s. 202(1).

CA 06 s. 201(2) prohibits public companies and private companies that are *connected* to public companies, from entering into a credit transaction with their directors, the directors of their holding companies, or persons connected to such directors, unless the credit transaction is approved by ordinary shareholder resolution. However, this is subject to the following exceptions:

- Credit transactions worth less than £15,000 do not require shareholder approval CA 06 s. 207(2)(b).
- Credit transactions that are in the ordinary course of the company's business, and are not on more favourable terms than would be provided to an unconnected person, do not require shareholder approval CA 06 s. 207(3).

Sanctions for non-compliance

Under CA 06 s. 213, if a company contravenes any of the above sections, the transaction will be voidable at the instance of the company unless:

- Restitution is no longer possible;
- The company has been indemnified for the loss or damage resulting from the transaction; or
- Bona fide rights that have been acquired by a third party who was not party to the transaction would be affected.

Alternatively, shareholders can affirm the transaction by ordinary resolution CA 06 s. 214.

In addition, the director/person connected to them that was involved in the transaction, and any other directors who authorised the transaction, must: (a) account to the company for any gain (direct or indirect) made; and (b) indemnify the company for any loss or damage resulting from the transaction. This is the case regardless of whether the transaction is avoided or affirmed by shareholders CA 06 s. 214(3)+(4).

Company A is a public company with two directors, Sean and Raj. Company A has one wholly-owned subsidiary: Subsidiary Z. Subsidiary Z has two directors, Sofia and Ragna. None of the directors are "connected" to one another. Which of the following transactions requires approval?

1. **Company A sells a car to Sofia for £30,000 on the understanding that Sofia will pay Company A back in instalments.**

   This is a credit transaction. As Sofia is not a director of Company A or of Company A's holding company, member approval is not required.

2. **A bank lends Sean £20,000 to undertake building work on his home and Company A agrees to repay the bank on Sean's behalf. Sean will repay Company A at a later stage.**

   This is a quasi-loan from Company A to one of its own directors and the loan is not for less than £10,000, so shareholder approval is required.

3. **Subsidiary Z guarantees a loan worth £20,000 given by a bank to Raj so that Raj can furnish his house.**

   This is a guarantee. Subsidiary Z is a *wholly-owned* subsidiary of Company A, so approval of Subsidiary Z's shareholders is not required. Instead, Company A's shareholders must approve the transaction. This would also be the case if Subsidiary Z had made the loan to one of its own directors (as opposed to Raj, who is a director of its holding company).

4. **Company A lends £100,000 to Sean's mother.**

   This is a loan. A parent is a "connected" party and the loan is not for less than £10,000, so approval from Company A's shareholders is required.

Business Law — *members* ↑

Shareholders

There are certain rights available to protect shareholders' interests. Shareholders can, for instance, hold directors accountable for their actions by removing them from office, or bring unfair prejudice or derivative claims where their interests have been neglected or their rights infringed.

Removal of a Director

CA 06 s. 168(1) entitles the company (including shareholders) to remove a director by ordinary resolution before the expiration of his period of office (regardless of any agreement made to the contrary). Note, a written resolution cannot be used to remove a director from office CA 06 s. 288(2)(a). There is a special procedure that shareholders must follow if they wish to propose the removal of a director in a general meeting. This is set out below.

Procedure for removal of a director

Special Notice

To remove a director, shareholders must first send to the board "special" notice of the proposed resolution to remove that director CA 06 s. 168(2). "Special notice" means notice that must be given at least 28 (CA s. 312) *clear* (CA 06 s. 360) days before the intended date of the general meeting at which the resolution to remove the director will be voted on.

Upon receipt of this notice, the board is obliged to send a copy to the relevant director and decide whether or not to put the resolution to remove the director on the agenda of the next general meeting (or to schedule a general meeting for the purpose of voting on the resolution). The board is not legally obliged to convene the necessary general meeting in order to pass the Resolution Pedley v Inland Waterways Association Ltd. However, if the board decides not to, this may have further ramifications (set out below).

Shareholders' power to require directors to call a general meeting

If the board decides not to put the resolution on the agenda:

- CA 06 s. 303 gives shareholders the power to call general meetings. Shareholders can therefore request that a general meeting is arranged specifically to enable them to vote on the resolution to remove the director. This request must be made by shareholders representing at least 5% of the company's paid up share capital. Note that shareholders can submit CA s. 312 and CA 06 s. 303 requests at the same time to place additional pressure on the board.

- Once a valid CA s. 303 request has been made, the board is *required* to call a general meeting to vote on the resolution CA 06 s. 304. Notice of the general meeting must be sent out within 21 days of the date on which the board received the members' CA s. 303 request and the general meeting must take place not more than 28 days *after* the date the notice is issued. These are *not* "clear" days, as CA 06 s. 304 is not one of the "clear day" provisions listed under CA 06 s. 360.

- If the board does not call a general meeting within the timescales listed above, shareholders become entitled to call a general meeting at the company's expense CA 06 s. 305.

- Note that shareholders could theoretically agree to call a general meeting themselves in accordance with CA 06 s. 305 as soon as the 21 day period expires, giving the usual 14 day notice period (so long as 28 *clear* days have passed since initially serving the CA 06 s. 312 request). This means that the board could delay the general meeting more by *complying* with the CA 06 s. 304 request, as it is entitled to schedule the general meeting for up to 28 days after the notice was served (whilst shareholders could schedule it after only 14 clear days). See the below timelines for clarification.

Prior to the general meeting

- The board must notify all other shareholders about the proposed resolution to remove the director and give at least 14 clear days' notice of a general meeting called to vote on the resolution.

- The directors whose removal is proposed are legally entitled to take steps to defend themselves. They can make representations in writing to be circulated to the shareholders prior to the general meeting CA 06 s. 169(3)(b).

Voting at the general meeting

- A majority of shareholders (i.e. more than 50%) would need to vote in favour of removing the director to pass the resolution (this is the threshold for an ordinary resolution).

- A director whose removal is proposed *can* vote on the resolution calling for his/her own removal, but only in their capacity as shareholder (if they hold shares). In Bushell V Faith, the court upheld a provision in a company's Articles that conferred weighted voting rights upon a director/shareholder in circumstances where a CA 06 s. 168 resolution was proposed. The director was able to block the resolution calling for his removal, as he was entitled to 3 votes for each share he held. Provisions such as this are now sometimes called "Bushell v Faith" clauses.

- Note that shareholders' agreements could also regulate voting (see the *Shareholder Rights and Minority Shareholders* section later in this chapter).

Timelines for removing a director

Co-operative board

Day 1: Shareholders wishing to remove a director submit a notice to call a general meeting CA 06 s. 303(1) and propose an ordinary resolution to remove the director CA s. 168(1)

Day 22: Directors serve "special" notice of the general meeting and the proposition to remove the director on the other shareholders (i.e. the shareholders who did not partake in the serving of a notice pursuant to CA s. 303(1))

Day 50: General meeting held at which an ordinary resolution to remove the director will be voted on

Directors must call a general meeting within 21 days of receiving the notice CA s. 304(1)(a)

The date of the general meeting cannot be more than 28 days after the date of the notice CA s. 304(1)(b)

Non-co-operative board (the board does not call a general meeting)

Day 1: Shareholders wishing to remove a director submit a notice to call a general meeting CA s. 303(1) and propose an ordinary resolution to remove the director CA s. 168(1)

Day 23: If directors do not call a general meeting on day 22, the shareholders can now serve notice of a general meeting and the proposition to remove the director on the other shareholders (i.e. the shareholders who did not partake in the serving of a notice pursuant to CA s. 303(1))

Day 38: General meeting held at which an ordinary resolution to remove the director will be voted on

Directors have 21 days to call a general meeting after receiving the notice CA s. 304(1)(a) at which point the shareholders can call one at the expense of the company instead

The earliest date the shareholders can specify for the general meeting is 14 clear days after the notice is served (CA s. 307(1) and CA s. 360(2))

Compensation

- If removed, the relevant ex-director(s) may be entitled to compensation. This could be for unfair dismissal and/or breach of contract (for early termination of his employment).

- Shareholder approval for the payment of compensation will not be required under such circumstances, although if the ex-directors are offered compensation for other reasons and that compensation exceeds £200, shareholder approval will be required CA 06 s. 217.

Employment Law

Employment law tends to be covered in greater detail in LPC electives such as *Employment Law/Corporate Transactions/Private Acquisitions* etc. However, it can also come up as part of the Business Law module, especially in the context of director removals (which is why we have included this section here). Remember that directors are employees. Where a director has been dismissed, you may have to advise that director on their potential remedies (or the company on the potential consequences).

Wrongful Dismissal

Wrongful dismissal is a common law claim that can entitle a dismissed employee to damages where they have been dismissed in breach of the terms of their employment contract. The breach usually involves:

(a) Failure to give the employee the period of notice stipulated in the contract when dismissing that employee; or

(b) Failure to make the stipulated payment to the employee in lieu of notice when dismissing that employee.

> **Payment in lieu of notice ("PILON") clause**: employment contracts may contain clauses that entitle the employer to dismiss an employee without notice, as long as the employer makes a payment to that employee to compensate them for the amount they would have earned had they actually worked during their notice period. This may be preferable for employers, as it means the employees will not be able to engage in disruptive behaviour in the office if they are disgruntled following the dismissal (e.g. complaining to other employees, downloading confidential information, attempting to solicit clients etc.).

Unfair dismissal

Unfair dismissal is a statutory claim that can be brought by an employee that has been unfairly dismissed, so long as that employee has worked for the company for at least two years (one year if employment began pre-6th April 2012) Employment Rights Act 1996 ("ERA 96"). Claims are based upon an employer's:

(a) Failure to follow a fair procedure; and/or

(b) Failure to dismiss the employee for a fair reason.

To avoid liability for unfair dismissal, the employer must therefore prove that both: (a) the reason for dismissal; and (b) the procedure followed were fair.

Fair reason

Fair reasons for dismissing employees include: incompetence or incapability; conduct (e.g. disobedience or abusive language); redundancy (e.g. if the job no longer exists); statutory illegality (e.g. if the employee's work permit expires); or "some other substantial reason" ERA 96 s. 98.

Fair procedure

A dismissal must also be fair in all the circumstances, meaning that the procedure followed must have been fair. Factors to consider include: the consistency of the employer's actions; whether the employee was given sufficient explanations as to why their conduct/performance was unsatisfactory; whether the employee was warned that failure to improve could result in their dismissal; and whether the employee received a fair hearing and the opportunity to appeal ERA 96.

Where a company brings a director's employment contract to an end quickly for commercial reasons, it is unlikely that the company would have had the time to follow a "fair" procedure. Accordingly, it is likely that a company would pay a dismissed director a sum (compensation) in settlement of any potential unfair dismissal claim that the director would otherwise be entitled to bring (in addition to, for instance, payment in lieu of notice).

Remedies

Compensation is the most common remedy for unfair dismissal. However, instead/in addition to compensation, a court can order reinstatement (obliging the company to give the director his/her old job back) or re-engagement (obliging the company to give the director a different job within the company). However, these remedies are less common. Note that employment contracts may also oblige employers to make payments to directors to compensate for their loss of directorship (known as "payments for loss of office").

Shareholder Rights and Minority Shareholders

The general rule, as set out in Foss v Harbottle, is that courts will not interfere with the way a company is managed. This case also clarified that when a wrong has been committed against a company, the *company* is the proper claimant (i.e. not the shareholders). However, various exceptions have eroded this rule, giving rise to a series of statutory remedies and other options available to shareholders that are seeking to have some impact upon the way a company is managed.

Membership rights in the Articles

A company's Articles bind the company and its shareholders. They confer various rights ("membership rights") upon members and if these rights are infringed, members can sue the company under CA 06 s. 33. Key membership rights include:

- The right to receive a dividend once it has been lawfully declared by the company.
- The right to share in surplus capital if the company is wound up (and there is any capital remaining).
- The right to receive notice of general meetings and annual general meetings.
- The right to vote at meetings.

Non-membership rights are not enforceable against the company under CA 06 s. 33 however. In order to protect shareholders, it is therefore important that any essential non-membership rights are set out in a separate contract that confers personal obligations upon other parties (rather than the company's Articles).

Membership rights were considered in Ely v Positive Government Security Life Assurance. In this case, the company's Articles contained a provision stipulating that the claimant shareholder would be appointed as the company's solicitor, although the appointment never occurred. The court held that the plaintiff could not sue, as the right to be appointed as a solicitor was *not* a "membership right".

Dividends

> **Dividend:** a dividend is a sum paid by a company to its shareholders (typically annually) out of its retained profits.

Companies are *not* legally obliged to declare dividends (except in the case of preference dividends, explained later), but once declared, the legal obligation arises to pay. If companies repeatedly fail to declare dividends (or declare dividends that are much smaller than could reasonably have been expected by their shareholders), the share price of those companies may decrease. This could reduce companies' attractiveness to investors and hinder their ability to raise finance in the future.

Companies can only pay dividends out of distributable profits (profits that remain once they have paid all their expenses):

- **It's a Wrap v Gula** confirmed that the financial status of a company needs to be considered each time a dividend is declared. Dividend payments may be deemed illegal if at the date of each payment the management accounts show that the company is losing money or its profits cannot support the dividend payment.

- **Bairstow v Queens Moat Houses plc** confirmed that where a dividend has been paid illegally, the CA 06 s. 847 provisions apply and the directors will be expected to repay the company the amount distributed "illegally".

> **Interim dividend**: a dividend paid throughout the year by the company. Interim dividends usually represent a portion of the company's profits of the year so far, based on an estimate of what the year-end results will be.

Paying an interim dividend does not involve as many procedural formalities as paying a final dividend. Only a board resolution is required to make the payment. Recipient shareholders have no legal right to the payment until it is actually paid **Potel v IRC**, meaning no "debt" arises for the company until payment is made.

> **Final dividend**: a dividend paid after the final year-end results have been assessed. The final dividend can add an appropriate amount to any interim dividend paid to make the total dividend reasonable for the year.

The process of declaring a dividend first involves the directors calling a board meeting, in which they will resolve to recommend an amount to the shareholders to be paid by way of a final dividend. The directors will then call a general meeting, at which point the *shareholders* will vote on whether to approve the dividend that has been recommended by the directors. The directors then hold another board meeting to resolve to pay the dividend.

Unlike interim dividends, final dividends become a legal obligation (a "debt") once they have been declared by the shareholders in a general meeting **Leclerc Ltd v Pouliot**. Only then can the shareholders sue the company if the dividend is not paid.

Shareholders' Agreements

> **Shareholders' agreements**: these are legally binding agreements between shareholders that are typically entered into to regulate the way each party will vote in a certain scenario. Shareholders' agreements are distinct from a company's Articles. For instance, if four friends start a business together, each acting as directors and equal shareholders, they could agree that one party may only be removed as a director if all four of them consent to the removal (thus protecting their interest in remaining as directors). This means that although 3 out of 4 votes would be enough to pass an ordinary (or special) resolution under the Companies Act 2006, the parties agree not to pass the required resolution unless all parties agree that it should pass. If a shareholder breaches the agreement, this will constitute a breach of contract, entitling the injured parties to sue those in breach for any losses they have incurred as a result.

Having a shareholders' agreement in place can give rise to various benefits:

- They are confidential, unlike a company's Articles.

- They can confer certain rights and obligations that could not be enforced if included in the Articles. For instance, shareholders have the freedom to contractually agree to vote a certain way.

- They can be enforced against other shareholders under the general principles of contract law, whereas a company's Articles can only be enforced against the company. Damages and/or injunctions may be available if a breach has occurred/is threatened.

- They can be amended without the need to pass a special resolution in a general meeting/a written resolution. The parties to the agreement simply need to all agree to amend the contract. This can protect minority shareholders, as the requirement for unanimous consent means minority shareholders will have the power to veto decisions.

Russell v Northern Bank

- In this case, the plaintiff was a party to a shareholders' agreement to which the company was also a party. The agreement included a clause preventing any increase in the share capital of the company without the written consent of all the parties to the agreement. Some of the parties intended to increase the share capital of the company without the unanimous consent of all the shareholders, so the plaintiff sought an injunction to restrain them from doing so. The defendants argued that the shareholders' agreement was void in its entirety because the company was a party to it and it thus amounted to an unlawful and invalid fetter on the company's statutory powers.

- The court reiterated that an agreement outside the Articles between shareholders as to how they would vote on a resolution to alter the Articles was enforceable, in so far as it amounted merely to a private agreement between shareholders. The House of Lords held that the part of the agreement between the company and the shareholders, which was void as being contrary to statute, could be severed from the rest of the agreement between the shareholders. The remainder of the agreement was valid and enforceable and therefore an injunction could be granted to prevent other shareholders from breaching that agreement.

Note that one or more of the shareholders will often also be directors. It is important to draft the provisions of the shareholders' agreement carefully, so as to avoid binding such shareholders to vote a certain way when acting in their capacity as directors. Any restrictive provisions that fetter directors' discretion could amount to a breach of the directors' duty to exercise independent judgment CA 06 s. 173.

Unfair prejudice

CA 06 s. 994 gives shareholders the right to bring a claim against the company if its affairs are being conducted in a manner that is unfairly prejudicial to shareholders. Examples of such behaviour include: directors not recommending dividends, overpaying themselves, or purposely holding regular meetings when certain shareholders cannot attend.

CA 06 s. 994 also applies to parties in a quasi-partnership that have been prejudiced. This is on the basis that such parties have a legitimate expectation to be involved in the management of the company and this expectation should thus be upheld (or those being prejudiced should be bought out).

> 📖 **Quasi-partnerships**: organisations that are effectively run as partnerships but have been incorporated as a company (e.g. five friends that run a company and are co-directors and equal shareholders).

If an unfair prejudice claim is successful, courts are likely to order those prejudicing the injured shareholders to buy the shares of the injured shareholders. This is seen as a solution that is the least disruptive to the business. Note that CA 06 s. 994 petitions are expensive, time consuming and complicated. In addition, courts have full discretion, meaning that the petitioner may not succeed. For this reason, negotiated settlements tend to be the preferred option in practice.

Derivative claims

CA 06 s. 260 gives the right to bring a claim for an act or omission involving a wrong committed against the company. Claims are brought on behalf of, and for the benefit of, the company (*not* the shareholders). Claims can be brought against directors (including former directors and shadow directors) or third parties that have wronged the company.

There is no requirement to show that the wrongdoer benefitted from the breach of duty, but the right to bring a derivative claim is confined to the company's shareholders. Shareholders can bring claims regardless of the number of shares they hold and regardless of whether they held shares at the time the wrong was committed (although they must be a shareholder when bringing the claim). However, the court will look at the size of the shareholding in deciding whether or not to exercise its discretion to permit a derivative claim to proceed.

Court permission

Permission of the court must first be sought to continue a derivative claim CA 06 s. 261(1). Courts will scrutinise whether claims satisfy the statutory preconditions and ought to be permitted to continue. CA 06 s. 263(2) requires the court to refuse permission if any of the following applies:

- People acting in accordance with CA 06 s. 172 (duty to promote the company's success) would not continue the claim (see Franbar Holdings v Patel below for examples of the factors courts will consider when assessing this); or
- The act or omission had been authorised before it occurred or has been ratified since.

Franbar Holdings v Patel

- In this case, the court refused permission to continue a derivative claim and set out a number of factors that a person acting in accordance with CA 06 s. 172 would consider when deciding whether to continue the claim.
- These factors include: the value of the claim; the likelihood of the claim succeeding; the cost of the proceedings (and the company's ability to fund the proceedings); the ability of the intended defendant(s) to satisfy a judgment; the impact on the company if it lost the claim and had to pay its own costs and those of the defendant; the potential disruption to the company's activities while the claim is pursued; whether pursuing the claim could damage the company in other ways (e.g. by losing the services of a valuable employee or alienating a key customer or supplier) etc. The court will also show particular regard towards the opinion of shareholders that have no personal interest in the action.

Where the preconditions for continuing a derivative claim are satisfied, the court still has discretion to prevent a member from continuing the claim. This discretion must be exercised having regard to all relevant matters, including the following non-exhaustive list of factors set out in CA 06 s. 263(3)+(4):

- Whether the member is acting in good faith.
- The importance that a person acting in accordance with CA 06 s. 172 would accord to the proposed claim.
- Whether a proposed/past act or omission would likely be authorised/ratified.
- Whether the company has decided not to pursue the claim.
- The views of the members of the company who have no personal direct or indirect interest in the matter.
- Whether the member has a cause of action that he may pursue in his own right rather than on behalf of the company.

Ratification

Certain acts cannot be ratified. These include unlawful acts, ultra vires acts, fraudulent acts and acts prejudicing the interests of creditors.

> 📖 **Ultra vires**: this is Latin for "acting beyond your powers/authority". For example, if a company has a restriction in its Articles on the number of shares it can issue and it exceeds this, it will have acted outside of its powers, or "ultra vires".

On any resolution to ratify a breach of duty by a director, if the director in breach is also a shareholder, his/her votes will not count towards the resolution. The same applies to the votes of any parties connected to that director CA 06 s. 239(4).

> 📖 **"Connected parties"**: to reiterate, a person is "connected" with a director when that person is: (a) a family member of the director CA 06 s. 252(2)(a), defined in CA 06 s. 253(2) as including spouses, civil partners, children and parents (but not siblings, uncles/aunts, nephews/nieces and grandparents CA 06 s. 253(3)); (b) a body corporate connected to the director CA 06 s. 253(2)(b), defined in CA 06 s. 254 as including any company in which the director and persons connected to him/her hold 20% or more of that company's share capital; (c) a business partner of the director CA 06 s. 252(2)(d).

Costs

- The court can grant permission to continue the derivative claim together with an order that the claimant (shareholder) be indemnified for costs by the company Civil Procedure Rule 19.9E.

> 📖 **Civil Procedure Rules**: these are rules that govern the civil litigation process. You will cover them in more detail on the *Civil Litigation* module.

Wallersteiner v Moir (No 2)

- In this case, the court held that it would normally be appropriate to grant an indemnity where:

    (a) The claim is one that would have been reasonable for the board of directors to have pursued; and

    (b) The claimant member has no interest in the outcome other than in his capacity as a shareholder of the company; and

    (c) All benefits reaped from the action will accrue to the company.

Petition for the winding up of the company

Another option for shareholders is to apply for the winding up of a company on the grounds that it is just and equitable to do so under the Insolvency Act 1986 ("IA 86") s. 122(1)(g). If the shareholders are successful in their petition, the company will have to cease trading.

Joint Ventures

Businesses acquire, merge with or cooperate with other businesses for a variety of reasons, many of which relate to the synergies that can arise. However, a less permanent solution may be to engage in alliances, partnerships or joint ventures, which give rise to similar benefits but also enable parties to retain some autonomy.

> **Joint Venture**: when two or more businesses agree to pool their resources and work together on a specific task or project, such as the development or launch of a product. The parties typically share the costs, risks and rewards.

> **Synergies**: synergies refer to the benefits that can result from the interaction between two companies. Examples of synergies include: the sharing of resources to reduce costs and the sharing of knowledge/human resources to improve product offerings. Synergies can ensure that the value generated by companies that have been combined exceeds the overall value that those companies could produce separately.

Below are some of the general advantages and disadvantages of acquiring/merging with/cooperating with other companies:

Advantages	Disadvantages
- **Access to new markets and customers:** this should facilitate an increase in sales. - **Access to complementary resources:** organisations can boost their own capabilities. For instance other businesses or partners may possess physical, financial or technical resources, expertise (market specific knowledge), complementary skills, supply chain relationships (for instance access to suppliers and distributors), or networks and contacts that enable firms to circumvent barriers to entry and compete more effectively. - **Economies of scope:** firms may benefit from collaborations that will enable them to diversify their product range. Selling a greater range of products could attract new customers and consequently increase sales. Bundling products with those of complementary businesses (for instance a mobile phone manufacturer linking with an Internet service provider or mobile game creator) could also improve a business' product offering. - **Efficiency:** if organisations combine and enlarge their operations, this could enable them to buy, produce and sell in greater quantities, consequently giving rise to increased economies of scale and thus lower costs. Integrating into the supply chain (by acquiring or partnering with supply chain actors) could reduce external costs. In addition, combining knowledge, expertise and resources could enable firms to increase operational efficiency and thus reduce internal costs. - **Savings:** companies could share costs such as infrastructure rent, marketing or research and development. - **Reputation:** organisations may influence others' perceptions of their capabilities through gaining external legitimacy, which can in turn increase trust from suppliers, lenders and customers. Linking with an established organisation in a new market (for instance Tesco partnering with Tata in India) may reduce consumer suspicion, encouraging consumers to make purchases. - **Innovation:** increasing access to resources and capabilities may foster innovation. - **Competition:** forming alliances with, merging with, or acquiring other businesses reduces direct competition in the market. This can increase a firm's market power, which lessens its need to reduce prices in order to compete.	- **Loss of control/conflict:** profits and decisions may have to be shared. Reaching an efficient consensus on decisions may be difficult if the motives or objectives of the parties involved do not align. - **Administration/costs:** coordinating and integrating different businesses can be a complex and costly process. - **Inefficiency:** communication issues may arise if an organisation becomes more complex. In addition, multiple alliances with similar partners may yield fewer benefits than partnerships with differentiated partners. - **Expropriation:** a larger, more powerful company may steal customers, expertise, assets or processes and then terminate the agreement. Ensuring intellectual property rights are sufficiently protected can mitigate this risk.

Joint Venture Agreements

Key documents

- **Articles of Association:** if the joint venture is set up as a company, it will need to have Articles. These could be based upon the Model Articles, or tailored to suit the particular wants and needs of the parties involved.

- **Confidentiality Agreement/Non-Disclosure Agreement (NDA):** the parties to a proposed joint venture will want to ensure that all other parties enter into a Confidentiality/Non-Disclosure Agreement so that sensitive information discovered by those parties during the due diligence process and whilst the joint venture is in operation cannot be disclosed to potential competitors/the market (for instance if the joint venture then falls through).

- **Exclusivity Agreement/Lockout clause:** parties may request exclusivity over a proposed joint venture for a period of time so that they do not waste time and money undertaking due diligence and negotiating only to then be excluded from the joint venture and replaced by another party.

- **Memorandum of Understanding/Heads of Terms:** before the Joint Venture Agreement is formalised, parties will draw up Heads of Terms. This document will provide an overview of the terms the parties have agreed. Most of it will not be legally binding, although certain provisions (notably confidentiality, lock out and jurisdiction clauses) are usually stated in the document to be legally binding and it can be difficult for parties to depart too far from the heads of terms in practice.

- **Shareholders' Agreement:** if the joint venture is set up as a company, the respective parties will be shareholders in the new joint venture company. A Shareholder Agreement may be drawn up to govern the relationship between those shareholders.

- **Supply Agreement/Asset Purchase Agreement:** depending on the type of joint venture, other agreements may need to be in place. If the joint venture will be purchasing assets from the parties involved (or third parties), Asset Purchase Agreements may need to be drawn up. Similarly, if the joint venture requires goods or services from the parties involved/third parties, Supply Agreements may need to be drawn up.

- **Joint Venture Agreement:** once the parties have agreed the Heads of Terms, these will be documented in a legally binding Joint Venture Agreement, which is typically drafted by solicitors. This will include the finer details, such as provisions relating to investment and exiting the joint venture.

Key terms in a Joint Venture Agreement

Below are common examples of key terms that relate to the operation of a joint venture ("JV") and will usually be included in a Joint Venture Agreement. Note that these terms may be heavily negotiated by the parties.

Object(s), time frame and scope of the JV

- What is the purpose of the JV (i.e. is it for a one off project or something more permanent)? Are there limitations to the activities in which the JV can engage? For how long do the parties envisage the JV will operate?

Contributions of each party

- Which assets will each party be expected to contribute? Will key personnel be seconded from the JV parties or recruited? Which intellectual property/know-how/expertise will be shared?

Financing and profits

- How much capital will each party invest in the JV? Will further investment be required down the line? How and when will profits be split between the parties?

Control, approval and conflict

- Will the parties have equal control over decisions concerning the JV? Will one party have more control over day-to-day activities, e.g. can one party appoint more directors than the other(s)? Are there specific matters that require unanimous (or majority) approval from the JV parties?

- How will conflicts be resolved if there is a deadlock? For instance, the JV Agreement could confer a casting vote to the chairman, could refer to forms of alternative dispute resolution, or could include a cooling off period (e.g. 14 days for parties to reconsider before terminating).

Employment law

- If employees are being transferred from the JV parties' own businesses to the JV, the Transfer of Undertakings (Protection of Employment) Regulations 2006 must be considered. This is dealt with in more detail in LPC electives, but it essentially means the employees will likely be entitled to retain the benefit of their existing employment terms and conditions.

Risks

- JV parties must have adequate procedures in place to ensure the avoidance of money laundering and bribery. Future risks, including the insolvency of a JV party or competition law issues should also be accounted for. If JV falls within the definition of "concentration", and has a "community dimension" it would need to be notified to the European Commission and approved before the JV Agreement could be implemented. Competition law is covered in more detail in the Corporate Transactions elective.

Tax and regulation

- How will the JV be taxed? What are the tax consequences of the parties contributing their assets to the JV? How will the parties' interests be taxed? What is the expected tax treatment of the JV on termination (i.e. how will the transfer of any remaining JV assets be taxed)?
- Which regulatory consents (e.g. competition clearance) are required? In which jurisdiction(s) will the JV operate and which laws apply?

Transfer, exit and termination

- How can parties exit the JV and transfer their interest to another party, or force another party to exit? There may be a buyout clause, giving an existing party the right to buy the exiting party's interest. However, on which terms and at what price? There are mechanisms that can deal with this, including the "Russian Roulette" and "Mexican/Texan Shoot-out" mechanisms.

- 📖 **"Russian Roulette" mechanism:** Party A can serve notice to Party B offering either to sell all of its shares to Party B or to buy all of Party B's shares (but not both) at a price specified by Party A. Party B can either accept the offer, or reverse it (i.e. offer to buy Party A's shares or sell its shares to Party A at the price specified in Party A's original notice). If the offer is reversed, the original offeror (i.e. Party A) is bound to accept it.

- 📖 **"Mexican (or Texan) Shoot-out" mechanism:** this is similar to the "Russian Roulette" mechanism, but can involve the parties submitting sealed bids in the form of an auction, with the highest bidder winning the right to buy all the shares.

- A JV Agreement will entitle the parties to terminate without repercussion in certain circumstances. These typically include circumstances where another JV party has: committed a material breach of the Shareholders' Agreement and has failed to remedy this within a set time; attempted to transfer its shareholding in the JV in breach of the Shareholders' Agreement; become insolvent; or changed ownership (i.e. been acquired by another party). Termination will also typically be available where the agreed term of the JV has expired or the project for which the JV was set up is complete or has failed.

Joint Venture Legal Structures

Joint ventures can be set up using a variety of legal forms, or can operate more informally. The options and the respective advantages and disadvantages are set out below.

Contractual Joint Venture

The simplest way to set up a joint venture is for the participants to enter into an arrangement under which they agree to associate as independent contractors (rather than as shareholders in a company or partners in a legal partnership). This type of agreement is often referred to as a "consortium" or "co-operation" agreement. The rights and duties of the participants and the duration of the joint venture will derive from the provisions of the contractual agreement (and any associated agreements, e.g. with third parties) and general common and civil law rules.

Advantages	Disadvantages
- **Flexibility:** can be quick to set up and easy to dismantle as no separate entity is created. Contractual JVs can therefore be useful for short term, single goal ventures. - **Ownership:** JV parties retain ownership of their own assets. - **Liabilities:** one JV party is not typically liable for the debts of other JV parties (although they may agree to share specific liabilities on contracts with third parties). - **Tax:** each JV party will be individually taxed on its share of profits and given relief for its share of losses. - **Regulation:** governed by less onerous regulation. - **Confidentiality:** contractual joint ventures offer more confidentiality than joint venture companies, as companies are subject to greater disclosure/reporting requirements.	- **Structure/identity:** contractual JVs do not operate through separate legal entities, so can suffer from a lack of clear structure and identity. This may affect both internal operations and dealings with 3rd parties. - **Risk of creating a partnership:** if a partnership is inadvertently created, this would give rise to unlimited joint and several liability, so each of the JV parties would be liable for all the JV's losses/liabilities. - **Raising finance:** potentially difficult to raise external loan finance as the JV is not a legal entity and therefore will not own assets over which security can be taken.

Joint venture company ("JVC")

Joint ventures can operate through a limited company structure if they incorporate under the ==Companies Act 2006==. If a company is set up for the JV to operate through, shares representing ownership will be distributed between the parties in the proportions agreed. Equal shareholding between two JV parties would usually mean that decision-making could only be made with unanimous consent.

Advantages	Disadvantages
<ul><li>**Separate legal entity:** a JVC has a familiar, universally-recognised structure with a clear corporate identity and corporate governance regime. A JVC can act in its own name, own its own assets, have its own independent management team/employees, sue and be sued, and enter into contracts in its own right.</li><li>**Legal framework:** a comprehensive legislative framework supports contractual arrangements between JV parties.</li><li>**Limited liability:** a JVC would have its own distinct legal personality and would enjoy limited liability. This would effectively shield the parties from liabilities that arise in the course of the JV (subject to a small number of exceptions, most notably if either party engages in fraud). This means the parties' liability would be limited to their investment in the JVC's shares.</li><li>**Additional financing:** if the JVC requires additional financing in the future, it could (if demand permits) raise capital through listing the company on a stock exchange and selling shares/bonds.</li><li>**Shares:** the parties can easily reflect their contributions and motivations by distributing shares in different proportions.</li><li>**Employees:** as a JVC will have shares, it will be able to offer employee share incentive schemes.</li><li>**Exit:** JV parties can realise their investments by selling shares, which will not necessarily disrupt the legal ownership or operations of the underlying business.</li><li>**Tax:** a JVC will be taxed on its own profits. This may be more advantageous where the JVC is liable to a lower rate of tax or a more favourable basis of taxation than the individual JV parties.</li></ul>	<ul><li>**Double taxation:** there is the potential for double taxation, as (1) the JVC may be taxed on its profits, then (2) an individual JV party may be subsequently taxed once they transfer the (already taxed) profits out of the JVC. Note that companies do not pay tax on dividends received, so double taxation is only a disadvantage where the JV parties are individuals.</li><li>**Flexibility:** the comprehensive legislative framework that governs companies can restrict operational flexibility.</li><li>**Administration:** more onerous reporting and compliance requirements bring increased administration and greater public disclosure requirements.</li><li>**Limited liability may be undermined:** the JVC's limited liability may be undermined in practice if the JVC takes advantage of debt financing. This is because the JV parties may have to provide guarantees and security on their own behalves to support external financing and third party contracts (exposing the parties to some risk).</li></ul>

Partnership

JVs can also be set up using a partnership structure, which would be governed by the ==Partnership Act 1890==. This could involve the JV parties negotiating and entering into a bespoke written agreement that sets out the terms of the partnership. Tailoring the agreement in this manner will typically be more appropriate than adopting the terms implied by the ==Partnership Act 1890== (which would be the default position in the absence of a written agreement).

Advantages	Disadvantages
<ul><li>**Flexibility**: the JV partnership will be governed primarily by the agreement made between the parties and will therefore be less restrained by the rigid legislative regime that governs companies.</li><li>**Fiscal transparency**: the individual JV parties will be taxed directly (the partnership is not taxed on its profits), reducing the risk of double taxation.</li><li>**Confidentiality**: sensitive details of the JV can remain completely confidential between the JV parties, as JV partnerships are not subject to the disclosure requirements of companies.</li><li>**Regulation**: partnerships are subject to less onerous rules and regulations than companies.</li></ul>	<ul><li>**Unlimited liability:** limited liability is not available to partnerships. Each JV party is jointly and severally liable for the whole of the JV's obligations and liabilities, which could enable creditors to pursue any (or all) of the JV parties if the JV partnership were to go into liquidation.</li><li>**Raising finance:** potentially difficult to raise external loan finance as the JV is not a legal entity and therefore will not own assets over which security can be taken.</li><li>**Administration:** any change in identity of the JV parties will require a new Partnership Agreement, which can be time-consuming and expensive to negotiate and draft.</li></ul>

> 📖 **Liquidation:** liquidation usually occurs when a company is insolvent. It refers to the process under which a company's operations are brought to an end and its assets (if it has any remaining) are divided among its creditors and (if any still remain) its shareholders.

Limited liability partnership

JVs can instead be set up using a limited liability partnership ("LLP") structure, which would be governed by the Limited Liability Partnerships Act 2000. LLPs fall somewhere in between a company and a partnership. LLPs are subject to less onerous rules and regulations than a company, but the parties do benefit from limited liability. LLPs are being used more often as vehicles for commercial ventures (they are no longer used solely for professional partnerships such as law firms).

Advantages	Disadvantages
- **Tax:** LLPs are treated as partnerships for tax purposes. Each JV party will therefore be individually taxed on its share of the profits and given relief for its share of losses. - **Separate legal entities:** like JVCs, LLPs benefit from a clear corporate identity/familiar, universally-recognised structure. - **Limited liability:** LLPs have their own distinct legal personality and have limited liability, shielding the parties from liabilities that arise in the course of the JV. - **Regulation:** the legislative framework for LLPs is not as comprehensive as for limited companies, which allows for greater operational flexibility. For example, the rules governing distributions of profits/dividends are less strict than they are for companies.	- **Structure:** the roles and responsibilities of LLP members are less defined and familiar than the roles of directors and shareholders (of companies). - **Less confidentiality:** there are public filing requirements (particularly in relation to financial accounts), although these are less extensive than for companies. - **Limited liability may be undermined:** the JVC's limited liability may be undermined in practice if the JVC takes advantage of debt financing. This is because the JV parties may have to provide guarantees and security on their own behalves to support external financing and third party contracts (exposing the parties to some risk).

Societas Europaea

There is an alternative JV vehicle that you may come across briefly on the LPC known as the Societas Europaea. However, this option has not yet been utilised by many businesses and thus its full advantages and drawbacks in practice may not yet have come to light.

Which of the above JV vehicles best suit the client's (JV party's) needs in each of the below scenarios?

Commercial needs of the client	Contractual JV	JVC	Partnership	LLP
The client wants to limit its liability for losses made by the JV.		☐		☐
The client wants the JV to be able to contract in its own name.		☐		☐
The client wants a JV with a management structure that is familiar to its managers.		☐		
The client wants the JV's profits to be taxed as if those profits were the client's own.	☐		☐	☐
The client wants to keep matters involving the JV confidential.	☐		☐	
The client wants to retain direct ownership of the assets it contributes to the JV.	☐		☐	
The client only wants to collaborate on a specific project.	☐			

Allotting Shares

Companies generally allot (or "issue") shares to raise capital, although shares may also be allotted to afford an ownership stake in a business to another party (e.g. key employees as part of incentive schemes, the parties to a joint venture that is to operate using a company structure etc.). There are various rules governing how, and under which circumstances, companies can allot shares. These are set out in this chapter.

Key Concepts

- **Share issue:** this is where a company sells ("issues") its shares. Investors provide money in exchange for shares that represent an ownership stake in a company, with the aim of reaping returns in the form of capital growth (if those shares are later sold at a profit) and dividends (if the company elects to pay dividends).

- **Initial Public Offering (IPO):** this is where a company lists its shares on a stock exchange for the *first* time (hence the phrase *initial* public offering) in order to sell those shares through the equity capital markets. Listing through a stock exchange also facilitates the subsequent trading of those shares.

Different Types of Share

There are many different types of shares and certain rules may not apply to all types. Familiarise yourself with these.

- **Ordinary shares:** ordinary shares will all rank equally and it will not be necessary to set out the share rights attaching to those shares in the company's Articles. Unless the Articles specify otherwise, each holder of ordinary shares in the company will be entitled to vote at a general meeting and will be equally entitled to any dividend declared or capital available if the company is wound up.

- **Preference shares:** give the holders a right to some form of preferential treatment, for instance a preferential right (in advance of the other shareholders) to receive a dividend and/or recover capital when the company is being wound up. Note that preference share dividends are usually paid at a predetermined fixed rate. Preference shares do not typically give the shareholder a right to vote at general meetings.

- **Participating preference shares:** in addition to having the preferential rights referred to above, shareholders will also be entitled to "participate" in (i.e. receive some of) any ordinary dividend declared, in addition to any preferential dividend payment received.

- **Deferred shares:** these carry no voting rights and do not entitle the holder to be paid any dividend. Occasionally a class of deferred shares will entitle the holder to a share of any surplus profits on the winding up of a company once all the other shareholders have received the amounts due to them. More usually deferred shares carry very few rights and are used in specific circumstances where "worthless" shares are required.

- **Redeemable shares:** CA 06 s. 684(1) enables (only) private companies to issue redeemable shares. Redeemable shares come with rights entitling the company (issuer) to redeem (i.e. buy back) those shares at the option of the company (or the shareholder), according to a pre-determined formula or price. The rights are either set out in the company's Articles at the time the redeemable shares are issued, or are determined by the directors before the time of issue CA 06 s. 685(3). Redeemable shares can only be redeemed if they are fully paid up CA 06 s. 686(1), meaning that shareholders must have paid the price in full for their redeemable shares. Note that once non-redeemable shares have been allotted, they cannot be converted into redeemable shares.

- **Convertible shares:** the rights attaching to convertible shares will usually carry an option (for the company or a shareholder) to convert the shares into shares of a different class under particular circumstances.

Procedure for Allotting Shares

Both private and public companies can allot (or "issue") shares. Before shares can be allotted, there are various restrictions and rules that a company must consider. For instance, the number of shares a company can issue may be capped in its Articles, the company's directors may lack sufficient authority to allot shares and/or the company may have to disapply pre-emption rights depending on the shares it intends to issue.

1. Is there a cap on the number of shares that can be issued?

Companies incorporated pre-2006

A company incorporated before the Companies Act 2006 came into force will have an "authorised" total amount of share capital that can be in issue at any one time. This would have been set out in its Memorandum of Association and essentially means that there was a cap placed on the number of shares that it could issue. This cap would be deemed to have automatically transferred to its Articles after the Companies Act 2006 came into force as a result of CA 06 s. 28.

To remove this cap (i.e. if the proposed amendment would cause the cap to be exceeded), an ordinary resolution is required paragraph 42(2)(b) of Schedule 2 to the 8th Commencement Order. Note that where an ordinary resolution is passed in this particular context, a copy of the ordinary resolution must be filed with Companies House (this is unusual for ordinary resolutions).

Therefore in an exam, be sure to check: (1) whether the company was incorporated pre-2006; and if so (2) whether the company has since adopted the Model Articles or amended its Articles to remove the cap (in which case, no ordinary resolution will be required as there will no longer be a cap that must be removed).

Companies incorporated under the Companies Act 2006

Companies that have adopted the Model Articles with no amendments will not have a cap in place. If there is no cap, then briefly acknowledge this and move on to the next step. If there *is* a cap in place (i.e. the Model Articles were amended at an earlier stage to impose such a cap) and the proposed allotment would cause this cap to be exceeded, then the company in question would need to amend its Articles by special resolution to raise/remove the cap CA 06 s. 21.

If there is no cap, or the cap has been raised/removed, then proceed to the step below.

2. Do the directors have the authority to allot?

Directors must have authority to allot all types of shares CA 06 s. 549.

Automatic authority to allot

The directors of a company incorporated under the Companies Act 2006 will *automatically* have authority to allot the shares under CA 06 s. 550 if:

1. The company is a *private* company;
2. It has only *one* class of share in issue (e.g. *only* ordinary shares);
3. It is proposing to issue only shares of *that* class (e.g. it has *only* ordinary shares already in issue and plans to allot *only* ordinary shares); and
4. It has not opted out of CA 06 s. 550 in its Articles.

> **Class of share**: in this context, shares with different rights attached to them are sometimes referred to as different "classes" of shares. For instance, ordinary shares count as a different class of shares to preference shares.

The notes to CA 06 s. 550 specify that the directors of companies that were incorporated *pre-1st October 2009* will only have automatic authority to allot shares if an ordinary resolution has been passed to *opt in* to CA 06 s. 550 (this ordinary resolution must be filed). The above criteria must also be fulfilled.

Authority to allot given by shareholders

If a company does not fall within the above criteria (e.g. if it has in issue/plans to allot more than one class of share, or was incorporated pre-1st October 2009 and has not opted in to CA 06 s. 550) its directors may only allot shares if authorised to do so by the company's Articles or by resolution of the company CA 06 s. 551(1). Where an ordinary resolution is passed, this must be filed with Companies House CA 06 s. 551(9) + CA 06 s. 29(1)(e). This must be done within 15 days CA 06 s. 30(1) and the relevant fees must be paid. Note that this is unusual for ordinary resolutions.

Authorisation under CA 06 s. 551 must state the *maximum* amount of shares that the directors are being given authority to allot CA 06 s. 551(3)(a), and the date on which the authorisation will expire (this date cannot be more than 5 years from the date on which authorisation is given) CA 06 s. 551(3)(b). In an exam, if you are told that shareholders previously passed an ordinary resolution or amended the company's Articles to give the directors authority to allot, be sure to check whether:

(a) The time limit has passed; and/or

(b) The proposed allotment will exceed the maximum number of shares that the directors have existing authority to allot.

Such authority may be revoked at any time by *ordinary* resolution CA 06 s. 551(4)(b). This applies even if the authority exists in the company's Articles CA 06 s. 551(8). Note that if directors were to allot shares in the company without the required authorisation, the allotment would still be valid CA 06 s. 549(6). However, doing so would constitute a criminal offence and the directors would be liable to a fine CA 06 s. 549(4)+(5).

3. Is it necessary to disapply pre-emption rights?

> **Pre-emption rights:** a company's existing shareholders may have the right (in advance of parties that do not hold shares) to purchase new shares in proportion to their existing shareholding if the company allots new shares CA 06 s. 561. This enables existing shareholders to retain their proportion of control (which would otherwise be diluted if the company issued shares to new shareholders). A company may not want to offer new shares only to existing shareholders however, for instance if it wants to attract investors with particular expertise.

Pre-emption rights arise where:

1. The shares being issued are "equity securities"; and
2. Those "equity securities" are being allotted in exchange for *cash*.

> **"Equity securities":** this is defined in CA 06 s. 560. It refers to shares that entitle a shareholder to a benefit that is uncertain, i.e. a dividend that is linked to company performance or the right to surplus capital assets in a winding up. Shares are not "equity securities" if they afford only a fixed (certain) right to receive dividends *and* a fixed right to receive capital assets. Preference shares are therefore not typically "equity securities" as they tend to offer a fixed return. If a share has the word "participating" in it (e.g. *participating* preference shares), it will constitute an "equity security", as the "participating" element gives the shareholder the right to receive part of (i.e. to "participate" in) the ordinary dividend. In an exam, check the company's Articles (if possible) to ascertain the specific rights attaching to the shares in question.

> **"Cash":** for pre-emption rights to apply, the company must be receiving money in exchange for its shares; pre-emption rights do not apply if shares are to be paid for wholly or partly otherwise than in cash CA 06 s. 565. Therefore, if a party were to be given shares in exchange for (as an example) transferring some business equipment to the company, the company would not have to offer shares pre-emptively to existing shareholders before offering them to that party.

Disapplying pre-emption rights

Companies will *not* need to disapply pre-emption rights if: (a) pre-emption rights have already been disapplied and the disapplication still applies; or (b) they want to offer shares to existing shareholders in proportion to those shareholders' existing shareholding (this would be a "pre-emptive" issue, which therefore upholds the pre-emption rights given to existing shareholders by CA 06 s. 561). Where such circumstances do not exist, the action that must be taken will depend on whether the directors were given authority automatically under CA 06 s. 550 or by shareholders under CA 06 s. 551.

Authorisation under CA 06 s. 550

- If directors are automatically authorised to allot shares under CA 06 s. 550 and wish to disapply pre-emption rights, then the company must give effect to the disapplication by either passing a special resolution or amending its Articles CA 06 s. 569. The disapplication will apply for so long as the company has in issue (and allots) only one class of share.

Authorisation under CA 06 s. 551

- If directors are authorised by shareholders to allot shares under CA 06 s. 551 and wish to disapply pre-emption rights, the company must give effect to the disapplication by either passing a special resolution or amending its Articles in accordance with CA 06 s. 570.

4. Are new class rights being created?

If a new class of share is being created, the company must pass a special resolution (under CA 06 s. 21) to amend its Articles to include the rights attached to shares within that new class.

Kaikoura Ltd operates whale watching boat tours for tourists. The board of directors is comprised of Kaikoura Ltd's only two shareholders, Mr Whale and Mr Dolphin, both of whom hold one ordinary share each. Both parties are in agreement that the company should raise finance by way of an issue of ordinary shares to Mr Fish, in exchange for £1 million, so that a new dolphin-watching boat can be added to its fleet. Kaikoura Ltd was incorporated in 2011 and adopted the Model Articles (these have not been amended). Briefly outline the issues that must be considered and the resolutions required to give effect to the issue.

1. **Cap**: the company was incorporated under the Companies Act 2006 and has adopted the unamended Model Articles, so there will be no cap on the number of shares it can allot.
2. **Director authority to allot**: no resolution is required to allot, as Kaikoura Ltd is a private company with only one class of share and it is not proposing to issue shares of a different class. The directors will therefore have authority to allot under CA 06 s. 550.
3. **Pre-emption rights**: the shares that the company intends to issue are "equity securities" (as ordinary shares give the right to *participate* in dividends declared by the company and any remaining assets following a winding up, and the potential of this right is uncertain) and these shares will be issued in exchange for cash. Pre-emption rights will therefore apply, so the directors are under a duty to either offer the shares first to Kaikoura Ltd's existing shareholders in proportion to their existing shareholding under CA 06 s. 561, or to disapply pre-emption rights. Because authorisation to allot was given under CA 06 s. 550, if pre-emption rights are to be disapplied, this must be done by special resolution or amending Kaikoura Ltd's Articles of Association under CA 06 s. 569.

    However, the directors are also the sole shareholders and both want to allot the shares to external parties. There would therefore be no point (practically speaking) in disapplying pre-emption rights, as both shareholders can simply decline the offer to purchase the shares pre-emptively, at which stage they (in their capacity as directors) can then allot the new shares to other parties.

4. **New class of share**: there is no new class of share being issued, so this needs no further consideration.
5. **Board resolution**: a board resolution is required to allot the shares and instruct the secretary (or director if the company has no secretary) to carry out post-meeting matters.

Procedure Plan

General meeting procedure plan for allotting shares

This is a procedure plan for a company (incorporated under the Companies Act 2006) that only has ordinary shares in issue and now wishes to allot a new class of ordinary shares. The Articles currently cap the number of shares the company can issue and this cap will be exceeded following the issue. The directors also currently lack sufficient authority to allot. In addition, the company does not want to offer shares to its existing shareholders (meaning pre-emption rights must be disapplied). You may be required in an exam to explain *why* certain resolutions must be passed. If this is the case, you should add in the detail included in the 4 steps above to your procedure plan.

Board Meeting 1

1. **Who calls the meeting?**

   Any director can call the meeting MA 9(1).

2. **Notice**

   Reasonable notice must be given Browne v La Trinidad.

3. **Quorum**

   The default position is that two or more serving directors must be present, unless the directors have agreed to a higher quorum (by board resolution) MA 11(2) or the company's Articles set a higher quorum. However, if the company has only one director (and the Articles do not require it to have more than one director), the quorum will be one director MA 7(2). Directors with a personal interest in the outcome of resolutions will not count towards the quorum when those resolutions are voted on MA 14.

   State who is present and who is in attendance, then conclude on the facts whether the quorum has been met.

4. **Agenda**

   Call a general meeting CA 06 s. 302. The directors must:

   - Approve form of notice of the general meeting. This notice should include:
     - (i) The time, date and location of the meeting CA 06 s. 311.
     - (ii) The precise wording of any special resolutions that will be voted on in the general meeting CA 06 s. 283(6).
     - (iii) A statement that a member may appoint a proxy CA 06 s. 325(1).
   - Direct company secretary to give notice of the general meeting in accordance with CA 06 s. 308. It should be given to shareholders CA 06 s. 310(1)(a), directors CA 06 s. 310(1)(b) and (if already appointed) the company's auditors CA 06 s. 502(2).
   - It is also good practice (but not required) to set out the precise wording of any ordinary resolution(s) to be proposed at the general meeting.

5. **Voting**

   The board must agree by board resolution (either unanimous decision or simple majority on a show of hands) on the issues set out in the agenda MA 7(1) + MA 8. If there is deadlock, the Chairman has the casting vote MA 13.

6. **Adjourn/close board meeting**

   If the board meeting will reopen within 24 hours, it will "adjourn" at this stage. If the board meeting will not reopen for more than 24 hours (e.g. if the general meeting will not take place for a few days) then the meeting will "close" (rather than "adjourn") at this stage.

Post Board Meeting 1 Matters

1. **Draw up minutes**

   Draw up minutes from the board meeting and keep these for at least 10 years CA 06 s. 248(2).

   Note that these matters can be dealt with after Board Meeting 2 if the general meeting is held on short notice (see below) as the 14 day time limit will not have passed by the time Board Meeting 2 takes place.

General Meeting

1. **Open general meeting**

2. **Notice**

   The default notice that must be given for a general meeting is 14 days CA 06 s. 307(1). However, CA 06 s. 360(1)+(2) clarifies that in this context, 14 days means 14 "clear" days, so you do not count the day on which notice is given and the day of the general meeting itself as part of the 14 days.

   However, if consent to hold the meeting on short notice is given, the general meeting can be held earlier CA 06 s. 307(5). Explain this in an exam, noting that if only a few shareholders exist, consent to short notice should be easy to secure.

3. Quorum

Where a company has only one shareholder, the quorum will be one CA 06 s. 318(1). Where there is more than one shareholder, the default position is that the quorum is two CA 06 s. 318(2). However, check the company's Articles in case a higher quorum has been set.

4. Agenda

Propose and (shareholders) vote on the resolutions required to undertake the allotment of new ordinary shares.

5. Voting

(a) An ordinary resolution to authorise the directors to allot shares is required under CA 06 s. 551. More than 50% of those voting must approve the decision in accordance with CA 06 s. 282(1).

(b) A special resolution is required to amend the Articles in order to: raise the cap on the number of shares that can be allotted and set out the new class rights being created CA 06 s. 21(1). These special resolutions must be passed by at least 75% of those attending and entitled to vote CA 06 s. 283(1).

Shareholders (including corporate representatives and proxies) can vote by a show of hands MA 42 unless a poll vote is demanded (in accordance with MA 44).

6. Close general meeting

You do not "adjourn" the meeting, as it will not be reopened.

Board Meeting 2

1. Reconvene/open board meeting

If board meeting 1 was "adjourned", then "reconvene" the meeting. If it was "closed", then "open" the meeting.

2. Who calls the meeting?

Any director can call the meeting MA 9(1).

3. Notice

Reasonable notice must be given Browne v La Trinidad.

4. Quorum

Same as for board meeting 1.

5. Agenda

(a) Chairman report that the ordinary and special resolutions were passed at the general meeting.

(b) Propose board resolution to allot shares.

(c) Direct the company secretary to deal with post meeting matters.

6. Voting

The board must agree by board resolution (either unanimous decision or simple majority on a show of hands) on the issues set out in the agenda MA 7(1) + MA 8. If there is deadlock, the Chairman has the casting vote MA 13.

7. Close board meeting

Post Board Meeting 2 Matters

1. Make the relevant filings at Companies House

(a) File a copy of the ordinary resolution granting authority to allot CA 06 s. 551(9) + CA 06 s. 29(1)(e). Usually ordinary resolutions need not be filed, but here there is an exception. This must be done within 15 days CA 06 s. 30(1) and the relevant fees must be paid.

(b) File a copy of the special resolutions to remove the cap and amend the Articles within 15 days and pay the fees CA 06 s. 30(1).

(c) File a copy of the new Articles within 15 days CA 06 s. 26(1).

(d) File **form SH01** to notify Companies House of the share allotment within one month CA 06 s. 555(2).

(e) If applicable, file **forms PSC02 and PSC07** to notify Companies House of changes to the PSC register within 14 days of updating the PSC register CA 06 s. 790VA.

(f) File a Statement of Capital within 1 month (this must be sent with **form SH01**) CA 06 s. 555(3)+(4).

2. Draw up minutes

(a) Draw up minutes from the general meeting and keep these for at least 10 years CA 06 s. 355(1).

(b) Draw up minutes from the board meeting and keep these for at least 10 years CA 06 s. 248(1).

3. Other tasks

(a) Update Register of Members so that it includes details of new shareholders CA 06 s. 554.

(b) Issue new share certificates to new shareholders CA 06 s. 769.

Calculating Voting Rights

On the LPC, you may be required to make fairly simple calculations to work out how many shares need to be issued to a particular shareholder to enable that shareholder to receive a certain percentage of the total voting rights or a certain dividend. Below are examples to help familiarise you with the process.

Queenstown Ltd intends to allot shares, each with a nominal value of £1. It currently has 280,000 shares in issue. The following parties own these shares in the following proportions:

- Director A: 30% (84,000 shares)   280,000 × 30% = 84,000

- Director B: 25% (70,000 shares)

- Director C: 20% (56,000 shares)

- Other employees: 10% (28,000 shares)

- Friends and family: 15% (42,000 shares)

Mr Tekapo (a new party) is willing to invest £6 million in exchange for 30% of the voting rights. How many new shares would the company have to allot to Mr Tekapo (a new party) to entitle him to 30% of the voting rights at a general meeting?

There are numerous ways of completing this calculation. We prefer the following method, but if you are taught a different method on the LPC, check whether you are expected to use that method in the exam before using the below method.

Start by working out the percentage that the *current* shares in issue must represent post-allotment in order to give Mr Tekapo the 30% he requires.

- 100% (the 280,000 shares *currently* represent 100% of the shares in issue) - 30% (Mr Tekapo requires 30% of the shares/voting rights post-allotment) = 70%. This means that the shares currently in issue will have to represent only 70% of the company's shares in issue *after* the new allotment.

- If 280,000 shares must equal only 70% post-allotment, then 1% will equal 4,000 shares (280,000 shares/70).

- If 1% (post-allotment) equals 4,000 shares, then 30% will equate to 120,000 shares (4,000 shares x 30)

- If Mr Tekapo is going to pay £6 million for 120,000, the price per share will be £50 (£6 million/120,000 shares = £50 per share). £1 of this represents the nominal value of the share, whilst the other £49 represents a premium.

Therefore, Company A must allot **120,000 shares to Mr Tekapo for £50 each** to give effect to the proposed deal.

What *percentage return* per share would Mr Tekapo require in order to receive a dividend of £300,000 per year?

If Mr Tekapo has 120,000 shares, he will need to earn £2.50 per share to reach £300,000 in total (£300,000/120,000 shares).

To work this out as a percentage, divide this amount by the price Mr Tekapo is paying for each share: £2.50/£50 = 5%. Mr Tekapo will therefore require a **5% return** on each share annually if he is to receive a dividend of £300,000.

Preference shares can *entitle* a shareholder to a fixed percentage, so Mr Tekapo could invest in 5% preference shares in order to ensure he receives his desired dividend (subject to Queenstown Ltd remaining solvent).

Debt and Equity Finance

In its early stages, a business may take out small loans, apply for government grants, or receive investment from venture capital firms/business angels. As a business grows and matures, it may use its cash resources to fund day-to-day operations and increasingly use debt (where the investors are lenders) or issuances of equity (where the investors become part or full-owners of the company). Large businesses may combine multiple forms of financing, for instance issuing shares (equity) whilst also taking on multiple layers of debt from different sources (for instance, taking out loans or issuing bonds). Note that businesses may borrow money even if they have cash available. For instance, a business may choose to invest available cash in a new venture and borrow money to fund day-to-day operations (or use available cash to fund day-to-day operations and use money borrowed to invest in a new venture) in the hope that the profits generated by that new venture will exceed the cost of borrowing money to use in place of the available cash.

- **Cash reserves**: financing operations using existing cash resources (for instance, retained profit).

- **Capital markets:** these are financial markets that link organisations seeking capital and investors looking to supply capital. Securities, including shares and bonds, are traded in the capital markets between governments and companies seeking capital, banks, private investors and other investors such as hedge funds and pension funds.

- **Debt security:** refers to debt instruments used by companies to raise finance, most notably overdrafts, loans and bonds. Ensure you do not confuse this with the "security" taken over assets by lenders in order to support loan.

- **Bank loan:** firms can borrow from banks and then pay back the loans in instalments, plus interest. The interest rate can be fixed (making it easier for a business to predict its costs) or floating, in which case the rate may be linked to the fluctuation of a benchmark interest rate (for instance LIBOR), which could in turn end up costing less than fixed rate repayments if interest rates happen to fall. A bank may be persuaded to issue a loan on the strength of a well-prepared business plan, a strong previous relationship with the borrower, a financial guarantee from another party, or a company's ability to provide collateral.

- **Bond issue:** this is where a company (the "issuer") sells bonds through the debt capital markets. Bonds are purchased by investors and entitle them to a periodic interest payment (a "coupon") in addition to a lump sum repayment of the principal amount after a set period of time (when the bond "matures").

Debt vs. Equity

Debt Finance

Advantages (from the borrower's perspective)	Disadvantages (from the borrower's perspective)
<ul><li>**Tax**: interest payments made by the borrower to the lender count as "expenses" and can be offset against the borrower's profits. They are therefore tax deductible.</li><li>**Control**: investors do not acquire an ownership stake or voting rights in the borrower's business.</li><li>**Cost:** interest payments are generally fixed (although floating rates may apply), meaning there is greater certainty as to costs for the borrower.</li></ul>	<ul><li>**Risk:** if the borrower defaults on the terms of the loan, the lender may be able to enforce its security (if security has been taken), which could entitle the lender to take possession of and/or sell the borrower's assets.</li><li>**Control:** lenders can exert control over borrowers by including onerous terms in the security documents, e.g. terms that prohibit borrowers from selling/replacing assets (this is not applicable to floating charges however) or taking new loans without lender consent.</li><li>**Cost:** borrowers will be obliged to make interest payments and loan repayments regardless of their financial performance, which could land them in financial difficulties. Setting up Loan Agreements is also a costly process.</li><li>**Procedure:** debt finance typically involves security. Security documents can be complex and expensive to produce as they are often heavily negotiated. Shareholder approval may also be required if a borrower's Articles restrict it from taking on additional debt.</li><li>**Gearing:** taking on additional debt would increase a company's gearing ratio. This could make the company less financially stable and make it harder for it to raise additional finance in the future.</li></ul>

Equity Finance

Advantages (from the issuer's perspective)	Disadvantages (from the issuer's perspective)
- **Cost:** no obligation on the issuer to pay dividends. The obligation only arises if profit is made and the company *decides* to declare a dividend. This means that if the company makes a loss, it will not accumulate further debt (unless it has issued preference shares entitling the preference shareholders to dividends regardless of the company's financial performance). However, not paying a healthy dividend may result in the company's share price reducing, which could make it more difficult for that company to raise further finance. In addition, the equity capital (the amount originally paid for the shares) will not have to be returned to the shareholders unless the company is wound up or it buys back its shares. - **Risk:** security will not need to be provided in exchange for the equity investments of shareholders. This means the company is at less of a risk (than with a loan) of losing assets if it underperforms. - **Experience:** a company could benefit from the skills, experience, relationships and resources that a new investor could bring to the company. If an investor has shares, this could motivate him/her to make meaningful contributions to the company, as they stand to benefit more if the company prospers. - **Gearing:** an equity investment into the company will strengthen its Balance Sheet and decrease its gearing.	- **Tax:** dividends are paid out of profits *after* tax has been deducted, so are not tax deductible. - **Control:** shareholders have an ownership stake in the company and may acquire voting rights. This can enable large investors to exert some control over the company (e.g. veto proposals), which could disrupt its business. - **Cost:** there is less certainty for the issuer as to costs. If preference dividends have been issued, these may oblige the company to make payments regardless of whether it has generated profit (or the amount owed to preference shareholders may accumulate over time). - **Risk:** failure to pay dividends could reduce the company's share price, and thus its attractiveness to shareholders. - **Procedure:** it can be more costly to set up a share issuance, especially if the company is required to produce a prospectus. Note that prospectuses are not required if the share issue does not constitute an "offer to the public" (this is covered in much more detail by the LPC Equity Finance module). A company may require shareholder approval depending on whether there are restrictions on allotting shares in its Articles or whether it has to disapply pre-emption rights (see the *Allotting Shares* section of this chapter).

Debt Finance

Debt finance is not usually covered in much detail as part of the *Business Law* LPC module, so do not take this section as a comprehensive overview of debt finance. The *Debt Finance* and *Corporate Finance* electives go into much more detail.

- **Term loan:** a bank loan (defined above) for a fixed period (or "term"). Term loans are typically used to fund particular investments (e.g. the purchase of a new factory) or long-term projects (e.g. expansion into new markets).

- **Overdraft:** a flexible form of lending that involves the lender making a certain amount of money available that the borrower can access as and when necessary. Overdrafts are usually more useful for companies' short-term cash flow requirements.

- **Conditions precedent:** conditions that must be fulfilled before full performance under a contract becomes due. Notable examples of conditions precedent include the verification (through due diligence) of all the key promises made by the seller prior to the transaction and the receipt of clearance from the relevant competition authorities.

> **Gearing:** if a company has a high ratio of debt in comparison to equity, this means it is "highly geared" and indicates it may lack sufficient assets to support debt repayments if additional debt is taken on. Lenders may therefore perceive highly geared companies as more risky borrowers and consequently charge them higher interest rates (or even refuse to lend).

	Overdrafts	**Term Loans**
Documentation required?	• Usually very little documentation: overdrafts are typically subject to the lender's standard terms and conditions and do not involve security/guarantees etc.	• Term Sheet: provides a (predominantly non-binding) overview of the negotiated terms of the loan. • Loan Agreement: heavily negotiated and binding. • Security documentation: if security is provided.
How quickly can the arrangement be put in place?	• Timing: overdrafts can usually be arranged immediately.	• Timing: term loans can take much longer to set up, as they can involve extensive negotiation, the drafting of security documents, and delays whilst conditions precedent are fulfilled.
Costs for the borrower?	• Interest rates: tend to be higher to reflect the fact that the money lent is unsecured. • Legal costs: costs of setting up tend to be low.	• Interest rates: may be lower if the borrower is perceived as low risk and/or gives security. • Legal costs: costs of setting up are usually much higher due to the amount of negotiation and documentation typically involved.
Certainty that all the funds will be made (and remain) available to the borrower?	• Less certain: the lender can typically terminate the loan at its own discretion and any money lent is usually repayable on demand. This can cause cash flow issues if repayment is demanded earlier than expected.	• More certain: as lenders are usually bound to lend once the Loan Agreement has been signed and the conditions precedent have been met. The lender remains contractually bound *not* to recall the loan early, unless a pre-agreed circumstance arises.
Can the lender exert control over the borrower's business?	• Limited control: the lender's control is limited to its power to recall the money at any time. This does mean however that the borrower has an incentive to comply with requests (e.g. for financial information) made by the lender.	• Depends on the terms: the lender's control depends on the terms of the Loan Agreement. If the lender has taken security, this will usually involve restrictions on the borrower's freedom to deal with the secured assets.

Procedure for setting up a term loan (overview)

Once a borrower has decided that a term loan would best suit its needs/business, it will approach the "relationship manager" at a bank to discuss the possibility of taking out a loan.

The lender's credit committee will undertake a credit check on the borrower based upon its financial accounts and may (if relevant) consider its previous relationship with the borrower. The lender will also follow its internal compliance procedures, undertaking (for instance) money laundering checks on the potential borrower (this is known as "Know Your Customer", or "KYC" for short). The borrower's solicitor will check the company's constitutional documents do not restrict the company and its directors from borrowing and (if relevant) granting security.

The term sheet, Loan Agreement and security documents will then be negotiated. Once agreed, a board meeting will need to take place so that the directors can resolve to enter into the relevant agreements (a Loan Agreement should be executed as a deed). Note, no general meeting is usually required for a business to enter into a Loan Agreement or set up an overdraft. This would only be required if a company's Articles included a specific requirement that shareholder approval is secured under such circumstances.

Once the conditions precedent have been fulfilled, the money should be made available for the borrower to draw down (withdraw/use) and the borrower will subsequently make interest payments and loan repayments as agreed. The security must then be registered at Companies House and the security documentation must be made available for inspection at the borrower's registered office.

> **Deed:** a type of contract. Consideration is not required for a deed to bind the parties. For a deed to be validly executed, it must be signed by either: two directors; one director and a company secretary; or one director in the presence of a witness.

Key Clauses

There are key provisions that you would find in most Loan Agreements, including: indemnities, representations, undertakings, warranties, acceleration clauses and grace periods.

> **Acceleration clause:** if the lender is in default, an "acceleration" clause will enable the lender to require the borrower to immediately repay the loan and accrued interest (but not interest that would have been due in the future however, as this would constitute an invalid penalty clause).

> **Grace period:** if an interest payment is missed due to a technical or administrative error, the Loan Agreement may include a "grace period" during which the borrower will be given the chance to remedy the breach. The lender will not be able to terminate or seek other contractual remedies if the breach is subsequently remedied within this period.

Business Law

- 📖 **Indemnities:** promises to pay the other party pound for pound compensation if specified scenarios take place. For instance, if the target company is in the middle of a law suit at the time it is acquired, the seller can agree to reimburse the buyers in the future for any money that the target company is required to pay out in relation to the law suit once it comes under the buyer's control. Indemnities may be subject to financial caps, i.e. limits on the amount that the seller will have to pay out if a claim relating to the circumstances covered by the indemnity is made. Indemnities may also be subject to time limitations, meaning that after a pre-agreed period of time post-acquisition, the buyer can no longer rely upon the indemnities.

- 📖 **Representations:** like warranties, representations are typically statements made about a company. However, whilst warranties are given in a contract, representations are usually made *before* the contract is entered into. Representations (unlike warranties) may be statements of *opinion* (i.e. not only statements of existing *fact*) and may not actually be included in the contract itself (although parties can agree to include representations as actual contractual terms). The remedies available also differ to the extent that a party can bring a claim for misrepresentation if they were induced to enter into a contract by a representation on which they relied, and this representation was untrue. Only claims for breach of contract are available for breaches of warranties.

- 📖 **Undertakings:** statements, given orally or in writing, promising to take/refrain from taking certain action in the future. The statements must be given in the course of business/legal practice by someone held out as representing the firm (i.e. including secretaries and trainees), to a party that reasonably places reliance on them. For instance, a seller may undertake (to a buyer) that it will settle any pending litigation before completion of an acquisition and to reduce the purchase price by any amount it pays out as part of that settlement agreement. It does not matter whether the undertaking explicitly includes the word "undertake", although statements of *intention* do not constitute undertakings.

- 📖 **Warranties:** statements of existing fact contained in a contract. These amount to assurances or promises relating to the present condition of an object or entity, the breach of which may give rise to a legal claim for damages. For instance, a seller may provide a warranty (to a buyer) that it is not currently involved in any litigation.

Note that when drafting/giving undertakings, take care to ensure that they are:

- **Specific:** it must be clear what the undertaking is referring to/requiring.

- **Measured:** it must be possible to deduce precisely what is required and when the undertaking has been fulfilled.

- **Agreed:** both sides must agree on the wording of the undertaking.

- **Realistic:** the action/inaction promised as part of the undertaking must be within the control of the person giving the undertaking.

- **Time-limited:** the undertaking must not operate for an indefinite period of time.

It is worth remembering that lenders will typically want to build strong relationships with borrowers in order to attract future business and gain a strong reputation in the market. For these reasons, lenders may in practice be willing to negotiate and provide more flexible options than those set out in the contract if borrowers do commit minor breaches of Loan Agreements.

Security

What is "security"?

Security is an essential form of protection for lenders. When giving a loan, a lender may take "security" over a borrower's assets in order to increase its chances of receiving back its money in full if the borrower defaults on the loan (fails to repay the loan as agreed), thus making that lender feel more *secure*. Lenders with no security ("unsecured creditors") will almost always be in a worse position than lenders with security ("secured creditors") if a borrower becomes insolvent.

- 📖 **Secured creditors:** lenders that have been granted security over a borrower's assets.

- 📖 **Unsecured creditors:** lenders that do not have the benefit of security over any of a borrower's assets.

"Security" in this context refers to a right given by a borrower to a lender. This right usually relates to some (or all) of the borrower's assets, and typically entitles the lender to sell enough of those assets to repay itself if the borrower fails to repay the loan as agreed. However, the lender can *only* invoke its right to sell the borrower's assets if pre-agreed circumstances arise, most notably if the borrower defaults on the terms of the loan (e.g. fails to make an interest payment on time). Security may also entitle lenders to exert some control over the borrowers' assets (e.g. a borrower may be prohibited from selling an asset over which the lender has been granted security). A borrower will offer security to persuade a lender to lend, or to persuade a lender to charge lower interest rates (in recognition that there is a lower risk of that lender not receiving back the money lent in full).

Over which assets can security be taken?

Security can be taken over a variety of assets. A purchaser of a home gives a lender a mortgage (this is a type of security) over his or her house in exchange for a loan. In simple terms, if that purchaser fails to repay the lender as agreed, the mortgage (security) entitles the lender to sell the house and repay itself out of the sale proceeds. In larger commercial transactions, there may be multiple lenders that collectively provide a loan (a "syndicated" loan), and the amounts lent may be in the hundreds of millions rather than the hundreds of thousands. However, the basic premise is the same.

> **Syndicated loan:** where multiple banks work together to contribute funds in order to provide the required capital. The syndicate of banks shares both interest payments from the borrower and risk. Syndicated loans are more viable where the borrower requires a large amount of capital, as these loans can be complicated and expensive to administer.

Borrowers in commercial transactions will typically be companies that own a wide range of assets. Lenders will usually take security over one or more of these assets (as they would over a house when lending to the purchaser of a home). These assets typically include factories, machinery and stock.

Types of security

There are various types of security, for instance "fixed charges" and "floating charges". This section provides a simplified overview of how different types of security (known as "charges") can operate, although you are unlikely to be expected to discuss the concepts outlined in any real detail in an interview. However, understanding the basic principles can help if you end up interning in a banking/debt finance-related department of a commercial law firm.

> **Mortgage/fixed charge:** a fixed charge (or mortgage) gives the lender a legal right to claim and sell the asset(s) over which security is taken (the 'secured assets') in order to recover the funds loaned out, in instances where a loan has not been repaid in accordance with the terms under which the security was taken. The borrower cannot sell the secured assets without the lender's consent, so fixed charges will not usually be suitable for assets such as stock (which companies need to be able to sell to consumers in order to make a profit), but can be suitable for fixed assets such as factories, photocopiers, cars, intellectual property, computers etc. Note, mortgages and fixed charges are not identical in all respects.

> **Floating charge:** defined in the case of Re Yorkshire Woolcombers, a floating charge operates in a similar manner to a fixed charge, but is different in that the assets over which the floating charge is taken can be freely sold unless the charge "crystallises". The parties can agree in advance the circumstances under which the charge will "crystallise" and these circumstances will usually include the borrower becoming insolvent. This ability to freely sell assets makes floating charges more suitable for assets over which it would be commercially impractical for the borrower to relinquish control to the lender, e.g. stock, or cash in a current account. A floating charge offers less protection for lenders however. This is because lenders that have the benefit of a floating charge are not repaid in the event of insolvency until certain other parties (such as fixed charge holders, the liquidator and unpaid employees) have been repaid in full. This often means that there is little left for floating charge holders after borrowers become insolvent.

> **Guarantees:** instead of giving an asset to a lender as security, the lender could request that another party guarantees the loan. Guarantees can be upstream (provided by the borrower's parent company), downstream (provided by a subsidiary of the borrower), cross-stream (provided by an affiliate of the borrower) or personal (e.g. given personally by a director). A guarantee would oblige the guarantor (person giving the guarantee) to pay the lender if the borrower fails to make a repayment.

> **Liquidator:** a party often appointed when a company becomes bankrupt. Functions include: collecting money the (bankrupt) company is owed, collecting and selling that company's assets, then distributing the proceeds to parties that are entitled to receive payment (e.g. existing lenders that have not been fully repaid).

Note that borrowers may not want to give banks security over assets worth more than the actual loan. This is because borrowers may want to raise additional finance and may need to offer other assets as security to support new loans.

Registration

Certain types of security must also be registered. Fixed charges for instance must be registered at Companies House within 21 days starting the day after the security was granted CA 06 s. 859A. Failure to register may mean that the security is void against a liquidator, administrator or creditor of the company and the debt will become immediately repayable CA 06 s. 859H. This can have dire consequences for lenders (as they will therefore rank beneath secured creditors in the order of priority and may thus not receive back any of the money they are owed).

To register a fixed charge, **form MR01** must be sent to Companies House, along with a certified copy of the document setting out the charge and the fee charged by Companies House.

Business Law

Acquisitions

Although acquisitions are dealt with in more detail on electives such as Corporate Transactions and Private Acquisitions, you are expected to know certain key concepts in some detail for the Business Law module. This will obviously vary between LPC courses/institutions, so be sure to attend your classes and check the areas that are most relevant for your exams.

Financial Assistance

There are restrictions on the extent to which a company is allowed to assist another company to acquire shares.

> **Financial assistance**: the term "financial assistance" encompasses the giving of gifts, guarantees, security, loans, indemnities, reliefs or waivers to other companies for the purpose of helping those other companies to purchase the shares of the company giving the "financial assistance" (or companies within its group). The giving of financial assistance is prohibited by the Companies Act 1985/2006 under certain circumstances.

The question of financial assistance becomes relevant when conducting due diligence on a target, because if the target in the past was acquired using illegal financial assistance, there may be an issue relating to the title to the shares. The Companies Act 2006 and the Companies Act 1985 deal with financial assistance differently. It is therefore important that you check when a particular transaction occurred, as the relevant rules are the rules that applied *at the time* the transaction occurred. For instance, a transaction that took place in 1992 would be subject to the financial assistance rules set out in the Companies Act 1985.

Financial assistance under the Companies Act 2006

Prohibited companies

The Companies Act 2006 allows financial assistance to be given between *private* companies, although this is of course subject to the overarching directors duties already explained in this module. There are however restrictions upon the freedom of *public* companies to give financial assistance, as set out below:

- CA 06 s. 678(1) where a person/company is acquiring or proposing to acquire shares in a *public* company, that public company (or its subsidiaries) cannot give financial assistance, directly or indirectly, for the purpose of the acquisition.
- CA 06 s. 679(1) where a person/company is acquiring or proposing to acquire shares in a *private* company, any subsidiaries of that private company that are *public* companies cannot give financial assistance, directly or indirectly, for the purpose of the acquisition.
- CA 06 s. 679(3) the above rules also prohibit the giving of financial assistance *after* the shares have actually been acquired.

Types of financial assistance

The types of transactions to which the financial assistance rules apply are set out in CA 06 s. 677(1) and include:

- Financial assistance given by way of gift;
- Financial assistance given by way of guarantee, security, indemnity, release or waiver;
- Financial assistance given by way of loan or similar agreement;
- There is also a "catch all category" in CA 06 s. 677(1)(d): any financial assistance given by a company that results in the net assets of that company reducing to a material extent.

Note that it is not enough that the transaction falls within any of the above categories. The company giving the assistance must have *intended* to facilitate the acquisition by giving that assistance, and no other exceptions must apply.

Exceptions

Even if a prohibited company has undertaken a transaction that constitutes financial assistance, exceptions exist that may render the transaction legal. The relevant exceptions are:

- **Purpose exceptions:** the "purpose" exceptions apply where the principal purpose in giving the assistance is not to fund the acquisition (i.e. the acquisition is only an incidental part of some larger purpose). The exceptions are contained in CA 06 s. 678(2), s. 678(4), s. 679(2) and s. 679(4), which apply to the rules set out in CA 06 s. 678(1), s. 678(3), s. 679(1) and s. 679(3) respectively. Note however that the court in Brady v Brady clarified that this exception has a very narrow application and will therefore rarely be applied by the courts.
- **Specific exceptions:** CA 06 s. 681 lists specific transactions to which the financial assistance rules do not apply (e.g. dividend payments and share buy-backs).
- **Conditional exceptions**: CA 06 s. 682 lists certain transactions that will be excepted if certain conditions are met.

Consequence of breaches

Breach of the above rules constitutes a criminal offence and the directors of the company in breach could be liable to a fine, imprisonment, or both CA 06 s. 680. Case law has also suggested that if an acquisition has been carried out using illegal financial assistance, the acquisition might be void or unenforceable. To avoid breaching these restrictions, companies could:

- Ensure financial assistance is only given from *private* limited companies; or
- Convert any public companies that are required to give financial assistance into private companies before doing so (including public subsidiaries of a private parent company).

Applying the Companies Act 2006 financial assistance rules

When applying the financial assistance rules to a scenario given to you in an exam, consider the following structure:

1. Draw a structure diagram *post-acquisition*

Draw a diagram of the ownership structure of the companies involved as it would look *after* the acquisition has taken place. This will help you to understand the application of the financial assistance rules. Consider the following example: Orange Ltd is proposing to acquire the shares of Banana Ltd from Banana Ltd's current holding company, Passion Fruit Ltd. Banana Ltd has two subsidiaries, Kiwi Ltd and Pear plc.

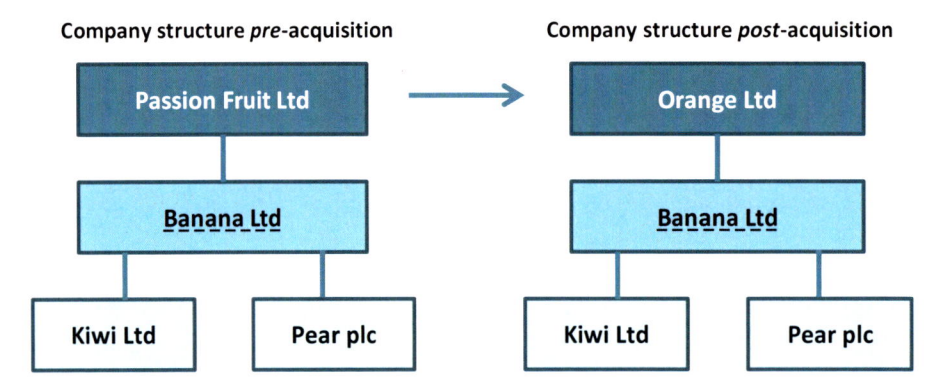

Company structure *pre*-acquisition

Passion Fruit Ltd → Banana Ltd → Kiwi Ltd, Pear plc

Company structure *post*-acquisition

Orange Ltd → Banana Ltd → Kiwi Ltd, Pear plc

2. Identify the target and the applicable CA 06 provision

Make sure you know which company is the *target* company in your structure diagram. In the above example, the target is Banana Ltd.

- If the target is a public company (plc), CA 06 s. 678 applies.
- If the target is a private company (Ltd), there are no relevant CA provisions that apply; the financial assistance rules will not be an issue.
- If the target is a private company but has a subsidiary that is a public company, CA 06 s. 679 applies. In our example, this is the relevant CA 06 provision: Banana Ltd is a private company with a subsidiary that is a public company (Pear plc).

3. Is the company that wishes to give assistance "prohibited" from doing so?

The CA 06 financial assistance rules only apply to the target company and its subsidiaries, which has two important implications: (1) any companies *above* the target in the *post*-acquisition structure diagram (i.e. Orange Ltd) are never "prohibited companies"; and (2) the *seller* (i.e. Passion Fruit Ltd) is never a "prohibited company".

- **If the *target* is a public company:** CA 06 s. 678 prohibits the target *and* its subsidiaries from giving financial assistance (they will be classed as "prohibited companies").
- **If the *target* is a private company, but has a subsidiary that is a public company**: that public company subsidiary is prohibited from giving financial assistance CA 06 s. 679.

This means that in our above example: Pear plc is a "prohibited company" as a result of CA 06 s. 679, so cannot give financial assistance; and Passion Fruit Ltd, Banana Ltd and Kiwi Ltd are not prohibited companies, so could give financial assistance to Orange Ltd (the buyer).

4. Which type of financial assistance is being proposed/has been given?

You should establish which type of transaction has occurred and whether it falls under the definition of "financial assistance" set out in CA 06 s. 677(1). Using our above scenario, the following are examples of transactions that would be classified as constituting "financial assistance" (and would therefore be prohibited):

- Pear plc pays Orange Ltd's solicitors' and accountants' fees in relation to the acquisition, with the result that Pear plc's net assets are reduced to a material extent (note that this would not constitute "financial assistance" if Pear plc's net assets had not been reduced to a *material* extent).
- Orange Ltd borrows money from a building society to fund the acquisition and Pear plc guarantees the loan.
- Pear plc lends Orange Ltd money, which Orange Ltd uses to fund the acquisition.

5. Exceptions

If you have established that a prohibited company has given financial assistance, you should consider whether any of the exceptions apply (see above for an outline of the relevant exceptions).

Companies Act 1985: financial assistance rules

Remember, transactions that occurred *before* Companies Act 2006 came into force will be subject to the rules in Companies Act 1985 (which deals with financial assistance differently). CA 85 s. 151 prohibits public companies under any circumstances from giving financial assistance to another company in order to finance the purchase of shares in itself or its parent company (as does Companies Act 2006). However, unlike Companies Act 2006, Companies Act 1985 prohibits *private* companies from giving financial assistance unless the statutory "whitewash" procedure is used.

Whitewash Procedure

This is set out in CA 85 s. 155-158 and entitles private companies to give financial assistance where the following criteria are met:

Business Law

1. **Statutory declaration:** the directors of the company make a statutory declaration of solvency, confirming their opinion that the company was solvent at the time and the giving of financial assistance would not prevent the company from paying its debts for the following 12 months.
2. **Auditors report:** the company's auditors confirm the opinion given by the directors.
3. **Special resolution:** the company's shareholders consent to the giving of the financial assistance by special resolution. If the company is a *wholly-owned* subsidiary, then its shareholder (i.e. parent company) does not need to consent; instead the shareholders of the *parent* company must consent.
4. **Net assets:** the giving of financial assistance will not reduce the overall net assets of the company to a *material* extent.

Breach

If a company incorporated under the Companies Act 1985 gives financial assistance and fails to use the whitewash procedure, this constitutes a criminal offence. The company's directors could then be liable to a fine, imprisonment or both CA 85 s. 151(3). There is also a risk that the transaction (e.g. the acquisition for which financial assistance was given) will be void, meaning the buyer would not have acquired good title to the target's shares.

Share Sale vs. Asset Sale

When deciding how to purchase a business, buyers/sellers must consider whether a share or an asset purchase/sale best suits their needs. Below are some of the advantages and disadvantages of different methods of purchasing a business.

- **Share Sale/Purchase:** this involves a purchaser buying either all of another company's shares, or a controlling stake in another company. For share sales, the sellers are the shareholders of the target company (e.g. if the target company is a subsidiary, the seller would be its parent company).

- **Asset Sale/Purchase:** this involves a purchaser buying specific assets owned by another company, such as buildings or intellectual property. For asset sales, the seller is the company that owns the assets (i.e. the target).

Share Sale	Asset Sale
Advantages for the Buyer	**Advantages for the Buyer**
Control: easier for purchasers to gain full control of a company, including its human capital, tangible assets (plant and machinery) and intangible assets (including knowledge of internal processes, business relationships, good will/brand loyalty and IP rights).	**Can be selective:** buyer can leave behind unknown liabilities (e.g. tax/litigation) and/or onerous assets and cherry pick the most useful/desirable/relevant assets. This can make the transaction more financially efficient.
Quicker and cheaper: there is only one type of asset to transfer (shares), so the transaction *may* be easier/quicker/cheaper to administer.	**Due diligence:** due diligence relating to specific assets may be quicker and easier to conduct than firm-wide investigations.
Continuity: it is easier to preserve continuity for the target's business post-sale. Third party contracts will remain in operation, as non-assignment clauses are not triggered by share sales (although change of control clauses could cause some problems).	**Valuation**: valuation of the target may be less subjective, as intangible assets such as customer loyalty need not be considered (such assets would usually only transfer as part of a share sale).
Less disruption: the target will retain its assets post-completion (unless the buyer decides to transfer any), meaning the target's business can continue as usual post-acquisition.	
Disadvantages for the Buyer	**Disadvantages for the Buyer**
Risk: buyer acquires all actual and potential liabilities (including tax and pension scheme liabilities etc.) and will take on the target's existing obligations.	**Time/Cost:** more complicated transaction if many assets are being purchased, which can involve more negotiation (and thus increased time/cost since each asset must be negotiated/transferred separately).
Due diligence: more detailed due diligence usually required, which can increase time and cost.	**Control:** purchasers may not gain full control over the entire company and may thus fail to benefit from certain employees and/or internal knowledge and processes that may have helped to facilitate efficient and effective utilisation of the assets.
Valuation: harder to value company as due diligence may not cover all potential liabilities/opportunities.	**Less continuity:** contracts with third parties may include non-assignment clauses, enabling those third parties to terminate if the seller tries to assign the benefit of those contracts as part of the asset sale.
Stamp duty: payable on the full value of the shares by the buyer.	**Assignments/novation/consents:** may be required for key contracts and leases. This could delay/prevent completion.
Shareholders: it may be difficult for purchasers to persuade a sufficient proportion of shareholders to agree to a sale (not an issue if there is one shareholder that wants the sale to go ahead, e.g. a parent company).	**Stamp duty land tax (SDLT):** this is payable on the sale of land/properties and is subject to higher rates than stamp duty (which is payable on shares).

Share Sale	Asset Sale
Advantages for the Seller	**Advantages for the Seller**
• **Clean break:** the seller will not be subject to any of the liabilities of the business sold. It will only be liable for warranties/indemnities etc. given in the sale agreement. • **Consideration**: will go directly to the sellers (e.g. the parent company selling the shares of its subsidiaries). Where a subsidiary's asset is sold, the money goes to the *subsidiary* instead of the parent. • **Simpler and cheaper:** there is only one type of asset to transfer (shares) so the transaction may be easier/quicker/cheaper to administer. • **Lower tax:** individual sellers may be able to benefit from Business Asset Disposal Relief and/or their annual exemption to reduce/eliminate any gain made on the sale of shares. Note that corporate sellers will pay corporation tax at 20% on any gain (as they would on an asset sale). • **Tax:** may be able to take advantage of Business Asset Disposal Relief, significantly reducing the tax burden on the sale. This is not available for asset sales.	• **Element of choice:** the seller can divest itself of loss-making/non-core divisions and carry on with/focus upon the rest of its business.
Disadvantages for the Seller	**Disadvantages for the Seller**
• **Nothing left:** seller retains no business interests. • **Subsequent restrictions:** the seller may face restrictions post-sale if it is required to sign, for instance, non-compete/non-solicit agreements etc.	• **Liabilities:** the seller could be left with a shell company that has liabilities. • **Time/Cost:** more complicated transaction if many assets are being purchased, which can involve more negotiation (and thus increased time/cost). • **Consideration:** the *target* will receive the consideration. It will have to declare a dividend or be wound up for the shareholders (e.g. parent company) to benefit. • **Double taxation:** proceeds from the sale will first be taxed under the corporation tax regime, as the proceeds go to the *company* (not the *shareholders*). If some of those proceeds are then distributed to shareholders via dividends, those shareholders may have to subsequently pay tax on those dividends.

📖 **Change of control clause/break clause:** such clauses can enable parties that are contracted to work with a company to terminate the contract without incurring any liability for breach of contract if control of the company changes hands.

📖 **Non-assignment clause:** prohibits one party from assigning their rights and obligations under the contract to another party. For instance, Company A may purchase goods from Supplier A, partly on the basis of the relationship it has had with Supplier A for a number of years. Company A may not want Supplier A to assign the contract to Supplier B, as Company A may not trust the level of service/flexibility that Supplier B would offer. Below is an example clause.

📖 **Non-compete Agreement:** a promise from the seller that if the deal goes ahead, the seller will not start up a similar business and emerge as a competitor of the business being acquired. Such agreements will usually apply for a limited period of time (typically 3 years) and/or apply only to regions in which the business being acquired already operates.

📖 **Non-Solicit clause:** a contractual promise from a seller to a buyer not to approach and attempt to poach, for instance, certain key employees, suppliers, distributors or customers of the newly purchased company for a given time period or in a particular jurisdiction.

Due Diligence

When conducting due diligence, companies (or their solicitors) will usually be afforded access to a "data room" (nowadays this is typically an online database) containing comprehensive information relevant to the transaction including commercial contracts, financial records and information on existing assets and liabilities. This helps bidders to understand in greater detail that which they are considering purchasing and provides advisers with an opportunity to discover (and subsequently mitigate) any potential issues.

The extent of the due diligence required will depend on the value of the target, the time available, the client's instructions/budget, the type of business operated by the target, the type/extent of the target's assets, and the extent to which the seller is willing to give warranties (the concept of warranties is explained in more detail below). Due diligence will typically look at the following elements:

Legal due diligence

- **Title:** does the seller have good title to the assets/shares being sold? Who owns any relevant intellectual property? Which assets are owned by the target (and thus included in the sale)?
- **Key contracts:** are there clauses of which the buyer should be wary, for instance change of control or non-assignment clauses? Are key contracts due to expire shortly and if so, will the counter-parties enter new contracts with the target?
- **Employees/pensions:** is there a pension deficit? Which employees will remain with/transfer to the target post-sale?
- **Liabilities:** what are the actual and potential liabilities of the target? Is it facing any litigation claims?

Financial due diligence

- **Accounts:** do the target's financial accounts indicate strong financial performance?
- **Debt:** has the target taken on a lot of debt? How will this impact on its ability to borrow more/generate future profits?

Limitations on due diligence

Sellers may put restrictions in place to prevent potential buyers (which may well also be existing competitors) from discovering too much about the company, thus reducing the ability of potential buyers to use such information to their own advantage if the deal falls through at a later stage. A Confidentiality Agreement could mitigate this risk.

However, it may not be economical for a buyer to scrutinise every part of a business, including its past activities and activities planned for the future. There are various ways in which the buyer can limit the amount of due diligence it conducts whilst still protecting its position. As explained in the *Debt and Equity Finance* section above, warranties (statements of existing fact), undertakings (promises to take certain action in the future) and indemnities (promises to reimburse the other party if certain costs arise) can be included in the contract to allocate/mitigate risk. Breach of these can result in the party that committed the breach having to pay damages (compensation) to the other party.

Warranties

As mentioned, warranties are statements of existing fact on which the buyer is entitled to rely. Warranties typically involve the seller stating that it has complied with previous obligations (e.g. attained the relevant consents before building properties/paid its tax bills on time etc.) and that certain statements about the target's business is true (e.g. that it owns good title to the target's shares/the target is not involved in any litigation). Consider the following benefits of warranties for buyers:

1. **Warranties can reduce the extent of the due diligence that the buyer must carry out**: this is because buyers can to some extent rely on sellers' warranties in the knowledge that they can sue the sellers if the target business is not in the state promised by the sellers, or if, contrary to the relevant warranty, a liability arises in the future in respect of an issue that arose pre-acquisition. A buyer would not want to rely solely on warranties however, as there is still the risk that an issue may be identified that would not have been covered by a seller's warranties. Moreover, there is always the risk that a seller will in the future become bankrupt and therefore be unable to fulfil a subsequent breach of warranty claim.

2. **Warranties can encourage the seller to make full disclosures**: this is for the reasons set out in the disclosure section below.

Limitations on warranties

There are limitations on warranties however. Warranties are typically subject to de minimis clauses, de maximus caps, and time limitation clauses that restrict the extent to which a buyer is free to claim against the seller. These are covered in greater detail in the *Drafting* section of this module. Warranties also usually contain restrictions against double recovery. In addition, a buyer may not be able sue under a warranty in relation to an issue that had already been disclosed (see the *Disclosure* section below for more detail).

> 📖 **De minimis clause:** this restricts the ability of an injured party to bring a claim unless that claim is worth at least a minimum specified amount. This prevents potential defendants from having to deal with the hassle of administering relatively small claims.

> 📖 **De maximus cap:** de maximus clauses place a cap on the maximum amount that can be claimed under the warranties. It therefore provides the defendant with a degree of comfort, as their liability will not be unlimited.

> 📖 **Double recovery:** a buyer's loss may be covered by both an indemnity and a warranty, by multiple warranties, or by an insurance policy. For instance, the seller may warrant that no contamination has taken place and also indemnify the buyer for any loss that arises as a result of any contamination that occurred before the sale. The buyer may also take out an insurance policy to cover any loss arising as a result of any contamination that is found on the property (for instance, to cover the risk of the seller becoming insolvent and thus being unable to pay the cost of clearing up any contamination that is later discovered). A double recovery clause prevents the buyer from recovering the same loss multiple times, meaning the buyer could not recover its loss from the seller under the warranty that was breached, then that same amount again under an indemnity covering the same issue and/or from their insurer.

Remedies for breaches of warranty

Damages

- The most commonly pursued/available remedy is damages. For a breach of warranty claim, the measure of damages is the difference between the true value of the asset and the value that would have been attributed to that asset had it been of the quality warranted.
- The buyer can claim the difference between the price it paid for the business and the value that would have been attributed to the business had the warranty been true. The usual rules of contract still apply, so the buyer must prove (1) loss; (2) that the loss was not too remote; and (3) that action was taken by the buyer to mitigate the loss. Note, the *buyer* receives the damages if there is a breach, *not* the target. This is because the warranties are given in favour of the buyer. If they were given in favour of the target, it would be more difficult for the buyer to access (and thus benefit from) the damages awarded.

Rescission

- Rescission may be available, but may not be commercially viable, especially if the buyer has already started to integrate the target into its own business.

Misrepresentation

> **Misrepresentation:** an inaccurate pre-contractual statement (representation) made by the seller about the company on which the buyer relied and which induced the buyer to enter into the contract.

- Misrepresentation claims offer the buyer an alternative remedy for breaches of warranties. In fact, a buyer will often seek to ensure that an acquisition agreement expressly states that the seller "warrants and represents" certain facts. Misrepresentation claims are tortious claims, so the measure of damages is the difference between the true value of the asset and the price actually paid.
- An effective entire agreement clause will make it difficult (or impossible) for a buyer to bring an action in misrepresentation against the seller for pre-contractual statements however, as entire agreement clauses indicate pre-contractual statements/representations were not intended to form part of the contract.

> **Entire Agreement clause:** clause stating that only the terms contained within the contract apply to the agreement and thus any previous negotiations or oral statements that are not recorded in the contract do not apply or bind the parties. This type of clause is covered in greater detail in the *Drafting* section of this module.

Negligent misstatement

- The remedy of rescission is not available for successful negligent misstatement claims, so damages are the most common remedy awarded. Damages are calculated on the basis of the tort of negligence (the principles of which are set out in ==Hedley Byrne v Heller==), meaning defendants will only be liable for damages that are *reasonably foreseeable*.
- The scope of negligent misstatement extends to advice and opinion, which is broader than actions for misrepresentation (which can only be founded on a statement of fact). Someone who is not a party to a contract could possibly be made liable for misstatements to a buyer (e.g. a director of the target company), although the buyer would have to show that the person owed them a duty of care, which can be difficult.

Disclosure

Warranties are subject to any corresponding disclosures made by the seller. Sellers are therefore motivated to disclose issues in the knowledge that the buyer may otherwise be entitled to sue under the warranties given in the sale agreement. For instance, a seller may warrant that the target is not currently facing any litigation, pending or threatened, other than the claims disclosed. The seller could then *disclose* any specific claims that do exist so as to avoid the buyer being able to claim that the relevant warranty has been breached. You may need to draft/amend clauses relating to disclosure in your exam, so the below may be relevant for your drafting assessment.

Disclosure Letter

All disclosures should be recorded in a formal disclosure letter, with copies of relevant documents annexed. This should be prepared by the seller's legal team and should disclose everything relevant, including matters of which the buyer is aware (just to be safe).

Signing and completion are different stages in the acquisition process. Signing indicates that the parties have finished negotiations, reached an agreement and agreed to be bound by that agreement *subject to* the completion of certain tasks/fulfilment of conditions precedent. Once those additional tasks/checks have been completed, "completion" then takes place and the deal is done. Things can change during the period between signing and completion; the disclosure letter should thus be updated as and when circumstances change during this period, then delivered in its final form at completion.

Remember, as warranties are *existing* statements of fact, a seller will not have breached a warranty made a few weeks before completion just because the circumstances changed at a later stage (so long as the warranty was true *at the time it was given*). For this reason, buyers may require sellers to repeat their warranties at completion, meaning those sellers would need to make additional disclosures (by updating the disclosure letter) to qualify those warranties if circumstances have changed.

Buyers will try to reserve the right to terminate the agreement or renegotiate the purchase price/indemnities if something is disclosed at completion that, if not disclosed, would have constituted a *material* breach of warranty. This effectively means that if particularly pertinent issues come to light after signing, but before completion, the buyer can terminate without facing penalties. The agreement will also typically prohibit the seller from rectifying errors in earlier drafts of the disclosure letter (any errors would be breaches of warranty); only new matters/changes in circumstances may be disclosed to qualify warranties.

Standard of disclosure

There is no objective standard of disclosure and buyers should not assume that the seller is required to give full, clear and accurate disclosures. Courts will look at the strict drafting of the documentation between the parties to ascertain whether parties intended the standard of disclosure to be "fair"; if the documentation does not indicate that the parties intended a fair disclosure standard, the court may decide that the parties intended to accept disclosures below a fair standard Infiniteland. The below drafting would likely cause the court to deduce that a fair standard of disclosure had been agreed between the parties:

"The seller is required to disclose matters fairly, with sufficient detail to identify the nature and scope of the matter disclosed."

"The parties agree that disclosures must be full, fair, accurate and clear."

Buyers should not accept clauses stating that mere references to documents constitute deemed disclosure of the full contents of those documents, as this could indicate to the court that a lower standard of disclosure had been agreed.

Fair disclosure

To meet the standard for fair disclosure, disclosures made by the seller must be sufficiently clear and precise. The below cases provide examples of disclosure that failed to meet this standard.

Levison v Farin

- In this case, the seller argued that it had given satisfactory disclosure to the buyer despite failing to disclose the fact that its profits were substantially below the figure predicted in its accounts. This was argued on the basis that the buyer knew the target's head designer was ill and should thus have deduced that the target's profitability would diminish.

- The court disagreed, holding that the disclosure was insufficiently precise to meet the agreed standard of fair disclosure. On this basis, stating that "all matters and documents referred to in the documents disclosed are deemed to be disclosed" would also fail to meet the standard of fair disclosure.

- In summation, it is not considered enough to put the buyer on enquiry or give it the means or knowledge to enable it to work out the facts and conclusions for itself. The seller must actually disclose the precise details. Using the above case as an example, the seller should have disclosed that the head designer's illness was likely to adversely affect its profitability.

New Hearts

- In this case, the seller referred to a 120-page document instead of disclosing specific contents from within that document. The court held that this was not sufficient to constitute fair disclosure of all the content of that document.

General disclosures

- Sellers can make more general disclosures to cover matters that appear in the public domain/matters of which the buyer should be aware on the basis of pre-contractual enquiries and searches.

- Sellers will try to phrase general disclosures as broadly as possible, for instance "the buyer is deemed to have knowledge of all matters in the public domain". However, buyers should strive for a narrower definition, as it may not be able to search out every piece of publicly available information relating to the target/seller. For instance, public records for a company may stretch back multiple decades. Rather than having to read through 40 years' worth of records on the seller/target, the buyer may insist that any relevant matters that occurred (for instance) 9 months or longer before completion must be specifically disclosed. In addition, a buyer could require that the seller references specific public records, as "anything in the public domain" is incredibly broad.

Knowledge

If a seller has failed to make a particular disclosure, a claim by the buyer for breach of warranty may fail if the undisclosed matter was within the buyer's knowledge. There are different types of "knowledge" for these purposes and the type of knowledge may determine the success of such a claim.

Actual knowledge

- This is knowledge the buyer actually has. If a buyer has *actual* knowledge of a breach of warranty, this will likely prevent the buyer from bringing a claim.

- Many acquisition agreements have a clause stating buyer knowledge will not prevent a claim for non-disclosure/breach of warranty, which suggests the buyer will still have a remedy if (for instance) a single employee had knowledge and did not pass it on. However, case law (e.g. Eurocopy Plc) suggests the effectiveness of such a clause is doubtful. As a compromise, the buyer could state that the "knowledge of the buyer" means the actual knowledge of certain named individuals only (e.g. directors) and excludes the knowledge of its agents and advisers.

Constructive knowledge

- This is information that the buyer *should* know, for instance information available from standard pre-acquisition searches/Companies House etc. Obiter in Eurocopy Plc suggested that constructive knowledge would not frustrate a claim.

Imputed knowledge

- This includes the knowledge of the buyer's agents (e.g. its solicitors). This knowledge of third parties is "imputed" to the buyer. Eurocopy Plc confirmed that imputed knowledge would *not* preclude a buyer from bringing a claim for breach of warranty, on the basis that it cannot be assumed that agents pass on all relevant information.

Knowledge-saving clause

- It is now common for buyers to insist that acquisition agreements expressly provide that knowledge imputed to a buyer, in addition to actual and constructive knowledge, should not prejudice that buyer's ability to bring a claim for breach of warranty (although it is still unclear whether a court would uphold this in relation to "actual" knowledge).

Knowledge-prevention clause

- Depending on the bargaining power of a seller, it may be able to insist on a "knowledge-prevention" clause, which would preclude the buyer from bringing a claim if it has knowledge (the type of knowledge covered would depend on negotiations).

Indemnities

As already mentioned, indemnities are essentially promises made by the seller to reimburse the buyer for any loss in connection with a specific liability which may arise in the future. Indemnities are used to mitigate risks that come to light as a result of the issues disclosed by the seller. They will therefore usually be agreed *after* the warranties have been given and the seller has made disclosure to qualify those warranties. If for instance it comes to light that the seller is currently facing litigation proceedings for supplying a faulty product to a third party, the buyer could require an indemnity to cover any costs incurred by the target as a result of those litigation proceedings. This may be a more favourable option for the buyer than simply waiting for the litigation to conclude and reducing the purchase price to reflect the pay-out made by the target (as litigation can take years to resolve). The buyer would only lose out after the sale if the seller becomes insolvent, or the indemnity is subject to a cap that is lower than the pay-out that is eventually made.

Like warranties, indemnities may also be subject to de minimis, de maximus and double recovery restrictions, and to time limitations. In addition, as with warranties, indemnities must be given in favour of the *buyer*, not the seller. It was confirmed in the case of ==Zim Properties v Proctor== that damages payable under an indemnity may otherwise be subject to tax.

To summarise...

1. **Warranty:** makes a general statement, e.g. Target is not involved in litigation.
2. **Disclosure:** qualifies the general statement in the warranty, e.g. Target is involved in claim ABC.
3. **Indemnity:** mitigates risk arising from the issues disclosed, e.g. Target will indemnify Buyer if costs arise out of claim ABC.

Other than negotiating warranties and indemnities, there are other actions buyers can take to protect their positions. They could impose conditions precedent that make completion dependent on the seller rectifying certain issues (e.g. settling outstanding litigation claims). A reduction in the purchase price could be negotiated. Waivers could be sought in advance from third parties that have change of control clauses in their contracts, confirming they will not invoke their right to terminate upon the sale of target.

Listed Companies and Acquisitions

The obligations that a company must comply with once its shares are listed are known as "continuing obligations". These continuing obligations are found in the ==Listing Prospectus Disclosure Transparency Rules (LPDTRs)==. You are not typically expected to know these rules in great detail as part of the Business Law module. However, if an acquisition involves a listed company, you may have to allude to the fact that certain obligations exist under these rules.

Announcements

Disclosure obligations

A listed company must announce to the market, as soon as possible, any inside information that directly concerns the issuer (i.e. the listed company).

- "Inside information" is any information held by a listed company that is likely to affect that listed company's share price in the opinion of a "reasonable investor".
- For instance, if a listed company were considering making an acquisition, a reasonable investor would arguably believe that the listed company's share price could be affected by the anticipation of that acquisition. This is because the market could anticipate that the acquisition could affect that listed company's profitability.

Delaying announcements

Companies can delay such announcements if making them would prejudice their legitimate interests, so long as they maintain confidentiality (i.e. ensure all parties with knowledge sign a Confidentiality Agreement). For instance, neither the buyer or the seller of a company would want the public to know that the acquisition of that company is being discussed, as this could affect the share price of either party, as well as the actions of stakeholders such as employees and suppliers.

Shareholders

Shareholder approval is required for particularly large transactions involving listed companies. This obligation must therefore be considered in the context of acquisitions. To secure approval, listed companies must send out a "circular" (a document that must be approved by the FCA) to its shareholders explaining its intentions, at which point those shareholders can indicate their approval/reject the proposition in a general meeting. Therefore, if one of the parties to a proposed acquisition is a listed company, the requirement that shareholders approve the acquisition could cause considerable delay.

Drafting

There are a variety of drafting tasks that you may encounter on the LPC. Some courses have exams dedicated solely to drafting. Other courses include drafting sections within the exam paper for other modules and your grade for that section will count towards both your drafting grade and your grade for that module. You may be required to write out memorised sections from boilerplate clauses. You may be required to comment upon the impact of clauses given to you in the exam and perhaps suggest amendments. You may be required to write a clause from scratch to achieve a given outcome. Ensure your drafting is as clear as possible so as to avoid ambiguity as to what is required by the parties to the contract.

Referencing

There are methods you can use to keep your clauses clear and concise, most notably using defined terms and attaching documents to a contract that can be referenced within contractual clauses. Contractual clauses would become cluttered and more difficult to read if, for instance, you repeatedly wrote out the full names of the parties to the contract, the agreed means for delivery, or a detailed account of the services one party is providing to another throughout the contract, Instead, you could simply write "Buyer"/"Seller", "Delivery" or "Services" in the relevant contractual clauses (the capital letters indicate to the reader that the term has been defined elsewhere in the contract), then define these terms. For example:

The Seller will provide the Services to the Buyer on the first day of each month.

"Buyer" means Ecotrip Ltd. "Seller" means Soap King Ltd.

"Services" means the Delivery and installation of 1000 bags of eco-friendly hand soap.

"Delivery" means the Seller delivering the soap to the Buyer's nominated warehouse, at the seller's expense, by 10am.

Moreover, using defined terms for elements such as the purchase price and the completion date would enable you to draft the contract before such details have been set in stone. You could then simply define the term(s) at a later stage (rather than having to amend multiple clauses throughout the contract).

You could also reference fictional schedules or attachments to the contract in order to make clauses more concise. For instance, if you are referencing the condition of a fleet of vehicles included in a sale, you could refer to "the Vehicles" in the contractual clauses, then in the defined term for "Vehicles", you could write "the vehicles listed in Schedule 1 to this Agreement".

Proof reading

Defined terms

- It is important to check that your defined terms are correct. If there are multiple documents, ensure the defined terms are consistent (if this is appropriate).

Format

- Ensure the numbering of clauses is consistent and aligns with references made in other clauses in the contract.

Contact details

- Are the parties' names spelt correctly? Are the contact details, dates, products/land listed for sale accurate? Keep these considerations in the back of your mind, as some of your drafting marks will simply be given for accurate proof reading/amending.

Payment/delivery

- Check the purchase price, deposit, currency, time/place for payment and delivery is as agreed. Have any items been left out (e.g. a piece of land or a factory)? Is VAT included/supposed to be included?

Drafting Key Terms

When drafting a clause, you must consider the **Who? What? When? Where? W**ho does the obligation relate to? **W**hat must be done? **W**hen must it be done? **W**here does the obligation take place? Below are examples of some of the other variables you should consider when drafting or commenting on contractual terms.

Payment

How much is due? When is payment due? Will payment be made in instalments? How should payment be made? Do prices change depending on order size? Is delivery/VAT included in the purchase price?

Delivery

When should delivery take place? Is the delivery obligation triggered by a particular event? Where should delivery take place? Who arranges delivery? Who pays for delivery?

Installation, removal, repair or replacement of chattels/equipment

What should be replaced/installed? Subjective terms such as "old" (e.g. to describe items to be replaced) or "good condition" (e.g. to describe the standard of work that must be carried out) are not helpful. Who should pay for the required work? What is the time frame? Does one party have to give the other "reasonable access" upon "reasonable notice"?

Risk/insurance

When does risk pass? For instance, if goods are being shipped, does risk pass to the buyer when the goods are loaded onto the boat, when the boat is at sea, or when the goods are delivered? This will determine when the buyer should have insurance in place. On this note, who pays for insurance? Who is responsible for arranging insurance?

When does title pass? If title passes to the buyer before the seller has received payment and the buyer then goes insolvent, the goods will be available for the buyer's creditors and the seller may not receive payment.

Termination/extension of the contract

Under which circumstances can the parties decide to terminate/extend the contract and on which terms?

Compromises

Learning certain stock phrases may help you to amend language to improve the position of your fictitious client in an exam scenario. You may be asked to use language that *both* parties are likely to feel comfortable with, so it is important to understand the different connotations of the words you choose to use. Below are key words and phrases to remember.

Knowledge

When drafting warranties, the seller may want to insert "as far as the seller is aware" before certain warranties, thus limiting liability to matters which are within the seller's actual knowledge. However, the buyer may not accept this.

A compromise could be to then insert "(having made reasonable enquiries of Specified Persons)" after "as far as the seller is aware", in order to place greater onus on the seller to check the validity of the statements it makes. The parties would then need to define "Specified Persons" and could agree on a list of people that must be consulted. For example:

As far as the seller is aware (having made reasonable enquiries of Specified Persons), no key contracts are due to expire within the next 12 months.

"Specified Persons" means all directors and senior managers of [name of Target].

Materiality

A seller may want to limit the extent to which it will be liable against the warranties it gives. The buyer may want the seller to warrant that the target is not involved in any litigation. This could include litigation worth a few hundred pounds and would thus require the seller to disclose insignificant litigation proceedings each time they arose (for fear that they would otherwise have breached the warranty). Imagine an airline having to disclose every small claim brought against it for spilt coffee or a delayed flight!

Instead, the word "material" could be inserted to place some limit on this. "Material" should then be defined, either in accordance with a cash amount, or a percentage of the value of the deal.

The Seller warrants that the Target is not engaged in any Material Litigation.

Definitions section: "Material Litigation" means litigation that could result in the Target having to pay damages worth more than £10,000.

The Seller warrants that no Material Client has since the last Accounts Date ceased to contract with the Target or given the Target written notice to terminate an existing contract.

Definitions section: "Material Client" means any client that is responsible for 5% or more of the Target's revenue.

Reasonableness

If the parties are required to take certain action under the contract, qualifying the clause using reasonableness may provide a compromise. If a clause requires a party to use their "best" endeavours to do something, for instance find out whether there could be any claims brought against the company, the onus on that party is much higher than if they are required to use only their "reasonable" endeavours. Accordingly, "reasonable endeavours" is more likely to strike a compromise that the parties will accept (although always remember that a negotiation will depend somewhat on the relative bargaining power of parties).

- If a party is required to make enquiries of third parties, they could use "reasonableness" to limit their obligation:

    Party A will, as far as *reasonably* practical, make enquiries of suppliers and employees to ascertain whether…

- Parties may also use "reasonableness" to limit the extent to which one party may make requests of the other, for instance:

    Party A will supply the documents that Party B *reasonably* believes to be of relevance.

Limitation clauses

Maximum cap on claims (de maximus clauses)

The common law places no cap on the amount of damages that a party may be awarded (subject to the ordinary principles of contract). Parties may therefore want to limit their liability in contract, using a de maximus clause. For example:

The Seller's aggregate liability for all claims shall not exceed the lower of £[x] or the Purchase Price.

The de maximus clause is typically set at the purchase price, although it may be lower depending on the parties' bargaining power.

Minimum threshold on claims (de minimis clauses)

The common law places no lower limit on the amount for which one party can bring a claim against another. The parties may want to limit this in contract to avoid the hassle and cost of having to administer a low value claim. For example:

The Seller shall not be liable for a Claim unless the value of that Claim is equal to or exceeds £[x].

The minimum threshold is usually in the region of 1% of the purchase price of a Target.

Minimum aggregate threshold on claims

Parties may also/instead include a minimum claim threshold that applies to *aggregated* claims. This provides slightly better protection for an injured party. For instance, if the minimum threshold were set at £10,000, a party would not be able to pursue claims worth £9,000, even if there are ten such claims. The "aggregation" element of the clause would change the position and enable them to do so, as all the claims combined would amount to more than £10,000. For example:

The Seller shall not be liable for a Claim unless the sum of such Claim together with any connected Claims exceeds £[x].

Buyers would want to ensure that the minimum/maximum thresholds apply only to claims for warranties (not indemnities). This is because the point of indemnities is to enable buyers to claim *pound for pound* payment where a risk covered by those indemnities materialises. Sellers with strong bargaining power are unlikely to agree however.

Time limits

Under the Limitation Act 1980, contractual claims must be bought within 6 years of the date of the relevant breach (12 years for claims relating to deeds). The parties may however wish to depart from this default position by contractually agreeing to different limitation periods (their ability to do so will depend on their bargaining power). The parties may also want to set out the procedure under which claims must be brought, thus ensuring the position of both parties remains clear. For instance:

The Seller shall not be liable for a Claim unless it receives written notice from the Buyer summarising in reasonable detail the nature of the Claim (in so far as it is known to the Buyer) and, as far as is reasonably practicable, an estimate of the amount claimed:

(a) In the case of a Claim made under the Tax Warranties or Tax Indemnities, within the period of 7 years commencing on the Completion Date; and

(b) In any other case, on or before the last day of the period of three years commencing on the Completion Date.

Standard time limits typically agreed by parties are:

- 2-3 years (from the end of the accounting period in which completion occurred) for breaches of warranties and indemnities that do not relate to the target's tax liabilities; and

- 6-7 years for tax indemnities and tax warranties (as this covers the period during which HMRC could bring a claim against the target, which in turn would affect the new *owner* of the target).

Double recovery

If the buyer is insured for a particular loss that also happens to be covered by one of the seller's warranties, it would be unfair if the buyer could claim from both the insurance company and the seller (and consequently recover twice for the same loss). Similarly, if a tax investigation results in HMRC suing the target for damages, the buyer could theoretically claim against the seller for (1) breach of the tax warranties; and (2) breach of warranties that no litigation is pending/has commenced. Double recovery clauses make sure that this type of scenario can be avoided. For instance:

The Buyer shall not be entitled to recover damages, or obtain payment, reimbursement, restitution or indemnity more than once in respect of the same loss, shortfall, damage, deficiency, breach or other event or circumstance.

This is however somewhat of a moot point, as the common law serves to restrict double recovery. We have only included it for completeness as it can come up on the LPC and you need to understand its purpose.

"Boilerplate" Clauses

By "boilerplate" clauses, we simply mean standard clauses that are commonly found in contracts and require little or no amendment. You must consider the connotations of these clauses in the context of exam question scenarios.

Entire Agreement

> **Entire Agreement clause:** clause stating that only the terms contained within the contract apply to the agreement and thus any previous negotiations or oral statements that are not recorded in the contract do not apply or bind the parties.

Entire Agreement clauses are typically made up of four elements, as set out below.

1. This Agreement constitutes the entire agreement between the parties and supersedes any previous discussions and/or agreements reached between the parties in relation to the subject matter of this Agreement.

2. Each party acknowledges and agrees that in entering into this Agreement it has not relied on, and shall have no remedy in respect of, any statement, representation, undertaking or warranty, whether oral or in writing, save as expressly set out in this Agreement.

3. Each party acknowledges and agrees that the only remedy available to it for breach of this Agreement shall be for breach of contract under the terms of this Agreement.

4. Nothing in this clause shall limit or exclude liability for fraud.

The forth element is a "carve out" for fraud. It clarifies that the parties are *not* attempting to exclude liability for fraud in the entire agreement clause. Thomas Witter Ltd v TBP Industries Ltd suggested that if this fourth element is not present, then the whole clause would be invalid. This is on the basis that the clause would effectively be attempting to exclude liability for fraud, which is deemed unreasonable under the Misrepresentation Act 1967. However, the case of Grimstead v McGarrigan suggests that the carve out for fraud may *not* be necessary, and in any event, the buyer may be estopped from claiming misrepresentation. The law in this area is therefore somewhat uncertain.

Exclusion of rights of third parties

Under the Contracts (Rights of Third Parties) Act 1999, certain individuals/companies may acquire rights under a contract even if they were not parties to the agreement. To prevent this from happening, many contracts include a clause expressly excluding this Act. For example:

No term of this Agreement shall be enforceable under the Contracts (Rights of Third Parties) Act 1999 by a third party.

Specific names of third parties that are intended to have rights under the contract may be expressly included if the parties agree. However, precluding other parties from acquiring rights under the contract removes the risk of one of the parties to the contract becoming bound to perform obligations to an unforeseen counterparty.

Force Majeure

> **Force Majeure clause:** predetermines the allocation of risk and frees each party from liability if specified circumstances beyond the control of the parties arise that prevent either party from fulfilling their obligations. Examples of such circumstances include strikes, riots, wars, or "acts of God" (including hurricanes, floods or volcanic eruptions).

Note that if an event outside the control of the parties would make fulfilment of the contract more expensive (but not impossible), this would not automatically qualify as an event of force majeure Blyth & Co v Richard Turpin & Co. However, it has become increasingly common for parties to expressly agree that such events constitute an event of force majeure.

When drafting a force majeure clause, you must consider:

- How/when does the party seeking to rely on the force majeure clause give notice to the other party?
- Should the other party be on a duty to mitigate the circumstances?
- Must the parties pay any balance due for goods/services received?
- How long should the period during which the force majeure applies last? When should obligations resume/be discharged?

Neither party is responsible for any failure to perform its obligations under this contract if it is prevented from performing those obligations by an event of Force Majeure. Where an event of Force Majeure has occurred, the party prevented from performing its obligations must immediately notify the other party giving full particulars of the event and how it has affected its ability to perform its obligations. Upon completion of the event of Force Majeure the party affected must as soon as reasonably practical recommence the performance of its obligations. If the event of Force Majeure has not ceased within 12 months the parties are discharged from any further obligations under the contract. This clause does not relieve the parties from liabilities that arose before the occurrence of the Force Majeure event.

Defined term: "Force Majeure" means: acts of God (including but not limited to fires, explosions, earthquakes, drought, tidal waves and floods); acts or threats of terrorism; war; riots; and strikes.

Notice

A party may under certain circumstances need to give notice to another party. For instance, if one party wants to terminate the agreement, they will have to give notice to the other party. Notice clauses set out the details of how the parties have agreed that notice must be served. For instance, a termination clause may state that a party must give 30 days' notice to the other party if it wishes to terminate. That clause may not however set out *how* notice should be given.

Notice clauses set out: (1) the place at which the parties agree that notice is to be served; (2) the agreed method of service; and (3) the time at which any notice is *deemed* to be served.

Any notice required to be given under this Agreement shall be in writing and may be delivered personally, by e-mail or by first class post to the registered business address of the recipient. Any notice given shall be deemed to have been received: (1) if delivered personally, at the time of delivery; (2) if sent by email, on the day of transmission provided it is sent during business hours on a business day, otherwise on the next business day; or (3) if sent by post, two business days after the date of posting, not including the date on which notice was posted.

Governing law and jurisdiction

A governing law clause sets out which law applies to (and therefore governs) the agreement. A jurisdiction clause sets out the jurisdiction in which any dispute arising out of the contract should be heard. Note that the applicable law does not have to be the law of the chosen jurisdiction (e.g. if the governing law is German but the chosen jurisdiction is England and Wales, the case would be decided by the courts of England and Wales under German law).

The parties irrevocably agree that the courts of England and Wales shall have exclusive jurisdiction to settle any claim or dispute arising out of this Agreement.

This Agreement shall be governed by and construed in accordance with German law.

Severance

A severance clause tries to ensure that if any *part* of the agreement is declared to be illegal, invalid or unenforceable, that part will automatically sever from the agreement. This effectively safeguards the validity of the remaining parts of the agreement.

If any provision of this Agreement shall be found by any court to be invalid or unenforceable, such invalidity or unenforceability shall not affect the remaining provisions of this agreement. The remaining provisions shall remain in full effect. The parties agree that should a provision be severed, it shall be substituted by an enforceable provision that achieves to the greatest possible extent the same effect as would have been achieved by the severed provision.

Non-assignment

As mentioned earlier, a non-assignment clause prohibits one party from assigning their rights and obligations under the contract to another party. For example:

Neither party shall be entitled to assign or sub-contract this Agreement or any part of this Agreement to any person.

Do not confuse non-assignment with change of control: change of control clauses relate to the owner/parent company of a party to the contract. A non-assignment clause cannot be invoked following the share sale of a company that is a party to a contract that contains such a clause. This is because any rights/obligations under that contract will *remain* with that company (no assignment has occurred); the *owner* of that company will simply have changed hands. If the company that was sold attempts to subsequently assign the contract however, then the third party could terminate.

Conditions Precedent

You may be required to identify a conditions precedent clause or draft one in accordance with your client's instructions. As explained earlier, conditions precedent are conditions that must be fulfilled before full performance under a contract becomes due. For example:

This Agreement is subject to the Buyer acquiring all the necessary licenses and the parties receiving clearance from the relevant competition authorities.

Restrictive Covenants

Restrictive covenants are contractual clauses that restrict the seller from taking certain action following an acquisition. They are designed to protect the buyer from the seller taking certain action that could adversely impact the operations and profitability of the newly acquired target. Restrictive covenants must be reasonable for the protection of a buyer's legitimate business interests. If they are unreasonable (i.e. they are more restrictive than is commercially necessary), then they may be deemed invalid by a court. In particular, when drafting restrictive covenants, remember that they must be reasonable in:

- **Geographical scope:** restrictive covenants must only apply to territories in which the buyer/target operate. For instance, if the buyer and target only operate in the UK, it would most likely be unreasonable to restrict the seller from operating in the US (this would be unnecessary to protect the buyer's legitimate business interests).

- **Business scope:** restrictive covenants should only relate to the type of business undertaken by the buyer/target. For instance, if the target is a sandwich shop, it would be unreasonable to prevent the seller from setting up an IT company.
- **Duration:** restrictive covenants can never be indefinite. They must only last for a reasonable period of time (i.e. long enough to protect the buyer's legitimate interests).

No specific guidelines as to what is reasonable exist. Reasonableness will depend on the particular clause and circumstances.

Non-compete Agreements

> **Non-compete Agreement:** a promise from the seller that if the deal goes ahead, the seller will not start up a similar business and emerge as a competitor of the business being acquired. Such agreements will usually apply for a limited period of time (typically 3 years) and/or apply only to regions in which the business being acquired already operates.

The Seller covenants with the Buyer that it will not carry on or be employed by any business which would be in competition with the Buyer and/or any of the Buyer's subsidiaries in [*geographical location of the buyer/target*] at any time during the period of [*number*] years beginning on the Completion Date.

Non-solicit clauses

> **Non-solicit clause:** a contractual promise from a seller to a buyer not to approach and attempt to poach, for instance, certain key employees, suppliers, distributors or customers of the newly purchased company for a given time period or in a particular jurisdiction.

The Seller covenants with the Buyer that it will not deal with or seek the custom of any person who is a client of the Buyer or any of its subsidiaries at the Completion Date (or was a client of the Target in the 12 month period immediately preceding that date) at any time during the period of [*number*] years beginning on the Completion Date.

The Seller covenants with the Buyer that it will not at any time during the period of [*number*] years beginning on the Completion Date offer employment to or enter into a contract for the services of any person who at the time of the offer, and was at the Completion Date, an employee of the Target or any of its subsidiaries.

Confidentiality Agreements / Non-disclosure Agreements

> **Confidentiality Agreement/Non-Disclosure Agreement (NDA):** Non-disclosure Agreements (or "Confidentiality Agreements") are designed to restrict and control one party's access to and use of sensitive/confidential information that relates to another party. A seller will typically require a potential purchaser to sign an NDA before granting that potential purchaser access to a data room. This is to ensure that the potential purchaser is deterred from using or disclosing sensitive, confidential information about the seller/target that is discovered during the due diligence process.

Each party undertakes that it shall not at any time disclose to any person any confidential information concerning the business, affairs, clients, suppliers or customers of the other party, unless the disclosure is made: (a) to employees, officers or advisors who agree to comply with this clause and need to know such information for the purposes of carrying out that party's obligations under this agreement; or (b) to comply with the law or a court order.

Warranties and Indemnities

Warranties

For the reasons discussed in the *Warranties* section of the *Acquisitions* chapter of the *Business Law* module in this handbook, buyers may require warranties from sellers. You may have to identify/draft/explain warranties in an exam. Examples include:

The Seller warrants that it owns full title to [*name of property/land*].

The Seller warrants that it will discharge in full the mortgage attached to [*name of property/land*] by the Completion Date.

The Seller warrants that there is no litigation against the target, including actual, pending or threatened litigation.

The Seller warrants that it will settle any outstanding litigation claims by the Completion Date.

The Seller warrants that the target's pension scheme is fully paid up.

Indemnities

Buyers may require indemnities from the seller against, for instance, damages that may arise as a result of pending litigation, fines that may be imposed by HMRC/environmental agencies, or past breaches of contracts/covenants by the target company. Remember to ensure indemnities are given in favour of the *buyer* (not the target). For example:

The Seller shall indemnify the Buyer from and against all liabilities, cash, expenses, damages and losses (including any direct, indirect or consequential losses, loss of profits and loss of reputation) suffered or incurred by the Buyer arising out of or in connection to...[*insert issue or scenario here*].

Termination

You may have to draft or amend clauses setting out the circumstances under which one or more parties can terminate a contract. Some of these are considered below. Note that a force majeure clause may be invoked to terminate an agreement (depending on its wording). It has been dealt with above, so is not listed again below.

Insolvency/administration

Companies do not generally want to continue supplying goods/services to another party once that other party is experiencing financial difficulties. This is because once a company becomes insolvent, it may not have enough money left to fully repay its creditors (including companies to which it owes money for goods/services). Parties will therefore want the freedom to terminate an agreement if a counterparty becomes insolvent (or insolvency becomes likely).

Either party may terminate this Agreement immediately by notice in writing if any corporate action, legal proceedings or other procedure or step is taken in relation to the appointment of a liquidator, receiver, administrator, administrative receiver or other similar officer in respect of either party or any of its assets.

Breach of contract

Parties will generally want the freedom to terminate an agreement if a counterparty commits a breach of contract. Such breaches could include non-performance of that counterparty's contractual obligations, non-payment (or very late payment) for goods/services received, or the provision of sub-standard products/services (for instance, goods that are not fit for purpose/not of satisfactory quality).

Parties will want this ability to terminate, as such breaches can indicate that the counterparty may be experiencing financial difficulties and/or the counterparty cannot be relied upon to provide the goods/service expected from it. However, parties are likely to agree that only *material* breaches of contract can result in termination (to prevent one party taking advantage of a minor breach, simply to relinquish itself of contractual obligations) and may insist on the inclusion of a grace period to enable the offending party to rectify a breach.

Either party may terminate this Agreement immediately by notice in writing if the other party commits a breach of this Agreement (and this breach, if capable of remedy, has not been remedied within [x] days of the non-breaching party giving the breaching party notice in writing to remedy the breach).

Change of control

> **Change of control clause/break clause:** such clauses can enable parties that are contracted to work with a company to terminate the contract without incurring any liability for breach of contract if control of the company changes hands.

Party A may only have agreed to contract with Party B if Party B has a parent company that has demonstrated willingness to support Party B's contractual obligations if Party B is unable to do so. A change of control clause would enable Party A to terminate the contract if Party B was subsequently sold (i.e. to a new parent company that was unwilling to support Party B's contractual obligations).

The Company may terminate this Agreement immediately by notice in writing if there is a change of control (as defined in section 450 of the Corporation Tax Act 2010) of the Contractor.

Break clause (termination on notice/agreement)

Parties will generally want the ability to terminate a contract without reason, otherwise the obligations would go on indefinitely, giving little scope for the parties to adjust their strategies. The parties would need to agree a notice period that must be given before such termination could take effect, and the method by which counterparties should be notified of the intention to terminate.

Either party may terminate this Agreement by giving to the other party not less than 90 days' prior notice in writing.

Consequences of termination

If a party terminates in a manner that is not permitted by the contract, it may have to pay damages to the counterparty for breach of contract. Certain accrued obligations may also remain in place post-termination (e.g. payment for goods already delivered), whilst new obligations may arise (e.g. destroy confidential documents, refund deposits etc.). It is important to expressly set out the consequences of termination in accordance with the contract so as to avoid confusion/argument at a later stage.

The termination of this Agreement for any reason shall be without prejudice to the rights and duties of the parties accrued prior to termination.

Survival clauses

After termination, certain clauses must continue to operate in order to protect the parties' interests. This includes the clause stating which clauses remain operational post-termination (obviously). In particular:

- **Confidentiality:** this must remain operational so as to prevent one party revealing sensitive information about a counterparty.
- **Governing Law and Jurisdiction:** these clauses should remain in place in case the parties need to sue for breaches of the contractual obligations before the parties ceased to be bound by those obligations.
- **Post-termination obligations:** any obligations (if relevant) upon one or more parties to take certain action post-termination, for instance the obligation to refund sums received in respect of goods/services that were not provided by a contractual party as a result of the termination. One party may be required to remove hardware/equipment or reinstate a premises to its original state. When drafting such a clause, consider: within which time period must the action take place? Who will pay? Must reasonable access be granted by one party to its premises/land?

Dealing With Common Issues

This section gives examples of how you could apply the principles above to specific issues. Remember, you can usually pick up a majority of drafting marks if what you write achieves the required purpose. Unless you are told otherwise, you do not need to memorise entire clauses. This section simply gives suggestions; do not neglect examples you are given throughout the LPC.

Litigation

The seller will want to limit the warranty to *material* litigation that is *within its existing knowledge*. The buyer will want the seller to warrant that no litigation (actual, pending or threatened) is outstanding, as if the target is sued, this will diminish the profits that the seller will make from the target's activities. This is because the *target* company will have to pay any claims, not the seller (even if the issues arose whilst the target was under the seller's control). The buyer will also want the warranty to cover arbitration, mediation and expert determination, as these proceedings can also be very costly. Below is a potential compromise:

As far as the seller is aware (having made all reasonable enquiries of Specified Persons) the Target is not engaged in any Material litigation, arbitration, mediation or expert determination, whether actual or pending.

"Material" means claims that are equal to or greater than £30,000 in value.

If there is actual or pending litigation, the seller could still give the above warranty, so long as it also discloses against the warranty in the contract. If the seller does make such a disclosure, the buyer would want an indemnity from the seller to cover any claims that the target is required to settle post-completion:

The Seller indemnifies the Buyer against any existing or future claims brought against the Target that relate to the Target's activities whilst under the Seller's control.

Employee dismissals

If employees have been dismissed by the target, the buyer will want to ensure that the dismissed employees will not have cause to bring a claim against the target in the future. The buyer will also want to be indemnified for any losses incurred if such a situation does arise.

The Seller warrants that it followed the relevant statutory procedures when dismissing the employee.

The Seller indemnifies the Buyer against any claim brought by the Dismissed Employee against the Target.

Tax/pension scheme liability

If there are outstanding liabilities (i.e. the seller has disclosed against warranties stating otherwise), the buyer could request further information in order to consider whether the outstanding liability is a real issue. If so, it could request a cheaper purchase price or even walk away from the deal.

Stock

If the purchase price takes into account stock currently held by the target, the buyer will want some assurances as to the condition of the stock. The buyer may want the seller to warrant that the stock is in "excellent condition" and is "capable of being sold at its full current list price". However, the seller will likely feel that goes too far. What qualifies as "excellent" condition? How can the seller know whether consumers will be willing to pay the full list price in the future? Below is perhaps a greater compromise:

As far as the Seller is aware (having made all reasonable enquiries) all of the stock owned by Target is in satisfactory condition and is suitable for sale.

Book debts

Book debts – i.e. money owed to the target company – may constitute a substantial asset (if a lot of money is owed). For this reason, the buyer will want to know that the value of book debts stated in the Target's accounts is accurate and that the book debts are collectible. The buyer could require the seller to warrant that it will use its reasonable endeavours to collect all book debts that are due, within an agreed time frame.

Plant, machinery and vehicles

If the buyer is purchasing equipment that must pass certain safety standards, it may require an indemnity from the seller against any costs incurred in ensuring that the equipment meets those safety standards. The seller could ensure that only costs "necessarily" or "reasonably" incurred are covered, to ensure that the buyer shops around for a reasonable price and only requires reimbursement for costs relating to improvements/repairs that are legally required.

The Seller indemnifies the Buyer against any costs necessarily incurred to ensure the Vehicles pass the Relevant Tests.

"Vehicles" means the fleet of vans listed out in Schedule 1 to this Agreement. "Relevant Tests" means the tests that the equipment is required to pass so as to meet the safety standards required by English law.

Accounts

The buyer will rely heavily on the target's financial accounts in order to value the target and ascertain whether the purchase price is likely to give a satisfactory return on investment. The buyer would therefore want the seller to warrant that the target's accounts for the past few years are "accurate". However, when auditors prepare accounts, they are only required to ensure that those accounts are "true and fair" CA 06 s. 393. Sellers would therefore want to avoid giving a warranty that their accounts are "accurate", as this is not the standard required by law; their auditors will only have ensured that the accounts are "true and fair", which is a lower standard. For this reason, "true and fair" is generally used instead of "accurate" in practice. Sellers will also want to limit the warranty to cover only accounts from the past two or three years, i.e. the accounts that are most relevant to the buyer.

The Accounts for each of the last two accounting periods show a true and fair view of the state of affairs of the Target.

Suppliers, customers and employees of the target company

Change of control clauses can enable third parties/employees to terminate their contract with a company if the owner of that company changes. Buyers will therefore want assurances that (1) key parties do not plan on terminating important contracts with the target once it has been taken over; and (2) the target is not too reliant on only a small group of suppliers/customers (as this will place the target at greater risk if change of control clauses are exercised).

No senior employee of the Target will leave their employment as a result of the acquisition of the Target by the Buyer.

Not more than 10 per cent of Target's turnover has in the previous two financial years (ending on the Accounts Date) been attributable to any single client and as far as the seller is aware (having made all reasonable enquiries) no person who was a client or supplier of Target at the Accounts Date has since ceased to contract, or intends to cease contracting, with Target.

- 10 per cent may be a reasonable figure, as this can contribute significantly to a company's profit/input. Similarly, two financial years seems to be a fair limit (any longer could be irrelevant and thus unnecessarily onerous on the seller). Make practical suggestions in the exam. If a supplier has threatened to invoke a change of control clause, consider how important that supplier is to the business and whether finding alternative suppliers is a viable option.

- Remember to distinguish between non-assignment and change of control clauses. Whilst a share sale will trigger a change of control clause, it will not generally trigger a non-assignment clause as contracts remain with the target after a share sale (and therefore do not need to be assigned).

Execution Clauses

Certain types of contract must be executed in different ways in order to properly bind the parties. The manner of execution will depend on whether the parties are individuals or companies, whether the agreement is a simple contract or deed, and the jurisdiction(s) of incorporation of the contractual parties. Foreign companies must execute in accordance with the law in their own territories. If a contract is not executed properly, it may not be binding (subject to the common law rule of estoppel). In an exam, you may need to draft execution clauses or identify which execution clauses are the most appropriate for certain types of contracts.

Simple contracts

A simple contract (i.e. a contract that is not a deed) is binding from the date that the contracting parties *intend* for it to come into effect, which is typically the moment at which the parties sign the agreement. There is no requirement for the signature to be witnessed.

Execution of simple contracts by individuals

Each party to the contract will sign separate, identical copies of the same document. The signed copies together form a single binding agreement.

Signed by [*name of individual*]: *Signature of individual*

Execution of simple contracts by companies

A simple contract may be effectively executed by the signature of a person authorised to contract on a company's behalf; this is usually (but not always) a director. In most cases the directors will have authority (usually in the Articles) to bind the company in contract. Note that simple contracts and deeds can be signed *by* a company or *on behalf of* a company.

Signed *by* a company

Where a simple contract is signed *by* a company, this means that the company itself is taken to have signed the agreement. There are three options for this:

1. **Affix the company seal in the presence of two directors or one director and a company secretary, both of whom will sign to evidence that they were present.**

    Executed by affixing the common seal of [*name of company*] in the presence of:

    Signature of director   *Signature of director/secretary*

    Director   Director/Secretary

2. **Signed by two authorised signatories.**

   Signed by [*name of company*] acting by [*name of authorised signatory 1*], a director and [*name of authorised signatory 2*], a [*director/secretary*]:

   Signature of director   *Signature of director/secretary*

   Director   Director/Secretary

3. **Signed by a director in the presence of a witness (who will also sign).**

   Signed by [*name of company*] acting by [*name of* director], a director, in the presence of [*name of witness*]:

   Signature of director   *Signature of witness*

   Director   Name, address and occupation of witness

Signed *on behalf of* a company

Where a simple contract is signed *on behalf of* a company, this means that the company has authorised a person to sign on its behalf. In such circumstances, the company will be bound in the same way as if the signature had been given "by" the company:

Signed by [*name of director*] for and on behalf of [*name of* company]:

Signature of director

Director

Execution of simple contracts under power of attorney

> **Power of Attorney:** a Power of Attorney is a legal document that lets the person/company delegating the power (the "donor") appoint one or more people (known as "attorneys") to help them make decisions or make decisions on their behalf. The "attorney" may sign his or her own name or the donor's name.

Signed by [*name of attorney*] acting for [*name of donor*] under a power of attorney dated [*date*]:

Signature of attorney

Attorney for [*name of donor*]

Deeds

Deeds are required by law in certain circumstances, for instance where real estate is transferred, powers of attorney are granted and binding agreements are made for no consideration (remember, simple contracts will only bind the parties if consideration exists). Deeds have a longer statutory limitation period than simple contracts: 12 years. Note that a deed may instead take effect as a simple contract if the requirements for the execution of a deed are not met in full, but the (lesser) requirements for a simple contract are satisfied.

Execution of deeds by individuals

Deeds must be in writing and will typically be executed in the presence of a witness.

Signed as a deed by [*name of individual*] in the presence of [*name of witness*]:

Signature of individual   *Signature of witness*

                                    Name, address and occupation of witness

Execution of deeds by companies

A deed must be *expressed* to be signed as a deed. Deeds may be effectively executed in the following ways:

1. **Signed by two authorised signatories.**

   Signed as a deed by [*name of company*] acting by [*name of authorised signatory 1*], a director and [*name of authorised signatory 2*], a [*director/secretary*]:

   Signature of director   *Signature of director/secretary*

   Director   Director/Secretary

2. **Signed by a director in the presence of a witness (who will also sign).**

   Signed as a deed by [*name of company*] acting by [*name of director*], a director, in the presence of [*name of witness*]:

   Signature of director   *Signature of witness*

   Director   Name, address and occupation of witness

Execution of deeds under power of attorney

Signed as a deed by [*name of attorney*] acting for [*name of donor*] under a power of attorney dated [*date*] in the presence of [*name of witness*]:

Signature of attorney   *Signature of witness*

Attorney for [*name of donor*]   Name, address and occupation of witness

Foreign companies

Signed *by* a foreign company

A foreign company may execute contracts by (a) affixing its common seal; or (b) by any manner permitted by the laws of its territory of incorporation.

Signed *on behalf of* a foreign company

Contracts may be executed *on behalf of* a foreign company using the following execution clause:

Signed on behalf of [*name of company*], a company incorporated in [*jurisdiction*], by [*name of authorised signatory*] being a person who, in accordance with the laws of that territory, is acting under the authority of the company:

Signature of attorney   *Signature of witness*
Attorney for [*name of donor*]   Name, address and occupation of witness

Share Buybacks

A company under certain circumstances can purchase back its own shares from investors that have previously purchased that company's shares (either from the company directly or through the capital markets). Completing a share buyback may improve the marketability of companies, as it can indicate that the company has generated sufficient retained earnings. Buybacks can also enable shareholders (including venture capital funds) to offload their shareholding in circumstances where there would not otherwise be a market for their shares. "Share buyback" is a term that covers both an "own share purchase" and a "redemption of shares". The procedure for undertaking a share buyback will depend on whether:

(a) The shares being bought back are *redeemable* shares, i.e. shares that were issued with rights entitling the company to "redeem" (buyback) those shares at a later stage; and

(b) The own share purchase/redemption of shares is to be funded using retained profits, a fresh issue of shares or capital.

> **Own share purchase:** the buyback of shares *other than* redeemable shares.

> **Redemption of shares:** "redemption" in this context means the buyback of *redeemable* shares.

CA 06 s. 690 sets out the circumstances under which companies can buyback ordinary shares, whereas CA 06 s. 684 covers the buyback of redeemable shares. If the correct procedure is not followed, the own share purchase or redemption of shares is void and the company/the directors involved will have committed a criminal offence CA 06 s. 658(2).

Note that share buybacks do not constitute "substantial property transactions" for the purposes of the Companies Act 2006, so the provisions of CA 06 s. 190 do not apply in this context. This is because CA s. 192(a) provides a carve out for directors with an interest in the shares being bought back, as those directors would be acting in their capacity as *shareholders*.

Off-market own share purchases

The LPC focuses on "off-market" own share purchases. An "off-market" own share purchase involves buying back shares otherwise than through a recognised investment exchange CA 06 s. 693(2)(a). Therefore all share buybacks conducted by private companies will be "off-market" (as private companies cannot sell - and thus cannot buyback - their shares through recognised investment exchanges such as the London Stock Exchange).

For off-market purchases, the buyback contract must be approved in advance by ordinary resolution CA 06 s. 694(2)(a) or must provide that no shares may be bought back until its terms have been authorised by ordinary resolution CA 06 s. 694(2)(b). In addition, the contract must be available for inspection at the company's registered office for not less than 15 days prior to the general meeting and at the meeting itself CA 06 s. 696(2)(b), or in the case of a written resolution it must be sent out with the written resolution CA 06 s. 696(2)(a).

Funding a Share Buyback

1. **Distributable profits**

   Companies can use distributable profits to fund buybacks CA 06 s. 692(2)(a)(i) and redemptions (the buyback of redeemable shares) CA 06 s. 687(2)(a).

2. **Fresh issue of shares**

   Companies can use the proceeds from a fresh share issue to fund buybacks CA 06 s. 692(2)(a)(ii) and redemptions CA 06 s. 687(2)(b). This involves the company issuing new shares in exchange for capital, then using that capital to buy back other shares.

3. **Cash**

   If authorised by their Articles to do so, companies can use cash to fund buybacks, up to an amount in a financial year not exceeding the lower of £15,000 or the value of 5% of its share capital CA 06 s. 692(1)(b).

4. **Capital**

   Private companies CA 06 s. 709(1) can use capital to fund buybacks CA 06 s. 692(1) and redemptions CA 06 s. 687(1). However, capital may *only* be used once *all* distributable profits/profits from a fresh issue of shares have been exhausted CA 06 s. 710. The amount of capital that a company is able to use is referred to as the "permissible capital payment". There are even stricter rules governing the use of funds in the share *premium* account in the context of a buyback/redemption.

Using funds in the share premium account

The funds in the share *premium* account are classed as "capital" and may only be used to fund a share buyback/redemption if the aforementioned CA 06 s. 710 criteria are satisfied *and* the following additional criteria are fulfilled (these are set out in CA 06 s. 692(4) for an own share purchase and CA 06 s. 687(5) for a redemption of shares:

1. The purchase is being funded out of a fresh issue of shares;

2. The shares being bought back had to have been originally issued at a premium themselves;

3. The shares being bought back must be bought back at a premium.

Capital Redemption Reserve

The way in which a share buyback is recorded in a company's balance sheet is dealt with in the *Share buyback/Capital Redemption Reserve* section of the *Business Accounts* chapter in the *Taxation & Accounts* module.

Calculating Changes in Voting Rights

After a share buyback, the percentage voting rights of the remaining shareholders will change. You may have to calculate these percentages in an exam. Consider the following example:

> **Ireland Ltd has 1.1 million £1 ordinary shares in issue. The shareholding is split up as follows:**
>
> - **Ali:** 385,000 shares (35% shareholding)
> - **Maive:** 220,000 shares (20% shareholding)
> - **Sarah:** 25% shareholding, **Clodagh:** 6% shareholding, **Jake:** 6% shareholding
> - **Employees:** 8% shareholding
>
> Calculate how the following scenarios would affect these percentages and whether the changes would have any significance.
>
> 1. **Ali sells 100,000 shares to Maive:**
>   - 100,000 shares = 9.09% of the total shareholding (100,000/1.1 million shares = 9.09%)
>   - Maive therefore would have 29.09% in total. This would enable her to block special resolutions, as the remaining shareholders would be unable to accumulate 75% in a vote.
>
> 2. **Alternatively, Ireland Ltd buys back 100,000 of Ali's shares:**
>   - If Ireland Ltd buys back Ali's shares, then all existing shareholders will see an increase in their voting rights. This is because post-buy back, Ali's shares will be cancelled CA 06 s. 706(6), leaving fewer shares (1 million) in circulation.
>   - Maive's shareholding would increase to 22% (220,000/1 million shares = 22%), which would not enable her to single-handedly block special resolutions. This is because the other shareholders could together carry 78% of the vote.

Procedure Plans

The below procedure plans are referring to "off-market" share buybacks, as these are typically the focus of the LPC.

General meeting procedure plan for a buyback of *non*-redeemable shares out of capital

In your exam, you may be asked to set out the procedure for buying back non-redeemable shares (e.g. ordinary shares) either out of retained profits or out of capital. **In the below example, the elements of the procedure plan that must be added *only* in the case of a capital purchase have been highlighted in purple.**

Board Meeting 1

1. **Who calls the meeting?**

   Any director can call the meeting MA 9(1).

2. **Notice**

   Reasonable notice must be given Browne v La Trinidad.

3. **Quorum**

   The default position is that two or more serving directors must be present, unless the directors have agreed to a higher quorum (by board resolution) MA 11(2) or the company's Articles set a higher quorum. However, if the company has only one director (and the Articles do not require it to have more than one director), the quorum will be one director MA 7(2). Directors with a personal interest in the outcome of resolutions will not count towards the quorum when those resolutions are voted on MA 14. State who is present and who is in attendance, then conclude on the facts whether the quorum has been met.

4. **Disclosure**

   Directors' duties must be considered. Directors that own shares that will be purchased as part of the share buyback should disclose their interests in the buyback contract in accordance with CA 06 s. 177(1) in *both* board meetings CA s. 177(6)(b).

5. Agenda

(a) Report on the proposed purchase of the company's own shares. Agree the proposed terms of the buyback contract (e.g. the price that will be offered to buy back shares).

(b) Call a general meeting to move an ordinary resolution to approve a buyback of shares and the proposed terms of the buyback contract, as required by CA 06 s. 694(2)(a).

(c) Approve the form of the special resolution required to approve payment out of capital CA 06 s. 716(1).

(d) Call a general meeting CA 06 s. 302. The directors must:

- Approve form of notice of the general meeting. This notice should include:
    (i) The time, date and location of the meeting CA 06 s. 311.
    (ii) The precise wording of any special resolutions that will be voted on in the general meeting CA 06 s. 283(6).
    (iii) A statement that a member may appoint a proxy CA 06 s. 325(1).
- Direct company secretary to give notice of the general meeting in accordance with CA 06 s. 308. It should be given to shareholders CA 06 s. 310(1)(a), directors CA 06 s. 310(1)(b) and (if appointed) the company's auditors CA 06 s. 502(2).
- It is also good practice (but not required) to set out the precise wording of any ordinary resolution(s) to be proposed at the general meeting.

6. Voting

The board must agree by board resolution (either unanimous decision or simple majority on a show of hands) on the issues set out in the agenda MA 7(1) + MA 8. If there is deadlock, the Chairman has the casting vote MA 13. Directors with an interest in the transaction *can* vote at this stage, as the matters covered in the meeting are purely procedural.

7. Close board meeting

The board meeting will "close" (not "adjourn") as the proposed buyback contract must be made available for inspection for at least 15 *clear* days before the general meeting takes place CA 06 s. 696(2)(b).

Post Board Meeting 1 Matters

Draw up minutes

Draw up minutes from the board meeting and keep these for at least 10 years CA 06 s. 248(1).

In-between Meetings

1. Buyback contract

The proposed terms of the buyback must be set out in the proposed buyback contract CA 06 s. 694(1). The proposed buyback contract must then be made available for inspection for at least 15 *clear* days before the general meeting takes place and must also be put on display at the meeting CA 06 s. 696(2)(b).

2. Prepare and execute (sign) directors' solvency statement

Before shares can be bought back out of capital, directors must provide a solvency statement confirming that the company is solvent and will continue to be so for 12 months following the buyback CA 06 s. 714(3). The statement must be made no longer than 1 week before the special resolution is passed CA 06 s. 716(2).

Copies must be made available to shareholders at the general meeting (or sent with a written resolution if this process is used) CA 06 s. 718 and made available for inspection at the company's registered office for 5 weeks after the resolution approving the buyback is passed CA 06 s. 720. If the statement contains inaccuracies, the directors responsible may face criminal sanctions.

3. Commission auditor's report

The company's auditors must produce a statement confirming that nothing unreasonable has been included in the directors' solvency statement CA 06 s. 714(6). Copies must be made available to shareholders at the general meeting CA 06 s. 718 and made available for inspection at the company's registered office for 5 weeks after the resolution approving the buyback is passed CA 06 s. 720.

4. Companies House

Give notice to Companies House of the place at which the directors' solvency statement and auditor's report are to be made available for inspection CA 06 s. 720(3).

File a copy of the directors' solvency statement and auditor's report CA 06 s. 719(4).

General Meeting

1. Open general meeting

2. Notice

The default notice that must be given for a general meeting is 14 days CA 06 s. 307(1). However, CA 06 s. 360(1)+(2) clarifies that in this context, 14 days means 14 "clear" days, so you do not count the day on which notice is given and the day of the general meeting itself as part of the 14 days.

Short notice would not generally be of use in this context, as the general meeting cannot be held until the buyback contract has been available for inspection for at least 15 days.

3. Quorum

The default position is that two or more serving directors must be present, unless the directors have agreed to a higher quorum (by board resolution) MA 11(2) or the company's Articles set a higher quorum. However, if the company has only one director (and the Articles do not require it to have more than one director), the quorum will be one director MA 7(2). Directors with a personal interest in the outcome of resolutions will not count towards the quorum when those resolutions are voted on MA 14.

4. Agenda

(a) Place the proposed buyback contract on display at the meeting CA 06 s. 696(2)(b).

(b) Place the directors' solvency statement and the auditor's report on display CA 06 s. 718(2)(b).

(c) Propose and (shareholders) vote on the resolutions required to approve the share buyback.

5. Voting

(a) Ordinary resolution to approve the proposed terms of the share buyback contract CA 06 s. 694(2)(a). More than 50% of those voting must approve the decision in accordance with CA 06 s. 282(1).

(b) Special resolution to approve a purchase out of capital CA 06 s. 716(1).

- This must be passed by at least 75% of those attending and entitled to vote CA 06 s. 283(1).

(c) Shareholders (including corporate representatives and proxies) can vote by a show of hands MA 42 unless a poll vote is demanded (in accordance with MA 44).

(d) A shareholder whose shares are being purchased can vote on a show of hands, provided that their vote does not *carry* the resolution (i.e. if the resolution only passes because of their vote, the resolution will be invalid). If a poll vote is demanded, shareholders can only vote in respect of the shares they hold that will *not* be bought back if the resolution is passed CA 06 s. 695(3)+(4).

- Advise interested directors only to vote with the shares that are *not* being purchased if the vote is on a poll and not to vote at all if voting is on a show of hands, as a director's show of hands vote would technically encapsulate all that director's shares (including the ones being sold).

- Note, resolutions would only be ineffective if interested directors exercised their votes in relation to their shares that are being bought back and the resolution would not have been passed had he not done so.

6. Close general meeting

Board Meeting 2

1. Open board meeting

2. Who calls the meeting?

Any director can call the meeting MA 9(1).

3. Notice

Reasonable notice must be given Browne v La Trinidad.

4. Quorum

Same as for board meeting 1.

5. Disclosure

Directors' duties must be considered. Directors that own shares that will be purchased as part of the share buyback should disclose their interests in the buyback contract in accordance with CA 06 s. 177(1) in *both* board meetings s. 177(6)(b).

6. Agenda

(a) Chairman report that the ordinary resolution and special resolution were passed at the general meeting.

(b) Resolve to enter into the contract to buy-back the company's shares. Directors with an interest can attend this meeting but cannot vote or count as part of the quorum when the board decides on whether to enter into the buyback contract and appointing someone to execute the agreement on the company's behalf.

(c) Direct the company secretary to deal with post meeting matters.

7. Voting

The board must agree by board resolution (either unanimous decision or simple majority on a show of hands) on the relevant issues set out in the agenda MA 7(1) + MA 8. If there is deadlock, the Chairman has the casting vote MA 13.

Directors with an interest in the transaction (i.e. directors who hold shares that are being bought back) will not count towards the quorum for, and cannot vote on, the board resolution to enter into the in board meeting 2 (or sign the contract on the company's behalf) MA 14.

8. Sign buyback contract

The board should appoint a corporate representative to sign the buyback contract on the company's behalf CA 06 s. 323 and this appointment should be evidenced in a board minute.

9. Close board meeting

Post Board Meeting 2 Matters

1. **Make the relevant filings at Companies House**
    (a) File a copy of the return using **form SH03** within 28 days of the share buyback CA 06 s. 707(1). This notifies Companies House that the share buyback has taken place.
    (b) File a notice of cancelation of the shares using **form SH06** within 28 days of the share buyback CA 06 s. 708(1).
    (c) File the statement of capital using **form SH19** within 28 days of the share buyback CA 06 s. 708(2).
    (d) File the special resolution within 15 days of it being passed CA 06 s. 30(1).

2. **Notice to creditors**
    (a) Within one week following the resolution approving the payment out of capital, the company must:
    - Publish a notice in the Gazette that the payment out of capital has been approved and that creditors may within 5 weeks apply for an order preventing the payment CA 06 s. 719(1); and
    - Publish a notice in an appropriate national newspaper to the same effect or give notice in writing to that effect to each of its creditors CA 06 s. 719(2).

3. **Draw up minutes**
    (a) Draw up minutes from the general meeting and keep these for at least 10 years CA 06 s. 355(1).
    (b) Draw up minutes from the board meeting and keep these for at least 10 years CA 06 s. 248(1).

4. **Company books/share certificates**
    (a) Amend Register of Members to reflect the changes to the shareholders CA 06 s. 113. If the company is left with only one shareholder, this must also be stated in the Register of Members CA 06 s. 123.
    (b) New share certificates must be issued to remaining shareholders within 2 months and the share certificates relating to the shares bought back must be cancelled CA 06 s. 776 (shares bought back are treated as cancelled CA 06 s. 706).
    (c) Keep a copy of the buyback contract at the company's registered address for 10 years CA 06 s. 702(3).

    The actual share buyback must take place 5-7 weeks after the passing of the special resolution if funded using capital CA 06 s. 723(1), as this is after the period during which creditors have a right to object.

Procedure plan for the buyback of redeemable shares

To recap, only private companies can issue redeemable shares CA 06 s. 684. Redeemable shares are issued with rights entitling the company to redeem them (i.e. buy them back) at the option of that company (or its shareholder) according to a pre-determined formula or price. Remember, redeemable shares can only be redeemed if they are fully paid up CA 06 s. 686(1), meaning that shareholders must have paid the price in full for their redeemable shares. You may need to make this point in an exam.

Procedure

The procedure for buying back redeemable shares is simpler than for non-redeemable shares since no contract for the buyback needs to be approved. Instead, the terms of the redemption are set out in the company's Articles CA 06 s. 685(1). The shareholders will effectively have consented to these terms when originally buying the shares. Remember that only shares that are *issued* as "redeemable" shares may be "redeemed" by the company using this simpler procedure.

When setting out a procedure plan for the buyback of redeemable shares, remember to make the following changes to the above/below procedure plans:

1. **Resolutions**
    - No ordinary resolution is required to approve the buyback contract if the company is funding the purchase using distributable (retained) profits/a fresh issue of shares, so no general meeting/second board meeting will be required.
    - If capital is being used to fund the purchase, then a special resolution will still be required however (meaning a general meeting will also be required) CA 06 s. 716, along with a directors' solvency statement and auditor's report CA s. 714. The rules relating to whether capital *can* be used are the same as those set out in the above *Funding a Share Buyback* section.

2. **Post meeting matters**
    - **Relevant filings at Companies House:** once a buyback of redeemable shares has taken place, Companies House must be notified within one month and a statement of capital must be filed (at Companies House) CA 06 s. 689.
    - **Minutes:** minutes must be drawn up for the relevant meetings and filed, as explained in the above procedure plan. Remember, there will be no general meeting unless the redemption is funded using capital.
    - **Company books/share certificates**: these must be dealt with as explained in the above procedure plan, although there will be no buyback contract to retain at the company's registered address.
    - If capital is used to fund the redemption, then the post meeting matters set out in purple above apply.

Written resolution procedure plan for a buyback of *non*-redeemable shares out of capital

In the below example, the elements of the procedure plan that must be added only in the case of a capital purchase have been highlighted in purple.

Pre-Board Meeting 1

1. **Prepare proposed buyback contract**

2. **Prepare and execute the directors' solvency statement**

    Before shares can be bought back out of capital, directors must provide a solvency statement confirming that the company is solvent and will continue to be so for 12 months following the buyback CA 06 s. 714(3). The statement must be made no longer than 1 week before the special resolution is passed CA 06 s. 716(2). If the statement contains inaccuracies, the directors responsible may face criminal sanctions.

3. **Commission auditor's report**

    The company's auditors must produce a statement confirming that nothing unreasonable has been included in the directors' solvency statement CA 06 s. 714(6). Copies must be sent with the written resolution CA 06 s. 718 and made available for inspection at the company's registered office for 5 weeks after the resolution approving the buyback is passed CA 06 s. 720.

4. **Companies House**

    Give notice to Companies House of the place at which the directors' solvency statement and auditor's report are to be made available for inspection CA 06 s. 720(3).

    File a copy of the directors' solvency statement and auditor's report CA 06 s. 719(4).

Board Meeting 1

1. **Who calls the meeting?**

    Any director can call the meeting MA 9(1).

2. **Notice**

    Reasonable notice must be given Browne v La Trinidad.

3. **Quorum**

    The default position is that two or more serving directors must be present, unless the directors have agreed to a higher quorum (by board resolution) MA 11(2) or the company's Articles set a higher quorum. However, if the company has only one director (and the Articles do not require it to have more than one director), the quorum will be one director MA 7(2). Directors with a personal interest in the outcome of resolutions will not count towards the quorum when those resolutions are voted on MA 14.

    State who is present and who is in attendance, then conclude on the facts whether the quorum has been met.

4. **Disclosure**

    Directors' duties must be considered. Directors that own shares that will be purchased as part of the share buyback should disclose their interests in the buyback contract in accordance with CA 06 s. 177(1) in *both* board meetings CA s. 177(6)(b).

5. **Agenda**

    (a) Propose a written resolution.

    - Directors can do this under CA 06 s. 288(3)(a) and must follow the procedure set out in CA 06 s. 291.

    (b) Approve the form/content of the written resolution document (to be sent out to shareholders).

    - Include an ordinary resolution to approve the contract and a special resolution to approve funding from capital.
    - Attach a copy of the buyback contract to the written resolution (**there is no requirement to display it for 15 days** when using the written resolution procedure) CA 06 s. 696(2)(a).
    - Attach a copy of the directors' solvency statement and auditor's report to the written resolution CA 06 s. 718(2)(a).
    - Include instructions on how to vote CA 06 s. 291(4)(a).
    - State the last date by which votes must be submitted (the lapse date) CA 06 s. 291(4)(b).
    - The default time period before the opportunity to vote will lapse is 28 days CA 06 s. 297(1) but check whether the company's Articles specify a different time period (the time period specified in the Articles will override the default position). Note that the time period is *not* 28 *clear* days, as CA 06 s. 297 is not listed under CA 06 s. 360 (which sets out the provisions to which the "clear day" counting rule applies).

    (c) Resolve to send the resolution to all *eligible* members CA 06 s. 291(2) and the company's auditors CA 06 s. 502(1).

    - "Eligible members" means all shareholders who would be entitled to vote on the resolution(s) on the date on which the written resolution is circulated CA 06 s. 289.
    - If all eligible members are present (e.g. if there is only one shareholder), the written resolution can be approved immediately.
    - Note that a shareholder with an interest in the transaction (i.e. a member who holds shares to which the resolution relates) is not an "eligible" member for these purposes CA 06 s. 695(3).

6. Voting

The board must agree by board resolution (either unanimous decision or simple majority on a show of hands) on the issues set out in the agenda MA 7(1) + MA 8. If there is deadlock, the Chairman has the casting vote MA 13. Directors with an interest in the transaction *can* vote at this stage, as the matters covered in the meeting are purely procedural.

7. Adjourn/close board meeting

If the board meeting will reopen within 24 hours, it will "adjourn" at this stage. If the board meeting will not reopen for more than 24 hours (e.g. if the written resolution will not lapse for 28 days and the company has to wait for a number of shareholders to return their vote during this period) then the meeting will "close" (rather than "adjourn") at this stage.

Between board meetings...

Pass the written resolution

To pass a written resolution, shareholders representing the required percentage of the total voting rights of eligible members must vote in favour CA 06 s. 296(4). Shareholders can vote by sending an authenticated document (e.g. the written resolution document) to the company identifying the relevant resolution and indicating their agreement/disagreement CA 06 s. 296(1).

- An ordinary resolution to approve the proposed terms of the share buyback contract CA 06 s. 694(2)(a). More than 50% of those voting must approve the decision in accordance with CA 06 s. 282(1).
- If capital is being used, a special resolution is also required to approve the buyback out of capital CA 06 s. 716(1). This must be passed by at least 75% of those attending and entitled to vote CA 06 s. 283(1).

The written resolution must be passed within a week of the directors' solvency statement being made CA 06 s. 716(2).

Board Meeting 2

1. Reconvene/open board meeting

If board meeting 1 was "adjourned", then "reconvene" the meeting. If it was "closed", then "open" the meeting.

2. Who calls the meeting?

Any director can call the meeting MA 9(1).

3. Notice

Reasonable notice must be given Browne v La Trinidad.

4. Quorum

Same as for board meeting 1.

5. Disclosure

Directors' duties must be considered. Directors that own shares that will be purchased as part of the share buyback should disclose their interests in the buyback contract in accordance with CA 06 s. 177(1) in *both* board meetings CA 06 s. 177(6)(b).

6. Agenda

(a) Chairman report that the ordinary resolution and special resolution were passed by written resolution.

(b) Enter into the buyback contract (by signing it).

(c) Directors to be given authority to carry out the buyback within 5-7 weeks from the date the written resolution was passed CA 06 s. 723(1). Directors must wait at least 5 weeks, as creditors have 5 weeks to object.

(d) Direct the company secretary to deal with post meeting matters.

7. Voting

The board must agree by board resolution (either by a unanimous decision or a simple majority on a show of hands) on the relevant issues set out in the agenda MA 7(1) + MA 8. If there is deadlock, the Chairman has the casting vote MA 13. Directors with an interest in the transaction cannot vote on whether to enter into the buyback contract MA 14.

8. Close board meeting

Post Board Meeting 2 Matters

1. Make the relevant filings at Companies House

(a) File a copy of the return using **form SH03** within 28 days of the share buyback CA 06 s. 707(1). This notifies Companies House that the share buyback has taken place.

(b) File a notice of cancelation of the shares using **form SH06** within 28 days of the share buyback CA 06 s. 708(1).

(c) File the statement of capital using **form SH19** within 28 days of the share buyback CA 06 s. 708(2).

(d) File a copy of the special resolution within 15 days of it being passed. CA 06 s. 29(1)(a) states that s. 30(1) applies to written resolutions.

2. Notice to creditors

Within one week following the resolution approving the payment out of capital, the company must:

(a) Publish a notice in the Gazette that the payment out of capital has been approved and that creditors may within 5 weeks apply for an order preventing the payment CA 06 s. 719(1); and

(b) Publish a notice in an appropriate national newspaper to the same effect or give notice in writing to that effect to each of its creditors CA 06 s. 719(2).

3. Company books/share certificates

(a) Amend Register of Members to reflect the changes to the shareholders CA 06 s. 113. If the company is left with only one shareholder, this must also be stated in the Register of Members CA 06 s. 123.

(b) New share certificates must be issued to remaining shareholders within 2 months and the share certificates relating to the shares bought back must be cancelled CA 06 s. 776 (shares bought back are treated as cancelled CA 06 s. 706).

(c) Keep a copy of the buyback contract at the company's registered address for 10 years CA 06 s. 702(3).

4. Draw up minutes

Draw up minutes from the board meeting and keep these for at least 10 years CA 06 s. 248(1).

5. Written resolution

Keep a record of the written resolution for at least 10 years CA 06 s. 355(1)(a).

The actual buyback must take place 5-7 weeks from the passing of the special resolution if funded using capital CA 06 s. 723(1) as this is the period during which creditors have a right to object.

Insolvency

UK insolvency law focuses on helping businesses to survive. There are various strategies businesses can pursue to try to avoid becoming insolvent, including: cost cutting, restructuring or selling off/closing down loss-making subsidiaries, renegotiating prices with suppliers, more efficiently chasing debtors for money owed etc. However, if a business passes the point of no return (i.e. insolvency becomes inevitable), insolvency law requires that the business ceases to trade and takes action to ensure creditors receive as much as possible of the money that they are owed. Often this is very little however.

When Is a Company "Insolvent"?

A company is "insolvent" if it is unable to pay its debts IA 86 s. 122(1)(f). A company is deemed to be unable to pay its debts if any one of the following applies:

1. **Failed to pay a debt exceeding £750:** the company owes a creditor more than £750, that creditor has served a written demand in the prescribed form requiring the company to pay the sum owed, and the company has failed to pay for a period of three weeks after the notice was served IA 86 s. 123(1)(a).
2. **Failed to pay following a judgment:** a creditor has obtained judgment against the company, attempted to execute the judgment, yet the debt remains outstanding (in full or in part) IA 86 s. 123(1)(b).
3. **Cash flow:** the company is unable to pay its debts when they fall due IA 86 s. 123(1)(e).
4. **Balance sheet:** the value of the company's assets is less than the amount of its liabilities IA 86 s. 123(2).

Directors' Obligations

When the risk arises that a company will become insolvent, there is an obligation on that company's directors to take appropriate action. Directors cannot simply ignore the fact that the company is experiencing financial difficulties. In an insolvency situation, the directors' duty to promote the success of the company (CA 06 s. 172) becomes subject to a higher duty to consider the interests of the company's creditors CA 06 s. 172(3). When doing so, there are various strategies that directors should consider pursuing:

- **Finance:** directors should liaise with creditors to avoid the risk of loans being suddenly and unexpectedly accelerated. Directors could try to renegotiate the terms of existing loans with creditors in order to give the company more time to repay those loans. The company should, where possible, avoid taking on additional debt as this could increase the company's gearing and consequently make the company even less financially stable. Issuing new shares (perhaps with enhanced rights to encourage demand for those shares) could provide a more viable source of additional finance, if demand for the company's shares still exists (which may be unlikely).
- **Profitability:** every effort should be made to improve profitability, including cost cutting and undertaking regular and thorough reviews of the company's business plan/objectives/accounts. Directors should try to improve cash flow (e.g. by trying to extend credit periods with existing suppliers or finding cheaper alternative suppliers). Customer debts should be collected more effectively (perhaps by offering shorter periods of credit) and dividend payments should be temporarily suspended. Regular board meetings should take place to review the company's accounts/financial situation.
- **Turnaround specialists:** directors could also consider consulting with turnaround specialists (who are responsible for helping companies to recover from financial difficulties).

However, if a company is insolvent or there is no reasonable prospect that it can avoid becoming insolvent, the directors must cease trading IA 86 s. 214 or could face legal action (e.g. a claim for "wrongful trading").

Financial Difficulties: Procedures

There are various arrangements that can be put in place when a company is struggling financially to try to avoid that company becoming insolvent. These arrangements may be initiated by a company's directors or creditors and involve placing differing levels of external control upon the company's operations. The arrangement(s) chosen will depend on the aims of a company, the extent of its financial difficulties and the intentions of its creditors.

Informal agreement: negotiated settlement

A negotiated settlement is the most common outcome in the first instance. This involves a company agreeing to a set of terms with its creditors in order to avoid those creditors calling in its debts or petitioning to have it wound up. Such terms could require a company to sell part of its business or reduce/temporarily suspend the payment of salaries in order to pay back a percentage of its debts. A company could have to grant additional security to its creditors and/or allow its creditors to monitor its activities more closely. Creditors in return could agree to extend the deadline(s) for repayment.

Negotiated settlements are typically quicker and cheaper than formal proceedings, can increase the likelihood of the company continuing as a going concern (which would be especially beneficial for unsecured creditors as they are unlikely to receive any money if the company becomes insolvent), and are private (thus avoiding the adverse effects publicity can have on goodwill, staff morale etc.). However, negotiated transactions require the support of *all* secured creditors and major unsecured creditors and no moratorium will be put in place.

Business Law

📖 **Moratorium:** a moratorium is a temporary prohibition on the certain claims/actions being pursued against the company, including winding up proceedings, the appointment of administrative receivers and the enforcement of debt. If the company appoints an administrator, an "immediate" moratorium ensues, whereas if the court appoints an administrator, an "interim" moratorium ensues.

Formal agreement: Scheme of Arrangement or Company Voluntary Arrangement

📖 **Scheme of Arrangement:** a *court-approved* agreement between a company and its shareholders or creditors (e.g. lenders or debenture holders) pursuant to CA 06 ss. 895-901. Before a court can approve the arrangement, a majority of each class of the company's creditors must agree to it. Once a court has approved a Scheme of Arrangement, it will bind *all* creditors (including dissenting and unknown creditors). Schemes of Arrangement only tend to be used for complex group insolvencies (e.g. to restructure the debts of large, complex groups of companies) and are more costly than Company Voluntary Arrangements.

📖 **Restructuring plan:** introduced by the Corporate Insolvency and Governance Bill 2020, the restructuring plan procedure works in a similar way to a scheme of arrangement, with the key distinguishing feature being that a court can approve the arrangement even if one or more classes of creditors voted against it, provided that certain conditions are met.

📖 **Company Voluntary Arrangement (CVA):** a CVA is an arrangement reached between a company and its creditors pursuant to IA 86 ss. 1-7. A CVA binds *all* the company's creditors, who will have agreed *self-imposed* terms regarding the enforcement/repayment of debt. A CVA aims to rescue a company if possible, or enable assets to be better realised than they would in a winding up.

	Company Voluntary Arrangement (CVA)
Procedure	Directors draft a proposal and then appoint an insolvency practitioner to consider it. Shareholders and creditors meet to consider/approve/reject the proposal, although the view of creditors prevails if these conflict. Administrators and liquidators can also propose CVAs. CVA proposals must be approved by at least 75% (by value) of a company's creditors. A timetable is put in place for the repayment of creditors. Creditors may agree to avoid enforcing their debt for a specified period, or to accept a percentage of their debt in full settlement of the whole. Alternatively, creditors could be offered shares in the company in exchange for relinquishing the debt (a "debt for equity swap"). A CVA is implemented and supervised by an insolvency practitioner, but directors continue to run the company under the terms of the CVA proposals. If the company does not fulfil its CVA obligations, the insolvency practitioner can petition for the company to be wound up.
Moratorium?	An optional moratorium is available for small companies following a court application CA 06 s. 382(3). This covers the period leading to the creditors'/shareholders' meeting. No moratorium is available for larger companies, meaning other creditors could still initiate proceedings. If a CVA was initially proposed by an administrator, then an administration moratorium will be in place (see the *Administration* table below).
Challenging transactions	Directors/insolvency practitioners are unable to challenge any voidable transactions, other than transactions defrauding creditors. Wrongful/fraudulent trading proceedings cannot be brought.
Advantages/ disadvantages	CVAs can be quicker and cheaper to arrange than other types of proceedings, can increase the likelihood of the company surviving (increasing the chances of creditors recovering debts owed), and involve limited publicity (thus reducing the adverse effects publicity can have on goodwill, staff morale etc.). CVAs can also lead to the company having more assets to distribute on a winding up. Remember, only liquidators and administrators can challenge floating charges, so if the CVA involves no liquidator/administrator, floating charge holders are not at risk of having their floating charge rendered invalid.
	CVAs require the support of secured creditors and (if applicable) major unsecured creditors, since CVA proposals must be approved by at least 75% (by value) of a company's creditors. If secured creditors do not support a CVA proposal, those secured creditors could instead choose to enforce their security and require the company to sell the secured assets and distribute the proceeds to repay the secured debts, which would likely undermine the aims of the CVA (in particular, saving the company). This is an advantage from the point of view of secured creditors, but not for companies/unsecured creditors.

Administration

	Administration
Procedure	**Out of court procedure:** the following can apply for administration proceedings to commence using the out of court procedure: (1) the company (i.e. its shareholders voting at a general meeting); (2) the company's directors; or (3) "qualifying" floating charge holders with floating charges that were granted on or after 15th September 2003 *and* relate to a debt that is expected to be worth *less* than £50 million.
	Court procedure: alternatively, the company, its directors, its creditors, Company Voluntary Arrangement supervisors or liquidators can apply to commence administration proceedings using the court procedure.
	Administrators take over the running of the company and owe their duty to the court. They must act in the interest of *all* creditors (including unsecured creditors). Appointment of an administrator terminates automatically after 12 months, but can be extended by 6 months on one occasion if the creditors agree.

📖 **Administration:** administration proceedings involve an administrator taking over the running of the company, pursuant to IA 86 s. 8 + Schedule B1 paragraph 3. Administration proceedings must pursue one of three cascading objectives: (1) to rescue the company as a going concern; if this is not possible (2) to achieve a better result for the creditors than would be likely if the company was wound up; and as a last resort (3) to realise property in order to make a distribution to secured or preferential creditors, without unnecessarily harming the interests of the creditors as a whole.

Moratorium?	A moratorium comes into force immediately. There is also an interim moratorium in place from the date of the court application until the appointment of an administrator occurs. Whilst a company is in administration, creditors cannot try to have it wound up, enforce security over its property or institute other legal proceedings against it. This is useful for creditors as a whole if some of the creditors could otherwise bring winding-up proceedings (which can result in less money overall for creditors as a whole).
Challenging transactions	Administrators can challenge all voidable transactions, including preferences, transactions at an undervalue, avoidance of floating charges and transactions defrauding creditors (these are explained in more detail later). Wrongful/fraudulent trading proceedings cannot be brought by an administrator however.
Advantages/ disadvantages	Administration can increase the likelihood of the company surviving/being sold as a going concern, which can result in creditors receiving back a greater portion of the debt they are owed. For this reason, administration is preferable to administrative receivership for the company, as the primary objective of the latter is to maximise assets in order to repay the creditor(s) that appointed the administrative receiver. If proceedings do not involve the court, administration could be cheaper than liquidation. Lenders may avoid adverse publicity if a business goes into administration (conversely, if the business is wound up because of the lender, this may motivate other borrowers not to borrow from that lender).
	Administration requires the support of secured creditors. There are requirements to publicise administration proceedings, which could negatively impact upon the company's internal/external relationships. Administration proceedings can be expensive, especially if the court is involved. Floating charge holders have no control over whether floating charge assets will be sold for their benefit (which from their perspective is a disadvantage).

📖 **"Qualifying" floating charge holder (QFCH):** a party that has been granted a floating charge over the whole or substantially the whole of the company's assets IA 86 Schedule B1 paragraph 14(3). The QFCH can appoint an *administrative receiver* (discussed below) if the charge was created before 15th September 2003. If the charge was created on or after 15th September 2003, then the QFCH can only appoint an *administrator*.

Administrative receivership

📖 **Administrative receivership:** proceedings in which certain "qualifying" floating charge holders can appoint an administrative receiver to take control of and (typically) sell any of the company's assets that are subject to a "qualifying" floating charge. The company's debts to those creditors will subsequently be repaid out of any sale proceeds.

Administrative Receivership	
Purpose	Administrative receivers can be appointed by the holders of "qualifying" floating charges that either: (a) were granted before 15th September 2003; or (b) granted on or after 15th September 2003 *and* relate to a debt that is expected to be worth at least £50 million.
	Administrative receivers owe their duty to the charge holder who appointed them, although there is a limited duty to act in good faith and not to act recklessly to the detriment of other creditors. Their role is to take control of the company's assets and realise secured property in order to repay the secured creditor(s) that appointed them.
Moratorium?	No moratorium is available.
Challenging transactions	Administrative receivers are unable to challenge voidable transactions and cannot bring wrongful/fraudulent trading proceedings.
Advantages/ disadvantages	There are no real advantages from the company's perspective, although creditors that have appointed the administrative receiver will have a greater likelihood of receiving secured debts that they are owed. The cost of appointing an administrative receiver is generally cheaper than administration proceedings however.
	It is unlikely that the company will survive as a going concern, so unsecured creditors are less likely to receive debts owed once an administrative receiver has been appointed. The holder of a pre-15th September 2003 floating charge can block the appointment of an administrator by appointing their own administrative receiver. This will decrease the chances of the company surviving, potentially to the detriment of other creditors. Lenders that appoint administrative receivers may receive adverse publicity if the company is consequently wound up.

Fixed charge receivership

📖 **Fixed charge receivership:** proceedings in which fixed charge creditors appoint a fixed charge receiver to take control of and (typically) sell any of the company's assets that are subject to a fixed charge. The company's debts to those creditors will subsequently be repaid out of any sale proceeds.

Business Law

Fixed Charge Receivership

Procedure	Fixed charge receivers can be appointed by lenders that have been granted fixed charges over the company's assets. The fixed charge receiver only becomes the receiver and manager of the company's assets that are subject to fixed charges (they cannot deal with the company's other assets). They therefore have no involvement in the running of the business.
	Fixed charge receivers will have certain limited powers set out in the Law of Property Act 1925 and additional powers that are set out in the debenture (these powers tend to be more extensive, including for instance the power of sale).
Moratorium?	No moratorium is available.
Challenging transactions	Fixed charge receivers are unable to challenge voidable transactions and cannot bring wrongful/fraudulent trading proceedings.

Liquidation

> **Liquidation (or "winding up") of a company** IA 86 ss. 73-229: the realisation and distribution of a company's assets to its creditors in the order of priority set out in IA 86 s. 175, s. 176A + s. 176ZA. Three months after Companies House receives notice that a company has been liquidated, the company will be "dissolved", meaning it will cease to exist.

Liquidation/Winding Up

Procedure	**Compulsory liquidation:** can be *initiated* by creditors, the company, the directors, an administrator, an administrative receiver, or the supervisor of a CVA if one of the IA 86 s. 122(1) tests for insolvency has been met. Compulsory liquidation must subsequently be *approved* by court order however.
	Members' voluntary liquidation IA 86 ss. 91-96: initiated by shareholders. Shareholders must pass a special resolution to approve the voluntary liquidation and an ordinary resolution to appoint a liquidator. This procedure can only be utilised if the company is solvent (i.e. where enough assets remain to repay *all* the company's creditors). The directors will be required to make a statutory declaration of solvency, which is a statement that the company will be able to pay its debts in full within a period specified in the declaration IA 86 s. 89(1). A *notice of intention* to put a resolution for voluntary liquidation to the shareholders must be given to any "qualifying" floating charge holders in advance.
	Creditors' voluntary liquidation IA 86 ss. 97-104: commenced by resolution of the shareholders, but proceeds under the effective control of the creditors (creditors can choose the liquidator). Creditors' voluntary liquidation is more appropriate where there is a shortfall in the assets available to repay creditors.
	Liquidators owe their duty to creditors. Their aim is to maximise the value of a company's assets and then distribute these assets to the company's creditors in the statutory order of priority. Liquidators also have the power to disclaim onerous property (e.g. contracts that are costing the company money) IA 86 s. 178.
Moratorium?	No moratorium is available, but a stay on proceedings against the company is put in place.
Challenging transactions	Liquidators can challenge all voidable transactions and can pursue directors for wrongful and fraudulent trading. Consent from creditors or the court may be required before the liquidator can take certain action however.
Advantages/ disadvantages	There are no advantages from the company's perspective. For creditors, liquidation will prevent the company from further depleting its assets, although by this stage there is often little left for the creditors anyway.
	The company ceases trading and employees will be made redundant. The business is likely to be sold on a break-up basis, meaning there is often little left for unsecured creditors.

Priority

Priority was explained in the *Debt and Equity Finance* chapter of this module in the context of security. A creditor's place in the order of priority in an insolvency can determine the extent to which it will receive moneys owed. There is a statutory order of priority set out in IA 86 s. 175, s. 176A + s. 176ZA that liquidators use as a framework when distributing an insolvent company's remaining assets. This is set out below, starting with the highest priority creditors:

1. **Liquidator's fees for realising the sale of fixed charge assets (e.g. land)**

2. **Creditors with a fixed charge over the company's assets**

    If any funds remain, these will first go to creditors with fixed charges. However, fixed charge creditors will only be repaid in priority out of the sale proceeds from the assets over which they hold those fixed charges. This means that if a fixed asset is sold for an amount that does not fully cover the debt owed to the relevant fixed charge holder, the fixed charge holder will not be repaid *in full*; the fixed charge holder will rank alongside unsecured creditors for any additional amounts owed.

3. **Other liquidator costs and expenses**

   If any funds remain, these will next be used to cover other costs and expenses incurred by the liquidator.

4. **Preferential creditors**

   If any funds remain, these will next go to debts owed to preferential creditors. IA 86 Schedule 6 grants preferential status to certain creditors. For instance, employees can claim up to £800 for wages due in priority to the creditors mentioned below. Employees will be classed as unsecured creditors for any additional amounts due however.

5. **Ring-fenced fund**

   If any funds remain that are subject to a floating charge (and/or there are funds resulting from the sale of assets that were subject to a floating charge), a prescribed portion will be set aside for the "ring-fenced" fund. Funds in the "ring-fenced" fund are set aside for the benefit of unsecured creditors. The Enterprise Act 2002 introduced this initiative in order to partially redress the balance in favour of unsecured creditors (who typically received little or nothing following a liquidation).

   The amount that is set aside is calculated in the following way: 50% of the first £10,000 available and 20% of any remaining funds (up to a maximum of £800,000) will be set aside IA 86 s. 176A. If less than £10,000 is available once the preferential creditors have been paid, then the ring-fencing provisions do not apply, so no ring-fenced funds will be available for unsecured creditors.

6. **Creditors with floating charges**

   If any funds remain that are subject to a floating charge (and/or there are funds resulting from the sale of assets that were subject to a floating charge), creditors with floating charges will have priority over these funds. If there are insufficient assets to repay floating charge creditors in full at this stage, those creditors will rank as unsecured creditors for the remainder of what they are owed.

7. **Unsecured creditors**

   Unsecured creditors are creditors that have not taken any security. They rank equally (referred to as "*pari passu*"), regardless of the amount they are owed and when the debt arose. Unsecured creditors are very rarely repaid in full following an insolvency, although their position has been slightly improved by the introduction of the ring-fencing provisions (mentioned above).

8. **Interest on unsecured debts**

   If any funds remain once unsecured creditors have been repaid, then those funds will be used to pay interest that has accrued on debts owed to unsecured creditors from the commencement of the winding up.

9. **Shareholders**

   Shareholders are entitled to any assets remaining once all creditors have been repaid in a winding up (which is very unlikely). Shareholders with different classes of shares may be entitled to priority over other shareholders following liquidation proceedings, so the company's Articles must be checked to determine shareholders' rights. For instance, holders of preference shares will typically have priority over ordinary shareholders.

   Below is an example of how the statutory order of priority is applied in practice.

Following a downturn in popularity, **Red Lion Street Tuition Ltd (RLST Ltd)** is being liquidated and dissolved. The balance sheet shows that the company's outstanding liabilities include:

- £200,000 loan from Accelerated Ltd secured by way of fixed charge (the fixed charge has been duly registered).
- £150,000 loan from Fast-track Ltd secured by way of (a valid) floating charge over *all* Red Lion Street Tuition Ltd's remaining assets.
- £10,000 outstanding salaries owed to 10 employees (they are owed £1,000 each).
- £312,800 owed to various unsecured creditors (assume for the purposes of this example that there is no interest outstanding on this debt).

It will cost the liquidator £1,000 to realise the sale of the assets over which fixed charges have been taken. The liquidator's other expenses amount to £20,000. The assets over which Accelerated Ltd has a fixed charge are now worth only £150,000. RLST Ltd's other assets are worth £200,000 in total. How will its assets be distributed?

1. The liquidator will first be able to claim the £1,000 spent on realising the cost of the fixed assets (leaving £349,000 of total assets remaining).
2. Accelerated Ltd will recover the £150,000 generated by the sale of the assets over which they have a fixed charge (leaving £199,000 worth of total assets remaining). They will rank as an unsecured creditor for the remaining £50,000 they are owed.
3. The liquidator will next recover in full their £20,000 worth of expenses (leaving £179,000 worth of total assets remaining).
4. Employees count as "preferential" creditors in a liquidation, but can only claim back up to £800 worth of wages in priority to creditors with floating charges and unsecured creditors. Each of the 10 employees can claim £800 at this stage - a total of £8,000 - but will rank as unsecured creditors for the remaining £200 that they are each owed (leaving £171,000 worth of total assets remaining).
5. 50% of the first £10,000 + 20% of any remaining funds that are subject to a floating charge (and/or funds resulting from the sale of assets that were subject to a floating charge) at this stage will be "ring-fenced" for unsecured creditors (up to a maximum of £800,000). This equates to £5,000 (50% of £10,000) + £32,200 (20% of £161,000) = £37,200 to be set aside for unsecured creditors (leaving £133,800 worth of total assets remaining).
6. As a floating charge holder, Fast-track Ltd comes next in the order of priority. Although they are owed £150,000, there is only £133,800 worth of non-ring-fenced assets remaining. Fast-track Ltd will therefore receive £133,800 and will rank as an unsecured creditor for the outstanding £16,200.
7. The unsecured creditors, including Accelerated Ltd (still owed £50,000), Fast-track Ltd (still owed £16,200) and the employees (still owed £2,000 in total) are owed £381,000 in total (£312,800 + £50,000 + £16,200 + £2,000). These unsecured creditors will rank equally when it comes to distributing the £37,200 in the ring-fenced fund, so they will be repaid in proportion to the amounts they are owed. £37,200 assets remaining/£381,000 debt owed = ~0.10. This means that for every £1 owed to unsecured creditors, they will receive only £0.10.

Challenging Transactions

Voidable transactions (sometimes referred to as "antecedent" transactions, meaning past transactions) can be challenged under certain circumstances. The main types of voidable transactions covered on the LPC are preferences, floating charges and transactions defrauding creditors. In addition, proceedings for wrongful trading, fraudulent trading, misfeasance and the disqualification of directors may also be brought. In your exam, you may have to identify the claims that may be brought against directors/the company and explain the implications.

Voidable Transactions

Transactions at an undervalue

Under IA 86 s. 238 transactions that have been concluded for no consideration, or consideration worth significantly less than the value of the transaction, may be challenged and reversed under certain circumstances. Consider the below steps when assessing whether a transaction is at risk of being voided.

1. Who can bring a claim to challenge a transaction at an undervalue?

Only a liquidator or an administrator can apply to the court to challenge transactions at an undervalue IA 86 s. 238(1).

2. Was the transaction at an undervalue?

Did the transaction involve no consideration (including gifts, i.e. payments a company is not contractually bound to make) IA 86 s. 238(4)(a) or consideration worth significantly less than the value of the transaction IA 86 s. 238(4)(b)?

3. Did the transaction take place within the "relevant time"?

Transactions at an undervalue can only be challenged if they took place within the two year period prior to insolvency IA 86 s. 240(1)(a). Note that this is the relevant time period *regardless* of whether the transaction is made with a connected person (in contrast to other voidable transactions set out below, e.g. preferences). The date on which "insolvency" is deemed to have occurred depends on the circumstances (see IA 86 s. 240(3)).

4. Was the company unable to pay its debts at the time of the transaction, or did it become so as a result IA 86 s. 240(2)?

The applicant must prove that the company was insolvent at the time the transaction took place, or became insolvent as a result of the transaction IA 86 s. 240(2)(a)+(b). This requirement is presumed to be satisfied if the transaction at an undervalue is entered into with a person who is "connected" to the company IA 86 s. 240(2).

> 📖 **"Persons connected with a company"**: a person is "connected" with a company if they are:
> (a) a director or shadow director of the company or an associate of such a director IA 86 s. 249(a); or
> (b) an associate of the company CA 06 s. 249(b).

> 📖 **"Associate"**: includes spouses, civil partners, children, parents, siblings, uncles/aunts, nephews/nieces, grandparents, other "lineal ancestors", and employers/employees IA 86 s. 435. Note that this definition is wider than the definition of "connected persons" in the Companies Act 2006 (e.g. for the purposes of substantial property transactions).

5. Are there any defences available?

The parties to the transaction may have a defence if:

- The transaction was entered into in good faith and for the purpose of enabling the company to carry on its business IA 86 s. 238(5)(a); and
- There were reasonable grounds at the time for the parties to believe the transaction would benefit the company (e.g. the transaction was entered into to resolve a dispute with a dismissed employee) IA 86 s. 238(5)(b).

6. What action is the court likely to take if the above criteria apply and no defence is available?

The court has full discretion to make such orders as it thinks fit to restore the company to the position it would have been in had the transaction not taken place IA 86 s. 238(3). IA 86 s. 241 sets out a non-exhaustive list of restoration orders that the court might make. For instance, the court may order the party that received company property at an undervalue to return that property to the company.

Preferences

A "preference" in this context refers to a preferential repayment made by the company of a debt owed to one of its creditors or a guarantor of its liabilities. Under IA 86 s. 239, transactions that give an unfair preference to another party may be voided where the following criteria are fulfilled:

1. Who can bring a claim to challenge the preferential repayment of a debt?

Only a liquidator or an administrator can apply to the court to challenge preferential transactions IA 86 s. 239(2).

2. Was the relevant creditor/guarantor placed in a better position than they would have been in post-insolvency had the payment not been made?

You should check when the payment was contractually due when assessing whether this is the case.

3. Did the preference take place within the "relevant time"?

The "relevant time" is **6 months** prior to the onset of insolvency for preferences given to **unconnected parties** IA 86 s. 240(1)(b) and **2 years** for preferences given to **connected parties** IA 86 s. 240(1)(a). Remember, connected parties include directors, shadow directors, associates of such directors and associates of the company (see above) IA 86 s. 249 + s. 435.

4. Was the company unable to pay its debts when the preference was given, or did it become so as a result IA 86 s. 240(2)?

The applicant must prove that the company was insolvent at the time the transaction took place, or became insolvent as a result of the transaction IA 86 s. 240(2)(a)+(b). Unlike with transactions at an undervalue, this requirement is *not* presumed to be satisfied purely because the preference was given to a connected party.

5. Was the company influenced by a desire to prefer the relevant creditor/guarantor IA 86 s. 239(5)?

The company must also have been influenced by a *desire* to give a preference IA 86 s. 239(5). If the preference is given to a connected person, there exists a rebuttable *presumption* that such a desire existed IA 86 s. 239(6). If the preference is given to an unconnected person, the terms of the agreement should therefore be assessed when determining whether the transaction should be unwound. The test for "desire" is subjective. It is not necessary to prove an "intention" to prefer; it is "desire" that must be proved (i.e. the preference may well have been given *deliberately* (meaning the *intention* to give was there), but the company may not have *wanted* (desired) to make the payment and only did so in response to some external pressure outside of its control Re MC Bacon. For instance, if the payment was made in response to genuine commercial pressure, it is unlikely that the requisite "desire" to give the preference existed.

6. Which action is the court likely to take if the above criteria apply?

The court can make such orders as it thinks fit to restore the company to the position it would have been in had the preference not been given IA 86 s. 239(3). IA 86 s. 241 sets out a non-exhaustive list of the types of restoration orders that the court might make (e.g. the court may order the party that was given preferential treatment to repay the company).

Rum Ltd went into liquidation 3 weeks ago. 4 weeks ago, it repaid a majority of the money it owed Harry Ltd. The payment was not due until next week. The Managing Director of Rum Ltd, Sarah Crimmens, is a good friend of a director of Harry Ltd and these two negotiated the settlement of Rum Ltd's debt to Harry Ltd. Explain whether a claim can be brought and if so, by whom.

The transaction in question may constitute a preference given by Rum Ltd in favour of Harry Ltd. Preference claims may be brought by liquidators or administrators pursuant to IA 86 s. 239(1). In this case, we know Rum Ltd has gone into liquidation, so a liquidator would bring the claim if the relevant criteria apply.

1. **Is Harry Ltd in a better position than it would have been in had the payment not been made?**

    As Rum Ltd has gone into liquidation and creditors rarely recover a majority of the funds that they are owed in a liquidation, it appears that Harry Ltd is in a better position than it would have been in had the payment not been made.

2. **Did the payment take place within the "relevant" time period?**

    "Good friend" does not constitute a "connected person" under IA 86 s. 249 + s. 435. The relevant period is therefore 6 months prior to the onset of insolvency. The debt was settled 4 weeks ago, so the transaction occurred within the relevant period.

3. **Was Rum Ltd insolvent at the time the payment was made or did it become insolvent as a result IA 86 s. 240(2)?**

    To give a certain answer, Rum Ltd's accounts would need to be analysed. However, as the payment was made 1 week before Rum Ltd went into liquidation, it appears likely that Rum Ltd was insolvent or became so as a result of the payment.

4. **Was Rum Ltd influenced by a desire to prefer Harry Ltd IA 86 s. 239(5)?**

    There is no rebuttable *presumption* that a desire exists in this scenario, as "good friends" are not "connected parties" for the purposes of the Insolvency Act 1986. However, on the facts, there appears to be no legitimate commercial reason for giving the preference and the payment was not due at the time it was made.

It appears likely that the court will classify the payment as a preference. It may order Harry Ltd to repay the money to the liquidator, to then be distributed to creditors in the statutory order of priority.

Floating charges

Remember, a floating charge will not fully secure the charge holder unless it has been duly registered CA 06 s. 859A, so check whether the charge has been registered when answering an exam question. Under IA 86 s. 245, floating charges may be voided (even if duly registered) if the following criteria apply:

1. Was the consideration (e.g. loan) given by the lender in exchange for the floating charge less than could have been expected at the time the charge was supplied IA 86 s. 245(2)?

A floating charge will be valid to the extent that *new* money or other fresh consideration is brought into the company in exchange for the company granting that floating charge. Therefore, a floating charge will likely be valid if granted in exchange for a *new* loan or the extinguishment of existing debts. *Existing* loans cannot be retrospectively secured by a floating charge, as the "consideration" requirement would not be met (i.e. no *new* consideration would be given for that floating charge).

2. Was the floating charge granted within the relevant time period?

The "relevant time" is **12 months** prior to the onset of insolvency for floating charges granted to **unconnected parties** IA 86 s. 245(3)(b) and **2 years** for floating charges granted to **connected parties** IA 86 s. 245(3)(a). Connected parties include directors, shadow directors, associates of such directors and associates of the company (see above) IA 86 s. 249 + s. 435.

3. Was the company unable to pay its debts when the floating charge was granted, or did it become so as a result IA 86 s. 245(4)?

This criterion does not need to be fulfilled in the case of *connected* parties: if a floating charge is granted to a connected party and criteria 1 and 2 above are satisfied, then that floating charge is invalid regardless of whether the company could pay its debts at the time/after the floating charge was granted. This would mean that the relevant creditor will rank equally in priority with other unsecured creditors.

This criterion *does* need to be fulfilled in the case of unconnected parties: if the company *was* able to pay its debts when the floating charge was granted, and the floating charge did not subsequently render the company unable to pay its debts, then the floating charge will remain valid. If all the above criteria are fulfilled, the floating charge will be invalid and the relevant creditor will rank equally in priority with other unsecured creditors.

Interpretation of "new" consideration by the courts

If a bank continues to provide an overdraft to a company and takes out a floating charge, this floating charge will only be valid over funds subsequently lent. This means that any payments made by the company out of the overdraft after this date will be covered by the floating charge, but funds owed before the floating charge was taken out would not be secured by the floating charge. The below cases set out how the courts have decided whether "new" consideration has been given in the context of companies using overdrafts.

Clayton's Case (Devaynes v Noble)

- Where a person (the debtor) owes a creditor multiple debts, if that person repays that creditor an amount of money but does not specify which debt it applies to, the repayment is appropriated to the earliest debt owed. For instance, if a company borrows £20,000 in January, £10,000 in March and £30,000 in May, then repays £25,000, the company will be deemed to have paid off the £20,000 lent in January and half of the money lent in March.
- Alternatively, the debtor can specifically allocate their repayment to a particular debt or (if the debtor fails to do so) the creditor can allocate the payment to a particular debt.

Re Yeovil Glove Co Ltd

- In this case, the company's current account was in overdraft by approximately £67,000. This amount was unsecured. The lender refused to let the company continue to use the overdraft without first granting the lender a floating charge, which the company subsequently did (at a time when it was insolvent). During the next 8 months of trading, the company had paid approximately £110,000 into the account, and had drawn out a similar amount (the account was continuously in overdraft however), leaving £67,000 still due to the lender under the overdraft. The lender then appointed an administrative receiver to enforce its floating charge. Later, the company's trade creditors petitioned for the company's winding up and the liquidator applied for a declaration that the floating charge was invalid on the grounds that it related to the unsecured (pre-floating charge) debt of £67,000 (as opposed to *new* consideration).
- It was held that the floating charge *was* valid for the entire £67,000 overdraft, meaning the trade creditors would not receive any of the money they were owed (the assets secured by the floating charge were of insufficient value to repay all creditors). This was based on the following reasoning:
    1. Each time the lender allowed the company to draw on its overdraft, "new money" (approximately £110,000 in total) was deemed to have been given by the lender to the company *by reason of* the floating charge.
    2. Payments made by the company into the bank account *first* discharged the unsecured pre-floating charge debt (i.e. the £67,000), rather than the "new money" advanced by the lender post-floating charge. This was an application of the rule in Clayton's Case that in the absence of contrary agreement/intention, payments made into a bank account are deemed to discharge the oldest debts. Therefore, the £67,000 outstanding when the lender appointed the administrative receiver constituted a portion of the £110,000 lent to the company (through its overdraft) *after* the floating charge had been created.

Transactions defrauding creditors

Under IA 86 s. 423, transactions that are held to have defrauded creditors may be challenged by the defrauded creditors, administrators, supervisors of a CVA or liquidators. Such transactions must be at an undervalue and it must be shown that by making a particular payment, the company *intended* to put the funds beyond the reach of present or future creditors, or to prejudice the interests of such creditors.

There is no time limit to bringing such an action, although such transactions are difficult to prove in practice due to the requirement of "intent". For this reason, it is unlikely that this option would be pursued unless the options discussed above do not exist. If a claim is successful, the relevant directors may be held to have breached their statutory duty to promote the success of the company, leading to action being brought for misfeasance (explained below) under IA 86 s. 212.

Wrongful/Fraudulent Trading, Misfeasance and Director Disqualification

Wrongful trading

If a company is insolvent or there is no reasonable prospect that it can avoid becoming insolvent, the directors/non-executive directors/shadow directors IA 86 s. 214(7) must cease trading IA 86 s. 214. The aim is to ensure that once directors become aware that insolvency is inevitable, they do everything possible to minimise the potential losses to the creditors.

- If a director continues trading but knows or ought to have concluded that there was no reasonable prospect that the company would avoid going into insolvent liquidation, they could face a claim for wrongful trading.
- A company is "insolvent" for these purposes if its assets are insufficient to cover its debts, other liabilities and expenses IA 86 s. 123. A claim for wrongful trading can be brought only by liquidators (IA 86 s. 214) and administrators (IA 86 s. 246ZB).

Defence

If the relevant directors knew or ought to have known that there was no reasonable prospect that the company would avoid going into insolvent liquidation, they may still have a defence if they can prove that they took every step that ought to have been taken to minimise the potential loss to the company's creditors IA 86 s. 214(3). This is consequently sometimes referred to as the **"every step" defence.**

- IA 86 s. 214(4) sets out the test to determine whether a director "knew or ought to have concluded" that insolvency would ensue. Directors are assessed against the "reasonably diligent person", a hypothetical threshold that assumes those directors have:
    1. The general knowledge, skill and experience that may reasonably be expected of a person carrying out the same functions as are carried out by that director in relation to the company *(the objective element)*; and
    2. The general knowledge, skill and experience that that director actually has *(the subjective element)*.
- Directors should make sure board minutes are taken/records are made to evidence that all steps that ought to be taken were actually taken. They could for instance seek professional independent advice (solicitors/accountants/insolvency practitioners), express their concerns to the board and to key shareholders (to get them on side), take positive steps to cut costs, and avoid taking on more debt/reduce current debt etc.
- A claim can be brought against any person who was *at the relevant time* a director. Therefore if one director resigns in the knowledge that the others will continue to trade in breach of IA 86 s. 214, this will not necessarily provide them with a defence. They must first take every possible step to try to persuade the board to stop trading.

Penalties

- If found guilty of wrongful trading, directors may have to personally contribute to the company's assets to compensate for the adverse effect their conduct had on the depletion of those assets IA 86 s. 214(1). The court can order the relevant director(s) to make such contributions to the company's assets as it sees fit. Directors would have to compensate for losses arising between the date that they *ought* to have concluded that the company could not avoid insolvent liquidation and the date the company actually went into liquidation.
- Directors could also face disqualification for a minimum of 2 years/maximum of 15 years if the court makes such an order under the Company Directors Disqualification Act 1986 s. 10.

Fraudulent trading

Directors could also be held liable for fraudulent trading under IA 86 s. 213. Fraudulent trading involves a party carrying on the business of a company with the *intent* of defrauding its creditors. If found guilty, those directors may be required to make such contributions to the company's assets as the court thinks fit. Criminal sanctions can also be brought under CA s. 993.

The test for dishonesty is subjective. The court considers what the particular director *knew* or *believed* at the time. If a director genuinely believed that the company's financial situation would improve, then that director has a defence regardless of how objectively unrealistic their belief was. This is known as the **"sunshine" defence.** Claims for fraudulent trading can only be brought by liquidators (IA 86 s. 213) and administrators (IA 86 s. 246ZA) but are therefore rarely brought in practice, as it is very hard for liquidators or administrators to prove that there existed actual intent to defraud.

Misfeasance

Misfeasance is a tort. It creates no new liabilities or rights, but simply provides a general procedure available in a liquidation for the enforcing of rights (for instance breach of directors' duties). Claims can be brought against directors (or other specified parties) that have misapplied, retained or become accountable for a company's money/property or have breached any fiduciary or other duty in relation to the company.

If found guilty, the relevant parties can be compelled to repay, restore or account for the money/property (or any part of it), with interest at such a rate as the court thinks fit. Those parties can also/alternatively be compelled to contribute to the company's assets financially in respect of the misfeasance/breach. Note that only liquidators can bring a claim for misfeasance under IA 86 s. 212.

Disqualification of directors

Under the Company Directors Disqualification Act 1986 ("CDDA 86"), directors may be disqualified from acting as a director for up to 15 years if they are found to have engaged in fraud, are convicted for an indictable offence, or have committed persistent breaches of company legislation. In the context of an insolvency, key grounds for director disqualification include:

- **Fraud in a winding up** CDDA 86 s. 4.
- **Unfit conduct of a director of an insolvent company** CDDA 86 s. 6: finding of misfeasance and/or responsibility for the company entering into a voidable transaction are relevant factors to which a court shall have regard when considering whether to make a disqualification order.
- **Fraudulent and wrongful trading** CDDA 86 s. 10: where the court makes a contribution order against a director, it has the discretion to also make a disqualification order against that director.

The court can disqualify directors for a minimum of 2 years and a maximum of 15 years; the period of disqualification will depend on the severity of the offence(s).

Taxation & Accounts

Taxation & Accounts

Business Taxation — 87
Taxation of individuals • different types of income • allowances and reliefs • capital gains tax • taxation of companies • total taxable profits • capital allowances • rollover relief • offsetting losses • close companies • summary

Business Accounts — 98
Key accounts • Income Statement/Profit and Loss Account • Balance Sheet/Statement of Financial Position • recording key transactions on the Balance Sheet • depreciation • accruals • prepayments • bad and doubtful debts

Solicitors' Accounts — 106
Double entry bookkeeping (debits and credits) • client money vs. office money • ledgers • recording various types of transactions • disbursements • property transactions (deposits and mortgages) • Value Added Tax (VAT) • abatements of costs • bad debts • interest • financial statements (in the context of property transactions)

Business Taxation

The *Business Taxation* module on the LPC does not typically require candidates to know specific provisions of tax legislation. For this reason, statutory provisions have been omitted throughout this section. However, ensure you check your specific course requirements in case there are particular references that you are expected to know.

There are different types of taxation that apply to different types of financial gain. Examples include:

- **Income tax**: an individual that earns a salary or makes a profit trading as a sole trader will pay income tax on the income received/profit generated (subject to allowances/reliefs).
- **Capital gains tax**: if an individual sells an asset (e.g. a house) for a profit, then that individual will (subject to exemptions) pay *capital gains* tax on the difference between the price paid for the asset (including the amount spent on any improvements) and the amount for which the asset was sold (minus any costs involved in selling that asset, for instance estate agent or auctioneer fees).
- **Corporation tax:** in contrast, companies pay *corporation* tax on trading profits (profits generated as a result of trade) and capital gains. There are different reliefs and exemptions available depending on the type of profit/gain generated.

> Melbourne Ltd earned £1 million in trading profits. Melbourne Ltd has three employees, Johan, Sara and Anders, each of whom were paid £100,000 (this amount has *already* been deducted as an expense of Melbourne Ltd's). Johan recently sold some land for £50,000 more than he originally paid for it, taking into account all selling fees etc. How will the parties be taxed?
>
> - Melbourne Ltd will pay corporation tax on the £1 million trading profits.
> - Johan, Sara and Anders will each pay income tax on the £100,000 salaries received.
> - Johan will also pay capital gains tax on the £50,000 gain made from the sale of the land.

Taxation of Individuals

Income

An individual can generate income in a variety of ways. Different types of income must be distinguished, as they are taxed in different ways. Below is an overview of the different types of income that you need to understand for the LPC:

- **Trading (or "non-savings") income**: income received from the sale of the goods and/or services offered by an individual.
- **Savings income:** interest received by individuals on the money held in bank accounts.
- **Dividend income**: money received from dividends paid out on shares held by individuals.

Individuals pay income tax on their **total *taxable* income**.

> **Total income:** a tax payer's gross income from all sources, i.e. the sum of the tax payer's trading (non-savings) income, savings income and dividend income. The meaning of "gross" will become apparent when dealing with savings and dividend income below. Exempt income must not be included in the total income figure (see below for an explanation of "exempt income").

> **Exempt income:** some types of income are non-taxable, which means they should not be included in the taxpayer's "total income". Forms of exempt income include: gaming and betting winnings; income from Individual Savings Accounts (ISAs); income from a child trust; redundancy payments; and compensation for loss of employment.

> **Net income:** to calculate an individual's net income, deduct any charges on income and pension contributions from the total income.

> **Charges on income:** charges on income incurred by a person should be deducted from that person's total income. This reduces their net income figure, which consequently reduces their tax liability. Charges on income include interest payments made on certain loans that have been taken out.

> **Pension contributions:** financial contributions that a person puts into their pension scheme (either occupational and/or personal pension schemes) can be deducted from that person's total income, thus reducing their net income figure.

> **Total Taxable Income:** to calculate an individual's total taxable income, deduct that individual's personal allowance from the net income (if possible). Personal allowances are explained below.

Personal allowance

Unlike companies, individuals are typically entitled to earn a certain amount of money tax-free. This is known as a "personal allowance", which is £12,570 for the 2021/2022 financial year. Note that this allowance changes every year so be sure to check the personal allowance figure that you are expected to use on the LPC. The personal allowance is deducted from an individual's net income to reduce their *total taxable* income.

When applying an individual's personal allowance, you should first offset as much of it as possible against non-savings income (as this is taxed at the highest rates). If the individual has not earned enough non-savings income to utilise all £12,570 of their personal allowance, then any remaining personal allowance may be offset against savings income, then dividend income (in that order). However, if an individual earns over £100,000 per year, that individual's personal allowance is reduced by the equivalent of *half* of any amount earned over £100,000 (capped at £0 personal allowance). See the below example to clarify this concept.

> **Yash earns £110,000 per year in total. What is Yash's personal allowance for the 2021/2022 tax year?**
>
> The default personal allowance for the 2021/2022 tax year is £12,570. Yash is earning £10,000 more than the £100,000 threshold. His personal allowance will be reduced by half of this £10,000 excess: £10,000/2 = a £5,000 reduction. Yash's personal allowance will therefore be **£7,570** (£12,570 - £5,000).

Trading (or "non-savings") income

Trading income is income generated by an individual, for instance through earning a salary. When calculating an individual's income tax, first deal with their non-savings income. If an individual has earned £12,570 or less, this will all be covered by their personal allowance, meaning they will not have to pay any income tax. If an individual earns more than £12,570:

- Every pound earned that takes the individual into the £0 - £37,700 bracket (*after* the personal allowance has been deducted) will be taxed at 20%.

- Each pound earned over £37,700 (up to £150,000, and after deducting the personal allowance) will be taxed at 40%.

- Each pound earned over £150,000 will be taxed at 45%.

Tax bands (2021/2022)	Tax rate
Basic rate: £0- £37,700	20%
Higher rate: £37,701 - £150,000	40%
Additional rate: over £150,000	45%

Therefore, an individual will only pay the higher (40%) tax rate on taxable income that falls within the "higher rate" bracket, and the "additional" (45%) tax rate on taxable income over £150,000.

Note that these brackets change annually; sometimes you are taught tax in one tax year, but your LPC exams take place in the next financial year, so it is important to check which rates your LPC institution wants you to apply in your exam.

> **Carly earned £30,000 of non-savings income in this tax year. How much income tax will she pay?**
>
> 1. **Taxable income:** Carly's taxable income will be her net income less her personal allowance. Carly has not earned more than £100,000, so her personal allowance will remain at £12,570. Her taxable income is therefore £30,000 – £12,570 = £17,430.
> 2. **Basic rate:** Carly' taxable income does not exceed £37,700, so all £17,430 of her taxable income will be taxed at the basic rate of 20%, i.e. £17,430 x 20% = **£3,486 income tax.**
>
> **Terry earned £60,000 of non-savings income in this tax year. How much income tax will he pay?**
>
> 1. **Taxable income:** Terry's *taxable* income will be his net income less his personal allowance. Terry has not earned more than £100,000, so his personal allowance will remain at £12,570. His *taxable* income is therefore £60,000 - £12,570 (personal allowance) = **£47,430**.
> 2. **Basic rate:** Terry will pay 20% on the first £37,700 of his *taxable* income. £37,700 x 20% = **£7,540**.
> 3. **Higher rate:** Terry's taxable income is more than £37,700 but less than £150,000. The remaining £9,730 of his income (£47,430 *taxable* income – £37,700 already accounted for in step 2 above) must therefore be taxed at 40%. £9,730 x 40% = **£3,892**.
> 4. **Total income tax payable:** £7,540 (see step 2 above) + £3,892 (see step 3 above) = **£11,432**.

Savings income

As mentioned above, savings income is interest received from banks on the money saved in those banks. When calculating an individual's taxable income, deal with their savings income only once you have dealt with non-savings income.

Grossing up

Unlike non-savings income, savings income is received *net* of tax. This means the bank, before paying interest into your account, automatically deducts tax at the basic rate of 20% (this is known as "tax deducted at source"). When dealing with savings income, you must first *gross up* the figure you are given in order to work out the actual income you were entitled to before tax was deducted. This is because you may in fact be a higher rate taxpayer and thus have to pay more tax than the amount automatically deducted from your savings income "at source" (or not have to pay tax at all, for instance if your savings income would be covered by your personal allowance). To work out what your savings income was before the 20% was deducted, you multiple the *net* savings income figure by 100/80 or 1.25 (these give the same result).

> **Ed received £10,000 savings income *net* of tax. How much did he earn *gross* (i.e. *before* tax was automatically deducted)?**
>
> £10,000 x (100/80) = £12,500 gross savings income
>
> This means Ed has already paid £2,500 tax. If his total tax liability was lower than this, he would receive a rebate from HMRC. If however he is a higher rate tax payer (and is therefore obliged to pay 40% tax on his savings income) he will have to pay an additional amount of tax to HMRC.

Tax relief on savings income

If an individual has earned £12,570 or more non-savings income, then their personal allowance will have been used up. If an individual's non-savings income has not used up all the personal allowance (i.e. they earned less than £12,570 income), then any remaining personal allowance can be offset against savings income.

In addition to an individual's personal allowance, a new **Personal Savings Allowance** was introduced in 2016 to offer further tax relief specifically for savings income:

- If an individual's taxable income categorises them as a basic rate taxpayer (i.e. their total taxable income is £37,700 or less), then the first £1,000 of *savings* income is tax-free.
- If an individual is a higher rate taxpayer, only the first £500 of *savings* income is tax-free.
- If an individual is an additional rate taxpayer, none of their *savings* income is tax-free.

Subject to the above, taxable savings income will be taxed based on the same tax bands as for non-savings income.

> **Kathleen earned £30,000 non-savings income and £8,000 (net) savings income in this tax year. How much income tax is due?**
>
> 1. **Non-savings income**: Kathleen will be able to deduct the full £12,570 personal allowance from her non-savings income, leaving her with £17,430 (£30,000 - £12,570) *taxable* non-savings income. £17,430 x 20% = **£3,486** income tax.
>
> 2. **Savings income:** we first work out Kathleen's *gross* savings income. £8,000 x (100/80) = **£10,000**. This means Kathleen has already paid £2,000 tax on her savings income (£10,000 *gross* savings income - £8,000 *net* savings income = £2,000 of tax, which would have been deducted at source). Remember this for later in the calculations.
>
>   The basic rate (20%) tax bracket only applies to income up to £37,700, so we must check whether Kathleen's savings income falls fully within this bracket. £37,700 (basic rate threshold) - £17,430 (the amount of income that has already been accounted for – see step 1 above) leaves £20,270 worth of income that can still be taxed at the basic rate of 20%. Kathleen has only earned £10,000 savings income (gross) and she is entitled to a Personal Savings Allowance of £1,000 as she is a basic rate taxpayer. Only £9,000 of her savings income will therefore be taxable at the basic rate (the remaining £1,000 will be tax-free).
>
>   Kathleen will pay £9,000 x 20% = **£1,800** income tax on her savings income.
>
> 3. **Total tax liability: £3,486** (non-savings income) + **£1,800** (savings income) = **£5,286 income tax.** Kathleen has already paid £2,000 of this at source however, so will only have to pay **£3,286** (£5,286 - £2,000).
>
> **Brittney earned £40,000 non-savings income and £24,000 (net) savings income in this tax year. How much income tax is due?**
>
> 1. **Non-savings income**: Brittney will be able to deduct the full £12,570 personal allowance from her non-savings income, leaving her with **£27,430** (£40,000 - £12,570) *taxable* non-savings income. £27,430 x 20% = **£5,486** income tax.
>
> 2. **Savings income:** Brittney's gross savings income is £24,000 x (100/80) = **£30,000** (meaning **£6,000** tax was already paid at source). Brittney's total *gross* income of £70,000 (£40,000 non-savings + £30,000 savings) means she is a higher rate taxpayer (as even after deducting her personal allowance, she still earns more than £37,700). This means she will only receive a £500 Personal Savings Allowance. Therefore, **£29,500** of her savings income is taxable (£30,000 – the £500 Personal Savings Allowance).
>
>   The basic rate (20%) tax bracket only applies to the first £37,700 of taxable income earned, £27,430 of which has been "used up" by her non-savings income (see step 1 above). Therefore, £10,270 (£37,700 - £27,430) of her savings income can be taxed at 20%, whilst the remaining £19,230 (£29,500 - £10,270) will be taxed at the higher rate of 40%. Note that her total income does not exceed £150,000, so she will not pay the additional (45%) rate on any of her income.
>
>   (£10,270 x 20% = £2,054) + (£19,500 x 40% = £7,692) = **£9,746**
>
> 3. **Total tax due: £5,486** (on non-savings income) + **£9,746** (savings income) - **£6,000** (tax already paid at source) = **£9,232** income tax.

Dividend income

This is money received through dividends paid by a company to an individual shareholder. When calculating an individual's income tax, deal with their dividend income only once you have dealt with non-savings and savings income. An individual's personal allowance is likely to have been fully used up by the time you come to working out the tax on their dividend income, but if that individual's non-savings and savings income total less than £12,570, then the remaining personal allowance may be offset against their dividend income.

Tax bands for dividend income (2021/2022)	Tax rate
Basic rate: £0 - £37,700	7.5%
Higher rate: £37,701 - £150,000	32.5%
Additional rate: £150,000+	38.1%

The first £2,000 worth of dividend income is tax-free, regardless of whether the personal allowance has been used up and irrespective of the tax band in which an individual's income falls. Any dividend income over £2,000 can be offset by any remaining personal allowance. Any remaining dividend income will be taxed at a rate that is dependent on the individual's total taxable income. Although the tax bands are the same for dividend income, the actual *rates* of tax differ (these are set out in the table at the bottom of the previous page).

Remember: (a) these tax bands refer to an individual's *total taxable* income (i.e. income minus personal allowance); and (b) the tax due on dividend income will be calculated *after* the tax due on non-savings and savings income has been calculated.

Grossing up

Dividend income, like savings income, is received by individuals *net* of tax. Like with savings income, tax is automatically deducted at the basic rate, although this rate is 7.5% for individuals (not 20% as is the case with savings income). To work out what the dividend income was before the 7.5% was deducted, multiply the *net* dividend income figure by (100/92.5).

> Ben earned £20,000 of non-savings income, £4,000 of savings income (net) and £10,000 of dividend income (net) in this tax year. How much income tax is due?
>
> 1. **Non-savings income**: Ben will be able to deduct the full £12,570 personal allowance from his non-savings income, leaving him with £7,430 (£20,000 - £12,570) *taxable* non-savings income. £7,430 x 20% = **£1,486** income tax.
>
> 2. **Savings income**: £4,000 x (100/80) = **£5,000** *gross* savings income (meaning £1,000 tax on this savings income was paid at source). Ben is a basic rate taxpayer, so will receive a £1,000 Personal Savings Allowance. His total *taxable* savings income is therefore £4,000.
>
>   £37,700 (basic rate threshold) - £7,430 (the amount of non-savings income already accounted for) leaves £30,270 worth of income that can still be taxed at the basic rate of 20%. He will therefore pay 20% tax on the full £4,000 taxable savings income. £4,000 x 20% = **£800** income tax.
>
> 3. **Dividend income**: £10,000 x (100/92.5) = **£10,810** *gross* dividend income (meaning £810 tax was deducted at source). £2,000 of *gross* dividend income is tax free, leaving £8,810 *taxable* dividend income.
>
>   So far, £11,430 (£7,430 + £4,000) of Ben's *taxable* income has been accounted for. £37,700 (basic tax rate threshold) - £11,430 leaves £26,270 income that can be taxed at the basic tax rate. All of Ben's £8,810 taxable dividend income can therefore be taxed at 7.5%. £8,810 x 7.5% = **£660.75** income tax.
>
> 4. **Total tax due**: **£1,486** (on non-savings income) + **£800** (on savings income) + **£660.75** (on dividend income) – **£1,000** (tax on savings income deducted at source) - **£810** (tax on dividend income deducted at source) = **£1,136.75**

Tax deducted at source

As mentioned in the above examples, under certain circumstances, tax is deducted automatically before an individual receives their income. For instance, when you receive interest on your savings, the bank will typically have paid tax to HMRC on your behalf before paying you that interest (meaning that you receive that interest *net* of tax). If part of your income comes from a salary, your employer is likely to have paid tax on your behalf before paying you your salary (this is how the Pay As You Earn (PAYE) system operates). This is known as "tax deducted at source".

Tax deducted at source should be ignored when you are initially calculating an individual's total taxable income and total tax liability. This is because the tax deducted at source is based on an estimate of the individual's earnings and may not reflect the individual's actual tax liability. An individual may in fact be a higher rate tax payer and thus have to pay more tax on the income that they received *net* of tax, or may instead qualify for a tax rebate (for instance if their gross income would be covered by their personal allowance). For this reason, always start by *grossing up* figures you are given that are *net* of tax.

However, once you have worked out an individual's *total* tax liability (i.e. what their actual tax liability would have been had no tax been deducted at source), you *then* deduct the tax they have already paid, which gives the final figure that they must pay to HMRC. If their total tax liability is *higher* than the tax deducted at source, the individual must pay the excess. If it is *lower*, the individual will qualify for a tax rebate (refund). Do not forget this step in an exam.

Summary: taxation of income

When calculating an individual's tax liability, follow the below steps:

1. Categorise different types of income into "non-savings income", "savings income" and "dividend income".
2. Deduct any available personal allowance. First deduct this from "non-savings income" then if there is any allowance, deduct it from "savings income" and then "dividend income" in this order.
3. Apply any relevant tax reliefs.
4. Apply the relevant rates of income tax.
5. Deduct the tax already paid at source (e.g. on savings or dividend income).

Business Taxation

The taxable income calculation is summarised in the below table:

Total income (gross)	X
- charges on income/pension contributions	(X)
= Net income	X
- personal allowance	(X)
= Total taxable income	X
Apply the relevant tax rate(s) (you may have to apply multiple tax rates depending on which tax bands the income falls across)	X
= Total tax liability	X
- Tax deducted at source	(X)
= Tax payable to HMRC	X

Capital Gains Tax

If an individual or a company sells an asset (e.g. a machine or a factory) for more than that asset originally cost, then a "capital gain" has arisen. The profit ("gain") made on the sale ("disposal") of that asset is what is subsequently taxed. "Disposal" includes transferring assets to other people as gifts and swapping them for alternative assets.

Capital gains are treated differently to income for tax purposes. Individuals pay "capital gains" tax on capital gains, the rates of which differ from the "income tax" rates. Companies pay "corporation tax" on their capital gains (as they do on income), but different reliefs are available to reduce the amount of gain that will be subject to tax (the "chargeable" gain). These reliefs are considered in more detail below. It is the *gain* that is taxed, not the *total* amount received for the asset. This means that the cost of purchasing/subsequently improving an asset, and the costs of selling that asset (e.g. estate agent, solicitor or auctioneer fees) will be deducted from the amount that is to be taxed.

Capital gains tax calculation

The formula for calculating taxable chargeable gain is set out below:

Sale price of asset (or *market value* if asset was received as a gift or from a "connected" person)

- Costs involved in disposing of the asset (e.g. auctioneer fees)

= Net Sale Proceeds

- Price paid to originally acquire the asset

- Incidental costs of originally acquiring the asset (e.g. solicitor's fees)

- Subsequent expenditure on *enhancing* the asset (e.g. funding an extension) or defending title if the asset is land

= Total Chargeable Gain

- Tax reliefs and exemptions (explained in detail later on)

- Capital losses carried forward/across (see below for an explanation)

= Taxable Chargeable Gain

> **"Enhancing"**: in this context, "enhancing" does not include expenditure on, for instance, routine repairs or costs involved in maintaining the asset. It must be something that would increase the value of the asset. Therefore, the building of an extension would constitute "enhancement" (it would increase the value of the asset) whereas the reparation of a fence would not.

> **"Connected person"**: in this context, examples of a "connected person" include an individual's: husband/wife, brother/sister, parent, grandparent or lineal descendant.

Capital losses

If an individual or a company sells an asset and makes a loss, tax relief may be available to reduce that individual's or company's tax burden. Capital losses may only be offset against capital gains (not income/trading profit) and the following rules must be followed:

1. Any capital losses must first be offset against capital gains that have arisen in the *same* accounting period.

2. If there are no capital gains in the same accounting period, or there are capital losses remaining once capital losses have offset *all* capital gains that arose in the same year, the taxpayer can carry forward the remaining capital losses to offset against future capital gains. Capital losses can *never* be carried back or be used to offset trading profits. The carrying back/forward of losses is explained in more detail in the *Taxation of Companies* section of this chapter.

Capital gains tax for individuals

The tax rate that an individual must pay on a chargeable gain will depend on the individual's total income. The thresholds are the same as the basic, higher and additional rate tax bands used for the purposes of calculating income tax.

- If an individual is a basic rate taxpayer, they must pay **10%** on their capital gains (subject to exemptions/allowances) unless the gain arises on the sale of a *residential* property, in which case the tax rate is **18%**.

- If an individual is a higher or an additional rate taxpayer (for income tax purposes), they must pay **20%** on their capital gains (subject to exemptions/allowances), unless the gain arises on the sale of a *residential* property, in which case the tax rate is **28%**.

There are various reliefs and exemptions available to reduce an individual's tax burden. Remember these figures change each tax year, so be sure to check the figures you are taught during your tax course.

Annual Exemption

Individuals (but not companies) receive an annual exemption that precludes them from having to pay tax on capital gains worth up to £12,300 in a year. *Note that this amount changes annually, so be sure to check the amount for the tax year on which your Business Tax course is based. The £12,300 figure is for the 2021/2022 tax year.*

> **Hayley earned £60,000 worth of taxable income in this financial year. She also sold a machine for £30,000 (she had purchased this machine for £10,000). How much capital gains tax must Hayley pay?**
>
> Hayley has made a capital gain of £20,000 (£30,000 - £10,000). Her annual exemption is £12,300 leaving her with a taxable chargeable gain of £7,700 (£20,000 - £12,300). As she has earned £60,000 worth of income, we know that she is a higher rate taxpayer, so the capital gains tax rate that applies is 20%.
>
> £7,700 x 20% = **£1,540** capital gains tax payable by Hayley.

Business Asset Disposal Relief

Business Asset Disposal Relief (known as Entrepreneurs' Relief prior to 6 April 2020) may be available to reduce an individual's (but not a company's) capital gains tax liability where that individual has made a gain as a result of selling shares. If the following criteria apply, then that individual will pay a flat rate of 10% on the taxable chargeable gain arising in relation to the sale of those shares (this percentage does not change for basic and higher/additional rate taxpayers):

1. The individual has not already used up their £1 million lifetime allowance (Business Asset Disposal Relief will only apply up to the first £1 million of qualifying capital gains that arise in an individual's lifetime; this limit was previously £10 million); and

2. For the 24 months prior to the disposal of the shares (12 months in respect of disposals made prior to 6 April 2019):

    (a) The person disposing of the shares must have been involved in the running of the company as a director or an employee;

    (b) The person disposing of the shares must have owned (and held voting rights representing) at least 5% of the company's ordinary shares;

    (c) The person must also have been entitled to at least 5% of the company's distributable profits and net assets (i.e. the assets that would be available on the winding up of the company) prior to the sale of the company's shares; and

    (d) The company must have been a trading company or the holding company of a trading company.

Capital gains and companies

As mentioned above, companies do not pay "capital gains" tax. Instead they pay corporation tax on capital gains that arise. Capital gains in the context of companies is therefore covered in the following *Taxation of Companies* section.

Taxation of Companies

Note that by "company" in this section, we mean a company that has been incorporated (either a private limited company or a public limited company). The profits of businesses run by sole traders are treated as the individual sole traders' profits/income and are thus taxed under the regime discussed in the previous section.

There are various differences between the treatment of income for individuals and companies. For example:

- **Personal allowance:** companies do not have a personal allowance, so tax is paid on *all* its taxable profits.
- **Savings income:** companies receive savings income *gross* (i.e. without having had tax deducted at source), so you do not need to "gross up" the savings income figure when calculating a company's total income.
- **Dividend income:** dividends received by a UK company will nearly always be exempt from tax. Therefore, for the purposes of this handbook, a company that receives a dividend from another company will not pay tax on that dividend.
- **Tax rates:** companies' profits are taxed at a flat rate of 19%; the rate does not increase in tandem with profit increases.

Calculating the Total Taxable Profits ("TTP")

Below is a summary of the calculation required to find a company's Total Taxable Profits figure. This is the amount to which the corporation tax rate is applied in order to calculate the amount of tax that the company must pay.

Total Taxable Profits = chargeable gains + income profits	
Chargeable gain	**Income profits**
Sale proceeds	Income receipts
- Allowable expenditure	- Deductible expenditure
- Indexation allowance	- Capital allowances
- Capital/Trading losses	- Trading losses
= Chargeable gain	**= Income profits**

Income profits

Income receipts

"Income receipts" refers to revenue that a company generates which is of an income nature (i.e. arises from trading activity).

Deductible expenditure

Only "expenses" that meet *all* the following criteria may be deducted from income before tax is calculated:

1. **Expenses that are incurred *wholly* and *exclusively* for the purposes of trade**: therefore, a company could not purchase a laptop for one of their shareholders and then deduct that as a business expense.
2. **Expenses that are not prohibited by statute from being deducted from revenue for tax purposes**: for instance, alcohol purchased to entertain clients cannot be deducted from revenue in order to reduce a company's tax burden.
3. **Expenses that are of an income nature**: this essentially means that expenses must relate to the day-to-day running of the business (for instance utility bills, rent, manufacturing costs, wages etc.) or to the purchase of items that the individual/company is in the business of buying and/or selling. Large one-off investments, such as the purchase of factories or machinery, *cannot* be treated as "expenses" (unless, for instance, the individual/company is in the business of buying and selling machinery). Such investments would instead be classed as "capital expenditure" and are taxed under the capital gains rules.

Capital allowances

Where a company purchases an asset to use as part of its business (e.g. equipment, machinery or business vehicles), this is known as **"capital expenditure"** (assuming the expenditure does not fulfil the "expenses" criteria for business expenditure). Let us use the purchase of a business laptop or a piece of machinery as an example. Both are examples of capital expenditure. Neither purchase is of an "income" nature (they are one-off purchases of fixed assets) so cannot simply be offset against the company's profits in the same way as expenses. Instead, companies can benefit from "capital allowances", which enable them to offset some or all of the value of the item(s) purchased from their profits for the purposes of reducing their tax liability.

Capital allowance rules

The rules governing capital allowances are complex, but for the purposes of the LPC a simplified overview should suffice. Note that only **"qualifying assets"** can give rise to capital allowances. Plant and machinery investments qualify, whereas land and buildings do not for instance. Whether an asset is qualifying is usually made quite clear on the LPC. The capital allowance rules allow businesses to offset 18% (or 6% under limited circumstances) of capital expenditure against their profits each year, until either: (1) the entire original cost of the assets purchased has been deducted for tax purposes; or (2) the assets have been sold/rendered defunct, in which case the loss/gain will be dealt with under the capital gains rules.

Business Taxation

..s, the first £1 million of any *new* capital expenditure can be *fully* offset against profits for the purposes of reducing a ...ity. This £1 million is known as the **Annual Investment Allowance**, which provides an incentive for businesses to invest. ...hases of new capital assets, you should first deduct the Annual Investment Allowance and *then* deduct 18% from the ... of that asset. You cannot use the Annual Investment Allowance to offset capital expenditure from previous years.

To illustrate the above, assume Company A has purchased a machine for £1,100,000. Company A's Annual Investment Allowance will enable it to offset £1,000,000 of the cost of this machine against its profits for that year, thus reducing its tax liability. This leaves £100,000 of the cost of the machine that has not yet been accounted for. Company A will also be able to deduct 18% of this £100,000 against its profits in that year (18% of £100,000 = £18,000). The following year, Company A could then offset another 18% of the value that has not yet been accounted for (£1,018,000 of the cost of the asset has already been accounted for, so Company A could only deduct 18% of the remaining £82,000 = £14,760).

Note that the Annual Investment Allowance could change on either 1st January or 1st April every year, so be sure to check which figure you are expected to use on the LPC. Although individuals and partnerships can also take advantage of capital allowances, the LPC tends to focus on companies in this context, which is why we have included this section here.

> 📖 **Capital allowance:** in summary, this is the amount that a business can offset against its profits to reduce its tax liability. It is comprised of (1) the Annual Investment Allowance; and (2) 18% of any additional capital expenditure not covered by the Annual Investment Allowance.

Written Down Value (WDV)

Once a business has offset some or all of the cost of qualifying assets that it has purchased, it must record the value of any remaining capital expenditure not yet offset, as this can then give rise to new capital allowances in the next financial year. The amount not yet offset is referred to as the "written down value". When calculating capital allowances, the below example may provide a useful reference point.

In Year 1, Bored Ltd purchased a machine for £1,300,000. It is a "qualifying asset" for tax purposes. It claims its full capital allowances for both Year 1 and Year 2. Bored Ltd owns no other "qualifying assets". What is the Written Down Value of the machine at the end of Year 2?

	Capital Allowance	**Written Down Value: end of year**
Year 1	Cost of the machine: £1,300,000 - Annual Investment Allowance (AIA): £1,000,000 can be offset against Bored Ltd's income profits. - Remaining capital allowance: a further 18% of £300,000* can be offset against Bored Ltd's income profits = £54,000 = **Total capital allowance for the year: £1,054,000**** £1,054,000 can be offset against Bored Ltd's income profits. * £1,300,000 cost of machine - £1,000,000 Annual Investment Allowance already offset = £300,000 ** £1,000,000 AIA + £54,000 further capital allowance = £1,054,000	Price originally paid: £1,300,000 - accumulated capital allowances: £1,054,000 = **Year 1 Written Down Value: £246,000*** * £1,300,000 cost of machine - £1,054,000 accumulated capital allowances relating to that machine = £246,000
Year 2	Year 1 Written Down Value: £246,000 - Remaining capital allowance: a further 18% of the £246,000 not yet accounted for can be offset against Bored Ltd's income profits = £44,280 = **Capital allowance for the year: £44,280*** £44,280 can be offset against Bored Ltd's income profits. * If Bored Ltd had bought another qualifying asset in Year 2, it could have taken advantage of its Annual Investment Allowance for Year 2 in relation to that new asset.	Price originally paid: £1,300,000 - accumulated capital allowances: £1,098,280* = **Year 2 Written Down Value: £201,720**** * £1,054,000 capital allowances relating to that machine in Year 1 + £44,280 capital allowances relating to that machine in Year 2 = £1,098,280 ** £1,300,000 cost of machine - £1,098,280 accumulated capital allowances relating to that machine = £201,720

Trading losses

If a company (or an individual) makes a trading loss (i.e. its expenses exceed its income), tax relief may be available to reduce that company's tax burden for previous or subsequent years where profit was/is generated. The following rules must be followed:

1. Trading losses should first be offset against trading profits and/or capital gains that have arisen *in the same accounting period*.

2. If there are still trading losses available to offset after step 1 has been followed, these losses may be *carried back* to the previous accounting period and offset against trading profits and/or capital gains. This could give rise to a tax rebate for the company. Note that the company must have been carrying out the *same trade* (i.e. the trade from which the losses arose) in both years to be able to carry back the losses to be offset against the previous year's profits.

3. If there are still trading losses that have not been offset at this stage, these losses may be *carried forward* to the next accounting period and offset against trading profits *arising from the same trade* (future capital gains *cannot* be offset).

Chargeable gain

A company will only pay tax on its *chargeable* gain and the formula on how to calculate this amount is set out in the *Capital Gains Tax* section above. Sale proceeds and allowable expenditure work in the same way as outlined in that section.

The main differences between the treatment of capital gains for individuals and companies are the reliefs and exemptions available and the rate of tax paid. Companies pay a flat rate of corporation tax (19%) on any taxable chargeable gain. Companies do not have an Annual Exemption and do not qualify for Business Asset Disposal Relief. Instead, they get the benefit of an "indexation allowance" and may be able to take advantage of the Substantial Shareholding Exemption and/or rollover relief.

Indexation allowance

The indexation allowance is a mechanism that takes into account the effect of inflation on the value of assets. This serves to reduce a company's chargeable gain on the disposal of an asset. LPC providers do generally not expect students to calculate the indexation allowance; the "indexation allowance" figure is usually given to you (i.e. it has already been calculated).

Substantial Shareholding Exemption ("SSE")

SSE is relevant where the assets being sold are shares in a company. If SSE applies, the company will not have to pay tax on any of the capital gain arising on the sale of those shares. For SSE to apply, the following criteria must be met:

1. The asset sold for a gain must be *shares* (i.e. not machinery, vehicles etc.);

2. The seller of the shares must be a *company* (i.e. not an individual);

3. The selling company must have owned at least 10% of the ordinary share capital of the subsidiary whose shares are being sold, for 12 *consecutive* months within the 6 year period prior to the disposal; and

4. The subsidiary whose shares are being sold must have been a *trading* company (or a member of a trading group) throughout the 12 month period prior to (and immediately after) the sale.

> **Juicy Ltd sells luxury campervans. Three years ago, it set up Wicked Ltd, a wholly-owned subsidiary, which sells budget campervans. Juicy Ltd has just sold all of the shares in Wicked Ltd, making a gain of £1 million. What is its corporation tax liability in relation to this gain?**
>
> On the facts, it seems that Juicy Ltd will qualify for the Substantial Shareholding Exemption, and will therefore not have to pay any tax on the gain. This is for the following reasons:
>
> - The disposed asset that gave rise to the gain was Wicked Ltd's *shares*.
>
> - The "Ltd" in Juicy Ltd's name indicates it is a *company* (not an individual).
>
> - Wicked Ltd has been a "wholly-owned" subsidiary (indicating Juicy owned 100%) for three years. This indicates the "10%+ shareholding for at least 12 consecutive months during the 6 years prior to the disposal" requirement is fulfilled.
>
> - Wicked Ltd was a trading company for at least 12 months prior to the sale, and nothing in the facts suggests it will stop trading immediately after the sale.

Where SSE is not available, rollover relief may be available. Rollover relief is available for a company if it is replacing an asset with another asset, so long as those assets both fall within the list of "qualifying assets" set out by HMRC. If a gain has arisen on the sale of the asset that is being replaced, the company can elect to postpone its liability to pay capital gains tax by "rolling over" the gain on the asset sold into the cost of the new asset being purchased. Note that rollover relief is a *deferral* mechanism; it does *not* permanently absolve the company of having to pay tax on the relevant gain.

The availability of rollover relief is subject to the following two rules:

1. The replacement asset must be purchased no earlier than 12 months before and no later than three years after the sale of the replaced asset.

2. If, when the cost of the replacement asset is deducted from the sale proceeds of the original asset, the resulting figure is greater than the amount of the gain that arose from the sale of the original asset, no rollover relief can be claimed.

Remember, when calculating the taxable chargeable gain, you deduct the *original* purchase price of the asset being sold from the sale price to ascertain the *taxable* gain. When a company has sold Asset A, replaced it with Asset B, and taken advantage of rollover relief, the gain "rolled over" will be deducted from the purchase price of Asset B (giving a lower "deemed" purchase price) for the purpose of calculating the capital gains tax due if/when Asset B is later sold for a gain.

> In 2012 Apollo Ltd sold Camper Field, a piece of land used to store its campervans, making a gain of £2 million. Apollo Ltd had been expanding steadily and bought a new larger plot of land, Camper Meadow, to replace Camper Field. What tax reliefs (if any) were available on the sale?
>
> The asset in question is land (not shares), so SSE is not available. Land is a "qualifying asset" for the purposes of rollover relief and Apollo Ltd replaced this asset with another qualifying asset, so rollover relief would have been available.
>
> Assume that Apollo Ltd took advantage of rollover relief to defer its tax liability on the sale of Camper Field and that it paid £5 million for Camper Meadow. If Apollo Ltd now sold Camper Meadow for £8 million and did not plan to replace it with another qualifying asset, what would its chargeable gain be on this disposal?
>
> First, we must deduct from the purchase price of Camper Meadow the £2 million (rolled over) gain on the sale of Camper Field. This gives us a "deemed" purchase price (for the purposes of calculating the chargeable gain) of £3 million for Camper Meadow (£5 million - £2 million). If Camper Meadow was sold for £8 million, its chargeable gain would be **£5 million** (£8 million sale price - £3 million "deemed" purchase price). As you can see, the earlier rollover relief claimed has increased Apollo Ltd's tax liability at this later stage to reflect the £2 million gain on the sale of Camper Field. If Apollo Ltd purchased *another qualifying* replacement asset at this stage, it could continue to defer its tax liability on the sale of both Camper Field and Camper Meadow, provided that new replacement assets purchased are expensive enough to cover the gains rolled over from previous sales.

Although rollover relief is less advantageous than SSE in the sense that the company will *eventually* have to pay tax on the gain, deferring the tax liability can have positive consequences for a company's cash flow and can free up funds to invest in additional assets. As mentioned in the example, companies can continue to rollover their gains from asset to asset until they sell an asset for a gain and do not replace it with a qualifying asset (subject to the above rules).

Trading losses

As mentioned above, if a company (or an individual) makes a trading loss, tax relief may be available. The rules for offsetting trading losses against profits and/or capital gains have been set out earlier in this section.

Capital losses

If a company sells an asset and makes a loss, this can be used to reduce that company's tax burden. Capital losses may only be offset against capital gains (not income profits) and the following rules must be followed:

1. Any capital losses must first be offset against capital gains that have arisen in the *same* accounting period.
2. If there are no capital gains in the same accounting period, or there are capital losses remaining once they have been offset against all capital gains, the company can carry *forward* the remaining capital losses to offset against future capital gains. Note, capital gains *cannot* be carried back or applied against trading profits.

> Over the past three years, Sydney Ltd has generated income and capital gains and incurred trading losses and capital losses as set out in the below table. How can the losses be offset to reduce Sydney Ltd's taxable profits?
>
> | Financial Year | Trading Profits (Trading Losses) | Capital Gains (Capital Losses) |
> |---|---|---|
> | 6th April 2018 – 5th April 2019 | £500,000 profit | £0 |
> | 6th April 2019 – 5th April 2020 | (£1,000,000 loss) | £20,000 gain + (£30,000 loss) |
> | 6th April 2020 – 5th April 2021 | £2,000,000 profit | £300,000 gain |
>
> **Capital gains/losses**
>
> 1. Offset the £30,000 capital loss incurred in the 2019-2020 financial year against the £20,000 gain made in that same year.
> 2. Carry forward the remaining £10,000 of capital losses (£30,000 losses - £20,000 gain) to the 2020-2021 financial year. This reduces the £300,000 capital gain to £290,000 for that year (thus reducing the tax Sydney Ltd will have to pay).
>
> **Trading profits/losses**
>
> 1. Offset the £1,000,000 trading loss incurred in 2019-2020 against the £500,000 profit generated in 2018-2019 financial year. This will reduce the taxable profit for 2018-2019 to £0. As Sydney Ltd will have already paid tax for the 2018-2019 year, it will receive a tax rebate for the amount paid.
> 2. This leaves £500,000 worth of trading losses to offset (£1,000,000 losses - £500,000 profit in the previous year). This £500,000 should next be carried forward and offset against the £2,000,000 trading profits generated in the 2020-2021 financial year, leaving £1,500,000 of trading profits to tax in respect of that year.
>
> **Total Taxable Profits for 2020-2021:** £290,000 capital gains + £1,500,000 trading profits = **£1,790,000**

Calculation and payment to HMRC of corporation tax

Corporation tax must be *paid* within **9 months and 1 day of the end of the previous accounting period if the company's total taxable profits are £1,500,000 or less**. However, if a company's total taxable profits figure is higher than £1,500,000, it must make corporation tax payments *quarterly* (i.e. every 3 months). Tax returns must be submitted within 1 year of the previous accounting period and Her Majesty's Revenue & Customs ("HMRC") has 6 years from this point to investigate whether the correct tax has been paid.

Paying interest on a loan

Note that if a company subject to UK corporation tax pays interest on a loan taken out from an individual, it will pay the interest *net* of tax. However, interest payments made to other companies and banks that pay UK corporation tax are made *gross* of tax (i.e. the borrower company need not deduct corporation tax on the lender's behalf before paying interest to the lender).

Close companies

The concept of a "close company" is relevant when, for instance, considering loans given by a company to its directors. A close company is defined in Corporation Tax Act s. 439. A company will be a close company if it fulfils either of two tests:

1. The company is *controlled* by five or fewer *participators*.
2. The company is *controlled* by any number of participators *who are also directors*.

> **Participator:** a person with an interest in/entitlement to a share of the capital or income of the company. "Participators" are typically shareholders, but may also be certain types of creditors.

> **Control:** a company is *controlled* by participators in this context if those participators collectively own more than 50% of the issued share capital or are entitled to the greater part (more than 50%) of the company's assets on a winding up.

If a close company gives a loan worth £15,000 or more to one of its participators, the company may have to pay corporation tax at a rate of 25% of the value of the loan. This will be the case if the borrower is a participator with a "material interest", which is defined as either: (a) indirect control of more than 5% of the company's ordinary shares; or (b) an entitlement on a winding up to more than 5% of the company's available assets. Such tax must be paid no later than "9 months and one day" from the end of the accounting period in which the loan was given.

Summary

Below are some of the key distinctions that you must remember to make when applying concepts in an exam.

Remember...

- **Total Taxable Income** is not the same as *revenue* or *net income*. Total Taxable Income is the amount of income that qualifies to be taxed once all relevant expenses have been deducted and the relevant tax exemptions and reliefs have been applied.
- **Capital gains** arise when assets have been *disposed of* for a profit. Capital gains are subject to different taxation rules for individuals and companies.
- **Capital allowances** can only be applied in relation to "qualifying" assets. Capital allowances give companies tax relief against profits, to encourage capital expenditure.
- **Tax rates** change for individuals depending on the amount they earn, the type(s) of income they receive and whether they have made a capital gain. Companies in contrast pay a flat rate of 19% corporation tax on their Total Taxable Profits (for companies, Total Taxable Profits includes both income profits and chargeable gains).

Individuals

- **Grossing up:** income tax is paid on an individual's *net* income. When calculating this, do not forget to *gross up* savings interest and dividend income (if you have been given the *net* savings/dividend income figures).
- **Tax relief for income:** ensure an individual's personal allowance has been applied and that any charges on income (e.g. pension contributions) have been dealt with.
- **Tax relief for capital gains:** if an individual has made a capital gain, ensure their annual exemption and (if applicable) Business Asset Disposal Relief have been applied. Any available capital losses should also be offset.
- **Other ways to reduce tax liabilities:**

    Tax relief is given for contributions made to personal pension schemes (as explained above), so an individual could make greater contributions out of their income in order to reduce their net income and thus pay less tax (although they will then have less disposable income).

    If a person owns shares that pay large dividends and has a spouse that is a lower rate taxpayer, that person could transfer their shares to their spouse so that a lower rate of tax will be paid on those dividends. The spouse would receive those shares on a "no gain, no loss" basis, and (as a lower rate tax payer) would pay less tax on any gain if the shares were subsequently sold.

    Individuals could make contributions to tax efficient savings vehicles such as Individual Savings Accounts (ISAs), as gains (i.e. interest) made on valid contributions to such accounts are exempt from tax (thus reducing the taxable savings income).

Companies

- **Tax relief for income:** ensure any trading/capital losses have been offset, and any qualifying capital allowances are claimed in order to reduce a company's income tax liability. Remember, **companies do not have a personal allowance**.
- **Tax relief for capital gains:** if a company has made a capital gain, it should take advantage of the substantial shareholding exemption where possible and if this is not available, consider whether rollover relief is available. Remember, **companies do not have an annual exemption.**

# Business Accounts

Companies are required by law to submit annual accounts to Companies House. These will show, in particular, the company's profits, losses, assets, liabilities and capital and give shareholders an indication of the company's financial performance. These accounts are typically not examined in any great detail on the LPC, but there are key elements that you may be required to assess/amend, notably: depreciation, accruals, prepayments and bad and doubtful debts.

You will usually be given a "trial balance" as part of a question examining your knowledge of business accounts. A trial balance sets out a number of items, including: revenue, various assets and liabilities, and a range of different expenses. You should start by categorising these items into: (1) items that appear in the Income Statement; and (2) items that appear in the Balance Sheet.

Key Accounts

In the UK, all registered companies are required to file financial accounts. Under CA 06 s. 477, publicly listed companies and private companies are required to publish more substantial, fully audited accounts if two or more of the criteria in CA 06 s. 382(3) apply: (a) the company's turnover exceeds £10.2 million; (b) the company assets are worth more than £5.1 million; and/or (c) the company has more than 50 employees on average.

For investors, financial accounts may indicate the viability of different investment options. They provide an insight into a company's financial performance and financial standing. Financial accounts are thus the building blocks for an analysis of a company's ability to generate profit and meet interest repayments (for example, payments to banks that have lent the company money). There are two key financial statements that you should aim to understand:

1. **The Income Statement** (or **"Profit and Loss Account"**): this measures a company's revenue, expenses (including interest and taxes) and after-tax profit over a year; and

2. **The Balance Sheet** (or **"Statement of Financial Position"**): this provides a snapshot of a company's financial position at a particular date (usually the end of the year).

Note that the third key financial statement is the Cash Flow Statement. However, this falls outside the scope of this handbook, as it does not tend to get covered in any detail on the LPC.

Income Statement/Profit and Loss Account

The Income Statement (known historically in the UK as the Profit and Loss Account) details a company's financial performance resulting from its day-to-day operations over a defined period of time (typically one year). It shows the income generated from a firm's operations within a period of time; the expenses relating to those operations; and the net profit (also known as the "bottom line" as it appears at the bottom of the Income Statement). Different companies may report their Income Statements in slightly different ways. The below example provides a *very* simplified illustration of an Income Statement, including an outline of the key elements. Brackets have been used to indicate that the amount is to be deducted from the revenue/profit before tax figures.

Income Statement	
Revenue/Turnover/Sales	**£ XX.XX**
– Cost of Goods Sold	£ (XX.XX)
– Selling, General & Administrative Costs	£ (XX.XX)
= Profit Before Tax	**£ XX.XX**
– Tax	£ (XX.XX)
= Net Profit	**£ XX.XX**

> 📖 **Cost of goods sold:** also referred to as "variable costs", this category of costs includes the direct costs associated with each sale. These costs will therefore change in relation to the number of units produced or sold and might include, for example, the cost of manufacturing, packaging and delivering each individual product.

> 📖 **Selling, General & Administrative costs / fixed costs:** these costs include general expenses that do not directly relate to each individual sale. Examples include: the rent paid for an office or a factory; the cost of paying utility bills; or the cost of fuel for an aeroplane flight. These costs will all remain the same (or almost the same) regardless of whether a business sells 0 or 1,000 units.

> 📖 **Net profit:** refers to the amount of money remaining from the revenue after all related expenses have been subtracted.

Business Accounts

Note that your LPC may use different terminology for different elements of the income statement and may split the above categories into sub categories. For instance, instead of being given a value for "Selling, General & Administrative Costs", you may be given a breakdown of costs within this category, such as: rent, utility bills, postage expenses etc.

Analysing elements of the Income Statement

You may be presented with basic financial accounts from the current year and the previous few years. If this is the case (depending on the issues you are asked to consider), start by analysing the profit figures to see how the company's performance has changed.

Profit

- If profits have increased year on year, this could indicate that the company could continue to thrive. Conversely, if the net profit has decreased, this could, on the face of it, suggest it may eventually run into financial difficulties. At this stage you should then try to discover (through looking at the accounts) *why* the net profit has decreased.

Revenue

- Check how revenue has changed year on year. Increases in revenue could indicate the company is growing and financially stable. Conversely, a decrease in revenue (which could cause a corresponding decrease in net profit) could suggest consumers are purchasing less of the company's products, which in turn may indicate that new competitors have entered the market (or that existing competitors have developed a similar or superior product, perhaps at a more favourable price).

Costs

- If the revenue has remained the same or increased but the net profit has decreased, look at whether the costs have increased (which would also decrease the net profit). If costs have increased, does this suggest the company has failed to implement effective mechanisms to control costs? If this seems to be the case, think of potential solutions, for instance laying off staff or looking for cheaper suppliers. Has the cost of raw materials increased? For example, if the company produces apple juice, has the price of apples increased?

- Alternatively, has the company made an investment (e.g. purchased a factory or invested in advertising) that has increased costs in the current year (and thus reduced the net profit)? Could this investment contribute to an increase in net profit in the future? Similarly, if there are costs associated with redundancies, this could mean that new equipment has been purchased to replace staff. This could lead to cost savings (and thus greater profit margins) in the future, even if profits are negatively affected in the short-term.

Balance Sheet/Statement of Financial Position

The Balance Sheet, also known as the Statement of Financial Position, provides a snapshot of a company's financial situation. It is an essential tool for analysing a company's finances, as it contains information on the company's capital structure.

> **Capital Structure:** this refers to the proportion of a company's capital (financial resources) that is attributable to debt and the proportion of the company's capital that is attributable to equity. This in turn can affect a company's ability to raise additional capital or its attractiveness to investors. For instance, a company that is highly in debt will be perceived as a riskier investment by potential lenders or investors.

Dual effect of transactions

All financial events in the life of a company must be accounted for through the recording of two corresponding entries in the Balance Sheet (each transaction has a **"dual effect"** on the Balance Sheet). These entries should be recorded using the **"double entry"** system. A company's assets (which are detailed on the top of the Balance Sheet) must have been supported through the use of some sort of financing, either through the company taking on debt ("liabilities") or equity/capital.

> **Asset:** something of value to a company. Tangible assets include machinery and factories. Intangible assets include intellectual property rights, customer loyalty and knowledge. On a Balance Sheet, it is generally the tangible assets that are accounted for.

For example, if a company raises £1 million through selling shares, and also takes out a loan of £1 million, its total assets will amount to £2 million.

- This £2 million will be recorded as:
    (a) £2 million cash in the "Current Assets" section of the Balance Sheet; and
    (b) £1 million in the "Equity" section and £1 million in the "Liabilities" section.

- If the company subsequently purchases a building for £500,000, then cash (on the "Assets" side) will reduce to £1.5 million and a new category will be created (also on the "Assets" side), typically called Plant, Property & Equipment, the value of which will be £500,000.

- In the meantime, the "Equity and Liabilities" side of the Balance Sheet will remain unchanged as no new share capital has been received and no new debt has been taken on.

- If £500,000 of the loan is then paid off using cash, the "Assets" section will decrease by £500,000 (to reflect the fact that cash has been spent on paying off the debt) and there would be a corresponding decrease in the "Liabilities" section (to reflect the fact that the value of the outstanding loan has reduced to £500,000).

The dual effects of various transactions are explained in the next section. On the next page is a simplified overview of a Balance Sheet.

Business Accounts

Balance Sheet/Statement of Financial Position	
Assets	
Current Assets	£XX.XX
Cash, receivables/debtors (payments due from customers), prepayments (explained later) inventory and other assets that will either be sold or removed from the Balance Sheet within a year.	
Non-Current (or "Fixed") Assets	£XX.XX
Machinery, land and buildings, long-term investments (including stakes in other companies), and other assets that will remain on the Balance Sheet for longer than a year. Accumulated depreciation is also set out here to reflect the net book value of the company's assets (explained below).	
Liabilities	
Current Liabilities	£XX.XX
Short-term debt (hence "current" liabilities), accruals (explained below), creditors (money owed to suppliers etc.), tax liabilities and other liabilities that will be removed from the Balance Sheet within a year.	
Non-Current Liabilities	£XX.XX
Long-term debt and equivalents (e.g. pension liabilities) and other liabilities that will remain on the Balance Sheet for longer than a year.	
Total Assets – Total Liabilities = Net Assets	**£XXX.XX**
Equity (sometimes referred to as "**Capital**")	
Retained Earnings	£XX.XX
Net profit minus dividends.	
Share Capital	£XX.XX
The *nominal* value of a company's shares multiplied by the number of shares sold.	
Share Premium	£XX.XX
Any *premium* paid by shareholders for their shares.	
Revaluation Reserve	£XX.XX
Sets out any changes in the value of company property.	
Capital Redemption Reserve	£XX.XX
This is created only when a company buys back or redeems its own shares (explained below).	
Total Equity	**£XXX.XX**

In the above Balance Sheet, **Assets – Liabilities (i.e. "Net Assets") = Equity**. The Net Assets figure *must* be the same as the Equity figure. If the figures are not identical, then the Balance Sheet does not "balance" and this means that there has been an error or omission in the recording of transactions and/or the preparation of the Balance Sheet. Note that sometimes only Assets are recorded on the top half of the Balance Sheet, with both Equity and Liabilities being recorded on the bottom half. When this is the case, Assets = Equity – Liabilities.

Recording transactions on the Balance Sheet

Share issue

Where a company issues new shares, the actual *money* it receives in return for those shares counts as an asset. The corresponding entry (or entries) will be within the "Equity" section of the Balance Sheet.

- If the shares are issued at nominal value, the corresponding entry will be recorded in the "share capital" account, which is listed within the "Equity" section of the Balance Sheet.
- If the shares are issued at a premium, there will have to be *two* corresponding entries: (1) an entry reflecting the *nominal value* of the shares issued, recorded in the "share capital" account; and (b) an entry reflecting the premium paid by shareholders for the shares, which will be recorded in the "share premium" account (also within the "Equity" section of the Balance Sheet).

> **Nominal value**: the face value of a share without taking into account any premium charged by the issuer or any increase in market value since the share was issued.

> **Share capital**: the funds that a company has raised by issuing shares.

> **Share premium account:** any premium paid by shareholders for their shares must be recorded separately in the "share premium" account. In this context, "premium" simply means any amount paid in excess of the "nominal" value. Do not confuse this with the "share capital" account, which only represents the nominal value of shares issued (not any additional premium charged by the company for those shares).

Dual effect on the Balance Sheet

- **Current assets ↑** The "Assets" section of the Balance Sheet increases. Money received would be recorded as cash (or "cash at bank"), which constitutes a current asset.

- **Share capital account ↑** The "Share Capital" account increases by the *nominal value* of the shares that have been issued. This account is listed in the "Equity" section of the Balance Sheet.

- **Share premium account ↑** Any premium paid by shareholders for their shares must be recorded *separately* in the "share premium" account (which is listed in the "Equity" section of the Balance Sheet). Note that no entry needs to be made in the share premium account if the shares are *not* issued at a premium.

Bonus issue of shares

A "bonus issue" of shares involves a company issuing shares to its existing shareholders *pro rata* (in proportion) to their existing shareholding, *without charging* those shareholders for the new shares. This means the company receives *no* consideration. A company may choose to do this to: (a) keep shareholders happy if that company lacks the cash to pay a reasonable dividend; and (b) increase the liquidity of its shares in the market (i.e. make it easier for shareholders to be able to sell their shares on the market). Liquidity would increase because the introduction of new shares will inevitably reduce the price of each individual share. Note that because shareholders will have a greater *number* of shares following the issue, this drop in the value of each individual share should not affect the overall value of their shareholdings.

Dual effect on the Balance Sheet

Note that as the company receives no consideration for the shares, the "Assets" section of the Balance Sheet is unaffected.

- **Share capital ↑** The "share capital" account increases by the *nominal value* of the bonus shares that have been issued.

- **Share premium account or retained profits ↓** CA 06 s. 610(3) states that the company may fund a bonus issue of shares using either its retained profits or funds from its share premium account (note this is one of the only circumstances under which funds in the share premium account may be used). Therefore, the "share premium" account or "retained profits" figure will reduce by the amount added to the "share capital" account, thus balancing the Balance Sheet.

Taking out a loan

Where a company takes out a loan, this will increase the amount of cash it has (meaning assets will increase), whilst also increasing its liabilities on the Balance Sheet (as debt is a "liability" that must eventually be repaid).

Dual effect on the Balance Sheet

- **Current assets ↑** The "Assets" section of the Balance Sheet increases (as cash is a current asset).

- **Liabilities ↑** The "Liabilities" section of the Balance Sheet will also increase (by the amount of the loan). Whether the "Current Liabilities" or "Non-Current Liabilities" increase will depend on whether the loan must be repaid in the short-term or long-term. As **Assets − Liabilities = Equity**, the increase in "Liabilities" will balance out the increase in "Assets", ensuring the "Net Assets" figure remains as it was before the loan was taken out.

Paying a dividend

Remember, dividends can only be paid out of retained (or "distributable") profits. Also remember that once declared, a dividend becomes a legally enforceable "debt" (and thus a liability for the company). This debt is only discharged once the dividend is paid.

Dual effect on the Balance Sheet when a dividend is *declared*

- **Current liabilities ↑** The current liabilities figure increases, as once a dividend is declared, it becomes a legally enforceable "debt", due in the short-term.

- **Retained profits ↓** The retained profits figure will reduce by the amount that the current liabilities have increased, thus ensuring the Balance Sheet balances (remember, the "Current Liabilities" figure *reduces* the "Net Assets" figure, and it is the *"Net Assets"* figure that must match the *Equity* figure at the bottom of the Balance Sheet).

Dual effect on the Balance Sheet when a dividend is *paid*

- **Current assets ↓** The current assets figure decreases by the amount paid to shareholders as a dividend.

- **Retained profits ↓** The retained profits figure will reduce by the amount that the current assets have reduced, thus ensuring the Balance Sheet balances.

Share buyback/Capital Redemption Reserve

As mentioned in the *Share Buybacks* section of the Business Law module, share buybacks may involve own share purchases or redemptions, and may be funded using retained profits, capital or a fresh issue of shares. Assets will always decrease to reflect the funds used to finance the share buyback (i.e. the money paid to shareholders for their shares). The corresponding entry will depend on how the buyback was funded, and there may be multiple corresponding entries if the buyback was funded using multiple forms of finance (e.g. retained profits and – once those profits have all been used – capital).

> 📖 **Capital Redemption Reserve**: once shares have been bought back, they are typically "cancelled", meaning the nominal value of those shares must be subtracted from the "share capital" section of the Balance Sheet (thus reflecting the fact that the company has a smaller number of shares in circulation post-buyback). To ensure the Balance Sheet still balances, an artificial entry is made in the Balance Sheet called "Capital Redemption Reserve". If shares are bought back out of retained profits or the proceeds of a fresh issue of shares, the Capital Redemption Reserve is *increased* by the amount by which the share capital has been reduced CA 06 s. 733 (thus ensuring the Balance Sheet balances). You do not study the Capital Redemption Reserve in any great detail on the LPC, so this section is providing a simple overview.

Dual effect on the Balance Sheet

- **Share capital** ⬇ If the shares that were bought back are cancelled, the share capital figure in the "Equity" section of the Balance Sheet must decrease by the nominal value of the cancelled shares.
- **Capital Redemption Reserve** ⬆ The "Capital Redemption Reserve" is created in the "Equity" section of the Balance Sheet and its value should reflect the value of any cancelled shares.
- **Current assets** ⬇ The current assets figure decreases by the amount paid to shareholders for their shares (to reflect the cash that has left the company to finance the purchase of those shares).
- **Retained profits** ⬇ Assuming the share buyback was funded using retained profits, the retained profits figure will reduce by the amount that the current assets have reduced, thus ensuring the Balance Sheet balances.

Volcano Ltd has bought back 100,000 of its shares using distributable profits, at a price of £225 per share, equalling £22.5 million. The shares were originally issued at their nominal value of £1 per share. The shares have been cancelled. How would you adjust the Balance Sheet?

The following adjustments must be made:

- Note that funds from the share premium account cannot be used to fund the share buyback, as the shares being bought back were not originally issued at a premium. In addition, liabilities have been left out of the below Balance Sheet, since they are not affected by the purchase.
- Reduce the net assets by £22.5 million, as this is the amount of cash that was used to purchase the shares.
- Reduce the retained profits by the amount spent on the buyback (£22.5 million). Remember, the distributable profits on the bottom half of the Balance Sheet correspond to some of the net assets on the top half of the Balance Sheet.
- Reduce the share capital figure by the nominal value of the shares bought back (£100,000) so that the Balance Sheet reflects the fact that Volcano Ltd now has a lower share capital (the shares that were bought back have been cancelled).
- Add the amount that you have deducted from the share capital account (£100,000) to the capital redemption reserve (an artificial account), purely to ensure that the Balance Sheet balances.

These changes are represented below. Remember, the net assets figure must match the equity figure if the Balance Sheet is to "balance". Note that this is a simplified Balance Sheet that does not take into account other forms of assets/capital.

Accounts	Before share buyback	After share buyback
Assets		
Total net assets	£147.2 million	£124.7 million (£147.2 million - £22.5 million)
Equity		
Share capital	£1.1 million	£1 million (£1.1 million - £100,000 nominal value of shares bought back)
Share premium account	£22.2 million	£22.2 million
Capital Redemption Reserve	N/A	£100,000 (artificial entry so the Balance Sheet balances)
Retained profits	£123.9 million	£101.4 million (£123.9 million - £22.5 million worth of distributable profits)
Total Equity	£147.2 million	£124.7 million

Revaluing company property

Sometimes a company may have its property revalued so that the true value of its assets can be reflected in its financial statements. For instance, if the company owns land and the land increases in value, it will want its Balance Sheet to reflect the fact that it now owns assets with a higher value (and is thus in a better position financially). Such an increase in value would be noted in the "Assets" section of the Balance Sheet. However, the increase in value cannot be attributed to the company raising any additional finance or spending its capital/retained profits. Without there being some corresponding entry elsewhere in the Balance Sheet, the Balance Sheet would no longer balance. The revaluation reserve is created to resolve this issue.

> **Revaluation Reserve:** the "Revaluation Reserve" is an artificial entry in the "Equity" section of the Balance Sheet. It is created to record a corresponding entry where the "Assets" section of the Balance Sheet has changed as a result of the revaluation of company property. Its value mirrors any changes in the value of company property resulting from a revaluation, ensuring that the Balance Sheet will still balance.

Dual effect on the Balance Sheet

- **Non-current assets ↑** The "Assets" section of the Balance Sheet increases (land counts as a non-current asset and as the land has increased in value, the overall "Assets" figure should increase to reflect this).
- **Revaluation reserve ↑** The "Revaluation Reserve" is created in the "Equity" section of the Balance Sheet and its value should reflect the increase in value noted in the Assets section.

Depreciation, Accruals, Prepayments and Bad and Doubtful Debts

Depreciation

> **Depreciation:** refers to the decrease in value of tangible (physical) assets over time. An older asset that has been regularly used will typically be worth less than a newer version of the same asset, as it is more likely to break or work with reduced efficiency. Accordingly, accountants typically record an asset's estimated loss in value (which has occurred as a result of the use of that asset over the accounting year) as a cost in the company's accounts. For example, assume a tractor owned by a farmer has an expected useful life (before it is likely to mechanically break or operate with unsatisfactory inefficiency) of approximately 30 years. If it costs £30,000 new, it is more sensible for accountants to reduce the value of the asset gradually year on year rather than state that the asset's value is £30,000 until the day before it is 30 years old, then the very next day record its value as £0. In this example, the cost of depreciation (on a straight-line basis) would be £30,000 / 30 = £1,000 per year for 30 years.

There are various methods that companies can use to estimate and record depreciation in their accounts, including the "straight line" method and the "reducing balance" method.

- **Straight line:** you deduct a percentage from the *original cost* each year. For example, if a tractor cost £50,000 and is depreciated by 10% each year using the straight line method, you will deduct a fixed amount of £5,000 (10% x £50,000) *every* year. Therefore, the tractor's value (as stated on the balance sheet) will decrease by £5,000 each year.
- **Reducing balance:** you deduct a percentage from the *Net Book Value* (cost – accumulated depreciation) each year.

> **Net Book Value (NBV):** the Net Book Value can be found by deducting any depreciation recorded in previous years from the original cost of the asset. For instance, if a tractor cost £50,000 and the depreciation percentage used is 10%, you would deduct £5,000 depreciation in year 1. This leaves you with a Net Book Value of £45,000 (£50,000 - £5,000 depreciation). In year 2, you would deduct 10% from £45,000, which would give you £4,500 depreciation and a new Net Book Value of £40,500 (£50,000 - £5,000 depreciation from year 1 - £4,500 depreciation from year 2). In year 3, you would deduct 10% depreciation from £40,500, giving £4,050 depreciation and a Net Book Value of £36,450 (and so on).

Dual effect on the Balance Sheet

- **Non-current assets ↓** The "Non-current Assets" section of the Balance Sheet decreases, as the depreciation for the year reduces the value of the company's non-current assets. Remember, the company's cash remains unaffected, since although depreciation is deemed an "expense" for the purposes of the company's financial accounts, the company has not *spent* cash to meet this "expense".
- **Retained profit ↓** Retained profit decreases in the "Equity" section of the Balance Sheet, as depreciation counts as an expense, which in turn reduces the company's retained profit figure.

Equipment that originally cost £34,000 will be depreciated using the straight line method at a rate of 10% per annum. Since the original purchase, the equipment has already depreciated in value by £20,000.

Category of fixed assets	Depreciation charge for this year	Accumulated depreciation at the start of this year	Accumulated depreciation at the end of this year
Equipment	£3,400 (10% x £34,000)	£20,000	£23,400
	This figure should be recorded in the Income Statement as an "expense".	This figure will be given in the trial balance.	This figure should be recorded in the "Assets" sections of the Balance Sheet.

Accruals

📖 **Accruals:** these are liabilities that a company has accrued to third parties. They arise when the company has used goods or services that it has not yet paid for (and will thus have to pay for in the future). For example, a company may use electricity before actually receiving (and paying) the bill for that electricity. Before the bill has been paid, the money owed for the electricity used will constitute an accrual in that company's financial accounts.

Dual effect on the Balance Sheet

- **Current liabilities ↑** Current liabilities increase in the "Liabilities" section of the Balance Sheet (as the money owed must be repaid in the short term).

- **Retained profit ↓** Retained profit decreases in the "Equity" section of the Balance Sheet (as expenses increase, thus reducing profit).

The Balance Sheet will "balance", as the increase in "Liabilities" will reduce the "Net Assets" figure (on the top half of the Balance Sheet) by the same amount as the reduction in "Equity" (on the bottom half of the Balance Sheet).

Leather Ltd used £500 worth of electricity in its current accounting period, but has not yet paid for it. Show how the Profit and Loss Account and Balance Sheet for that accounting period will need to be adjusted.

Accrual Item	Expense given in trial balance	Amount of accrual	Expense in Profit and Loss Account	Balance Sheet adjustment
Electricity	£7,500	£500	£8,000	£500
			We increase the expense to account for the fact that the electricity has been used in the year for which the accounts are being prepared. As this expense was incurred in the process of generating the profit shown in the trial balance, the expense must be accounted for even though it has not yet been paid (£8,000 reflects the true value of electricity used in that year).	*The Current Liabilities figure in the Balance Sheet must be increased by £500, as the money owed for electricity constitutes a liability that must be paid in the near future.*

Prepayments

📖 **Prepayments:** these are assets that a company will stand to benefit from in the future. They arise when the company has paid in advance for goods or services that it has not yet used (and will thus be entitled to use at no additional charge in the future). For example, a company may pay rent for its offices 6 months in advance. Before the offices have been used for the period paid for in advance, the money paid for rent will constitute a prepayment in that company's financial accounts.

Dual effect on the Balance Sheet

- **Current assets ↑** Current assets in the "Assets" section of the Balance Sheet increase (the entitlement to use the goods/services that have been prepaid for constitutes an asset).

- **Retained profit ↑** Retained profit increases in the "Equity" section of the Balance Sheet (this is because the expenses figure reduces, thus increasing profit).

Leather Ltd paid £12,000 for 12 months' rent (at £1,000 per month), commencing on 1 May 2021. Leather Ltd's accounting year ends on 31 December 2021. Show how the Profit and Loss Account and Balance Sheet will need to be adjusted.

Prepayment Item	Expense given in trial balance	Prepayment made	Expense in Profit and Loss Account	Balance Sheet adjustment
Rent	£42,000	£4,000	£38,000	£4,000
			We decrease the expenses figure in the Profit and Loss Account to reflect the fact that some of the amount was paid for rent that will not be used until the next financial year (as it will benefit the company in the next financial year, it should be offset against next year's profits, hence the adjustment to this year's Profit and Loss Account).	*The Current Assets figure in the Balance Sheet must be increased by £4,000, as the money paid in advance for future rent (rent for January 2021 – April 2021) constitutes an asset.*

Bad and doubtful debts

- **Bad debts:** these are debts owed to the company that have been written off, usually because the debtor (e.g. a customer that owes money to the company) has become insolvent.

- **Doubtful debts:** these are debts that the company believes will be written off, for instance if it is aware some of its debtors are in financial difficulty. A company will usually make provision for doubtful debts, recording in its accounts a percentage that it believes it will have to write off. This percentage may be adjusted from year-to-year and it is this adjustment that must be recorded in the company's financial accounts (by adjusting the company's "expenses" figure).

Dual effect of *bad debts* on the Balance Sheet

- **Assets ↓** "Receivables" in the "Assets" section of the Balance Sheet decreases to reflect the fact that the money owed by the creditor will not actually be paid.
- **Retained profit ↓** Retained profit decreases in the "Equity" section of the Balance Sheet, as the business' income for the accounting year will now be lower than it had previously expected.

Explanations of each adjustment are set out in the table below. When making an adjustment on the LPC, always deal with the bad debts before you deal with the doubtful debts (as illustrated below).

Provision for Doubtful Debts: *start* of year	Provision for Doubtful Debts: *end* of year	Increase/ decrease in provision for Doubtful Debts	Bad Debts	Bad and Doubtful Debts expense *(this affects the Profit and Loss Account)*	Adjusted "debtors" figure *(this goes in the Balance Sheet)*
This figure should be given to you either in the trial balance or in the question.	You may be given (1) a specific provision and (2) a general provision, expressed as an estimated % of the "debtors" figure. Before calculating this, ensure your "debtors" figure takes into account any new debts that the company is owed this year.	Here you note the change in provision from the start of the year to the end of the year.	You should be told this figure. Note, you only need to adjust the "debtors" figure if you are told about an *additional* year-end bad debt. All other bad debts should have already been taken into account and thus reflected in the "debtors" figure in the trial balance.	Add / subtract the increase / decrease in the provision for doubtful debts (given in column 3) to/from the "bad debts" figure given in column 4. The figure you get should be included in the Profit and Loss Account and will either increase or decrease the company's expenses.	Deduct the year-end provision for doubtful debts figure from the "debtors" figure given in the trial balance. This figure should be included in the Balance Sheet

---

Make the necessary calculations/state the required adjustments to the Profit and Loss Account and Balance Sheet based on the following:
- Provision for doubtful debts (start of year): £6,000
- Provision for doubtful debts (end of year): £4000 (specific provision) + 1% of debtors (general)
- Bad debts: £5,000 has already been written off in the course of the accounting period.
- Debtors figure in the trial balance: £304,000

Provision for doubtful debts: start of year	Provision for doubtful debts: end of year	Increase/ decrease in provision for doubtful debts	Bad debts	Bad and doubtful debts expense	Adjusted "debtors" figure
£6,000* *This figure is given to you in the question	£7,000 *£4000 (specific provision for doubtful debts) + 1% of £300,000 = £3,000 (general provision for doubtful debts). Note: the "debtors" figure given was £304,000. We should only calculate the general provision (1%) from what is left of the debtors figure after the specific provision (£4000) has been accounted for (i.e. £304,000 - £4000 = £300,000, which we then multiply by 1%)	£1000* *£7,000 - £6,000 = £1,000 increase in provision for doubtful debts	£5,000* *This figure is given to you in the question	£6,000* *£1,000 (change in provision) + £5,000 (bad debts)	£304,000* *You only need to adjust the "debtors" figure given in the trial balance if you are told about an additional year-end bad debt. The £5,000 bad debt mentioned in the facts of this question will already be reflected in the £304,000 "debtors" figure. If the £5,000 bad debt had been stated to be an additional/new bad debt, then you would first deduct it from the debtors figure (e.g. £304,000 - £5000) before calculating the provision for doubtful debts in the second column (i.e. multiplying the figure by 1%).

0# Solicitors' Accounts

This module covers how a law firm/solicitor should account for: (a) money held on behalf of clients; and (b) money that belongs to the solicitor. There are various rules and frameworks that must be followed when recording any transactions involving client money and firm money. The Solicitors Regulation Authority Accounts Rules (the "Rules") © *The Law Society 2019* is one of the main sources you will use in this context.

- Law firms will have a "client" bank account, in which money belonging to their clients will be held. Clients will deposit money into this account and solicitors will then use it to pay any expenses incurred on behalf of that client (e.g. the deposit/purchase price of a property, the cost of carrying out due diligence searches, and the cost of the legal advice itself). The objective underpinning these rules is to keep money belonging to clients of the firm safe.

- Law firms will also have an "office" bank account for their own money. Sometimes payments will/must be made from the office account on behalf of clients, and money from the client account will later be transferred to the office account to reimburse the firm.

It has been assumed throughout this chapter that the standard rate of Value Added Tax (VAT) is 20%. However, as this rate sometimes changes, make sure you check the rate that you are expected to apply in your LPC exams. VAT is ignored throughout this chapter until the *VAT and Abatement of Costs* section.

Key Concepts

Double entry bookkeeping: Debits and Credits

Although not often taught alongside Solicitors' Accounts, a basic understanding of "double entry bookkeeping" will make it much easier to understand the rules governing how a firm must record transactions using client and office money. Like with most forms of financial accounting, solicitors' accounts are based on the double entry bookkeeping method of recording transactions, which involves recording "Debit" and "Credit" entries in an account "ledger".

> **Ledgers:** a "ledger" (sometimes referred to as an "account ledger") groups together transactions of a similar type so that those transactions can be recorded in the same place. The word "recorded" is important here: a ledger is essentially a report that shows which transactions have occurred and how money/assets/liabilities have been moved between parties/bank accounts.

Different ledgers can be used to record, for instance, different types of income received, expenses incurred, assets received/transferred, and liabilities that arise/have been discharged. For example, a *Rent Expense* ledger is a statement/report that records/shows the firm's expenditure on rent, whilst a *Bank Account* ledger is a statement/report that records/shows how much money has gone into and out of a particular bank account (it also states the new balance of the bank account after each transaction).

Two entries must *always* be made when recording a particular transaction: a "Debit" entry and a "Credit" entry (hence the term "*double entry bookkeeping*"). If you ever find yourself recording (for instance) two Debit entries and no Credit entry when dealing with a particular transaction, this means something is not right.

How do I know when to record a "Debit" entry and when to record a "Credit" entry?

When deciding whether to record a transaction as a "Debit" or a "Credit" in a ledger, follow the basic rules:

- **Ledgers relating to assets:** increases in assets should be recorded as "Debit" entries (and decreases as "Credit" entries). Notable examples of ledgers relating to assets include the Bank Account ledger, Petty Cash ledger and Receivables ledger. In this context, the "asset" is typically money in a bank account, or money *owed* to a solicitor ("receivables").

- **Ledgers relating to liabilities:** increases in liabilities should be recorded as "Credit" entries (and decreases as "Debit" entries). Notable examples of ledgers relating to liabilities include the Payables ledger (which records money the solicitor *owes* to someone else) and the VAT Account ledger.

- **Ledgers relating to income/revenue:** increases in income/revenue should be recorded as "Credit" entries (and decreases as "Debit" entries). Notable examples of ledgers relating to income/revenue include the Profit Costs ledger and the Sales ledger.

- **Ledgers relating to expenses/losses:** increases in expenses/losses should be recorded as "Debit" entries (and decreases as "Credit" entries). Notable examples of ledgers relating to expenses/losses include the Rent Expense ledger and the Bad Debt ledger.

Therefore, whether an entry is going to be a Debit or a Credit entry depends on the type of ledger you are using. The below example illustrates this concept.

Record the following transactions:

(a) As a starting point, the firm has £1,500 in its bank account.

Bank Account ledger				
DATE	DETAILS	DEBIT	CREDIT	BALANCE
				1,500 Debit

This shows that the firm has £1,500 in its bank account (the balance of the Bank Account ledger is 1,500 Debit). No double entry is needed, as we have not been required to show where this money came from originally.

Solicitors' Accounts

(b) The firm pays **£500 rent out of its bank account on 1 February 2021**. The firm records rental payments in its **"Rent Expense"** ledger.

Bank Account ledger				
DATE	DETAILS	DEBIT	CREDIT	BALANCE
				1,500 Debit
1 Feb 2021	Rental payment		500 Credit	1,000 Debit

(handwritten: take away)

The Bank Account ledger relates to (i.e. records the movement of) assets (the funds in the bank account to which the ledger relates). Therefore, in accordance with the above rules, any decrease in the value of this asset must be recorded using a "Credit" entry. The £500 rent paid from the bank account has accordingly been shown in the Bank Account ledger by recording "500" as a "Credit" entry. This reduces the remaining balance of the bank account to £1,000 (shown by the 1,000 Debit balance recorded in the "Balance" column of the Bank Account ledger).

(handwritten: take away)

As we have made a "Credit" entry in relation to the transaction, there must be a corresponding "Debit" entry. As stated above, money has come *out* of the Bank Account (hence the "Credit" entry, as the asset has decreased). The "Debit" entry is required to show where the money has gone:

(handwritten: credit money out — debit where gone)

Rent Expense ledger				
DATE	DETAILS	DEBIT	CREDIT	BALANCE
1 Feb 2021	Rental payment	500 Debit		500 Debit

The Rent Expense ledger relates to expenses. Therefore, in accordance with the above rules, any increase in expenses recorded must be recorded using a "Debit" entry. The £500 rent expense has accordingly been shown in the Rent Expense ledger by recording "500" as a "Debit" entry. The "500" shown in the "Balance" column shows that £500 is the total amount that the firm has spent on rent since this ledger was opened.

To summarise, always ask yourself: (1) does the ledger relate to an asset, a liability, a source of income or an expense; and (2) is the balance recorded in the ledger increasing or decreasing? Only then can you ascertain whether you should record the transaction using a Debit or a Credit entry.

Client money vs. office money

- **Client money:** money held or received on behalf of a client, including legal fees and unpaid disbursements prior to the delivery of a bill in respect of those fees and disbursements Rule 2.1. Client money must generally be held separately to "office money" Rule 4.1 in a "client account", subject to the limited exceptions in Rule 2.2.

- **Office money:** money that belongs to the firm. This must generally be held in an "office account".

Client money or office money?

Client money

- **Money received "on account of costs".** This is the money that a solicitor will ask a client to provide when that solicitor is first instructed, to cover future costs incurred in connection with the legal matter for which the firm has been retained (e.g. court fees or charges for carrying out searches). This money initially *belongs* to the client, as the solicitor will not yet have incurred the costs for which the money was transferred to cover Rule 2.1(d).

- **Money received for unpaid disbursements** Rule 2.1(d). This is when the client pays an amount to the firm to cover a *specific* future disbursement that the firm will have to pay on that client's behalf in the future (in contrast, money paid "on account of costs" is a general pool of money to be used by the firm on the client's behalf as and when necessary).

Office money

- **Money received in settlement of fees and disbursements.** This would usually include money paid in consideration for legal services already provided, as well as money to reimburse the solicitor for disbursements paid on the client's behalf. Note that a solicitor must deliver a bill to the client before transferring funds from the client account to the office account Rule 4.3.

- **Bill of costs:** for the purpose of this chapter, this is the invoice sent to a client for the legal services provided and disbursements paid for by the solicitor.

- **Disbursements:** in the context of this chapter, disbursements are payments made by a solicitor on a client's behalf. Note that a solicitor's usual office overheads (e.g. postage, courier and photocopying costs) do not count as "disbursements".

Exceptions

There are very limited exceptions to the general rule that client money should always be paid into/held in a client account and that office money should always be paid into/held in an office account. In particular, if money received from a client is a "mixed payment" (i.e. if a single payment represents partly client money and partly office money, for example money owed in respect of legal services delivered), the full amount can be paid into a client account if the "office" money is promptly transferred to the office account Rule 4.2.

Solicitors' Accounts

Paying money out of the client account

Under Rule 5, client money may only be withdrawn from a client account if sufficient funds are held on behalf of that client to make the payment, you appropriately authorise and supervise the withdrawals, and:

- The money is withdrawn for the purpose for which it is being held;
- The client (or a third party for whom the money is held) instructs you to make the withdrawal; or
- The SRA gives you prior written authorisation (or certain circumstances prescribed by the SRA arise).

Solicitors' Accounting System

Ledgers

Ledgers were explained in detail in the *Key Concepts* section at the start of this chapter. The following are key ledgers for the Solicitors' Accounts module:

"Office Cash": ledger showing how much money there is in the firm's bank account.

- The Office Cash ledger relates to assets (money in the firm's bank account).
- When assets (money) go into the firm's bank account, this is recorded using a Debit entry. When assets come out of the firm's bank account (i.e. the solicitor makes a payment), this is recorded using a Credit entry.

"Office Ledger": ledger showing how much money the client owes the firm.

- The Office Ledger relates to assets from the firm's perspective, as it records money that the firm is *entitled* to receive from the client ("receivables"). This *entitlement* is an "asset" from the *firm's* perspective.
- When the firm's entitlement to money in the future increases (e.g. when it sends a bill of costs to a client), this is recorded using a Debit entry. When the firm's entitlement to money in the future decreases (e.g. when the solicitor receives the money owed by his/her client), this is recorded using a Credit entry.

"Client Cash": ledger showing how much money there is in the bank that belongs to the firm's clients.

- The Client Cash ledger relates to assets (money in the firm's client bank account).
- When money goes into the firm's *client* bank account (a bank account opened by a solicitor/firm to hold money on behalf of its clients), this is recorded using a Debit entry. When assets come out of the firm's client bank account (e.g. the solicitor makes a payment on the client's behalf), this is recorded using a Credit entry.

"Client Ledger": ledger showing how much money the firm holds *on behalf of* a client.

- The Client Ledger relates to *liabilities* from the *solicitor's* perspective. This is because the firm technically "owes" the amounts recorded to the client, in the sense that the firm would have to return this money to the client if no further costs are incurred on behalf of that client (and no further legal fees arise).
- Liabilities that arise/increase are recorded in the Client Ledger using Credit entries and liabilities that are reduced/discharged are recorded in the Client Ledger using Debit entries.

For simplicity, the four ledgers described above are often combined into pairs: (a) Office Cash/Client Cash; and (b) Office Ledger/Client Ledger (see below).

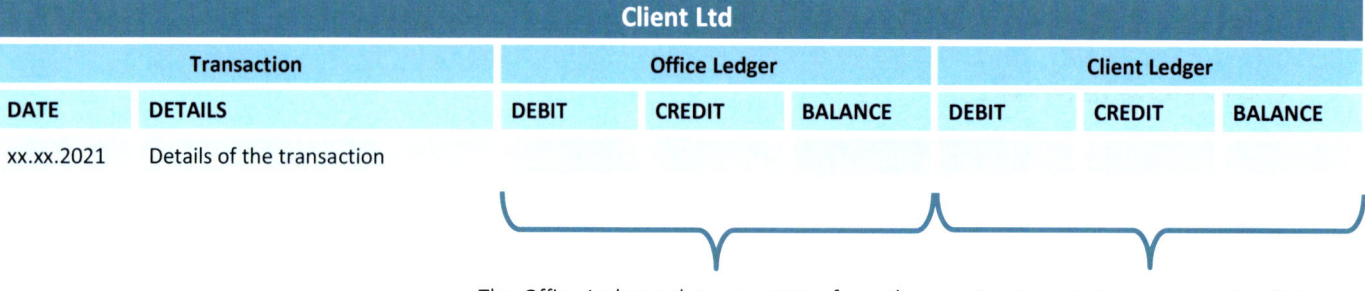

Client Ltd							
Transaction		**Office Ledger**			**Client Ledger**		
DATE	DETAILS	DEBIT	CREDIT	BALANCE	DEBIT	CREDIT	BALANCE
xx.xx.2021	Details of the transaction						

The Office Ledger relates to *assets* from the firm's perspective, as it records money that the firm is entitled to receive from the client. Increases in value are recorded using Debit entries, whilst decreases are recorded using Credit entries.

The Client Ledger relates to *liabilities* from the firm's perspective, as it records money that is technically owed by the firm to its clients. Increases in liabilities are recorded using Credit entries, whilst decreases are recorded using Debit entries.

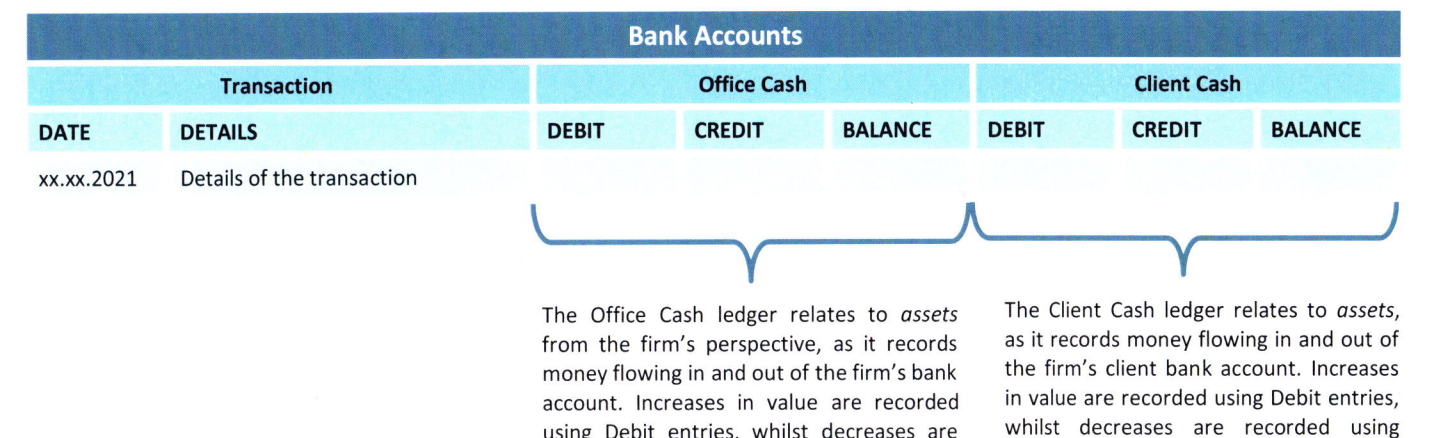

Solicitors' Accounts

Bank Accounts						
Transaction		**Office Cash**			**Client Cash**		
DATE	DETAILS	DEBIT	CREDIT	BALANCE	DEBIT	CREDIT	BALANCE
xx.xx.2021	Details of the transaction						

The Office Cash ledger relates to *assets* from the firm's perspective, as it records money flowing in and out of the firm's bank account. Increases in value are recorded using Debit entries, whilst decreases are recorded using Credit entries.

The Client Cash ledger relates to *assets*, as it records money flowing in and out of the firm's client bank account. Increases in value are recorded using Debit entries, whilst decreases are recorded using Credit entries.

Recording transactions: money "on account of costs"

Consider a scenario where a client (Client Ltd) pays the firm £5,000 on account of costs on 6 January 2021. Remember, this means that money is being placed into the client's cash account to cover future costs that may arise. This transaction will be accounted for in the following way:

1. **The Client Cash ledger will be Debited £5,000**. This reflects the fact that money is being put *into* the firm's client bank account. As the Client Cash ledger relates to assets (money in the firm's client bank account), increases in value are recorded using *Debit entries*.

2. **Client Ltd's Client Ledger will be Credited £5,000.** This reflects that the solicitor *owes* the client the money that is going into the firm's client bank account until that money is used on the client's behalf. As the Client Ledger relates to a liability, increases in value are recorded using *Credit entries*.

Note that in the "details" section of a particular ledger, you must provide details of the transaction that you are recording and note the ledger in which you have made a corresponding entry. For instance, in the first of the two ledgers below (the Bank Accounts ledger) we have written, "Client Ledger: Client Ltd…" in the details section to show that a corresponding Credit entry has been made in Client Ltd's Client Ledger (the second ledger below).

Bank Accounts						
Transaction		**Office Cash**			**Client Cash**		
DATE	DETAILS	DEBIT	CREDIT	BALANCE	DEBIT	CREDIT	BALANCE
6 Jan 2021	Client Ledger: Client Ltd Money paid to the firm on account of costs				5,000		

Note that you are *not* usually expected to record the "Balance" of the Client Cash account on the LPC.

Client Ltd						
Transaction		**Office Ledger**			**Client Ledger**		
DATE	DETAILS	DEBIT	CREDIT	BALANCE	DEBIT	CREDIT	BALANCE
6 Jan 2021	Client Cash Money paid to the firm on account of costs					5,000	5,000 Credit

Recording transactions: payment *out of* the client account

If the solicitor in the above example uses some of the money in the firm's client bank account to pay for a Land Registry search fee of £13 on behalf of Client Ltd on 7 July 2021, this will be recorded in the following way:

1. **The Client Cash ledger will be Credited £13**. This reflects the fact that funds have been taken out of the firm's client bank account. As the Client Cash ledger relates to assets, decreases in value are recorded using Credit entries.

Bank Accounts						
Transaction		**Office Cash**			**Client Cash**		
DATE	DETAILS	DEBIT	CREDIT	BALANCE	DEBIT	CREDIT	BALANCE
6 Jan 2021	Client Cash Money paid to the firm on account of costs				5,000		
7 July 2021	Client Ledger Client Ltd (Land Registry search fee)					13	

2. **Client Ltd's Client Ledger will be Debited £13.** This reflects the fact that the solicitor *owes* less money to the client following the payment, meaning the solicitor's *liability* has decreased (or in other words, the solicitor no longer hold that money *for* the client). As the Client Ledger relates to liabilities, any decrease in value is recorded as a Debit entry.

Client Ltd							
Transaction		Office Ledger			Client Ledger		
DATE	DETAILS	DEBIT	CREDIT	BALANCE	DEBIT	CREDIT	BALANCE
6 Jan 2021	Client Cash Money paid to the firm on account of costs					5,000	5,000 Credit
7 July 2021	Client Ledger: Client Ltd Land Registry search fee				13		4987 Credit

Recording transactions: recording the issue of a bill of costs

A bill of costs is an invoice sent by a solicitor to their client for the legal services carried out. When an invoice is sent, no *money* is actually transferred between the client and the solicitor at this stage. For this reason, the Client Cash and Office Cash ledgers remain unaffected. Instead, a new ledger must be introduced called "Profit Costs". This ledger relates to *income*, as it is used to record the fees to which the solicitor becomes entitled as a result of legal services rendered. When a bill of costs is issued, this is recorded in the following way:

1. **Client Ltd's Office Ledger will be Debited.** This reflects the fact that the client now *owes* the solicitor more money. As the Office Ledger relates to assets (it records money to which the solicitor has become entitled), any increases in value are recorded using Debit entries. Remember, the "asset" in question is the *right* to be paid by (i.e. the right to receive an asset from) the client.

2. **The firm's Profit Costs ledger will be Credited.** This reflects the fact that the solicitor has become entitled to receive a payment (income) from the client. As the Profit Costs ledger relates to income, increases are recorded using Credit entries.

Continuing the above example, imagine now that the solicitor has sent Client Ltd a bill of costs requesting £180 on 14 July 2021.

Client Ltd							
Transaction		Office Ledger			Client Ledger		
DATE	DETAILS	DEBIT	CREDIT	BALANCE	DEBIT	CREDIT	BALANCE
6 Jan 2021	Client Cash Money paid to the firm on account of costs					5,000	5,000 Credit
7 July 2021	Client Ledger: Client Ltd Land Registry search fee				13		4,987 Credit
14 July 2021	Profit Costs Bill of costs to Client Ltd	180		180 Debit			

Profit Costs			
DATE	DETAILS	DEBIT	CREDIT	BALANCE
14 July 2021	Office Ledger: Client Ltd Bill of costs to Client Ltd		180	180 Credit

Recording transactions: transferring money from a client account to the office account

When the client pays for ("settles") a bill of costs sent by their solicitor, the transfer of money from the firm's client bank account to the firm's ("office") bank account must be recorded using four entries. First, the transfer *out of* the firm's client bank account must be recorded using two entries, then the transfer of this money *into* the firm's ("office") bank account must be recorded using another two entries.

(a) Recording the transfer *out of* the firm's client bank account.

1. **The Client Cash ledger will be Credited.** This reflects the fact that the amount of money being held in the firm's client bank account (i.e. money held on the *client's* behalf) has decreased. As the Client Cash ledger relates to assets (the money in the firm's client bank account), the reduction in value is recorded using a Credit entry.

2. **Client Ltd's Client Ledger will be Debited.** This reflects the fact that the solicitor owes less money to the client (less money is being held on the client's behalf). As the Client Ledger relates to liabilities (the money held by the firm on the client's behalf), the reduction in value must be recorded as a Debit entry.

Solicitors' Accounts

(b) Recording the transfer *into* the firms "office" bank account.

3. **The Office Cash ledger will be Debited**. This reflects the fact that additional funds have gone into the firm's office bank account. As the Office Cash ledger relates to assets (i.e. money in the firm's office bank account), the increase in value is recorded using a Debit entry; and

4. **The Office Ledger will be Credited**. This reflects the fact that the client has effectively paid off a debt and therefore no longer owes that amount to the solicitor. As the Office Ledger relates to assets (i.e. it records money to which the solicitor has become entitled), the reduction must be recorded as a Credit entry.

Note that you can never carry out a double entry consisting of only one "office" entry and one "client entry". This is why the above transaction must be accounted for in two steps.

Recording transactions: solicitors paying money to their clients

Once the work for a client has been completed, a solicitor must repay to that client any remaining funds held on that client's behalf. This is accounted for in the following way:

1. **The Client Cash ledger will be Credited**. This reflects the fact that money is being transferred out of the firm's client bank account (in order to repay the client). As the Client Cash ledger relates to assets, you record any decrease in value using a Credit entry.

2. **Client Ltd's Client Ledger will be Debited**. This reflects the fact that money is no longer being held on the client's behalf (the firm no longer owes this money to the client). Remember, as the ledger relates to liabilities, any reduction in value is recorded using a Debit entry.

Recording transactions: disbursements

You saw above that when a solicitor incurs a disbursement on behalf of a client, the solicitor can use client money to pay for that disbursement if the client has money in its client account (i.e. there is a Credit balance in its Client Ledger). However, if the solicitor incurs a disbursement on behalf of a client but that client has not yet paid any money to the solicitor, or the solicitor is acting as principal when incurring the disbursement (this is explained in the *VAT and disbursements* section below), the solicitor must use office money to pay for the disbursement and later reclaim the money from the client.

To record a transaction where a disbursement has been paid on behalf of a client out of the office cash account, the following double entry should be made:

1. **The Office Cash ledger will be Credited.** This reflects the fact that money is leaving the office bank account. As the Office Cash ledger relates to assets, any decreases are recorded using Credit entries.

2. **The Office Ledger will be Debited.** This reflects the fact that the client now *owes* the solicitor more money. As the Office Ledger relates to assets (it records money to which the solicitor has become entitled), any increases in value are recorded using Debit entries.

Paid vs. incurred

Disbursements should be recorded either when they are *incurred* or when they *are paid* (whichever is earlier). The exception to this is for professional disbursements (e.g. the fees of a barrister who was instructed by the firm to work on the client's case); these should *only* be recorded when they are actually paid.

Recording transactions: split receipt of money from client

This section relates to situations in which a client pays a solicitor an amount of money that represents both client money *and* office money. For instance, if you are acting for Client Ltd, Client Ltd has not provided any money on account of costs, and you incur and pay a disbursement of £500 on their behalf, Client Ltd will owe you this money (meaning there will be a Debit balance in Client Ltd's Office Ledger). If Client Ltd then sends a cheque for £1,000, the entire amount cannot be put into the office cash account, as £500 of it will still be "client" money (remember, client money can almost *never* be put in the office account - see the *Client money vs. office money* section above). The rules therefore allow the solicitor to either:

(a) Promptly pay all of it into the client account and transfer the £500 into the office account; or

This option would be recorded by first transferring the money in the manner set out in the *Recording transactions: money on account of costs* section above. The £500 of office money would then be transferred to the office in the manner set out in the *Recording transactions: transferring money from the client account to the office account* section above.

(b) Split the money and pay £500 into the office account and £500 into the client account.

1. **The Office Cash ledger will be Debited.** This reflects the fact that money is going into the office bank account. As the Office Cash ledger relates to an asset (bank) account, any increase in value is recorded using a Debit entry.

2. **The Office Ledger will be Credited.** This reflects the fact that the client no longer owes the solicitor £500. As the Office Ledger relates to assets (it records money to which the solicitor has become entitled), decreases in value are recorded using Credit entries.

3. **The Client Cash ledger will be Debited.** This reflects the fact that money is going into the firm's client bank account. As the Client Cash ledger relates to an asset (bank) account, any increase in value is recorded using a Debit entry.

4. **Client Ltd's Client Ledger will be Credited.** This reflects the fact that the solicitor now holds the money on behalf of the client (i.e. would have to pay it back to the client if no further costs/legal fees arise). As the Client Ledger relates to a liability, increases in value are recorded using Credit entries.

Recording transactions: petty cash

A solicitor will sometimes, for the sake of ease, pay disbursements using cash rather than by cheque/e-transfers. Where this is done, a new ledger must be introduced: the "Petty Cash" ledger. This ledger relates to assets (cash held by the firm that is not in a bank account). To illustrate how transactions using petty cash should be recorded, consider the following example:

On 25 October 2021 the solicitors' firm withdrew £200 from the office account to keep as petty cash. On 4 November 2021, a solicitor working at the firm took a taxi costing £40 to Client Ltd's office. The solicitor paid using petty cash. This should be recorded in the following way:

The withdrawal of money from the office account to keep as petty cash (25 October 2021)

1. **The Office Cash ledger will be Credited.** This reflects the fact that money is leaving the bank account. As the Office Cash ledger relates to assets, any decreases are recorded using Credit entries; and

2. **The Petty Cash ledger will be Debited.** This reflects the fact that the firm is effectively transferring money out of the office bank account, to be held as "petty" cash. The firm will therefore hold a larger amount of "petty" cash, meaning the value recorded in the Petty Cash ledger will increase. As the Petty Cash ledger relates to assets, increases in value must be recorded using Debit entries.

The use of £40 petty cash to pay for a taxi to Client Ltd's offices (4 November 2021)

1. **The Petty Cash ledger will be Credited**. This reflects the fact that money has been taken from the Petty Cash account. As the Petty Cash ledger relates to assets, decreases in value must be recorded using Credit entries.

2. **Client Ltd's Office Ledger will be Debited.** This reflects the fact that Client Ltd now owes the firm £40. As the Office Ledger relates to assets (it records money to which the solicitor has become entitled), any increases in value are recorded using Debit entries.

Property Transactions: Deposits and Mortgages

Seller's solicitor receiving deposit funds

When a client buys a property, it will typically be required to pay a deposit (expressed as a percentage of the purchase price) when the contracts are exchanged. The buyer will send money to its solicitor, which the solicitor will then hold in a client bank account. The buyer's solicitor will then pay the money to the seller's solicitor. When the seller's solicitor receives the deposit money, the recording of that transaction will depend on whether, under the contract for sale of the property, that solicitor is acting as a "stakeholder" for the seller or as the seller's "agent".

Note that the rest of this section applies to the *seller's* solicitor in a property transaction. For an explanation of the difference between exchange and completion in a property transaction, please see the *Property Law* module in this handbook.

Solicitor acting as stakeholder

> **Acting as stakeholder:** when a solicitor acts as stakeholder for the seller, the solicitor holds any deposit funds received on trust for both the seller and the buyer until it is clear to whom the money should be paid. Therefore, the money cannot be handed over to either the buyer or the seller without the consent of the other, or until completion of the property transaction. The deposit money received by the seller's solicitor is "client" money but it cannot be *paid* to the seller since the seller does not have the power to freely use those funds until the sale has completed.

When a solicitor is acting as a stakeholder, the transfer to them of deposit funds is recorded in the following way:

(a) At exchange of contracts

We must now introduce a new type of ledger called "Stakeholder Ledger". This ledger relates to *liabilities*. This will be used instead of the seller's own Client Ledger at exchange, since at this point the money does not *belong* to the seller.

1. **The Stakeholder Ledger will be Credited.** This reflects the fact that the solicitor has received money in their capacity as stakeholder for their client. As the Stakeholder Ledger relates to liabilities, the increase in value is recorded using a Credit entry.

2. **The Client Cash ledger will be Debited.** This reflects the fact that the money is being placed into the firm's client bank account. As the Client Cash ledger relates to assets, the increase in value is recorded using a Debit entry.

(b) On completion

1. **The Stakeholder Ledger will be Debited.** This reflects the fact that the money is being transferred from the Stakeholder Ledger to the seller's Client Ledger. As the Stakeholder Ledger relates to liabilities, the decrease in value is recorded using a Debit entry.

2. **The seller's Client Ledger will be Credited**. The solicitor now owes this money to the seller client (meaning a liability has arisen). As the Client Ledger relates to liabilities, the increase in value is recorded using a Credit entry.

The money is already in the firm's client bank account, which is why no entry needs to be made in the Client Cash ledger at stage (b) above.

Solicitors' Accounts

Solicitor acting as agent

When a solicitor is acting as the seller's agent, that solicitor can hand over the deposit money to the seller as soon as it is received from the buyer (the deposit money will *belong* to the seller from the time of exchange). The seller's solicitor's receipt of the deposit money will be recorded in the following way:

1. **The Client Cash ledger will be Debited.** This reflects the fact that the money is being placed into the firm's client bank account. As the Client Cash ledger relates to assets, the increase in value is recorded using a Debit entry.

2. **The seller's Client Ledger will be Credited.** This reflects the fact that the money received by the firm from the buyer actually belongs to the seller. The solicitor therefore *owes* this money to the seller client. As a liability has arisen (the liability to eventually pay the money to the seller client), the increase is recorded using a Credit entry.

Mortgages

When a buyer has borrowed money (taken out a mortgage) to purchase a property, the lender (e.g. a bank or a building society) will pay the mortgage funds to the buyer's solicitor just before completion. One solicitor/firm will often represent both the buyer and the lender. The mortgage funds will *belong* to the lender until completion, but in certain circumstances those funds can be recorded in the buyer client's Client Ledger.

Note that the rest of this section applies to the *buyer's* solicitor in a property transaction. When the solicitor is acting for both the buyer and the lender, the receipt of mortgage funds on behalf of the buyer from the bank can be recorded in either of two ways: (1) recording the receipt of the mortgage funds in the *buyer's* Client Ledger; or (2) recording the receipt of the mortgage funds in a ledger set up specifically for the *lender* client.

Recording the receipt of the mortgage funds in the *buyer's* Client Ledger

When the lender forwards the money to the buyer's solicitor (which must be done in time for completion), that money will go into the firm's client bank account and, provided that the funds are clearly identifiable, this can be recorded as follows:

1. **The Client Cash ledger will be Debited.** This reflects the fact that money is going into the firm's client bank account. As the Client Cash ledger relates to assets, any increase in value is recorded using a Debit entry.

2. **The buyer's Client Ledger will be Credited.** This reflects the fact that the solicitor now holds the money on behalf of one of its clients (i.e. would have to pay it back to the client if no further costs/legal fees arise). As the Client Ledger relates to liabilities, increases in value are recorded using Credit entries. It will be noted in the ledger that the money constitutes mortgage funds received from the lender. Remember, the mortgage funds technically still belong to the lender until completion has occurred.

Here is an example to help illustrate this. On **2 January 2021**, the bank - Lender Ltd - **forwards £500,000 to fund your client's** - Buyer Ltd's - property purchase:

Bank Accounts						
Transaction		**Office Cash**			**Client Cash**	
DATE	DETAILS	DEBIT	CREDIT	BALANCE	DEBIT	CREDIT	BALANCE
2 Jan 2021	Client Cash Receipt of mortgage funds from Lender Ltd.				500,000		

Buyer Ltd						
Transaction		**Office Cash**			**Client Cash**	
DATE	DETAILS	DEBIT	CREDIT	BALANCE	DEBIT	CREDIT	BALANCE
2 Jan 2021	Client Ledger: Buyer Ltd Receipt of mortgage funds from Lender Ltd.					500,000	500,000 Credit

Recording the receipt of the mortgage funds in the *lender's* Client Ledger

If this method is used, the solicitor will open up a new ledger for the lender (rather than using Buyer Ltd's existing Client Ledger). The transfer of funds will first be recorded in Lender Ltd's Client Ledger and then transferred to the buyer client. This will be recorded in two steps as follows:

(a) Record the funds in Lender Ltd's Client Ledger

1. **The Client Cash ledger will be Debited.** This reflects the fact that money is going into the firm's client bank account. As the Client Cash ledger relates to an asset (bank) account, any increase in value is recorded using a Debit entry.

2. **Lender Ltd's Client Ledger will be Credited.** This reflects the fact that the solicitor now holds the money on behalf of one of its clients (i.e. would have to pay it back to Lender Ltd if no further costs/legal fees arise). As the solicitor's *liability* (to Lender Ltd) has increased, this will be recorded using a Credit entry.

Solicitors' Accounts

(b) Transfer the funds to the buyer client's Client Ledger

1. **Lender Ltd's Client Ledger will be Debited.** This reflects the fact that the solicitor's liability to Lender Ltd no longer exists, as the money is now held on behalf of *Buyer Ltd* not Lender Ltd. As the *liability* has *decreased*, this will be shown using a Debit entry.

2. **Buyer Ltd's Client Ledger will be Credited.** This reflects the fact that the solicitor now holds the money on behalf of Buyer Ltd. As the solicitor's *liability* to Buyer Ltd has increased, this increase is recorded using a Credit entry.

Note that the Client Cash ledger will not need to be amended at this stage. The funds were transferred into Buyer Ltd's bank account in step (a) above and will remain there throughout step (b). Step (b) simply records the transfer of the *entitlement* to the money.

Recording payment of the lender's costs

Remember, "Profit Costs" refers to the ledger used to record the payment of legal fees. If a solicitor is acting for both the buyer *and* the lender, legal fees will arise in relation to both parties. In property transactions, a buyer will typically pay both their own legal costs *and* the lender's legal costs. As in the above section, how this is recorded depends on whether the solicitor has set up a separate Client Ledger for the lender or whether the solicitor simply uses the buyer's existing Client Ledger.

Recording payment of the lender's costs in the *buyer's* Client Ledger

Using this method, the legal fees (or profit costs) for *both* the buyer and lender will be recorded in the buyer's Client Ledger, using a separate entry for each. First however, the solicitor must send an invoice (or bill of costs) to the buyer. This process will be recorded in the following way:

1. **The Profit Costs ledger will be Credited with the value of *Buyer Ltd's* bill of costs.** This reflects the fact that the solicitor has become entitled to receive a payment (income) from the buyer client. As the Profit Costs ledger relates to income, increases are recorded using Credit entries.

2. **Buyer Ltd's Office Ledger will be Debited with the value of *Buyer Ltd's* legal fees.** This reflects the fact that Buyer Ltd now owes the solicitor money for the legal work completed on their behalf. As the Office Ledger relates to assets (it records money to which the solicitor has become entitled), any increases in value are recorded using Debit entries.

3. **The Profit Costs ledger will be Credited with the value of *Lender Ltd's* bill of costs.** This reflects the fact that the solicitor has become entitled to receive a payment from Buyer Ltd (for work done on behalf of *Lender Ltd*). As the Profit Costs ledger relates to income, increases are recorded using Credit entries.

4. **Buyer Ltd's Office Ledger will be Debited with the value of *Lender Ltd's* legal fees.** This reflects the fact that Buyer Ltd now owes the solicitor money for the legal work completed on behalf of the *lender*. As the Office Ledger relates to assets (i.e. money to which the firm has become entitled), any increases in value are recorded using Debit entries.

Recording payment of the lender's costs in the *lender's* Client Ledger

Step 1

The first step is to record profit costs in the standard way. To recap, you would make: (a) two Credit entries in the solicitor's Profit Costs ledger (one relating to Buyer Ltd's bill of costs and one relating to Seller Ltd's bill of costs); and then (b) a Debit entry in Buyer Ltd's Office Ledger and another in Lender Ltd's Office Ledger recording the value of the legal fees owed to the solicitor.

Step 2

The second step is to transfer the liability to pay Lender Ltd's costs to Buyer Ltd (this is all on the assumption that the parties have agreed that Buyer Ltd will pay Lender Ltd's legal costs). The liability to pay the cost of the legal work carried out on behalf of Lender Ltd (i.e. the cost shown in Lender Ltd's bill of costs) will be "transferred" from Lender Ltd's Office Ledger to Buyer Ltd's Office Ledger. This is recorded in the following way:

1. **Lender Ltd's Office Ledger will be Credited.** This reflects the fact that Lender Ltd no longer owes a debt to the solicitor as Buyer Ltd has taken on the obligation to pay Lender Ltd's legal fees. As the Office Ledger relates to assets (it records money to which the solicitor has become entitled), the reduction must be recorded as a Credit entry.

2. **Buyer Ltd's Office Ledger will be Debited with the value of *Lender Ltd's* legal fees.** This reflects the fact that Buyer Ltd now owes the solicitor money for the legal work completed on behalf of the *lender*. As the Office Ledger relates to assets (it records money to which the solicitor has become entitled), any increases in value are recorded using Debit entries.

Value Added Tax (VAT)

Solicitors must *charge* VAT on the fees they charge for their legal services if they have (or their firm has) registered for VAT. This means that solicitors are expected to collect VAT from their clients on behalf of Her Majesty's Revenue and Customs (HMRC). This is called "output" VAT. Solicitors will also typically have to *pay* VAT when they pay disbursements on behalf of their clients. This is called "input" VAT. This section sets out how to deal with VAT in the context of common transactions. For the purpose of this handbook, the rate of VAT is assumed to be 20% (although check whether this rate has changed when revising for your LPC exam).

VAT and profit costs

When a solicitor charges for their legal services (i.e. sends a bill of costs to a client), they must charge VAT. For instance, if the client has incurred legal fees of £2,000 *excluding* VAT, the solicitor must add an additional £400 VAT (20% of £2,000) to that client's bill of costs. The solicitor must then pass on the £400 received from the client to HMRC.

Solicitors' Accounts

To properly account for VAT, a new ledger must be created: the "VAT Account" ledger. This ledger relates to liabilities, as it records money that the solicitor *owes* to HMRC. Increases in the liability are recorded using Credit entries, and decreases using Debit entries. To illustrate how this works, when a solicitor sends the client a bill of costs, this is recorded using the following four steps:

(a) Recording the legal fees owed to the solicitor *excluding* VAT.

1. **The client's Office Ledger will be Debited with the amount of the solicitor's legal fees *excluding* VAT.** This reflects the fact that the client now owes the solicitor money for the legal work completed. As the Office Ledger relates to assets (it records money to which the solicitor has become entitled), any increases in value are recorded using Debit entries.

2. **The Profit Costs ledger will be Credited with the amount of the solicitor's legal fees *excluding* VAT.** This reflects the fact that the solicitor has become entitled to receive a payment from the client for the legal work carried out. As the Profit Costs ledger relates to the solicitor's *income*, increases are recorded using Credit entries.

(b) Recording the amount of the VAT charged on the legal fees.

3. **The client's Office Ledger will be Debited with the amount of VAT payable on the legal fees.** This reflects the fact that the client now owes VAT to the solicitor (who in turn will owe that money to HMRC). As the Office Ledger relates to assets, any increases in value are recorded using Debit entries.

4. **The VAT Account ledger will be Credited with the amount of VAT payable on the legal fees.** This reflects the fact that the solicitor now *owes* HMRC VAT. As the VAT Account ledger records the solicitor's *liability* to HMRC, increases are recorded using Credit entries.

VAT and abatements of costs

> 📖 **Abatement of costs:** when a client feels they have been charged too much, they might dispute the amount in the bill of costs. A solicitor may consequently reduce ("abate") that client's bill by writing off some of the fees.

When a client's bill of costs is abated (assuming that the original bill of costs had already been recorded), the abatement is recorded using the following four steps:

(a) Reducing the amount the client owes the firm.

1. **The client's Office Ledger will be Credited with the amount of the abatement *excluding* VAT.** This reflects the fact that the client now owes *less* money to the solicitor for the legal work completed. As the Office Ledger relates to assets (it records money to which the solicitor has become entitled), any decreases in value are recorded using Credit entries.

2. **The Profit Costs ledger will be Debited with the amount of the abatement *excluding* VAT.** This reflects the fact that the income (payment from the client) to which the solicitor is entitled has decreased. As the Profit Costs ledger relates to the solicitor's *income*, decreases are recorded using Debit entries.

(b) Reducing the VAT the client must pay on the cost of their solicitor's legal fees.

3. **The client's Office Ledger will be Credited with the amount by which the VAT payable on the bill of costs has reduced.** This reflects the fact that the amount of tax that the solicitor must charge on the legal fees has decreased. As the Office Ledger relates to assets, any decreases in value are recorded using Credit entries.

4. **The VAT Account ledger will be Debited with the amount by which the VAT payable on the bill of costs has reduced.** This reflects the fact that the solicitor's liability to HMRC has reduced (as less tax will be payable). As the VAT Account ledger records the solicitor's *liability* to HMRC, decreases are recorded using Debit entries.

VAT and disbursements

For VAT purposes, "disbursements" means costs or expenses paid by a firm to another party which the firm passes on to clients but on which no VAT is chargeable to the client. When recording disbursements paid for by a solicitor, consider the following four steps in order to establish if, when, and by whom, VAT is payable:

1. Is VAT chargeable on the service/good purchased by the solicitor?

If the business providing the service is not VAT registered, or if the service is exempt from VAT, no VAT will be chargeable.

- **Exempt supplies:** these include court fees, stamp duty land tax (SDLT) and some search fees (including Local Authority searches, Central Land Charges Registry searches and Land Registry searches).
- **Taxable supplies:** these include expert witness' fees, counsel's fees, surveyor's fees, estate agent fees, and the cost of environmental and coal searches.

2. If VAT is chargeable, does the client or the solicitor pay that VAT?

It is always the *supplier* of a good or service that will charge VAT.

- For the supplier, this counts as "output" VAT, as it is being charged on goods/services that the business is outputting. The person to whom that good or service is *supplied* will have to pay this VAT to the supplier (who in turn will account for that VAT to HMRC).
- For the person that has purchased the good/service, the VAT paid constitutes "input" VAT. If that person then creates new products using the good/service supplied to them, they will then have to charge "output" VAT on those new products, and the cycle goes on.

It is important to distinguish between input and output VAT, because businesses can offset the cost of input VAT against the output VAT that they charge to/collect from customers (in order to lower their overall VAT liability to HMRC). A solicitor will only account for input VAT that arises on disbursements when they are acting as "principal" for a particular arrangement (e.g. when instructing counsel), as opposed to when they are acting as their client's "agent".

Solicitors' Accounts

(a) Solicitor acting as principal

The solicitor acts as "principal" where a taxable supply is supplied directly to *them* (in their name), as opposed to the client. For instance, consider a property transaction where the solicitor decides to carry out an environmental search as part of their work. Although this search is being carried out on the client's behalf, the *solicitor* actually carries out the search and the cost of that search will initially be charged to the *solicitor* (even though the solicitor will inevitably recoup the cost from the client at a later stage). Therefore, the solicitor should record the input VAT charged by the supplier on this transaction (and can later use this to offset output tax payable to HMRC).

A solicitor is acting as "principal" when: (a) instructing counsel or other solicitors; and (b) paying for searches in the context of property transactions. Note that when a solicitor pays for a disbursement as principal, the payment must be made from the firm's bank account (and thus recorded in the Office Cash ledger and Office Ledger).

(b) Solicitor acting as agent

When the solicitor acts as the client's "agent", the relevant supply is being made directly to the *client* (not the solicitor). For instance, when the *client* instructs a third party (e.g. a surveyor) and the solicitor simply pays the third party's bill on that client's behalf, the solicitor is said to be acting as the client's "agent". Under such circumstances, the solicitor will not need to account for the input VAT charged (by the supplier) on the disbursement.

3. If the solicitor is accounting for the VAT, how is it accounted for and at which point should the cost be passed on to the client?

To record a transaction that involves a solicitor having to account for the input VAT paid on a disbursement, two sets of entries are required. Assume that the solicitor has instructed counsel (and has thus acted as principal) and has now been invoiced for counsel's fees:

(a) The solicitor incurs the cost and records the payment to counsel of their fees.

1. **The Office Cash ledger will be Credited with the amount charged by counsel *excluding VAT***. This reflects the fact that money has come out of the office bank account to pay counsel. As the Office Cash ledger relates to assets, the decrease in value is recorded using a Credit entry.

2. **The Office Ledger will be Debited with the amount charged by counsel *excluding* VAT**. This reflects the fact that the client owes the solicitor money as the solicitor has paid counsel's fees on the client's behalf. As the Office Ledger relates to assets (it records money to which the solicitor has become entitled), the increase must be recorded as a Debit entry.

    The reason VAT is excluded at this stage is because the client does not become liable to pay the VAT until they *receive* the solicitor's bill of costs (which will include a request for money to cover the amount paid to counsel). This is because VAT is always chargeable at the point of *supply* (which, in the case of a solicitor's firm, is when they issue a bill of costs to a client).

3. **The Office Cash ledger will be Credited with the amount of VAT paid on the disbursement (counsel's fees)**. This reflects the fact that money has come out of the firm's bank account to pay VAT on counsel's fees. As the Office Cash ledger relates to assets, the decrease in value is recorded using a Credit entry.

4. **The VAT Account Ledger will be Debited with the amount of VAT paid on the disbursement (counsel's fees)**. This is because this amount can be offset against the output VAT that the solicitor charges the client on top of the solicitor's legal fees. Therefore their *liability* to HMRC is effectively decreasing (and decreases in liabilities are recorded using Debit entries).

(b) The solicitor sends the client a bill of costs. The bill of costs will include counsel's fees plus VAT payable on those fees. This is because the work undertaken by counsel is classed as part of the overall legal services provided (or "supplied") by the solicitor to the client.

1. **The client's Office Ledger will be Debited with the value of legal fees shown on the bill of costs *excluding VAT.*** Note that the counsel's fee was recorded in the Office Ledger in the previous step (also excluding VAT), which is why only the legal fees are recorded at this stage. This reflects the fact that the client now *owes* the solicitor more money. As the Office Ledger relates to assets (i.e. it records money to which the solicitor has become entitled), any increases in value are recorded using Debit entries.

2. **The Profit Costs ledger will be Credited with the value of legal fees shown on the bill of costs *excluding VAT.*** This reflects the fact that the solicitor has become entitled to receive a payment (for the legal work carried out) from the client. As the Profit Costs ledger relates to income, increases are recorded using Credit entries.

3. **The client's Office Ledger will be Debited with the amount of VAT payable on the bill of costs.** This will be the amount of VAT charged on the legal fees *and* the disbursement (counsel's fee). This reflects the fact that the client now owes VAT to the solicitor. As the Office Ledger relates to assets, any increases in value are recorded using Debit entries.

4. **The VAT Account ledger will be Credited with the amount of VAT charged on the *legal fees only***. This is because we have already accounted for the VAT charged on the counsel's fee (in step (a) above). As the VAT Account ledger records the solicitor's *liability* to HMRC, increases are recorded using Credit entries.

The following example illustrates how a solicitor should account for VAT when acting as principal.

A solicitor undertakes an environmental search for £100 (+£20 VAT) whilst working on a property transaction for Client Ltd on 20 August 2021. On 3 September 2021 the solicitor issues a bill of costs to Client Ltd, which includes the solicitor's own legal fees of £2,000 (+£400 VAT). This will be recorded in the following way:

Bank Accounts

	Transaction		Office Cash			Client Cash	
DATE	DETAILS	DEBIT	CREDIT	BALANCE	DEBIT	CREDIT	BALANCE
20 August 2021	Office Ledger: Client Ltd Environmental Search		100				
20 August 2021	VAT Account VAT on cost of environmental search		20				

Solicitors' Accounts

The supply of the environmental search to the solicitor is recorded in the Office Cash ledger (the solicitor is acting as principal and therefore the firm must pay for the disbursement using the firm's bank account) and the Office Ledger. Note that on 20 August 2021 the VAT on the disbursement is not yet accounted for in the Client Ledger; this cannot be accounted for in the Client Ledger until 3 September 2021 (this is the point of *supply* from the solicitor to the client).

Client Ltd

	Transaction	Office Cash			Client Cash		
DATE	DETAILS	DEBIT	CREDIT	BALANCE	DEBIT	CREDIT	BALANCE
20 August 2021	Office Ledger: Client Ltd Environmental Search	100		100 Debit			
3 September 2021	Profit Costs Bill of costs sent to Client Ltd	2000		2100 Debit			
3 September 2021	VAT VAT on bill of costs sent to Client Ltd	420		2520 Debit			

Note that on 3 September the client will be charged for the VAT paid on the environmental search *and* the legal fees, so the total VAT included in the bill of costs will be £400 (VAT on legal fees) + £20 (VAT on environmental fees) = £420.

VAT

DATE	DETAILS	DEBIT	CREDIT	BALANCE
20 August 2021	Office Cash VAT on environmental search	20		20 Debit
3 September 2021	Office Ledger: Client Ltd VAT on profit costs to Client Ltd		400	380 Credit

Here the £20 of input VAT has been offset against the £400 of output VAT, meaning the overall liability to HMRC is £380.

Profit Costs

DATE	DETAILS	DEBIT	CREDIT	BALANCE
3 September 2021	Office Ledger: Client Ltd Bill of costs to Client Ltd		2000	2000 Credit

Bad Debts

"Bad debts" refer to amounts owed to the solicitor that the solicitor will be unable to recover (for instance, money owed by a client that has gone insolvent). When a solicitor "writes off" a bad debt, they can recover the VAT charged on that debt if it is older than six months (i.e. they can get it back from HMRC).

To record this, a "Bad and Doubtful Debts" ledger needs to be introduced. This ledger relates to *expenses*, since the money that a solicitor will be unable to recover is classified as an "expense" for that solicitor. Where a bad debt is being written off, this must be recorded using two sets of entries:

(a) Writing off the debt *excluding* VAT

1. **The client's Office Ledger will be Credited with the amount of the bad debt *excluding* VAT.** This reflects the fact that the client no longer *owes* the solicitor the amount that has been written off (this is purely procedural, as the fact that the debt has been written off means the client was unable to pay the debt anyway). As the Office Ledger relates to *assets* (it records money to which the solicitor has become entitled), decreases in value are recorded using Credit entries.

2. **The Bad and Doubtful Debts ledger will be Debited with the amount of the written off ("bad") debt *excluding* VAT.** As this ledger relates to an "expense", increases in value are recorded using Debit entries.

(b) Writing off the *VAT* element of the debt

1. **The client's Office Ledger will be Credited with the amount of the VAT attributable to the legal fees that were written off.** This reflects the fact that the client no longer *owes* the solicitor the VAT, as VAT is only payable if the legal fees are *paid*. As the Office Ledger relates to *assets*, decreases in value are recorded using Credit entries.

2. **The VAT Account ledger will be Debited with the amount of VAT attributable to the legal fees that were written off.** This reflects the fact that the solicitor's liability to HMRC has reduced (as less tax will be payable). As the VAT Account ledger records the solicitor's *liability* to HMRC, decreases are recorded using Debit entries.

Interest

When a client puts money into a firm's client bank account, interest will accrue on that money. As that money belongs to the client (the solicitor is holding the money on the client's behalf), the interest also belongs to the client. Firms must therefore account to clients or third parties for a "fair sum" of interest on any client money held on their behalf Rule 7.1, unless the client or third party gives their informed consent in respect of an alternative arrangement Rule 7.2.

In the Solicitors' Accounts exam, you will not typically be expected to determine the amount of interest due to a client. Instead, a question dealing with interest will tell you how much interest is due and ask you to show how the transaction (i.e. paying that interest to the client) should be accounted for.

How interest is accounted for depends on whether the client in question has their money in the firm's general client bank account or whether the client has its own separate designated client bank account. A firm is more likely to have a separate designated client bank account for a client if a large sum of money is being held for that client, or if that client is a long-standing client of the firm.

General client account

Where a client's money is in a general client bank account, we must introduce two new ledgers to record the accrual and payment of interest: the "Interest Received" ledger (which relates to income) and the "Interest Paid" ledger (which relates to expenses). The transaction will be recorded in two stages:

(a) The bank will pay interest earned on the general client account into the firm's office account.

1. **The Office Cash ledger will be debited with the amount of interest paid by the bank**. This reflects the fact that money has come into the office bank account. As the Office Cash ledger relates to assets, the increase in value is recorded using a Debit entry.

2. **The Interest Received ledger will be credited with the amount of interest paid by the bank**. This reflects the fact that the solicitor has received a payment of interest. This ledger relates to income, so the increase in value will be recorded using a Credit entry.

(b) A "fair sum" (a fair portion of the amount paid by the bank) will be paid to the individual client in question. As stated earlier, you are typically not expected to calculate a "fair sum".

1. **The Interest Paid ledger will be debited with the "fair sum" due to the client**. This reflects the fact that an expense has arisen that must be paid by the solicitor. The Interest Paid ledger relates to expenses, so the increase in value will be recorded using a Debit entry.

2. **The Office Cash ledger will be credited with the amount of the "fair sum" due to the client**. This reflects the fact that money is going out of the firm's bank account to pay the interest to the client. As the Office Cash ledger relates to assets, the decrease is recorded using a Credit entry.

3. **The Client Cash ledger will be debited with the amount of the "fair sum" due to the client**. This reflects the fact that money is going into the firm's client bank account. As the Client Cash ledger relates to assets, the increase is recorded as a Debit entry.

4. **The Client Ledger will be credited with the amount of the "fair sum" due to the client.** This reflects the fact that an additional sum is now owed to the client (more money is now being held on the client's behalf). As the Client Ledger relates to liabilities, the increase is recorded using a Credit entry.

Separate designated client account

Where a client's money is in a separate designated client account, recording the payment of interest is more straight forward (as the interest will be paid directly into the separate designated client account by the bank). We must introduce a new "Client Cash" ledger, which will relate only to the separate designated bank account for the particular client.

1. **The separate designated Client Cash ledger will be Debited**. This reflects the fact that money has been deposited into the client's separate designated bank account. As the Client Cash ledger relates to assets, the increase in value is recorded using a Debit entry.

2. **The Client Ledger will be credited.** This reflects the fact that an additional sum is now owed to the client (more money is now being held on the client's behalf). As the Client Ledger relates to liabilities, the increase is recorded using a Credit entry.

Financial Statements (Property Transactions)

A financial statement is usually sent by a solicitor to their client towards the end of a property transaction to show either: (1) how much money is due from the client to complete the purchase of the property (if the client is a buyer); or (2) how much money the solicitor will pay the client following the sale of the property (if the client is a seller). In addition to detailing how much money is due, it will also detail any payments made by the client to the solicitor during the course of the transaction (e.g. it would set out any payments made by the client "on account of costs" and any payments made to cover legal fees).

The financial statement must show details of all payments made over the course of the transaction. You should use the information recorded in the ledgers that we have introduced to you throughout this module to put together the financial statement.

Financial statement example for a client that is *buying* a property

To: [*name of buyer client*] Re: [*address of property being purchased*] Completion date: [*contractual completion date*]	
Contractual purchase price of property	**£X**
Add:	
Legal fees	X
Disbursements	X
Total costs for the buyer client	**£X**
Less:	
Money already received from the buyer client	(£X)
Mortgage monies from the lender	(£X)
Interest due to the buyer on money held in the firm's client bank account	(£X)
Balance required from the buyer to complete the sale	**£X**

Add to the financial statement

Legal fees and disbursements are the main costs that typically need to be *added* to the financial statement when acting for a *buyer* in the context of a property transaction, including:

- Legal fees charged by the solicitor to the client + VAT.
- Legal fees charged by the solicitor to the lender + VAT (if the client has agreed to pay the lender's legal costs).
- Surveyor's fees (if these were initially paid for by the solicitor on the client's behalf). Note that the solicitor will not be acting as "principal" when paying surveyors fees, so will not need to account for VAT (the client will do this instead).
- Search fees (e.g. Land Registry, Local Authority or environmental searches) + any applicable VAT.
- Stamp Duty Land Tax payable on the purchase.
- Fees charged by the Land Registry to register the purchase.

Deduct from the financial statement

Money already received from the client must be *deducted* from the financial statement when acting for a *buyer* in the context of a property transaction, including:

- Any deposit monies paid.
- Money received from the client on account of costs.
- Any other payments received from the client in respect of disbursements/legal fees that have arisen.

Financial statement example for a client that is *selling* a property

To: [*name of seller client*] Re: [*address of property being sold*] Completion date: [*contractual completion date*]	
Contractual purchase price of property	**£X**
Less:	
Legal fees	(X)
Disbursements	(X)
Amount required to redeem any mortgage to which the property is subject	(X)
Net sale proceeds	**£X**
Add:	
Money already received from the seller client	£X
Interest due to the seller on money held in the firm's client bank account	£X
Balance required from the buyer to complete the sale	**£X**

Legal fees and disbursements (+ any applicable VAT) are the main costs that typically need to be *deducted* from the financial statement when acting for a *seller* in the context of a property transaction. These costs are deducted from the money sent by the buyer to the seller's solicitor.

VAT and financial statements

VAT must be recorded in a separate entry on a financial statement where:

1. The solicitor is charging VAT on the service they are providing to their client; and/or
2. Where the solicitor must account for VAT on services supplied to them as principal (e.g. counsel's fee). Where the solicitor is paying disbursements as "agent" (e.g. surveyor's fees), the VAT need *not* be recorded in a separate entry on the financial statement.

Consider the following example to illustrate *how* to record VAT as a separate entry. Note that you use the middle column to record VAT as a separate amount, and the right column to show the total amounts payable *including* VAT.

To: Client Ltd Re: Purchase of 1 LPC Street Completion date: 25 August 2021		
Contractual purchase price of property		£500,000
Add:		
Our fees	£1,000	
VAT thereon	£200	£1,200 (fees + VAT)
Environmental search	£500	
VAT thereon	£100	£600 (search + VAT)
Surveyor's fee (including VAT)		£2,000
Our fees acting for Lender Ltd (including VAT)		£200
Total costs for the buyer		**£504,000**
Less:		
Deposit money already paid by the buyer		(£50,000)
Mortgage monies from High Street Bank Limited		(£450,000)
Interest due to the buyer on money held in the firm's client bank account		(£15)
Money already paid by the buyer on account of costs		(£2,000)
Balance required from the buyer to complete the sale		**£1,985**

Property Law

Property Law

Introduction to Property Law — 123
Key concepts

Title Investigation — 124
Investigating the Official Copies • the Property Register • the Proprietorship Register • the Charges Register • unregistered interests which override registered dispositions

Pre-contract Searches — 128
Local Land Charges Search • Local Authority enquiries • Commercial Property Standard Enquiries • other searches that must always be carried out • company searches • other searches carried out only in certain circumstances

Planning Law, Building Regulations and Environmental Law — 130
Planning law • listed buildings and conservation areas • building regulations • environmental law

Drafting and Exchanging the Contract for Sale — 133
Structure of the contract for sale • issues dealt with in the contract for sale • conditional contracts • conditional contracts • drafting a contract for sale • pre-exchange of contract for sale • exchange • risks between exchange and completion

Completion — 138
Pre-completion • completion • post-completion • issues and remedies

Drafting — 143
Drafting form TR1 • drafting form AP1

Unregistered Land — 145
Deducing title to unregistered land • burdens affecting unregistered land • the seller • first registration and post-completion

Commercial Security of Tenure — 149
Tenant protection • terminating a protected tenancy • statutory grounds of opposition • interim rent • the new tenancy

Terms of a Lease — 153
Key covenants • repair • insurance • rent and service charge • alteration clauses • user clauses

Alienation — 158
Privity of estate • privity of contract • assignment • underletting/subletting • alienation provisions in the lease

Rent Review — 163
Procedure • assumptions and disregards

Landlord's Remedies — 164
Non-payment of rent • breach of repair covenant

Introduction to Property Law

The first 8 chapters in this module relate to the purchase/sale of a freehold interest in land. These chapters are: Title Investigation; Pre-contract Searches; Planning Law, Building Regulations and Environmental Law; Drafting and Exchanging The Contract For Sale; Completion; Drafting Form TR1; Drafting Form AP1; and Unregistered Land. The stages involved in a transaction relating to the purchase/sale of a freehold interest in land are set out below:

Investigation of the title and the property → Negotiation of and drafting the contract for sale → Exchanging and signing the contract → Pre-completion → Completion → Post-completion

The final 5 chapters in this module relate to leasehold transactions. These chapters are: Commercial Security of Tenure; Terms of a Lease; Alienation; Rent Review; and Landlord's Remedies.

Key Concepts

There are a few key concepts you need to be aware of prior to this module. These should have been taught to you during your law degree or law conversion, therefore they have been included briefly to refresh your knowledge. For the purpose of this handbook, it will be assumed that you are familiar with these concepts.

- **Dominant land/benefiting land:** land which has been granted a right over other land, e.g. a right of way.

- **Servient land/burdened land:** land over which a right has been granted for the benefit of other land.

- **Easement:** a right enjoyed by a landowner (the owner of the dominant land) to cross or otherwise use someone else's land (the servient land) for a specified purpose.

- **Restrictive covenant:** an agreement whereby the owner of the burdened land is required to refrain from doing a certain act, e.g. refrain from building anything on the property with a height exceeding 2 metres.

- **Positive covenant:** an agreement whereby the owner of the burdened land is required to do some positive act, e.g. maintain a boundary fence in good repair.

- **Lease:** a lease grants the lessee (the tenant) exclusive use of a property for a period of time.

- **License:** unlike a lease, a licence does not confer any legal interest in the land. Instead, licenses confer *personal* rights to use the property to which the licence relates. A license is therefore a "permission" granted to the licensee to use the licensor's land in a manner that, without a licence, would constitute trespass.

- **Registered land:** registered land is land that has been registered at the Land Registry. The Land Registry keeps a record of matters relating to ownership, possession and other rights in land.

- **Unregistered land:** this is land that has not been registered at the Land Registry. The aim is that all land should be registered and pursuant to Land Registration Act 2002 s. 4, if certain transactions take place, the land *must* be registered. Such transactions include the sale of the land or the granting of a lease over the land for a period of more than 7 years.

- **Title:** when a person has "title" to land they have a bundle of rights in a piece of property. The main rights include exclusive possession and exclusive use of the property as well as conveyance (the right to transfer the title).

- **Mortgage:** a mortgage is a type of fixed charge that gives the lender a legal right to claim and sell the asset(s) over which security is taken (the "secured assets") in order to recover the funds loaned out, in instances where a loan has not been repaid in accordance with the terms under which the security was taken. In the context of the Property Law module, the asset will be a house or building, although mortgages can also be taken over other assets.

Title Investigation

A prospective buyer of a property (or rather, their solicitor) must investigate the seller's title to that property prior to the purchase. The buyer must make sure there are no defects to the seller's title, as this could affect the value of the property and also the *buyer's* ability to sell the property on in the future. Title investigation is carried out by checking the "Official Copies" of the property and any ancillary documents that are referred to in the "Official Copies".

> **Official Copies:** this is a document issued by the Land Registry that contains copies of any entries made on the registered title of a property. It records all matters that affect the property, such as who owns the property and if anyone else (for instance, a tenant) has any rights over the property.

Investigating the Official Copies

There are three main parts to the Official Copies and the buyer's solicitor must carefully examine each part in order to assess whether there is anything present that could create problems for the buyer. This section outlines each part of the Official Copies and issues you should look out for when investigating title to a property. It also explains how you can try to solve the more commonly found issues.

The Header

The top section of the Official Copies contains information on the date and time of the issue of the Official Copies, and sets out the title number of the property. It is important to check whether:

- The title number of the property corresponds with other documentation, such as: the heads of terms, the contract for sale and **form TR1** (explained later); and

- The Official Copies are recent. The buyer's solicitor should not accept and review old versions of the Official Copies, otherwise he/she risks missing more recent entries.

The Property Register

1. Description of property

The property will be described by its address and by reference to a title plan.

2. Rights benefiting the property

The most common form of rights benefiting the property is an easement (see *Key Concepts* in the introductory chapter to this topic for a definition). If an easement is included in the Property Register, you should examine its suitability for the buyer by considering the following four factors:

(a) **Adequacy:** is the easement adequate for the buyer's intended use?

- Does the easement only allow access by foot, or does it allow for vehicles as well?
- Does the easement only allow access at certain times of the day?
- Does the easement run from the property to a public highway? If the road to which the easement attaches is not public, it is arguably useless for the buyer. A CON29 search and/or a Highways search will confirm whether this is the case (these searches are explained in the chapter *Pre-contract searches*).

If the easement is inadequate for the buyer's intended use, the buyer has the option to ask the person who owns the servient land to vary the easement using a "Deed of Variation" (the servient owner is likely to require payment in return). The owner of the servient land can be found using a SIM search (this search is explained in the *Pre-contract searches* chapter).

(b) **Maintenance:** is there an obligation for the owner to maintain/pay towards the maintenance of the relevant land?

Sometimes the owner of the land that benefits from the easement has to contribute towards the cost of maintaining and/or repairing the plot of land over which the easement has been granted. This is something the buyer would want to know about in advance.

Even if the entry in the Property Register detailing the easement mentions nothing about maintenance/repair costs, this does not mean the buyer will definitely have no obligation to pay for maintenance/repair in the future. For instance, if the seller has paid towards maintenance in the past, this may have given rise to an obligation to do so in the future (including future buyers).

To find out whether the seller has contributed financially in the past, the buyer should consult the Commercial Property Standard Enquiries ("CPSEs" this is explained in the chapter *Pre-contract searches*). If the seller has only owned the property for a short period of time, the buyer may also want to consider the CPSEs given to the current seller by the previous seller when the current seller purchased the property.

Property Law

(c) **Adoption:** has the relevant road been adopted or are there plans to adopt it in the future?

Private roads can be "adopted" by (i.e. brought under the control of) local authorities. When a road is "adopted", the authority that has adopted the road can require those with property abutting the road to contribute towards the cost of bringing it up to an "adoptable" (appropriate) standard.

Bringing a road up to adoptable standard can be very costly, so the buyer should be advised of this risk when they have an easement over a private road that abuts their property. A CON29 search will reveal whether the local authority has any plans to adopt the road or whether it has in the past been adopted.

(d) **Registration:** has the easement been registered over the servient land?

Easements should be registered over the servient land so as to protect that interest. A buyer's solicitor is responsible for ensuring this is the case. How an easement is registered depends on whether the servient land is registered:

- If the servient land is unregistered: a "caution against first registration" must be entered against the servient land.
- If the servient land is registered: the buyer should ensure the easement is registered in the Charges Register of the servient land.

A SIM search can be used to check whether the servient land is registered or unregistered.

> **Caution against first registration:** this protects an interest over unregistered land. When the Land Registry receives an application for first registration of land and that land is the subject of a caution, the interest (e.g. easement) will be noted on the Charges Register for that land.

3. Other forms of rights benefiting the property

- **Drainage:** the buyer would want to make sure that the foul and service water from the property drains to a public sewer. If such access is inadequate, the buyer should consider approaching the person who owns the burdened land to have the right varied (extended).
- **Right to light:** where a right to light is established, and then interrupted by a new building, the owner of the dominant land is entitled to a flow of adequate light for the use and enjoyment of their land.

The Proprietorship Register

1. The registered proprietor

The registered proprietor is the owner of the property and therefore, in the context of a property transaction, typically the seller. The seller may however also be a bank (if the property has been repossessed) or a personal representative of a deceased owner. There are some things a buyer must consider depending on who the seller is.

(a) Where the seller is a company

A company's identity lies in its company number, *not* its name. A buyer should therefore carry out a search using the company seller's company number (found in the Proprietorship Register) at Companies House, to check what the company seller's *current* company name is. It is the *current* name that should be used in heads of terms/the contact for sale (even if the Proprietorship Register uses the old name).

Where the seller is a company, the buyer should make sure that the person signing the relevant contracts (e.g. the director) has authority to sign on behalf of the company.

(b) Where the seller is a joint owner

A property can be owned by more than one owner at the same time. An issue could arise where one owner has died and the remaining owner(s) is (are) selling the property. Where a joint owner has died, the consequences depend on whether the property was owned as "tenants in common" or "joint tenants".

> **Tenants in common/joint tenants:** where land is owned by multiple people, they must own the property either as "tenants in common" or as "joint tenants". The main distinction between the two is the operation of "survivorship". If a joint tenant dies, the surviving joint tenant(s) will have the legal right to the deceased's share. If a tenant in common dies, their interest in the property will be transferred to their estate (and not to the other joint owners).

If the seller is a sole surviving tenant in common:

- It is necessary to "overreach" the deceased beneficial interest. This is done by appointing a second trustee and ensuring that the payment for the property is made to both the surviving owner and the second trustee. Both (i.e. the surviving tenant in common and the appointed second trustee) must then execute the contract and purchase deed. The Land Registry will require evidence of the deceased joint tenant's death and the appointment of the second trustee when completing the sale: an official copy of the deceased tenant in common's death certificate and the deed of appointment of the second trustee will be necessary.

If the seller is a sole surviving joint tenant:

- The operation of survivorship means that the surviving joint tenant can execute the contract and purchase deed alone, meaning the deceased's interest will not need to be "overreached". The Land Registry will only require an official copy of the deceased joint tenant's death certificate when completing the sale.

Where the seller is a personal representative:

- The buyer must ensure that the personal representative has been properly appointed. The evidence of this is a grant of representation. Payment to a personal representative will overreach the beneficial interest of the deceased. The Land Registry will require an official copy of the grant of representation when completing the sale.

> **Personal representative:** will be appointed when an estate owner has died and will be responsible for bequeathing that owner's title interest. Such appointment will be evidenced by a "grant of representation".

2. Indemnity covenants

An "indemnity covenant" relates to positive covenants over land. Positive covenants are noted on the Charges Register (see below) but it will also be noted that the owner has given an indemnity covenant in relation to those covenants in the Proprietorship Register. This note could for instance read: *'The transfer to the Proprietors contains a covenant to observe and perform the covenants referred to in the Charges Register and of indemnity in respect thereof'*.

3. Class of title

The Proprietorship Register notes which class of the title the owner possesses. There are three types of classes of ownership (referred to as "titles to freehold estates"), which are found in the Land Registration Act 2002 s. 9 + s. 10. These are:

- Absolute title
- Qualified title
- Possessory title

It is important that the seller has "absolute title". Any other class of title should be flagged as a potential problem. For instance, banks (when providing a mortgage) and insurance companies will not normally accept any class of ownership other than title absolute.

The Charges Register

The Charges Register sets out any third party rights that burden the property. The following are the most common third party rights that may appear on the Charges Register:

Mortgages

There are normally two entries in the Charges Register to indicate that a bank/building society has been granted a mortgage over the property. Lenders can also put in an entry in the Proprietorship Register to further protect their position, to emphasise that the property cannot be sold without their consent. When a buyer buys the property, it is important that they do not take the property subject to a mortgage, so their solicitor must ensure that any mortgages are discharged before the sale completes (the discharge of mortgages and the relevant documentation are dealt with in more detail in the *Completion* chapter of this module).

When a buyer is buying only part of a plot of land, it is important that the lender (of the person who is selling part of their land) has given its consent to the sale. This is not necessary when the whole of the land is being sold (as the mortgage will be discharged).

Leases

A buyer would need to be advised that if any leases have been granted over the property, they might be buying the property *subject* to those leases; any existing leaseholders would retain the rights connected to their lease after the sale.

Restrictive covenants

If you need a reminder as to what a restrictive covenant is, please refer to the *Key Concepts* section at the start of this module. Case law has established that the burden of restrictive covenants "runs with the land". This means that the owner of the dominant land will be able to enforce any restrictive covenants even when the servient land has been sold, thus binding the buyer. Problems may arise if: (a) the current owner (or a previous owner) has breached a restrictive covenant in the past (even if the new buyer does not breach it); or (b) if the buyer intends to use the land in a way that would constitute a breach of the restrictive covenant(s) in the future.

(a) Past breach of a restrictive covenant

If you establish that there has been a breach of a restrictive covenant in the past, the following advice should be given to the client (in order of preference):

- If the breach is remediable, it should become a term of the contract that the seller should remedy the breach prior to completion.
- If the breach is not remediable and the restrictive covenant is old (created more than 50 years ago), restrictive covenant insurance should be purchased prior to completion. It is normally the seller that will have to pay for this. Insurance companies are more willing to insure against past breaches of restrictive covenants if: (a) the restrictive covenants are old; and (b) the owner of the dominant land has not yet complained, as these factors indicate a lower risk of any complaints arising in the future. Bear in mind that as a solicitor you cannot advise on insurance Financial Services and Markets Act 2000 s. 19.

- If the restrictive covenant is new (created less than 50 years ago), restrictive covenant insurance may be expensive (because of the greater risk of complaints arising) and therefore unsuitable. Therefore, if the restrictive covenant is new, it may be better to seek retrospective consent from the owner of the dominant land. Note that the owner of the dominant land should only be approached once the insurance option has been ruled out, as the approach will effectively tip them off about the breach (meaning an insurance company would probably refuse to subsequently provide insurance).

- The last option is to apply to the Lands Tribunal pursuant to Law of Property Act 1925 s. 84 to modify, discharge or waive the restrictive covenant. This is the last resort as it is time consuming, expensive and offers no guarantee of success.

(b) Future breach of a restrictive covenant

If the buyer is intending to breach the covenant in the future once they own the property, the same order of preference of potential actions apply as for a past breach. However, any insurance is likely to have to be paid for by the buyer and it is likely to be more expensive. This is because even though the covenant may be old, if there has been no past breach it will be difficult for the insurance company to assess the likelihood of the owner of the dominant land suing in the future if/when the covenant is breached.

Positive covenants

Unlike with restrictive covenants, positive covenants do *not* run with the burdened land. Therefore, a buyer of a property that is subject to a positive covenant at the time of sale will not necessarily be legally bound by that positive covenant.

It is possible for a buyer however to *become* bound by the positive covenant, if they contractually promise to observe it when they buy the land. It is important for the seller to include such a promise from the buyer in the contract for sale, as otherwise the seller would remain liable for the new owner's compliance with the positive covenant (and the new owner would not be bound to observe/uphold it). For this reason, it is standard for positive covenants to bind successive buyers contractually; this is known as a "chain" of indemnity covenants.

- The actual *covenant* (setting out what the owner of the land must do to comply with it) is set out in the Charges Register.

- The *indemnity covenant*, which is the promise to adhere to the positive covenant, is contained in the Proprietorship Register.

Problems may arise if (a) the current owner (or a previous owner) has breached a positive covenant in the past (even if the buyer has done nothing wrong); or (b) if the buyer intends to use the land in a way that would constitute a breach of the positive covenant in the future.

(a) Past breach of a positive covenant

This is dealt with in the same way as with past breaches of restrictive covenants:

- If the breach is remediable, the buyer should ask the seller to remedy the breach.

- If the breach is not remediable and the covenant is old (created more than 50 years ago), the buyer should ask the seller to purchase insurance.

- If the breach is not remediable and the covenant is new (created less than 50 years ago), it may be better to ask the owner of the dominant land for retrospective consent.

- Note that an application to the Upper Tribunal (Lands Chamber) is not available for positive covenants.

(b) Future breach of a positive covenant

The same applies as for past breaches (with the exception that the buyer would typically be the one to pay for any insurance purchased).

Unregistered Interests Which Override Registered Dispositions

When investigating title to a property, from a buyer's perspective it is also important to consider interests in land that are not noted in the Official Copies, but may still affect the property. This is because some interests in land can bind subsequent owners despite not being registered. Unregistered interests that override a registered transfer of land (i.e. unregistered interests that will bind a buyer) include:

- **Legal easements** pursuant to Land Registration Act 2002, Schedule 3, paragraph 3.

- **Leases of not more than 7 years** pursuant to Land Registration Act 2002, Schedule 3, paragraph 1. This is because leases that are granted for more than 7 years must be registered and would therefore appear in the Official Copies. Shorter leases would not appear in the Official Copies, but would still bind a buyer.

- **Interest of persons in actual occupation** pursuant to Land Registration Act 2002, Schedule 3, paragraph 2. It is therefore important to investigate, prior to purchasing the property, whether anyone is unofficially living on the premises as a non-owner. If there are, the buyer must ensure such occupiers sign a waiver of any rights to the property and agree to leave the property prior to completion.

Pre-contract Searches

The seller in a commercial property transaction has a very limited duty of disclosure, giving rise to the principle of *"caveat emptor"* (meaning "buyer beware"). It is therefore crucial for a buyer to make proper investigations of a property prior to committing to purchase it. As part of such investigations, the buyer's solicitor will undertake a range of different searches to identify any issues and report to his/her client whether there are any issues that indicate the purchase should be avoided/renegotiated.

Some searches should always be carried out, whilst others will only be required under certain circumstances. This chapter outlines the different searches, common problems to look out for, and potential solutions to these problems.

Searches That Will Always Be Carried Out

Local Land Charges Search (LLC1)

The LLC1 search mainly shows information in relation to planning law. The main purpose (for the purposes of the LPC) of carrying out an LLC1 search is to establish what planning permission has been granted in the past, in order to establish whether any past building works have breached any relevant planning law. The search will reveal:

- Planning permission granted in the past.

- Whether the property is in a Conservation Area and/or has Listed Building status.

- Any changes in registered use that have been permitted (i.e. given planning permission).

- Whether the property is subject to a "Smoke Control Order".

- Whether any parts of the Town and Country Planning (General Permitted Development) (England) Order 2015 ("GPDO 15") have been disapplied (see the *Planning Law, Building Regulations and Environmental Law* chapter).

Enquiries at the Local Authority (CON29)

The CON29 search provides information about the property's planning history and surrounding areas. There is some overlap between the information provided by CON29 enquiries and LLC1 searches. A CON29 search takes the form of a questionnaire, with numbered enquiries to which the local authority replies systematically. CON29 searches will reveal:

- Information about planning permissions and consents, including consents that were applied for but refused.

- Information relating to Building Regulations approval.

- Details of whether any private roads have been adopted or if there are any plans to adopt them.

- Information about contamination: the enquiries will reveal whether the local authority has served any notices under environmental legislation requiring action on the part of the owner to clean up their land.

Highways search

A highways search will detail any boundaries between public highways and the private land that the buyer is looking to buy. It is important to ensure that the property abuts a highway or that the property has a right of way over a road that abuts a public highway (otherwise there could be no legitimate access to the property/land).

Commercial Drainage and Water search (CON29DW enquiries)

A buyer needs to establish whether a property is connected to water and drainage/sewer systems. It may be necessary to make further investigations into who provides such services to the property if it is not connected to the main sewer system.

Desktop Environmental search

A desktop environmental search is carried out to reveal any contamination present at the property (in particular from former industrial use). It also reveals information on the likelihood of flooding or subsidence occurring. It is particularly important to find any contamination issues at the pre-contractual stage of the property transaction, as liability to clean up contaminated land can be incredibly expensive and may rest with the *owner* of the property (even if they did not originally *cause* the contamination). This is discussed further in the *Environmental law* section in the *Planning Law, Building Regulations and Environmental Law* chapter in this module.

If a desktop environmental search reveals that contamination exists/may exist, further investigations should be carried out:

- **Phase 1:** this involves a surveyor physically inspecting the land.
- **Phase 2:** if the surveyor deems it necessary to investigate further, this should be carried out. This involves taking and analysing soil samples.

Commercial Property Standard Enquiries (CPSEs)

This is a standard set of enquiries sent from a buyer to a seller. The enquiries cover a wide range of information that would otherwise be known only to the seller. They could for instance reveal:

- Whether the owner has taken any action that could potentially be in breach of a covenant.
- Whether there are any non-owners occupying the property.
- Whether there are any other third party rights affecting the property that are not required to be registered (i.e. they will not show on the Official Copies).
- Whether there are any barriers to access the property.
- Details about the physical condition of the property (e.g. issues with damp or rot).

Index Map Search (SIM)

- **Registered land:** a SIM search is carried out to establish whether any third party interests are registered against the title to the property. A SIM search can also reveal the owner of the neighbouring land and whether that land is registered or unregistered.
- **Unregistered land:** a SIM search is essential in order to establish whether any *part* of the land has already been registered or whether the land is subject to a caution against first registration.

A SIM search could, for instance, be used to find out who owns the neighbouring (dominant) land if a prospective buyer is looking into the possibility of varying an easement.

Searches Carried Out Only In Certain Circumstances

Company search

If the seller is a company, a search at Companies House should be undertaken to confirm the seller's company number and official name. Buyers must also ensure that there are no insolvency proceedings affecting the property.

Optional Enquiries at the Local Authority (CON29O)

If the property is close to large fields or parks, it is important to establish that there are no rights that will interfere with the buyer's use of the property. This is where a CON29O enquiry should be made, as it will reveal:

- Information about public footpaths, common land and village greens surrounding the property.
- Information about rights in common, such as rights of grazing or rights of access. Rights in common are historic rights exercised by a group of people (e.g. the residents of a town).

Waterways search

This should be conducted where there is a river passing through the property. The search will reveal:

- Who is liable to maintain the riverbanks and to keep the river free from obstruction.
- Any rights of way along the riverbanks or towpaths.
- Any drainage rights.
- Any fishing rights.

A buyer would be bound by these rights and obligations subsequent to purchasing the property, which could affect their intended use of the property (and result in them incurring additional costs).

Coal mining search (CON29M enquiries)

This is necessary where the property is located on a former mining site. It will reveal any subsidence risk, in addition to past and planned future uses of the site for mining.

Planning Law, Building Regulations and Environmental Law

There are a variety of laws affecting how, where and what individuals can build/demolish on their property. A buyer must establish (a) whether there are any restrictions that could affect their intended use of the property; and (b) whether there have been any past breaches of planning law, environmental law and/or building regulations. This is because a subsequent owner can still be liable for breaches made by past owners.

Planning Law

Planning law relates to planning permission. The rules relating to planning permission determine when an intended development or use of land requires permission from the relevant local authority. Buyers must ensure that any past or current developments or uses of the land have been carried out with the correct permission. The fundamental principle is that planning permission is required for any *development* of land Town and Country Planning Act 1990 ("TCPA 90") s. 57(1).

> **"Development" of land**: is defined in TCPA 90 s. 55(1) as:
> (1) The carrying out of building, engineering, mining or other operations in, or under land (this includes the demolition of buildings TCPA 90 s. 55(1A); or
> (2) The making of any material changes in the use of any buildings or land.

Planning permission can therefore be required in relation to: (a) building operations; (b) demolition; and (c) the use of land.

> **Use of land:** "use" here relates to what the property is being used for, e.g. used as a restaurant or as a shop. An example of a *change* of use could be, for instance, changing the use of property from a casino to a museum.

Planning permission for building works

When establishing whether a particular building work requires (or required, if it has been done in the past) planning permission, the following is a useful structure to follow:

1. Do the building works fall within the definition of "development" in TCPA 90 s. 55(1A)?

If the building works do not fall within the definition of "development", no planning permission is necessary TCPA 90 s. 57(1)

"Development" includes "building operations" (see above definition). "Building operations" is defined in TCPA 90 s. 55(1A) as including:

- Demolition.
- Rebuilding.
- Structural alterations or additions.

The following types of building works are *not* "developments" TCPA 90 s. 55(2)(a):

- Alterations that affect only the *interior* of the building (e.g. temporary partitioning walls).
- Alterations that do not materially affect the external appearance of the building.

2. Is planning permission granted automatically?

In certain circumstances no application for planning permission is required even though the building works fall within the definition of "development". Planning permission is deemed to have been automatically granted for "permitted developments", which are listed in the GPDO 15:

- For private dwelling houses, the permitted developments include enlargements and improvements GPDO 15 Schedule 2, Part 1.
- For commercial properties, the permitted developments include erecting a fence and painting a building GPDO 15 Schedule 2, Part 2.

To summarise: if the building works fall within the definition of "development" and do not count as "permitted developments" (in which case planning permission would automatically be granted), planning permission is required.

Planning permission for demolition

Demolition is dealt with in a slightly different way to other building operations. If you are dealing with a past or intended future demolition, the following structure will help to establish whether planning permission is necessary.

1. Does the demolition fall within the definition of "development" in TCPA 90 s. 55(1A)(a)?

The following do *not* fall within the definition of "development" pursuant to The Town and Country Planning (Demolition – Description of Buildings) Direction 2014 and thus do not require planning permission:

- The demolition of a *whole* building, the volume of which when measured externally, does not exceed 50 cubic meters; or
- The demolition of the whole or any part of any gate, fence, wall or other means of enclosure, so long as the relevant means of enclosure is *not* situated inside a conservation area.

If the demolition does not fall within these exceptions, planning permission is required.

2. Is planning permission granted automatically?

Even if planning permission is required, it can be granted automatically by the GPDO 15 if the demolition constitutes a "permitted development". Planning permission is automatically granted for the following "permitted developments":

- Any demolition that is *not* the demolition of: (1) buildings that have been rendered unsafe or uninhabitable as a result of the owner's actions/inaction; or (2) unlisted buildings in Conservation Areas GPDO 15 Schedule 2, Part 11, Class B.
- Any building operation consisting of the demolition of the whole or any part of any gate, fence, wall or other means of enclosure, unless the structure in question is an unlisted structure in a Conservation Area (GPDO 15 Schedule 2, Part 11, Class C).

To summarise: if the demolition falls within the definition of "development" and does not count as a "permitted development" (in which case planning permission would automatically be granted), planning permission is required.

Note that the partial demolition of a building will *always* fall under the definition of "development" under TCPA 90 s. 55(1A)(a) and is not granted automatic planning permission under any circumstances, so will *always* require planning permission.

Planning permission for change of use

1. Is it a *material* change of use (meaning it therefore falls within the definition of "development")?

TCPA 90 s. 55(1) defines "development" to include a "material change of use".

- TCPA 90 s. 55(2)(f) clarifies that where a change of use occurs within the same use class, this is *not* considered to be a "material change of use" and therefore does *not* fall within the definition of "development".
- Use classes are listed in the Town and Country Planning (Use Classes) Order 1987. Each distinct "use class" is identified by a combination of a letter and a number (e.g. A1). A "material change of use" occurs where the use (i.e. purpose) of a property changes from a use listed in one "use class" to a use listed in another (e.g. the property was originally used for a purpose listed in use class A1 and is now being used for a purpose listed in use class A3).

2. Is planning permission granted automatically?

Even if there is a change of use from one class to another, planning permission may still be automatically granted if that change falls under those listed in GPDO 15 Schedule 2, Part 3. It is an extensive list and includes, for example, a change from use class A5 (hot food takeaways) to A1 (shops).

To summarise: If the change of use is a "material" change of use, and it does not fall within GPDO 15 Schedule 2, Part 3 (in which case planning permission would automatically be granted), planning permission is required.

Breach of planning legislation and enforcement periods

Enforcement periods

- **Material change of use**: for a material change of use made without the required planning permission, enforcement action can be brought for up to ten years following the date on which the change of use took effect (TCPA 90 s. 171B(3)). There is one exception however: changes to a *dwelling house* can only be challenged for four years.
- **Building works:** for building works carried out without the required planning permission, enforcement action can be brought for up to four years following *substantial* completion of the works (TCPA 90 s. 171B(1)).
- **Concealment**: however, if either of the above types of breach has been deliberately concealed (e.g. the owner put up fences to hide a new building or change of use), there is *no time limit* for enforcement.
- **Planning permission conditions:** it is also important to consider whether the conditions of any planning permission granted have been complied with. If a property has been built, or its use has changed, in a way that does not accord with the conditions contained in the planning permission granted, the enforcement period is ten years (from the date on which the breach occurred). It is therefore important for a buyer to obtain copies of any planning permissions granted in the past, so that they (or their solicitor) can check that any conditions imposed were complied with in relation to any developments that were subsequently carried out or changes of use that subsequently took place.

Consequences

A breach of planning legislation could result in the local authority serving:

- An enforcement notice, which is an order to restore the land. There are criminal sanctions if this is not complied with.
- A stop notice, which is an order to stop all activities that are held to be in breach.
- A planning contravention notice, intended to flush out information about potential breaches before an enforcement notice is served.

If the buyer's solicitor establishes that past building works or changes of use have occurred without planning permission (under circumstances where planning permission would have been required), it is important that this is dealt with before completion. The buyer should request that the seller obtains retrospective planning permission; this should be made a special condition in the contract (the contract for sale and special conditions are explained in the *Drafting and Exchanging the Contract for Sale* chapter of this module).

Listed Buildings and Conservation Areas

Special planning law rules apply when the property is a listed building or in a conservation area. These rules are complicated and you must therefore check with your LPC provider which assumptions you can make and in what detail you are expected to know them. This is just a brief overview of the potential consequences of making alterations in a conservation area/to a listed building.

Listed buildings

> **Listed buildings**: buildings that have been placed on the Statutory List of Buildings of Special Architectural or Historic Interest.

These are buildings that have a special historical or architectural merit and are therefore protected by more stringent planning laws and controls. The relevant consent that will sometimes be required is called Listed Building Consent and is needed in addition to any planning permission. This consent is needed for exterior and interior works if it affects its character. This is very subjective, so it is advisable to assume that any building works on a listed building will require Listed Building Consent. There is no time limit for enforcement for a breach where works have been carried out without Listed Building Consent. The breach carries criminal sanctions and subsequent owners may become liable to rectify the building to its original state.

Conservation areas

> **Conservation areas**: defined in statute as areas that are of "special architectural or historical interest, the character or appearance of which it is desirable to preserve or enhance".

Planning laws are stricter for buildings that are situated in conservation areas. The GPDO 15, which affords automatic planning permission for certain building works (see above *Planning Law* section), is normally disapplied for properties in conservation areas. Building works or changes of use will therefore typically require planning permission if the property is situated in a conservation area. Whether a property is situated in a conservation area/whether the GPDO 15 has been disapplied for the property can be ascertained using an LLC1 search. Note that this also applies to trees – any tree in a conservation area cannot be felled or lopped.

Demolition of a listed building in a conservation area

- *Total* demolition of a listed building in a conservation area will be automatically granted planning permission if it complies with GPDO 15 Class B Part 11 Schedule 2. Listed Building Consent will also be required.
- *Partial* demolition of a listed building in a conservation area will always need planning permission and Listed Building Consent (it is assumed for the purpose of this handbook that any demolition affects the building's character).

Sanctions

There are no time limits for enforcement following breaches of planning law in conservation areas. Criminal sanctions may also be available against perpetrators, but not subsequent owners (although subsequent owners may be required to rectify breaches).

Building Regulations

Building regulations are rules relating to the construction and alteration of buildings. Building regulations approval, recorded in a "Building Regularisation Certificate", is an additional requirement to planning permission. Such approval may be required even where planning permission is not (e.g. where planning permission is granted automatically by the GPDO 15). There is no time limit for enforcement, meaning that it is particularly important to ensure that building regulations approval has been obtained and complied with for any building works previously carried out on the property. It may be possible to obtain a retrospective "Building Regularisation Certificate" for building works carried out without approval in the past. The buyer should make it a special condition of the contract that the seller will obtain one of these if it transpires that the seller has failed to obtain building regulations approval in the past.

Environmental Law

The relevant legislation to consider for LPC purposes is the Environmental Protection Act 1990 ("EPA 90"). There are strict laws governing pollution and contamination. These apply to owners and, in certain circumstances, subsequent owners (even if a previous owner is the responsible party for the relevant pollution/contamination). It is therefore important for the buyer's solicitor to consider any potential environmental liability.

Remediation Notices

A local authority can issue remediation notices on an "appropriate person", which means that person is liable to clean up the relevant pollution/contamination.

The appropriate person: Class A and B persons

- **Class A person**: the person who caused or knowingly permitted the pollutant to be in the land OR a person who buys land with knowledge of the pollution/contamination and does nothing to remedy it.
- **Class B person**: the person who owns or occupies the relevant property. If no Class A person can be found following an investigation by the local authority, the Class B person will be liable for the remediation of the pollution/contamination.

Remedying pollution/contamination can be very expensive and contaminated land will be difficult to sell, let or mortgage. Because a buyer could be a Class B person (or a Class A person if they had knowledge of the pollution/contamination at the time of purchase), it is crucial to carry out environmental searches at the investigation stage (these are dealt with in the *Pre-contract Searches* chapter of this module).

Drafting and Exchanging the Contract for Sale

When the buyer's solicitor has completed the investigation of the title and the property, a contract for sale will be drafted and exchanged. The contract for sale in a property transaction is the agreement that the seller is to sell and the buyer is to buy the relevant property. The *Purchase Deed* (**form TR1**) is a separate agreement that actually transfers the ownership of the land. The purchase deed is signed (and dated) *after* the contract for sale has been exchanged/signed.

Structure of the Contract for Sale

The seller's solicitor usually prepares the first draft of the contract. It normally includes three sections:

1. A front page that states the parties' details (such as name and address), the address and particulars of the property, any incumbrances, the price (and the deposit), and the relevant dates for the transaction.

   Incumbrances: a general term for anything that burdens a land (e.g. mortgages, easements, restrictive covenants etc.).

2. The second section of the contract normally incorporates either the Standard Commercial Property Conditions ("SCPC") for commercial property transactions, or the Standard Conditions of Sale ("SCS") for residential property transactions. These are standard form contracts that are pre-printed and include terms covering a range of issues that could arise in a property sale (such as what happens if completion is delayed).

3. The third section of the contract contains any special conditions, which are used to amend and/or exclude terms from the standard form contract, and/or create new terms covering matters/issues that are not covered in the standard form contracts. For instance, special conditions may cover issues that have come to light as a result of the searches and investigations carried out on the land/property (e.g. that the seller is to obtain a retrospective Regularisation Certificate in respect of building work previously carried out without Buildings Regulations approval).

Issues Dealt With in the Contract for Sale

Specified incumbrances

A sale is subject to incumbrances specified in the contract; incumbrances discoverable by inspection pre-contract; incumbrances the seller does not know and could not reasonably have known about; those (other than monetary charges/incumbrances) disclosed or which would have been identified by searches/enquiries that a prudent buyer would have made before entering into the contract; and public requirements (e.g. public rights of way) SCPC 4.1.2.

In commercial property transactions (where the SCPC are incorporated) the onus is therefore on the buyer to carry out all the relevant searches and enquiries – they will be deemed to be taking subject to matters that would be revealed by such searches/enquiries even if they did not make them.

Defects in title

If a previous seller did not properly pass legal title to a subsequent buyer and there is a break in the chain of ownership (and this defect cannot be remedied), the seller should disclose the problem in the contract by using an appropriate special condition that reveals the nature of the defect and states that the buyer accepts the defect and will raise no objection to it. This is referred to as a "Faruqi clause".

Fixtures and chattels

The default position is that fixtures (items that are *attached* to the property such as sinks, radiators and kitchen units) are included in the sale unless they are explicitly excluded in the contract for sale. In contrast, specific reference must be made in the contract to any chattels (moveable items such as curtains, chairs and tables) that the buyer wishes to acquire.

Where the parties are using the SCPC, they have two options for dealing with the inclusion of chattels: (1) use SCPC Special Condition 3 and attach to the contract a list of fixtures excluded from/chattels included as part of the sale; or (2) draft a new special condition setting out that which the parties intend to be included in/excluded from the sale. Where the parties are using the SCS, the standard form contract for sale includes a box titled "Contents price" in which the parties can state the price to be apportioned to any chattels that the buyer is acquiring.

Stamp Duty Land Tax (explained later) is not paid on the price of chattels, so separating the price of the property and the price of the chattels can give rise to tax savings for a buyer. However, a buyer cannot apportion an inflated price to chattels so as to reduce their Stamp Duty Land Tax liability (as established in the case of Orsman).

Indemnity covenant

SCPC 7.6.5 allows the seller to demand an indemnity covenant in relation to the positive covenant to maintain the fence. The seller could otherwise be perpetually bound to perform this previously agreed obligation. The importance for a seller to be given an indemnity covenant is explained in the *Charges Register* section of the *Title Investigation* chapter of this module.

VAT

Under SCPC 2.1 and SCPC 2.2, the seller warrants that the transaction is a taxable supply and the buyer must pay VAT in return for a VAT invoice. Therefore, if the parties do not intend the transaction to involve VAT, they should instead include a warranty (under SCPC Optional Condition A) from the seller that (a) the sale does not constitute a supply that is taxable for VAT purposes; and (b) the seller will not elect to waive this exemption. If VAT is to be charged (for either of the two reasons mentioned above), Part 2 Condition A1 will be expressly incorporated in the SCPC.

Title guarantee

SCPC 7.6.2 states that the seller transfers the property with full title guarantee. If the seller wants to instead give limited title guarantee or no title guarantee at all, this is done by way of special condition.

- **Full title guarantee**: a guarantee that the seller has the right to sell and that the property is free from all charges/incumbrances and other third party rights other than: (a) those disclosed in the contract; and (b) those the seller could not reasonably have known about. This is usually given if the seller is an absolute owner.

- **Limited title guarantee**: this gives no guarantee from the seller that the property is free from all third party rights, charges and incumbrances. It is simply a guarantee that since the last sale, the *seller* has not created any incumbrances and is not aware that anyone else has.

- **No title guarantee**: this means if any difficulties with title arise following completion, the buyer will have no remedy against the seller. This may be given if the land is being gifted or a lender is exercising its power of sale.

Conditional Contracts

Conditional contracts are contracts that contain one or more conditions that must be satisfied before the deal can be completed. The full purchase price will not typically be paid until the condition(s) has (have) been satisfied. Conditional contracts may be used:

- Where the contract is dependent upon planning permission being granted.
- Where the results of environmental/local authority searches are not available by the date of exchange.
- Where the buyer has not yet secured finance (e.g. a bank loan) for the purchase.

Points to consider when drafting conditional clauses

- What is the contract conditional upon?
- Define the obligations on each party. Whose job is it to fulfil the various conditions? For example:

    "The Buyer must apply for planning permission within 14 days of exchanging contracts".

- If the condition is fulfilled, when must completion take place?
- Include time limits for satisfaction of the condition, including a final "long-stop date" to avoid uncertainty (i.e. a date on which parties can walk away from the deal if the condition is not yet satisfied).
- If the condition is not fulfilled, how will parties rescind and who gets to keep the deposit?

Drafting a Contract for Sale

Some LPC providers may require students to draft or re-draft a contract. The following section comments on which information should be included in each section of the contract when drafting.

Contract incorporating the Standard Commercial Property Conditions (Second Edition)

Date	This should remain blank until contracts are exchanged. At exchange a date will be noted here, at which point a legal contract is formed. The parties are bound to complete at that point.
Seller	Ensure the seller's name is spelt correctly and if it is a company, that the company number is accurate.
Buyer	Ensure the buyer's name is spelt correctly and if it is a company, that the company number is accurate.
Property (freehold/leasehold)	Strike through the option that does not apply to the sale (i.e. if it is a freehold sale strike through "leasehold"). If the address seems too vague, use the description from the property register from the Official Copies. Ensure the title number is inserted here as well.
Title Number/Root of Title	For registered land, the title number should be inserted here. Check the Official Copies to ensure that the correct title number is used. You should also strike through "root of title" as this would only be used for an unregistered property.
Specified incumbrances	Standard drafting practice in registered land is to disclose latent incumbrances by referring to the relevant entries in the Charges Register of the Official Copies (instead of listing all incumbrances affecting the property), e.g. *"the matters set out at Item 1 of the Charges Register of title number 12345"*. You should check that this doesn't, for instance, refer to the Proprietorship Register or the Property Register instead of the Charges Register and that the entry numbers of the incumbrances match those in the Official Copies.
Title Guarantee	This will be either full guarantee, limited guarantee or no guarantee at all. See the *Issues Dealt With in the Contract for Sale* section (above) for an explanation of this concept.
Completion Date	This date will be filled out at exchange and should therefore be left blank until that point. At exchange, the parties will agree on the final completion date. SCS 6.1.1 and SCPC 9.1.1 imply completion is 20 working days from exchange, although parties in practice usually agree a specific date that is inserted into the front of the standard form contract upon exchange, which overrides SCS/SCPC.
Contract Rate	The contract rate is typically around 4%. If the contract rate is not specified, SCPC 1.1.1(e) applies, which means the Law Society interest rate applies (this is 4% above Barclays Bank's base rate).
Purchase Price	Check that the purchase price matches the one given to you in the facts.
Deposit	Make sure the deposit is the correct % of the purchase price. SCPC 3.2.1 states that the deposit will be 10% unless otherwise agreed, however special conditions could amend/override this if the buyer and seller agree a different deposit amount.
Balance	The balance will be the purchase price, less contents price, less the deposit.

Special conditions

Pre-printed special conditions

The back page of the Standard Commercial Property standard form contract contains a series of pre-drafted special conditions. Examples include special conditions relating to vacant possession and VAT. The parties can strike through the special conditions that they do not want to include as part of the Sale/Purchase Agreement ("SPA").

Tailored drafting of special conditions

When drafting special conditions from scratch, you should aim to cover "**who does what by when**?" This will help to ensure that your special conditions are clear, concise and unambiguous. Below are some examples of special conditions drafted using this technique:

"The Seller will repair the Fence at his own expense before completion so that it is in good and sufficient condition."

"The Seller will purchase restrictive covenant insurance in the form of the attached draft policy before completion."

"The Seller shall provide the Buyer with a Regularisation Certificate in respect of building regulations for the construction of a new wing on the property in 2008 on or before Completion."

Pre-exchange of Contract for Sale

When parties exchange contracts they become legally bound by the terms of the contract. It is therefore crucial for each party to ensure they will be able to discharge their contractual obligations before exchanging contracts. The following table is a brief summary of what each party must consider before exchange.

Pre-exchange: buyer's solicitor	Pre-exchange: seller's solicitor
• **Searches and documentation**: any issues that have arisen from searches made must have been dealt with and incorporated into the contract. Send enquiries to the seller's solicitor if any further issues are outstanding. • **Survey**: the buyer should also carry out a physical survey of the property to ensure the property is in a satisfactory condition. • **Deposit**: there must be clear funds available in the buyer's solicitor's client account so that the deposit can be transferred to the seller at exchange. The buyer's solicitor must also ensure that a deposit cheque has been requested from the accounts department (payable to the seller's solicitor). • **Price**: confirm the final purchase price and that everything necessary has been taken into account (e.g. the inclusion of any chattels). • **Mortgage**: confirm with the bank that the funds will be available at completion and that the offer of finance is binding. For commercial mortgages, lenders will require draft *certificates of title* at this stage (the final versions will be sent on the day of completion). • **Completion money**: the solicitor should draw up a draft financial statement to check that the client has enough money to complete (a final version will be prepared nearer completion). For an explanation of the use of financial statements in a property transaction, see the *Financial Statements (Property Transactions)* chapter in the *Solicitors' Accounts* module in this handbook. • **Buyer's signature and instruction**: the solicitor must ensure that the buyer gives authority to exchange and signs the contract.	• **Mortgage**: obtain a provisional redemption figure from the existing lender to ensure that the sale proceeds will be sufficient to pay off all loans/mortgages that relate to the property. If the proceeds will not be sufficient to discharge the mortgage over the *whole* property (of if the seller does not want this), the lender's consent will be needed to release the part being sold from the mortgage (otherwise the buyer takes the property subject to the mortgage). • **Enquiries**: reply to any enquiries made by the buyer's solicitor and make any final amendments to the contract. • **Contract**: once the contract has been agreed, the seller's solicitor will prepare "engrossments" (final versions) of the contract. • **Pre-contract package**: this includes the draft contract, the evidence of title and the results of any searches the seller's solicitor has been asked to undertake. It is prepared by the seller's solicitor and a copy is sent to the buyer's solicitor.

Exchange

The most common procedure for exchanging contracts is called "Formula B", which involves exchange by telephone. This is one of three formulae approved by the Law Society for exchanging contracts. Formula B is the only one outlined in this handbook so you must check with your LPC provider whether you are required to know the other potential methods of exchange.

Exchange occurs when each solicitor agrees to hold his/her client's signed part to the other's order (i.e. the solicitors confirm to each other that their respective clients have signed the contract and that they will exchange those contracts via post/in person). The Formula B exchange procedure is summarised in the below flow chart:

| Solicitors confirm they hold the same version of the contract and that their clients have signed it. | → | Completion date is inserted into the contract. | → | The specific phrase as set out in Formula B must be said over the telephone. | → | Date of exchange is inserted into the contract by the solicitors. | → | Both parties undertake to send the signed contract to the other and the buyer's solicitor undertakes to send the deposit to the seller's solicitor. | → | An attendance note should be filed as a record that exchange has taken place. Contracts are sent via post. |

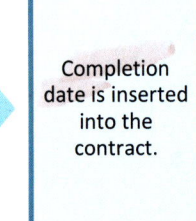

Risks Between Exchange and Completion

Risk and insurance

Even though contracts have been exchanged and the parties are as such legally obliged to complete, there are still some risks that may materialise in the interim period between exchange and completion.

The risk of anything happening to the property (e.g. damage as a result of a fire) passes to the buyer on exchange. SCS 5.1 explicitly states that the risk passes to buyer upon exchange. The SCPC is silent on the matter, but the common law position is the same (the risk passes on exchange). It is therefore crucial that the buyer insures the property so that such insurance takes effect on the date of exchange.

However, the seller will still owe the buyer a duty of care to exercise reasonable care in the upkeep of the property in the interim period. Thus if the seller deliberately damages the property/negligently permits damage, the buyer may be able to claim damages for breach of this duty.

Occupation by buyer before completion

Occasionally a buyer will request permission to occupy the property prior to completion (e.g. to carry out works or start using the property for its intended purpose), for instance if completion is delayed as a result of outstanding third party consents that are sought.

If the buyer is allowed to occupy the property before completion, there is a risk that the buyer may then lose its incentive to complete. If completion does not take place, the seller may consequently have to resort to obtaining a possession order from the court to regain possession. To avoid this, the buyer's occupation should only be as a licensee (SCS 5.2 provides for this, although if the SCPC are used, this would have to be negotiated and included as a special condition).

Death of buyer or seller after exchange but before completion

This does not affect the validity of the contract. The benefit/burden of the contract passes to the deceased's personal representative who is bound to complete.

- **Deceased single seller**: the personal representative must obtain a grant of representation before they can complete the sale.

- **Deceased joint seller:** if the property was held as tenants in common, the deceased tenant in common's interest must be overreached by the appointment of a second trustee.

- **Deceased buyer:** the personal representative must complete the purchase (after they have been granted a grant of representation). Where the purchase was to be funded by a mortgage, it is likely that the offer of finance will be revoked, leaving the personal representative with insufficient funds to complete the purchase. Despite the revocation of the mortgage offer, the personal representative is bound to complete.

Insolvency of buyer or seller after exchange but before completion

- **Single seller's bankruptcy:** the bankrupt party's assets (including any legal estates in property) vest in the trustee in bankruptcy. The buyer must from thereon deal with the trustee instead of the seller.

- **Joint seller's bankruptcy**: trustee in bankruptcy would join in the sale with the solvent co-owner.

- **Single buyer's bankruptcy:** the benefit of the contract passes to the buyer's trustee in bankruptcy, who may either continue with the purchase or disclaim the contract (a trustee in bankruptcy has the right to disclaim any onerous contracts). However, completion may not be possible if the purchase was dependent on a bank loan, as a bank is likely to revoke the offer of finance following an insolvency.

- **Co-buyer's bankruptcy:** similarly, if a co-buyer becomes bankrupt, the benefit of their share of the contract passes to their trustee in bankruptcy. The trustee can disclaim the obligation to complete if they so wish. However, the remaining co-owners are still contractually obliged to complete (although they may have difficulty doing so if a bank revokes its offer to provide finance).

Completion

Once contracts have been exchanged, the parties are legally bound to purchase/sell the relevant property. The contract will reference the "completion date", which is the date on which legal title to the property is to be transferred to the buyer (and thus the date on which "completion" occurs). In the interim period between exchange and completion, the parties can make practical arrangements (e.g. packing up their belongings and booking a removal company) in the knowledge that the other party is bound to go ahead with the sale/purchase. This is the reason why exchange and completion do not typically occur simultaneously (although the parties can choose to exchange and complete on the same day if they so wish).

Pre-completion

Pre-completion steps: buyer's solicitor

Prepare the Purchase Deed (form TR1)

The buyer's solicitor will draft the purchase deed after the contracts have been exchanged, and send it to the seller's solicitor. **Form TR1** is used for the transfer of both freehold and leasehold land where the *whole* of the land is being sold. Some LPC providers ask students to draft or re-draft **form TR1**. You will find an annotated version of **form TR1** at the end of this chapter, explaining how to fill it out.

Completion Information and Undertaking Form

This form can be either the **Law Society's Transaction Form: TA13** or a law firm's own in-house version of this form. This form is sent by the buyer's solicitor to the seller's solicitor to obtain practical information about completion so as to ensure completion will run smoothly. The form will also make a request for:

- An undertaking from the seller's solicitor that any outstanding mortgages will be redeemed (and therefore discharged) prior to or at completion.
- A completion statement from the seller that sets out the balance of funds required to complete (i.e. the purchase price plus any chattels minus the deposit already paid).
- Details of the seller's solicitor's bank account (to which the completion funds will be transferred).
- Information on how to obtain the keys to the property

Finance

The buyer's solicitor will send the buyer a final financial statement outlining what the buyer must pay for completion to go ahead (the buyer should ensure they have the money ready). The buyer's mortgage provider should also be contacted to ensure that the funds will arrive in time for completion.

Pre-completion searches

Pre-completion searches: registered land	Pre-completion searches: unregistered land
1. Land Registry priority search using **form OS1**: this is to ensure that no further entries have been made on the register since the date of the Official Copies (that have been used in the transaction so far). The search also affords the buyer a 30 working day "priority period"; the buyer will take priority over any new entries placed on the register during this period. The priority will be lost if the buyer does not register the purchase within those 30 working days however.	**1. K15 search** to the Central Land Charges (CLC) Department to ensure there are no new or unexpected third party rights burdening the property (CLC searches are dealt with in more detail in the *Unregistered* Land chapter of this module). The K15 search also affords the buyer a 15 working day protection period where the buyer will take priority over any new entries placed. The purchase should therefore be completed within this period.
2. Solvency search on the seller (*only* if the seller is a company). This is done at Companies House.	**2. Solvency search on the seller** if the seller is a company (same as for registered land)
3. Solvency search on the buyer where the buyer's solicitor is also acting for the bank providing the buyer's mortgage (this is the same as for unregistered land). The search is for the benefit of the bank. Send **form K16** to the Central Land Charges (CLC) Department to carry out a solvency search on individual buyers. Carry out a Companies House search to check the solvency of company buyers.	**3. Solvency search on the buyer** where the buyer's solicitor is also acting for the bank providing the buyer's mortgage (this is the same as for registered land). The search is for the benefit of the bank. Send **form K16** to the CLC Department to carry out a solvency search on individual buyers. Carry out a Companies House search to check the solvency of company buyers.

Pre-completion steps: seller's solicitor

1. Approve/amend the Purchase Deed (form TR1)

The seller's solicitor will receive the draft **form TR1** from the buyer's solicitor and should approve it or make any necessary amendments. Once approved by the seller's solicitor, the buyer's solicitor will prepare an engrossed **form TR1**, which is the purchase deed document in its final form.

Property Law

Rules for the execution of the Purchase Deed (form TR1)

The seller must *always* execute **form TR1**.

The buyer must only execute **form TR1** when:

- The buyer is entering into new restrictive or positive covenants;
- The buyer is giving the seller an indemnity covenant;
- A trust is declared (e.g. where joint purchasers declare that they are holding the property as tenants in common); or
- A second trustee is being appointed (e.g. where a deceased joint owner's interest is overreached).

2. Completion Information and Undertaking Form

The seller's solicitor should reply to the Completion Information and Undertaking form sent to them by the buyer's solicitor (see the above *Pre-completion steps: buyer's solicitor* section in this chapter). SCS 4.3.1 and SCPC 7.3.1 require the seller's solicitor to reply to this form within 4 working days of receiving it.

3. Finance

The seller's solicitor should send the buyer's solicitor a final completion statement, which states the total amount due from the buyer on completion and how this has been calculated. The seller's solicitor should also obtain a final redemption figure from the seller's lender so they know how much is required to discharge (pay off) any outstanding mortgage(s) over the property. It is important that the sale proceeds will cover this amount, as the seller will otherwise be in negative equity. The seller's solicitor will undertake to the buyer's solicitor that the seller's mortgage will be discharged at completion (the buyer's solicitor, as explained above, will request this in the "Completion Information and Undertaking Form").

The seller's solicitor will also give the seller a final financial statement showing what funds are due to the seller from the seller's solicitor after the transaction is completed (see the *Financial Statements (Property Transactions)* chapter in the *Solicitors' Account* module in this handbook for an explanation of the financial statements used in property transactions).

Completion

The completion date would have been agreed by the parties at exchange (it is included in the contract that was signed at exchange). Completion typically takes place over the phone.

Buyer's solicitor ensures they have received the funds (from the buyer and lender) required to complete. Seller's solicitor ensures the TR1 is signed and that a redemption figure has been obtained by the bank.	First phone call: seller's solicitor confirms their undertaking to redeem the seller's mortgage and to send the buyer form DS1 (proof of discharge). Buyer's solicitor undertakes to send the completion funds.	Between first and second phone call: buyer's solicitor transfers the completion funds to the seller's solicitor's client account. Seller's solicitor receives confirmation from its accounts department that funds have been received.	Second phone call: buyer's solicitor agrees to complete and consents to the seller's solicitor releasing funds to the seller. Seller's solicitor agrees to complete and dates the TR1.

Post-completion

Post-completion steps: seller's solicitor

Informing concerned parties

The seller's solicitor will inform the seller, the seller's lender and any third parties (e.g. tenants) of the completed sale.

Mortgage

The lender's charge must now be discharged (as per the undertaking given by the seller's solicitor to the buyer's solicitor at completion). The required funds (from the sale proceeds) needs to be sent from the seller to their lender to redeem the mortgage on the same date as completion. The balance of the sale proceeds can then be sent to the seller.

The seller's solicitor will receive a **DS1 certificate** (a certificate to prove that the seller's mortgage has been discharged) and this must be forwarded to the buyer's solicitor as proof that the buyer will not take subject to the seller's mortgage. This form will also be sent to the Land Registry (see below).

Purchase Deed (form TR1)

The seller's solicitor sends **form TR1** (that was dated at completion stage) to the buyer's solicitor.

Post-completion steps: buyer's solicitor

Informing concerned parties

The buyer's solicitor will inform the buyer and the buyer's lender that the sale has been completed.

Stamp Duty Land Tax (SDLT)

> **Stamp Duty Land Tax (SDLT):** SDLT replaced "stamp duty" on UK land and buildings. SDLT is charged as a percentage of the value of the property being sold, and is paid by the *buyer*.

Residential property		Non-residential property	
Property value	**SDLT rate**	**Property value**	**SDLT rate**
Up to £125,000	Zero	Up to £150,000	Zero
£125,001 to £250,000	2%	The next £100,000 (the portion from £150,000 to £250,000)	2%
£250,001 to £925,000	5%	The remaining amount (the portion above £250,000)	5%
£925,001 to £1.5 million	10%		
More £1.5 million	12%		

The buyer (or their solicitor on their behalf) must pay Stamp Duty Land Tax by submitting **form SDLT1** to HMRC together with the required payment within 30 days of the "effective date" (i.e. the completion date). HMRC will return an **SDLT5 certificate** as an acknowledgement of receipt. The **SDLT5 certificate** will then be sent to the Land Registry (see below).

Mortgage

- The legal charge (meaning the mortgage and the debenture) should be dated on the date that completion takes place.

- The debenture must be registered at Companies House within 21 days commencing the day after the date on which the charge was created. Registration is done by submitting **form MR13** and paying the relevant fee. Failure to register the charge means that the debt due to the bank becomes payable on demand and the security will not be valid.

- Subsequent to the registration of the debenture, Companies House will return a Certificate of Registration to the buyer's solicitor. This must later be sent to the Land Registry (see below).

Registration at Land Registry

The transfer of ownership of land must be registered with the Land Registry using **form AP1**. The application to register must be submitted within the priority period of 30 working days from the date of the OS1 search (for the reasons explained above in the *Pre-completion steps: buyer's solicitor* section of this chapter). The following must be sent together with the application:

- Land Registry fee.
- **SDLT5 certificate.**
- **DS1 certificate** in relation to the seller's (now discharged) mortgage.
- The Purchase Deed (**form TR1**).
- Copies of the documentation relating to the new mortgage/debenture, including the Companies House Certificate of Registration.
- Any other documents relevant to the transfer, such as death certificates, deeds of appointment of second trustees, grants of representation etc.

Some LPC providers require students to draft or re-draft **form AP1**. An example **form AP1**, annotated with instructions as to how to complete it, is provided later in this module.

Issues and Remedies

Delayed completion

If completion is delayed (i.e. it occurs after the contractually agreed date for completion or not at all) the SCS and SCPC offer remedies to the non-defaulting party.

Normally the contract will set out a specified completion date. If no date is specified, the default completion date is 20 working days after the date of exchange SCS 6.1.1/SCPC 9.1.1. The time for completion should also be specified in the contract, but if it has not been, the default time for completion is 2pm SCS 6.1.2/SCPC 9.1.2. Therefore if completion takes place *after* 2pm on the completion date, completion is deemed to have taken place the following working day.

If one party fails to complete, there are three possible remedies available to the non-defaulting party:

1. Contractual compensation

- For commercial transactions, where the SCPCs have been incorporated into the contract, *only the seller* is entitled to receive compensation for a delay caused by the other party (i.e. the buyer) SCPC 10.

- For residential transactions, where the SCSs have been incorporated into the contract, *both* parties are entitled to receive compensation for a delay caused by the other SCS 7.2.

Compensation is set at the "contract rate" (the rate specified in the contract). This is normally 4% above the base rate of a specified bank (e.g. Santander plc) per annum. If there is no contract rate specified in the contract, the Law Society Interest Rate will apply by default SCS 1.1.1(e) and SCPC 1.1.1(e). This is 4% above Barclays Bank's base rate. The contract rate is a daily rate of interest that must be paid by a defaulting party to the non-defaulting party. It is a percentage that is applied to: (1) the whole purchase price, if the seller is the defaulting party; or (2) the outstanding balance of the purchase price (i.e. subtracting any deposit already paid) if the buyer is the defaulting party.

To establish what compensation is due, use the following step-by-step calculation:

1. Calculate what the *annual* compensation would be: this is the contract rate multiplied by the purchase price (if the seller is defaulting) or the outstanding balance (if the buyer is defaulting).

2. Divide the *annual* compensation by 365, which gives you the *daily* compensation payable under the contract.

3. Establish how many days for which compensation should be paid. For this purpose, count the day on which completion *should* have taken place, but *not* the day that completion *actually* takes place SCPC 10.3.1 – 10.3.2. Note that you count *all* days, not only working days. Remember that if completion takes place after the time specified in the contract (or after 2pm if no time is contractually agreed), completion is deemed to have taken place the *next* working day.

4. Multiply the number of days for which compensation should be paid by the daily compensation payable. This will give you the total compensation payable.

Contractual compensation for delayed completion

UMAB Ltd is purchasing a property, 4 Old Street, from GAIS Ltd. The completion date has been specified in the contract as 10 July 2021. The purchase price is £1,000,000, including a deposit of £100,000 that UMAB Ltd has already paid. The contract rate is 4% above the base rate of Barclay's Bank plc from time to time. UMAB Ltd is having a problem with processing the funds through its account department however, and as a result, will not be able to complete until 18 July 2021. What contractual compensation will be available to GAIS Ltd? Assume that the base rate of Barclay's Bank plc is 1%.

The amount of compensation due to GAIS Ltd *annually* from UMAB Ltd will be 5% x £900,000(£1,000,000 purchase price - £100,000 deposit) = £45,000. The *daily* compensation is therefore equal to £45,000/365 = £123.29.

If completion takes place *before 2pm* on 18 July 2021, then the number of days for which compensation is due is 8 days. Compensation will therefore amount to 8 x £123.29 = £986.32

If completion takes place *after 2 pm* on 18 July 2021, completion is deemed to actually have occurred on the 19 July, and then the number of days for which compensation is due is 9 days. Compensation will therefore amount to 9 x £123.29 = £1109.61

---

2. Rescinding the contract

Rescission is not available as a remedy for delayed completion unless time is of the essence. One party can specify that time is of the essence by serving the other party with a "notice to complete". Once such notice is deemed served, the parties have 10 working days to complete (excluding the day of service) SCS 6.8.2/SCPC 9.8.2, otherwise rescission will be available to the non-defaulting party.

Property Law

SCSs and SCPCs govern the service of the notice and how to calculate the deemed date of service:

If the SCSs are used, notice to complete can only be sent after the time specified for completion (e.g. after 2pm on the date of completion). If the SCPCs are used, notice to complete can be sent at any time on the date of completion (e.g. even before 2pm).

- SCS/SCPC 1.3 states that notice may be sent by post, fax or email.
- SCS/SCPC 1.3.5 governs the *deemed* date of service. If notice is received *after* 4pm on a working day, that notice is deemed to have been served on (i.e. received by) the other party on the *next working* day. Do not confuse this with the 2pm rule for *completion* (i.e. the rule that if completion takes place *after* 2pm on the completion date, completion is deemed to have taken place the following working day).
- SCS/SCPC 1.3.7 governs the deemed *time* of service. For instance, if the notice is sent by fax, it is deemed received one hour after the transmission, whilst if the notice is sent by email, it is deemed received one hour after dispatch of the email.

Failing to complete when a notice to complete has been served can result in the following consequences:

- SCS 7.4/SCPC 10.5: if the buyer fails to comply with a notice to complete (i.e. fails to complete within 10 working days, excluding the day on which the notice was deemed to have been served), the seller can rescind the contract, and keep the deposit, resell the property and claim damages for breach of contract.
- CS 7.5/SCPC 10.6: If the seller fails to comply with a notice to complete, the buyer can rescind the contract and require the seller to return the deposit with interest.

> **GAIS Ltd sends a notice to complete to UMAB Ltd by fax at 3.30pm on Friday 16 July 2021. What is the earliest date on which GAIS Ltd could rescind the contract?**
>
> The notice is sent by fax at 3.30pm and is therefore deemed to be received at 4.30pm (SCPC and SCS 1.3.7). As this is *after* 4pm, the notice is *deemed* to have been served on the next *working* day: Monday 19 July 2021. Completion would need to take place at any time within 10 working days (not including 19 July, as the day the notice is deemed served is excluded).
>
> The 10th working day after 19 July 2021 is 2 August 2021. If UMAB Ltd has not sent GAIS Ltd the completion funds by this date, GAIS Ltd can send notice to UMAB Ltd the following day (3 August 2021) to rescind the contract.

Misrepresentation

> 📖 **Representations:** statements made by a seller about the property *before* the contract is entered into. Representations may be statements of *opinion* and may not actually be included in the contract itself (although parties can agree to include representations as actual contractual terms). If the seller makes an untrue representation, the buyer may be able to bring a claim for misrepresentation.

> 📖 **Misrepresentation:** an inaccurate pre-contractual statement (representation) made by the seller about the property on which the buyer relied and which induced the buyer to enter into the contract.

An issue can arise where it transpires that the seller made a misrepresentation about the property prior to the sale. As explained previously, the principle of *caveat emptor* ("buyer beware") applies to property transactions; however this does not mean that the seller has no duty to disclose whatsoever:

- A seller cannot either actively conceal physical defects or answer enquires from the buyer dishonestly. Doing so will amount to misrepresentation Gordon v Selico.
- What constitutes a *representation* was discussed in William Sindall plc v Cambridgeshire County Council. It was held that if a buyer enquires about whether something relating to the property is true (e.g. "are there any boundary disputes currently in progress?") and the seller replies with "not so far as the seller is aware", this counts as a representation by the seller that they have made reasonable inquiries into the matter. If the statement turns out to be incorrect (i.e. there *are* boundary disputes currently in process), the seller can therefore be sued for misrepresentation unless they *had* made reasonable enquiries.

Remedies for misrepresentation

The remedies available for a buyer if the seller has made a misrepresentation are set out in SCS 7/SCPC 10:

- If there is a *material* difference (meaning a difference that is capable of being remedied by money) between the property as represented by the seller and the *actual* property, the buyer is entitled to damages only. The buyer cannot rescind the contract on this basis.
- If the seller's misrepresentation results from fraud or recklessness, or there is a *substantial* difference (meaning more than a "material" difference) in quality, quantity, or tenure between the property as represented by the seller and the *actual* property, the buyer can rescind the contract.

It is preferable to pursue remedies under the Standard Conditions instead of pursuing remedies under the common law misrepresentation, because there is no need to prove that the buyer was induced to enter into the contract by the seller's pre-contractual statements (this is however required for common law misrepresentation).

Drafting Form TR1

Form TR1 contains 11 "panels". The following is an outline of how to fill out each panel:

1. Title number

This should only be the title number (not the name). **Form TR1** can sometimes be used as the purchase deed for transfers of unregistered land, in which case you leave this panel blank (there will be no title number as the property is not registered).

2. Property

This should be a description that references the address of the property for that title number (if the land being sold is registered). If the property is unregistered, you would also need to refer to a description in a previous conveyance, preferably with a plan (conveyances for unregistered land are explained in more detail in the *Unregistered Land* chapter of this module).

3. Date

At the drafting stage this should be left blank. The date will be filled out at completion (see above in the *Completion* chapter of this module for an explanation of when **form TR1** will be dated).

4. Transferor

This should be the name of the seller. Remember that in the event of a sale by a sole surviving tenant in common it will have been necessary to appoint a second trustee whose name should also appear in this panel together with the seller.

5. Transferee for entry in the register

This should be the name of the buyer. If the buyer is a company, ensure that the company number is included (and accurate).

6. Transferee's intended address(es) for service for entry in the register

This is the address to which the buyer will receive future related correspondence. If the property is to be used as residence, it is likely this address will be the address of the property being purchased. If the buyer is a company, then consider whether it would be more appropriate to use the buyer's registered business address as opposed to the address of the property actually being purchased.

7. The transferor transfers the property to the transferee

This panel merely sets out the wording that gives effect to the transfer (no drafting is necessary here).

8. Consideration

The correct box must be ticked (if the buyer has paid money in consideration, the first box *"The transferor has received from the transferee for the property the following sum"* should be ticked). The purchase price must be written out in numbers *and* words.

9. Title guarantee

Title guarantee was covered in more detail in the *Issues dealt with in the contract for sale* section of the *Drafting and Exchanging the Contract for Sale* chapter in this module. Full title guarantee is expected in most cases (so this should be used if you have been given no facts suggesting the contrary).

10. Declaration of trust

If the buyer is a single entity this will be left blank. A declaration of trust will only be necessary where there is more than one buyer.

11. Additional provisions

The following should be included here:

- The wording of any new restrictive or positive covenants being created.
- If the buyer is giving the seller an indemnity covenant (in relation to *existing* positive covenants), it should be included here. Note that even if the parties forget to include a special condition to the effect that the buyer is to give the seller an indemnity covenant, SCPC 7.6.5 allows the seller to require inclusion of the indemnity covenant in **form TR1** in any event. An example indemnity covenant is:

    "The Transferee covenants with the Transferor to observe and perform the covenants contained or referred to in entry X of the Charges Register of title number [XXX] and to indemnify the Transferor against any liability for any future breach or non-observance of those covenants."

- Exclusion of third party rights. Third party rights should always be excluded. The provision could read (for instance):

    "Unless otherwise expressly stated nothing in this contract will create rights pursuant to the Contracts (Rights of Third Parties) Act 1999 in favour of anyone other than the parties to the contract."

12. Execution

To ascertain who needs to execute **form TR1**, see the *Pre-completion (seller's solicitor)* section in the *Completion* chapter of this module.

- If a *company* is executing, this is done by either: (1) affixing the company seal in the presence of two directors or one director and one secretary; or (2) signed by two directors (or one director in the presence of an attesting witness).
- If an *individual* is executing, this is done by signing in the presence of an attesting witness.

Drafting Form AP1

Form AP1 contains 15 "panels". The following is an outline of how to fill out each panel:

1. Local authority serving the property
Write here the council that the buyer will pay council tax to.

2. Title number
Check that the title number is accurate and matches the one in the Official Copies.

3. Application affects
When dealing with the whole land (which is normally the case on the LPC), the first box should be ticked.

4. Application, priority and fees
Here the buyer should list all the applications they are making (e.g. discharge of a mortgage). Under the value column, the buyer should note how much is being paid for the property. If it is a transfer by way of gift or assent, then the property's financial worth should be noted instead.

5. Documents lodged
All the documents being sent to the Land Registry should be listed here.

6. The applicant
This should be the name of the person(s) who is(are) actually applying to change the register.

7. Application sent to Land Registry by
This should be the name and address of the person with whom the buyer wants the Land Registry to deal (this could be, for instance, the buyer's solicitor).

8. Third party notification
This only needs to be filled out if the buyer wishes for the Land Registry to notify a third party that the application has been completed (e.g. a tenant).

9. Address for service for proprietors of the registered estate
If an address has already been put down for service in panel 7, you only need to tick the second box.

10. Name and address for service of the proprietor of any new charge to be entered
You will not need to fill out this panel unless you are registering a new mortgage.

11. Disclosable overriding interests
The Land Registry should be informed of certain interests that affect the land (to which the registration relates). Such interests include, for instance (but are not limited to): leases for 1-7 years, interests of people in actual occupation and certain easements.

12-14. Evidence of identity
These panels only need to be completed if the property is being assented to someone other than the person registering the transfer. The names of each beneficiary to whom the property is being assented should be listed in the left hand column of panel 14(1). The name and address of any conveyancer acting for such beneficiaries should be noted in the right hand column.

15. Execution
The applicant noted in panel 6 should sign the form and insert the date.

Unregistered Land

Since 1 December 1990, all land in the UK is subject to "compulsory first registration". This means that there are certain transactions that *trigger* first registration (if a piece of land is not already registered). These transactions include when land is sold or mortgaged. This means some land still remains unregistered (i.e. if the land has not been subject to any transaction triggering first registration since the requirement of compulsory first registration was introduced). This chapter explains the process of a property transaction relating to unregistered land, including how unregistered land is registered.

Deducing Title to Unregistered Land

The buyer's solicitor must "deduce title" to the unregistered land. "Deducing title" simply means: (1) ensuring that the seller actually owns the property and that they are entitled to sell it; and (2) establishing what burdens/benefits affect the land. Because there are no Official Copies to consult for unregistered land (Official Copies only exist in relation to registered land), a variety of documents ("title deeds") must be checked to deduce title. The bundle of relevant title deeds is referred to as the *epitome of title*. The seller's solicitor will send the buyer's solicitor the epitome of title so that the latter can make the necessary investigations. The epitome of title is therefore the bundle of documents that the buyer's solicitor needs to see in order to deduce title.

Documents to be included in the epitome of title

Not all historical documents relating to the property need to go into the epitome of title. The seller only has to go as far back as the "good root of title". If the seller has a document that meets the requirements for a good root of title, then that is the foundation document of the seller's title. Subject to certain exceptions, the buyer need not consider, and in any event cannot require the seller to provide, any documents that were created prior to the good root of title LPA 25 s. 45. The exceptions are: (1) documents granting Power of Attorney under which any documents included in the epitome of title have been executed; and (2) any pre-root document referred to by a document in the epitome of title LPA 25 s. 45(1)(b)(i)-(iii).

Root of title

The root of title is the document that proves the seller's ownership of the property. This is the conveyance to the current seller and will therefore be referred to as the "root conveyance" throughout the rest of this chapter.

> **Conveyance:** a legal document (a deed) effecting the transfer of property.

In order for a conveyance to be deemed a "good" root of title, the following must be established:

- **Conveyance must be dated prior to 1 December 1990**: this is because if the sale took place subsequent to the 1 December 1990, the property (and the transfer) should have been registered (the land should therefore no longer be unregistered). If the seller did not register their title (when they should have done so), legal title to the property would have remained with the previous owner. Therefore, this would mean that the seller does not currently have legal title to the property he/she is selling (and thus the root of title is not "good").

- **Description**: the conveyance must include a sufficient description of the land (for identification purposes). The conveyance will typically have described the land by reference to a plan. In order for the use of a plan to constitute a sufficient description, you must consider the language used. For instance, "9 Steel Lane, *more particularly* delineated on the plan annexed hereto and thereon edged in red..." will be deemed sufficient description for the conveyance to be a good root of title. However, "9 Leather lane, *for identification only* delineated on the plan annexed hereto and thereon edged in red..." will not be sufficient, as the use of "for identification only" as opposed to "more particularly" suggests that the map is not drawn to scale. Note that it is sufficient if the root of title refers to an earlier conveyance (e.g. "said property is more particularly described in a conveyance dated the 23rd day of May One Thousand Nine Hundred and Eighty Three..."), so long as that earlier conveyance is also included in the epitome of title.

- **Whole interest**: the conveyance must deal with the whole of the legal and beneficial interest in the land. This will be the case where the conveyance is by deed and has been validly executed and stamped (see below for rules regarding this).

- **Cast no doubt as to the seller's title**: doubt could be cast if, for instance, the epitome of title is missing a power of attorney, grant of probate or marriage certificate where this is necessary to prove that the current seller is the same person as the buyer in the root conveyance.

Other documents to be included in the epitome of title

- **Any documents *referred* to in the root conveyance.** For example, if the root conveyance refers to a plan of the property in an earlier conveyance, that earlier conveyance must be included in the epitome of title. This is one of the exceptions to the general rule that the buyer cannot see any documents that were created earlier than the root conveyance.

- **Any conveyances that are older than the root conveyance and contain a restrictive covenant.** The root conveyance could for instance contain wording such as *"the Seller conveys the property subject to the restrictive covenant contained in the conveyance dated 1975 between Smith and Keran"*. If this is the case, the 1975 conveyance must be included in the epitome of title. This is because the 1975 conveyance contains the actual details of the restrictive covenant that affects the property being sold. This is one of the exceptions to the general rule that the buyer cannot see any documents that were created earlier than the root conveyance.

- **Documents evidencing any name changes of the seller, death certificates of an owner, or grants of probate.** This is to show any links between the people in the last conveyance and the people who are now selling the property. For instance, if the root conveyance documents a sale to a "Miss Blue" but she (the seller) is now known as "Mrs Red", the epitome of title must include Mrs Red's marriage certificate to prove that the seller is the same person as the person noted as the buyer in the root conveyance.
- **Deeds of easement.**
- **Leases.** However, expired leases where the tenant has vacated the property do not need to be included since they no longer burden the land.
- **Post-root mortgages.** These must be included regardless of whether they have been discharged. In particular, this includes the mortgage taken out by the current seller when they bought the property, even though this mortgage will be discharged at completion. Mortgages that were discharged before the good root of title came into existence need not be included however.

Procedural concerns

Execution of documents

Conveyances of a legal estate must have been executed correctly, otherwise title to the property would not have passed properly to the buyer.

Documents executed by individuals before 31 July 1990	Documents executed by individuals from 31 July 1990	Documents executed by companies before 31 July 1990	Documents executed by companies from 31 July 1990	Documents executed under Power of Attorney
Signed, sealed, delivered, witnessed.	Signed and delivered as a deed in the presence of a witness who attests the signature.	Company seal affixed in the presence of two directors or one director and company secretary.	Either: 1. Company seal affixed in the presence of two directors or one director and company secretary; *or* 2. Signed as a deed by two directors or one director and the company secretary.	Signed as a deed and delivered by the attorney in the presence of a witness who attests the attorney's signature.

Stamps and Certificates of Value

All conveyances in the epitome of title must have either an **"ad valorem"** stamp or a **Certificate of Value** (or both).

All conveyances must also have a **PD stamp** (this stands for "Particulars Delivered").

If a deed lacks the required stamps, the seller must rectify it. This is done by applying for late stamping and paying a penalty. An unstamped deed is inadmissible as evidence in a civil court, which means it would be hard for the buyer to prove their ownership of the land in the future. The parties can agree, as a special condition, that the seller is to rectify it (see the *Drafting and Exchanging the Contract for Sale* chapter in this module for an explanation on how to draft special conditions).

Burdens Affecting Unregistered Land

As with transactions involving registered land, it is important for the buyer to understand which burdens affect the land he/she is looking to buy and whether these would affect their intended use of the land.

Registered burdens

Even though the land itself is not registered, a system exists which allows the registration of third party rights (*burdens* from the buyer's perspective) over unregistered land. These rights are registered as Central Land Charges at the Central Land Charges Registry. Central Land Charges are registered against the name of the owner that owned the land when the third party right was created. For instance, if Martha owned a piece of unregistered land between 1987 - 1989 and in 1988 a restrictive covenant was created (burdening Martha's land), that restrictive covenant would have been registered at the Central Land Charges Registry against Martha's name. Note that in order to bind future purchasers, the covenant need only to have been registered against the name of the *original* covenantor (i.e. the person that originally granted that right). It does not need to be registered against the name of subsequent owners.

Central Land Charges searches ("CLC searches") are carried out to reveal whether any such third party rights burdening the land exist. The buyer must therefore ensure that the correct searches have been carried out so that he/she will be aware of all third party rights.

CLC search results will reveal the existence of, for instance: puisne mortgages (second mortgage), estate contracts (contracts in which the owner of land agrees to create a legal estate in that land, e.g. granting a lease), and restrictive covenants.

Property Law

Establishing that the correct CLC searches have been made

Typically the buyer will receive the results of CLC searches carried out by previous buyers. The buyer must ensure that these are sufficient. The searches must:

(a) Have been carried out against the correct names, i.e. the names in the searches must match the names of previous owners as written in the conveyances. Note that sometimes people may appear to have different or shortened names, for instance person may be referred to as "Matilda Sweetling" in a conveyance, but the past CLC search may have been made against "Tilda Sweetling". If this is the case, a search for each version of the name should be made.

(b) Go back as far as 1926 (this is the year in which the CLC Registry was first used).

(c) Specify the years during which each estate owner in question owned the property.

- If there is no information as to when an owner *bought* the property, the search on his/her name must be carried out all the way back to the date on which the property was sold to the previous (known) owner.
- If there is no information as to when an owner *sold* the property, the search must be made to the date on which the next known owner bought it.

When a prospective buyer makes a CLC search, that buyer is afforded a "protection period" (see the *Pre-completion steps: buyer's solicitor* section of the *Completion* chapter in this module for an explanation of this concept). You must ensure that each conveyance has been dated within the protection period of the relevant CLC search. If any sale was completed after the protection period, the relevant CLC search must be carried out again.

Note that there may be burdens affecting the property that do not show up on a CLC search. If this is the case, the buyer will still be bound by that burden, but the buyer will be entitled to state compensation if they suffer a loss as a result Law of Property Act 1969 s. 25.

CLC Searches

You are acting for a buyer that is purchasing a property from Hannah Watson, the title to which is unregistered. The current year is 2021. The seller's solicitor has provided you with the epitome of title, which contains the following documents: (1) a conveyance dated 1966 between Matilda Jones and Sean Baker; (2) a conveyance dated 1981 between Sean Baker and Liam Gregson; and (3) a conveyance dated 1988 between Liza McKenna and Hannah Watson. Which CLC searches should be carried out (ignoring any searches carried out by the seller's solicitor)?

Name of Estate Owner	Period for CLC Search
Matilda Jones	1926 – 1966 (because we do not know when Matilda bought the property, we must search against her name all the way back to 1926).
Sean Baker	1966 – 1981 (we can deduce from the conveyances provided both when Sean bought and sold the property).
Liam Gregson	1981 – 1988 (we know Liam bought the property in 1981 but we do not know when he sold it. The next conveyance is dated 1988, so the latest he *could have* sold is the day before the 1988 conveyance. Remember that we need to search for the maximum possible period of ownership).
Liza McKenna	1981 – 1988 (we know Liza sold the property in 1988, but we do not know when she bought it. The previous conveyance is dated 1981, so the earliest she *could have* bought it is the day after the 1981 conveyance).
Hannah Watson	1988 – 2021 (we know Hannah bought the property in 1988 and since she is the seller, we know she is selling now).

Unregistered burdens and benefits

Restrictive and positive covenants

- Normally a restrictive covenant should be registered as a D(ii) land charge against the original covenantor and should therefore appear on a CLC search (see above). If a restrictive covenant has not been correctly registered, it will not run with the land. It will not be automatically binding on subsequent buyers, but may be binding as a matter of *contract law* if there has been an unbroken chain of indemnity covenants (i.e. in the way in which *positive* covenants bind subsequent owners). The epitome will not necessarily contain all conveyances since the covenant was created. If our seller gave an indemnity covenant when he bought the land, then he will insist that the buyer is giving one too. Therefore it will be enough to check whether the conveyance to the current owner contains an indemnity covenant.

- Positive covenants will only bind successors in title indirectly and only if a chain of indemnity covenants exist from the original covenantor to the current seller (as is the case with registered land).

Unregistered interests overriding first registration Land Registration Act 2002 Schedule 1:

These are interests that will bind buyers even though they are not registered (and would thus not show up on a CLC search):

- Leases not exceeding 7 years.
- Interests of persons in actual occupation.
- Legal easements.

Easements

If there are any easements that benefit the unregistered land, that benefit must be protected by the buyer immediately after the purchase has been completed. The process depends on whether the servient land is registered or unregistered (a SIM search can be used to check whether the servient land is registered or unregistered):

- **If the servient land is registered:** the buyer should ensure any easements are registered in the Charges Register of the servient land.
- **If the servient land is unregistered:** a "caution against first registration" must be entered against the servient land.

> **Caution against first registration:** this protects an interest over unregistered land. When the Land Registry receives an application for the first registration of land against which a caution against first registration has been lodged, the interest (e.g. an easement) will be noted on the Charges Register for that land as part of the registration process.

The Seller

Like with registered land, a buyer must consider who the seller is and whether any additional documents and/or procedures are necessary to facilitate investigations into the property.

Co-owners

If it transpires that more than one person owns or has owned the property at the same time, it must be established whether they owned that land as joint tenants or tenants in common. This is important because it affects how the property can be transferred.

If the relevant conveyance is silent as to whether the owners are joint tenants or tenants in common, it can be presumed that they purchased the property as joint tenants. Furthermore, it can be presumed that they *remained* as joint tenants if *all* of the following conditions are met Law of Property (Joint Tenants) Act 1964 s. 1:

- There is no Memorandum of Severance
- None of the joint tenants were declared bankrupt at any point. A bankruptcy would be revealed by a **K15** CLC search on the individuals; if previously declared bankrupt, the letters 'PA(B)' or 'WO(B)' would appear next to their name.
- In the conveyance to the new buyer, the surviving joint tenant sells as "beneficial owner" or as "solely and beneficially interested".

Once it is established whether the co-owners were joint tenants or tenants in common, the same rules apply as for registered land in a situation where one of the co-owners has died (i.e. a surviving joint tenant can execute a purchase deed by himself/herself, whereas a surviving tenant in common must have the deceased owner's interest "overreached"). This, and the proof required by the Land Registry, is explained in the *Proprietorship Register* section of the *Title Investigation* chapter in this module.

Other unusual sellers

The land may also be sold by personal representatives, mortgagees (if the borrower defaulted on the loan and the mortgagee repossessed the property), a company or people with Power of Attorney to sell. The same principles apply and the same procedures are relevant as for registered land. This is explained in more detail in the *Proprietorship Register* section of the *Title Investigation* chapter in this module.

First Registration and Post-completion

When unregistered land is sold, it must be registered (it will be the land's first registration). The requirements are set out in Land Registration Act 2002 s. 4 + s. 27. The application to the Land Registry for first registration must be made within 2 months of completion Land Registration Act 2002 s. 6(4). The application is made using **form FR1** and the following evidence must be sent together with the application:

- A conveyance that constitutes good root of title.
- Document's showing the seller's title to the property.
- Any CLC search results.
- Contract for sale.
- Purchase deed (**form TR1**).
- **SDLT5 certificate** (this is proof of payment of Stamp Duty Land Tax). Note that Stamp Duty Land Tax must be paid within 30 days of completion, as is the case with registration of registered land.
- If a mortgage is entered into, the debenture and the registration certificate from Companies House (see the *Completion* chapter in this module for details of how to register a mortgage post-completion).

Commercial Security of Tenure

> **Security of tenure:** a legal protection afforded to a commercial tenant, which allows that tenant to occupy a property after the lease expires except in certain specified circumstances.

Tenant Protection

The tenant protection that stems from commercial security of tenure is two-layered and is found in Landlord and Tenant Act 1954 ("**LTA 54**") s. 24(1):

1. A tenancy will continue past the Contractual Expiry Date ("CED") unless it is terminated in one of the ways specified by the LTA 54. Where the tenancy continues despite the contract coming to an end, this is referred to as the tenant "holding over".
2. A tenant has the right to apply for a new tenancy when the current tenancy is about to be, or has been, terminated.

LTA 54 s. 23(1) sets out the requirements that must be met for a tenant to be afforded this statutory protection:

1. Tenancy LTA 54 s. 23(1)

A "tenancy" must exist, whether oral or written, periodic or fixed, and it must not be excluded by LTA 54 s. 43. Excluded tenancies are:

- Agricultural holdings (these are protected by a different statute).
- Mining leases.
- Tenancies where the tenant is a service provider (e.g. a gatekeeper may be a tenant of a flat on the property for which he/she is gatekeeper).
- Fixed term tenancies that do not exceed six months. However, if the same business is a continuous tenant for more than 12 months, the tenancy will not be excluded (and will thus benefit from the statutory protection mentioned above). Similarly, if the tenancy is renewable beyond 6 months at the tenant's option it will not be an excluded tenancy.

2. Occupation LTA 54 s. 23(1)

The tenant wishing to rely on the protection in LTA 54 s. 24(1) must *occupy* the relevant property that they are leasing from the landlord. Therefore, if the property is subject to a sub-lease, the original tenant (the sub-lessor) will not be protected.

3. Business purpose LTA 54 s. 23(1)

The property must be occupied for a *business* purpose, i.e., it must be used for a trade, a profession or employment. This is widely interpreted however. The sole purpose of the tenancy need not be a "business" purpose, so long as the "business" purpose is significant.

4. The parties have not contracted out of the protection LTA 54 s. 23(1)

Under LTA 54 s. 38(A), a landlord and a tenant can contractually agree that the tenant will not be afforded the protection of LTA 54 s. 24(1). Such agreements are typically entered into where a landlord is only letting the property for a short period of time and wants to be certain that they can regain the property at the end of the tenancy. This agreement is referred to as the tenant "contracting out" of the protection. Contracting out may be advantageous to tenants, as landlords typically have to charge a lower rent to incentivise tenants to give up their rights.

In the interest of protecting tenants, the LTA imposes a strict procedure that must be followed in order to effectively contract out of the LTA 54 s. 24(1) protection. This procedure is set out in the Regulatory Reform (Business Tendencies) (England and Wales) Order 2003:

"Slower" process for terminating a tenancy	"Quicker" process for terminating a tenancy
<ul><li>The landlord must serve a **warning notice** on the tenant at least 14 days before the tenant becomes bound to sign the lease/agreement for a lease.</li><li>The tenant must sign a "**simple declaration**" that they agree to giving up the protection in LTA 54 s. 24(1).</li><li>The lease must contain a written confirmation that the parties have agreed to exclude security of tenure and such confirmation must contain a reference to both the warning notice and the tenant's simple declaration.</li></ul>	<ul><li>If the parties do not have 14 days before the tenant is to agree to enter into the lease, the tenant can instead make a "statutory declaration" that they have received the warning notice and that they agree to contract out of the protection.</li><li>A statutory declaration must be made in front of an independent solicitor.</li></ul>

Terminating a protected tenancy

A protected tenancy can be terminated by either the landlord or the tenant by serving a notice on the other party to the lease. An LTA 54 s. 25 notice (landlord's notice) cannot be served after an LTA 54 s. 26 notice (tenant's notice) has already been served and vice versa. This rule exists because both parties have ways of opposing notices/requests sent by the other.

Termination by the landlord LTA 54 s. 25

Hostile notice

> **Hostile notice:** the landlord wants to terminate the tenancy and does not wish to renew the tenant's lease.

The landlord must serve a notice on the tenant and set out the statutory ground(s) on which they are relying to refuse the granting of a new lease (the statutory grounds on which the landlord can terminate a protected lease are explained below). The landlord must specify a "Specified Termination Date" ("STD"), which is the date the landlord wishes the tenancy to end. The rules for which STD the landlord can choose are set out in LTA 54 s. 25(2):

- The STD cannot be less than 6 months and not more than 12 months from the date on which the notice is served; and
- The STD must not be before the CED.

Friendly notice

> **Friendly notice:** the landlord wants to terminate the tenancy but is open to negotiate a new lease with the tenant to commence immediately after the current one.

A landlord may wish to serve a friendly notice for a number of reasons, such as: to ensure that the tenant is tied into a future term to guarantee the stream of rental income; and to increase the rent if rental rates in the area have risen (a tenant will typically pay the same level of rent as specified in their original lease if they are holding over). The landlord must include an STD when serving a friendly notice on the tenant. The same rules as above (LTA 54 s. 25(2)) apply as to which date the landlord can choose. If the landlord wishes to change the terms of the lease, such changes should also be outlined in the notice.

Competent landlord

Notices in this context, whether hostile or friendly, must be served on the tenant by a "competent landlord" and must be in a prescribed from (pre-printed versions are available).

> **Competent landlord:** the "competent landlord" for these purposes is either: (a) the freeholder or (b) a tenant (who is subletting) with at least 14 months left until the contractual expiry date of their lease. A tenant will still qualify as the "competent landlord" if the contractual expiry date of their lease is less than 14 months away but they benefit from security of tenure and thus have the right to extend the lease to last for at least 14 months. If no tenant has 14 months or more remaining, only the freeholder can be the competent landlord.

Court application

If a hostile notice has been served on a tenant, the tenant can apply to court to challenge the statutory grounds upon which the landlord is relying to terminate the tenancy LTA 54 s. 24(1). If the tenant is successful, the lease will be renewed. A court application can be made by either party at any time after notice has been served, but must be made by the STD (which will be stated by the landlord in his/her hostile notice) LTA 54 s. 29A. This deadline can be extended by written agreement between the parties LTA 54 s. 29B. If the tenant fails to apply to court within this time, they lose the right to be granted a new lease. A landlord can then apply to court to have the lease terminated LTA 54 s. 29(2).

Termination by the tenant LTA 54 s. 26 and s. 27

This is when a tenant wishes to terminate the current lease and request a new lease to commence immediately after. There are various reasons why a tenant would do this (and not rely on commercial security of tenure and simply hold over), for instance: the rents in the area have decreased and the tenant wishes to lower their contractual rent; as a pre-emptive tactic where the tenant suspects that the landlord is about to serve a notice pursuant to LTA 54 s. 25 (the tenant, by serving their notice first, will have the benefit of specifying the start date of the new lease); or if the tenant wants to assign or sublet the lease (since a lease with a longer contractual term remaining is more attractive).

The tenant must serve notice on the landlord if they want to request a new lease, and must follow the procedure in LTA 54 s. 26. Such notice must include a "Proposed Commencement Date" ("PCD"), which is the date on which the tenant wishes the new lease to commence. It should also include the proposed new terms of the lease. The rules to determine which PCD the tenant can choose are set out in LTA 54 s. 26(2):

- The PCD must be not less than 6 months and not more than 12 months from the date that the notice is served; and
- The PCD cannot be before the CED.

When a tenant has served a notice, the landlord has two months to serve a "counter-notice". In a counter-notice, the landlord should indicate whether they are approving the tenant's request for a new lease or whether they wish to oppose the granting of a new lease. In the case of the latter, they must specify the statutory ground(s) that entitle them to do so (see below for an explanation of these statutory grounds). Any notice sent by the tenant to the landlord pursuant to LTA 54 s. 26 must be in a prescribed from (pre-printed versions are available) and should be served on the "competent landlord".

Complete termination

If a tenant wishes to terminate the tenancy and does not want to commence a new one, they can serve a notice pursuant to LTA 54 s. 27 on the immediate landlord (i.e. the landlord that is the counterparty to their existing lease, and therefore not necessarily the *competent* landlord). An LTA 54 s. 27 notice must be served at least 3 months before the date the tenant wishes to leave. If a tenant has served an LTA 54 s. 27 notice they cannot later serve an LTA 54 s. 26 notice.

Court application

If a landlord fails to serve counter-notice within two months, they will lose their right to apply to court to oppose the grant of a new lease.

Interpretation of time limits/notice periods

Calculating the expiry of a notice period: "Corresponding date" rule

A notice period will end on the corresponding date of a future month. For instance, if you need to calculate when a 6-month notice period expires and the notice was given on the 5 January 2021, the expiration date will be 5 July 2021. Where the months have different numbers of days, the last date in the month in which it is due to expire should be used. For example, if a 6-month notice is served on 31 August 2021, the notice will expire on 28 February 2021.

Calculating the CED: "From and including"/"Commencing on"

When this wording is used in a tenancy, the tenancy will expire on the day *before* the corresponding date in the relevant future month/year. For instance, if the tenancy is for 15 years "from and including 24 February 2021", or the tenancy is "commencing 24 February 2021", the tenancy will expire on 23 February 2036.

Calculating the CED: "From"

When this wording is used in a tenancy, the tenancy will *commence* the day *after* the date specified in that tenancy. For instance, if the tenancy is for 7 years "from 24 February 2021", it will commence on 25 February 2021 and expire on 24 February 2028.

Statutory Grounds of Opposition

As stated before, if the landlord wishes to end a tenancy (by either serving a hostile notice under LTA 54 s. 25 or serving counter-notice to a tenant's request for a new tenancy under LTA 54 s. 26) they can only do so if one (or more) of the statutory grounds of opposition exists. These are found in LTA 54 s. 30(1). There are both mandatory grounds (which, if established by the landlord, means the court *must* terminate the tenancy) and discretionary grounds (which, if established by the landlord, gives the court the *authority* to terminate the tenancy, but may refuse to do so). This section only focuses on the three most common mandatory grounds, so you must double check with your LPC provider whether there are other grounds that you need to be familiar with.

- **Alternative accommodation** LTA 54 s. 30(1)(d): the landlord has offered and is willing to provide alternative accommodation for the tenant, and such accommodation is suitable for the tenant's requirements (including the preservation of the tenant's goodwill with third parties, for instance business customers). Therefore, if the current tenancy is for a shop located on Oxford Street in London, the landlord cannot rely on this ground if the accommodation they are offering as an alternative is located in an industrial area in Milton Keynes.

- **Reconstruction/demolishing** LTA 54 s. 30(1)(f): the landlord intends to demolish or reconstruct the premises (or a substantial part of it) or intends to carry out *substantial* construction work to it. Such construction must be of a nature that it could not possibly go ahead without the landlord obtaining vacant possession of the property (i.e. granting the landlord a mere right of entry whilst the tenant is still occupying would be insufficient). The intention could, for instance, be shown by the landlord's obtaining planning permission for the concerned developments.

- **Landlord occupation** LTA 54 s. 30(1)(g): the landlord intends to occupy the property for the purpose (or partly for the purpose) of carrying out a business or using it as their primary place of residence. This is subject to LTA 54 s. 30(2), which states that the landlord *cannot* rely on this ground if they purchased the property less than five years before the STD contained in the LTA 54 s. 25 notice that they gave to the tenant.

Saving provision

LTA 54 s. 31(2) contains a saving provision for a landlord that wishes to terminate the lease in circumstances where the ground on which they intend to rely has not yet occurred. For grounds 30(1)(d) and 30(1)(f), the court must refuse the new tenancy if the landlord can prove that they *would* have proven the ground on which they are seeking to rely if the STD had actually been up to 12 months later.

Compensation for tenants

A tenant (that enjoys commercial security of tenure) may be compensated if they are refused a new tenancy LTA 54 s. 37. Compensation is only available if the landlord has opposed the granting of a new lease on the grounds set out in in LTA 54 s. 30(1)(e), s. 30(1)(f) and/or s. 30(1)(g) (these are referred to as the "compensatory grounds"). If both a "compensatory ground" and a "non-compensatory ground" have been proven, no compensation will be available. It is therefore in a landlord's interest to prove a "non-compensatory ground".

The amount of compensation available for a tenant is calculated by multiplying the "rateable value" of the property by a "multiplier" (a figure set by the local authority). If the tenant's business has occupied the property for 14 years or more, twice the rateable value will be used to calculate the compensation LTA 54 s. 37(2).

Interim Rent

Interim rent may be charged by the landlord throughout the period in which the tenant is "holding over". Either party can have an incentive to delay the commencement of the new tenancy: if the rents in the market have decreased, the landlord would want to delay a new tenancy as the new rent is likely to be lower; whilst if the rents in the market have increased, the tenant would want to delay a new tenancy as the new rent is likely to be higher. Such "delay" can be caused when the landlord or the tenant choose a new commencement date when giving their notice.

To create a fairer balance between the parties, the law entitles either party to apply for "interim rent". Interim rent will be payable from the earliest STD or PCD (depending on whether a landlord's s. 25 LTA notice or a tenant's s. 26 LTA notice has been used) that *could* have been specified in the relevant notice LTA 54 s. 24C.

There are two ways in which the interim rent can be determined, depending on the circumstances:

- If the landlord is willing to grant a new lease, the interim rent will be set at market level LTA 54 s. 24C.

- If the landlord is not willing to grant a new lease, the interim rent will usually be 10-15% below the market level LTA 54 s. 24D.

> **Commercial security of tenure and interim rent**
>
> Today's date is 10 December 2021. A lease has a CED of 1 December 2021 (i.e. the tenant is currently "holding over"). Market rents have increased in the area but the landlord has not served an LTA 54 s. 25 notice, so the tenant is still paying a relatively low rent. The tenant wishes to serve an LTA 54 s. 26 notice today to request a new tenancy, and wants to propose a PCD 12 months from today's date, i.e. 10 December 2022 (this is the longest period the tenant can specify, which means that they pay the lower rent for as long as possible). If the landlord was to apply for interim rent, from which date would such interim rent be payable?
>
> Because the earliest PCD the tenant *could* have specified in their s. 26 notice is 10 June 2022 (six months from the date of the notice), interim rent (if applied for by the landlord) would be payable from 10 June 2022.

The New Tenancy

After the landlord or tenant has served their notice, they will negotiate the terms of the new tenancy that is to commence after the current one has terminated. Even though the parties both agree that a new tenancy should be granted, it is not certain that they will agree on the terms of that tenancy. It is therefore important that a court application is made after either party has served notice (even if everything appears amicable). The court application will proceed "in the background" just in case the parties do eventually need to consult the court; the pending application provides a good fallback position for the tenant, as the court can step in if the parties fail to agree the terms of the new tenancy. If the court is called upon to decide the terms of the new tenancy, the principal terms will be those contained in LTA 54 s. 32-35:

- **Premises:** the premises being leased will be the same as at the date of the court order.

- **Term**: the court can decide any duration for the lease so long as the duration decided does not exceed 15 years.

- **Rent**: the rate of rent will be ascertained using a valuation formula contained in the LTA.

- **Commencement:** the term of the lease will begin when the current tenancy comes to an end.

- **O'May v City of London Real Property:** any other terms will be determined using the terms of the current tenancy as a starting point. The court will consider any amendments suggested by the parties but will determine the terms of the new tenancy in a just and fair way, taking all the circumstances into account. The court will not necessarily incorporate every term of the current tenancy however, as some may be outdated.

> **Commercial security of tenure**
>
> Poppy Ltd is a tenant of (and occupying) Oak House and has a lease with a contractual expiry date ("CED") of 29 October 2021. Poppy Ltd is using the property for a business purpose and has not contracted out of the tenant protection afforded by s. 24(1) Landlord and Tenant Act 1954. Poppy Ltd believes market rents are falling and is thus looking to renew its lease pursuant to the Landlord and Tenant Act 1954. Assume that today's date is 1 March 2021 and that Poppy Ltd wants the new lease to commence as soon as possible. What is the earliest Proposed Commencement Date ("PCD") they could suggest and at what date must they serve their request to the landlord pursuant to s. 26 Landlord and Tenant Act 1954?
>
> The CED (29 October 2021) is 8 months away from today's date. The CED (which is the earliest date on which the new lease can commence) is less than 12 months but more than 6 months away from today's date and therefore, the s. 26 request could (and should) be served by Poppy Ltd today and specify a PCD of 29 October 2021. This means the new lease will commence on the same date as the current lease expires, i.e. the PCD will be the same as the CED.

Terms of a Lease

This section deals with some of the terms that are typically found in a contract for a lease between a landlord and a tenant. The landlord and tenant will negotiate the different clauses making up the lease. Certain wording will be "landlord-friendly", whilst some will be "tenant-friendly". Whether the terms will be beneficial to the tenant or the landlord comes down to the bargaining strength of the parties and those parties' particular objectives. Below are examples of different clauses relating to repair and insurance, including examples of how these can be drafted in a manner that is either "tenant-friendly" or "landlord friendly".

Key Covenants

Absolute covenants

An "absolute" covenant completely prohibits a tenant from undertaking the relevant action covered by that covenant. For instance, *"The Tenant covenants with the Landlord not to make any external or structural alterations to the Premises"*.

Qualified covenants

A "qualified" covenant restricts a tenant from undertaking the type of action covered by that covenant, whereby the tenant can only carry out the action with the landlord's consent. For instance, *"The Tenant covenants with the Landlord not to make any internal non-structural alterations to the Premises without the Landlord's consent"*.

Fully qualified covenants

A "fully qualified" covenant prohibits a tenant from undertaking the type of action covered by that covenant without the landlord's consent. However, unlike with "qualified" covenants, landlords cannot *unreasonably* withhold their consent to actions covered by *"fully* qualified" covenants. For instance, *"The Tenant covenants with the Landlord not to paint any walls in the Premises without the Landlord's consent, such consent not to be unreasonably withheld or delayed"*.

Repair

A commercial lease typically contains a "repair covenant".

> **Repair covenant:** an agreement whereby the tenant promises to keep the rented property in good condition. Such covenants have three elements: (1) the tenant's obligation to repair the premises during the term; (2) the tenant's obligation to return the premises back to the landlord in repair (see below); and (3) tenant's obligation to decorate the premises throughout the term at pre-decided intervals.

"Keeping" or "maintaining" a property in repair

Common law has established that if a tenant has an obligation in their Tenancy Agreement to "*keep* the property in good repair", then this will automatically give rise to the obligation for that tenant to put the property back into good repair, even if they take it on in a state of disrepair. Therefore, if the lease contains an obligation on the tenant to "keep the property in good repair", this will be landlord-friendly and should thus be challenged by the tenant's solicitor.

To make such a clause more tenant-friendly, the obligation should instead be to "*maintain* the property in good repair". A good way to provide additional protection for the tenant in this respect is to include a "Schedule of Condition".

> **Schedule of Condition:** the tenant will employ a surveyor who will create a report on the state of repair prior to the commencement of the lease. This will be included in a "Schedule of Condition", which can then be attached to the lease to evidence the state of repair at the time the tenant moved into the property. The repair covenant in the Tenancy Agreement could then specify that the tenant's obligation to repair does not include a requirement to put the property in any better state of condition than that evidenced by the Schedule of Condition.

Landlord-friendly drafting:

"The Tenant shall keep the Premises in good and substantial repair and condition."

Tenant-friendly drafting:

"The Tenant shall maintain the Premises in good and substantial repair and condition but the Tenant shall not repair the Premises where the disrepair is caused by an Insured Risk and provided that the Tenant shall not be required to put the Premises in any better state of condition or repair than as evidenced by the Schedule of Condition attached to this lease".

The standard of repair

A landlord would want to ensure that a tenant has an obligation to repair damage that is caused by "fair wear and tear", whereas the tenant would want to avoid any such obligation. A landlord would, in addition, want to impose an obligation on the tenant to replace/renew/rebuild (which extends the liability beyond merely repairing something). This would be disadvantageous to the tenant.

Fixtures and fittings

A tenant could also be obliged to repair or replace any of the property's fixtures and fittings. Where this is the case, it is advisable for a tenant to ensure that the obligation is not to replace fixtures/fittings with "identical" items, as this could be virtually impossible. A more tenant-friendly clause could instead oblige a tenant to replace fixtures/fittings with:

"...articles of a kind and quality that are substantially the same as the articles being replaced".

Latent defects

If the property being sold is a new (or fairly new) building, the tenant's solicitor would want to exclude from their repair liability any damage caused as a result of latent defects.

> **Latent defects:** defects to a property caused by faulty design, materials or workmanship that could not be discovered by inspecting the property prior to completion. Such defects are typically not apparent or readily detectable until some years after completion of the building (at which point a tenancy will likely already be in existence).

"Yielding up"

A tenant may be required to covenant to return the property to the landlord in a state that accords with the repair obligations contained in the lease. The landlord will want such a covenant to be judged "to the satisfaction of the Landlord". A tenant would want to qualify this however, for instance through amending the clause to read:

"...to the satisfaction of the Landlord's surveyor, acting reasonably".

Insurance

A tenant will typically covenant to pay insurance for a property during their tenancy. Sometimes the cost of this insurance will be included in the contractually agreed rent (rent clauses are discussed further below). Because of this, it is important that a tenant explicitly excludes any liability to repair damage caused by a risk that is insured under the insurance policy (as they will have paid insurance so as to avoid such costs).

It is in the interest of both parties to ensure the list of risks covered by the insurance is wide-ranging. A landlord may also want to include "such other risks as the Landlord from time to time may reasonably consider necessary", but a tenant should attempt to reject such wording. The landlord could otherwise insist on unreasonable risks being insured at the cost of the tenant.

The tenant would ideally want for the insurance to be in both the tenant's and the landlord's name. This would mean that any proceeds are payable to both parties. It would also ensure that the tenant avoids subrogation (if the insurance company is allowed to be subrogated, it means that the insurance company could pursue the tenant for losses they have contributed towards). If the insurance premium is not in both parties' names (it is rare), the tenant could instead ensure that the insurance company has waived its right of subrogation against the tenant.

The tenant will want to make sure that the insurance clause imposes an obligation on the landlord to:

- Insure the "Insured Risks" (this is often a defined term);
- Make a claim if any insured risk materialises and causes damage;
- Reinstate the property (a tenant would want to delete any term allowing the landlord to use insurance proceeds "as they deem necessary"); and
- Make up any shortfall out of their own money.

Rent and Service Charge

Rent

Rent is typically paid in four equal instalments every year. The standard quarter days for a commercial lease are 25 March, 24 June, 29 September and 25 December.

It is in the interest of the landlord to ensure that as many payments as possible are defined as "Rent" in the lease (such as insurance premiums paid by the tenant to the landlord and/or the service charge). This is because the landlord can take advantage of the (better) remedies available for non-payment of rent (this is explained in the *Landlord's Remedies* chapter in this module).

Rent suspension

The default position under the common law is that a tenant must continue to pay rent even if a property has been subject to damage of such a degree that the property is rendered unfit for use. It is therefore crucial that the tenant insists on including a clause entitling them to suspend the payment of rent in the event that an insured risk materialises and renders the property unfit for use. The landlord, in order to ensure that they will receive payment during that time, would want to include an obligation in the lease to take out insurance that covers the landlord for the loss of rent if such an event materialises.

Service charge

> **Service charge:** the landlord will incur costs relating to communal services that benefit all the tenants residing in a particular block of flats/offices, for instance, the cost of cleaning the communal areas, employing doormen and maintaining lifts. These costs are typically passed onto the tenants in the form of a "service charge" that is payable by all tenants (typically annually).

The landlord estimates the annual service charge for each tenant who then pays it quarterly (sometimes, as mentioned above, the service charge may also be included in the contractual definition of "Rent"). At the end of a year, the landlord will establish the *actual* cost for the services that they have provided during that year. If the actual cost is higher than the estimated charge, the tenants will have to pay an additional sum to make up the shortfall. If the actual cost is lower, any surplus paid by the tenants will carry forward to next year's service charge.

When drafting and negotiating the lease, there are a number of things that both the tenant and the landlord would want to consider in relation to the service charge:

- **Range of services covered:**

    It is in a landlord's interest to ensure that every tenant is obliged to pay for the provision of the widest possible range of services that may be required for the building. It is therefore in the interest of the landlord to include a widely drafted "sweep-up" provision containing wording such as "such other facilities as the Landlord sees fit".

    A tenant, however, would want a narrower range of services included so as to add a greater degree of certainty to the costs that they may have to contribute towards. The list of services should therefore, in the interest of the tenant, be clearly defined and ambiguous phrases such as the above should be avoided.

    Whilst negotiating the lease, the tenant's solicitor must consider the service charge provisions and establish (a) whether they seem fair; and (b) whether the tenant will actually use/need the services covered by the service charge. For instance, a tenant that leases a ground floor office would not want to pay towards lift maintenance.

- **Obligation:** the tenant would want an express covenant by the landlord to provide the services. If this is not the case, the landlord can decide which services are necessary.

- **Conditional services:** the tenant would attempt to avoid the provision of services being conditional on the service charge being paid.

- **Suspension:** the tenant will want to ensure that service charge payments (like with the rent payments) are suspended if an insured risk causes damage or destruction that renders the building inaccessible.

Alteration Clauses

A lease will typically contain alteration clauses, which restrict the type of building works that the tenant is allowed to carry out on the premises. This is important for a landlord, since in the absence of any agreement to the contrary, a tenant is allowed to carry out any alterations to the property as long those alterations do not devalue the property. The agreement can also contain provisions to the effect that alterations are allowed, but only to the extent that they have been approved by the landlord in advance. However, a landlord will not (from a commercial standpoint) want to place too may limitations on alterations in the lease, as this would mean that the rent they can charge will be lower (the landlord would effectively have to compensate for such restrictive terms by charging a lower rent, otherwise they may struggle to find tenants willing to take on the lease).

Effect of the Landlord and Tenant Act 1927

The Landlord and Tenant Act 1927 ("LTA 27") s. 19(2) will affect any *qualified* covenants in the Lease Agreement that relate to alterations (see the beginning of this chapter for an explanation of the difference between an absolute prohibition, a qualified covenant and a fully qualified covenant). LTA 27 s. 19(2) implies into qualified covenants against "improvements" that the landlord is *not* to unreasonably withhold consent. This is referred to as "upgrading" the qualified covenant into a fully qualified covenant.

> **Improvement:** it is important to note the language of LTA 27 s. 19(2), since it only applies to qualified covenants against "improvements" (i.e. not "alterations"). However, the case of Lambert v FW Woolworth defined "improvements" widely and clarified that whether an alteration is an improvement should be decided using the tenant's perspective. Therefore, when a tenant is proposing an alteration, it will usually constitute an "improvement". In Iqbal v Thakrar the landlord was held to be reasonable when he withheld consent on the basis that there were serious concerns that the suggested alterations would have a negative effect on the building (therefore not even from the tenant's perspective could the alteration constitute an improvement).

LTA 27 s. 19(2) somewhat redresses the balance between landlord and tenant however, by entitling the landlord to make their consent conditional upon the tenant agreeing to: pay compensation for any damage or diminution in value of the premises that arises as a result of the improvements; pay compensation for any legal or other expenses properly incurred in connection with the giving of consent; and undertake to reinstate the premises to its original condition before ceasing to become a tenant.

> **Operation of s. 19(2) Landlord and Tenant Act 1927**
>
> **Poppy Ltd is leasing Oak House. The lease contains the following term: "The Tenant covenants with the Landlord not to make any internal non-structural alterations to the Premises without the Landlord's consent". Poppy Ltd is now looking to make the premises open plan and as such needs to remove some non-structural walls. Would Poppy Ltd require the landlord's consent to make these changes and if so, is the landlord likely to give their consent?**
>
> The lease contains a qualified covenant against internal non-structural alterations, which are the type of alterations that Poppy Ltd is looking to carry out. If the proposed alterations count as "improvements", then s. 19(2) Landlord and Tenant Act 1927 will upgrade this qualified covenant to a fully qualified covenant: the landlord would consequently have to act reasonably when deciding whether or not to grant consent in relation to Poppy Ltd's proposed alterations.
>
> Whether the alterations constitute "improvements" is to be decided from the tenant's perspective (Lambert v Woolworth). It is assumed that Poppy Ltd considers the removal of the non-structural wall to be an improvement (as they want to operate using an open plan premises), and accordingly it is unlikely that the landlord will be able to unreasonably withhold their consent. An instance where the landlord would be deemed reasonable in withholding consent could, for instance, be if there is a serious concern that Poppy Ltd's suggested alteration would have a negative effect on the building (Iqbal v Thakrar).

Licence to alter

If the lease contains an absolute covenant that prohibits a specific type of alteration, LTA 27 s. 19(2) will have no effect on that provision. This does not mean that the landlord is legally prohibited from giving consent; they merely do not have to be *reasonable* when making their decision whether or not to give their consent.

The consent to alter is typically contained in a "licence to alter".

> **Licence to alter:** if the lease contains a fully-qualified covenant, then the landlord will not be obliged to give consent to alterations covered by that covenant. If the landlord decides to give consent anyway, then such consent will take the form of a "license to alter" (i.e. a license to carry out alterations). Both the landlord and the tenant will be a party to the licence.

The tenant will covenant to:

- Carry out the alteration works (typically defined by reference to a plan attached to the licence) in accordance with the landlord's requirements (the landlord will typically have requirements as to the quality of materials used and the standard of workmanship);

- Obtain all required consents (such as planning permission);

- Reinstate the property to its original state at the end of the lease;

- Pay the landlord's costs and expenses relating to the giving of consent (i.e. the application for a licence to alter).

The tenant will also seek to include a proviso that ensures that any improvements are disregarded if/when the rental rate is reviewed. Otherwise, the tenant could end up funding improvements that improve the quality of the premises and then paying a higher rent as a result of their own investment. Rent review and "disregards" are explained in the *Rent Review* chapter of this module.

Deed of variation

If the landlord is happy to consent to an alteration that is currently prohibited by an absolute covenant, the parties may instead choose to change the terms of the lease so as to remove that absolute covenant from its terms. This will enable the tenant to make the prohibited alterations at any time during the remainder of the term, rather than in accordance with a specific license that must be granted by the landlord each time such alterations are to be carried out. To remove an absolute covenant from the lease, a "deed of variation" will be required (i.e. a deed that serves to vary the lease). Note that if the lease is registered, this variation must be registered at the Land Registry.

User Clauses

A "user clause" restricts how, and for which purpose(s), a tenant may use the property. In the absence of a user clause, the tenant may use the property in whichever way they like (subject to statutory requirements, for instance those restricting noise pollution at certain times of the day). User clauses typically take the form of restrictive covenants, as they are usually expressed as *prohibiting* forms of use (e.g. "the tenant agrees not to use the property other than as/to..."), rather than permitting forms of use.

The way "use" is typically set out in the lease is as follows:

- The tenant will covenant not to use the premises other than for the "Permitted Use" (this being a defined term in the lease).

- In the Definitions section, "Permitted Use" will be defined either by: (1) using descriptive wording, e.g. "as a restaurant"; or (2) by reference to the Town and Country Planning (Use Classes) Order 1987, e.g. "uses falling within Class A1 or A2 in the Town and Country Planning (Use classes) Order 1987".

Effect of the Landlord and Tenant Act 1927

The relevant section when dealing with user clauses is the Landlord and Tenant Act 1927 ("LTA 27") s. 19(3). This does *not* imply a reasonableness requirement to qualified covenants in relation to user clauses (the way in which LTA 27 s. 19(2) works in relation to qualified covenants against improvements). Instead, in the context of "user" clauses, LTA 27 s. 19(3) prohibits landlords from charging tenants in exchange for their consent. The only situation in which a landlord is allowed to require a payment in exchange for consent is if the change of use will require a *structural* change to be made to the property. The prohibition does not stop the landlord from recovering their costs in relation to the tenant's application for consent however (e.g. legal fees).

Licence to change use

> **Licence to change use:** If there is a qualified prohibition against a proposed (by the tenant) new use, then this type of licence can be used to grant the tenant consent to change to the new use. Both the landlord and the tenant will be parties to this licence.

A qualified prohibition would typically be found in the definition of "Permitted Use" and could for instance read "Permitted Use means any use falling within Class A1 of the Town and Country Planning (Use classes) Order 1987 or such other use falling within Class B2 of the Town and Country Planning (Use classes) Order 1987 to which the Landlord gives its written consent, such consent not to be unreasonably withheld".

The tenant will covenant to:

- Pay any increase in the insurance premium that may be a consequence from the change of use; and
- Obtain all the relevant consents (such as planning permission).

Deed of variation

If there is an absolute prohibition against the intended new use (proposed by the tenant), the lease *must* be varied in order to allow the change of use. Note that if the lease is registered, this variation must be registered at the Land Registry.

Operation of s. 19(3) Landlord and Tenant Act 1927

Poppy Ltd is leasing Oak House and using the premises for their shop selling coffee machines. The lease contains the following term: "The Tenant covenants with the Landlord not to use the premises other than for the "Permitted Use". The lease also contains a definition of "Permitted Use" which states: "Any uses falling within Class A1 in the Town and Country Planning (Use classes) Order 1987 or such other use falling within Class A3 of the Town and Country Planning (Use classes) Order 1987 to which the Landlord gives its written consent." Poppy Ltd is now looking to change the use from a shop to a restaurant selling hot food (for consumption on the premises). Would Poppy Ltd need the landlord's consent to such a change and if so, can the landlord charge a premium for the granting of such consent?

The lease contains a qualified covenant prohibiting Poppy Ltd from using the premises for any purpose other than a shop (class A1), but the landlord can give their consent to using it as a restaurant (class A3). The Landlord and Tenant Act 1927 s. 19(3) does not upgrade this to a fully qualified covenant and accordingly, the landlord does not have to be reasonable when deciding whether to give consent to the proposed change of use.

Section 19(3) Landlord and Tenant Act 1927 does however preclude the landlord from charging a premium or a fine in return for giving their consent, unless the change of use requires any structural alteration to the property. Therefore, if Poppy Ltd needs to make any structural changes as part of changing the shop to a restaurant, the landlord would be allowed to charge a premium for the granting of his consent.

Alienation

> **Alienation:** where the tenant disclaims his interest in a lease by, for instance, underletting or assigning it.

Although there are terms in a lease that relate to alienation, for the sake of clarity this handbook deals with alienation separately. This section deals with: assignment and underletting; clauses in a lease that determine whether (and if so, under which circumstances) a tenant may alienate their lease; and the ways in which a landlord can limit a tenant's ability to alienate his/her lease. It also outlines some drafting considerations for licences to assign and licences to underlet.

Privity of Estate and Privity of Contract

When considering alienation, you must understand the following contractual concepts:

> **Privity of contract:** "privity of contract" refers to the contractual link that exists between parties who have signed a contract containing rights and obligations. Only parties to the contract can sue for breach of contract.

> **Privity of estate:** "privity of estate" refers to the link that exists between parties who both hold an interest in the same piece of land. Where privity of estate exists, one party can sue the other for non-observance of any covenants that relate to the land. This is not as useful as the right to sue for breach of contract.

Assignment

> **Assignment:** this is the term used where the tenant (the "assignor") transfers their remaining interest in a lease to another person (the "assignee"). The assignee will become the *immediate* tenant under the landlord. After an assignment has occurred, privity of estate will exist between the landlord and the assignee. However, privity of contract in relation to that same lease remains between the landlord and the *assignor*. No new lease has been created and it is not possible to change the terms of the lease unless the landlord consents to a change.

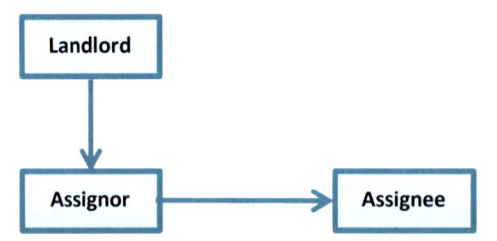

```
         Landlord
            │
            ▼
        Assignor  ──────▶  Assignee
```

Procedure for assigning a lease

Investigation of title (the assignee)
The assignee will investigate the landlord's freehold title and any relevant documents relating to the lease that they are to take on by way of assignment (such as rent review memorandums and/or any deeds of variation that may have been executed). Rent review memorandums are explained in the *Rent Review* chapter of this module.

Landlord's consent and licence to assign
Sometimes a lease will prohibit the current tenant (i.e. the intended assignor) from assigning their lease without the landlord's consent (this is dealt with in more detail below, under "alienation provisions in a lease"). Such consent is recorded in a "licence to assign".

> **Licence to assign:** the document in which a landlord grants permission to the current tenant to assign their lease.

The parties to a licence to assign are the current tenant (the assignor), the assignee and the landlord. This ensures that privity of contract is created between the landlord and the assignee (therefore the landlord can sue the assignee directly in the event that the assignee defaults on any terms in the lease).

The assignee will make the following covenants to the landlord:
- To observe and perform the covenants in the lease (i.e. the original lease between the landlord and the assignor).
- To notify the landlord when the assignment has been completed.

The tenant will make the following covenants to the landlord:
- To ensure the assignee does not take possession prior to the assignment being completed. If the assignee takes possession before having signed their covenants, the assignee could be protected by security of tenure (since occupation is one of the requirements for the imposition of security of tenure).
- To pay the landlord's costs in relation to the giving of consent (such costs could be, for instance, legal advice and the drafting of the licence and/or surveyors employed to give advice on the suitability of the proposed assignee).

Lender's consent

If the landlord's title and/or the current tenant's title are subject to mortgages, consent of the lender may be required before the lease can be assigned.

Documentation and registration

The sale of an *interest* in land must be made by deed LPA 1925 s. 52. Assignment constitutes the sale of an *interest* in land and must therefore be effected by deed (if the original lease was registered, **form TR1** should be used to record the assignment).

Assignment of a *registered* lease

This must always be registered at the Land Registry. This is done using **form AP1** (together with the relevant fee) and the following documents are required:

- The Deed of assignment (**form TR1**).
- A copy of the lease.
- If the assignee is mortgaging the lease, the mortgage deed or the debenture and the Companies House registration certificate if the tenant is a company.
- **SDLT5 certificate** (if Stamp Duty Land Tax has been paid – see below).
- Consent from any relevant lender (e.g. the landlord's or the tenant's lender) or evidence that any mortgage has been discharged.

Assignment of an *unregistered* lease

An assignment of an unregistered lease must only be registered if the lease has more than seven years left to run. This is done using **form FR1** if the landlord's title is also unregistered, and **form AP1** if the landlord's title is registered. The following documents are required for the registration of an unregistered lease (together with the relevant fee):

- The Deed of Assignment (**form TR1**).
- A copy of the lease.
- **SDLT5 certificate** (if Stamp Duty Land Tax has been paid – see below).
- Consent from any relevant lender (e.g. the landlord's or the tenant's lender) or evidence that any mortgage has been discharged.
- If the assignee is mortgaging the lease, the mortgage deed or the debenture, and the Companies House registration certificate if the tenant is a company.

Stamp Duty Land Tax

Stamp Duty Land Tax will only be paid by the buyer if any premium is paid by the assignee to the assignor for the assignment (although this is rarely the case for commercial assignments).

Original tenant liability and Authorised Guarantee Agreements ("AGAs")

For leases granted prior to 1 January 1996 ("old leases"), the original (first) tenant that assigned their lease (the assignor) remains liable for the lease. This meant that if an assignee failed to pay rent to the landlord, the landlord could pursue the *original* tenant instead, even though that tenant no longer has anything to do with/benefits from the lease. This doctrine is known as "original tenant liability".

For leases granted from and including 1 January 1996 ("new leases"), the position is now different as a result of the changes brought in by the Landlord and Tenant (Covenants) Act 1995. For new leases, a tenant will be automatically released from all covenants in the lease following the effective (lawful) assignment of that lease.

It is therefore important to differentiate between "old leases" and "new leases" for the purpose of establishing who can be held liable for a tenant's failure to observe the covenants in a lease. To illustrate: consider an example where a tenant ("Tenant 1") has assigned their lease to "Tenant 2". "Tenant 2" then assigns the lease to "Tenant 3":

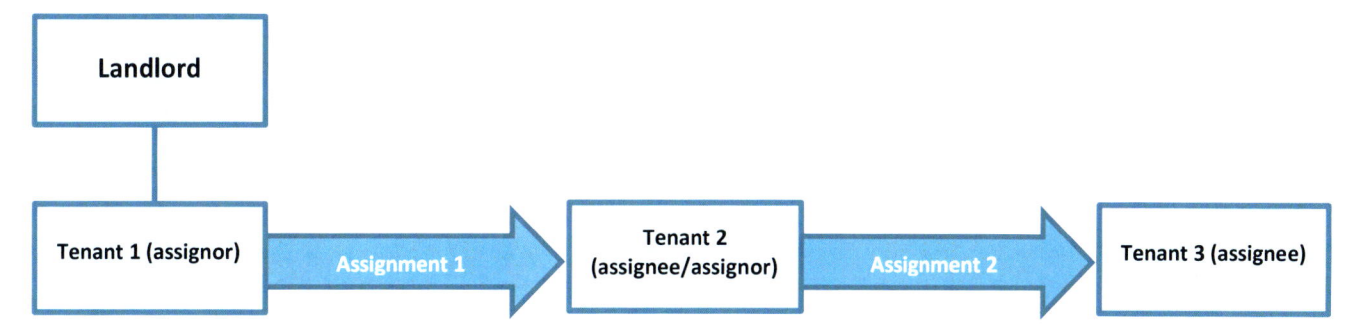

```
Landlord
   |
Tenant 1 (assignor) --Assignment 1--> Tenant 2 (assignee/assignor) --Assignment 2--> Tenant 3 (assignee)
```

If the lease is an "old lease": this would mean that Tenant 1 will be liable together with the current tenant (Tenant 3). The same applies if Tenant 3 then assigns to a new tenant, "Tenant 4": Tenant 1 would always remain liable.

If the lease is a "new lease" (and an AGA has been provided by each assignor – see below**):** this would mean that Tenant 2 will be liable together with the current tenant (Tenant 3).

Note that leases granted on or after 1 January 1996 (which are on the face of it "new" leases) will still give rise to original tenant liability if those leases were entered into pursuant to an agreement for a lease that was made prior to 1 January 1996 (i.e. be an "old lease").

Authorised Guarantee Agreements

As a condition for consenting to the assignment of a lease, a landlord will typically require their tenant (i.e. the proposed assignor) to enter into an Authorised Guarantee Agreement.

> **Authorised Guarantee Agreement ("AGA"):** an agreement in which the assignor guarantees the obligations of the immediate assignee. This allows the landlord to pursue the assignor should the immediate assignee default on one of the covenants in the lease.

However, an AGA will only remain in effect until the lease is next assigned (i.e. if the assignee assigns their interest to a *new* assignee, the AGA between the landlord and the original assignor will no longer bind that assignor). Therefore, a landlord will only ever be able to hold the following parties liable: (a) the *current* tenant; and (b) the tenant that assigned their lease to the current tenant (i.e. the previous tenant). This still provides the landlord with *some* degree of protection for the loss of original tenant liability in "new leases" however.

Landlord and Tenant (Covenants) Act 1995 s. 16 is the statutory provision that allows a landlord to incorporate a requirement into the lease that the tenant must give an AGA if that tenant wants to assign their lease.

Underletting/Subletting

> **Underletting/subletting:** whilst assignment involves a tenant transferring their entire interest in their existing lease, underletting (or "subletting") in contrast involves a tenant granting a new lease out of their own lease. A tenant may for instance transfer their interest in the property to a new tenant (the "undertenant") for only *part* of the duration for which the lease is due to run (e.g. if they have the lease for another 10 years, they may transfer their interest to another party for only the next three years). Alternatively, a tenant may transfer an interest in only *part* of the property that they are themselves leasing. Such transfers of a tenant's interest involve the tenant effectively granting a new lease (the "underlease") out of their own lease (which is subsequently referred to as the "headlease"). The term of an underlease must *always* be less than the headlease, otherwise the underletting will take effect as an assignment Milmo v Carreras. The headlease (i.e. the lease between the landlord and the original tenant) also typically requires that the terms of any underlease must at least match the headlease (or be more onerous). Both privity of contract and privity of estate will exist between the tenant and the undertenant, but no privity at all will exist between the landlord and the undertenant. This is because the agreement between the original tenant and the landlord remains in place. See the below diagram for clarification.

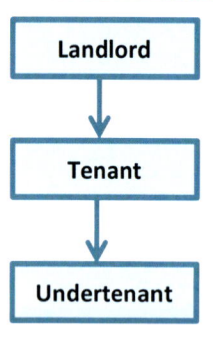

```
Landlord
   ↓
 Tenant
   ↓
Undertenant
```

Procedure for underletting a lease

Investigation of title (the undertenant)

The undertenant will investigate the landlord's freehold title, the existing tenant's lease and any other relevant documents relating to the lease out of which their underlease is to be granted.

Landlord's consent and licence to underlet

Sometimes a lease will prohibit the current tenant from underletting their lease without the landlord's consent (this is dealt with in more detail below in the *Alienation provisions in a lease* section of this chapter). Such consent is typically recorded in a licence to underlet.

> **Licence to underlet:** the document in which a landlord grants permission to the current tenant to underlet. There will be three parties to a licence to underlet: the landlord, the tenant and the undertenant. This is because the landlord will want the benefit of privity of contract with the subtenant (this gives the landlord a better range of rights, including the right to sue the undertenant directly in the event that they default on any terms of the underlease and the tenant does not enforce that term).

The undertenant will make the following covenants to the landlord:
- To observe and perform the covenants in the underlease (the lease signed between the tenant and the undertenant).

The tenant will make the following covenants to the landlord:
- Not to grant the sublease before the undertenant has made a formal declaration that they are contracting out of the protection afforded by the Landlord and Tenant Act 1954 s. 24. This is the protection of commercial security of tenure, which is covered in full detail in the *Commercial Security of Tenure* chapter of this module. This is to avoid the undertenant acquiring the right to occupy the property subsequent to the expiration date of the underlease.
- Not to allow the undertenant to occupy the property until the underlease (and the licence to underlet) has been completed.
- To pay the landlord's costs in relation to the giving of consent (such costs could be, for instance, legal advice and the drafting of the licence and/or surveyors employed to give advice on the suitability of the proposed undertenant).

Lender's consent

If the landlord's title and/or the current tenant's title are subject to mortgages, consent of the lender may be required before the lease can be underlet.

Documentation and registration

An underlease is created by granting a Lease Agreement between the current tenant and the undertenant. The underlease therefore replaces **form TR1**/the Deed of Assignment, which would otherwise be required when assigning a lease. The rules that apply to the granting of "normal" leases also apply to the granting of an underlease:

Underlease for 7 years or more: must be registered at the Land Registry using **form AP1** Land Registration Act 2002 s. 27(2). The following must be sent to the Land Registry together with **form AP1**:

- The underlease.
- The Land Registry fee.
- If the underlease is being mortgaged, the mortgage deed or the debenture, and the Companies House registration certificate if the tenant is a company.
- Consent of any relevant lender (e.g. the landlord's or the tenant's lender).
- **SDLT5 certificate** (if Stamp Duty Land Tax has been paid).
- The licence to underlet (if relevant).

Underlease for less than 7 years: this type of lease does not require registration at the Land Registry.

Alienation Provisions in the Lease

A landlord will typically seek to limit the circumstances under which a tenant can alienate their lease, as in the absence of such limitations the tenant will be free to do what they want with the lease (and therefore won't require a licence to assign or underlet/sublet). For this section it is important to be able to distinguish between absolute covenants, qualified covenants and fully qualified covenants. Please refer to the *Key terms: types of covenants* section in the *Terms of a Lease* chapter of this module if you do not remember these distinctions. Statutes have imposed certain rules relating to alienation provisions that are contained in a lease and these are covered below.

Landlord and Tenant Act 1927 s. 19(1)(a)

Application

The Landlord and Tenant Act 1927 ("LTA 27") s. 19(1)(a) applies to all types of alienation (i.e. assignment *and* underletting/subletting).

Function

If a lease contains a qualified covenant that restricts alienation (e.g. "the Tenant covenants with the Landlord not to assign the whole of the Premises without the prior written consent of the Landlord"), LTA s. 19(1)(a) upgrades this qualified covenant into a *fully* qualified covenant (i.e. the covenant will be deemed to include that consent is not to be unreasonably withheld, for example: "the Tenant covenants with the Landlord not to assign the whole of the Premises without the prior written consent of the Landlord, *such consent not to be unreasonably withheld*"). LTA s. 19(1)(a) also allows a landlord to charge a reasonable sum to compensate for legal or other expenses incurred as a result of giving of consent.

Law of Property Act 1925 s. 144 clarifies that the landlord may only charge a fine or premium as a condition for the giving of consent if the lease contains a provision that explicitly entitles the landlord to do so. Unless the landlord has very strong bargaining power, it is unlikely that such a provision will be accepted by a tenant's solicitor when the lease is being negotiated.

Reasonableness

The question of when it is reasonable for a landlord to withhold consent has been dealt with in case law:

- International Drilling Fluids v Louisville Investments: a landlord can only refuse to give their consent for a reason that relates to the tenant-landlord *business* relationship. A legitimate reason could be, for instance, that the landlord does not think the proposed "new" tenant is financially secure and may therefore struggle to pay rent. Conversely, the landlord disliking the proposed "new" tenant's personality would not constitute a legitimate reason to refuse consent.

- Moss Bros Group v CSC Properties: it is deemed reasonable for a landlord to refuse consent on the basis that the proposed "new" tenant's business does not align with the landlord's policy as to the mix of tenants they want on their premises (e.g. the landlord of a shopping centre may want to ensure that the shopping centre is comprised of a wide variety of stores, so could refuse to allow assignment to tenants that run businesses of a type already in existence in that shopping centre). The existence of such a policy must however be rational and be made known to tenants.

- Ashworth Frazer v Gloucester City Council: if the landlord is aware that the proposed "new" tenant is looking to use the property in a way that would amount to a breach of covenant existing between the landlord and the current tenant (and that therefore would be included in the underlease), it is reasonable for them to refuse consent.

- Crestford v Tesco: a landlord is allowed to incorporate pre-conditions to consent in the lease. Such pre-conditions are still subject to the reasonableness rule under LTA s. 19(1)(a) and if the tenant does not meet the pre-conditions, the landlord is not even obliged to consider the application for consent.

Landlord and Tenant Act 1927 s. 19(1A)

Application

This provision applies *only* to clauses relating to assignment.

Function

LTA s. 19(1A) allows the landlord to specify a list of *circumstances* which, if they exist at the time a tenant requests consent to assign their lease, will enable the landlord to refuse consent (the refusal of consent will automatically be deemed "reasonable"). Such circumstances could, for instance, include situations in which the proposed assignee is not of sufficient financial standing or where the proposed assignee is not resident in a jurisdiction where the landlord can easily enforce the covenants of the lease.

LTA s. 19(1A) also allows the landlord to specify in a lease (e.g. the lease they agree with their current tenant) a list of *conditions* that will automatically attach to any consent that they choose to give for that tenant to assign the lease to a sub-tenant. Such conditions will automatically be deemed reasonable. The conditions could include, for instance, that the tenant must execute and deliver an Authorised Guarantee Agreement to the landlord in respect of the proposed assignee prior to the assignment, and/or that an assignment cannot proceed until any requisite consent has been obtained (e.g. consent from any relevant lenders).

Landlord and Tenant Act 1988 s. 1

Application

The Landlord and Tenant Act 1988 ("LTA 88") s. 1 applies to all types of alienation (i.e. assignment *and* underletting/subletting).

Function

This section applies to *fully* qualified covenants contained in a lease that prohibit alienation. When the tenant makes a written application for the landlord's consent, the landlord owes a duty to reply within a reasonable time, either: giving consent; giving conditional consent; or refusing consent and providing reasons as to why. In Dong Bang Minerva v Davina, a period of 28 days from the date the landlord received the tenant's application was held to constitute "a reasonable time". The case also emphasised that a tenant must provide their landlord with sufficient particulars of the proposed assignment so as to enable the landlord to make a sensible, informed decision regarding consent.

Property Law

Rent Review

"Rent review" refers to a mechanism that can be used to vary the amount of rent charged under a lease. Rent review can be in the interest of a landlord where market rents have increased (as it could enable the landlord to charge higher rent) or in the interest of a tenant where market rents have decreased. All commercial leases with a term of 10 years or more will typically contain a "rent review" clause. There are various forms of rent review, but this handbook focuses on "open market" rent review. It is important that you check with your LPC provider whether you need to understand any other forms of rent review.

> **Open market rent review:** the rent will be reassessed periodically on the basis of what the rent *could* have been had the property been a new let at the date of the rent review. This means that the rent will be changed (if necessary) to reflect the *current* rental market.

Rent review is typically "upwards only" (unless the tenant is in a very strong bargaining position), meaning rent *cannot* be decreased under any circumstances. "Upwards only" open market rent review means that if, upon review, it is found that rents in the market are higher than the rent currently charged by the landlord, the rent will increase. However, if rents in the market are lower, the rent will stay the same (it will not reduce in line with current market rates). Although this seems unfair on the tenant, it reflects general market practice.

Procedure

Most rent review clauses require the landlord and tenant to first attempt to agree a new rent by themselves. If those parties fail, a valuer will typically be called in to determine the new rent. The valuer will take a range of considerations into account, including the size, location and quality of the premises, in addition to whether the lease is currently tenant-friendly or landlord-friendly (a tenant-friendly lease for instance would be more attractive to tenants and would therefore cost more).

Assumptions and Disregards

A valuer will also base their valuation on certain "assumptions" and "disregards"; the lease will specify factors that the valuer must *assume* to be true (even if they are not) and factors that they must *disregard* (even though they exist) when making their valuation. The purpose of assumptions and disregards is to ensure that the valuation of the property is as fair as possible to both parties.

For instance, if a property is in a state of disrepair, a valuer is likely to attribute a lower value to the lease. Assume that the obligation is on the *tenant* to keep the property in a good state of repair. It would be unfair on the landlord if the property is in a state of disrepair as a result of the *tenant's* actions. By operating under the "assumption" that the tenant has complied with all repair covenants, the valuer can set a rate of rent that would reflect the quality of the property had the tenant *actually* complied. The tenant will not therefore be rewarded for failing to look after the property.

Conversely, it would be unfair if the tenant has made improvements to the property, at their own expense, and are then made to pay a higher rent as a result of the consequent improvement in the quality of the property. To avoid this, the lease could specify that any improvements made at the tenant's expense must be "disregarded" for the purposes of rent review. The assumptions and disregards give rise to what is referred to as a "hypothetical letting". The tenant's solicitor would want to ensure that the hypothetical lease contains fair assumptions and disregards.

Would the following assumptions and disregards favour the landlord or the tenant for the purposes of rent review?

1. A lease contains the following clause: "The Tenant covenants not to use the Premises other than as a restaurant". The valuer will make the following assumption: "The Tenant may use the Premises as a restaurant or for any other use within Classes A1, A3, A4 or A5 of the Town and Country Planning Act (Use Classes Order) 1987".

2. The valuer will make the following assumption: "The rent review provisions contained in the lease are to be disregarded".

1. This assumption would favour the landlord. The actual lease is more restrictive than the hypothetical letting created by this assumption. A less restrictive lease is more tenant-friendly, which could cause the valuer to raise the rent.

2. This disregard would favour the landlord. Rent review provisions typically favour the landlord (as they can increase, but not decrease, the rent). Provisions that favour the landlord make leases less "tenant-friendly", which in turn can give rise to lower rental rates. If the valuer disregards the rent review provision whilst valuing the property, this will make the hypothetical letting more tenant-friendly than the actual lease, which could therefore cause the valuer to increase the rent.

Landlord's Remedies

If a tenant breaches a provision in a lease, there are a variety of options available to the landlord (the availability of these options depends on a number of factors). When establishing which remedies will be available to a landlord, it is advisable to first consider which type of breach has occurred (hence the structure of this chapter).

Non-payment of Rent

Forfeiture

> **Forfeiture:** a tenant's loss of their lease as a penalty for a wrongdoing or breach of contract. This means a tenant will have to vacate the property over which they had the lease.

A lease may contain a forfeiture provision, which allows the landlord to end the lease, evict the tenant, re-enter the premises and let the premises to another party. It is important for a landlord to expressly include a forfeiture provision in the contract, as otherwise they will not have the right to forfeit the lease as a remedy.

When a landlord is exercising their right to forfeit the lease (pursuant to a forfeiture clause in the lease contract) because of a tenant's failure to pay rent, the special kind of notice outlined in LPA 25 s. 146 *does not* have to be given to the tenant. This type of notice will therefore be explained in the next section (*Breach of repair covenant*).

Damages

A landlord can also seek contractual damages as a remedy when their tenant has failed to pay rent. Note that the normal rules on limitation periods apply, and a landlord must therefore issue proceedings within the six-year period commencing on the date that the unpaid rent became due.

Deposit

The landlord can also choose to deduct from the tenant's deposit any unpaid rent that is due.

Breach of Repair Covenant

Forfeiture

As explained above, a forfeiture clause must exist in the contract for this remedy to be available to the landlord.

LPA 25 s. 146 Notice

Unlike with non-payment of rent, if the tenant has breached a repair covenant, a special kind of notice must be given to the tenant. Before exercising their right to forfeit the lease (pursuant to a forfeiture clause in the lease contract), the landlord must serve a notice on the tenant in accordance with LPA 25 s. 146. There are three requirements for a s. 146 LPA notice set out in LPA 25 s. 146(1)(a)-(c):

- The notice must set out the breach on which the landlord has based his right to forfeit the lease.
- The notice must require the tenant to remedy the breach within a reasonable time.
- The notice must require the tenant to pay compensation for the breach.

Only if the tenant does not remedy the breach or give reasonable compensation to the landlord will the landlord be entitled to forfeit the lease.

Note that, as explained above, if the landlord is seeking to forfeit the lease on the basis that the tenant failed to pay rent on time, no notice is required (LPA 25 s. 146(11)). In all other circumstances, the landlord must comply with this section.

Leasehold Property (Repairs) Act 1938 s. 1

If the breach is of a repair covenant, the tenant has a further layer of protection before the lease can be forfeited. This protection exists if:

- The lease in question was originally granted for at least seven years; and
- At the date that the notice is served, three years or more of the term of the lease remain unexpired.

The act states that the landlord must, when giving notice of their intention to forfeit the lease, set out the tenant's right to serve a counter-notice on the landlord within 28 days requiring the landlord to secure court approval prior to forfeiting the lease. If the lease does not fulfil the above criteria (i.e. it was originally granted for less than 7 years and/or it has less than three years left to run), then only the "normal" LPA 25 s. 146 notice need to be sent to the tenant.

Damages

The landlord can seek contractual damages as a remedy for a tenant's breach of a repair covenant, but the right to do so is limited by Landlord and Tenant Act 1927 s. 18. This limitation means that the landlord can only recover damages up to an amount that is equivalent to any reduction in the value of the landlord's property. The landlord is therefore likely to receive only a small amount of damages if the value of his/her property is not significantly affected by the tenant's failure to comply with a repair covenant.

For instance, consider a situation where the tenant leases a central London property and the repair covenant contains an obligation on the tenant to repaint the exterior of the building on a regular basis. The cost for the landlord to repaint the building (if the tenant has failed to) will be significant, yet the value of the property is likely to remain largely unaffected by the lack of a new coat of paint. The landlord would not therefore be adequately compensated for having to paint the property. Consequently, pursuing damages is not typically a favourable option for landlords in the context of breaches of repair covenants.

Self-help

This remedy will allow the landlord to enter the premises to repair or make good any damage that the tenant should have dealt with pursuant to a repair covenant. The cost of doing so then becomes a debt, which the landlord can recover from the tenant. The advantage of this cost being classified as a "debt" is that the limitations imposed by s. 18 Landlord and Tenant Act 1927 (see above) do not apply and the landlord is therefore likely to be able to claim for the full sum of the repair should the tenant fail to pay the debt. The availability of this remedy was confirmed in the case of Jervis v Harris and as such, the clause granting the remedy is sometimes referred to as a "Jervis and Harris clause". Like with forfeiture, the remedy of "self-help" is only available if it is expressly included in the lease.

Tenant-friendly drafting:

"The Landlord may enter the Premises on reasonable notice during normal business hours, except in an emergency, to inspect its condition and may give the Tenant notice of any breach of the tenant covenants in this lease relating to the condition of the Premises. The Tenant shall carry out and complete any works needed to remedy that breach within the reasonable time required by the Landlord, in default of which, the Landlord may enter the Premises and carry out the works needed. The reasonable and proper costs incurred by the Landlord in carrying out any works pursuant to this clause shall be a debt due from the Tenant to the Landlord and payable within 14 days of written notice."

Landlord-friendly drafting:

"The Landlord may enter the Premises except in an emergency to inspect its condition and may give the Tenant notice of any breach of the tenant covenants in this lease relating to the condition of the Premises. The Tenant shall carry out and complete any works needed to remedy that breach within the time required by the Landlord, in default of which, the Landlord may enter the Premises and carry out the works needed. The costs incurred by the Landlord in carrying out any works pursuant to this clause shall be a debt due from the Tenant to the Landlord and payable on written notice."

Stig Ltd is the landlord of Oak House, which Poppy Ltd is leasing. Poppy Ltd's lease was originally granted for 15 years and it has 5 years left to run. Last week, Stig Ltd's surveyor noticed several large patches of missing paint on the exterior of the building.

The lease contains a repair covenants whereby the tenant covenants to keep the premises in repair and in accordance with the Schedule of Condition. The Schedule of Condition attached to the lease shows the exterior of the building in perfect condition.

The lease contains the following clause: "The Landlord may re-enter the Premises at any time after any of the following occurs: (1) any rent is unpaid for seven days after becoming payable; or (2) any breach of any condition or covenant of this lease; or (3) the Tenant is wound up or enters liquidation. If the Landlord re-enters the Premises pursuant to this clause, this Lease shall immediately end."

Explain whether Stig Ltd would need to serve a s. 146 Law of Property Act 1925 notice on the tenant to forfeit the lease for this breach, and if so, the information the notice must include.

The lease contains an express forfeiture provision; therefore forfeiture is available as a potential remedy to Stig Ltd. The forfeiture clause specifies that one of the events upon which the landlord may forfeit the lease is the tenant's breach of any covenant. The tenant has on the facts breached their repair covenant, as they have not maintained the property in accordance with the Schedule of Condition (they have failed to keep the paintwork in good condition).

An LPA s. 146 notice will first need to be sent to Poppy Ltd (remember, the only exception to this is if the tenant has not paid rent). The notice must specify the breach, require the tenant to remedy the breach within a reasonable period of time and explain whether any compensation is being sought. If Poppy Ltd does not remedy the breach or pays compensation, Stig Ltd may forfeit the lease.

However, because the lease is for a term of not less than seven years (it is for 15 years) and it has at least three years left to run (it has 5 years left to run), the provisions of the Leasehold Property (Repairs) Act 1938 must also be complied with. This means that the LPA s. 146 notice should also contain a statement that the tenant has the right to serve counter-notice on the landlord within 28 days requiring the landlord to secure court approval prior to forfeiting the lease.

Specific performance

> **Specific performance:** this is an equitable remedy whereby the court orders the party in default to perform a contractual duty (it is typically used in cases where damages would not be an appropriate remedy).

Although specific performance may be available to a landlord as a remedy pursuant to Rainbow Estates Ltd v Tokenhold, it is rarely used, as the courts do not wish to take on the burden of supervising such orders.

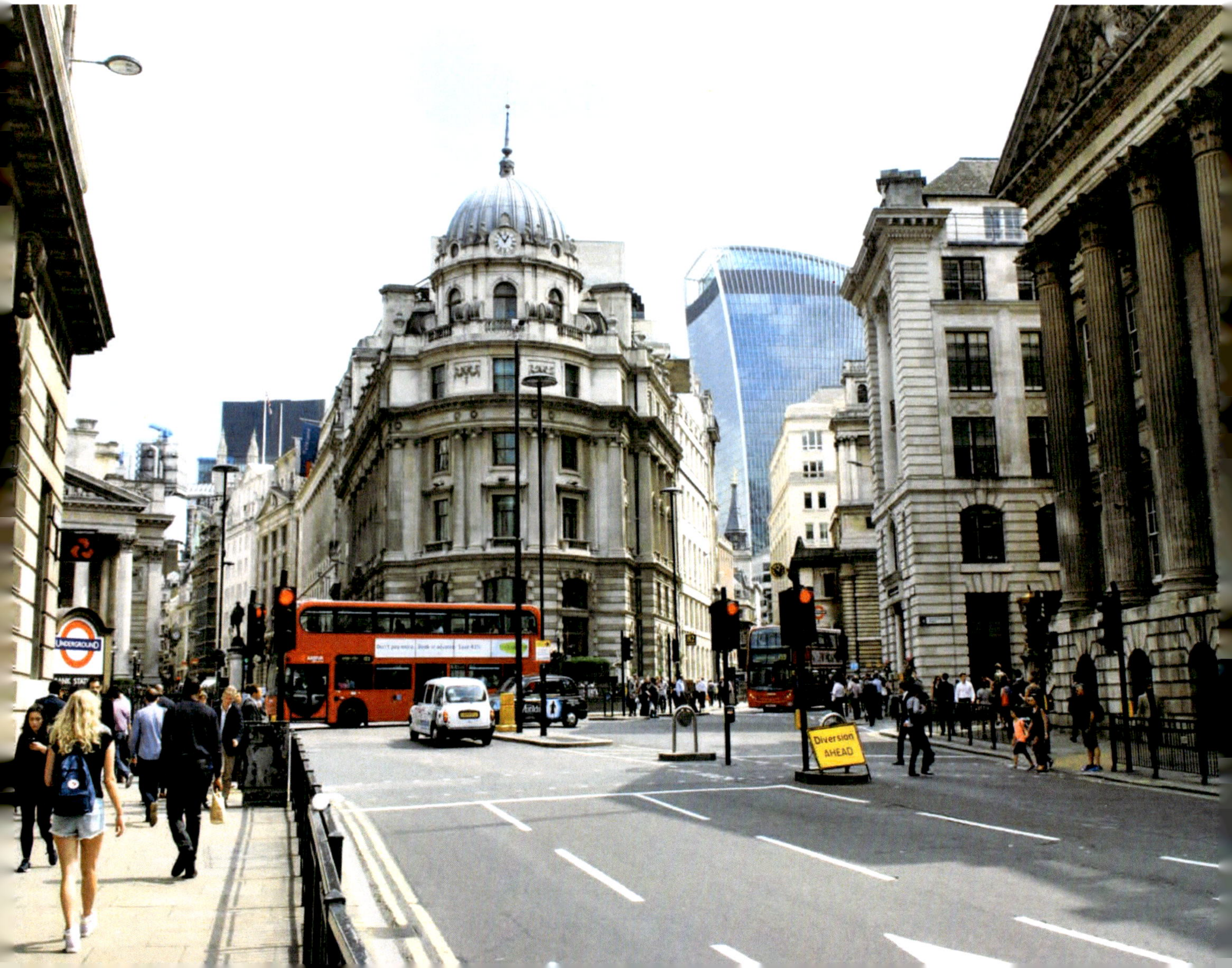
UNDERGROUND
Diversion
AHEAD

Civil Litigation

Civil Litigation

Introduction to Civil Litigation — 169

Understanding the Civil Procedure Rules • counting time • the overriding objective

Commencement of a Claim — 170

Pre-action considerations • choice of court • claim form • method and timing of service • Particulars of Claim • drafting a Particulars of Claim

Reply and Defence — 178

Reply • Acknowledgement of Service • judgment in default • Defence • drafting a Defence

Allocation and Case Management — 182

Directions • allocation to a track • court powers and sanctions • costs budgets

Disclosure and Inspection — 185

Standard disclosure • privilege • disclosure procedure

Witnesses — 188

Admissibility of witness evidence • witness statements • drafting a witness statement

Experts — 192

Role of experts in litigation proceedings • separate experts and single joint experts • expert reports

Settlement and Part 36 Offers — 194

Making and accepting a Part 36 Offer • consequences of rejecting a Part 36 Offer • settlement

Pre-trial, Trial and Costs — 198

Pre-trial • trial • costs

Interim Applications and Injunctions — 200

Applying for interim injunctions • security for costs • summary judgment • interim prohibitory injunctions • freezing injunctions • interim hearing cost orders

Foreign Jurisdictions — 205

The Brussels Regulation • the common law rules • foreign element: effect on proceedings

Alternative Dispute Resolution — 210

Mediation • expert determination • arbitration

Enforcement — 214

Investigating a judgment debtor's means • taking control of goods order • third party debt orders • charging orders • attachment of earnings • proceedings for insolvency

Appeals — 216

Grounds for appeal • permission • which court hears the appeal?

Introduction to Civil Litigation

Understanding the Civil Procedure Rules

The most important source of rules for the Civil Litigation course is the Civil Procedure Rules ("CPRs"). The CPRs contain chapters and each chapter has a variety of rules, which are numbered in accordance with the chapter number. For instance, Rule 3(a) in Chapter 14 can be written as "CPR 14.3(a)".

The CPRs also contain Practice Directions ("PDs"). Each chapter often has its own Practice Direction (some chapters have more than one). In this handbook, Practice Directions are referenced as follows: the chapter number to which the particular Practice Direction relates, followed by "PD" and the number of the relevant paragraph. For example: "16 PD 3" would mean paragraph 3 of the Practice Direction relating to Chapter 16.

> **Practice Direction:** a supplemental protocol that gives practical advice on how to interpret the rules.

Counting time

Many rules and frameworks in the CPRS require you to count days. These rules set out how to do this:

- "Days" in the CPRS always means "clear days" CPR 2.8(2).

- "Clear days" means that the day on which the period begins is not included CPR 2.8(3)(a).

- The day on which the period ends is *not* included if the end of the period is defined by reference to an event (e.g. "3 days before the hearing" would mean that the day of the hearing is *not* a clear day). In all other circumstances, the day on which the period ends is a clear day CPR 2.8(3)(a).

- Where the specified period is 5 days or less, Saturday, Sunday and Bank Holidays are not counted CPR 2.8(4).

Consider the following examples for illustration (do not worry if you do not understand the concepts now, this is only to help you understand how to interpret "days" in the CPRS):

- Particulars of Claim must be served within 14 days of service of the claim form. If the claim form is deemed served on 3 February, the last day for service of the Particulars of Claim is 17 February.

- Notice of an application must be served at least 3 days before the hearing. For example, if the hearing is fixed for Monday 18 July, the notice of application must be served on Tuesday 12 July.

Overriding objective

> **Overriding objective:** the overriding objective of civil litigation is that the court must ensure that cases are dealt with justly and at proportionate cost CPR 1.1.

The overriding objective is an overarching principle that the CPRs are designed to uphold. You will therefore see that it is referred to throughout the rules and practice directions.

Commencement of a Claim

This chapter explains how to commence a litigation claim in the civil courts of England & Wales. At this stage the claimant must: decide in which court it should commence the claim; have its claim form issued at the court; and serve the claim form and Particulars of Claim on the defendant. These steps are explained in more detail throughout this chapter.

Pre-action considerations

Pursuing a litigation claim should be viewed as a last resort for a potential claimant. Litigation should only be pursued after careful consideration, as the procedure involved is incredibly costly and time-consuming. The CPRs contain a section called the "**Pre-action protocols**". This includes a general pre-action protocol and protocols for specific types of claims. For instance, there is a specific protocol for professional negligence claims. The pre-action protocols set out "best practices" that should be adopted by parties before involving the court in their dispute. They outline the steps a potential claimant should take prior to commencing litigation, with the aim of solving the dispute without involving the courts.

In order to incentivise the potential claimant to actually carry out those steps, courts have the discretion to punish parties who fail to do so. The most important sanction available to a court is pursuant to CPR 44.2(5), which allows the court to consider any non-compliance with pre-action protocols when making costs orders. This essentially means that when the court decides which party/parties should be compensated for the costs of the litigation, and how much such compensation should amount to, they can decide to penalise a party if it has failed to follow the relevant pre-action protocol (this is dealt with in more detail in the *Pre-trial, Trial and Costs* chapter of this module). Because litigation can be very expensive, this is an efficient way of ensuring that the parties to a dispute consider the relevant pre-action protocol.

The court is also given the discretion to consider whether the parties have complied with the pre-action protocol when giving directions, pursuant to CPR 3.1(4). This could mean that the court will be stricter, and perhaps less accommodating, towards a party that has failed to comply with the relevant pre-action protocol throughout the litigation proceedings.

Key procedures in the pre-action protocol

Before issuing proceedings, courts will expect the parties to have, amongst other things (Practice Direction on Pre-action Conduct and Protocol ("PDPCP") paragraph 3):

- Exchanged sufficient information to understand each other's position;
- Considered alternative forms of dispute resolution to assist with settlement (thus avoiding involving the courts); and
- Reduced the costs of resolving the dispute PDPCP paragraph 3.

This should also ensure that, if proceedings *are* commenced, they are progressed expeditiously since the parties have already narrowed the issues in dispute through their pre-action communications.

Potential claimants should first send a **claim letter** (or **letter before claim**) to the potential defendant. The potential claimant must allow the potential defendant 14 days (if the claim is straight forward) or 3 months (if the claim is very complex) to reply PDPCP paragraph 6. Proceedings should not be subsequently issued until the defendant's letter of response denies the claim in its entirety and there is no letter of settlement, or this 3 month negotiation period has expired.

If a dispute has not been resolved after the parties have followed a pre-action protocol or the PDPCP, the parties should review their respective positions and consider whether proceedings can be avoided. They should at least seek to narrow the issues in dispute before the claimant issues proceedings PDPCP paragraph 12.

Pre-action protocols should not be used as tactical devices and costs incurred in complying with pre-action protocols or the PDPCP must be proportionate PDPCP paragraph 4-5.

Choice of Court

CPR Chapter 7 and 7A PD contain rules that help to determine the court in which a claimant should pursue its claim.

High Court or County Court

Claims worth more than £100,000 may be commenced in either the High Court or the County Court. Claims worth less than £100,000 should be commenced in the County Court 7A PD 2.1. For personal injury claims, this amount is reduced to £50,000 7A PD 2.2. If the claimant has a choice (i.e. the claim is worth more than £100,000), the following factors (listed in 7A PD 2.4) indicate the High Court to be the most appropriate court:

- The case has complex facts.
- The outcome of the case has an element of public interest.
- The claimant believes the High Court is the suitable court.

Civil Litigation

How to ascertain the value of a claim CPR 16.3(6)

The value of a claim is its financial worth (i.e. the loss that one party requires the other to make good), disregarding the following factors:

- Interest accumulated.
- The legal costs of pursuing the claim.
- The costs involved in pursuing any counterclaim(s).
- The effect a contributory negligence claim could have on the value of the original claim.

> **Counterclaim:** this is where the defendant makes a claim against the claimant that will form part of the defendant's defence. Counterclaims are governed in part by CPR 20. A counterclaim can be used to partially (or wholly) set-off the main claim, whereby the defendant argues that it has a right to withhold some of the funds that the claimant demands on the basis that the defendant is owed money by the claimant CPR 16.6. The claimant must reply to a counterclaim by serving a defence to the counterclaim on the defendant. Defences are covered below in the *Defence* section of this module.

Divisions of the High Court

The rules determining the High Court division in which a claim should be brought are set out in s. 61 Senior Courts Act 1981. Below sets out the types of cases typically heard in each division:

Chancery Division or Queen's Bench Division	
Chancery Division	**Queen's Bench Division**
<ul><li>Land</li><li>Mortgages</li><li>Trusts, Administration of Estates and Probate</li><li>Bankruptcy</li><li>Partnerships and Company matters</li><li>Intellectual Property</li></ul>	<ul><li>Contract</li><li>Tort</li><li>Commercial matters</li><li>Judicial review</li><li>Admiralty</li></ul>

Claim Form

The claim form is the document used to commence litigation proceedings (or *issue* proceedings). The claimant's solicitor prepares the claim form using **form N1** (7A PD 3.1) and files it at court. The court will then issue the claim by sealing the claim form (which halts the limitation period for the claim), and allocating a claim number to the claim. The claim form is then valid for four months and the "relevant step" (explained below in *Method and timing of service*) for validly serving it on the defendant must be completed within this period CPR 7.5(1). There can therefore be a four-month delay between the claimant filing the claim form at the court and the defendant receiving it.

Henderson v Merrett: a claimant can run concurrent claims in both contract and tort.

> **Limitation period:** the limitation period for a breach of contract claim ends 6 years from the date of the breach (excluding the actual date of the breach), even if the actual damage occurred sometime after the breach. The limitation period for a tortious breach ends 6 years from the date of the actionable damage (i.e. the date when the damage was suffered), although there are certain exceptions (e.g. the limitation period is only 3 years for personal injury claims).

> **Serving a document:** giving a document to another party to the proceedings in a way recognised by the court as valid.

> **Filing a document:** lodging a document at court.

The claim form is the first "statement of case".

> **Statement of case:** any document in which a party sets out their case. This includes (but is not limited to): the claim form, the Particulars of Claim, and the Defence. An amendment to a statement of case can be made at any time before it is served CPR 17.1. If it has already been served, it can only be amended with the consent of the other parties or the court.

Method and timing of service

The methods by which a claimant may *serve* the claim form on the defendant are set out in CPR 6.3. These methods determine the date on which the claim form will be *deemed* served CPR 6.14. The deemed date of service of the claim form will be the *second business day* after the "relevant step" has taken place (there are different "relevant steps" for each method of service). CPR 7.5 lists the "relevant step" for different methods of service. For instance, if the claimant uses fax, the "relevant step" will be completing the fax's transmission.

> **Deemed date of service:** this is the fictional date that will be used in the proceedings for the purpose of calculating future deadlines. Even though a document may have been received before or after the "deemed" date, the court - for the purpose of interpreting the deadlines set out in the Civil Procedure Rules – will presume that the relevant party received it on the "deemed" date of service.

CPR 6.17(1): where the *court* serves a claim form, the court will send the claimant a notice that includes the date on which the claim form is deemed served pursuant to CPR 6.14.

CPR 6.17(2): where the *claimant* serves a claim form, the claimant must then file a certificate of service within 21 days of service of the particulars of claim, unless all the defendants have filed acknowledgments of service.

Limitation period, deemed date of service and validity of a claim form:

C Ltd and D Ltd enter into a contract in which D Ltd agrees to deliver 15,000 computers to C Ltd in return for £150,000. The contractually agreed date of delivery is 24 February 2021. D Ltd delivered the computers a month late and C Ltd now wishes to sue D Ltd for breach of contract. C Ltd issued the claim form in the High Court on 23 June 2021 and posted the claim form to D Ltd on 2 July 2021. Assume that any relevant pre-action protocols have been complied with.

When does the limitation period for bringing a claim expire, what is the deemed date of service of the claim form, and was the claim form validly served?

Limitation period: D Ltd breached the contract when it failed to deliver the goods on the contractual date of delivery. The limitation period ends 6 years after the agreed contractual date of delivery (excluding the date of contractual delivery, as this is the date of the breach). C Ltd issued the claim form within this 6-year period and will thus not be barred from bringing the claim. Note that the limitation period stopped running when C Ltd issued the claim form.

Deemed date of service: C Ltd posted the claim form on 2 July 2021. To establish the deemed date of service, we use CPR 6.14, which in turn refers us to CPR 7.5. The "relevant step" (posting the claim form) is completed on 2 July. Therefore under the CPRs, the deemed date of service will be the second business day after that date, which is 6 July 2021.

Validity of the service of the claim form: when a claim form is issued, it must be served on the defendant within 4 months pursuant to CPR 7.5(1). C Ltd's claim form was served on D Ltd on 6 July 2021, which is within this 4-month period. The claim form was therefore validly served.

Particulars of Claim

This document is served by the claimant on the defendant either after or together with the claim form. Whilst the claim form contains a very brief summary of the claim (sometimes just a sentence), the Particulars of Claim sets out all material facts and details the elements of the claim brought by the claimant (i.e. the duty(ies) owed, the breach(es) of such duty(ies), causation and loss).

Method and timing of service

If prepared as a separate document

CPR 7.4(1)(b) states that, if prepared separately to the claim form, the Particulars of Claim must be served on the defendant within 14 days of the deemed date of service of the claim form. This is subject to the rule that once issued by the court, the claim form must be served within four months (discussed above) CPR 7.4(2).

CPR 6.26 is the applicable rule when ascertaining the deemed date of service of any document *other than* the claim form. This is thus the rule to use when the Particulars of Claim is prepared as a separate document. This CPR rule contains a table that helps you ascertain the deemed date of service for different forms of methods of delivery (such as post, personal delivery, fax etc.).

If served together with the claim form

Case law has established that although the wording of CPR 7.5 is specific to claim forms, it also applies to Particulars of Claim when served together with a claim form. Therefore, the rules in relation to the method and timing of service of claim forms also apply to Particulars of Claim when both are served together.

Contents of a Particulars of Claim

LPC providers may require students to re-draft a Particulars of Claim as part of the Civil Litigation examination. This section aims to provide you with the necessary tools to answer such a question effectively. It is advisable to consider this section in conjunction with the example of a Particulars of Claim found at the end of this section.

The content required for a Particulars of Claim is set out in CPR 16.4 and you will find further guidance in 16 PD 3. If your exam is open book, consider having these sections open whilst answering a question that requires you to re-draft a Particulars of Claim.

Civil Litigation

Title of proceedings

All statements of case must be headed with the title of the proceedings. This should state 7A PD 4.1:

- The number of proceedings.
- The full name of each party. 16 PD 2.6 further clarifies how the name should be written:
    - If the party is an individual, his/her full name and title;
    - If the party is an individual carrying on business in a name other than their own name, the full name of that individual, their title and "trading as [*name of business*]";
    - In the case of a partnership (other than an LLP): (a) where the partners are being sued in the name of the partnership, the full name by which the partnership is known together with the words "(A Firm)", or (b) where the partners are being sued as individuals, the full name of each partner and their respective titles;
    - If the party is a company or an LLP, its full registered name, including suffix (e.g. Plc, Limited, LLP etc.).
- Each party's status in the proceedings (i.e. claimant/defendant).

Material facts

The Particulars of Claim should first set out all material facts. You must analyse the scenario given to you in the exam question carefully to ensure everything is accurate and anything that is relevant in establishing the claim is included. The material facts should contain both the defendant's and the claimant's profession or business:

"At all material times, the Claimant [*description of the Claimant's profession/business*] and the Defendant [*description of the Defendant's profession/business*]."

Duty

Typically the drafting question relates to either a breach of contract and/or tort. You should therefore ensure you have a brief understanding of how to analyse each element of both a tortious and contractual claim.

Contract

The duty in contract arises as a result of the terms of that contract. The terms may be express and/or implied. Express terms are terms explicitly included in the contract whilst implied terms are terms implied by law. "Implied" for these purposes means that the contract "is to be treated as including" certain terms (even if it does not expressly do so). In the "duty" section of the Particulars of Claim, you must ensure that the contractual terms relevant to the defendant's alleged breach(es) are clearly set out.

- **Express term:** this could for instance be written in the following way:

    "It was an express term of the contract that the goods were to be delivered on 24 February 2021."

- **Implied term:** the relevant implied term typically dealt with for contractual claims on the LPC are the ones implied by the Sale of Goods Act 1986. When drafting clauses in an exam, ensure that you use any defined terms that have already been set out in the facts/contract (e.g. "the Computers") and tailor the wording to the given facts (e.g. use the *name* of the claimant rather than simply "the claimant").

    "It was an implied term of the contract that the [*goods*] would be of satisfactory quality."

    "It was an implied term of the contract that the [*goods*] would be fit for the purpose made known to [*name of defendant*] by [*name of claimant*]."

    "It was an implied term of the contract that the [*goods*] would correspond with the description included in the contract."

> 📖 **Satisfactory quality:** the Sale of Goods Act 1979 requires goods sold to be of satisfactory quality. A product will not be of satisfactory quality if it has defects or problems or if it does not last a reasonable time.

> 📖 **Fit for purpose:** the Sale of Goods Act 1979 requires goods sold to be fit for purpose. This includes any specific/special intended purpose that you made known to the seller before entering into the contract. It also includes obvious purposes for an item (e.g. if you have bought an apple peeler and the product received cannot peel apples).

Tort

The tortious duty could relate, for instance, to a professional service provider owing a duty of reasonable care and skill to its clients.

"As a result of their position, the Defendant owed the Claimant a duty of reasonable care and skill."

Breach

This section of the Particulars of Claim should explain *how* the duty owed has been breached. You should refer to the duties you have already outlined previously when doing so.

"In breach of the implied term outlined in paragraph X of these Particulars of Claim, the Defendant [*explain the breach*]."

"In breach of the duty of reasonable care and skill outlined in paragraph X of these Particulars of Claim, the Defendant [*explain the breach*]."

Sometimes the breaches are set out in a list headed "Particulars of Breach". In such cases, the breaches are not dealt with in separate paragraphs, but rather in one paragraph and could look like this:

In breach of the implied/express term(s) outlined in paragraph X above, the [*product*] was not of satisfactory quality.
PARTICULARS OF BREACH

(c) Reason 1 why the [*product*] was *not* of satisfactory quality.

(d) Reason 2 why the [*product*] was *not* of satisfactory quality.

(e) Reason 3 why the [*product*] was *not* of satisfactory quality.

Causation

In this section, you should explain *how* the breach(es) caused the loss, for instance:

"As a result of the breach set out in paragraph X above, the Claimant had to [*action taken to compensate for the breach*]."

Loss

This section outlines the losses the claimant claims it has suffered, both financial and non-financial (e.g. loss of reputation). They are normally outlined in a table under the title "Particulars of Loss and Damage" in a tabular format:

"As a result of the breaches referred to in paragraph X above, the Claimant has suffered loss and damage."

PARTICULARS OF LOSS AND DAMAGE

Cost A	£X
Cost B	£X
Cost C	£X
LESS	
(Deduction A)	(£X)
TOTAL	**£XX**

The claimant should also ask for interest in this section, after the Particulars of Loss and Damage have been outlined. The right to claim interest may be set out in the contract between the parties but if it is not, there is a statutory right to interest. The wording will vary depending on the court in which the claim is brought and whether the claim is specified or unspecified.

To calculate the daily rate of interest, multiply the sum on which interest is claimed by the percentage rate of interest and then divide the figure by 365. For instance, if you are claiming £100,000 and the percentage rate of interest is 10%, multiply £100,000 by 0.10 (i.e. 10%), which gives £10,000 (the annual interest), then divide £10,000 by 365 (to give the daily rate of interest). To calculate the total amount of interest, multiply the daily rate of interest by the number of days for which the claim has run.

Specified claim

This is where the sum of the damages sought is already agreed, such as a debt claim or a liquidated damages claim.

"The Claimant also claims interest pursuant to [*Clause X of the contract/Section 35A Senior Courts Act 1981 (if in the High Court)/Section 69 County Courts Act 1984 (if in the County Court)*] from the due date of the invoice to today's date at the rate of [X]% per annum in the total sum of £X."

Unspecified claim

This is where the court has a decision to make on the amount of damages because the parties do not agree the amount. This includes, for instance: loss of goodwill/reputation; loss in the value of an asset; loss of future profits/earnings; and any damages where remoteness, foreseeability and/or mitigation are disputed.

"The Claimant also claims interest on such damages as are awarded to it pursuant to [*Section 35A Senior Courts Act 1981 (if in the High Court)/section 69 County Courts Act 1984 (if in the County Court)*] at such rate and for such period as the court thinks fit."

Summary of remedies sought (the "prayer")

After setting out the breaches, causation and loss, you should then include a summary of what the claimant is actually seeking as a remedy. This summary is sometimes referred to as the "prayer".

Specified claim

AND THE CLAIMANT CLAIMS:

(i) The said sum of £X;

(ii) Interest under paragraph X above to today's date in the sum of £Y; and

(iii) Further interest under paragraph Y above at a daily rate of £Z until judgment or earlier payment.

Unspecified claim

AND THE CLAIMANT CLAIMS:

(i) Damages under paragraph X above.

(ii) Interest under paragraph Y above.

Statement of Truth

A Statement of Truth must be included in the Particulars of Claim. This must never be on a page of its own (to avoid fraud) so if it is on a separate page in your exam script, point this out. The wording depends on whether the person signing the document is the *actual party* to the proceedings. For instance, if the claimant is a company, and the managing director is signing the Particulars of Claim, the managing director will not be the actual party (the actual party would be the company).

If signed by a person other than the actual party

"The Claimant believes that the facts stated in this Particulars of Claim are true. I am duly authorised by the Claimant to sign this statement."

If signed by the actual party

"I believe that the facts stated in this Particulars of Claim are true."

General points

There are a number of format and consistency points you should look out for when re-drafting a Particulars of Claim. Here is a good checklist for format and consistency:

- Check that the name/division of the court is accurate.

- Check that "Defendant" and "Claimant" are used in the correct places and the "C"/"D" are capitalised where appropriate.

- Check that the dates in the Particulars of Claim correspond with the ones given in the facts.

- Check that the spelling of names and parties in the Particulars of Claim correspond with the ones given in the facts.

- Check that the name of the firm of solicitors that drafted the Particulars of Claim is inserted at the end of the Particulars of Claim (just before the Statement of Truth).

- If you refer to a contract/document, add "A copy of the [*relevant document*] is attached to these Particulars of Claim".

- Check that the Particulars of Claim refer to the same object/person/document in a consistent manner throughout the document. For instance, if an abbreviation has been set for a particular name, ensure it is used consistently.

Particulars of Claim: drafting example

IN THE HIGH COURT JUSTICE　　　　　　　　　　　　　　　　　　　　　　Claim number: 2021 HC 1712
QUEEN'S BENCH DIVISION

BETWEEN

HELLOWAY GOLF LIMITED

Claimant

- and -

GIPPON STEEL LIMITED

Defendant

PARTICULARS OF CLAIM

---

1. At all material times, the Claimant was a company engaged in producing and selling high-end golf clubs. The Defendant at all material times carried on a business as a manufacturer and seller of steel alloy used in the manufacture of golf clubs.

2. On 16 July 2016 the Claimant entered into a contract (the "Contract") with the Defendant whereby the Defendant agreed to supply the Claimant with 1 tonne of steel alloy (the "Steel Alloy"). This was to be used in the production of the Claimant's new line of golf clubs. The Claimant agreed to purchase the Steel Alloy for £100,000 (inclusive of VAT). A copy of the contract is attached. The Claimant spent £10,000 on rent for an exhibition stand at a trade show for golfing equipment, for the purpose of launching its new line of golf clubs. The Claimant did so in reliance on the Steel Alloy being available for use in the manufacture of the new clubs.

3. It was an express term of the Contract that the Steel Alloy would have a density of 7.9 kg/m^3.

4. It was an implied term of the Contract that the Steel Alloy would be fit for purpose and of satisfactory quality.

5. The Defendant duly delivered the Steel Alloy to the Claimant's premises in accordance with the contract.

6. The Claimant duly paid the contractually agreed price of £100,000 by telegraphic transfer on 31 August 2016 in accordance with the contract.

7. In breach of the express term in paragraph 3 above, the Steel Alloy did not have a density of 7.9 kg/m^3. When the production process for the golf clubs commenced, it turned out that the density was in fact 7.5 kg/m^3.

8. In breach of the implied term in paragraph 4 above, the Steel Alloy could not be used for the manufacture of the Claimant's new line of golf clubs. The functionality and intended quality of the golf clubs required the Steel Alloy to have the agreed density of 7.9 kg/m^3.

9. As a result of the breaches set out in paragraph 7 and paragraph 8 above, the Claimant could not use the Steel Alloy supplied by the Claimant and consequently had to purchase new steel alloy at the correct density of 7.9 kg/m^3 from another supplier. This additional steel alloy cost £120,000. The Claimant (as a producer of only high-end golf clubs) had no use for the Steel Alloy supplied by the Defendant, as the density of the Steel Alloy meant that it could only have been used in the production of low quality golf clubs.

10. In addition, the Claimant was also unable to manufacture the clubs in time for the trade show at which they had paid to exhibit the clubs. This meant the Claimant's competitors gained an advantage since they could present their new line of clubs before the Claimant.

11. Further, as a result of the breaches set out in paragraph 7 and paragraph 8 above, the Claimant has suffered damage to its reputation. The Claimant was unable to demonstrate innovation at the trade show mentioned in paragraph 10, which has adversely impacted its reputation as a producer of high-end golf clubs.

12. As a result of the breaches set out in paragraph 7 and paragraph 8, the Claimant has suffered loss and damage.

PARTICULARS OF LOSS AND DAMAGE

Cost of exhibition stand at trade show	£10,000
Cost of additional steel	£120,000
TOTAL	**£230,000**

13. The Claimant also seeks damages for damage to its reputation.

14. The Claimant is entitled to interest on such damages as are awarded to it under Section 35A Senior Courts Act 1981 at such rate and for such period as the court thinks fit.

AND THE CLAIMANT CLAIMS:

i. Damages as set out in paragraph 12 and paragraph 13; and

ii. Interest as set out in paragraph 14.

NORAH & CO LLP

Statement of Truth

The Claimant believes that the facts stated in these Particulars of Claim are true. I am duly authorised by the Claimant to make this statement.

Signed:

Henric Wood

Managing Director, Helloway Golf Limited

Served this day 17 August 2021 by Norah & Co LLP, Solicitors for the Claimant.

Reply and Defence

When the claimant has served the claim form and the Particulars of Claim on the defendant, the defendant has three choices: it can "admit" to the allegations and settle the claim; file an acknowledgement of service; or "deny" and file and serve a defence. If the defendant has served a defence, the claimant can choose to issue a reply (but there is no requirement for it to do so) CPR 16.7. This chapter sets out the procedure and relevant time limits for the defendant's response, and the potential consequences if the defendant fails to reply. It also includes a section on how to redraft a Defence.

Reply

Timing and methods of service

Once the defendant has been served with the Particulars of Claim, the defendant must either file an Acknowledgement of Service or a Defence with the court within 14 days of the deemed date of service of the Particulars of Claim CPR 15.4. Filing an Acknowledgment of Service at court gives the defendant 28 days from the deemed date of service of the Particulars of Claim to then admit to the allegations or file a Defence with the court. Acknowledgement of Service is dealt with in CPR Part 10. The court is responsible for notifying the claimant that the defendant has filed an Acknowledgement of Service.

If a Defence has been filed at court, the defendant must also serve it on the other parties CPR 15.6.

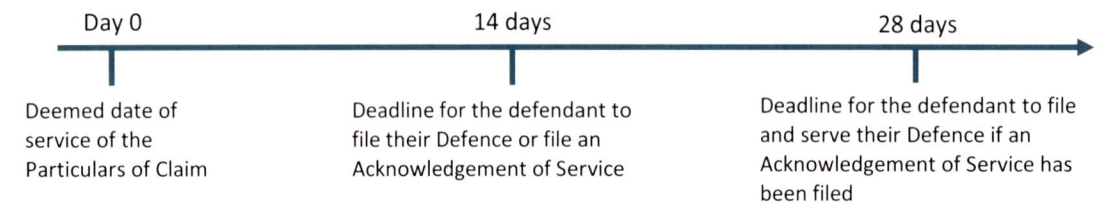

Day 0	14 days	28 days
Deemed date of service of the Particulars of Claim	Deadline for the defendant to file their Defence or file an Acknowledgement of Service	Deadline for the defendant to file and serve their Defence if an Acknowledgement of Service has been filed

Extension of time

CPR 15.5 allows the parties' solicitors to agree to extend the deadline for filing and serving a Defence by up to 28 days, but they must notify the court in writing if they do so.

If the defendant requires more time but the claimant does not consent, the defendant must apply to the court using an interim application to request an extension. Such an interim application will put the case on hold until the interim hearing, and the defendant will not be required to file a Defence during that period (even if the court subsequently dismisses the application at the hearing). Where an application for an extension is made, the defendant has to file and serve the Defence after the interim hearing in accordance with the court's directions. Interim applications are covered in more detail in the *Interim Applications and Injunctions* chapter in this module.

Judgment in default

If the defendant fails to reply to the claimant's Particulars of Claim, the claimant has the option to apply for default judgment (or "judgment in default") pursuant to CPR Part 12. This can only be done after any relevant deadlines have passed and the defendant has failed to file an Acknowledgment of Service or a Defence. If a claimant is successful with its application for default judgment, this means that the claimant has won the case.

The claimant must apply for default judgment promptly and provide evidence (e.g. a witness statement) showing that: the Particulars of Claim has been served; the time for filing a Defence or an Acknowledgment of Service has expired (taking into account any extension that may have been agreed); the claim has not been admitted, satisfied or denied; and no application for summary judgment has been made. Note that summary judgment is dealt with in more detail in the *Interim Applications and Injunctions* chapter in this module.

Setting aside or varying a default judgment

If a judgment in default is successful, the defendant can subsequently apply to have it varied or set aside pursuant to CPR Part 13. There are mandatory grounds and discretionary grounds upon which a court can set aside or vary a default judgment. The difference between the two categories is as follows: if the defendant can prove a mandatory ground, the court *must* set aside the default judgment. In contrast, if the defendant can only prove a discretionary ground, the court *may* set aside the default judgement, but is under no obligation to do so.

Mandatory grounds CPR 13.2

- The Defence or Acknowledgement of Service was served within the required time limits;
- The time limit for acknowledging service or serving a Defence had not expired when judgment in default was entered;
- The defendant had satisfied or admitted the claim before default judgment was entered; or
- Summary judgment had been applied for, or the case had been struck out, before default judgment was entered.

Civil Litigation

Discretionary grounds CPR 13.3

- The defendant has a real prospect of successfully defending the claim; or
- It appears to the court that there is some other good reason why judgment should be set aside or varied or the defendant should be allowed to submit a Defence.

Defence

Content of a Defence and drafting a Defence

Some LPC providers require candidates to re-draft a Defence to allegations set out in a Particulars of Claim. Typically the candidates will be provided with the claimant's Particulars of Claim, an outline of the facts from the defendant's perspective, and an unfinished draft of the defendant's Defence. Candidates are then asked to re-draft that unfinished Defence. This section explains how to tackle such a question.

The requirements for the content of a Defence are outlined in CPR 16.5. The structure of a Defence follows that of the Particulars of Claim, whereby the defendant "replies" to each allegation in the Particulars of Claim. If an allegation is not dealt with, the defendant will be deemed to have accepted the claimant's version of that particular event. Therefore, when drafting a Defence, you must ensure that every allegation in the Particulars of Claim has been dealt with.

It is advisable to consider this section in conjunction with the example Defence found below.

Admit, deny or require proof

CPR 16.5(1) sets out three options for dealing with an allegation:

1. Admit

This is when the defendant admits and completely accepts the claimant's version of events. In order to save time and costs, a defendant should admit any fact or allegation that is not disputed and that they know to be true. The defendant could "admit", for instance, the paragraph setting out the profession of both parties or (if it is a contractual dispute) that the contract on which the dispute is centred exists.

"The Defendant admits paragraph 3."

2. Deny

The defendant should deny any allegations and facts that are in dispute. Defendants cannot make bare denials, but must give reasons for why they are denying a particular fact or allegation. The defendant can also (as a way of giving reason for the denial) put forward a different version of events. Paragraphs mentioning alleged breaches in the Particulars of Claim will typically be denied, as otherwise the defendant will effectively be admitting that it was in the wrong.

For instance, consider a claim for breach of contract where the claimant argues that computers provided by the defendant were faulty. The defendant will deny that the duty to provide computers that were fit for purpose was breached, perhaps alleging in response that they were damaged during installation (which was not the responsibility of the defendant). They will, however, admit that the duty to provide computers that were fit for purpose existed.

"The Defendant denies paragraph 4. [*Reason for denial*]."

"The Defendant admits the first sentence of paragraph 4 but denies the second sentence of paragraph 4. [*Reason for denial*]."

3. Require proof

The defendant should require proof of any allegation or fact relating to something that the defendant did not know about (and could not have known about). The defendant will typically require proof of any causation points (such as any action taken by the claimant as a result of the alleged breach) or the quantification of the alleged loss/damage.

"The Defendant is unable to admit or deny paragraph 5 and as such requires proof."

Formatting

Introduction

In the introduction, the defendant should adopt the definition used in the Particulars of Claim so that the same defined terms can be used throughout (for sake of ease).

"The Defendant adopts the definitions used in the Particulars of Claim."

Main body

This is where the defendant will reply to the allegations made by the claimant in the Particulars of Claim (admit, deny or require proof).

Conclusion

At the end, the defendant should make a general statement to the effect that they are denying the claimant's right to the sum claimed. They could either be denying in full (they deny that anything is owed) or partially (if they are denying only in part).

"In the circumstances the Claimant is not entitled to the relief sought or any relief."

The name of the firm of solicitors who drafted the Defence should be inserted at the end of the Defence, before the Statement of Truth.

Statement of Truth

As with the Particulars of Claim, a Defence must contain a statement of truth. The same principle applies here as to the Particulars of Claim (see the *Particulars of Claim* section in the *Commencing a Claim* chapter in this module for more detail on Statements of Truth).

If signed by the actual party

"I believe that the facts stated in this Defence are true."

If signed by a person other than the actual party

"The Defendant believes that the facts stated in this Defence are true. I am duly authorised by the Defendant to sign this statement."

The example Defence on the next page is based upon the allegations made in the example Particulars of Claim included earlier in this module.

Civil Litigation

Defence: drafting example

IN THE HIGH COURT JUSTICE
QUEEN'S BENCH DIVISION

Claim number: 2021 HC 1712

BETWEEN

HELLOWAY GOLF LIMITED

Claimant

-and-

GIPPON STEEL LIMITED

Defendant

DEFENCE

1. The Defendant adopts the definitions used in the Particulars of Claim.

2. The Defendant admits paragraph 1.

3. The Defendant admits the first, second and third sentences of paragraph 2. The Defendant is unable to admit or deny the fourth and fifth sentences of paragraph 2 and accordingly requires proof.

4. The Defendant admits paragraph 3, paragraph 4, paragraph 5, and paragraph 6.

5. The Defendant denies paragraph 7. The Steel Alloy was of the agreed density of 7.9 kg/m^3. The Defendant submits that it was the way in which the Claimant subsequently dealt with the steel in its golf club production process that caused the Steel Alloy to decrease in density to 7.5m^3.

6. The Defendant denies paragraph 8 for the reasons set out in paragraph 5 of this Defence.

7. The Defendant cannot admit or deny paragraph 9, paragraph 10 and paragraph 11 and as such requires proof.

8. If, which is denied, the Defendant is found to be liable to the Claimant, the Claimant is required to prove the quantum of any loss and damage alleged to have been suffered. The Defendant therefore requires proof of paragraph 12 and paragraph 13.

9. In the circumstances, the Claimant is not entitled to the relief sought or any relief.

STRAND & OAK LLP

Statement of Truth

The Defendant believes that the facts stated in this Defence are true. I am duly authorised by the Defendant to make this statement.

Signed:

Larry Cox

Managing Director, Gippon Steel Limited

Served this day 28 August 2021 by Strand & Oak LLP, Solicitors for the Defendant.

Allocation and Case Management

This section continues where the previous left off; it covers the procedural aspects of a litigation claim once the claim has commenced and any Defence/Counterclaim has been issued and served. The court will first allocate the case to a track and give directions relating to the proceedings that will follow. This section will also outline the key management powers conferred upon the court in relation to costs and budgets.

Directions and Allocation

CPR Part 26 deals with the procedure governing the allocation of cases to particular tracks.

After the defendant has filed the Defence, the court will make an initial assessment of the track to which the claim should be allocated. Once the court has made a decision, it will serve a "Notice of Proposed Allocation" to both parties. This notice will contain a request that certain documents are sent back to the court, which will provide the court with the information necessary to properly evaluate the claim. These documents are:

1. **Directions Questionnaire**: the parties must file their Directions Questionnaire 28 days after the deemed service of the Notice of Proposed Allocation for the Fast-Track and Multi-Track and 14 Days for the Small Claims Track CPR 26.3(6).

2. **An agreed proposed directions order**: CPR 29.4 requires the parties to cooperate and attempt to agree on which directions they should request from the court. The agreed proposed directions (or, in the absence of agreement, each party's individual direction proposal) must be filed at the court no later than seven days before the case management conference.

3. **Costs budget:** parties must file (with the court) and exchange (with each other) their cost budgets 21 days before the first case management conference, unless the court orders otherwise CPR 3.13. Costs budgets are dealt with in more detail below under "Costs Management".

> **Track:** cases are allocated to a particular "track", depending on factors such as value and complexity. This is covered in more detail in the *Allocation to a track* section below.

> **Case Management Conference:** this is a meeting held to ensure that the real/significant issues have been identified and understood by the parties and the court. The aim is to narrow the issues before trial so that the case can be dealt with more efficiently. Case management conferences normally occur once a case has been allocated so that specific directions can be set for the conduct of the action that must be taken before trial.

Directions and the Directions Questionnaire

> **Directions**: directions are essentially instructions given to the parties by the court in advance to outline how the parties must prepare for the case. Directions will usually cover matters such as deadlines for the exchange and filing of documents, when and where hearings will take place, and how/when witness statements and/or expert reports should be exchanged. The court can also direct the parties to consider forms of alternative dispute resolution (and stay proceedings whilst they attempt to settle out of court).

The CPRs contain standard directions for the small claims track (found in the Appendix to PD 27) and the fast track (found in the Appendix to PD 28). No standard directions exist for the multi-track. It is advisable to skim through these appendices, as it will give you an idea of the matters usually covered by "directions".

The Directions Questionnaire is sent to each party and must be completed and returned to the court (as outlined above). The following issues are dealt with in the Directions Questionnaire:

- Which court the parties believe the case should be allocated to (this is where the parties can dispute the provisional allocation contained in the Notice of Proposed Allocation).
- The number of witnesses required (note that witness evidence is dealt with in the *Witnesses* chapter in this module).
- The type and number of experts required (note that expert directions and expert evidence are dealt with in the *Experts* chapter in this module).
- The estimated length of trial.
- Other facts and/or documents that the parties would like the judge to consider.
- A list of directions sought by the parties (the list should be agreed between the parties if possible).

Allocation to a track

There are three tracks to which a court can allocate a case: (1) the small claims track; (2) the fast track; and (3) the multi-track. The rules governing case allocation are set out in CPR 26.6. The court has full discretion to choose the track to which a case will be allocated, so there is no guarantee that a case will be allocated to a specific track purely because it fits the requirements.

Civil Litigation

Small Claims track

The small claims track is governed by CPR 26.6(1)+(2) + CPR 27. This track is suitable for:
- Personal injury cases.
- Certain cases between landlords and tenants.
- Any other case with a value of less than £10,000.

Fast track

The fast track is governed by CPR 26.6(4) + CPR 28. This track is suitable for:
- Claims worth more than £10,000 but less than £25,000.
- Cases that will not last longer than one day (5 hours).
- Cases in which only one expert per party will be necessary.

Therefore, if a case is worth £18,500 but two experts are required for each party, the fast track will not be suitable even though the value of the claim falls within the financial limit.

Multi-track

The multi-track is used for any case that does not fall within the other two categories.

Assessing the value of a claim

This is governed by CPR 26.8(2). The calculation of the value of a claim should disregard:
- Amounts not in dispute.
- Any claim for interest.
- Any alleged contributory negligence.

Court Powers and Sanctions

Key powers

The court has extensive powers to manage litigation proceedings. Below are some of the court's key case management powers:

General powers of management

CPR 3.1 contains a list of the court's case and cost management powers. Note that CPR 3.1(2)(m) is a "sweep-up" provision, furthering the extensive powers of the court by enabling it to take any step or make any order for the purpose of managing the case and furthering the overriding objective.

Power to make orders of its own initiative

CPR 3.3(3) allows the court to make orders on its own initiative, regardless of whether the parties have applied for the order or made representations in anticipation of an order being made.

Power to strike out a statement of case

The court has the power to strike out a statement of case pursuant to CPR 3.4(2)(a)+(b). Here, "strike out" means to exclude/eliminate the statement of case from the claim. This can be done it if it appears to the court that:
- The statement of case discloses no reasonable grounds for bringing or defending the claim (this is a high standard);
- The statement of case is an abuse of the court's process or is otherwise likely to obstruct the just disposal of the proceedings (this includes, for instance, vexatious claims or claims that have already been decided); or
- There has been a failure to comply with a rule, practice direction or court order (this could, for instance, include the failure to file or exchange documents on time).

Sanctions

The court has many options for sanctioning parties. For instance, it may sanction a party that has failed to comply with the CPRs, a court order and/or directions. Examples of such sanctions are:
- Striking out the whole or part of the case.
- Debarring a party from putting forward evidence CPR 35.13.
- Making costs orders (more details are contained in the *Pre-trial, Trial and Costs* chapter of this module).
- Decreasing or increasing interest on any sum.
- Order the party to pay a sum of money into court CPR 3.1(3)(a) + (5).
- Make an "unless" order.

> **"Unless" order:** the court will often not penalise a party immediately if that party breaches a rule/order/direction, and particularly not if it is that party's first misdemeanour. The court will instead make an "unless" order, stating that *unless* the party complies with the relevant rule within a specified time limit, the sanction will be enforced.

The court can also sanction a party that has failed to comply with a pre-action protocol and thus caused litigation to commence which might have been avoided had that litigant complied with that protocol.

Relief from sanctions (CPR 3.9)

If the court has sanctioned a party, CPR 3.9 contains a procedure by which that party can apply to be relieved from the sanction. An application for relief from sanctions must be supported by evidence CPR 3.9(2).

Guidance on how to apply CPR 3.9 was originally interpreted in the case of Mitchell v Newsgroup Newspapers, but was subsequently clarified in the case of Denton v TH White Ltd.

The court in Denton v TH White Ltd explained that the three-step test set out in Mitchell v Newsgroup Newspapers had been applied too harshly by the courts and set out the following steps for clarification:

1. **Assess the significance and seriousness of the party's non-compliance**: did the non-compliance affect or jeopardise the future conduct of the litigation? If the breach is not significant and serious → relief should be given. If it is, consider step 2.

2. **Did the party have a legitimate reason for the default?** The reason must be genuine, and simply lacking the time to properly comply is not a legitimate reason. If a legitimate reason exists → relief should be granted. If no such reason exists, consider step 3.

3. **Circumstances of the case:** if the breach is significant and serious, and the party lacks a genuine reason, the court must *only at this stage* evaluate all the circumstances of the case. The court must ensure that the case is dealt with justly and take into account the factors listed in CPR 3.9: litigation shall be conducted effectively and at a proportionate cost; and the court's role as enforcer of rules, orders and directions.

It is important to note however that courts do not view favourably parties who attempt to take advantage of minor breaches of the CPRs by opposing parties where such breaches have not prejudiced their position or jeopardised a hearing date.

Costs Management

The court manages costs throughout the proceedings. The purpose of the court's cost management powers is to ensure effective case management at a proportionate cost and to maintain transparency in line with the overriding objective. The court effectively decides which costs parties can incur (e.g. they can decide how much money a party can recover from money spent on legal advice, experts etc.). Costs are managed through the preparation and approval of costs budgets.

Costs budgets

> **Costs budget:** an estimate of the reasonable and proportionate costs (including disbursements) that the parties intend to incur during the proceedings CPR Glossary. The budget should cover the amount each party is likely to spend throughout the proceedings and should detail all anticipated costs, not just legal fees.

All parties must prepare a costs budget, file it at court and exchange it with the other parties. Unless the court orders otherwise, the costs budget will be filed with the Directions Questionnaire if the value of the claim is less than £50,000 CPR 3.13(1)(a), whilst in all other cases, the costs budget must be filed no later than 21 days before the first case management conference CPR 3.13(1)(b).

The budget is important, as it will be subject to approval by the court. If it is approved, this is an indication that the costs included in that budget will be recoverable, depending on the outcome of the case CPR 3.18. For instance, if the court makes a costs order in the claimant's favour, the claimant is likely only to be able to recover from the defendant the costs set out in its approved budget. For an explanation of the concept of costs orders, see the *Pre-trial, Trial and Costs* chapter of this module.

The approval of a costs budget is given in a cost management order. The court will state the extent to which the budgets prepared are approved CPR 3.15. If any part of the budget is not approved, this does not prohibit the parties from actually *incurring* the costs that have not been approved; they will however be very unlikely to recover those costs if proceedings are decided in their favour.

Revising the cost budgets

A party can revise (either increase or decrease) its budget in respect of future cost if significant developments in the litigation warrant such revisions, but those revisions must be submitted to the other parties and be agreed 3E PD 7.6. If the parties cannot agree, the amended budgets must be submitted to the court, together with a note of the changes made, the reasons for those changes, and any objections from the other parties. The court may approve, vary or reject the revisions.

Failure to file a cost budget

If a party fails to file a cost budget, the party will be treated as having filed a budget comprising only the applicable court fees CPR 3.14. This is a very draconian sanction, as court fees are very small in comparison to the costs a party will incur when receiving legal advice from solicitors and counsels.

Disclosure and Inspection

Disclosure and inspection are governed by CPR 31. During litigation proceedings, parties are under a duty to disclose certain categories of information so that each party is able to properly assess its position and likelihood of success. Note that there is an important distinction between "disclosure" and "inspection" in this context.

- **Disclosure:** telling the other party that you possess a particular document.

- **Inspection:** the other party actually accessing and reviewing the documents that have been disclosed.

Standard Disclosure

The court has a variety of options - a "menu" of sorts - for which method of disclosure should apply to proceedings. Depending on your LPC provider you may need a more thorough understanding of the different options included in this "menu". However, only "standard" disclosure is typically covered in detail on the LPC. This section will therefore focus on standard disclosure. However, make sure you recognise that other options exist, if only for the sake of comparison.

Standard disclosure is best dealt with by dissecting the relevant CPRs into 5 steps:

1. The meaning of *document*

"Document" is defined in CPR 31.4 as *"anything in which information is recorded"*. This is very wide and virtually anything is therefore a "document" for these purposes: an email, a letter, a USB stick etc.

2. Ascertain whether the document is within the party's control

Only documents within a party's control need to be disclosed. "Control" is defined in CPR 31.8 and this includes:

- Where the document is or was in the *physical possession* of the party.
- Where the party has or has had a *right to possess* the document.
- Where the party has or has had a legally enforceable *right to inspect or take copies* of the document.

3. Ascertain whether the document falls within the test for standard disclosure

The circumstances in which a party must disclose a document when standard disclosure applies are set out in CPR 31.6. A party is only required to disclose:

- Documents on which they will (or might) rely.
- Documents that adversely affect their own case, adversely affect another party's case, or support another party's case.
- Documents that they are required to disclose by a practice direction.

4. Does the party have a right to prevent another party from inspecting the document?

The general rule in CPR 31.3(1) is that *"a party to whom a document has been disclosed has a right to inspect it"*.

However, if the above criteria are fulfilled and the document is disclosed, there is still a possibility that the disclosing party can prevent the other party from "inspecting" it. Under such circumstances, although the other party will be informed of the relevant document's existence (i.e. "disclosure" will have taken place), they will be unable to look at (i.e. "inspect") it.

One exception to this (the most common exception dealt with on the LPC) is if the document is "privileged". See below for more details, including an overview of the different "heads of privilege".

5. In which part of the document list should the document be placed?

The disclosure procedure involves the parties exchanging a list of the documents that they are disclosing. An answer to an exam question dealing with disclosure should briefly set out in which part of the list a document should be referenced. The list has three parts.

- **Part 1:** documents over which the party has control and which they do not object to the other side inspecting.
- **Part 2:** documents over which the party has control, but which they object to the other side inspecting (e.g. on the basis that those documents are privileged).
- **Part 3:** documents that the party has had, but which are no longer in their control. For instance, if the party sent a letter to a bank, it no longer has control over the original version of that letter (the bank does). Therefore, even if the letter falls within the test for standard disclosure, the original letter should go in part 3 of the list. If the party has made an office copy however, the office copy of the letter should go in part 1 of the list.

Privilege

This chapter deals with the three most common heads of privilege. If a document falls within any of these three heads of privilege, the party will be able to prevent the other side from inspecting it. Privilege is one of the few Civil Litigation topics on the LPC that typically requires you to know some case law.

Legal advice privilege

> **Legal advice privilege:** communication between a lawyer and their client for the purpose of giving and/or receiving legal advice.

It is useful to break this definition down and apply case law to fully understand what documents will be caught by this head of privilege:

"Communication between lawyer and client"

- Parry v Newsgroup Newspaper: an attendance note (which is a non-confidential report) written by one party's solicitor concerning a conversation between the parties or anything that happened in court will not constitute "communication" for these purposes. "Communication" must be confidential to the party seeking to rely on this head of privilege.
- Three Rivers District Council v Governor of Bank of England (in the Court of Appeal): this case applied a narrow meaning to "client". The "client" for the purpose of legal advice privilege in this case was held to be a specific department within the bank, as opposed to the entire bank (meaning employees in other parts of the bank did not constitute "the client"). As a result, internal memorandums prepared by anyone/any department outside of the department that was a party to the proceedings did not constitute "communications between a lawyer and a *client*" and were thus not privileged.

"Purpose of giving and/or receiving legal advice"

- Balabel v Air India: introduced the principle of "continuum of communication". If a solicitor is retained to provide legal advice, any conversation between the lawyer and the client will be privileged. This is the case even if the conversation is ancillary to the purpose of giving legal advice. This applies so long as the nature of the information is confidential (see Parry v Newsgroup Newspaper above).
- Three Rivers District Council v Governor of Bank of England (in the House of Lords): a wide definition was given for "legal advice". It was concluded that this can include tactical, strategic and presentational advice. The lawyer gave "presentational advice" to their client. It was held that this was privileged as the lawyers had given the presentation through "legal spectacles" (the advice given in the presentation concerned tactics relating to the on-going litigation).
- Bank of Nova Scotia v Hellenic/"The Good Luck": if a client receives legal advice and then passes that information on to another individual within the company, the repetition of that advice will also be privileged communication (so long as it is not released publicly).

Litigation privilege

> **Litigation privilege:** communication between a lawyer and their client or between either of them and a third party, where the dominant purpose of such communication was to obtain advice, evidence or information relating to litigation which was reasonably in prospect at the time that the communication took place.

"Dominant purpose"

- Waugh v British Railway Board: if a document has two equal purposes, neither can be a dominant purpose (and therefore the document will not be privileged).
- Re Highgrade Traders: this case explained from whose perspective the "purpose" of a document should be established. It was held that it is the commissioner's purpose that is the relevant one for litigation privilege. The author's purpose is irrelevant.

"Litigation being reasonably in prospect"

- USA v Phillip Morris: there must have been a real likelihood that litigation would ensue on the matter at the time the communication took place. Foresight of a mere possibility of litigation at the time is not enough.

Without prejudice privilege

> **Without prejudice privilege:** "without prejudice" privilege typically applies to bona fide settlement offers made by one party to another, although it may also apply to communications made during pre-trial negotiations with the intention of reaching a settlement agreement. Solicitors typically write "without prejudice" on documents when they want this privilege to apply (although doing so does not guarantee that the document will be deemed privileged).

Rush and Tompkins v Greater London Council: the court will look to substance over form when establishing whether a document is a bona fide attempt to settle. The question to ask is whether the offer to settle is *genuine*: is the monetary amount reasonable in light of the total value of the claim? Is the timing of the offer reasonable? Does the tone and language suggest the party making the offer is genuinely open to negotiations or does it seem hostile? A document does not need to contain any *specific/standard* wording for this privilege to apply. Conversely, a document will not be privileged merely because it includes, for instance, *"without prejudice communication"* as a heading.

Waiver and redaction

Waiving privilege

A party can decide to waive privilege over a document (i.e. allow the other party to inspect the document despite it being privileged). If a particular document falls within any of the heads of privilege, but the party believes that the document would be a favourable one to disclose and use during the proceedings, they may decide to waive it for this reason.

Great Atlantic Insurance v Home Insurance established that a party can waive privilege over a whole document, but not only a part of it.

CPR 31.14 states that a party can inspect any documents mentioned in witness statements or expert reports. Privilege is therefore effectively waived if a privileged document is mentioned in a witness statement or an expert report.

Drafts of documents (e.g. draft defences or witness statements) are privileged. Once the final draft is submitted to the opposing party/the court, privilege is waived over that final version. However, the drafts remain privileged.

Redaction

Redaction means striking out a part/parts of a document that is being disclosed, preventing the other party from reading those specific parts whilst inspecting the document. There are strict and complex rules governing parties' freedom to redact. In summary, a party can redact:

- Irrelevant information in a document that is not privileged.

- Privileged parts of a document that contains both privileged and non-privileged information. Note that if a document contains both privileged and non-privileged information, the redacted version will be put in list 1, whereas the original version will be put in list 2 (see above concerning document lists).

Parties would typically want to redact commercially sensitive information. However, such information can only be redacted if it is either irrelevant or privileged.

Disclosure by mistake

If a party receives a privileged document by mistake, that document will only lose its "privileged" status if the receiving party reasonably thought (at the time of receiving it) that they were entitled to see it. The court's permission will be required to rely on such document in court however CPR 31.20.

Disclosure Procedure

The following is a simplified version of how the disclosure procedure works:

- Each party writes up a list of the documents that they are required to disclose. They then serve this list on the other party. The list must be in prescribed form (using **form N265**) and must contain a disclosure statement 31A PD.

- When a party receives the other party's document list, they must send a written notice if they wish to inspect any document(s) contained on the list. A party must allow inspection within 7 days of receiving a notice requesting inspection CPR 31.15.

- The duty to disclose documents applies throughout the proceedings, and it follows that if a party creates or comes across a new document that falls within the test of standard disclosure, they must serve a supplemental list on the other party CPR 31.11.

Witnesses

Witnesses and the evidence provided by them are important parts of the litigation proceedings. This section deals with what types of witness evidence are admissible in court, rules regarding hearsay evidence and the drafting of witness statements. Rules regarding witnesses are contained in CPR 32 and CPR 33.

Admissibility of Witness Evidence

Not all witness evidence can be admitted to the court in litigation proceedings. Admissibility of evidence is, in addition to the CPRs, also governed by the Civil Evidence Act 1995 ("CEA 95").

> **Admissible evidence:** evidence that a party is allowed to present in (and have considered by the) court.

The general rule is that all evidence relevant to the case is admissible. This rule, however, has important exceptions, particularly in relation to opinion and hearsay evidence.

Evidence can be given orally or otherwise (for instance, by video link CPR 32.3).

Opinion evidence

The general rule is that witnesses can only present evidence that is factual, and opinion evidence is therefore not admissible. There are two exceptions to this:

1. Perceived facts Civil Evidence Act 1972 s. 3(2)

Perceived facts are statements that help witnesses to recount their own perception of particular facts, although they are technically opinions. For instance:

- "The car was driving fast" • "It was hot outside" • "Tony seemed intoxicated"

2. Expert opinions Civil Evidence Act 1972 s. 3(3)

These are opinions given by an expert, for instance the opinion of a doctor as to the most likely cause of a patient's injury during a clinical negligence case. Expert evidence and opinion is dealt with further in the *Experts* chapter in this module.

Hearsay evidence

Rules regarding hearsay evidence are complicated and it is a difficult concept to understand. This handbook only provides a brief summary, and you must check with your LPC provider to find out the level of detail they expect you to know in relation to hearsay evidence. Courts treat hearsay evidence with caution, as it is less reliable than evidence given by the primary source. Hearsay evidence is governed by CPR 33.

> **Hearsay evidence:** hearsay evidence is a statement recounted in court to prove a matter relating to the case, where someone other than the witness presenting the statement originally made that statement. Imagine a trial where Mr Nandwani is a witness giving evidence in relation to whether a technician had been negligent when installing computers. Ms Patron was working with the technician when he installed the computers, but she died a week later. Prior to her death, she told Mr Nandwani that the technician had rushed his work and failed to install the computers properly. When Mr Nandwani presents Ms Patron's statement in court, this constitutes hearsay, as he is recounting/passing on someone else's statement/experience.

Admissibility of hearsay evidence

Hearsay evidence is admissible in civil proceedings pursuant to CEA 95 s.1 (note that it is not generally admissible in criminal proceedings however). The party seeking to use hearsay evidence must give notice to the other side that they intend to rely on evidence of a hearsay nature CEA 95 s.2. The rules governing such notice are set out in CPR 33.2. The notice must be included in the list of witnesses exchanged between the parties and must identify which pieces of evidence constitute hearsay (it is therefore not a *separate* notice but a note made in the list of witnesses).

Options for a party receiving notice of hearsay evidence

When a party receives notice that the other party intends to present and rely on hearsay evidence, there are a number of ways in which it can respond pursuant to the Civil Evidence Act 1995:

Civil Litigation

- Request further details or particulars of the hearsay evidence on which the other party is seeking to rely CPR 33.2(4)(b).

- Cross-examine the person who made the original statement CEA 95 s. 3 (in the example above, if Ms Patron had not died, the opposing party could have called for her to be cross-examined at trial).

- Challenge the weight the court attaches to the hearsay evidence CEA 95 s. 4. CEA 95 s. 4 sets out the factors to consider when assessing the weight of the hearsay evidence, such as whether it would have been reasonable for the party by whom the evidence was adduced to have produced the maker of the original statement as a witness.

- Attack the credibility of the person who made the original statement CEA 95 s. 5. A party who wishes to attack the original person's credibility must notify the party seeking to rely on the hearsay evidence that they intend to do so, no later than 14 days after the hearsay notice was served CPR 33.5.

Witness Statements

The parties will exchange witness statements prior to the trial and in accordance with the directions previously given by the court (in relation to how and when the exchange should take place). If a witness statement is not served before the deadline given by the court, the witness can only be called to give oral evidence if permitted to do so by the court CPR 32.10. Parties can, in accordance with CPR 29.5, agree between themselves (in writing) to extend any deadline given by the court for the exchange and filing of witness statements by up to 28 days without the need for court approval.

Witness statements are important. Witnesses are generally only allowed to present oral information at trial if that evidence was contained in the witness statements previously exchanged CPR 32.4. This is because the main purpose of a witness appearing at trial is to allow the opposing side to cross-examine him/her. The evidence to be presented by a witness at trial must therefore be outlined in a witness statement.

Drafting a witness statement

Some LPC providers commonly ask students to draft, or re-draft, a witness statement. This section provides an outline of what to consider when doing so. A majority of the formal requirements for a witness statement can be found in CPR 32.8 and 32 PD 17-20. The LPC typically deals with two types of witness statements: witness statements for the main proceedings and witness statements for interim applications (there are differences between these that must be considered). Note that interim applications are dealt with in the *Interim Applications and Injunctions* chapter of this module, and you may find it useful to read that chapter prior to studying this section on drafting a witness statement.

You will find an example witness statement after this chapter. It is advisable to consider the following points in conjunction with that example.

Heading

The heading contains the name of the parties, the court, and the following wording: "WITNESS STATEMENT OF [*first name and surname of witness*]". You should check that the names and titles of the parties are correct, and that the correct court is listed. For a witness statement for **an interim application**, the parties should be referred to as Applicant and Respondent. For a witness statement for the **main proceedings**, the parties should be referred to as Claimant and Defendant.

Corner endorsement

This is the same for both types of witness statement. In the upper right hand corner of the witness statement, six things should be noted:

1. The party for which the witness is giving evidence: Applicant (for **interim applications**)/Claimant (for **main proceedings**) or Respondent (for **interim applications**)/Defendant (for **main proceedings**).

2. Name of witness (first initial and last name).

3. Number of witness statement (if it is the witness' first witness statement for the proceedings/interim application, this should be "First").

4. Number of documents/exhibits: state the witness' initials and the number of documents. Here, "documents" means any documents annexed to the witness statement.

5. Date of witness statement.

6. Claim number.

Opening statement

A witness statement should contain an opening statement to the following effect:

"I [*name of witness*], of [*witness' address*] will say as follows:"

Some interim applications (e.g. freezing injunctions, explained in the *Interim Applications and Injunctions* chapter of this module) require witnesses to give evidence under oath. When this is the case, the opening statement should acknowledge this:

"I [*name of witness*], of [*address*] will make oath and say as follows:"

The address used should be the witness' place of residence, unless they are giving evidence in their professional capacity in which case it should be their business address/the business address of their employer.

Introductory paragraph

After the opening statement, the witness should introduce their role as a witness. The witness must acknowledge that they make any statements from matters within their own knowledge and belief, and that they will indicate where any statement is based upon knowledge they have received from another person or source.

"I make this witness statement from matters within my own knowledge and belief save where the contrary appears. Where I refer to matters of which I have been told by others, those matters are true to the best of my knowledge and the source of my information appears."

For **interim applications** only, the witness should also refer to the application that the party (applicant) is making and acknowledge that they are authorised by that party to make the witness statement.

"I am authorised by the Applicant to make this witness statement in support of an application for [*the purpose of the application should be briefly set out here*]."

Main body

The main body contains the evidence that the witness is to present orally at the trial. The following points are useful to consider when drafting or re-drafting the main body:

- The witness is effectively telling a story. Use the facts and dates provided to you and ensure that the witness statement presents the "story" in a logical and chronological order. Ensure paragraphs do not duplicate information.

- Ensure that all material facts are included in the witness statement and include any other relevant facts and dates.

- If the witness is referring to a document, this document must be annexed (i.e. attached) as an exhibit. Each exhibit will have a mark. Thus, if a document is mentioned, you should add: "I refer to copies of [*the document referred to, e.g. a contract*] marked [*exhibits are generally marked with the initials of the witness and the number of the exhibit*]."

- The witness statement must not contain any irrelevant or inadmissible information. Any statement that is irrelevant and/or inadmissible must be struck out (such as opinion evidence or privileged information).

Request (ONLY for interim applications)

In an interim application, the witness will end his/her statement by asking the judge to grant the application in favour of the Applicant. The party making the application will, together with the witness statement, provide the court with a draft of the order it is seeking the court to make. The witness should refer to this draft. Draft orders are dealt with in more detail in the *Interim Applications and Injunctions* chapter of this module.

"I would therefore ask this Honourable Court to make an order in the terms of the draft, including that the Respondent [*brief sentence on what the order is seeking to achieve, e.g. "pays security of costs to the court"*]."

Verification/statement of truth

The witness must verify that they believe the information they have provided is true.

"I believe the facts stated in this witness statement are true."

General points

There are a number of format and consistency points you should look out for when re-drafting a witness statement. Here is a good checklist for format and consistency:

- Check that the name/division of the court is accurate.

- Check that 'Defendant' and 'Claimant' is used in the correct place and the "C"/"D" are capitalised where appropriate.

- Check that the dates correspond with the ones given in the facts.

- Check that the spelling of names and parties correspond with the ones given in the facts.

- Check that it refers to the same object/person/document in a consistent manner (i.e. using the same word or phrase) throughout the document.

Civil Litigation

Witness statement: drafting example

Assume that Larry Cox, the managing director of Helloway Golf, believes the defendant's Defence to be weak and accordingly applies for summary judgment. This is a very simplified version of a witness statement and the issues covered, and is mainly to be used to understand the structure of a witness statement.

Claimant
L Cox
First
LC1
10.10.15
Claim number: 2021 HC 1712

IN THE HIGH COURT JUSTICE
QUEEN'S BENCH DIVISION

BETWEEN

HELLOWAY GOLF LIMITED

Claimant

-and-

GIPPON STEEL LIMITED

Defendant

WITNESS STATEMENT OF LARRY COX

I, Larry Cox, technical engineer, of 55 Downson Road, York, will say as follows:

1. I am the managing director of the Claimant. I make this witness statement from matters within my own knowledge or belief save where the contrary appears. Where I refer to matters of which I have been told by others, those matters are true to the best of my knowledge and the source of my information appears.

2. I am authorised by the Claimant to make this witness statement in support of an application for summary judgment.

3. It is clear to me that the Defendant has no real prospect of successfully defending the claim for the following reasons. *[The witness will set out their reasons].*

4. Moreover, there is no other compelling reason why the case should be disposed of at trial. *[The witness will set out their reasons].*

5. In the circumstances, I submit to this Honourable Court for the reasons set out above that the Defendant is liable for the sum claimed and that the Claimant's application should therefore be granted and judgment be given in favour of the Claimant for the full sum due together with interest on that sum.

Statement of Truth

I believe that the facts stated in this witness statement are true.

Signed:

Larry Cox

Managing Director, Gippon Steel Limited

Dated this day 10 September 2021

Experts

Parties may use experts and expert evidence throughout the proceedings. They need the court's permission to do so, and this section deals with the rules governing the appointment of experts and the use of expert reports. Experts and expert evidence is dealt with in CPR 35. "Guidance for the instruction of experts in civil claims 2014" published by The Civil Justice Council ("Expert Guidance 14") will be referred to in this chapter.

Role of Experts in Litigation Proceedings

The court only has knowledge about the law and thus typically needs help to assess cases by experts in various fields. For instance, if a party claims that land it has purchased is worth less than expected, the court is not in a position to decide what the value of that land is. The court will need to rely on an expert, such as a land surveyor, to ascertain what the value of the land is. Although it is the parties to the proceedings that *instruct* experts, any experts instructed have an overriding duty/obligation to aid the court CPR 35.3.

Adducing expert evidence in the court

A party can instruct as many experts as it likes, but it must receive permission from the court to present the evidence given by those experts at trial CPR 35.4. Using experts generates additional costs and can result in lengthier trials. The court is therefore under a duty pursuant to CPR 35.1 to only permit expert evidence that is reasonably required to resolve the proceedings (in the interest of fulfilling the overriding objective).

The Directions Questionnaire will ask the parties whether they wish to instruct experts and if so, whether they intend to adduce the evidence given by those experts at trial. At this stage, the parties must also inform the court of the estimated cost of using experts, the issues that experts will be instructed to resolve, the experts' field(s) of expertise and (if known) the names of any experts that the parties are considering instructing CPR 35.4(2). Direction Questionnaires are dealt with in more detail in the *Allocation and Case Management* chapter of this module.

Separate experts or a single joint expert?

> **Single Joint Expert:** defined in CPR 35.2(2) as an "expert instructed to prepare a report for the court on behalf of two or more of the parties (including the claimant) to the proceedings".

In the interest of the overriding objective, the parties should attempt to agree to instruct a "single joint expert" (SJE). It is possible to have a mix of both SJEs and individual experts, depending on the nature and variety of the issues at hand.

Even in the absence of an agreement between the parties, the court can direct that the evidence is to be given by an SJE CPR 35.7. When considering whether to make such direction, the court must consider:

- The overriding objective (the court will typically only allow individual experts in the absence of special circumstances).
- Factors in 35 PD 7. These include the amount in dispute, the complexity of the issues at hand and the importance of the particular issues to the parties.

Procedure

Expert directions

If the parties want to use experts, they will ask the court to give directions relating to such experts at the directions stage (the concept of directions is explained in more detail in the *Allocation and Case Management* chapter of this module). Below are examples of the types of expert-related directions that parties may seek from the court:

- **Single or separate joint experts**: can the parties instruct single or separate experts (or a combination of the two)?
- **Instructions:** when, by whom, and in relation to which issues, should experts be instructed?
- **Giving evidence:** will the expert(s) be required to provide a written report, oral evidence at trial, or both?
- **Timing:** when is the deadline for exchanging expert reports?
- **Meetings:** can the parties attend any meetings that are scheduled to occur between experts? See the *Discussions between experts* section below for more detail.

Expert reports

An expert (who has been permitted to adduce evidence in court) must produce an expert report. The parties must exchange reports made by their own experts, and this will be done in accordance with the directions given by the court. If a party fails to pass on an expert report to the other side, that party will only be allowed to use the evidence contained in that report with the court's permission CPR 35.13. 35 PD 3 contains the requirements for an expert report.

Civil Litigation

Each party provides instructions for its expert(s) and these instructions will be referred to by the expert(s) in the expert report. A party's instructions to an expert are *not* privileged. However, it is unlikely that the court will allow a party to inspect original instructions sent by the other side to one of its experts unless the court considers that the summary of those instructions in the expert report is either inaccurate or incomplete CPR 35.10(3)+(4). The possibility (albeit slight) that the other party will be able to inspect the original instructions will however serve to encourage parties to provide experts with accurate and unbiased instructions.

Discussions between experts

In order to save costs and unnecessary trial time, the court has the power to order the parties' experts to meet and identify the relevant issues in the case together CPR 35.12(1) and attempt to reach an agreed opinion on the issues requiring their expertise. The purpose of meetings between experts is not to usurp the role of judges by deciding the case. The conclusion of the meeting(s) is simply supposed to guide the judges in making their decision.

The courts can then ask the experts to produce a joint statement setting out the issues on which they agree/disagree CPR 35.12(3). Any agreement reached between experts as a result of discussions will not bind the parties, unless the parties have agreed to be bound CPR 35.12(5). However, Expert Guidance 14 paragraph 80 suggests parties should be wary of disagreeing to be bound, as any joint statement from the experts is admissible in court. If a party does not agree, this could lead to adverse consequences in terms of costs and that party's credibility.

35 PD 9.4 states that unless agreed by the court or all the parties and experts, the parties and/or their lawyers may not attend the discussions between experts.

Questions to experts

A party is allowed to ask the other party's expert(s) questions after exchange of the expert reports. Such questions must be sent in writing within 28 days of the expert report being served CPR 35.6. The purpose is mainly to clarify anything contained in the expert report. The expert receiving the questions does not have to reply within a particular time frame, but if he/she does not reply, the party seeking to rely on that expert's report could be prohibited from doing so CPR 35.6(4). That party could also be penalised by not being allowed to have that expert's fees recovered if they win the case.

Expert's change of opinion

If an expert changes his/her view after producing a report, this should be communicated to all parties without delay 35 PD 2.5. In addition, if a party decides not to rely on a certain expert's report, the other side may still rely on it CPR 35.11. If a party commissions an expert report and later believes that report is unfavourable to their case, that party may either try to discredit that report or attempt to convince the court to place less weight on it.

Unfavourable reports by a single joint expert

If the court has ordered the parties to use an SJE and their report is unfavourable to one of the parties, that party could:

- Challenge the SJE in cross-examination. It is acceptable to informally engage another expert in order to get ammunition for this cross-examination, although it may be difficult to recover the costs of doing so if the party is later successful (see the *Pre-trial, Trial and Costs* chapter of this module for more information on how costs work).

- The party could also informally commission another report from a different expert (advisory expert) and present this report to the SJE before the court hearing in an attempt to get him/her to change his/her mind.

- A party could instruct another expert, but would need the court's permission to have that evidence included at the trial CPR 35.4. Note that the court will only ever allow this in exceptional circumstances, and if the first report is also disclosed; this prevents parties from "expert shopping". It is also a costly way of dealing with this scenario.

If the court has ordered an SJE to be used, and it is favourable to one of the parties, that party could:

- Consider serving a "Notice to Admit Facts" on the other party.

- Consider commencing new rounds of informal negotiations.

> **Notice to Admit Facts**: CPR 32.18 allows a party to serve notice on the other requiring them to admit that certain proposed "facts" are true. If the party receiving such notice does not admit to the truth of those facts, and such facts are subsequently proven to be true at trial, the receiving party may face adverse costs consequences. Such notices must be served no later than 21 days before trial.

Settlement and Part 36 Offers

Part 36 Offers are aimed at encouraging parties to make/accept settlement offers. Settling a case saves both time and costs; the incentives to settle that underpin the litigation system therefore help to further the overriding objective. This chapter explains both claimants' and defendants' Part 36 offers, and how costs are likely to be awarded when such offers have been made. It also includes a brief section on Settlement Agreements.

Part 36 Offers, as the name indicates, are dealt with in CPR Part 36. They may seem confusing at first, but understanding the underlying logic will ensure you will be able to effectively answer a question on Part 36 offers in an exam.

Making and Accepting a Part 36 Offer

A Part 36 offer is simply an offer to settle a case, using a monetary incentive. For instance, the claimant can inform the defendant that they will accept £50,000 to settle the proceedings or the defendant could offer to pay the claimant £40,000 to settle the proceedings. If the other party accepts an offer, the proceedings will be stayed and the claim will not continue to trial CPR 36.14(5).

A Part 36 offer can be made by either party and must be in writing. To be valid, the offer must adhere to the specifications set out in CPR 36.5: it must be set out in writing; it must be clear that it is made pursuant to CPR 36; it must state whether it relates to all or part of the claim and whether it includes any counterclaim(s); and it must specify a "relevant period". If these requirements are not complied with, the offer might not have Part 36 consequences (see below for more information on these potential consequences). However, the court has discretion to order that Part 36 consequences apply regardless.

Part 36 offers are deemed to be "without prejudice save as to costs" CPR 36.16, meaning any admissions contained in such offers are privileged. Until the case has been decided, the parties must not communicate to the trial judge the fact that a Part 36 offer has been made or the terms of such offer, unless any of the exceptions set out in CPR 36.16(3) apply.

> 📖 **"Relevant period" in a Part 36 offer**: the "relevant period" must be 21 days or more, but can otherwise be specified by the offeror CPR 36.5(1)(c). This period is important for the purpose of withdrawing or amending an offer (see below) and for determining when any Part 36 cost consequences start applying. If the offer is not accepted, those cost consequences will start running from the expiry of the relevant period (this is illustrated below in the *Consequences of Rejecting a Part 36 Offer* section). Note that the relevant period will start once the offer is served on the other party.

The other party can then accept a Part 36 offer by serving a written notice of acceptance CPR 36.11(1).

Withdrawing or amending a Part 36 offer

It is not possible to withdraw or amend a Part 36 offer that has already been accepted. If a party wishes to withdraw or amend a Part 36 offer that has not yet been accepted, the offeror must serve a "notice of withdrawal" or "notice of amendment" to the offeree and following applies:

Withdrawing/amending before the end of the relevant period

- If the offeror wants to withdraw the offer or amend it to make it *less advantageous* to the offeree, and the offeree (after having received the notice of withdrawal/amendment) accepts the (non-amended) original offer before the end of the relevant period, the offer can only be withdrawn/amended if the court permits it CPR 36.10(2)(b). The court will typically not permit such withdrawal/amendment unless the offeror can prove a sufficient change in circumstances. However, if the offeree has not served notice of acceptance of the (non-amended) original offer by the *expiry* of the relevant period, the offeror's notice of withdrawal/amendment then takes effect.

- If the offeror wants to amend their Part 36 offer to make it *more advantageous* to the offeree, the offer will be treated as a *new* Part 36 offer, so a new relevant period will commence CPR 36.9(5).

Withdrawing/amending after the end of the relevant period

- The offeror can withdraw and amend (either to make it more or less advantageous) at any time.

Consequences of Rejecting a Part 36 Offer

Part 36 incentivises parties to make settlement offers by: (a) conferring a benefit on those who make sensible proposals that are subsequently rejected by the other party; and (b) penalising parties that reject reasonable settlement offers in favour of proceeding to trial. These benefits and penalties are discussed further in the *Consequences of Rejecting a Part 36 Offer* section below.

Civil Litigation

The incentivising element of Part 36 becomes clear when considering the consequences for parties that have wrongly rejected Part 36 offers. The consequences will depend upon the difference between the amount offered in settlement and the amount actually awarded at trial CPR 36.17 (this is how the court determines whether the rejection was reasonable).

Offer made by the claimant and rejected by the defendant

Consequences where the judgment against the defendant is *at least as advantageous* to the claimant as the claimant's Part 36 offer has been

This is the scenario addressed by CPR 36.17(1)(b). If the claimant has offered to settle for a sum that is *the same or less* than what they were subsequently awarded at trial, the defendant will be punished for being unreasonable. This is because the defendant could have avoided going to trial and would in no way have suffered adverse consequences from doing so (thus saving time and costs, in accordance with the overriding objective).

The defendant will be punished in accordance with CPR 36.17(4) for the period between the last day on which the defendant could have accepted the offer (the end of the "relevant period") and the day of the trial. For this period, the defendant may have to:

- Pay costs on an indemnity basis (see the *Pre-trial, Trial and Costs* chapter in this module for an explanation of the difference between costs on an indemnity basis and costs on a standard basis) CPR 36.17(4)(b)-(c).

- Pay interest on any sums awarded at a rate not exceeding 10% above the base rate CPR 36.17(4)(a).

- Pay an additional amount up to 10% of the amount awarded (not exceeding £75,000).

These are only maximum penalties however, and the court has full discretion to impose no penalties if it considers the imposition of penalties unjust in the circumstances.

For the period starting with the commencement of the claim and ending with the trial, the normal costs rules will apply in accordance with CPR 44.2, i.e. the unsuccessful party (the defendant) pays the successful party's (the claimant's) costs. Costs awards are explained in more detail in the *Pre-trial, Trial and Costs* chapter of this module.

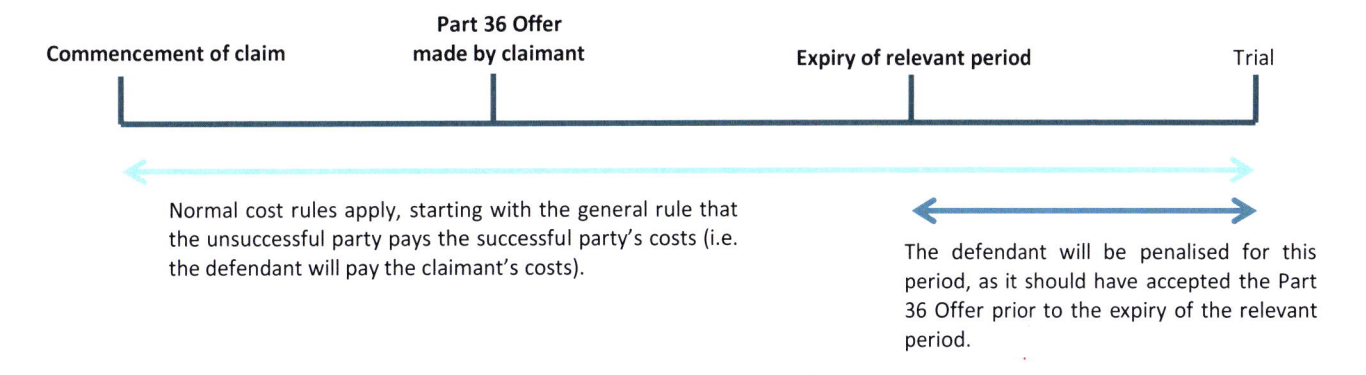

Commencement of claim	Part 36 Offer made by claimant	Expiry of relevant period	Trial

Normal cost rules apply, starting with the general rule that the unsuccessful party pays the successful party's costs (i.e. the defendant will pay the claimant's costs).

The defendant will be penalised for this period, as it should have accepted the Part 36 Offer prior to the expiry of the relevant period.

Where the judgment against the defendant is less advantageous to the claimant than in the claimant's offer

In this scenario there will be no adverse consequences for the defendant, as the result at trial indicates that the defendant was not unreasonable in rejecting the claimant's offer. Normal cost rules will apply for the period starting with the commencement of the claim and ending with the trial date, i.e. the unsuccessful party (the defendant) will pay the successful party's (the claimant's) costs CPR 44.2.

No judgment against the defendant

In this scenario there will be no adverse consequences for the defendant, as the result at trial indicates that the defendant was not unreasonable in rejecting the claimant's offer. Normal cost rules will apply for the period starting with the commencement of the claim and ending with the trial, i.e. the unsuccessful party (the claimant) will pay the successful party's (the defendant's) costs CPR 44.2.

Claimant's Part 36 Offer

A claimant has made a valid Part 36 offer to the defendant, stating that it will accept £100,000 to settle the proceedings. Consider the following two scenarios: (1) the judge awards the claimant £100,000 at trial; (2) the judge awards the claimant £80,000 at trial.

Scenario (1): the defendant has unreasonably rejected a sensible settlement offer. It could have paid the same following the claimant's Part 36 offer and consequently saved time and costs by avoiding trial. CPR 36.17(1)(b) therefore applies and the defendant will likely be penalised pursuant to CPR 36.17(4).

Scenario (2): the defendant has rejected a settlement offer that has proved to be unreasonable. The claimant's offer required a greater payment than was subsequently awarded at trial (the defendant would have had to pay more had they accepted the offer). Part 36 therefore has no effect and the defendant will not be penalised for rejecting the offer.

Offer made by the defendant and rejected by the claimant

Where the claimant fails to obtain a judgment *more advantageous* than a defendant's offer

This scenario is addressed by CPR 36.17(1)(a). If the claimant wins but is awarded the same amount or less than the defendant offered, the claimant will be punished for being unreasonable (even though they have won the case). This is because the claimant could have avoided going to trial and would in no way have suffered adverse consequences from doing so (thus saving time and costs, in accordance with the overriding objective).

The court may make a "split costs" order to punish the claimant, in accordance with CPR 36.17(3), for the period between the last day on which the claimant could have accepted the offer (the end of the "relevant period") and the trial date. Note that these are only maximum penalties however, and the court has full discretion not to award any penalties if it considers it unjust to do so.

> **Split Costs Order:** this involves the court ordering the defendant to pay the claimant's costs for the period between the commencement of the claim and the expiry of the "relevant period" (in accordance with the normal cost rules in CPR 44.2), and ordering the claimant to pay all costs thereafter up to the trial date. The claimant may also be further penalised by the court ordering them to pay interest on those costs. The claimant (despite being the successful party) has to pay costs for the later (wasted) part.

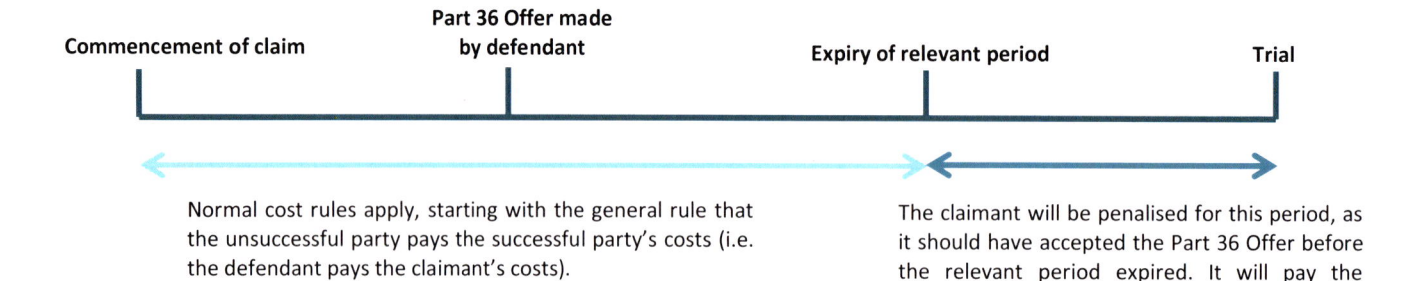

Commencement of claim	Part 36 Offer made by defendant	Expiry of relevant period	Trial

Normal cost rules apply, starting with the general rule that the unsuccessful party pays the successful party's costs (i.e. the defendant pays the claimant's costs).

The claimant will be penalised for this period, as it should have accepted the Part 36 Offer before the relevant period expired. It will pay the defendant's costs (plus interest) for this period.

Where the claimant obtains a judgment *more advantageous* than a defendant's offer

In this scenario there will be no adverse consequences for the claimant, as the result at trial indicates that the claimant was not unreasonable in rejecting the defendant's offer. Normal cost rules will apply for the period starting with the commencement of the claim and ending with the trial, i.e. the defendant (the unsuccessful party) will pay the claimant's (the successful party's) costs CPR 44.2.

No judgment against the defendant

If the claimant loses and is awarded nothing, the defendant has technically "won". Normal costs rules apply and the unsuccessful party (the claimant) will pay the successful party's (the defendant's) costs CPR 44.2. Arguably CPR 36.17(1)(a) applies here as well, since the claimant has failed to obtain a judgment more advantageous than the defendant's Part 36 Offer. Although the defendant is likely to have all of its costs paid, it may also be rewarded for making a reasonable offer to the claimant in the interests of avoiding a trial. For instance, the claimant may be ordered to pay interest on the defendant's costs for the period starting with the expiry of the relevant period and ending with the trial.

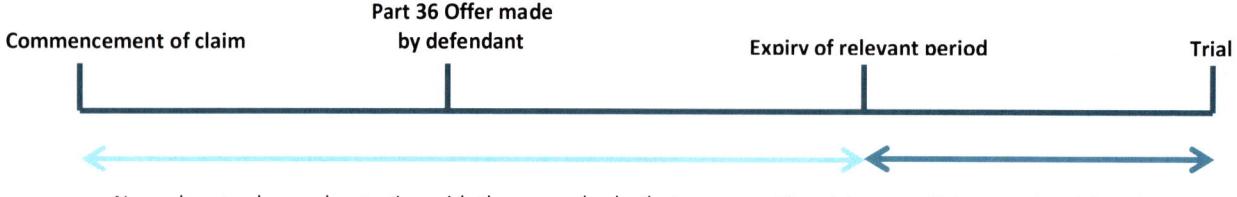

Commencement of claim	Part 36 Offer made by defendant	Expiry of relevant period	Trial

Normal cost rules apply, starting with the general rule that the unsuccessful party pays the successful party's costs (i.e. the claimant pays the defendant's costs).

The claimant will be penalised for this period, as it should have accepted the Part 36 Offer before the relevant period expired. For instance, it may have to pay interest on the defendant's costs for this period.

A defendant has made a valid Part 36 offer to the claimant, stating that it will pay £100,000 to settle the proceedings. Consider the following two scenarios: (1) the judge awards the claimant £100,000 at trial; (2) the judge awards the claimant £120,000 at trial.

In scenario (1), the claimant has unreasonably rejected a sensible settlement offer. It could have received the same amount without going to trial, consequently saving time and costs. **CPR 36.17(1)(a)** therefore applies and the claimant may be punished pursuant to **CPR 36.17(3)**.

In scenario (2), the claimant was not unreasonable in rejecting the earlier settlement offer, which was lower than the amount the claimant was subsequently awarded at trial (the claimant would have been paid less had they accepted the offer). Part 36 therefore has no effect and the claimant will not be punished.

Where both parties have made an offer

Where both parties have made an offer, and neither offer has been accepted, you must establish which offer takes effect.

Where the judgment against the defendant is at least as advantageous to the claimant as the claimant's offer

Here the claimant's offer will take effect and the defendant will be punished for unreasonably rejecting it (see above).

Where there is no judgment against the defendant or where the claimant fails to obtain a judgment more advantageous than a defendant's offer

Here the defendant's offer will take effect and the claimant will be punished for unreasonably rejecting it (see above).

Where the claimant has won less than their own offer, but more than the defendant's offer

Neither offer will take effect, as neither party has been unreasonable. Costs will be awarded under the CPR 44.2 principle.

Claimant's Part 36 Offer

The claimant has made a Part 36 offer of £200,000 and the defendant has made a Part 36 offer of £100,000. Both offers remain open at the time of trial. Consider these three circumstances: (1) the judge awards £300,000 to the claimant; (2) the judge awards £150,000 to the claimant; (3) the judge awards £100,000 to the claimant.

Scenario (1): the claimant has won more than the amount it previously offered to the defendant. The claimant's offer therefore takes effect **CPR 36.17(1)(b)** and the defendant may be punished in accordance with **CPR 36.17(4)**. The defendant's offer will not take effect since it offered less than the amount awarded to the claimant at trial.

Scenario (2): neither offer takes effect. The claimant has been awarded less than the amount in its Part 36 offer to the defendant, but more than the amount offered in the defendant's Part 36 offer. Neither party has therefore been unreasonable in rejecting the respective offers.

Scenario (3): the claimant has won an amount equal to that offered by the defendant in its Part 36 offer. Therefore the defendant's offer takes effect **CPR 36.17(1)(a)** and the claimant will be punished in accordance with **CPR 36.17(3)**. The claimant's offer does not take effect since its Part 36 offer was higher than the amount it was subsequently awarded at trial.

Settlement

The Part 36 procedure is not the only means by which parties can settle a claim. Settlement can also arise simply as a result of communication and negotiation between the parties. Settlement can also be the result of an alternative dispute resolution procedure, for instance mediation. Different types of alternative dispute resolutions are outlined in the *Alternative Dispute Resolution* chapter of this module.

What the court can order following a (non-Part 36) settlement offer:

- Stay the proceedings.

- Dismiss the claim. This would mean that the claimant could never commence proceedings on the same issue again.

- Make a consent order (see below).

- Discontinue the claim. If this is ordered, the claimant can later commence new proceedings on the same issue.

Nature of a Settlement Agreement

Whether a Settlement Agreement is binding is a question of normal contractual principles (i.e. offer, acceptance, consideration and intention to create legal relations). If a settlement is reached after proceedings have commenced, the court must be notified. In order to enforce the Settlement Agreement, the innocent party would have to sue the party in breach for breach of contract and apply for summary judgment. To avoid this, it is usually advisable for parties who have reached an agreement to request that the court makes a "consent order".

> **Consent order:** once the parties have agreed to settle a claim, a consent order can be used to set out the terms of the settlement for evidential purposes. If one party were to then breach these terms, the other party would have greater enforcement options available than would have been the case had the parties simply entered into a contractual settlement agreement (in which case, the only available remedy would be to pursue a claim for breach of contract).

If the parties are concerned about confidentiality, they may wish to use a "Tomlin order" instead.

> **"Tomlin" order**: a type of consent order used when the parties wish to keep the terms of the settlement agreement confidential. It is also used when the terms of the settlement go beyond that which the court can generally order as part of the proceedings. A Tomlin order will contain two parts: (1) the public part (40B PD 3.5 states that this part must contain details of any payment that is to be made out of court and details of the assessment and/or payment of costs); and (2) the private schedule (which should contain any terms of the agreement that the parties wish to keep confidential).

Pre-trial, Trial and Costs

Pre-trial

The following is a brief summary of the steps to take and the considerations to make in the period leading up to the trial:

Pre-trial checklist

A pre-trial checklist (**form N170**) will be sent to each party by the court at least 14 days before the deadline for filing it. The deadline for the filing of the pre-trial checklist will have been given as part of the court's directions earlier in the proceedings, and will be no later than 8 weeks before the start of the trial 29 PD 8.1.

If both parties fail to file a pre-trial checklist before the deadline, the court will make an "unless" order to the effect that if the parties do not file their pre-trial checklists within seven days of that order, the claim (including any defence and/or counterclaim) will be struck out CPR 29.6(3) and 29 PD 8.3(1). If only one party fails to file the pre-trial checklist, the court is unlikely to strike out the claim, and may instead give further directions CPR 29.6(4) + 29 PD 8.3(2).

Directions

Once both parties have filed their pre-trial checklist, the court will give final directions as to the date and place of trial, and any other directions in relation to pre-trial matters. These can either be given at a hearing or at a pre-trial review.

> **Pre-trial review**: this is a hearing conducted up to ten weeks before a trial. The purpose is to: ensure that the parties have complied with any court orders and directions; fix the trial timetable (if this has not already been done); and enable the court to give directions for the conduct of the trial.

Trial bundle

The claimant must file a trial bundle containing the documents to which references will be made at the trial or in other hearings. It must be filed by the claimant not more than 7 days and not less than 3 days before the start of the trial CPR 39.5(2).

Skeleton arguments and list of authorities

These are required for High Court trials and are prepared by both parties. The skeleton arguments provide summaries of the legal arguments that the parties will present at the trial, and each skeleton will include a list of the authorities that the parties intend to rely on whilst making their arguments.

Settlement

Settlements often occur close to the commencement of a trial, as this is when the parties have a better idea of the strengths/weaknesses of their cases and tend to contemplate the very substantial costs of trial. Parties should reconsider settlement and whether they should make a Part 36 offer.

Notices to Admit Facts

The parties should consider whether they should serve any notices to admit facts on the other side (this must be done at least 21 days before the hearing). See the *Experts* chapter of this module for an explanation of Notices to Admit Facts.

Summoning witnesses

Parties should ensure they summon reluctant witnesses who may otherwise fail to attend the trial. A witness summons is a document issued by the court that legally requires a witness to attend court to give evidence or produce documents for the court.

Brief to Counsel

The "brief" is the document given to counsel containing his/her instructions. The brief fee (the fee covering the preparation for, and first day of, trial) is normally not refundable. Parties therefore often reconsider settlement immediately before delivering briefs.

Trial

The general rule is that a hearing is to be held in public CPR 39.2(1). However, a hearing or any part of it may be in private in certain circumstances, for instance if it involves confidential information (including information relating to personal financial matters) and publicity would damage that confidentiality CPR 39.2(3)(c). Below is a brief summary of the trial procedure in civil proceedings.

Civil Litigation

Opening speech: by claimant's advocate. This is not necessary and can be dispensed with by the judge 29 PD 10.2.

⬇

Claimant's evidence called: the claimant's counsel will examine the claimant's witnesses, but cannot use leading questions. The defendant's counsel can then cross-examine those witnesses and may use leading questions when doing so. The claimant's counsel can then re-examine those witnesses, but still cannot use leading questions.

⬇

Closing speech: the defendant's counsel will make a closing speech.

⬇

Defendant's evidence called: the defendant's counsel will examine the defendant's witnesses, but cannot use leading questions. The claimant's counsel can then cross-examine those witnesses and may use leading questions when doing so. The defendant's counsel can then re-examine those witnesses, but still cannot use leading questions.

⬇

Judgment: The judge can give judgment immediately or reserve it. Once judgment has been given the judge will draw up an order and serve it on both parties.

> 📖 **Leading questions:** questions that prompt or encourage particular answers/responses. For instance, a leading question could begin with the phrase "isn't it right that...".

Costs

A judge must also make a decision as to who will pay the costs incurred by each party throughout the proceedings. The court will address this issue at a separate hearing, *after* judgment has been given. The judge can decide to make no order at all, in which case each party will have to pay for their own costs. Costs and cost orders are dealt with in CPR 44 and the following are the key rules that you should consider when answering questions on costs orders:

1. Discretion of the court

CPR 44.2(1) affords full discretion to the court to decide: whether costs are payable by one party to another; the amount of those costs; and when those costs are to be paid.

2. General rule

CPR 44.2(2) states that the general rule is that *the unsuccessful party pays the successful party's costs*. Thus, if there has been a judgment against the defendant, the defendant will usually pay the claimant's costs. If the defendant has successfully defended the claim and there is no judgment against the defendant, the claimant will usually pay the defendant's costs.

3. Factors to consider when exercising discretion

The factors a court should consider when exercising its discretion are outlined in CPR 44.2(4) and include: the conduct of all the parties; whether a party has succeeded on part of its case; and any admissible offer to settle made by a party which is drawn to the court's attention (note that Part 36 Offers are not admissible). "Conduct of the parties" is further clarified in CPR 44.2(5) and includes (for instance) compliance with any pre-action protocols.

4. Amount of costs payable

There are two "bases of assessment", meaning two sets of principles that can be used when calculating the value of costs that the unsuccessful party will have to pay:

> 📖 **Standard basis:** this is the most common method used. It is less severe than the indemnity basis method for the paying party (i.e. the party that has been ordered to pay the other party's costs). Using the standard basis, the court will allow costs that have been reasonably incurred and are proportionate in amount and any doubt will be resolved in favour of the paying party CPR 44.3(2). The receiving party (i.e. the party that is having its costs reimbursed by the other party) will normally recover 60-70% of their costs if the court is using the standard basis.

> 📖 **Indemnity basis:** this is more favourable to the receiving party. When using the indemnity basis, the court will allow costs that have been reasonably incurred and are reasonable in amount and any doubt will be resolved in favour of the receiving party CPR 44.3(3). The indemnity basis is typically used when the court wishes to punish the paying party, for instance if the court disapproves of an element of the paying party's conduct. The receiving party will normally recover 70-80% of their costs if this method is used.

Courts will use the receiving party's last approved cost budget when deciding which amount of costs would be reasonable to award. See the *Allocation and Case Management* chapter for an explanation on how costs budgets are used.

Interim Applications and Injunctions

Interim applications are applications made by either party to the court after the commencement of a claim, but before the trial (note, however, that some applications can also be made before the claim is commenced). The applicant is applying for the court to make an order or give directions. This handbook will deal with the following types of interim applications: summary judgment, security for costs, interim prohibitory injunctions and freezing injunctions. Interim applications are generally governed by CPR 23, but each type of interim application is also typically covered by a specific chapter in the CPRs.

Applying for Interim Applications

Interim applications must usually be made "on notice", meaning that the applicant gives notice of the application to the other party. In limited circumstances, an interim application can be made "without notice" (which means that only the applicant will be aware of the application; the respondent will not find out about it until the court has already made a decision on that application).

> **Applicant/Respondent:** the applicant is the party that makes an interim application in litigation proceedings. The respondent is the party against which the application is submitted.

"With notice" application procedure

```
The applicant applies to court and must produce the following documents:
 • Application notice (using form N244): the document stating the applicant's intention to seek a court order.
 • Draft order: this is a draft of the order the applicant wishes the court to make.
 • Evidence: this is normally in the form of a witness statement.
 • Skeleton arguments (if the application is to be heard before a High Court).
```
⬇
```
The court issues the application and notifies the parties of the time and date for the hearing (sometimes called the "return date").
```
⬇
```
The application notice and other documentation (i.e. the draft order and the witness statement) must then be served on the respondent at least 3 days before the hearing CPR 23.7(1)(b).
```
⬇
```
The respondent must then serve any evidence they wish to rely on as soon as possible (there is no set time frame for this, although the court can set one pursuant to 23 PD 9.4).
```
⬇
```
The applicant can then serve any evidence in reply to that provided by the respondent.
```

"Without notice" application procedure

An applicant will only be allowed to withhold knowledge of their application from the respondent under exceptional circumstances (where permitted by a CPR, a PD or a court order CPR 23.4(2)). This is because a lack of awareness of the application will deny the respondent the opportunity to present any opposing arguments or defend the application in court. Such exceptional circumstances include (but are not limited to): when the matter is urgent 23A PD 3(1); and when the purpose of the application would be defeated by giving notice to the respondent. Freezing injunctions, for instance, typically fall into the second category and are therefore often dealt with without the respondent receiving notice (freezing injunctions are dealt with later in this chapter).

Because of the inherent unfairness of without notice applications, the applicant also has an onerous duty of full and frank disclosure of all material facts Memory Corporation v Sidhu (No 2). This means that the applicant must set out all facts regardless of whether they are favourable to its application, so as to allow the court to consider the application in a way that is (at least to some extent) fair to both parties.

Once the court has made its decision on the application, the applicant must serve on the respondent the application notice, any evidence, the court order and a statement setting out the respondent's right to have the court order set aside CPR 23.9-10. All without notice hearings will be followed by a with notice hearing (again, to promote justice and fairness). Typically at the without notice hearing, the court will set a return date, which is the date for the with notice hearing and also the date until which the interim order/injunction will be effective.

Civil Litigation

Security for Costs

> **Security for costs:** security for costs applications are made by parties that are in defending positions (typically the defendant in the main proceedings). The aim of these applications is to ensure that the claimant would be able to meet any potential future costs orders made against it, for example if the defendant successfully defends the case. This is because defendants are effectively "dragged" into litigation, meaning it would arguably be unfair if they could not recover at least some of their costs from the claimant if the court subsequently establishes that the defendant was not in the wrong (and should thus not have been sued in the first place).

Conditions

The key conditions that must be fulfilled in order for an applicant to succeed in a security for costs application are set out in CPR 25.13(2). The applicant must prove *either* of the following:

1. **That the claimant is resident out of the jurisdiction** CPR 25.13(2)(a). If the claimant is a company, "residency" means the place at which it has its place of central management and control. "Out of the jurisdiction" does not have its literal meaning, but refers to jurisdictions in which it would be impossible or difficult to enforce an order/judgment. A claimant residing in a Brussels Regulation member state would therefore be unlikely to be classed as being "resident out of the jurisdiction" (the Brussels Regulation is dealt with in more detail in the *Foreign Jurisdictions* chapter in this module).

2. **That the claimant is a company/body and there is reason to believe that it will be unable to pay the defendant's costs if ordered to do so** CPR 25.13(2)(c). The meaning of this has been considered in the following cases:

    Re Unisoft Group: it is not enough to show that the company *may* not be able to pay; the court must be persuaded that the company *will not* be able to pay. This should be assessed at the time of the application being made, although future financial expectations may be taken into account.

    Jirehouse Capital v Beller: this clarified that the court should not apply the Re Unisoft Group test too strictly, making it easier for an applicant to satisfy the court that the respondent would be unable to pay the defendant's costs if ordered to do so. The court clarified that an applicant would not necessarily be required to satisfy the court that "on the balance of probabilities" the respondent would be unable to pay. A lower threshold may be acceptable.

Note that there are other conditions set out in CPR 25.13(2) but the LPC tends to focus on the above two conditions.

Court's discretion

The court is under no obligation to order security for costs despite either or both grounds being satisfied by the applicant. The court must consider the fact that a security for costs order may act as a barrier to justice for the respondent (if the respondent cannot comply with the order) Olatawura v Abiloye. The respondent's right of access to the courts must therefore be balanced with the applicant's need for financial security. The case of Sir Lindsay Parkinson v Triplan set out the main factors for the court to consider when undertaking this balancing act. These factors are:

- Is it a bona fide claim, or is the applicant using a security of costs application oppressively as a tactical device to stifle the claim? If the respondent has a reasonably good prospect of success, the claim is likely to be perceived as bona fide.

- Was there a delay in making the application?

- Was the claimant's want of means brought about by the defendant's conduct (i.e. has the claimant been impoverished by the actions of the defendant)? If so, it would arguably be unfair to impose a security for costs order on the claimant, as such an order could prevent the claimant from being able to continue with the claim (if the claimant would consequently lack the funds to do so).

Awards

The awards that may be made by the court following security for costs applications are set out in CPR 25.12(2). The court has complete discretion to determine the *amount* to be paid into court by the respondent as security (but the court should consider how much the respondent is realistically able to raise) CPR 25.12(3). In practice, the amount is typically 75-80% of what the defendant would reasonably expect to recover at trial. The potential orders include:

- The respondent must pay the sum into court.
- The respondent must pay the sum to the applicant's solicitor.
- The respondent must obtain a bank guarantee to cover the potential costs the defendant will incur.
- The respondent must give an undertaking to pay the defendant's costs if ordered to do so.

The procedure to follow is the one set out in the *"With notice" application procedure* section of this chapter (above).

Summary Judgment

> **Summary judgment:** successful applications for summary judgment result in all or part of cases being disposed of before trial. The aim is to save time and cost in situations where claims are unlikely to succeed for legal or evidential reasons. Either party can make an application for summary judgment.

Grounds

The grounds for summary judgment are set out in CPR 24.2. To succeed, the applicant must satisfy **both** of the following:

1. The respondent has (1) no real prospect of succeeding with the claim (if the respondent is the claimant); *or* **(2) no real prospect of successfully defending the claim** (if the respondent is the defendant).

The meaning of "real" has been considered in case law:

- Swain v Hillman: the case clarified that "real prospect" does not mean "substantial prospect". It follows that even if the respondent will "probably" not be successful, this will not be sufficient to prove that they have no "real" prospect. The respondent's prospect of success must be merely fanciful or imaginary in order for the applicant to fulfil this criterion.

- International Finance Corporation v Utexafrica: the word "real" was further clarified to mean "more than merely arguable".

2. There must be no other compelling reason why the case should proceed to trial.

Compelling reasons include the following:

- The facts are disputed.
- The case is complex and/or not straightforward.
- The defendant requires more time to sufficiently investigate the claim made against it.
- Expert evidence is required.

Awards

The court can make any of the following orders pursuant to 24 PD 5:

- **Judgment on the claim:** the court gives judgment in favour of the claimant (the claimant is successful with its claim and the case will not proceed to trial).

- **Dismissal of the claim:** the court gives judgment in favour of the defendant (the claim is struck out and the case will not proceed to trial).

- **Dismissal of the application:** the applicant has been unsuccessful, no summary judgment will be given and the claim will continue.

- **Conditional order:** the court can order that the claim may only continue if a particular condition has been fulfilled.

- **Costs orders:** the court can give costs orders following an application for summary judgement. Costs orders are dealt with in the *Interim Applications and Injunctions* chapter in this module.

Procedure

The procedure for a summary judgment application differs slightly from the one outlined in the *With notice application* section of this chapter (above). This diagram summarises the procedure for applying for summary judgment:

Applicant gives at least 14 days notice to the respondent **CPR 24.4(3)** → Respondent must serve any evidence within 7 days of the hearing **CPR 24.5(1)** → Applicant must serve any counter-evidence at least 3 days before the hearing **CPR 24.5(2)** → Both parties must file statements of costs at least 24 hours before the hearing **44 PD 9.5(4)(b)**

If the **claimant** wishes to apply for summary judgment, it cannot make its application until the defendant has served either a defence or an Acknowledgment of Service, unless the court gives permission CPR 24.4(1). If the defendant has not yet served a defence but the court has given such permission, it will not be required to do so before the hearing CPR 24.4(2).

If the **defendant** is applying, there is no requirement for it to file a Defence or an Acknowledgement of Service prior to an application for summary judgment.

Civil Litigation

Interim Prohibitory Injunctions

📖 **Interim prohibitory injunction ("IPI"):** an IPI is used when the applicant wishes to obtain a court order prohibiting the respondent from doing (or continuing to do) a specific act. For instance, consider a situation where a claimant is pursuing a claim for patent infringement against a defendant who is selling products that are allegedly infringing one of the claimant's existing patents. The claimant may wish to apply for an IPI to prohibit the defendant from selling those products during the period leading up to (and including) the trial.

Grounds

In *American Cyanmid v Ethicon* the court developed a set of guidelines to be used when assessing whether an IPI should be granted (note: these are not "requirements" – the court does not have to grant an IPI simply because the situation falls within the guidelines). These guidelines are summarised in the following flowchart:

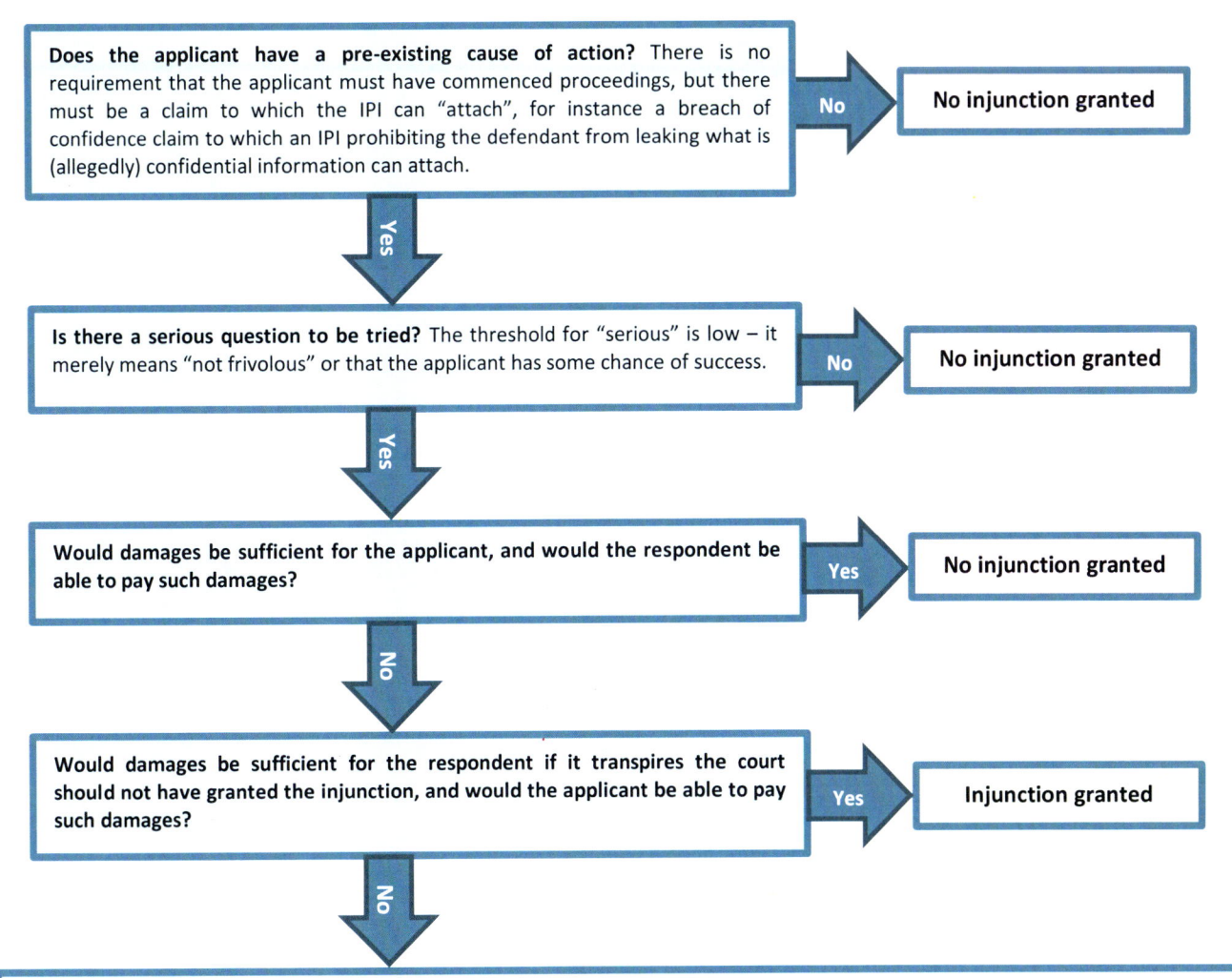

Does the applicant have a pre-existing cause of action? There is no requirement that the applicant must have commenced proceedings, but there must be a claim to which the IPI can "attach", for instance a breach of confidence claim to which an IPI prohibiting the defendant from leaking what is (allegedly) confidential information can attach. → **No** → No injunction granted

↓ Yes

Is there a serious question to be tried? The threshold for "serious" is low – it merely means "not frivolous" or that the applicant has some chance of success. → **No** → No injunction granted

↓ Yes

Would damages be sufficient for the applicant, and would the respondent be able to pay such damages? → **Yes** → No injunction granted

↓ No

Would damages be sufficient for the respondent if it transpires the court should not have granted the injunction, and would the applicant be able to pay such damages? → **Yes** → Injunction granted

↓ No

In this scenario the court can consider the following to assess the **balance of convenience** to decide whether the injunction should be granted. When deciding this, the court may consider:
- *Status quo ante* (what was the position of the respondent before the behaviour commenced?). This generally favours an injunction being granted unless the alleged wrong was committed by the *applicant*.
- Equitable factors (e.g. has the applicant delayed in bringing the claim/has the applicant acquiesced to the respondent's action?).
- Public interest (is there anything in the public interest suggesting the IPI should be granted/not granted?). For instance, could the decision result in a business being bankrupted and people being made redundant?
- Merits of the case - although this should always be a last resort.

📖 **Balance of convenience:** this part of the test asks the court to consider who suffers the greatest inconvenience: the applicant (if the injunction is *not* granted), or the defendant (if the injunction is granted).

Procedure

Refer to the sections above to clarify the procedure to be followed in the event that the application is made "with" or "without" notice.

Freezing Injunctions

> **Freezing injunction:** this is an interim prohibitory injunction that limits the respondent's ability to deal with its assets (e.g. by prohibiting the respondent from selling certain assets or spending money held in specific bank accounts). A freezing injunction can also be awarded against third parties, to obligate those third parties to prevent the respondent from disposing of assets (e.g. the court might order a bank to prohibit the respondent from accessing or depleting its bank accounts). The purpose of a freezing injunction is to protect any of the respondent's assets that may have to be handed over following a judgment made in favour of the applicant at trial. The total value of the assets that the applicant is seeking to "freeze" is therefore typically limited to the value of the applicant's claim.

Grounds

The grounds for freezing injunctions are set out in case law, and the leading case is Mareva v International Bulkcarriers (freezing injunctions are accordingly sometimes referred to as Mareva injunctions). The applicant must prove all of the following:

1. The applicant must have a pre-existing cause of action against the respondent

The applicant must have a cause of action against the respondent that is capable of being brought in England & Wales.

2. The applicant must have a good arguable case

Ninemia Maritime Corporation v Trave established that this means the applicant must have a case that is "more than barely capable of serious argument, and yet not necessarily one a judge believes to have more than a 50% chance of success at trial".

3. The respondent must have assets within the jurisdiction

4. There must be a real risk of the respondent dissipating the assets

The court will use a variety of factors when establishing whether such a risk exists, including whether the respondent: has been dishonest; has defaulted on any debts in the past; has already started to dispose of its assets; is based in a tax haven.

Procedure

Because of the nature of freezing injunctions, applications are typically made without notice. If notice is given, this could act as a "warning" to the respondent, which could lead to the respondent dissipating all/most of its assets (so as to frustrate the enforcement of subsequent judgments in favour of the applicant). The evidence that forms part of the application must be in the form of an affidavit (25A PD 3.1) due to the draconian nature of a freezing order. The applicant must also provide a bank guarantee demonstrating their ability to pay any damages if the injunction is wrongly granted.

> **Affidavit:** a sworn statement made under oath.

Interim Hearing Cost Orders

At the end of an interim hearing the judge will make an interim costs order. This will concern the costs incurred by the parties in relation to applying for/responding to the interim application. There are a variety of interim costs orders that the judge could make and these are listed in 44 PD 4.2:

- **Costs in any event:** the successful party in the interim application will recover their costs regardless of who is the successful party at the end of the trial.

- **Costs in the case:** the costs of the interim hearing will be dealt when costs are awarded at the end of the trial.

- **Costs reserved:** costs will be decided later (and if they are not, then costs in the case will apply).

- **No order:** each party will bear its own costs (this will usually be awarded if the judge is critical of both sides).

- **Wasted costs:** the lawyers have to pay their own costs (as punishment for poor conduct).

When deciding which order to make, the judge will consider the same factors as when the court is deciding on costs at the end of the trial. This is discussed in the *Costs* section of the *Pre-trial, Trial and Costs* chapter in this module.

Civil Litigation

Foreign Jurisdictions

This chapter deals with claims that have an international element, for instance claims involving companies that were incorporated outside of England & Wales. In order to make a binding judgment against a party, the court giving that judgment must have "jurisdiction" over the claim. Different regimes exist that allow parties and courts to establish in which jurisdiction a claim should be brought, and this handbook will focus on the Brussels Regulation and the common law rules.

The Brussels Regulation

The Brussels Regulation ("BR") refers to EU Regulation No 1215/2012, which deals with the recognition and enforcement of judgments in civil and commercial matters among EU member states. The current BR only applies to cases that commenced on or after 10 January 2015 (the previous Brussels Regulation applies only to cases that commenced before this date). The BR helps to establish which court has jurisdiction over a dispute involving two or more member states. The following section outlines how to apply the Brussels Regulation in order to ascertain whether the English courts have jurisdiction over a dispute.

Step 1: Does the Brussels Regulation apply?

The following three factors must be established for the Brussels Regulation to apply to a dispute:

1. International element

The dispute must have an international element. This simply means that the legal issue arising in the dispute must be of an international nature, for instance if one party is from Germany and another is from England.

2. Material scope

To establish a "material scope", the following two factors must exist:

(a) The claim must have a connection to a Member State

A claim will be connected to a BR member state if any of the following three applies:

- The defendant is domiciled in a Member State. An individual's domicile is ascertained using BR Article 62. A company's domicile is ascertained using BR Article 63, and BR Article 63(2) clarifies the situation in the United Kingdom.

    (a) If the defendant is an *individual*, his/her domicile will be ascertained in accordance with BR Article 62.

    (b) If the defendant is a *company*, its domicile will be ascertained in accordance with BR Article 63. This article states that a company is domiciled at the place where it has its: statutory seat; central administration; or principal place of business. BR Article 63(3) clarifies that for the purpose of the UK, "statutory seat" means the registered office (or, if none exists, the place of incorporation).

- The exclusive jurisdiction rules set out in BR Article 24 apply. This is where the conflict concerns a certain subject matter that by its nature means the claim is "connected" to a member state. These subject matters include, for instance, immovable property, validity of a company and validity of intellectual property rights.

- The parties have a choice of jurisdiction clause in the contract and a member state is the contractually chosen jurisdiction BR Article 25.

(b) The claim must be of a civil or commercial nature BR Article 1

The Brussels Regulation would therefore not cover a claim relating to (for instance) a will, taxation or family law.

3. Temporal scope

The claim must fall into the temporal scope of the Brussels Regulation. The Brussels Regulation only applies to disputes that arose/arise after a certain date: the proceedings must have been *instituted* on or after 10 January 2015. For the purposes of England & Wales, BR Article 66 clarifies that "instituted" means the date on which the claim form was issued.

Step 2: Do the courts of England & Wales have jurisdiction?

There are certain articles that will automatically confer jurisdiction upon the courts of a particular country. This means that even if the courts of England & Wales initially appear to have jurisdiction because the claim falls under the criteria of a particular article, courts in another country may still have priority. The highest "ranking" article takes priority over all other articles (and thus confers jurisdiction to the courts of the country indicated by that article). See the hierarchical flow chart and example below for clarification.

1. Do BR Articles 24, 26 or 25 apply?

BR Article 24
- **Exclusive jurisdiction:** As mentioned in the previous section, Article 24 applies where the subject matter of the dispute is significantly linked to a particular state. Such subject matters include ownership of property, validity of a company and intellectual property.

BR Article 26
- **Submission**: A court is given jurisdiction under this article where the defendant submits to a court, i.e. enters an appearance in that court (unless the appearance is to contest jurisdiction).
- In England & Wales, a defendant submits when they acknowledges service of a claim or files a defence.

BR Article 25
- **Choice of jurisdiction clause**: This article takes effect when the parties have a choice of jurisdiction clause in their contract. The jurisdiction that they have contractually agreed upon is acknowledged by this article. Note that it is irrelevant whether the parties have contractually agreed which *law* that is to apply to the contract. "Choosing a jurisdiction" refers to the choosing the *court* in which the case should be heard, not choosing the *law* that is to apply to the contract.

For instance, if a contract contains a choice of jurisdiction clause giving England & Wales jurisdiction over any dispute (i.e. BR Article 25 applies), but the subject matter of the dispute concerns the validity of a French company (i.e. BR Article 24 applies), France will have jurisdiction over the claim.

If Articles 24, 26 or 25 do not apply to the dispute, the claimant is left with a choice. They can either:

2. Use the *general rule* in BR Article 4; or

- This general rule is that the state in which the defendant is *domiciled* has jurisdiction.

3. Use one of the *special jurisdiction rules* in BR Articles 7+8.

- BR Article 7(1) applies to matters involving a contract. It allows a claimant to sue the defendant in the jurisdiction that is the *place of performance* of the contract. Place of performance is defined in the article as where the goods were due to be delivered (for the sale of goods), or where the service was due to be performed (for the provision of services).

- BR Article 7(2) applies to matters involving torts. It allows the claimant to sue the defendant in the jurisdiction in which the harm occurred (or may occur).

- BR Article 7(5) applies where the dispute relates to the operations of a branch or an agency. It allows the claimant to sue the defendant in the jurisdiction where the branch/agency is based. For instance, if the Swedish branch of a German company is the entity in breach, the claimant can sue in Sweden even though the defendant is domiciled in Germany.

- BR Article 8(1) applies where the proceedings have more than one defendant and the co-defendants are domiciled in different states. The defendant may be sued in the courts of the state in which the co-defendant is domiciled. Consider the following example for illustration. You were the passenger of a car that collided with a lorry carrying methanol in Italy. The driver of the car is domiciled in England and the company that owns the lorry and the methanol business is domiciled in Portugal. You want to sue both the driver and the company in the courts of England & Wales. You can sue the driver in England pursuant to BR Article 4 (the general rule) and BR Article 8(1) will allow you to join in the Portuguese company as a co-defendant, even though the company is not domiciled in England.

Step 3: Will the courts of England & Wales accept jurisdiction?

Even though it has been established in step 2 that the courts of England & Wales have jurisdiction, those courts will not necessarily accept that jurisdiction and allow the claim to be brought there. This is the case in two situations:

Civil Litigation

1. BR Article 29

A state must not allow a case to be brought in its courts if proceedings between the same parties, involving the same cause(s) of action, are already in existence in another member state (this rule is referred to as "*lis pendens*"). The court in which proceedings are first brought is known as the "court first seised".

> 📖 **Court first seised:** this phrase is explained in BR Article 32. A court is deemed to have been "seised" when a document instituting proceedings (or an equivalent document) is lodged with that court. In England, this would be when the claim form is issued at the court.

Note that BR Article 29 imposes an *obligation* – the court *must* not allow proceedings to continue if BR Article 28 applies (compare this to the discretionary nature of BR Article 30 below).

2. BR Article 30

A state *may* not allow a case to be brought in its court if related proceedings already exist in another member state. In other words, any court *other than* that first seised may stay its proceedings when related proceedings exist in another member state.

Note that BR Article 30, unlike BR Article 29, does not impose an obligation – the court *may* prevent proceedings from continuing if related proceedings exist elsewhere in a member state.

Application of the Brussels Regulation

On 20 January 2021, Old Street Limited (an English company) contracts with ICEA (a company incorporated in Denmark) to purchase a consignment of reclaimed wood to be used in its furniture design company. The wood is to be delivered to Old Street Limited's warehouse in Coventry. Old Street Limited is not happy with the quality of the wood received and wishes to sue ICEA. There is no choice of jurisdiction clause in the contract, but there is a clause stating that Danish law applies to any dispute. Can Old Street Limited sue ICEA in the English courts?

1. **The Brussels Regulation applies to this dispute:** the dispute has an international element (the parties to the dispute are from two different states and the contract involves shipping between the two states). There is material scope, as the defendant is domiciled in Denmark, a Brussels Regulation member state, and the dispute is of a commercial nature. There is temporal scope as the dispute arose after 10th January 2015.

2. **The courts of England & Wales have jurisdiction:** BR Article 24 does not apply since the subject matter of the dispute does not fall into any of the exclusive jurisdiction categories. BR Article 26 does not apply, as ICEA has not submitted to the jurisdiction. BR Article 25 does not apply because we are informed that the contract between the parties does not contain a choice of jurisdiction clause. It is irrelevant that the parties have chosen Danish law to be the governing law of any dispute; "choosing a jurisdiction" refers to the choosing the *court* in which the case should be heard, not choosing the *law* that is to apply to the contract.

Old Street Limited is therefore left with a choice. It can either: (a) rely on the general rule in BR Article 4 and sue in the defendant's jurisdiction (i.e. Denmark); or (b) rely on one of the special jurisdiction rules, the relevant one here being BR Article 7 as we are dealing with a dispute arising out of a contract. Because the place of contractual performance is England (the wood was to be delivered to Coventry), pursuant to BR Article 7(1) the courts in England & Wales will have jurisdiction over the dispute.

3. **Will the courts of England & Wales accept jurisdiction?** Nothing on the facts suggests any proceedings dealing with the same dispute already exist in a different member state. Nor does it appear that any related proceedings exist in another member state. Therefore, neither BR Article 29 nor BR Article 30 applies. This indicates that the courts of England & Wales would be likely to accept jurisdiction.

In conclusion, Old Street Limited is likely to be able to sue in the English courts.

The Common Law Rules

If it is established that the Brussels Regulation does not apply (i.e. Step 1 above is not fulfilled), the common law rules should instead be used to establish whether the courts of England & Wales have jurisdiction over a particular dispute. There are three circumstances under which the courts of England & Wales will have jurisdiction over a dispute involving a foreign defendant:

1. Presence

A claimant may commence proceedings against a foreign defendant if that foreign defendant is present in the jurisdiction when the proceedings are served (by serving a claim form on that foreign defendant). Such presence may be permanent (for instance if the defendant is a foreign company and has a branch office in London) or temporary (for instance if the foreign defendant is only in London for a day).

The defendant may however contest the claim's commencement in the English courts by arguing that it is not the "forum conveniens" (i.e. arguing that the English courts are not the most appropriate forum available to the parties to hear the claim). The burden of proof is on the defendant to prove that the English courts are not the "forum conveniens". They must therefore prove that there is another jurisdiction in which it is more suitable to bring the claim.

> **Forum conveniens**: the leading case on establishing whether or not a jurisdiction is a "forum conveniens" is Spiliada Maritime Corporation v Cansulex Limited. The courts shall consider all the circumstances of the case, which may include: applicable law (which law governs the dispute?); availability of witnesses (where are the majority of witnesses residing?); local knowledge (does the jurisdiction possess the local knowledge required to adequately assess the case?); cost (if the case were to be heard in the jurisdiction, would this involve higher costs than if the case were to be heard elsewhere? For instance, would experts have to be flown into the jurisdiction?).

2. Submission

If a foreign defendant *submits* to the English courts, then these courts will have jurisdiction over the dispute. There are two main ways in which a foreign defendant may submit to the English courts:

(a) Appointing an agent to accept service on its behalf

This is the case if, for instance, the foreign defendant instructs an English solicitor on whom proceedings may be served.

(b) Appearing in court/the proceedings

This simply means taking a step in the proceedings, such as filing a defence. If a foreign defendant has been served with a claim form (commencing proceedings in England & Wales) and does not want to submit to the English courts, it should *only*, at this stage, acknowledge service within the time limit and indicate that it wishes to contest the jurisdiction of the English courts. It should then apply pursuant to CPR 11(1) for an order declaring that the English courts lack jurisdiction.

3. Permission

A claimant must apply for permission from the court to serve proceedings on a foreign defendant who is not in the jurisdiction (i.e. if the defendant is not present in the jurisdiction and has not submitted). The application for such permission is made pursuant to CPR 6.36. This is a type of interim application and as such is governed by CPR 23 (for more information about interim applications see the chapter *Interim applications and Injunctions*). There are three requirements that must be fulfilled for the application to be successful, and the applicant must support its application with written evidence. The three requirements are set out in CPR 3.37 and are as follows:

1. Jurisdictional gateway

It must be established that the dispute falls within one of the grounds in 6B PD 3.1. These grounds are referred to as the "jurisdictional gateways".

6B PD 3.1(3) Necessary or proper party

If the claimant has served a claim form on a defendant, and there is between the claimant and the defendant a real issue which it is reasonable to try, that claimant may serve a claim form on another person who is a *necessary or proper party* to the claim. A necessary or proper party can be, for instance, a co-defendant (to the defendant on which the claim form has already been served).

Contract 6B PD 3.1(6)

A claimant may commence proceedings in the English courts against a foreign defendant if the claim is made in respect of a contract that:

(a) Was made within England & Wales;

(b) Was made through an agent residing within England & Wales;

(c) Is governed by English law; or

(d) Contains a choice of jurisdiction clause affording the English courts jurisdiction over the claim.

Tort 6B PD 3.1(9)

A claimant may commence proceedings in the English courts against a foreign defendant where:

(a) The damage was sustained (or will be sustained) within the jurisdiction; or

(b) Damage that has been (or will be) sustained results from an act that was (or is likely to be) committed within the jurisdiction.

2. Reasonable prospect of success

Pursuant to CPR 6.37(1)(b), the applicant must have a reasonable prospect of success in relation to the claim that they seek permission to bring in the English courts. "Reasonable prospect" is a relatively low threshold and can be equated to the test for refusing summary judgment (there is more detail on this in the *Interim Applications and Injunctions* chapter of this module).

3. Proper place ("*forum conveniens*")

England & Wales must be the proper place ("*forum conveniens*") in which to bring the claim. The court has discretion to refuse the bringing of a claim in England & Wales on the basis that the jurisdiction is not the *forum conveniens* CPR 6.37(3).

Civil Litigation

The burden of proof is on the claimant (the person applying for permission to bring a claim in England & Wales on a foreign defendant) to establish that England & Wales is the *forum conveniens*. If it is established that England & Wales is *not* the *forum conveniens*, this does not necessarily mean that the application to have the case heard by the courts of England & Wales will be refused. The court will also consider whether "substantial justice" requires that the case be tried in England & Wales. Factors that suggest "substantial justice" will not be achieved if the case is heard elsewhere include: if the alternative jurisdiction in question does not offer legal aid; there is an inherent risk of assassination; or the jurisdiction struggles with corruption and unfair trials.

> **Application of the Common Law rules**
>
> MakeFace is a company incorporated in Delaware, United States, where it also has its central administration. It manufactures organic make-up products. MakeFace does not have any subsidiaries in England, but exports to English beauty stores that sell the products to English customers. It transpires that some exported mascaras have been contaminated during the manufacturing process and have caused severe eye damage to a number of English customers. MakeFace is now being approached by English solicitors (on behalf of the customers affected) who wish to commence proceedings against it in the English courts. MakeFace has not appointed any English solicitors in relation to the matter and has not instructed anyone to accept service of proceedings on their behalf. Can the English claimants validly commence proceedings against MakeFace in the English courts?
>
> 1. **Presence:** MakeFace is not present in England (neither permanently nor temporary); it has no subsidiaries there.
>
> 2. **Submission:** There is no evidence to suggest that MakeFace has submitted to the jurisdiction of the English courts.
>
> 3. **Permission**: The English claimants therefore need permission to bring a claim against MakeFace in the English courts. To obtain permission, they must first establish a "jurisdictional gateway". 6B PD 3.1(9) will be the relevant gateway because we are dealing with a tortious claim. This allows a claimant to bring proceedings against a foreign defendant in England & Wales if the harm occurred within England & Wales. This appears to be the case on the facts, since the claimants suffered eye damage in England. Secondly, the claimants must show that they have a reasonable prospect of succeeding with the case. Nothing on the facts suggests the contrary so a reasonable prospect of success can be assumed here. Thirdly, the English courts must be the *forum conveniens* (the proper place to bring the claim). Two factors in particular suggest that the courts of England & Wales may conclude that England & Wales is the *forum conveniens*: (1) the claimants and the doctors that treated them, all of whom are key witnesses, are based in England; and (2) the mascara was sold in England. It is worth noting that the fact that the defendant is based in the USA would weigh against England & Wales being recognised as the *forum conveniens*.
>
> In conclusion, it is likely that the English claimants can validly commence proceedings against MakeFace in the English courts.

Foreign Element: Effect on Proceedings

Extended time frames

When dealing with a foreign defendant, the time periods for Acknowledgement of Service and the filing of a Defence are extended.

- **Claim form:** the claimant has 6 months (instead of 4 months) to serve the claim form on the defendant once the claim form has been issued by the court CPR 7.5.

- **Acknowledgement of Service:** the defendant will have longer than the standard 14 days to serve an acknowledgement of service or a Defence. The time period allowed will depend on the country in which the defendant is domiciled:

    (a) For countries that are Brussels Regulation member states, the time period for filing an Acknowledgment of Service or admission is 21 days after service of the Particulars of Claim CPR 6.35(3)(a). Where the defendant files an Acknowledgement of Service, the time period for the defendant to file their Defence is 35 days from the deemed date of service of the claim form CPR 6.35(3)(b).

    (b) For non-Brussels Regulation member states, the common law rules apply. Under these circumstances, the period of time is ascertained using the table in 6B PD, which lists the countries and their relevant time periods (CPR 6.37(5) directs that the table is to be used for this purpose). The number of days in the table refers to the time the defendant has to either acknowledge service or file a Defence. If the defendant acknowledges service, it then has the total number of days listed in the table, plus an additional 14 days to serve its Defence.

Permission

When a claimant wants to issues proceedings (i.e. serve a claim form) against an *English* defendant, there is no requirement to obtain permission from the courts to do so.

Likewise, if the Brussels Regulation applies to the dispute and the courts of England & Wales have jurisdiction, the claimant does not require prior permission from the court before serving a claim form on the foreign defendant CPR 6.33. This is the case even if the defendant is not physically in the jurisdiction when the claim form is served.

However, if the common law rules apply, and the defendant is not physically present in the English jurisdiction, the claimant will require prior permission before serving a claim form on the foreign defendant CPR 6.36+6.37. Therefore, if the claimant is relying on any of the jurisdictional "gateways" discussed above, the claimant must apply for permission to commence proceedings CPR 6.36.

Alternative Dispute Resolution

Parties are encouraged to consider alternative forms of dispute resolution throughout the litigation proceedings (in the interest of the overriding objective). This chapter outlines some of the main forms of ADR considered on the LPC.

Mediation

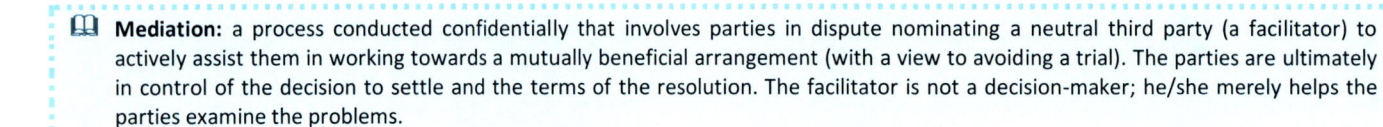

> **Mediation:** a process conducted confidentially that involves parties in dispute nominating a neutral third party (a facilitator) to actively assist them in working towards a mutually beneficial arrangement (with a view to avoiding a trial). The parties are ultimately in control of the decision to settle and the terms of the resolution. The facilitator is not a decision-maker; he/she merely helps the parties examine the problems.

Advantages and disadvantages of mediation

Advantages	Disadvantages
• **Cost and time:** mediation is a cheap and relatively quick method of dispute resolution. • **Preserving relationships:** the informal nature of mediation and focus on cooperation means it is an efficient form of dispute resolution in terms of preserving business relationships between the parties. • **Confidentiality:** the courts are not involved in mediation, so all discussions can take place in/remain private. • **Without prejudice:** discussions held throughout the mediation process are "without prejudice", meaning they will not be admissible in court should the mediation fail and the parties proceed to trial.	• **Precedent:** settlements/solutions resulting from mediation will not provide legal precedent for future disputes, meaning mediation does not contribute to the prevention/resolution of future disputes. • **Commitment:** mediation will only be appropriate/effective if both parties genuinely intend to resolve the dispute out of court. • **Complexity:** if the case involves complex legal or factual issues, mediation may not be appropriate. • **Uncertainty:** there is no guarantee that the parties will find a solution, so mediation could turn out to be a waste of time and money.

Expert Determination

> **Expert determination:** an independent expert in the subject matter of the dispute is appointed by the parties to resolve the matter. The parties can agree in advance to be legally bound by the expert's decision.

Advantages and disadvantages of expert determination

Advantages	Disadvantages
• **Confidentiality:** the courts are not involved in expert determination, so all discussions can take place in/remain private. • **Flexibility:** parties can decide which expert is used and how the procedure will work. • **Binding decision:** the parties will be bound by the expert's decision (unless they agree otherwise). • **Knowledge:** an expert is more suited than the court to deal with complex issues (e.g. technical or scientific). • **Time and cost efficiency:** expert determination is usually cheaper and quicker than litigation.	• **Disagreement:** parties may not agree on a particular expert. • **Relationship preservation:** compared to mediation, there is a higher risk of damage to commercial relationships. • **Inflexible procedure:** there is less scope for examining parties' evidence than there is at a trial (since there will not be a full hearing). • **Uncertainty:** there is no guarantee that the parties will find a solution, so expert determination proceedings could prove to be a waste of time and money.

Arbitration

> **Arbitration:** a process used by parties to settle disputes. An impartial arbitrator (which may be a tribunal or panel) is nominated who may, if the parties so choose, be an expert in the field of the relevant conflict. Unlike any decision or resolutions reached during mediation, decisions reached following arbitration proceedings will be final and binding on the parties (unless certain circumstances exist). This method of resolving disputes is therefore more contentious and adversarial than, for instance, mediation.

Advantages and disadvantages of arbitration

Advantages	Disadvantages
- **Confidentiality:** arbitration offers a more confidential dispute resolution process than litigation, as arbitration documents and hearings are private. - **Final solution:** a decision made by an arbitrator is generally not subject to an appeal procedure. - **International aspect:** the New York Convention ensures that decisions made by an arbitrator can be more easily enforced abroad. - **Flexibility:** parties can choose their arbitrators (e.g. experts in the field, rather than judges) and to some extent the rules governing the procedure (in contrast, parties to litigation must adhere to the Civil Procedure Rules). Parties can also stipulate that the arbitrator should make commercial (rather than legal) decisions.	- **Expensive:** recent research suggests that arbitration can be more expensive than litigation, as the parties have to pay for the arbitrator and the venue (as well as legal advisers). - **Adversarial:** unlike mediation, the arbitration process is not focused on finding a compromise and may therefore strain business relationships. - **Precedent:** decisions made by an arbitrator are not legal precedent for future disputes. - **Third parties:** the use of arbitration derives from an agreement between two parties. Unlike litigation, there is no power to join third parties to the dispute unless they agree.

Arbitration clause

Parties must agree to use arbitration as a dispute resolution procedure (unlike with litigation where one party can "drag" another to court). Parties can agree prior to any dispute arising (e.g. during the negotiation of a contract for the sale of goods) that should a conflict arise, it will be resolved by arbitration. This is usually done by inserting an arbitration clause into the contract between the parties. For an arbitration clause to be valid and legally binding, it must be evidenced in writing Arbitration Act 1996 ("AA 96") s. 5 and comply with the formality requirements in AA 96 s. 6.

The arbitration clause may deal with:

- The seat, language and governing law of the arbitration.
- How arbitrator(s)/the tribunal is to be appointed.
- The scope of the arbitration clause (i.e. which conflicts will be dealt with by arbitration). Where the conflict that has arisen falls within that defined scope, the parties must use arbitration before commencing any litigation proceedings.

Parties can also agree to use arbitration to resolve a dispute *after* it has arisen, although this is less common.

> **Arbitration seat:** the legal jurisdiction to which the arbitration is tied.

The Arbitration Act 1996

The AA 96 is the Act that governs arbitration procedure in England & Wales. Therefore, if the seat of the arbitration is England & Wales, the arbitration process will have to adhere to the rules in this piece of legislation. The parties can also create their own procedural rules so this legislation somewhat acts as a default set of rules (although, as you will see below, some rules contained in the AA *must* govern the arbitration procedure).

The Arbitration Act 1996 contains two types of provisions:

1. **The mandatory provisions**: these are rules that *must* apply to the arbitration process, so parties cannot agree to exclude them or agree to any rules that contradict them. All the mandatory provisions are listed in AA 96 Schedule 1.

2. **The Non-mandatory provisions**: these rules will only apply to the arbitration process if the parties have not explicitly excluded them (i.e. they are possible to exclude). Where the rules do apply, they will only apply to the extent that the Arbitration Agreement is silent on a particular aspect of the procedure.

The following section sets out some of the key provisions in the AA and explains their application:

Staying legal proceedings

Sometimes a party will bring court proceedings despite an Arbitration Agreement existing between the parties. If the defendant wishes to uphold the Arbitration Agreement (i.e. use arbitration rather than litigation to resolve the dispute), it must ensure that the legal proceedings are stayed. The defendant must:

- Acknowledge service of the Particulars of Claim so as to avoid the claimant obtaining a default judgment.

- Apply to the court pursuant to CPR 62.8, which deals with the mandatory provision AA 96 s. 9. This allows a party to an Arbitration Agreement against whom legal proceedings have been brought to apply to court to stay the proceedings. The court must grant a stay unless it is satisfied that the Arbitration Agreement is null and void, inoperative, or incapable of being performed AA 96 a. 9(4).

- The application mentioned in the above bullet point requires an application notice, a draft order and evidence in support of the legal proceedings being stayed (these must be issued at court when making the application). Such evidence should confirm that there is a binding Arbitration Agreement in existence and that the dispute falls within the scope of that agreement.

Duties of the arbitrator and the parties

The general duty of the arbitrator is set out in AA 96 s. 33, which is one of the *mandatory* provisions. The arbitrator must act fairly and impartially, adopt suitable procedures, and avoid unnecessary delays and costs. This includes declaring an interest in the case if one exists (i.e. the arbitrator should tell the parties if there is reason to believe that he/she may fail to be impartial, in which case another arbitrator should probably be used instead).

The general duty of the parties is set out in AA 96 s. 40, another *mandatory* provision. The parties must do all things necessary for the proper and expeditious conduct of the arbitral proceedings, such as ensuring their compliance with any orders from the tribunal.

Peremptory orders

The tribunal uses peremptory orders when a party fails to comply with directions. Such orders are made pursuant to AA 96 s. 41. It is similar to an "unless order" as used by the courts in litigation, as it prescribes a time limit for compliance by the party in default. Peremptory orders exist to incentivise the parties to adhere to any orders/directions made by the tribunal, although AA 96 s. 41 is a non-mandatory provision.

There are sanctions available for the tribunal should a party fail to comply with a peremptory order. These are listed in AA 96 s. 41(7) and include: refusing to allow the party in default to rely on a particular piece of evidence; drawing inferences; proceeding to a premature award; or making a costs order in favour of one of the parties.

The tribunal can also apply to court and request that a party is forced to comply with the peremptory order pursuant to AA 96 s. 42 (a non-mandatory provision). This effectively means that if a party continues to contravene the order, it will be in contempt of court.

Security for costs

The Arbitration Act 1996, like the Civil Procedure Rules, offers defendants the opportunity to apply for a security for costs order pursuant to AA 96 s. 38(3). However, unlike the security for costs procedure in the Civil Procedure Rules, a tribunal will not make such an order purely on the basis that the claimant is resident outside the jurisdiction of England & Wales. An application for security for costs is instead typically successful on the ground that the claimant is unlikely to be able to meet any awards as to costs. AA 96 s. 38 (and therefore the tribunal's power to make security for costs orders) is a non-mandatory provision.

Awards and appeals

A tribunal will make an award, which is comparable to a judgment at the end of litigation. The parties can agree to the basis on which the dispute shall be resolved. The award can be based on law (from any jurisdiction) or, for instance, commercial, religious or equitable considerations. The tribunal must decide the dispute on the principles chosen by the parties AA 96 s. 46. The arbitrator can also award costs and interest pursuant to AA 96 s. 61 and AA 96 s.49 respectively. Both provisions are non-mandatory.

Civil Litigation

There is limited opportunity to appeal arbitration awards. There are three key provisions to consider for parties wishing to challenge and/or appeal an award:

- **AA 96 s. 67** allows a party to appeal to the court to challenge an award on the basis that the tribunal lacked substantive jurisdiction. For instance, the party wishing to challenge the award could argue that the Arbitration Agreement/clause was invalid, or that the dispute was not within the scope of disputes covered by the Arbitration Agreement/clause. The court can either confirm the award, vary the award or set aside the award in whole or in part. This provision is *mandatory*.

- **AA 96 s. 68** allows a party to appeal to the court to challenge an award on the basis that there is (or has been) a serious irregularity affecting the tribunal, the proceedings or the award. The provision lists the kinds of irregularities that are deemed "serious" including, for instance, a failure of the tribunal to comply with its general duty. This provision is *mandatory*.

- **AA 96 s. 69** allows a party to appeal to the court on a question of law arising out of an award made in the proceedings. This provision is *non*-mandatory. Note that the parties typically agree to exclude this provision in the Arbitration Agreement, as parties often want an award to be final (this is one of the advantages of arbitration, as mentioned above).

AA 96 s. 70: if a party wishes to appeal an award under **AA s. 67**, **AA s. 68** or **AA s. 69**, that party must first exhaust any available arbitral process of appeal or review. Any appeal must be brought within 28 days of the date of the award or, if there has been any arbitral process of appeal, of the date when the party was notified of the result of that process. This provision is *mandatory*.

Enforcement

Parties can apply to the court to have an award enforced should a party fail to comply with it pursuant to **AA 96 s. 66**. This is a *mandatory* provision.

Arbitration procedure

Commence proceedings: the party wishing to commence proceedings will typically need to provide the other side with a written request including the details of the claim and the remedies sought.

⬇

Appoint an arbitrator: the arbitration clause will normally contain an agreed process for choosing an arbitrator. In the absence of such agreement, **AA 96 s. 16-18** applies. These sections impose time limits by which the parties must have agreed on an arbitrator(s).

⬇

Preliminary hearing: similar to the Case Management Conference in litigation, this hearing aims to establish: the preliminary issues, the rules that are to govern the procedure, a timetable; and how disclosure, witness and expert evidence is to be handled.

⬇

Hearing: this is typically in private and only the parties, their representatives and the arbitrator will attend.

⬇

Award/Appeal: see above for an outline of the procedure in relation to the award and any appeal.

Enforcement

Enforcement refers to the procedure by which a successful claimant (a "judgment creditor") can enforce a judgment obtained in its favour at the end of the litigation proceedings. It is effectively a way of forcing the unsuccessful defendant (the "judgment debtor") to pay the damages it owes if it has failed to do so within the time frame set out by the court. In any event, enforcement action cannot be commenced until the debt has become due. Enforcement is generally governed by CPR 70.

Investigating a Judgment Debtor's Means

Prior to commencing litigation proceedings against a potential defendant, a claimant will conduct an investigation into the potential defendant's means (i.e. it will check whether the defendant has enough assets to satisfy a potential claim). It is pointless to waste a large amount of money and time on litigation if the potential defendant will not be able to pay if the claimant obtains a judgment in its favour.

If the judgment creditor wishes to commence enforcement proceedings after the litigation has been concluded, it will typically conduct a second investigation into the judgment debtor's means in order to establish which assets the judgment debtor possesses. This will determine which method of enforcement will be the most appropriate. Investigating a judgment debtor's means could include, for instance, carrying out company searches, obtaining Official Copies from the Land Registry, and searching against other relevant registers. A judgment creditor can also apply to court to obtain an order requiring the judgment debtor to provide information about its means CPR 71.2(2).

Methods of Enforcement

The court will not automatically take enforcement action against a judgment creditor. Instead, a judgment creditor will have to rely on one (or a combination) of the below methods of enforcement. A typical exam question could list a judgment debtor's assets and ask you to set out which method(s) of enforcement would be the most appropriate for the judgment creditor to pursue. There is a list of the different methods of enforcement in 70 PD 1.1.

Taking Control of Goods Order ("TCG")

> 📖 **Taking Control of Goods Order:** a court order allowing the judgment debtor's assets to be seized and then sold at an auction to pay off the debt owed to the judgment creditor (and to pay off administrative expenses). CPR 83-86 set out detailed rules regarding TCGs, but this handbook will only provide a brief overview of the procedure.

TCG as a method of enforcement is suitable where the judgment debtor legally owns (in its own name) moveable assets. The judgment creditor will apply to court for the relevant court document (the document will be addressed to, and received by, an "enforcement officer"). If the High Court is used, the relevant court document is called a "writ of control" and if the County Court is used, the relevant document is called a "warrant of control".

To which court should the judgment creditor apply for a TCG order?		
Debts up to £600	**Debts between £600-£5000**	**Debts exceeding £5000**
County Court	County Court *or* High Court	High Court

The actual procedure for seizing and selling the assets takes place in three steps:

1. The enforcement agent will send advance written notice to the judgment debtor (at least 7 clear days before taking control of any goods, i.e. giving the judgment debtor 7 days to pay).

2. The enforcement agent will enter the judgment debtor's premises and seize the goods. There are certain restrictions to this action. For instance: the enforcement agent can only use reasonable force against the property (not a person); they can only enter between certain hours of the day; and they cannot enter when vulnerable persons are present at the property (e.g. children).

3. The judgment debtor shall be given notice after the entry, including an inventory of the goods seized.

An alternative at step 2 (above) is for the enforcement agent to offer the judgment debtor a "controlled goods arrangement". This gives the judgment debtor a last chance to pay the debt before its assets are seized, thus allowing it to retain custody over those assets in the interim.

Third Party Debt Orders

A third party debt order puts an obligation on a third party, such as a bank, to pay the judgment creditor money that the third party owes the judgment debtor. This method of enforcement is appropriate where the judgment debtor is owed money (e.g. he has a credit balance in a bank account). The legal title to the debt must belong to the judgment debtor for such an order to be possible.

To obtain a third party debt order, the judgment creditor must follow the procedure set out in CPR 72.2(2). An interim order against the judgment debtor will be made "without notice" (so as to avoid the risk of the judgment debtor emptying its bank accounts). This interim order will first be served on the *third party* debtor, to prevent that party from making any payments to the judgment debtor. The order will then be served on the judgment debtor and an "on notice" hearing will follow (the judgment debtor can make representations at this hearing). After that hearing, the court will decide whether the order should be discharged or upheld (and thus whether the third party/parties will be required to pay the judgment creditor).

Charging Orders

Charging orders are made pursuant to CPR 73. A charging order "attaches" to assets, for instance land or certain types of securities. The judgment claimant must, subsequent to making an application for a charging order, apply for a second order to have the assets sold; the charging order does not by itself produce any funds.

Often, land or other assets are already subject to mortgages/charges or are jointly owed. In such situations, a charging order would not be appropriate, since the judgment debtor would not be the owner/only owner of the whole of the land/asset. The procedure for obtaining a charging order is similar to that for obtaining a third party debt order: an interim application will first be made "without notice", subsequent to which an "on notice" hearing will be arranged.

Attachment of Earnings

This type of order requires the judgment debtor's employer to pay a sum from his/her salary towards the debt owed to the judgment creditor. The funds will be paid to the court for onward transmission to the judgment creditor. This order is only available in the County Court so the creditor must transfer its debt to the County Court prior to making an application.

This method of enforcement is appropriate if the judgment debtor does not have any assets of significant value, but earns a regular salary from employment.

Insolvency proceedings

A creditor that is owed more than £750 may petition for the debtor's bankruptcy or the winding up of the company at the local court. Due to the drastic consequences such action could have on a debtor, the mere threat of it is often enough to ensure the debtor pays the debt due. It is important to consider which other creditors a judgment debtor may have before commencing such action. Some creditors may be secured, and the judgment creditor will rank behind them equally ("*pari passu*") with other unsecured creditors. Consequently, the judgment debtor could be left with insufficient assets to repay the judgment debt (after secured creditors have been repaid). You will learn more about creditors and their ranking in the *Business Law* module within this handbook.

> Silver Ltd has obtained a High Court judgment against Bronze Ltd in the sum of £310,000. Bronze Ltd has not made any payment to Silver Ltd and Silver Ltd wishes to enforce the judgment. Silver Ltd has investigated Bronze Ltd's means and has discovered the following: the company has two directors, Eloise Zen and Mike Anderson; the company owns premises in Manchester from which it operates its business; Eloise Zen lives in Cheshire in rented accommodation and Mike Anderson owns a property in central Manchester. What method of enforcement and against which asset should Silver Ltd aim for in its enforcement proceedings?
>
> The most appropriate asset to pursue is the premises Bronze Ltd owns in Manchester. The judgment is against the company and therefore Silver Ltd can only have its judgment enforced against assets owned by the company (Bronze Ltd). The most relevant method of enforcement for real property such as the business premises is a charging order.

Appeals

Grounds for appeal

A party does not have an automatic right to appeal. Appealing in a higher court against a decision made in a lower court will only be allowed where the decision of the lower court was: (1) wrong; or (2) unjust because of a serious procedural or other irregularity in the proceedings CPR 52.21(3). Therefore, where the judge has exercised any discretion when making his/her decision, that decision cannot be appealed on the basis that the discretion was exercised "incorrectly". This is because when a judge exercises discretion, he/she is fundamentally deciding whose story is more credible.

New evidence

Unless it orders otherwise, the appeal court will not hear oral evidence or any evidence that was not put before the lower court CPR 52.21(2). The appeal court will typically only order that new evidence can be heard if: (a) the evidence in question could not reasonably have been obtained for use in the lower courts; (b) the evidence is credible; and (c) the evidence is likely to have an impact on the result. The court will also keep the overriding objective in mind when considering whether to allow new evidence to be heard.

Permission

An appellant requires permission to appeal, except in limited circumstances CPR 52.3(1). The application for permission may be made either: (a) to the lower court that made the decision that one of the parties wishes (or both parties wish) to appeal; or (b) to the appeal court CPR 52.3(2). If the application for permission is made to the appeal court (e.g. if the lower court refuses permission), an "appeal notice" must be filed CPR 52.3(2). An application for permission to appeal must be made within 21 days of the lower court's decision (unless the court orders otherwise) CPR 54(2)(b), together with the reasons for the appeal.

The test for whether permission should be granted is contained in CPR 52.3(6). The court must find that:

- The appeal has a real prospect of success; or
- There is some other compelling reason why the appeal should be heard.

Note that this test bears some similarities to the test for summary judgment in Swain v Hillman (this is dealt with in the *Interim Applications and Injunctions* chapter).

Which court hears the appeal?

The court to which an appeal should be made depends on: (1) the court that made the decision being appealed; and (2) who made that decision (e.g. a district judge or a master).

Blue arrows show the routes for a first appeal, whereas the orange arrows show the route for a second appeal. For instance:

Case first heard by a district judge in a County Court

It may first be appealed to a circuit judge in a County Court → if appealed again, it must be appealed to the Court of Appeal (as shown by the orange arrow).

Case first heard by a circuit judge in a County Court

The first appeal would be to the High Court (as shown by the blue arrow) → only after this could the appellant appeal to the Court of Appeal (as shown by the orange arrow).

Case first heard by a Master in the High Court

The first appeal would be to a High Court judge in the High Court → only after this could the case be appealed to the Court of Appeal. The Supreme Court would be the final option for appeal.

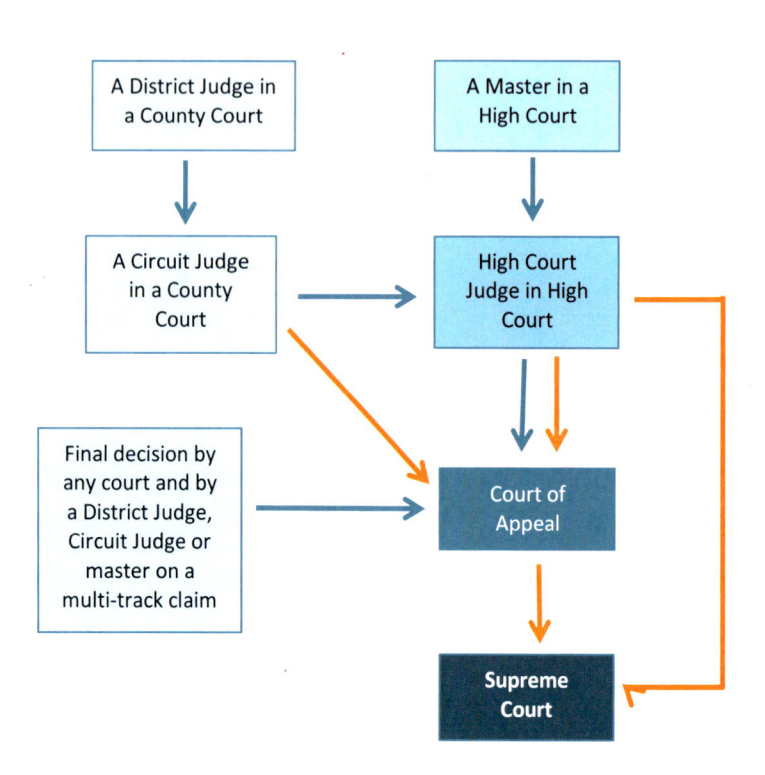

Criminal Litigation

Criminal Litigation

Police Powers — 219
Stop and search • arrest • detention • samples • lawful interviews • rights of a detainee

Advising a Client at the Police Station — 224
Remaining silent • the "DEAD" factors • answering questions • submitting a prepared statement

Bail — 227
General rule • exceptions to the general rule • conditions • abscondment

Allocation — 229
Plea before venue • court allocation

Evidence and Witnesses — 231
Competence and compellability of witnesses • admissibility • exclusion of evidence • identification evidence (Turnbull factors) • character evidence

Sentencing — 236
Types of sentences • sentencing powers of the courts • sentencing procedure: which sentence is likely to be imposed?

Criminal Litigation

Police Powers

The police have certain powers in relation to their handling of people suspected of committing a criminal offence. When police officers exercise such powers, they must be able to demonstrate that:

1. They had the legal authority to do so; and
2. That they do so lawfully.

This section outlines the power to stop and search, the power to arrest, the power to take samples, and the power to extend detention periods or delay the access to legal advice/another person.

Stop and Search

> **Stop and search powers:** the power of a police officer to stop a person and ask what they are doing, why they are in the area and/or where they are going.

Legal authority

Police officers are granted the power to stop and search by PACE 84 s. 1 (when the person being stopped is suspected of possessing stolen or prohibited articles) and Misuse of Drugs Act 1971 s. 23 (where the person being stopped is suspected of possessing illegal drugs). An inspector may also authorise a general power to stop and search in a particular area CJPOA 94 s. 60 (how this works is explained below).

Criteria for exercising stop and search powers

PACE 84 s. 1 and the Misuse of Drugs Act 1971 s. 23

PACE 84 s. 1 and the Misuse of Drugs Act 1971 s. 23 require that:

- The police officer using the power is at least of the rank constable;
- The stop and search must be carried out in a public place or a place to which the public has access; and
- The constable must have reasonable grounds for suspecting that he/she will find stolen or prohibited articles. Whether a constable did have reasonable grounds should be ascertained using COP A 1.1-2.9, and in particular COP A 2.2-2.11. These state, amongst other things, that:

    (a) The officer must have a *genuine* suspicion and there must be an objective basis for that suspicion.

    (b) The officer cannot base any suspicion on personal factors (e.g. mode of dress or skin colour).

    (c) The officer cannot base any suspicion on generalisations, stereotypes, or the fact that a person has previous convictions.

    (d) Suspicion should be based on intelligence or information about, or some specific behaviour by, the suspect, or information about a specific article being carried.

    (e) The officer can, however, base his/her suspicion on the suspect's behaviour even if no intelligence/information exists in limited circumstances. For example, if an officer encounters someone on the street at night who is obviously trying to hide something, the officer may (depending on the other surrounding circumstances) base such suspicion on the fact that this kind of behaviour is often linked to stolen or prohibited articles being carried.

CJPOA 94 s. 60

To authorise a *general* power to stop and search in a particular area, CJPOA 94 s. 60 requires that:

- Authority is granted by an officer of at least the rank of inspector;
- The police officer reasonably believes that incidents involving serious violence may take place in any locality in his police area; or
- The police officer reasonably believes that persons are carrying dangerous instruments/weapons in any locality in his police area without good reason.

Once the power has been granted, this means a police officer of at least the rank of inspector has already made the decision that there are reasonable grounds to stop and search. Therefore, the individual constables actually carrying out the stop and search do not need to have reasonable grounds themselves (which they would need if they undertook a stop and search under s. 1 PACE or s. 23 Misuse of Drugs Act).

How a stop and search should be carried out

The requirements for how the power to stop and search should be exercised are set out in s. 2 and 3 PACE and (in particular) COP A 3.2-3.11.

Location
- The power to stop and search can only be exercised in a public place or in a place to which the public has access (whether on payment or otherwise).

Etiquette
- The stop and search must be carried out with courtesy, consideration and respect.
- The police officer must seek the co-operation of the person in every case and can only use reasonable force as a last resort and only if necessary.

Clothing
- When conducting a stop and search, the officer has no power to require a person to remove any clothing other than an outer coat, jacket or gloves.
- A policeman can only require removal of face coverings PACE 84 s. 117.

Other steps to be taken prior to the search
- The individual must be told (COP A 3.8):
    (a) That they are being detained for the purpose of a search;
    (b) The officer's name;
    (c) Which legal search power is being exercised (e.g. s. 1 PACE, s. 23 Misuse of Drugs Act or s. 60 PACE);
    (d) The purpose of the search and the basis for reasonable suspicion; and
    (e) That they are entitled to a copy of the search record.

Consequences of failure to comply

Breaches of these rules might lead to evidence being excluded at trial (i.e. if the evidence was found as a result of an unlawful exercise of the power to stop and search). This is covered in more detail in the *Evidence and Witnesses* chapter of this module.

Arrest

Legal authority

The power to arrest a person without a warrant is found in PACE s. 24.

Criteria for carrying out an arrest without a warrant

Under PACE s. 23(1)+(4), a police officer may arrest a person without first obtaining a warrant if:

- The police officer carrying out the arrest is at least the rank of constable.
- The arresting officer must have reasonable grounds for suspecting that a person has committed, is committing or is about to commit an offence.
- The officer must have reasonable grounds for believing that it is necessary to arrest the person in question. The "necessity" grounds are set out in PACE s. 24(5). The most commonly used grounds are:
    (a) Necessary to facilitate the prompt and effective investigation of the offence or the conduct of the person in question PACE s. 24(5)(e).
    (b) Necessary to prevent any prosecution for the offence from being hindered by the disappearance of the person in question PACE s. 24(5)(f).
- COP G 2.4-2.9 contains further guidance on when it is deemed necessary to arrest a person.

How an arrest should be carried out

The person being arrested must be informed that they are under arrest as soon as practicable s. 28(1) PACE and must be told the ground(s) for their arrest s. 28(3) PACE.

- The person being arrested must be cautioned COP G 3.4/COP C 10.4.
- If necessary, an officer may use reasonable force to aid an arrest s. 117 PACE.

Criminal Litigation

> 📖 **Cautioned:** cautioning a person means informing them of their rights in relation to answering questions. The prescribed wording for this is found in COP G 3.5 and is as follows: *"You do not have to say anything. But it may harm your defence if you do not mention when questioned something which you later rely on in Court. Anything you do say may be given in evidence."*

The case of Lewis v Chief Constable of South Wales established that if an arrest is deemed unlawful as a result of a procedural irregularity (e.g. if the arresting police officer did not caution the person being arrested), this can be corrected at a later stage.

Detention

When an arrested suspect arrives at the police station, he/she will be put before the custody officer. The custody officer must be at least of the rank sergeant.

The custody officer will decide whether he/she has sufficient evidence to charge the arrested person with the offence for which that person was arrested, and may detain the arrested person at the police station for such period as is necessary to enable him/her to decide on the question of sufficiency of evidence PACE s. 37(1). If the custody officer determines that the evidence is insufficient, he/she must release the arrested person unless he/she has reasonable grounds for believing that it is necessary to detain the person without charge to:

1. Secure or preserve evidence relating to an offence for which the arrested person is under arrest; or

2. Obtain such evidence by questioning the arrested person PACE s. 37(3).

If such reasonable grounds do exist, the custody officer can authorise detention of the arrested person and open a custody record for them. The custody officer must inform the arrested person of the grounds for their detention PACE s. 37(5).

Reviews of detention

The detention of a person in connection with the investigation of an offence must be reviewed periodically by an officer who is not involved with the investigation of the case and is at least the rank of inspector (if the arrested person has not yet been charged) PACE s. 40(1)(b). The reviewing officer must be satisfied that the grounds for detention still exist.

- The first review must take place not later than **six hours** after the detention was first authorised; and

- The second review must take place not later than **nine hours** after the first review; and

- Subsequent reviews must take place with intervals of not more than nine hours PACE s. 40(3).

Extending the detention period

A person must not be kept in police detention for more than 24 hours without being charged (PACE s. 41). The time for these purposes starts running from the time the suspect first arrives at the police station (i.e. *not* the time at which the person was arrested or when their detention was *authorised*). This is referred to as the "relevant time".

By the end of the 24 hours, the person must either be released or charged, unless grounds exist to extend the detention period. Under PACE s. 42, a police officer of at least the rank of superintendent can authorise the extension of the detention period to 36 hours after the "relevant time" (i.e. extend the detention for a further 12 hours) if:

1. The offence in question is an indictable offence;

2. Authority is granted by an officer of at least the rank of superintendent; and

3. The officer that authorises the extension is satisfied that the extension is necessary because the original grounds for detention still exist and investigation is being conducted diligently/expeditiously.

- The authorisation to extend the detention period cannot be given before the second review has taken place. The officer authorising the extension is under a duty to inform the suspect of the grounds for his continued detention and allow him/her or his/her solicitor to make representations about the detention.

- PACE s. 43 and 44 allow the police under certain circumstances to apply to the magistrates' court for any further extension of the detention period, although under no circumstances can a person be detained without charge for longer than 96 hours in total (the magistrates' court can extend detention for another 2 x 36 hours to a maximum of 96 hours).

> **Cora has been arrested on suspicion of possession of a controlled drug on Wood Green high street on 14 December 2021 at 11am. The arrest was lawfully conducted in accordance with PACE. Cora is taken to the closest police station, and she arrives there at 11.50am. The custody officer authorises her detention at 12.30pm. How long can Cora be held in detention without being charged and when should she be released?**
>
> Cora can be held 24 hours without charge, starting with the time she first arrives at the police station (s. 41 PACE). She must therefore be released on or before 11.50am 15 December 2021, unless a delay has been authorised.

Samples

There are three types of samples that a police officer has the power (under certain circumstances) to take from a suspect: non-intimate samples, intimate samples and fingerprints.

> **Non-intimate samples:** samples of hair other than pubic hair, samples taken from a nail or from under a nail, saliva, skin impressions (this is *not* the same as fingerprints), swabs taken from any part of a person's body other than a part from which a sample would constitute an "intimate" sample (s. 65 PACE).

> **Intimate samples:** blood, semen, urine, tissue fluid, pubic hair, dental impressions, swabs taken from any part of a person's genitals PACE s. 65.

Authority to take samples

Non-intimate PACE s. 63	Intimate PACE s. 62	Fingerprints PACE s. 61
In order to take a non-intimate sample without consent from the suspect, the following must apply: • The offence must be a recordable offence. • The suspect must not already have had a non-intimate sample taken in the same investigation (or if they have, that sample must not have been good enough for the purpose for which it was taken).	Written consent from the suspect will *always* be required. The taking of an intimate sample must: • Be authorised by an officer with at least the rank of inspector. • The officer must have reasonable grounds for suspecting that the person from whom the sample will be taken was involved in a recordable offence, and that the taking of the intimate sample is likely to confirm or disprove their involvement.	Fingerprints can be taken without the consent of the suspect. The following must apply: • The offence must be recordable. • The suspect must not already have had their fingerprints taken in the same investigation (or if they have, that sample must not have been good enough for the purpose for which it was taken).

> **Recordable offence:** recordable offences are defined and listed in COP D NFG 4A.

How samples should be taken

Non-intimate PACE s. 63	Intimate PACE s. 62	Fingerprints PACE s. 61
• The suspect must be warned that samples may be subject to a speculative search. • The suspect must be informed of the reason why the sample is being taken and the authority on which the power to take the sample is based. • The taking of the sample must be recorded in the custody record. • Reasonable force can be used if necessary s. 117 PACE.	• The suspect must be warned that samples may be subject to a speculative search. • The suspect must be informed of the reason why the sample is being taken and the authority on which the power to take the sample is based. • The suspect must be warned that refusing to consent to the taking of the sample may lead to adverse inferences being made in court at a later stage. • The suspect must be reminded of his/her right to legal advice. • Intimate samples (other than urine) must be taken by a registered medical practitioner. • The relevant grounds and authorisation and the person's consent must be recorded in the custody record.	• The suspect must be warned that samples may be subject to a speculative search. • The suspect must be informed of the reason why the sample is being taken and the authority on which the power to take the sample is based. • The fact that a sample has been taken must be recorded in the custody record. • Reasonable force can be used if necessary s. 117 PACE.

Lawful Interviews

When a police officer interviews a suspect, there are certain procedural requirements that must be followed for the interview to be lawful. The definition of an "interview" is wide and is contained in COP C 11.1A: *"The questioning of a person regarding their involvement or suspected involvement in a criminal offence"*. The requirements for a lawful interview are:

- The interview must be recorded COP C 11.7.

- The suspect must be cautioned prior to the interview COP C 10.1.

- The suspect must be informed of his/her right to receive legal advice COP C 11.2.

- The interview must take place at the police station unless special circumstances exist COP C 11.1.

Rights of a Detainee

A suspect has the right to have someone informed of his/her arrest (PACE s. 56) and to consult privately with a solicitor (PACE s. 58). A person being arrested can only have these rights denied/delayed in very limited and special circumstances.

Delaying the right of a detainee to inform another of their detention

A detainee's right to inform another of their detention can be delayed pursuant to PACE s. 56 and COP C Annex B where:

- The person is detained on suspicion of an indictable offence;

- Authorisation for the delay is given by an officer of at least the rank of *inspector*; and

- The officer authorising the delay has reasonable grounds for believing that informing another would: lead to interference with evidence; lead to physical injury to another person; alert other offenders; or hinder the recovery of property.

The right can be delayed for a maximum of 36 hours.

Delaying the right to legal advice

The right to legal advice can be delayed pursuant to PACE s. 58. It is only the right to receive legal advice from a *named* solicitor that can be delayed however, not the general right to receive legal advice. COP C 6.4 further emphasises that a police officer should never attempt to dissuade a detainee from obtaining legal advice.

Because of the draconian nature of denying a person's right to legal advice, it has stricter requirements compared to the requirements for delaying the right of a detainee to inform another of their detention. The requirements are:

- The person is detained on suspicion of an indictable offence;

- Authorisation for the delay is given by an officer of at least the rank of *superintendent*; and

- The officer authorising the delay has reasonable grounds for believing that giving the detainee access to a particular (named) solicitor would: lead to interference with evidence; alert other people suspected of committing an indictable offence; and/or hinder the recovery of property.

- The right can be delayed for a maximum of 36 hours.

Advising a Client at the Police Station

A suspect will be interviewed as part of the investigation process. The aim is to obtain evidence that will form part of the case. Any evidence obtained in the interview will subsequently be used in court if the matter progresses to trial and thus anything the suspect says in an interview can be used against him/her. When being interviewed at the police station, the suspect has three options:

1. To answer questions;
2. To remain silent; or
3. To hand in a prepared statement.

> **Prepared statement:** a statement handed in before the interview that contains the suspect's defence. The suspect will still be asked questions by the police officer(s) but will remain silent or simply reply "no comment" to any questions asked.

Remaining Silent

A suspect always has a right to remain silent in police interviews and is under no obligation to provide any evidence in their own defence. This ties in with one of the fundamental principles of the English criminal justice regime: the suspect is deemed to be innocent until the prosecution has proven otherwise.

However, if a suspect chooses to remain silent in police interviews, this can have negative consequences for their case if it progresses to trial. This is because the judge and the jury may be allowed to draw "adverse inferences" from a suspect's decision not to answer the police's questions. Note that the case of R v Hoare clarified that a defendant cannot rely solely on the fact that they were advised to remain silent by their legal advisor to justify doing so; this will not necessarily preclude the judge/jury drawing adverse inferences.

> **Adverse inferences:** legal inferences that prejudice a defendant's case, drawn from the silence of, or failure to provide evidence by, that defendant. Put simply, the judge/jury may be entitled to assume that a defendant chose not to answer a question in order to cover up their guilt in relation to a particular accusation. However, it is important to note that adverse inferences alone can never be enough to prove a defendant's guilt at trial Criminal Justice and Public Order Act 1994 s. 39 ("CJPOA 94").

Adverse inferences may be drawn if the conditions set out in the following CJPOA provisions are satisfied:

1. Suspect fails to mention a fact in their interview on which they later attempt to rely CJPOA 94 s. 34

Adverse inferences can be drawn pursuant to this section where:

(a) The defendant, at any time before they were charged with the offence, fails to mention any facts at a police interview (carried out under caution) which they then later attempt to rely on in court as part of their defence; and

(b) In the circumstances existing at the time, it would have been reasonable for the defendant to have mentioned such facts. These circumstances could be, for instance, that:

- A sufficient amount of information had been disclosed to the suspect/their solicitor prior to the interview; and/or
- The suspect was in good mental and physical health and neither a child nor an elderly person.

Note the requirement that the interview must have been made under caution; this means that no inference can be drawn if the suspect was not interviewed under caution.

Adverse inferences that a judge/jury could make under this section include, for instance, that the explanation or defence given at trial has been fabricated and that at the time of the interview, the defendant had no reasonable explanation for their actions.

2. Suspect fails to explain an object, substance or mark CJPOA 94 s. 36

- Adverse inferences can be drawn pursuant to CJPOA 94 s. 36 where the defendant, at the time of their arrest, was found with an object, substance or mark on them and, when asked to explain that object, substance or mark, failed/refused to do so.

- In order to make adverse inferences pursuant to this section, the suspect must have been given a "special warning" when they were asked to provide an explanation at the time of their arrest CJPOA 94 s. 36(4). The wording of special warnings can be found in COP C 10.11.

3. Suspect fails to explain their presence at the place of arrest CJPOA 94 s. 37

- Adverse inferences can be drawn pursuant to this section where the defendant is arrested and, when asked to explain their presence at the place at which they were arrested, failed or refused to do so.

- In order to make adverse inferences pursuant to this section, the suspect must have been given a "special warning" when they were asked to provide an explanation at the time of their arrest CJPOA 94 s. 37(3). The wording of special warnings can be found in COP C 10.11.

Hannah is on trial for domestic burglary during which some expensive jewellery was stolen. She was arrested a couple of weeks after the burglary took place. The police found some of the stolen jewellery at Hannah's flat, but she was not present at the time the goods were discovered. During her police interview she answered "no comment" to all the questions put to her. Hannah has pleaded not guilty to the offence and has her trial tomorrow. She is now planning to give evidence and will say as follows:

"I did not commit the burglary. I was attending a gym class at the time the burglary took place, and the jewellery items found at my place have nothing to do with me. They belong to a friend who accidentally left them there."

Which types of adverse inferences might be relevant at Hannah's trial?

- CJPOA 94 s. 34 is relevant: Hannah is basing her defence on facts that she could reasonably have provided at the time of her arrest, but failed to do so. The judge/jury may therefore draw adverse inferences to the effect that Hannah has fabricated the story.

- CJPOA 94 s. 36 is irrelevant: the stolen jewellery was found in Hannah's house but not *at the time* of Hannah's arrest.

- CJPOA 94 s. 37 is irrelevant: Hannah was not arrested near the scene of the offence (i.e. not near the burgled house).

Advising a Suspect: the "DEAD" Factors

It is the solicitor's task to advise his/her client on which option they should choose, and when doing so they should consider a variety of factors, including the risk that adverse inferences may be drawn from silence. The factors a solicitor should consider are sometimes referred to as the "DEAD" factors: **D**isclosure, **E**vidence, **A**rgent, **D**efence.

1. Disclosure

- There is no general police duty to disclose to the suspect (or their solicitor) the nature (and amount) of evidence that exists in relation to the case. The only rights the suspect's solicitor has are: (a) the right to see the custody record COP C 2.4; and (b) the right to receive a copy of the suspect's description, if such a description was given by a potential witness COP D 3.1. However, the police will typically inform the suspect or his/her solicitor of the background to the offence and the facts on which the police have based their suspicion that the suspect is involved in the offence.

- The solicitor must therefore first decide whether they think sufficient information has been disclosed to justify the suspect answering questions. If insufficient evidence is available to properly advise the client, the case of R v Roble states that it is not appropriate for a court to draw adverse inferences pursuant to CJPOA 94 s. 34 if the client remains silent. In such a situation it may therefore be appropriate to advise the client to remain silent so as to avoid the risk of the client inadvertently incriminating himself.

2. Evidence

- The solicitor should consider which elements make up the criminal offence for which the suspect has been detained (i.e. the *mens rea* and the *actus reus*) and ascertain whether sufficient evidence exists to indicate that those elements of the offence exist. When answering a question relating to the DEAD factors, it is advisable to state what evidence exists (and assess the strength of this evidence) and whether any evidence is lacking (if so, perhaps allude to the types of additional evidence that would be necessary to establish that the offence had been committed by the subject).

- If the evidence against the victim is not very extensive or conclusive, it may be appropriate to advise your client to remain silent. Note however that R v Howell clarified that where the victim/complainant has not provided a witness statement, this does not automatically provide a good reason for advising your client to remain silent.

3. Argent factors

- If certain circumstances exist or the suspect has certain attributes, adverse inferences cannot be drawn at the trial from the suspect's silence at interview. This was established in the case of R v Argent. These circumstances include, for instance, where the defendant is of ill health, not sober, a child, an elderly person or not fully aware (these are therefore referred to as the "Argent" factors).

- If any of the "Argent" factors apply, the suspect should be advised to remain silent. Conversely, if none of these factors exist, the court may be entitled to draw negative inferences from any decision made by the suspect to remain silent.

4. Defence

- Consider the suspect's defence and whether it can be easily proven. If the suspect has a strong defence/alibi, it may be appropriate to advise the suspect to answer questions solely for the purpose of putting forward their defence/alibi (provided that the Argent factors do not apply and the suspect is therefore of strong enough character to do so).

Answering questions

Advantages	Disadvantages
• If a suspect answers questions (and therefore does *not* remain silent), they avoid the risk of adverse inferences being drawn. • If the suspect intends to make any admissions, it may be favourable to be cooperative at this stage (since an early admission can have a positive impact at the sentencing stage). • If the suspect has a legitimate defence/alibi that completely undermines the prosecution's case, it may be better to provide such explanation at an earlier stage (to avoid unnecessary detention).	• The suspect may incriminate himself/herself, for instance by inadvertently providing the police with new information/evidence. Anything the suspect says can be used as evidence against them at trial. • The suspect may become intimidated/nervous and inadvertently provide a poor/ambiguous/incorrect account of the event.

Remaining silent

Advantages	Disadvantages
• If a suspect remains silent, they will be able to control the content and extent of the information they provide to the police. This will avoid the risk of the suspect incriminating himself/herself or inadvertently giving evidence that will later be used again them. • Suitable where the police lack sufficient evidence to prosecute the suspect or where there has not been enough information disclosed.	• There is a risk of adverse inferences being drawn from the suspect's silence if the case progress to trial. This could negatively affect the suspect's case.

Prepared statement

Advantages	Disadvantages
• Submitting a prepared statement is suitable where the suspect is vulnerable but wishes to put forward a defence. • Doing so allows the suspect to raise a defence, whilst also controlling the content and extent of the information that is being provided.	• Adverse inferences can still be drawn where a prepared statement is given (unless the suspect maintains the account given in their prepared statement should the case proceed to trial). This was established in R v Knight.

Bail

Bail relates to the question of whether or not the court is likely to grant the suspect bail after he/she has been charged with an offence or, alternatively, whether they are to be detained in police custody before their first court appearance.

> **Bail:** the release of a person who will be under a duty to later surrender to custody.

The granting of bail is governed by the Bail Act 1976 ("BA 76"). Exam questions dealing with bail on the LPC could ask, for instance, whether a defendant is likely to be granted bail, or which submissions the defence/prosecution are likely to make in a bail application. When answering a question on bail, consider working through the relevant sections of BA 76 in the following order:

1. General rule

BA 76 s. 4, together with the European Convention of Human Rights Article 5(3), establishes that a defendant has a general right to be granted bail until they are convicted.

2. Exceptions to the general rule

The main exceptions to the general rule for the purposes of the LPC are outlined in BA 76 Schedule 1, Part 1, paragraph 2(1). Bail need not be granted if the court is satisfied that there are "**substantial grounds**" for believing that the defendant, if released on bail, would:

(a) Fail to surrender to custody;

(b) Commit an offence while on bail; or

(c) Interfere with witnesses or otherwise obstruct the course of justice, whether in relation to himself/herself or another person.

Note that the exceptions set out in BA Schedule 1, part 1, paras 2, 2A and 6 will not apply if it appears to the court that there is no real prospect that the defendant will receive a custodial sentence BA 76 Schedule 1, Part 1, paragraph 1A(1). The court will use the Sentencing Guidelines to establish the likelihood of a custodial sentence on conviction (the Sentencing Guidelines are explained in more detail in the *Sentencing* section of this module).

3. Meaning of "substantial grounds" BA 76 Schedule 1 Part 1 Paragraph 9

Whether the court has "substantial grounds" for believing that one of the above exceptions exists is a question of fact for the court to determine. When doing so, the court must take into account the factors set out below:

- The nature and seriousness of the offence.

- The character, antecedents, associations and community ties of the defendant.

- The defendant's record in respect of the fulfilment of his obligations under previous grants of bail.

- The strength of the evidence against the defendant.

- Any other factors which appear relevant.

For example, if the prosecution is trying to persuade the court to refuse the suspect bail on the grounds that the suspect will later fail to surrender to custody (exception (a) as listed above), the court will only do so if it is satisfied, in light of the above factors, that there are "substantial grounds" for the prosecution's concerns. If the suspect has in the past violated the conditions attached to a previous grant of bail, this could constitute "substantial grounds" for believing that the suspect would fail to surrender to custody if granted bail in the present case.

4. Conditions

Even if bail is granted, sometimes it will be subject to conditions (BA 76 s. 3 allows for this). Examples of common conditions include that the defendant must:

- Surrender his/her passport.

- Report to the police station at regular intervals.

- Have another person stand as surety for his/her surrender (i.e. that other person would have to pay a fine should the suspect not surrender).

- Live and sleep at a specified address.

- Refrain from entering a certain area.

- Refrain from contacting specified individuals.

- Remain indoors during certain hours (i.e. a curfew may be imposed).

5. Abscondment

Finally, you should set out what happens if the defendant fails to adhere to the conditions attached to their bail or fails to surrender to custody when required to do so at a later stage.

"Absconding" (failing to surrender) is an offence in its own right. The offence is committed if:

(a) The defendant fails to surrender to custody without having reasonable cause for doing so BA 76 s. 6(1); or

(b) The defendant had reasonable cause for initially failing to surrender, but subsequently failed to surrender without reasonable cause after the new (later) time limit for surrendering had passed BA 76 s. 6(2).

Bail applications and submissions

Danny is charged with an offence of burglary in a convenience store in Whetstone High Street and is currently held in police custody. He has one previous conviction of theft and two for burglary, but has never failed to surrender whilst on bail in the past. All previous offences were committed at night on Whetstone High Street. Danny is married, has three young children and lives at a permanent address. Danny is unemployed.

Danny appears before the magistrates today and his defence lawyer, Andrew, is making a bail application on his behalf. Which objections to bail is the prosecution likely to raise and which factors from Schedule 1, Part 1, Paragraph 9 will the prosecution use to support their arguments?

Although Danny has a general right to bail, it is likely that the prosecution will argue that the following two exceptions apply: (1) that Danny is likely to commit further offences whilst on bail; and (2) that he is likely to fail to surrender. The following paragraph 9 factors suggest that there are substantial grounds for believing that those exceptions will apply:

- Burglary is a serious offence which means Danny, if he is convicted, is likely to receive a custodial sentence. This means there are substantial grounds for believing that he will fail to surrender to custody.

- Danny's previous convictions mean that he has bad character and antecedents, which means there are substantial grounds to believe that he will commit similar offences whilst on bail.

Allocation

Allocation refers to the procedure under which a case is allocated to a particular court. Criminal cases will be dealt with either in the magistrates' court or the Crown Court (but note that the *allocation procedure* always takes place in the magistrates' court). There are three types of offences:

- **Summary only offences:** offences that can only be dealt with in the magistrates' court.

- **Either way offences:** offences that can be dealt with in both the magistrates' court and the Crown Court.

- **Indictable offences:** offences that can only be dealt with in the Crown Court.

It follows that if the offence is an "either way" offence, a decision must be made as to which court will hear the case (i.e. which court the case will be *allocated* to). As explained below, the question of sentencing power is an important one throughout the process of allocation. Sentencing is dealt with in more detail in the *Sentencing* chapter of this module.

Plea before venue

- **Plea before venue:** a preliminary hearing (always in the magistrates' court) where the defendant indicates whether he/she intends to plead guilty or not guilty. This is the first step in the allocation procedure.

Magistrates' Court Act 1980 s. 17A ("MCA 80") sets out the procedure of plea before venue:

The court will read out the charge to the defendant. The court will then ask the defendant to indicate whether he wishes to plead guilty or not guilty.

- **If the defendant pleads guilty:** the court will proceed immediately to sentencing.

- **If the defendant pleads not guilty:** the court will proceed to allocation.

Court allocation

MCA 80 s. 19 governs the second step in the allocation procedure. The court must decide whether the offence appears more suitable for summary trial or for trial on indictment, using the factors set out in MCA 80 s. 19(3). The court shall consider:

1. **The adequacy of the sentences that a magistrates' court has the power to impose.**

   When considering the adequacy of the magistrates' sentencing powers for a specific offence, you should assess the Sentencing Guidelines applicable to the specific offence and any aggravating or mitigating factors. Sentencing and aggravating/mitigating factors are explained in more detail in the *Sentencing* chapter of this handbook.

2. **Any representations made by the prosecution or the defence.**

   Both parties will be invited to make representation as to whether a summary or indictment trial is more appropriate.

The court will also have regard to the "allocation guidelines" published by the Sentencing Council. These guidelines emphasise that "either way" offences should be tried summarily (i.e. in the magistrates' court) unless the defendant (if found guilty) would likely deserve a sentence that is in excess of the magistrates' court's powers.

- If the magistrates' court accepts jurisdiction (i.e. establishes that the case can be tried summarily), the defendant can choose whether he/she wants to be tried in the Crown Court or in the magistrates' court.

- If the magistrates' court rejects jurisdiction (i.e. establishes that the case should be tried on indictment instead), the case will be sent to the Crown Court.

If the defendant can choose

As mentioned, if the magistrates' court has accepted jurisdiction, the defendant can choose whether to be tried in the Crown Court or the magistrates' court.

Indication

Before the defendant makes their decision as to whether they would like to be tried in the magistrates' court or in the Crown Court, they can ask the magistrates' court for an indication of whether it would impose a custodial sentence upon the defendant. The magistrates' court does not have to give such an indication, but if it does, it is bound by its indicated decision if the defendant subsequently chooses to be tried in the magistrates' court.

Factors to consider

When making their decision, the defendant should consider the following factors:

Cost:

- Trials in the magistrates' court involve fewer and lower costs than in the Crown Court.

Time:

- Trials in the magistrates' court are less time consuming, in particular as a result of such trials being scheduled more quickly and the fact that they involve fewer formal procedures than trials in the Crown Court.

Sentencing powers:

- The magistrates' court has weaker sentencing powers than the Crown Court, although they can commit the case to the Crown Court for sentencing (meaning this factor is less significant).

Acquittal rates:

- The Crown Court has a higher rate of acquittal than the magistrates' court.

Evidence/Voir dire:

- "Voir dire" is the process in the *Crown* Court whereby the jury is asked to leave the room when the judge considers the admissibility of a particular piece of evidence.

- In a magistrates' court however, the magistrates will hear evidence and then decide whether it is admissible; this means it may be difficult for the magistrates' to avoid being prejudiced by evidence that should not have been admitted to court.

- The Crown Court may therefore be more suitable if the defendant has made an application to exclude evidence and this application has not yet been settled. Note that the admissibility and exclusion of evidence is dealt with in more detail in the *Evidence and Witnesses* chapter of this module.

Jury:

- Unlike in the Crown Court, the defendant can avoid a trial by jury in the magistrates' court. This may particularly appeal to company defendants (as juries historically treat companies with a higher degree of suspicion).

Publicity:

- Cases in the magistrates' court typically attract less publicity (although they are still generally open to the public).

Criminal Litigation

Evidence and Witnesses

This chapter relates to the evidence that will be put before the court in order to determine whether the defendant is guilty.

Competence and Compellability of Witnesses

> **Witness competence:** a witness is "competent" if he/she is *permitted* to give evidence in the proceedings.

> **Witness compellability:** a witness is "compellable" if he/she can be *forced* to give evidence in the proceedings.

When dealing with the competence and compellability of witnesses, it is useful to first establish into which category the witness in question falls. The witness could be:

- The defendant
- A co-defendant;
- The spouse or civil partner of the defendant or a co-defendant; or
- A person that falls outside the above categories (known as an "ordinary" witness). Note that a policeman is categorised as an "ordinary witness".

Different rules apply to the different categories. The rules for competence and compellability also vary depending on the side for which the witness is to give evidence (i.e. the prosecution or the defence). The rules can be summarised as follows:

Ordinary witnesses

The general rule is that all ordinary persons are *competent*, as long as they are able to understand questions put to them and are capable of giving answers that can be understood Youth Justice and Criminal Evidence Act 1999 s. 53 ("YJCEA 99"). All competent witnesses are *compellable*.

The defendant as a witness

For the prosecution

- The defendant is *neither* competent nor compellable to testify for the prosecution YJCEA 99 s. 53(4).

For the defence

- The defendant is a *competent* witness for the defence, but is *not* compellable Criminal Evidence Act 1898 s. 1 ("CEA 98").
- Note however that the court may draw adverse inferences as a result of a defendant refusing to give evidence for the defence CJPOA 94 s. 34. Adverse inferences are explained in the *Advising a Client at the Police Station* chapter of this module.

The spouse or civil partner of the defendant or co-defendant as a witness

For the prosecution

- The defendant's spouse or civil partner is a *competent* witness for the prosecution YJCEA 99 s. 53(1).
- The defendant's spouse or civil partner is only compellable for the prosecution if the defendant is charged with a "specified offence" PACE 84 s. 80(2A)(b). These "specified offences" are outlined in PACE 84 s. 80(3) (see below definition box).

For the defence

- The defendant's spouse or civil partner is a competent *and* compellable witness for the defence, unless the spouse/civil partner is a co-defendant in the proceedings PACE 84 s. 80(2).

For the co-defendant (for both the defence and the prosecution)

- The spouse or civil partner of one co-defendant is only compellable to give evidence relating to another co-defendant's defence or prosecution if the offence is a "specified offence" PACE 84 s. 80(2A)(a).

> **Specified offences**: "specified offences" in the context of witnesses are listed in PACE 84 s. 80(3) and include: assault, injury or threat of injury to a spouse, civil partner or a child under 16; sexual offences on a person under 16; and conspiring, attempting, aiding or abetting any of the aforementioned offences.

The co-defendant as a witness

For the prosecution
- The co-defendant is neither competent nor compellable to testify for the prosecution YCJEA 99 s. 53(4).

For the defence
- The co-defendant is a competent witness for the defence, but is *not* compellable CEA 98 s. 1.

Admissibility

> **Admissible evidence:** evidence that a party is allowed to present to, and have considered by, the court.

For evidence to be admissible, it must be:

- Relevant to the case (irrelevant evidence is inadmissible);
- Evidence of facts (opinion evidence is generally inadmissible, unless given by an expert witness); and
- Not excluded by an application (see below).

Exclusion of Evidence

It is sometimes in the defendant's interest to try to exclude certain pieces of evidence (e.g. if the evidence incriminates them, or if it would be unfair to base their guilt upon them). As mentioned, the Crown Court and magistrates' court have different procedures for ascertaining whether evidence should be excluded:

- In the Crown Court, an application to exclude evidence takes place by way of "voir dire", whereby the jury will leave the room whilst the judge decides on the question of admissibility.
- In the magistrates' court, an application to exclude evidence takes place in front of the magistrates and if it is decided that the evidence is inadmissible, the magistrates must "put it from their minds" when deciding on the defendant's guilt (this leaves some room for bias permeating the minds of magistrates, as it can be difficult in reality to "forget" something already seen/heard when forming a judgment on a matter).

When deciding whether a piece of evidence may be excluded, you should consider the following:

1. General rule

In criminal proceedings, the general rule is that all evidence is admissible so long as it is factually relevant to the case.

2. Exclusion under PACE 84 s. 76 (confessions)

This rule should only be considered if the defendant is seeking to exclude a *confession* made by them that has been included as evidence. If a confession is excluded, this means that the confession must not be taken into account when deciding on the defendant's guilt.

> **"Confession":** this is defined as "any statement wholly or partly adverse to the person who made it, whether made to a person in authority or not and whether made in words or otherwise" s. 82(1) PACE.

The starting point is that confessions are admissible, pursuant to PACE 84 s. 76(1). Confessions can however be excluded in two circumstances:

(a) Oppression PACE 84 s. 76(2)(a)

- This exclusion applies if the defendant has confessed as a result of oppression from a third party. "Oppression" includes: torture, inhuman or degrading treatment, and the use or threat of violence (whether or not it amounts to torture) PACE 84 s. 76(8).

(b) Unreliability PACE 84 s. 76(2)(b)

- This exclusion applies if the defendant has confessed as a result of anything said or done which was likely, in the circumstances existing at the time, to render unreliable any confession that might be made by the defendant in consequence. "Things said or done" could include, for instance, a police officer breaching PACE when the confession was made, or a police officer inducing a confession by offering the suspect a grant of bail in return.

There is a "causal link" requirement for both the oppression and unreliability exclusion. This means that the oppression or the "thing said or done" must have *caused* the confession to be made. The most important factor when establishing a causal link is *time*: the confession must immediately follow from the oppression/"thing said or done" (there should be no or little delay, otherwise the element of "inducement" will be harder to prove).

If the defence has raised either oppression or unreliability as a potential ground for having a confession excluded, the prosecution must prove beyond reasonable doubt that the confession (notwithstanding that it may be true) was not obtained as a result of oppression/unreliability. If the prosecution is unable to do this, the court must rule the confession inadmissible (note that this requirement is mandatory).

3. Exclusion under PACE 84 s. 78

PACE 84 s. 78 applies to *all* types of evidence (whereas PACE 84 s. 76 only applies to *confession* evidence). PACE 84 s. 78 states that evidence may be deemed inadmissible by the court if it appears that the admission of evidence would have such an adverse effect on the fairness of the proceedings that the court ought not to admit it.

- Circumstances that may affect fairness to such a degree could be, for instance, that the evidence was obtained illegally, improperly or unfairly (e.g. if the evidence was obtained in a way that constitutes a breach of PACE or COP).

- However, the case of R v Walsh clarified that for evidence to be inadmissible pursuant to PACE 84 s. 78, the breach of PACE or COP must be significant and substantial. A minor failure by the police to observe the rules is not enough.

Note that unlike with PACE 84 s. 76, the rule under PACE 84 s. 78 is *discretionary*. This means that the judge has absolute discretion when deciding whether to exclude the evidence on this ground.

Regina tells her defence lawyer that she admitted to an offence for which she was arrested. She claims she did this only because the police officer that arrested her kept threatening her that unless she admitted to the alleged crime now, he would ensure that she would be sent to prison and would never see her daughter again. The police officer had this conversation with Regina in the police car on the way to the police station. What can Regina's defence lawyer do to attempt to exclude her admission from the evidence that will be put before the court?

The general rule is that Regina's confession is admissible as evidence against her at her trial. Reginas's defence lawyer can however use both PACE 84 s. 76 and PACE 84 s. 78 to try to exclude Regina's confession from the evidence.

- s. 76 PACE deals with the exclusion of confession evidence. Here it could be argued that Regina only admitted to the offence as a result of "things said and done" by the police officer that arrested her. The police officer acted in a threatening way and also breached COP, since he held an unlawful interview (the requirements for a lawful interview are outlined in the *Lawful Interviews* section of the *Police Powers* chapter of this module). It is therefore likely that PACE 84 s. 76(2)(b) applies. A causal link would need to be established, which will depend on whether Regina's confession immediately followed the policeman's actions.

- s. 78 PACE can be used to exclude evidence if it can be established that admitting the relevant evidence would have such an adverse effect on the fairness of the proceedings that the court ought not to admit it. Since the evidence was obtained through a breach of COP (an unlawful interview), the confession may also fall under this section (if it is deemed, pursuant to R v Walsh, to be a significant and substantial breach of COP).

Identification Evidence

> **Identification evidence:** evidence given by a witness relating to the identity of the defendant. This could take the form of, for instance, eyewitness accounts or photographic evidence.

One of the main issues in many cases is identifying who, as a matter of fact, actually committed the offence. There is an inherent risk that a witness can be genuinely mistaken in their identification of a defendant, but convincing in front of a jury.

Consider a scenario where a victim is mugged and threatened at knifepoint. An eyewitness says she saw the defendant run from the scene. That eyewitness later identifies the defendant in an identification procedure (e.g. through a Video Identification Parade Electronic Recording ("VIPER") procedure, where the witness is asked to pick the defendant out from a group of nine similar-looking individuals). If the defendant states that he was not at the scene, and no other evidence exits (such as CCTV evidence, forensic evidence or other witnesses), the case will effectively turn on whether that one eyewitness' identification was accurate. Wrongful identification can therefore cause great injustice.

Turnbull factors: "ADVOKATE"

The Turnbull factors become relevant where: (1) the defendant is disputing the identification evidence; and (2) there is little or no other evidence to be put before the court that implicates that particular defendant. The judge must establish that allowing the identification evidence to be put before the jury would not result in an unsafe conviction. When doing so, the judge will be guided by the factors set out in R v Turnbull:

- **Amount of time under observation**: for how long did the witness have the defendant in view?
- **Distance**: how far away was the witness from the defendant?
- **Visibility:** what was the visibility like at the scene? For instance, did fog or rain affect the witness' view, or was it dark?
- **Obstruction**: did anything obstruct the witness' vision (for instance, a dirty window or a lorry)?
- **Known to the witness**: had the witness seen the individual before? If so, when and how frequently? If the witness knew the defendant, this could suggest that the witness was more likely to have been accurate in their identification.
- **Any reason to remember**: were there any special reasons to remember the individual, such as tattoos and/or scars?

- **Time lapse**: how much time lapsed between the witness initially seeing the individual and the witness identifying that individual in an identification procedure (e.g. a VIPER procedure)? In general, the greater the lapse of time, the less reliable the witness' memory.

- **Errors**: are there any discrepancies or errors between the witness' description and the individual's actual appearance?

Remembering the word "**ADVOKATE**" can help you to remember the above (this represents the first letter of each factor).

Turnbull warning

If the judge (subsequent to their analysis of the situation using the Turnbull factors) establishes that it would be unsafe to admit the identification evidence, they must withdraw the case from the jury. This is because without the identification evidence, no other evidence exists that can be put before the jury, meaning the prosecution no longer has a case.

If the judge instead establishes that the identification evidence may be used, or that other evidence exists, the trial can proceed. However, when the judge is putting forward his summary to the jury, he/she must give them a "Turnbull warning":

- The judge must warn of the special need for caution before convicting the defendant, and explain the need for this warning. The judge should emphasise that a mistaken witness can still be a convincing witness.

- The judge should then direct the jury to examine the circumstances in which the identification was made (using the Turnbull factors).

- The judge should also remind the jury of any weaknesses in the identification evidence in light of the Turnbull factors.

Character Evidence

> **Character evidence**: evidence relating to the character or disposition of a defendant for the purpose of proving that they were more likely to have acted in a particular way on a particular occasion. There is both "good character" evidence and "bad character" evidence. Good character evidence is used to show that the defendant's character is not of a nature that would suggest they committed the crime of which they have been accused (e.g. evidence to show a defendant accused of a violent crime is in fact of a peaceful nature). Bad character evidence tends to show a defendant's disposition towards misconduct.

Good character

If the defendant is of previous good character, the defence may attempt to adduce this as evidence. This can be done by calling witnesses to testify to the defendant's good character or adducing evidence from the prosecution witnesses in cross-examination.

When good character evidence has been presented, the judge must make a "Vye direction" (named after the case of R v Vye). This involves the judge:

- Telling the jury (whilst summing up) to consider that the defendant's good character means it is less likely that he/she committed the offence; and

- Telling the jury (when the jury is considering the defendant's own testimony/pre-trial statements) that the defendant's good character is relevant to his/her credibility as a witness; the jury is effectively directed to consider that the defendant is more likely to be telling the truth.

Bad character

Bad character evidence cannot always be adduced. Consider the following structure when answering a question on whether bad character evidence can be presented in a particular situation:

1. Definition of bad character

The Criminal Justice Act 2003 ("CJA 03") s. 98 defines "bad character" evidence as evidence of *prior* misconduct by the defendant (not evidence relating to the *offence* with which the defendant has been charged and/or misconduct during the investigation). "Misconduct" is in turn defined in CJA 03 s. 112 as "the commission of an offence or other reprehensible behaviour". Bad character evidence therefore relates to a defendant's previous convictions.

2. General rule

CJA 03 s. 101 sets out the general rule, that evidence of a defendant's bad character is inadmissible except where one of the "gateways" contained in CJA 03 s. 101(1)(a)-(g) apply.

3. The "gateways"

Although there are seven "gateways" in CJE 03 s. 101(1), this handbook focuses on the first four. Check with your LPC provider whether you are expected to apply and understand the other three.

Criminal Litigation

Gateway A – CJA 03 s. 101(1)(a)

Bad character evidence can be adduced if *all* parties agree to that evidence being admissible.

Gateway B - CJA 03 s. 101(1)(b)

Bad character evidence can be adduced if the evidence of "bad character" was: (a) presented by the *defendant* himself/herself; or (b) given in answer to a question asked to the defendant in cross-examination that was intended to elicit it.

Gateway C – CJA 03 s. 101(1)(c)

Bad character evidence can be adduced if it provides important explanatory evidence. "Important explanatory evidence" is defined in CJA 03 s. 102 as evidence that, if not adduced, would make it difficult (or impossible) for the court or jury to understand other evidence in the case and its value for understanding the case as a whole is substantial.

Gateway D – CJA 03 s. 101(1)(d)

Bad character evidence can be adduced if it is relevant to an important "matter in issue" between the defendant and the prosecution. Most cases have two main matters "in issue": (1) the matter (or likelihood) of whether the defendant committed the crime; and (2) the matter (or likelihood) of whether the defendant is telling the truth when giving evidence CJA 03 s. 103(1).

1. **Likelihood of whether the defendant committed the crime:** when assessing the defendant's propensity to commit a certain type of crime, the court can consider the defendant's previous convictions (if any) for offences **of "the same kind" as the offence with which he/she has been charged** CJA 03 s. 103(1)(a). CJA 03 s. 103(2) clarifies that an offence of "the same kind" means an offence of:

   (a) **The same *description* as the offence with which the defendant has currently been charged**. There is some uncertainty as to the meaning of this, but the case of R v Hanson, Gilmore and Pickstone set out some guidelines:

   - The fewer and older the previous convictions, the weaker the bad character evidence;

   - "Description" can be viewed broadly. For instance, if the method used in the crimes for which the defendant was previously convicted shares significant features with the method used in the current alleged offence (even if the features are not identical), "propensity" to commit a certain type of crime may be inferred.

   - This would suggest (for example) that a previous conviction for common assault would be appropriate as bad character evidence for a defendant that is subsequently charged with threatening behaviour (assuming the previous conviction is not too old).

   (b) **The same *category* as the offence with which the defendant has been charged.** These categories are decided by the Secretary of State and currently only two exist: offences under the theft act and sexual offences against children. Thus, if the defendant has previously been convicted of an offence under the Theft Act, this can be used as bad character evidence in a current trial if the new offence also falls under the Theft Act.

2. **Likelihood that the defendant is telling the truth:** bad character evidence in this context can be important when the prosecution is seeking to discredit the defendant as a witness (i.e. by suggesting to the jury that the defendant is lying in his/her statements).

   - A defendant's propensity to be untruthful may be proven if the defendant has previously been convicted for offences involving "untruthfulness" (note that this is not the same as "dishonesty"), for instance perjury CJA 03 s. 103(1)(b).

   - If the prosecution tries to rely on bad character evidence in this context, the defence should try to draw the court's attention to R v Campbell. In this case, it was emphasised that the jury/judge should focus on the *current* charge, and whether *current* evidence indicates that the defendant has committed the alleged offence. The court felt previous convictions should not be relied upon too heavily.

4. Safeguards for the defendant

There are certain safeguards that defendants can use if the prosecution attempts to adduce bad character evidence. CJA 03 s. 103(3) states that the court must not admit evidence under gateway D or gateway G (on an application by the defendant to exclude that evidence) if it appears to the court that the admission of such evidence would have such an adverse effect on the fairness of the proceedings that the court ought not to admit it. When assessing whether this would be the case, the court will consider (in particular) the length of time between the "old" convictions and the offence with which the defendant has currently been charged.

5. Notice

CJA 03 s. 111 requires the prosecution to notify the defendant in advance of any intention to adduce bad character evidence in court (unless the defendant has agreed to the admission of any bad character evidence).

Sentencing

> **Sentencing:** the process by which a judge decides what punishment the defendant will incur after being convicted for committing a crime.

Types of Sentences

Non-custodial sentences

- **Fines**: these are imposed and fixed in accordance with a three-stage process set out in CJA 03 s. 164.

- **Community orders**: a defendant could be ordered to, for instance, carry out unpaid work for a set number of hours or undertake drug/alcohol rehabilitation. CJA 03 s. 177 contains a list of possible community orders that may be imposed.

- **Absolute or conditional discharge**: an absolute discharge completely discharges the defendant from punishment, whereas a conditional discharge means the defendant will avoid punishment subject to the condition that he commits no offence of any type during a specified period (this period can be set up to a maximum of three years). An absolute or conditional discharge may be suitable for a defendant whose circumstances are such that the recording of a criminal offence will be sufficient punishment in itself. Such orders are made pursuant to Powers of the Criminal Courts (Sentencing) Act 2000 ("PCC(S)A 00") s. 12.

- **Compensation to the victim**: if the offence involves personal injury, the court must give reasons if they do not order the defendant to pay compensation to the victim PCC(S)A 00 s. 130.

Custodial sentences

- CJA 03 s. 152 places certain restrictions on the ability of the courts (both the Crown Court and magistrates' court) as to when to impose custodial sentences on convicted defendants:

    (a) The court should only impose a custodial sentence where the offence (or series of offences) is (are) so serious that neither a fine nor a community sentence can be justified.

    (b) The court can also impose a custodial sentence where the defendant has been given a community order sentence and has failed to comply with any requirements in relation to that order.

- **Suspended sentences:** CJA 03 s. 189 allows for the suspension of prison sentences that are imposed for a period ranging from 14 days to two years.

> **Suspended sentence:** the judge suspends the defendant's serving of the custodial sentence. The defendant avoids going to prison immediately and is given a chance to "stay out of trouble" and comply with any conditions that may be attached to the suspended sentence. For instance, a defendant can be sentenced to one year's imprisonment but have it suspended so that they can attend drug rehabilitation/treatment. If the defendant breaches the terms of the sentence (e.g. if they fail to attend scheduled rehabilitation), the suspended sentence may consequently be activated (meaning the defendant will then have to serve time in prison).

Sentencing Powers of the Courts

The Crown Court and the magistrates' court have different sentencing powers (this was briefly mentioned in the *Allocation* section above).

1. Sentencing powers of the magistrates' court

PCC(S)A 00 s. 78 and Magistrates' Court Act 1980 s. 133 ('MCA 80') together govern the sentencing powers of the magistrates' court:

- The maximum custodial sentence that may be imposed for any single "either way" or "summary only" offence is six months.

- The maximum custodial sentence that may be imposed for a defendant convicted of committing *two or more* "either way" offences is 12 months. However, where a defendant is convicted of committing *multiple* "*summary only*" offences, the magistrates' court cannot impose a custodial sentence that exceeds six months.

- To illustrate, if a defendant has been convicted for ten summary only offences, the maximum imprisonment a magistrates' court can impose on them is six months. If they have instead been convicted for two either way offences, the maximum imprisonment the magistrates' court could impose on them is 12 months.

- If a defendant has been convicted in the magistrates' court for an either way offence, the magistrates' court can instead commit the defendant to the Crown Court for sentencing if it considers its maximum sentencing power to be insufficient PCC(S)A 00 s. 3.

2. Sentencing powers of the Crown Court

The Crown Court is not subject to any specific sentencing limitations in respect of adult offenders. The only limitations are those imposed by statute (offences usually state the maximum sentence that may be imposed following a conviction, as explained below).

Sentencing Procedure: Which Sentence Is Likely To Be Imposed?

When answering a question that requires you to assess which sentence a defendant is likely to receive, consider the various rules and guidelines set out below:

1. Identify the rules that the court will consider

- The magistrates' court will consider the Magistrates' Court Sentencing Guidelines.

- The Crown Court will consider the Crown Court Sentencing Guidelines.

- Courts will also consider the overarching principles and policies relating to sentencing, notably the need to: punish criminal behaviour; deter (and thus reduce) crime; protect the public; compensate victims of crime (and avoid the risk that people will "take matters into their own hands" in order to achieve "justice"); and rehabilitate offenders so that they can contribute to society.

2. Statutory aggravating factors

If any of the following CJA 03 s. 143 statutory aggravating factors apply, the offence in question is considered more serious and is therefore likely to attract a harsher sentence:

- Higher level of culpability of the offender in committing the offence.

- Higher level of harm caused by the offence.

- The offence was pre-mediated/planned.

- The offence was committed whilst the defendant was already on bail for another crime.

- The defendant had recently been convicted for a similar offence.

CJA 03 s. 145 and CJA 03 s. 146 contain additional statutory aggravating factors that can lead a court to impose harsher sentences where the crime in question was motivated by race, religion, disability or sexual orientation.

3. Establish a starting point and a range

There are different "categories" of offences. The category into which a particular offence falls will depend on the culpability of the offender and the harm caused by the offence. The Sentencing Guidelines provide the following guidance:

Category 1	Greater harm and higher culpability
Category 2	Greater harm and lower culpability *or* lesser harm and higher culpability
Category 3	Lesser harm and lower culpability

The Sentencing Guidelines also contain a list of factors that help a court to distinguish between greater/lesser harm and higher/lower culpability. Below is an example from the Magistrates' Court Sentencing Guidelines for the commission of domestic burglary (note the phrasing below is slightly different to the phrasing contained in the Sentencing Guidelines).

Factors indicating greater harm	**Factors indicating lesser harm**
• Theft of/damage to property causing a significant degree of loss to the victim (whether economic, commercial or personal value).	• Nothing is stolen from the property, or items stolen were of a very low value to the victim (whether economic, commercial or personal value).
• Property is soiled, ransacked or vandalised.	• There was limited damage and/or disturbance to the property.
• The offence is committed in the presence of the occupier(s).	
• Trauma is caused to the victim, beyond the normal inevitable consequence of intrusion and theft.	
• Violence is used or threatened against the victim.	

Factors indicating higher culpability	Factors indicating lower culpability
• The premises or victim had been deliberately targeted (thus indicating some degree of pre-meditation). Examples include targeting: pharmacies or doctor's surgeries, particularly vulnerable victims, or victims on the basis of their race, religion, disability or sexual orientation etc.	• The offence was committed on impulse, with limited intrusion into the property.
• There was a significant degree of planning or organisation.	• The offender was exploited by others (e.g. gang members).
• The offender was carrying a knife or other weapon at the time (this is not relevant if the offender was charged separately for carrying the weapon in question).	• The offender has a mental disorder or learning disability that is somehow linked to the commission of the offence.
• The offender was equipped for burglary (e.g. they were in possession of implements used to break into a house and/or had a getaway vehicle at their disposal).	
• The offender was a member of a gang or group.	

Each category of offence has a sentencing "starting point" and a sentencing "range". These are also set out by the Sentencing Council for England and Wales and in the courts' Sentencing Guidelines.

- The "starting point" may be a particular type/length of sentence, or a particular action that the court must initially take.

- The "range" sets out the minimum and maximum sentences that can be imposed for the sentence in question.

Below is an example taken from the Magistrates' Court Sentencing Guidelines for the commission of domestic burglary:

Offence Category	Starting Point	Category Range
Category 1	Crown Court (the Crown Court – not the magistrates' court – should be responsible for sentencing).	Crown Court (the Crown Court – not the magistrates' court – should be responsible for sentencing).
Category 2	1 year custodial sentence.	High Level Community Order – Crown Court (2 year's custody).
Category 3	High level Community Order.	Low Level Community Order – 26 weeks' custody.

4. Aggravating factors in the Sentencing Guidelines

The Sentencing Guidelines contain aggravating factors specific to particular offences. If an aggravating factor exists, this means that the offence is more serious and is thus more likely to result in a harsher sentence. As an example, the following are aggravating factors that can increase the sentence imposed for a person convicted of committing a domestic burglary:

- The offence was committed at night.

- The offence involved the abuse of a position of trust (e.g. a doctor committing the offence against a particularly vulnerable patient).

- The offence involved the unwarranted ("gratuitous") degradation of the victim(s).

- Steps were taken to prevent the victim(s) from: (1) reporting the incident or obtaining assistance; and/or (2) assisting or supporting the prosecution throughout the investigation.

- Established evidence of community impact.

- The offence was committed whilst the offender was under the influence of alcohol or drugs.

- The offence involved the offender's failure to comply with an existing court order (e.g. a curfew).

5. Mitigating factors

Where mitigating factors exist, the court may impose a more lenient sentence on the offender. CJA 03 s. 166 allows the court to consider the defendant's personal circumstances when assessing whether any mitigating factors exist, for example the defendant's community standing, job, family, health, education and (f relevant) efforts made to rehabilitate themselves following drug or alcohol addiction.

There are also mitigating factors that are specific to particular offences (these are set out in the Sentencing Guidelines). As an example, the following are mitigating factors that can reduce the sentence imposed for a person convicted of committing a domestic burglary:

- The offender voluntarily offered reparation to the victim.

- The offender had a subordinate role in a group or gang.

Criminal Litigation

- The offender had no previous convictions or no relevant/recent convictions.
- The offender has shown genuine remorse.
- There is evidence of the offender's good character and/or exemplary conduct.
- The offender has evidenced their determination to address their addiction (if relevant) and/or reform their offending behaviour (e.g. they have shown that they have taken steps such as attending a rehabilitation clinic).
- The offender is the sole or primary carer for dependent relatives.
- The offender has a serious medical condition that requires urgent, intensive or long-term treatment.

6. Credit for making a guilty plea and the defendant's remorse

If the defendant pleads guilty at an early stage, this may lead to a reduction in their sentence CJA 03 s. 144. The earlier in the proceedings a guilty plea is made, the higher the reduction in sentence that may follow. Showing genuine remorse may also work in the defendant's favour, but this is only relevant if the defendant has pleaded guilty; a court will not take into account a person's claim that they are remorseful following a conviction if that person claimed throughout the proceedings that they were innocent.

7. Conclusion on sentence

At this stage in an exam question, you should estimate the sentence that the court is likely to impose. Take into account the starting point, the range, any mitigating and aggravating factors, and (if relevant) any guilty pleas and evidence of remorse. If you conclude that a *custodial* sentence is likely to be imposed, then consider the possibility that the sentence may be "suspended" and the conditions that may be attached to the suspension.

8. Ancillary orders

Lastly, you should consider whether any ancillary orders are likely to be made alongside the sentence, for instance an order to pay compensation to the victim.

Charles has been convicted of a domestic burglary pursuant to the Theft Act 1968 s. 9(1)(b). He has three previous convictions, but for different offences (all were for the possession of cocaine). He is due to be sentenced today in the Crown Court.

- Charles specifically targeted 114 Maidrock Road, as he knew Rosa lives there alone and is 84 years old.
- He pretended to be a TV licence investigator and visited Rosa in the morning of the day on which he carried out the offence. He did this to get a first-hand view of the house so that he could formulate a proper plan for the actual burglary.
- Charles, at 11.45pm that night, broke in through a window and ransacked the downstairs living room. He eventually found a box containing £100 cash, which he stole. He also stole a small painting worth £400 that was a family heirloom.
- Charles was arrested as a result of his attempt to sell the painting to a pawnbroker (the pawnbroker knew Rosa and recognised the painting). The pawnbroker later identified Charles in court.
- Rosa claims that she has suffered some psychological harm following the burglary and consequently has to take sleeping pills in order to get to sleep at night.
- Charles was convicted at the end of the trial, having pleaded not guilty throughout.

What is the court likely to see as its starting point and range for sentencing? What are the aggravating and mitigating factors?

1. Starting point and range

The following factors indicate greater *harm* in light of the Crown Court Sentencing Guidelines for domestic burglary:

- Charles ransacked the property.
- Rosa was left traumatised.
- The occupier (Rosa) was at home when the burglary took place.
- One of the items stolen (the painting) was of high sentimental value.

The following factors indicate higher *culpability* in light of the Crown Court Sentencing Guidelines for domestic burglary:

- Charles deliberately targeted Rosa as a result of her vulnerability and age.
- Charles undertook a significant degree of planning.

To summarise the above, the offence involved a high level of culpability and caused a significant level of harm. The offence is therefore likely to be deemed a "Category 1" offence. The starting point (also found in the Crown Court Sentencing Guidelines) for a Category 1 domestic burglary is a 1-year custodial sentence, whilst the range is a custodial sentence lasting from 2 years to 6 years.

2. Aggravating and mitigating factors

The following factors are aggravating factors under the Crown Court Sentencing Guidelines for domestic burglary:

- The offence was committed at night.

No statutory aggravating factors apply (note that Charles' previous convictions cannot be used as an aggravating factor as they are not similar to this offence). Using the Crown Court Sentencing Guidelines for domestic burglary, no factors apply to this scenario that could reduce the seriousness (mitigating factors).

240

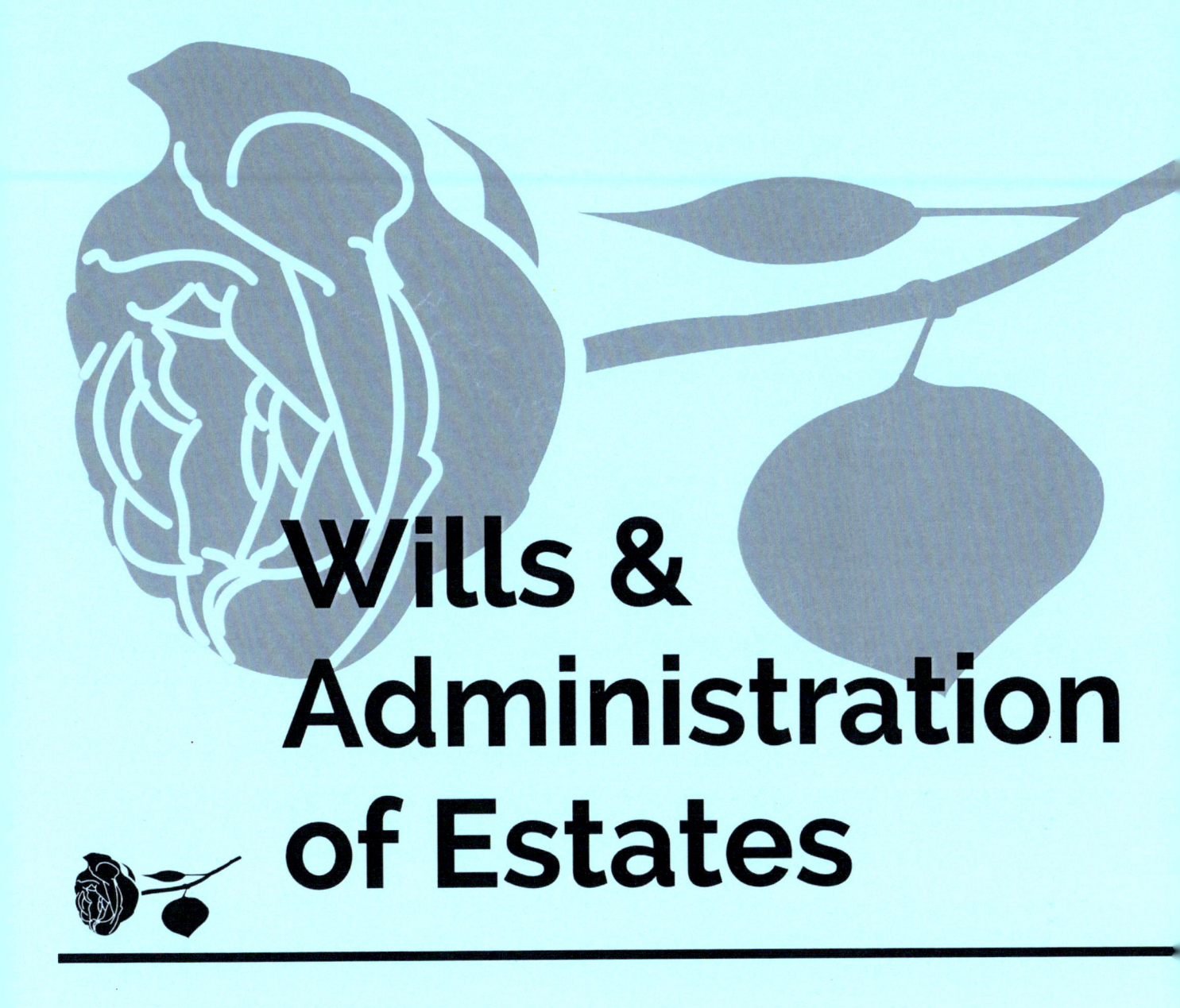

Wills & Administration of Estates

Wills & Administration of Estates

The Succession Estate and the Will — 243

The succession estate • validity of a will • incorporating documents into a will • altering a will • revoking a will • failure of legacies under a will

Distribution Under the Intestacy Rules — 245

Testate • intestate • flow chart setting out the intestacy rules

Inheritance Tax — 246

Chargeable transfers • exemptions and relief • identifying the taxable estate • valuing the taxable estate • cumulative total • nil rate band • inheritance tax rates

Grant of Representation — 249

Grant of probate • grant of letters of administration with the will annexed • grant of letters of administration

Administering the Estate: Duties and Powers of Personal Representatives — 251

Statutory powers • remuneration • powers granted by the will • duties of personal representatives • missing beneficiaries/creditors

The Succession Estate and the Will

The Succession Estate

> **Succession estate:** the assets owned by the deceased that will form part of the "pool" of assets that is to be distributed to the deceased's heir(s).

The following assets are *excluded* from a deceased's succession estate:

- **Property held with others as joint tenants**: this is because of the operation of "survivorship" (see the *Property Law* module in this handbook). Immediately upon the death of a joint tenant, the surviving joint tenant(s) will receive the deceased joint tenant's "share" of the property.
- **Life insurance policies written "in trust"**: life insurance policies are typically written "in trust" for the benefit of a nominated person (e.g. a spouse). That person (the beneficiary of the trust) will receive the insurance pay-out when the insured person dies.
- **Discretionary pension schemes and benefits**: in some circumstances, a person with a pension scheme will have nominated a named third party beneficiary that will be entitled to receive money from that pension scheme after the party with the pension scheme dies.
- **DMC ("*donation mortis causa*")**: this refers to a gift made by the donor in anticipation of their own impending death. The gift takes immediate effect upon the donor's death.
- **Trusts and settlements**: the distribution of trust property (other than life insurance policies) is governed by the deed that created the trust.

The Will

Validity of a will

The following must exist for a will to be valid:

1. Capacity

- The testator must be over the age of 18, unless they are executing a "privileged" will.
- The testator must have soundness of mind, memory and understanding. This means they must understand: what making the will means, what constitutes their property, and the moral claims they should consider (e.g. the needs of children they will leave behind).

> **Testator:** the person who is making the will/giving away their legacy after their death.

> **Privileged will**: privileged wills are valid even if the formalities are not met (for instance, if the testator was under 18). Privileged wills are usually made by men or women who are in "active military service", where it may not be possible to comply with the various formalities (e.g. the correct number of witnesses etc.).

2. Intention

- The testator must have both: (1) the *general* intention to make a *will* (as opposed to another type of document such as a contract); and (2) the *specific* intention to make the *particular* will they are writing and signing (i.e. they have not been coerced into signing something that does not reflect their true intentions).
- Intention is presumed if the testator is of sound capacity (but this presumption is rebuttable).

3. Compliance with the Wills Act 1837 ("WA 37")

The formality requirements are set out in s. 9 WA 37 and are as follows:

(a) The will must be in writing and signed by the testator;

(b) The will must be witnessed and signed by two or more witnesses;
   - Both witnesses must be present when the testator signs.
   - The testator must be present when each witness signs, but there is no requirement that the witnesses are present for each other's signature.

   Note that a beneficiary of a will (or a person who is a spouse of that beneficiary at the time of execution) should not act as a witness. If they do, that beneficiary will be unable to inherit under that will, although the rest of the will remains valid WA 37 s. 15.

(c) If a will contains an attestation clause (a clause explaining the circumstances under which the will was executed), there will be a presumption that s. 9 WA 37 has been complied with (if the explanation given suggests a valid procedure was used) and therefore that the will has been property executed.

Incorporating documents into a will

When a document is "incorporated" into a will, it means that the document will form part of the will (and will therefore be admitted to probate) even though it does not comply with the formality requirements explained in the above section. For a document to be incorporated:

- It must be clearly identified in the will;
- It must exist at the date of execution of the will; and
- Its existence at that date must be confirmed in the will.

> 📖 **Admitted to probate:** the word "probate" means to prove or validate. If a will has been *admitted* to probate this means the Court has approved it as valid (i.e. confirmed it is the last will of the testator and that it has been properly executed).

Altering a will

Alterations made *before* the will is executed will be valid if the will is valid. However, if alterations are made *after* the will is executed, such alterations must be attested (i.e. signed by both the testator and two witnesses). If there is no attestation, there is a rebuttable presumption that the alteration was made *after* the execution of the will and is therefore invalid (this is to avoid fraud, as it is difficult to prove when an alteration took place). To properly attest an alteration, it is sufficient for the testator and the two witnesses to sign their initials next to the alteration.

If an invalid alteration to a will has been carried out, the following rules will govern the next steps that must be taken:

- **Original wording still legible/apparent:** if the original wording can still be ascertained, these words will be valid and will take effect.
- **Original wording no longer legible/apparent:** if the original wording is no longer ascertainable (e.g. the original words were fully redacted and only the invalid alteration is legible), the original wording is deemed to have been "obliterated" (meaning those words will not take effect). This is the case even if other evidence exists that would help to establish the nature of the original gift.

    However, if it appears that the testator attempted to *substitute* (rather than completely override) the original wording using new amendments, the court may find that the "obliteration" was in fact *conditional* upon the new wording taking effect. In this scenario, the court may accept external evidence to help establish the nature of the original gift.

> 📖 **Codicil:** a valid amendment/alteration to an already executed will. The original will and all codicils are read together and the estate is distributed accordingly, with the most recent alterations overriding earlier conflicting bequeaths. To be valid, codicils must comply with the aforementioned formality requirements set out in s. 9 WA 37.

Revoking a will

A will will be revoked in the following circumstances:

- **Marriage**: if the testator marries or enters into a civil partnership after executing their will, that will will be automatically revoked unless the testator clearly expressed (in the will) that the will was in contemplation of a particular marriage WA 37 s. 18.
- **Destruction**: if the will is completely and deliberately destroyed by the testator (e.g. if it is burned), it will be taken to have been revoked provided sufficient intention to revoke can be ascertained WA 37 s. 20.
- **Revocation by later will or codicil**: the later document must contain a revocation clause, expressly revoking all wills previously executed. If there is no such express revocation clause, both wills will be valid. To the extent that they are inconsistent, the later will will take effect.

Failure of legacies under a will

> 📖 **Failure of legacy:** where a gift given in a will fails and thus does not take effect (i.e. the beneficiary will not receive it). Where a gift fails, the relevant asset will consequently form part of the residue of the estate.

- **Divorce:** if a testator divorces their spouse/civil partner, their will remains valid. However, when the estate is distributed, any gift to such ex-spouse/civil partner will fail and any appointment of such ex-spouse/civil partner as trustee or executor will be deemed ineffective.
- **Beneficiary predeceases testator:** if a beneficiary dies before the testator, the gift will fail, unless that beneficiary is a descendent of the testator and has their own issue. In such circumstances, the issue will receive the benefit under the will WA 37 s. 33.
- **Ademption:** this relates to the situation where a specific asset bequeathed by the will no longer forms part of the testator's estate at the time of his/her death (e.g. the testator has given a car to Maggie in his will, but at the time of death, that testator no longer owns that car). In such a scenario, the asset will be considered "adeemed" and the gift will fail.
- **Uncertainty:** a gift will fail if the asset cannot be identified from the description in the will. For instance, if the testator writes in his will "I give my ring to John" and the testator has multiple rings in his succession estate at the time of his death, "ring" will not be a sufficient enough description to ascertain precisely which ring John is to receive. The gift would consequently fail.
- **Disclaimer:** this refers to the situation where the beneficiary refuses to accept a gift given to him/her in the testator's will. Under such circumstances, the gift would fail.

Distribution Under the Intestacy Rules

Whether a person dies testate or intestate determines whether the intestacy rules will be followed (rather than a will) when distributing a deceased's estate.

> **Intestate:** a person dies "intestate" if they die without a valid will in place.

> **Testate:** a person dies "testate" if they die having made a valid will.

When a person dies intestate, the same rules as outlined above apply as to which assets will form part of the succession estate. However, as there is no will that sets out who will receive what from that succession estate, the distribution will instead be made in accordance with the statutory intestacy rules. These rules are summarised by the following flow chart:

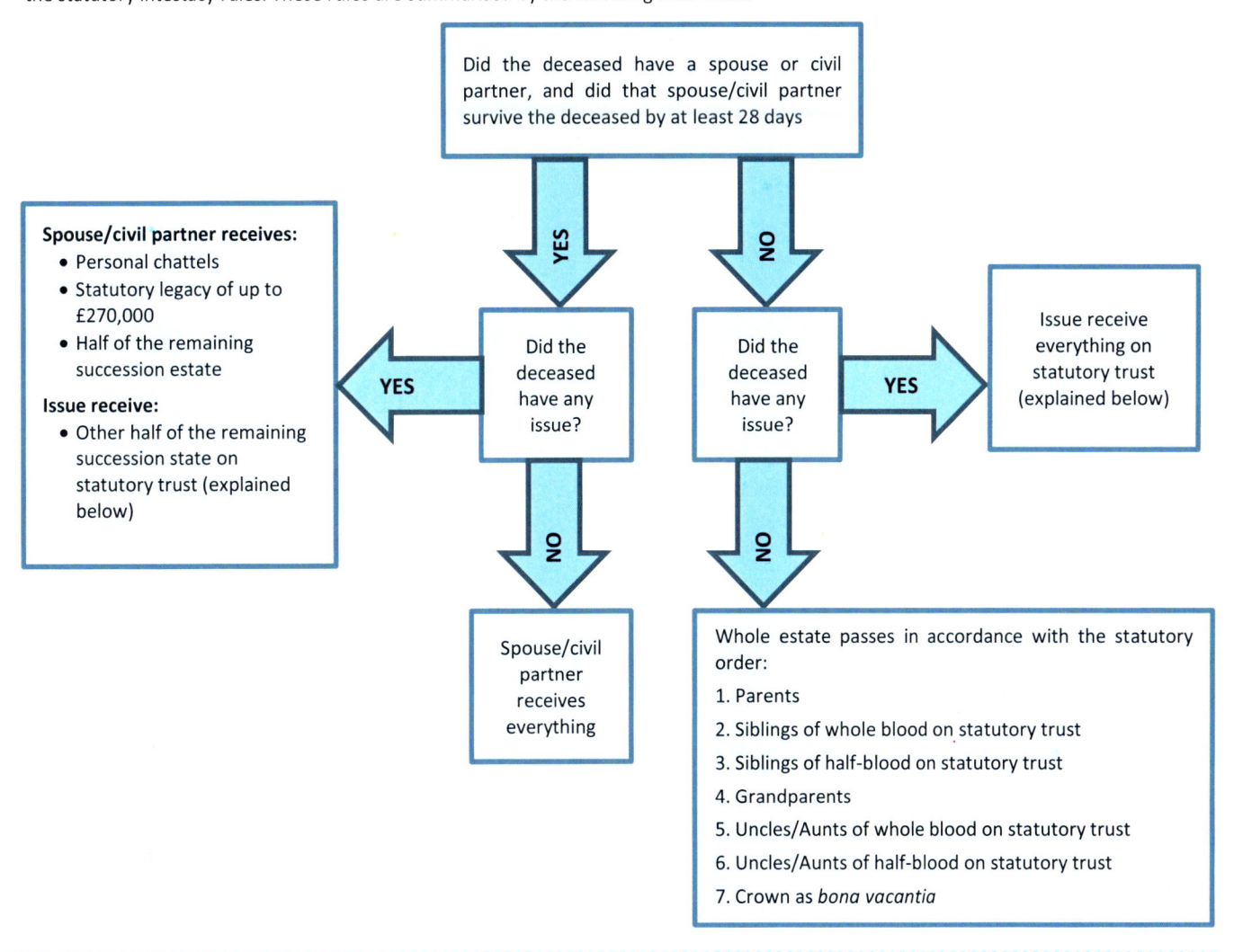

Flow chart:

Did the deceased have a spouse or civil partner, and did that spouse/civil partner survive the deceased by at least 28 days

- **YES** → Did the deceased have any issue?
  - **YES** → Spouse/civil partner receives:
    - Personal chattels
    - Statutory legacy of up to £270,000
    - Half of the remaining succession estate

    Issue receive:
    - Other half of the remaining succession state on statutory trust (explained below)
  - **NO** → Spouse/civil partner receives everything

- **NO** → Did the deceased have any issue?
  - **YES** → Issue receive everything on statutory trust (explained below)
  - **NO** → Whole estate passes in accordance with the statutory order:
    1. Parents
    2. Siblings of whole blood on statutory trust
    3. Siblings of half-blood on statutory trust
    4. Grandparents
    5. Uncles/Aunts of whole blood on statutory trust
    6. Uncles/Aunts of half-blood on statutory trust
    7. Crown as *bona vacantia*

> **Issue:** in this context, we mean a person's children or other lineal descendants.

Statutory trust

> **Statutory trust:** when a child is the beneficiary of a will, they cannot take direct ownership of the relevant asset. Instead, they will take assets on a statutory trust. Beneficiaries (other than parents or grandparents) also take their inheritance on statutory trust (see the above flowchart). This means that in order to inherit, the beneficiary must survive the intestate by at least 28 days and either: (a) reach the age of 18; or (b) if they are younger, be married. If the beneficiary is already 18 or married at the time of the intestate's death they will have a "vested interest", meaning they will inherit absolutely and immediately. If the beneficiary dies before the intestate, their issue can inherit provided that they reach the age of 18 or marry earlier.

Right of surviving spouse to take the family home

If the intestate was married and lived with their spouse in the matrimonial home, the surviving spouse has a right to receive that home if either: (a) the intestate solely owned the home; or (b) the intestate and the spouse owned the home as tenants in common. Remember that if the intestate and spouse owned the home as *joint tenants*, the deceased's share would automatically transfer to the spouse due to the operation of survivorship (i.e. the home would not have formed part of the succession estate anyway). If the value of the house is higher than the "statutory legacy" allowance of up to £270,000 and there are issue, the spouse must pay an amount equal to half of the amount in excess of £270,000 to the personal representatives to be held on statutory trust for the benefit of such issue.

Inheritance Tax

Chargeable Transfers

A chargeable transfer is a transfer between individuals that will be subject to inheritance tax. There are three such categories that are typically covered on the LPC:

1. Potentially Exempt Transfers ("PETs")

These are gifts made by the deceased during their lifetime (to another person) that are not taxable at the time, but may *potentially* become taxable at a later stage (e.g. a parent gifting a child £10,000 to help pay for that child's wedding).

- If the person giving the gift (the "transferor") dies within seven years of making that gift, the gift will be deemed a "chargeable transfer" and inheritance tax will consequently become payable on the value of the transfer at the full "death tax" rate of 40%. This is referred to as a "failed" PET.
- If the transferor survives for seven years after making the gift, the gift will be exempt and will therefore not constitute a chargeable transfer.

2. Lifetime Chargeable Transfer ("LCTs")

An LCT includes, for instance, gifts made from individuals to companies or transfers from individuals to discretionary trusts. These types of transfers are subject to 20% tax at *the time* of the transfer.

- If the transferor survives for at least seven years after the transfer is made, no further tax will be payable.
- However, if the transferor dies within seven years of making the transfer, the tax liability is assessed at the time of death and the value of the transfer will be subject to the full "death tax" rate of 40% (i.e. the additional 20% will have to be paid). This re-evaluation of tax due is subject to *taper relief*, which is explained in more detail below.

3. Transfer after death

If the transfer is made following the transferor's death (i.e. the transfer is given effect in a will or by virtue of the statutory intestacy rules), the full "death tax" rate of 40% will be payable on the value of the transfer (subject to the reliefs and exemptions outlined below).

Exemptions and Relief

Exemptions, allowances and reliefs for *lifetime* transfers only

Annual allowance

- An individual can make transfers of up to £3,000 tax free in any given tax year; this is known as the "annual allowance".
- This allowance can be carried forward to the following year (but not any subsequent years) and only a maximum of twice the annual allowance (i.e. £6,000) can be applied in any one tax year.
- The allowance is applied chronologically, meaning the first £3,000 given away in a year will automatically attract the annual allowance (the allowance cannot instead be allocated to subsequent sums gifted).
- Any unused annual allowance that has already been carried forward once will be lost.

Small gifts allowance

- An individual can transfer amounts worth up to £250 as often as they like without a risk arising that the amount will be subject to inheritance tax, so long as the same individual does not receive *more* than £250.
- If a gift exceeds £250, the *whole* gift will be subject to inheritance tax (if no other exemptions or allowances apply).

Normal expenditure out of income

- Transfers from income that do not affect the transferor's standard of living will not later be subject to inheritance tax.

Marriage exemptions

- Transfers made in consideration of a marriage are exempt subject to the following rules:
    - (a) Up to £5,000 is exempt if given by a parent to one of either party to the marriage.
    - (b) Up to £2,500 is exempt if given by one party of the marriage to the other.
    - (c) Up to £2,500 is exempt if given by a remote ancestor (e.g. a grandparent) of one of the parties.
    - (d) Up to £1,000 is exempt if given to either of the parties by anyone else.

Family maintenance

- Payments for the maintenance of a spouse/former spouse/child/dependent relative are exempt from inheritance tax.

Exemptions, allowances and reliefs for lifetime transfers and the death estate

Transfers between spouses/civil partners

- A person can transfer an unlimited amount to their spouse without the transfer attracting inheritance tax, both during the transferor's lifetime and at their death (i.e. through their will or by the intestacy rules).
- Note however that the inheritance must occur *immediately*. Therefore this exemption does not apply where the beneficiary of the transfer is a child for *life* with the *remainder* to the spouse.

Charity

- Transfers to charities (whether during the deceased's lifetime or through their will) are exempt from inheritance tax.

Agricultural Property Relief ("APR")

- If a person transfers a "qualifying agricultural property" during their lifetime or through their will/the intestacy rules, at least some relief from inheritance tax will be available if:
    1. The transferor *owned* and *occupied* the property for agricultural purposes for at least the two year period ending on the date of the transfer, 100% relief is available; or
    2. The transferor *owned* the property for at least the seven-year period ending on the date of the transfer but someone else occupied the property for agricultural purposes throughout that period.

Business Property Relief ("BPR")

- If a person transfers a relevant business property (whether during the deceased's lifetime or through their will), relief from inheritance tax will be available if the transferor *owned* the property for at least two years ending on the date of the transfer. The amount of inheritance tax relief available depends on the *nature* of the relevant business property:
    (a) A business or an interest in a business (e.g. a share of a partnership): 100% relief is available.
    (b) Shares in an unquoted (i.e. private) company: 100% relief is available.
    (c) *Controlling* interest in a *quoted* (i.e. public) company: 50% relief is available.
    (d) Land, plant or machinery *owned* by the transferor but *used* by, for instance, a partnership in which the transferor was a partner: 50% relief is available *if* the partnership was still using the relevant property up until the transferor's death.

Heritage assets

- Certain types of property are deemed to be of natural, historic, scientific or artistic value. An owner of such property can apply to HMRC for the transfer of that property to be exempt from inheritance tax.
- The approval of the exemption from HMRC is typically subject to the condition that the new owner must preserve and permit public access to the Property.

Exemptions and relief for the death estate only

Woodland relief

- The value of any timber transferred will be exempt from inheritance tax.

Quick succession relief

- This is available in the following situation. Person X leaves their taxable estate to Person Y (and Person Y pays inheritance tax on it). Person Y dies within 5 years and leaves their taxable estate to Person Z. A tax credit is available to reduce the amount of inheritance tax due on Person Y's estate (payable by Person Z).

Death in active service

- The estates of members of the armed forces will be exempt from inheritance tax if those members of the armed forces die whilst in service.

Taper relief

You will remember from above that if a person dies within seven years of making a PET and LCT, inheritance tax may be payable on PETs and the inheritance tax rate increases from 20% to 40% on LCTs.

To make this seven year rule less harsh, taper relief exists to reduce the inheritance tax liability if the transferor dies between three and seven years after making the transfer. The longer the period after the transfer was made, the larger the reduction:

- If the transferor survived for 3+ years, but for less than 4 years: 80% of the inheritance tax due will be payable.
- If the transferor survived for 4+ years, but for less than 5 years: 60% of the inheritance tax due will be payable.
- If the transferor survived for 5+ years, but for less than 6 years: 40% of the inheritance tax due will be payable.
- If the transferor survived for 6+ years, but for less than 7 years: 20% of the inheritance tax due will be payable.

Identifying and Valuing the Taxable Estate

Identifying the *taxable* estate

Note that the question of identifying the *taxable* estate is a different question to that of which property is included in a person's succession estate.

Property included in the estate for inheritance tax purposes	Property *not* included in the estate for inheritance tax purposes
Property subject to a reservation: this is where a donor transfers property but reserves the right to benefit from the asset (e.g. parents gifting a child a holiday house but retaining the right to use it free of charge).	**"Excluded" property:** the most common example is a reversionary interest in a trust (i.e. a remainder interest).
Property that has joint owners: this is regardless of whether such owners hold the property as joint tenants or tenants in common.	**Insurance policies written in trust:** the sum of such policies will have been written in trust for the benefit of another.
"Donatio mortis causa": a lifetime gift made conditional on the donor's death. **Life interests in trusts created by a will.** **All property that is not specifically excluded:** a catch-all category.	**Discretionary pension scheme contributions:** discretionary lump sum paid by a pension fund trustee.

Valuing the taxable estate

The general rule is that the value of property for the purposes of inheritance tax is the *market* value. This is subject to certain exceptions:

- **Related property:** some assets are worth more as a pair (e.g. a set of two antique candle sticks). To take account of this, HMRC will value (for instance) an individual item that is one of a set of two items, at half the value of the combined pair. This only applies between spouses.
- **Joint property (land):** because half a piece of land or half a house is difficult to sell, HMRC allows the value (for the purposes of inheritance tax) of an individual's share to be reduced by a set percentage where that share has been transferred to another. This does not apply where spouses own land together and it is transferred from one to the other.

Cumulative Total and Nil Rate Band

- **Cumulative total:** the cumulative total is the sum of all chargeable transfers made by the deceased in the seven years leading up to his/her death (this includes the transfer of property *at* death, i.e. through the deceased's will or the intestacy rules). Note that the cumulative total is calculated *after* exemptions and reliefs have been taken into account.

- **Nil Rate Band ("NRB"):** if the cumulative total falls below the "nil rate band", then no inheritance tax will be payable on the deceased's estate. For the 2021/2022 tax year, the nil rate band has been set at £325,000. This means that if the cumulative total is less than £325,000, no inheritance tax will be payable on the deceased's estate and, if it is more, no tax is payable on the first £325,000 (this is explained in more detail below).

Transfer of the nil rate band between spouses

If a person has an unused portion of their nil rate band at the time of their death (i.e. their cumulative total was less than £325,000), the unused percentage can be transferred to their spouse. For example, if a person dies and their taxable estate is only worth £100,000, an additional inheritance tax allowance worth £225,000 can be "transferred" to their spouse. This means that a spouse (in the seven years preceding their death and in their will/through the intestacy rules) can transfer up to £550,000, without the recipient(s) having to pay inheritance tax. In addition, if someone dies on or after 6 April 2017 and their estate is above the basic inheritance tax threshold, the estate may be entitled to an additional allowance before any inheritance tax becomes due. For 2021-2022, this amount is up to £175,000.

Inheritance Tax Rates

The inheritance tax rates for the 2021/2022 tax year are as follows (although the estate can pay Inheritance Tax at a reduced rate of 36% on some assets if a person leaves 10% or more of the net value to charity in his/her will):

Band	Tax rate
Deceased's estate valued at £0 - £325,000 (unless the nil rate band has been increased as a result of a transfer by a spouse of his/her remaining NRB)	0%
Above £325,000	40%

Grant of Representation

> **Personal representative:** this is the person appointed to administer a deceased's estate. If a personal representative is appointed by a will, they are referred to as an "executor". If a personal representative is appointed by statute, they are referred to as an "administrator". The personal representative's duty is to collect the property of the deceased and administer such property in accordance with law.

> **Grant of Representation:** a court order giving the personal representative(s) named in a will the authority to collect and distribute a deceased's estate.

There are three types of grant of representation: a Grant of Probate; a Grant of Letters of Administration with the Will Annexed; and a Grant of Letters of Administration.

Grant of Probate

This is the appropriate grant if the deceased had in place a valid will that appoints executors. Those executors must be able and willing to act as personal representatives and must not be minors. An appointed executor can "renounce probate" (i.e. formally step down), in which case the Grant of Probate will not be the appropriate grant.

If a person has died in partial intestacy (i.e. the will does not distribute *all* of the deceased's assets), a Grant of Probate may also be used so long as willing and able executors have been appointed.

A PR appointed by a will is referred to as an "executor".

Grant of Letters of Administration with the Will Annexed

This type of grant is appropriate where the deceased has left a valid will and:

- The will does not appoint executors; or

- The will does appoint executors, but those executors have all renounced power or are not *able* to act as a personal representative (e.g. they are minors); or

- The will does appoint executors, but those executors were outlived by the testator.

Entitlement to the grant of letters of administration with will annexed

When this type of grant is used, it will be unclear who the personal representative(s) should be. To resolve this, there exists a statutory order of priority of people to whom the grant can be made. This order of priority is contained in Rule 20 of the Non Contentious Probate Rules 1987 ("NCPR") and is as follows:

1. The executor.

2. A trustee of the residuary estate.

3. Any other residuary beneficiary (whether under the will or under the intestacy rules).

4. The personal representative(s) of any other residuary beneficiary other than a life tenant of the residue.

5. Any other beneficiary or a creditor.

6. The personal representative(s) of any other beneficiary or a creditor, other than a life tenant of the residue.

A personal representative that has been appointed by NCPR Rule 20 is referred to as an "administrator".

Grant of Letters of Administration

This is the appropriate grant where no valid will exists and the estate is therefore to be distributed in accordance with the intestacy rules.

Entitlement to the grant of letters of administration

When this type of grant is used, again it will be unclear who the personal representative(s) should be. To resolve this issue, there exists another statutory order of priority of people to whom the grant can be made. This order of priority is contained in Rule 22 of the Non Contentious Probate Rules 1987 ("NCPR") and is as follows:

1. The deceased's spouse or civil partner.

2. The deceased's children. If any of the deceased's children died before the deceased, then also the issue of those children.

3. The deceased's father and mother.

4. The deceased's brothers and sisters of whole blood. If any of the deceased's brothers and sisters of whole blood died before the deceased, then also the issue of those brothers and sisters.

5. The deceased's brothers and sisters of half-blood. If any of the deceased's brothers and sisters of half-blood died before the deceased, then also the issue of those brothers and sisters.

6. The deceased's grandparents.

7. The deceased's uncles and aunts of whole blood. If any of the deceased's uncles or aunts of whole blood died before the deceased, then also the issue of those uncles or aunts.

8. The deceased's uncles and aunts of half-blood. If any of the deceased's uncles or aunts of half-blood died before the deceased, then also the issue of those uncles or aunts.

9. The "Treasury Solicitor". This is when the crown claims *bona vacantia*.

10. The deceased's Creditors.

For people falling within categories 1 – 8, the person applying for the grant must have some beneficial entitlement to the estate in order for their application to be successful.

A personal representative that has been appointed by NCPR Rule 22 is referred to as an "administrator".

Administering the Estate: Duties and Powers of PRs

Powers of Personal Representatives

Personal representatives derive their powers primarily from: (a) the will; and (b) four main statutory sources. These statutory sources include: the Administration of Estates Act 1925 ("AEA 25"), the Trustee Act 1925 ("TA 25"), the Trustee Act 2000 ("TA 00") and the Trusts of Land Appointment of Trustees Act 1996 ("TOLATA 96").

Statutory powers

- **Power to advance capital:** TA 25 s. 32 allows trustees to use capital to pay out benefits to a beneficiary even where that beneficiary is not absolutely entitled to the asset (e.g. they have not married and marriage is a pre-condition to take absolutely). This is subject to restrictions: (1) any beneficiaries with a life interest must consent and; (2) the money that has been paid out must be taken into account at the time where the beneficiary in question becomes entitled to the asset (i.e. deduct any payments already made to that beneficiary).

- **Power to appropriate:** AEA 25 s. 41 affords trustees the power to decide which assets from the succession estate should be used to fulfil each beneficiary's entitlement. This power is subject to the following: (a) the trustees' decisions taken pursuant to this power must not prejudice any beneficiary; (b) beneficiaries must give their consent to the appropriation of the asset(s) in question; and (c) the value of any asset(s) being appropriated is ascertained at the time of the *transfer* (i.e. not at the time of the transferor's death).

- **Power of maintenance:** this relates to the power of dealing with income arising from a trust asset (e.g. rental income from a property). TA 25 s. 31 states that PRs have complete discretionary power to apply income generated from trust assets towards the maintenance, education or other benefits for minor beneficiaries. If any income is unused, that income must be invested.

- **Power to invest:** PRs have the power to make any kind of investment that *"he could make as if he were absolutely entitled to the assets"* TA 00 s. 3. This is subject to the rule in TA 00 s. 4 that PRs (as trustees) must have regard to the standard investment criteria (the suitability to the trust of the investments made and the need for diversification).

- **Power to insure:** TA 00 s. 34 gives power to the personal representatives to insure any property that is part of the succession estate and to pay for the premiums out of that estate's income or capital.

Remuneration

TA 00 s. 29 allows PRs who act in a professional capacity (i.e. are professional trustees) to receive reasonable remuneration out of the trust fund for the services they provide in relation to administering the estate. This is subject to some restrictions: (1) they must not be a sole PR; and (2) the other PRs must give their consent to such remuneration.

Non-statutory powers: powers granted by the will

Some common powers that are often included in a will (since they are not given to personal representatives by statute) include:

- **Running a business:** if the deceased owned a business, there is no statutory power given to personal representatives to continue running that business subsequent to the death. In the interest of selling that business as a going concern (which typically results in a higher price being obtained than if the assets of the business were sold separately), personal representatives may be granted the power to temporarily run the business in the will. This is especially important if the testator was a sole trader, as no one else would be able to help with selling the business as a going concern.

- **Indemnity clause:** this would allow the personal representatives to be indemnified by the beneficiaries for any losses suffered as a result of mistakes made by those personal representatives.

Duties of Personal Representatives

Personal representatives are subject to a variety of duties that are imposed on them by statute and the common law. Personal representatives must perform their duties with due diligence and in accordance with the powers that they have been given (either by statute or the will). This section outlines some of the key duties that you may need to know in your exam.

Duty to collect assets and administer the estate

As mentioned, personal representatives must collect the real and personal estate of the deceased and then "administer" that estate in accordance with the law AEA 25 s. 25. This includes:

- Paying outstanding debts owed by the deceased;
- Transferring assets to the correct beneficiaries; and
- Paying any residue to those entitled.

Personal representatives have a duty to take reasonable steps to preserve the value of the estate and to carry out the administration process within 12 months from the date on which the deceased died (this is sometimes referred to as the "executors' year").

Duty to comply with apportionment rules

A deceased's assets/investments can continue to produce income after death, for instance rental income relating to land owned by the deceased. The personal representatives are under a duty to "apportion" any accrued income appropriately. This means that they must decide whether what they are distributing is: (a) income that *belonged* to the deceased; or (b) income that arose after the death to which a particular beneficiary is entitled.

For instance, take the scenario where the deceased left a property to Doris and the residue of their estate to Sid. If the property provided rental income before the deceased's death and continued to do so afterwards, how should the personal representatives apportion this income?

- Any rental income which arose *before* Doris became entitled to the property (i.e. income relating to the period before the deceased died) would form part of the residue of the estate and could thus go to Sid; whilst
- Any income that arose *after* Doris became entitled to the property (i.e. income that accrued *after* the deceased died) could go to Doris, as from this point it was effectively *Doris'* property that was generating the income.

Note that this duty can be excluded in the will.

Statutory duty of care

Under the TA 00 s. 1, personal representatives must exercise such care and skill as is reasonable in the circumstances, having regard in particular:

- To any special knowledge or experience that they have or hold themselves out as having; and
- If acting as personal representative in the course of a business or profession, to any special knowledge or experience that it is reasonable to expect of such a person.

Note that a will can contain a clause that explicitly excludes or modifies this statutory provision (e.g. to protect the personal representatives from liability if they make any mistakes in good faith).

Breaches of duty

Personal representatives are personally liable for any loss resulting from a breach of duty that they have committed (they are not typically liable for loss resulting from breaches of duty by co-personal representatives). Breaches of duty could arise from:

- Incorrectly administering the estate: for instance, distributing assets to the wrong beneficiaries.
- Negligence: for instance, allowing the value of the estate to drop where the drop in value could easily have been avoided, or unreasonably delaying the administration of the estate.
- Misappropriation: for instance, a personal representative wrongly retaining property to which they were not entitled.

Where such a breach has occurred, a claim can be brought by either a creditor or a beneficiary that has suffered loss as a result. However, the court has the power to relieve personal representatives of liability where they have "acted honestly and reasonably and ought fairly to be excused" TA 25 s. 61.

Missing Beneficiaries/Creditors

One of the duties of a personal representative is to pay to all beneficiaries that which they are entitled to pursuant to the will or intestacy rules. As mentioned, personal representatives are personally liable for failing to distribute to an entitled beneficiary. This can be problematic where there are many beneficiaries and the specific identities or locations of some are unknown. There are a number of options available to PRs to protect themselves should such a situation arise:

Claims by *unknown* beneficiaries/creditors

An "unknown" beneficiary or creditor is a beneficiary or creditor of which the personal representative(s) had no notice at the time they were distributing the assets. TA 25 s. 27 enables personal representatives to protect themselves against claims by such parties (and thus to avoid personal liability arising) by:

- Advertising the intention to distribute the relevant property in the Gazette and, if the property in question is land, in a local newspaper relating to the locality in which the land is situated; and

- Following such advertising, allowing a period of at least 2 months for any person believing that they are beneficially entitled to provide details of their claim.

If the personal representatives distribute the estate after this process has been followed, an unknown beneficiary or creditor cannot claim against the personal representative (meaning the PR will avoid personal liability).

Claims by *known* beneficiaries

TA 25 s. 27 will not protect a personal representative if they have failed to distribute property to a *known* beneficiary. A "known" beneficiary is one whose identity is known by the personal representative, although the personal representative may not know their whereabouts or may have been unable to get in contact with them. If the personal representative cannot locate a particular beneficiary, there are certain measures that they can take to avoid personal liability for failing to distribute relevant assets to that missing beneficiary:

- **Benjamin Order:** personal representatives can apply to court for a "Benjamin Order", which permits trustees to distribute a missing beneficiary's share to other beneficiaries on the assumption that the missing beneficiary no longer qualifies for an interest under the will. If the missing beneficiary subsequently appears, the personal representatives will not be personally liable; instead, that beneficiary can recover their share from the beneficiaries that were originally given the missing beneficiary's share. Note that the court will only make a Benjamin Order if reasonable attempts to locate/contact the missing beneficiary have been made.

- **Indemnity:** the personal representatives can seek an indemnity from the other beneficiaries of the will before distributing the share of an unknown beneficiary. This means the other beneficiaries will cover the cost of any claims made against the personal representatives.

- **Insurance:** the personal representatives could purchase insurance that would pay out should a missing beneficiary appear and make a claim.

- **Payment into court:** the personal representatives could pay the missing beneficiary's entitlement into court.

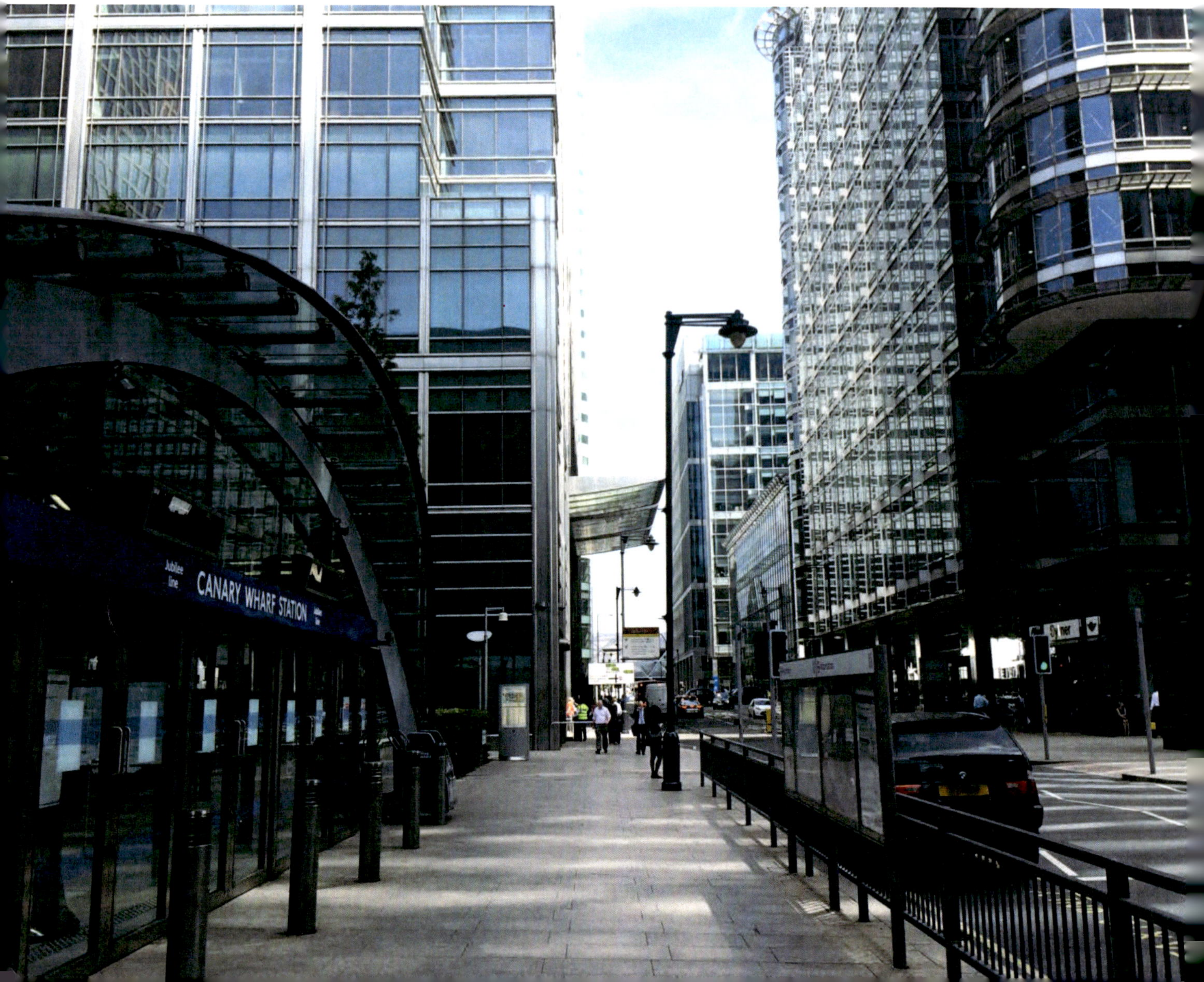
Jubilee line
CANARY WHARF STATION

Professional Conduct & Regulation

Professional Conduct & Regulation

Solicitors Regulation Authority Code of Conduct   257

SRA Principles • SRA Code of Conduct for Solicitors, RELSs and RFLs • SRA Code of Conduct for Firms • maintaining trust and acting fairly • dispute resolution and proceedings before courts, tribunals and inquiries • client care, client service and competence • referrals and introductions • confidentiality and disclosure • conflicts of interest • cooperation and accountability • advertising and publicity • managing your business

Money Laundering   269

Assessing risk • offences under the Proceeds of Crime Act 2002 • client due diligence

Financial Services and Markets Act 2000   274

The general prohibition • exclusions • exemption • the Scope Rules and Conduct of Business Rules • penalties • summary

Solicitors Regulation Authority Standards & Regulations

Professional services firms and their employees can face a wide range of severe sanctions if they fail to comply with regulation designed to govern their conduct. Professional conduct is therefore an incredibly important module on the LPC.

The previous "Solicitors' Regulation Authority Code of Conduct" – released in 2011 - was a single consolidated code for both solicitors and firms that was based on various "outcomes" and "indicative behaviours". The Solicitors Regulation Authority ("**SRA**") replaced this in 2019 with a new set of Standards and Regulations, which is comprised of a series of principles and two shorter codes of conduct: one for solicitors (and non-UK qualified lawyers) and another for firms. These principles and codes are together referred to throughout this chapter as the "**SRA Standards**" (© *The Law Society*). The new codes focus instead on "standards" and have stripped out many of the requirements that duplicate general legislation.

The SRA Standards codify the standards of professionalism that the SRA and the public expect from solicitors, non-UK qualified lawyers and SRA authorised firms, and apply alongside other legislative and regulatory obligations (such as requirements relating to referral fees Legal Aid, Sentencing and Punishment of Offenders Act 2012 s.56, anti-money laundering regulation and the law relating to counter terrorist financing).

Your LPC provider may focus on specific SRA Standards or particular elements of the codes, so be sure to check the requirements of your particular course. This handbook provides only an overview of the Professional Conduct & Regulation course, as much of the course content is fairly self-explanatory and is set out in your course materials. It is therefore essential that you study this guide alongside your course materials. Also note that various terms used throughout the SRA Standards have been defined in the SRA Handbook Glossary (the "**SRA Glossary**") (these terms tend to appear in italics in the Codes) and you might be expected to reference these definitions when answering exam questions.

SRA Principles

This section introduces the SRA Principles (the "**Principles**"), which are a set of seven mandatory principles that underpin the SRA Standards and Regulations and represent the foundation of this regulatory regime. The SRA states that these Principles "comprise the fundamental tenets of ethical behaviour that we expect all those we regulate to uphold" including "all individuals we authorise to provide legal services…as well as authorised firms and their managers and employees". Try to reference these Principles where possible when answering exam questions. According to the Principles, those regulated by the SRA should:

Principle 1: Act in a manner that upholds the constitutional principle of the rule of law, and the proper administration of justice

Obligations exist to the court, to clients and to third parties with whom regulated solicitors and firms have dealings on clients' behalves.

Principle 2: Act in a way that upholds public trust and confidence in the solicitors' profession and in legal services provided by authorised persons

Those regulated should avoid any behaviour within *or outside* their professional practice that could undermine the public's trust in them and the legal profession. For instance, acting for a client despite there being a conflict of interest could undermine public confidence in the legal profession.

Principle 3: Act with independence

Independence in this context refers to both the independence of a law firm and the independence of individual solicitors. Those regulated should avoid situations that could put their independence at risk.

Principle 4: Act with honesty

Honesty should underpin regulated individuals' and firms' professional dealings with clients (for whom solicitors are supposed to be *trusted* advisors), the public in general, other solicitors and the court.

Principle 5: Act with integrity

Integrity should underpin regulated individuals' and firms' professional dealings with clients, the public in general, other solicitors and the court. The SRA has stated that the concept of integrity is broader than simply acting honestly, and could include reckless disregard of, or indifference in relation to, the SRA Standards.

Principle 6: Act in a way that encourages equality, diversity and inclusion

This applies not just to regulated individuals and firms, but to all employees of regulated firms (i.e. not just senior employees).

Principle 7: Act in the best interests of each of their clients

Regulated individuals and firms should do their best for clients, observe confidentiality, avoid conflicts of interest and act in good faith.

Breach of the principles

The Principles (and the Code for Solicitors and Code for Firms, together the "**Codes**") are supported by the SRA's enforcement strategy, which sets out guidance around reporting solicitor conduct to the SRA. When considering taking action for breaches of the SRA Standards, the SRA will take into account the impact and harm that arises as a result of the conduct of those regulated.

Conflicting principles

Situations may arise where complying with one principle could contravene another. For instance, if you become aware that your client is involved in an illegal activity, your duty to uphold the rule of law and comply with legal requirements (by reporting your client) conflicts with your duty to act in that client's best interests (e.g. by helping them to hide their illegal activities). Where such a conflict arises, the principle that best safeguards the wider public interest (including the rule of law and public confidence in the profession) takes precedence. If you are faced with such a conflict scenario in an exam, consider structuring your answer as follows:

1. **State the issue:** explain that a conflict has arisen between the principles.
2. **Explain why the issue has arisen:** explain which specific principles conflict and why.
3. **Explain how the conflict should be resolved:** identify which principle best serves the wider public interest and explain why.

The Codes

This section briefly summarises the two new SRA Codes. We will then discuss the main concepts underpinning the Codes, with references to the relevant sections of each code.

SRA Code of Conduct for Solicitors, RELs and RFLs

The Solicitors Regulation Authority Code of Conduct for Solicitors, registered European lawyers and registered foreign lawyers (the "**Code for Solicitors**") applies to the conduct and behaviour of individuals authorised by the SRA and sets out a framework for acting ethically and competently. This framework applies regardless of the role each authorised individual is performing or the context within which they are working. The SRA states that these individuals must exercise their own judgement in applying these standards to the situations they are in, taking into account their role and responsibilities, areas of practice and the nature of their clients (which in an in-house context will generally include their employer). The Code for Solicitors is divided into eight paragraphs:

1. Maintaining trust and acting fairly
2. Dispute resolution and proceedings before courts, tribunals and inquiries
3. Service and competence
4. Client money and assets
5. Referrals, introductions and separate businesses
6. Conflict, confidentiality and disclosure
7. Cooperation and accountability
8. When you are providing services to the public or a section of the public

SRA Code of Conduct for Firms

The Solicitors Regulation Authority Code of Conduct for Firms (the "**Code for Firms**") applies to the conduct and behaviour of firms that are authorised by SRA and sets out the standards and business controls that both the SRA and the public expect of authorised firms, with a view to maintaining the right environment for the provision of competently and ethically delivered legal services to clients. If a firm fails to meet the SRA Standards or commits a serious breach of the regulatory requirements to which it is subject, this could lead to the SRA initiating regulatory action against either the firm itself, or specific individuals who are responsible for the firm's compliance (e.g. compliance officers, managers, employees responsible for breaches etc.). The Code for Firms is divided into nine paragraphs:

1. Maintaining trust and acting fairly
2. Compliance and business systems
3. Cooperation and accountability
4. Service and competence
5. Client money and assets
6. Conflicts of interest, confidentiality and disclosure
7. Applicable standards in the Code for Solicitors
8. Managers in SRA authorised firms
9. Compliance Officers

Maintaining Trust & Acting Fairly

Dealing fairly with third parties

CS 1 & CF 1.2 state that solicitors (in both their professional and personal capacity) must not abuse their positions by taking unfair advantage of third parties, including clients *and* non-clients. This includes taking advantage of another person's lack of legal knowledge if they have not instructed a solicitor.

Equality and diversity

It is not mandatory to have a *written* equality and diversity policy in place; doing so is simply seen as good practice and can help to evidence that the relevant SRA Standards have been compiled with. In particular, CS & CF 1.1 states that you (including firms, qualified lawyers, trainees and other individuals working for authorised firms) must not unfairly discriminate by allowing your personal views to affect your professional relationships and the way in which you provide your services, whilst CS 3.4 adds that you must "consider and take account of your client's attributes, needs and circumstances".

Pretty much all the SRA Principles come into play here, and individuals are also bound by the Equality Act 2010 not to discriminate against others based on a series of "protected" characteristics, including: age, disability, gender re-assignment, marriage, civil partnership, pregnancy and maternity, race, religion or belief, sex and sexual orientation.

SRA guidance on equality, diversity and inclusion ("SRA EDI Guidance") obligates authorised firms to make reasonable adjustments to ensure that disabled employees and clients are not put at a *substantial* disadvantage, and may not pass on the costs incurred in doing so. Authorised firms also have a responsibility to encourage diversity across the workforce (this is an objective in the Legal Services Act 2007) and must collect, report and publish data about this. In addition, those authorised by the SRA have a duty to take positive steps to ensure that disabled employees and clients have fair and equitable access to opportunities.

Note that there is no set definition of what is meant by "discrimination"; it is left for those authorised by the SRA to form a judgement in any given scenario. However, examples given by the SRA of what constitutes discrimination include: treating one person less favourably than another in the same (or similar) circumstances without legitimate reason; treating someone less favourably because of their sexual orientation; subjecting a person to harassment; victimising somebody (e.g. a whistle-blower); charging a disabled client a higher amount because their disability has resulted in it taking longer to take/carry out instructions; and putting into effect an internal process or procedure that places somebody at a disadvantage compared to others because of one of the factors listed in the Equality Act 2010.

Undertakings

> **Undertakings:** an undertaking is a "statement, given orally or in writing, whether or not it includes the word 'undertake' or 'undertaking', to someone who reasonably places reliance on it, that you or a third party will do something or cause something to be done, or refrain from doing something" SRA Glossary. Undertakings may be given by authorised individuals, individuals who work for authorised firms, other parties who work for such individuals, and anyone held out by the firm as representing the firm (including trainees and secretaries).

Certain undertakings are implied or may be given by unqualified staff during the usual course of everyday transactions (e.g. on exchange of contracts during a conveyancing process), whereas others – such as an undertaking to pay another party's costs – might be governed by much stricter internal procedures (e.g. some firms state that only partners can sign-off on certain types of undertakings).

The right to enforce an undertaking can be invoked directly against the firm (rather than the firm's client), and failure to honour an undertaking can constitute a serious disciplinary offence. Note that undertakings are specifically enforceable, so it is advisable for firms to keep a record of which undertakings have been given (including who has promised what to whom) and when they have been discharged.

Drafting undertakings

Undertakings should be clear about what needs to be done, capable of quantification and agreed by both sides; any ambiguity undermining an undertaking will be construed in favour of the person relying on the undertaking. The subject matter of an undertaking should be within the control of the person/firm giving it, and undertakings should not be of unlimited duration (all undertakings must be performed within an agreed timescale or, if such timescale has not been specified, within a reasonable period of time CS & CF 1.3).

Dispute Resolution & Proceedings Before Courts, Tribunals and Inquiries

This section relates to your duties to the client and to the court if you are exercising a right to conduct litigation or advocate. Solicitors deal with the court, both indirectly and directly. For example, solicitors often prepare documents (e.g. witness statements and other evidence) to be used in court and work alongside clients and barristers involved in court cases. In addition, upon qualification, solicitors automatically have the right of audience in (i.e. the right to advocate in front of) tribunals, Magistrates' Courts, County Courts and the European Courts, so they could find themselves dealing directly with "courts" for the purposes of the SRA Standards.

To appear as a "solicitor-advocate" in higher courts, solicitors must follow one of the qualification routes set out in the SRA Higher Rights of Audience Regulations 2011. Qualification is assessed in terms of ability rather than experience, although solicitors must have completed the required Continuing Professional Development (CPD) training in relation to the provision of advocacy services in the higher courts.

Misleading the court

Under Solicitors Act 1974 s.50(1), a solicitor is an "officer of the court", so should always conduct themselves in a manner that befits a member of the legal profession and recognise that their overriding duty is to the court. CS 2 (which also applies to firms by virtue of CF 7.1(a)) requires solicitors not to waste the court's time, to avoid placing themselves in contempt of court CS 2.5 & CF 7.1(a) and to only make assertions, representations or submissions that are properly arguable CS 2.4 & CF 7.1(a).

There is also a general obligation under CS & CF 1.4 not to mislead or attempt to mislead the court. Inadvertently misleading the court likely wouldn't constitute misconduct. However – based on the "indicative behaviours" set out in the previous SRA Code of Conduct – if a solicitor becomes aware that they have misled the court, or that their client has done so or committed perjury, they must stop acting for that client unless the client consents to the disclosure of the truth to the court.

Examples of what might constitute "misleading the court" include: submitting documents in support of a client's case that are not properly arguable; alleging that a crime, misconduct or fraud has occurred, unless you have reasonable grounds for such allegation and it is material to your client's case; and calling a witness whose evidence you know is untrue.

Evidence

There are various other SRA Standards that are designed to govern how those authorised by the SRA conduct themselves when dealing with evidence. For example:

- You must not misuse or tamper with evidence, or attempt to do so CS 2.1 & CF 7.1(a).

- You should not try to influence the substance of any evidence. This includes generating false evidence and attempting to persuade witnesses to amend their evidence CS 2.2 & CF 7.1(a).

- You should not provide (or offer to provide) any benefit to witnesses where such benefit is contingent on either the nature of their evidence or the outcome of the case CS 2.3 & CF 7.1(a).

- You should draw the court's attention to procedural irregularities of which you are aware, and which are likely to have a material effect on the outcome of the proceedings CS 2.7.

Client Care, Client Service & Competence

Accepting instructions

Before accepting instructions from a client, there are various obligations to consider:

- **Properly identify your client:** before accepting instructions, you must first identify who you are acting for Code for Solicitors 8.1 ("CS 8.1") and Code for Firms 7.1 ("CF 7.1").

- **Only act for clients on their instructions or the instructions of somebody properly authorised to provide instructions on their behalf.** If you are unsure whether the instructions represent your client's wishes, you should avoid acting until you are satisfied that they do CS 3.2 & CF 4.1. This requirement aligns with the overriding obligation to protect your client's best interests.

- **Do not take on a client if the fulfilment of their instructions would breach the SRA Standards.** You are generally free to decide whether to take on a particular client, provided that your decision is not founded upon unlawful discrimination (Paragraph 1.1 of the Codes). However, you cannot take on a client if the fulfilment of their instructions would breach the SRA Standards. Examples would include acting for the client despite there being a conflict of interest (CS & CF 6.1, 6.2 & 6.5) or helping the client to launder money (in breach of the Money Laundering Regulations 2017, dealt with later in this module).

Client care letters

Issuing clear, detailed client care letters can help you to meet your obligation to treat your clients fairly (in accordance with CS & CF Paragraph 1) and reduce the likelihood of complaints arising, although the SRA Standards do not *obligate* solicitors to send formal customer care letters as long as certain information is communicated in writing (e.g. information about their right to make a complaint CS 8 & CCF 7.1(c)).

> **Client care letter:** this is a letter typically sent from a solicitor to his/her client following the initial meeting between them. It usually confirms the client's instructions and options, explains the key issues, sets out the next steps and envisaged timeframes, and summarises the services that you will provide. Client care letters also usually explain who will be dealing with the matter (and if relevant, who will be supervising), the responsibilities of both you and your client, an estimate of how much the work is going to cost (including hourly rates, if applicable) and details of the firm's complaints procedure.

There is an ongoing obligation to keep clients informed about all relevant aspects of their matter, including any changes to the information provided in the client care letter (e.g. if the original costs estimate or scoping of the matter no longer reflects the current position). It is also seen as good practice to send out a new client care letter to an *existing* client when that client instructs the firm on a new matter, although these can typically omit some of the information that the client will already have received.

Professional Conduct & Regulation

Service and competence

The SRA Standards also govern the level of service that should be maintained by those authorised by the SRA. For example:

- **Delivering legal services:** you should ensure the service you provide is competent and delivered in a timely manner CS 3.2 & CF 4.2, and that you take into account clients' needs, attributes and circumstances CS 3.4 & CF 4.2.

- **Maintaining your own competence:** you should maintain your competence to carry out your role, including your professional knowledge and skills CS 3.3.

- **Maintaining others' competence:** firms are responsible for ensuring that their managers and employees are (and remain) competent to carry out their roles, that their professional knowledge and skills are maintained, and that they understand their legal, ethical and regulatory obligations CF 4.3. Managers are similarly responsible for those under their management CS 3.6.

- **Supervision:** firms should ensure that matters are supervised effectively CF 4.4. In addition to this, when managing or supervising others' provision of legal services, individuals must supervise them effectively and remain accountable for their work CS 3.5.

Client information and publicity

The Code for Solicitors sets out rules that govern the provision of information to clients (which also apply to firms by virtue of CF 7.1(c)).

- **Presentation of information:** you must present information in a way that clients can understand and ensure clients are in a position that enables them to make informed decisions about their options, the services they need and how their matter will be handled CS 8.6. You must also ensure clients understand whether (and if so, how) the services you intend to provide are regulated CS 8.10 and the regulatory protections available to them (if any) CS 8.11.

- **Transparency around costs:** you must be clear and transparent about the likely costs that each client will incur, both at the time of the engagement and, where appropriate, over the course of the matter CS 8.7 & CF 7.1(c).

- **Publicity:** any publicity relating to your practice must be accurate and not misleading, including information around your fees and interest payments CS 8.8.

Client money and assets

Authorised firms and individuals are also subject to various obligations relating to client money. In particular, they must safeguard money and other assets entrusted by clients and third parties CS 4.2 & CF 5.2, properly account for any financial benefits received by virtue of their instructions (unless the client has agreed otherwise) CS 4.1 & CF 5.1, and avoid personally holding client money unless authorised to do so by relevant regulations CS 4.3.

Claims and complaints

The Code for Solicitors sets out various obligations relating to the handling and regulation of complaints (which also apply to firms by virtue of CF 7.1(c)). To summarise:

- **Complaints handling procedure:** where appropriate, you should establish, maintain and participate in a procedure for handling complaints relating to the legal services you provide CS 8.2 and inform clients at the outset about their right to complain about your services and charges; how to raise a complaint and to whom; and when they may be able to escalate a complaint to the Legal Ombudsman CS 8.3 & CCF 7.1(c).

- **Complaints handling:** all complaints must be dealt with properly, fairly and free of charge CS 8.5.

- **Next steps:** if a client raises a complaint and you have not managed to adequately resolve it within 8 weeks, you should inform the client in writing about any right they have to complain to the Legal Ombudsman, how to raise such complaint, and any applicable timeframes for doing so CS 8.4. If your complaints procedure has been exhausted by this stage, you should also confirm in writing to the client that you cannot settle the claim, provide the details of an approved alternative dispute resolution body that would be competent to deal with the complaint, and confirm whether you agree with the scheme operated by that body CS 8.4.

Legal Ombudsman

- Once the firm's internal complaints procedure has been exhausted, clients may be able to take their complaint to the Legal Ombudsman. Only individuals, charities, micro-enterprises (very small businesses), clubs and trusts can complain to the Ombudsman (not large corporations). The Legal Ombudsman is competent to hear complaints relating to poor service and bills/fees, but *not* complaints relating to professional misconduct (which should instead be referred to the SRA – see below).

- The Legal Ombudsman can require parties to correct errors or omissions, give apologies, pay the costs of complaints, limit their fees, and provide compensation for loss (plus interest), inconvenience and/or distress (capped at £50,000, excluding interests and costs). Decisions of the Legal Ombudsman may be appealed by way of judicial review.

SRA

- Clients can complain to the SRA where allegations of misconduct and/or dishonesty arise. The SRA has the power to order a firm to refund its client's legal costs, to restrict or interfere with a firm's practice, to reprimand solicitors and to refer cases to the Solicitors' Disciplinary Tribunal. Note that going through the courts is a last resort and most complaints do not reach this stage.

Solicitors' Disciplinary Tribunal

- Clients cannot complain directly to the Solicitors' Disciplinary Tribunal; cases must be referred. Once referred, the tribunal has the power to strike off or suspend solicitors from practice, reprimand solicitors, fine solicitors (payable to HM Treasury) and award costs against a party to the proceedings. However, it cannot award compensation.

Solicitors' Compensation Fund (SCF)

- If an authorised solicitor has embezzled a client's funds, that client should be able to raise a claim for reimbursement directly with the Solicitors' Compensation Fund.

Terminating a retainer

The SRA Standards do not explicitly deal with termination of retainers. However, retainers cannot be terminated purely on the grounds of self-interest, as this would breach the requirement to treat clients fairly Paragraph 1 of the Codes, act in clients' best interests Principle 7 and act with honesty and integrity Principles 4 & 5. The following are examples of potentially acceptable reasons for terminating a retainer:

- If you are unable to obtain clear instructions (e.g. if you are given conflicting instructions from multiple people acting on behalf of a corporate client).

- If continuing to represent the client would result in you breaking the law or breaching the SRA Standards (e.g. if a conflict of interest arises).

- If your client has failed to pay its bill(s) in breach of your contractual arrangements with them.

Referrals & Introductions

Some firms have agreements in place with third parties, whereby the firm will introduce clients/work to the third parties or the third parties will refer clients/work to the firm, in exchange for a share of the fees or commission. The SRA's primary intention in such circumstances is to preserve the independence and integrity of firms and solicitors (in line with Principles 3 & 5), so referral fees may only be retained if firms and solicitors comply with the relevant SRA Standards (which include an obligation to obtain client consent).

The Codes

CS 5.1 & CF 7.1(b) deal with two types of scenarios:

- Circumstances in which law firms or solicitors wish to refer clients to third parties, such as other law or financial services firms; and
- Circumstances in which law firms or solicitors have arrangements with third parties under which those *third parties* introduce business to the firm or solicitor in return for a fee.

Such fee may be fixed, or calculated based on a percentage of the amount subsequently charged to the client. Note that the SRA Glossary defines "introducer" as "any person, business or organisation who or that introduces or refers clients to your business, or recommends your business to clients or otherwise puts you and clients in touch with each other."

In accordance with CS 5.1 & CF 7.1(b), when referring clients *to* a third party, or when accepting a referral *from* a third party who introduces business to you or with whom you share your fees, you must ensure that:

(a) Clients are informed of any financial or other interest which you or your business or employer has in referring the client to another or which an introducer has in referring the client to you CS 5.1(a) & CF 7.1(b);

(b) Clients are informed of any fee sharing arrangement that is relevant to their matter CS 5.1(b) & CF 7.1(b);

(c) The fee sharing agreement is in writing CS 5.1(c) & CF 7.1(b), although the SRA Standards cover even informal or implied agreements.

(d) You do not receive payments relating to a referral or make payments to an introducer in respect of clients who are the subject of criminal proceedings CS 5.1(d) & CF 7.1(b) or whose costs are publicly funded (in whole or in part); and

(e) any client referred by an introducer has not been acquired in a way which would breach the SRA's regulatory arrangements if the person acquiring the client were regulated by the SRA."

Analysis

In light of SRA Principle 7 (you should act in your client's best interests), those authorised by the SRA should only make introductions where they believe the referral is purely for the client's benefit, for example if the third party is genuinely best placed to advise or support the client. Any financial or other benefit should be wholly ancillary and not affect the decision to make the introduction, otherwise this might also give rise to an "own interest" conflict in accordance with CS & CF 6.1.

CS 5.1 & CF 7.1(b) also obligate those authorised by the SRA to properly inform clients about any financial or other interest they have in making an introduction, including any introducer fees they might receive as a result. Similarly, if carrying out "regulated activities" under Financial Services and Markets Act 2000 s. 327(3), you must account to your client for any pecuniary reward or advance received in relation to any financial products. When such a commission is paid, if the firm is not authorised by the Financial Conduct Authority, it must keep a record of such commission, including how the firm has accounted to the client in respect of that commission Financial Services (Conduct of Business) Rules 2019 Rule 5.1.

Note that solicitors are prohibited from giving or receiving a referral fee based on clients' damages claims in cases involving personal injury or death Legal Aid, Sentencing and Punishment of Offenders Act 2012 s. 56(1). This includes referrals through intermediaries, although genuine payments for services rendered are not prohibited (note however that the onus is on firms/solicitors to prove that payments received constituted genuine consideration for services, as opposed to referral fees Legal Aid, Sentencing and Punishment of Offenders Act 2012 s.57(7)).

Examples of fee sharing and referral arrangements include: a lawyer accepting a fee in return for sharing client work internally; an employee of an authorised firm accepting a payment from the firm in return for referring a new client; a law firm referring a client to another firm in return for a fee; agreeing to pay a lender a percentage of fees generated in return for the loan; paying third parties in return for them referring clients; and even donating a percentage of fees to charities.

Bribery Act 2010

One further consideration in the context of referral fees is the Bribery Act 2010, which makes it an offence for a UK citizen or resident to receive or pay a bribe (directly or indirectly). A law firm can also commit an offence under the Bribery Act 2010 if a bribe is paid on its behalf. There are various actions law firms should take/avoid in order to avoid risking liability. For starters, law firms should ensure that relevant stakeholders have anti-bribery policies in place (or are subject to anti-bribery policies). Firms should also prohibit the giving or receiving of gifts or hospitality where such giving or receiving is designed to influence a business decision (there is a fine line between legitimate business development and bribery).

The types of referral fees covered by CS 5 & CF 7.1(b) are not, on the face of it, illegal under the Bribery Act 2010. However, firms must consider the extent to which such referral fees are influencing the judgment of those involved.

Confidentiality & Disclosure

Confidentiality and disclosure is another topic that comes up frequently in exams. Key SRA Principles relating to this topic are: Principle 2: solicitors should act in a way that preserves public trust and confidence in them and the legal profession; Principle 3: solicitors should remain independent (which may be difficult where the duty of confidentiality to one client conflicts with the duty to disclose all material information to another client); Principle 5 solicitors should act with integrity; and Principle 7: solicitors should act in the best interests of each of their clients.

Confidentiality

CS & CF 6.3 stress that solicitors and firms (plus everyone working in those firms) must keep the affairs of their clients confidential – regardless of the sources of any information acquired - unless disclosure is required/permitted by law or the client consents. The duty of confidentiality continues to apply after the client has terminated their retainer and even extends to a deceased (ex-)client's personal representatives. This means that solicitors cannot disclose the content of a client's will after that client's death without the consent of that client's personal representatives. No duty is owed to non-clients however, and information that is already in the public domain (and therefore no longer confidential) may be disclosed.

Exceptions

Examples of where the law *may* permit or require a solicitor to disclose confidential client information include:

- Where a government body or regulator is legally empowered to demand such disclosure;
- Where such disclosure is permitted or required by statute or regulations (e.g. the Money Laundering Regulations 2017, the Proceeds of Crime Act 2002 or anti-terrorism legislation);
- Where the disclosure is required to support a solicitor's defence to a civil claim initiated against them by the client, or as part of a criminal trial; or
- Where the solicitor believes a child's mental or physical health is in danger following a discovery that the child has been sexually or physically abused (in such cases, disclosure may be permitted to an appropriate authority).

Duty of disclosure

CS & CF 6.4 impose a *personal* duty on every solicitor - regardless of whether they are acting individually or as part of a firm - to disclose to a client all information *material* to that client's retainer of which the solicitor is aware. The duty of disclosure applies only to a client's solicitor(s), not others within a solicitor's firm who may have knowledge of relevant information. Information that is not material need not be disclosed however (e.g. information that has no bearing on the client's retainer).

"Material" is not defined by the SRA in the Codes, but the 2007 SRA Code of Conduct defined "material" as meaning information that "might reasonably be expected to affect the client's decision-making with regard to their matter in a way which is significant having regard to the matter as a whole".

Exceptions

There are certain exceptions that might alleviate solicitors from having to comply with this duty of disclosure, including:

- Where disclosure is prohibited by legal restrictions imposed in the interests of national security or crime prevention CS & CF 6.4(a);

- Where the client gives informed written consent to such non-disclosure CS & CF 6.4(b) (more on this below);
- Where the solicitor has reason to believe that serious mental or physical injury will be caused to the client or another person if such disclosure is made CS & CF 6.4(c); or
- Where the material information is contained in a privileged document that was accidentally disclosed to the solicitor CS & CF 6.4(d).

Note that SRA Guidance indicates that the exceptions listed in (a), (c) and (d) will rarely apply in practice. SRA Guidance also indicates that it will be difficult for clients to give informed instructions to their solicitor if those clients are unaware of all matters that are relevant to their case. To give informed consent to non-disclosure, clients must have some level of understanding of the importance of the information that the solicitor cannot disclose, including the extent to which they may be prejudiced by such non-disclosure.

A solicitor must therefore at least broadly indicate the nature of the withheld information (being careful not to breach another client's right to confidentiality) and even if the solicitor does obtain consent, they will still need to ensure they are upholding Principle 7 (solicitors should act in the best interests of each of their clients).

Conflict between the duties of confidentiality and disclosure

At times, the duty of confidentiality may conflict with the duty of disclosure, for instance where you hold confidential information about Client A that is material to Client B. There may also be an overriding obligation to report to the National Crime Agency (e.g. if fraud occurred) or to report an impending criminal offence (e.g. if the client says they are going to assault another person). Alternatively, there may be an overriding obligation to disclose to supervisors anything representing a risk to the security of your firm's money/client funds.

Where these duties conflict in such a way, the duty of confidentiality overrides the duty to disclose. However, you cannot rely on a duty of confidentiality to excuse a failure to meet your duty of disclosure. If you do become privy to confidential information about Client A that constitutes information that is material to Client B, you have to either:

- Renegotiate the terms of your retainer with Client B to evidence their consent to you holding material information about their matter that you cannot disclose; or
- Refuse to act for Client B (or cease acting for them if you have already started).

However, if the conflict between these two duties cannot be overcome by the measures set out in CS & CF 6.5 (see below), you will likely have to cease acting for at least one of the clients.

Exception

Alternatively, there is an exception under CS & CF 6.5 that may enable you to act despite the conflicting duties. If your prospective client has an interest that is "adverse" to one of your (or your firm's) existing or former clients and you hold confidential information on behalf of that existing or former client that is material to the prospective client, you cannot act for that prospective client unless:

- Effective measures are taken which result in there being no real risk of disclosure of the confidential information CS & CF 6.5(a); or
- The existing or former client has given *informed* written consent to you acting for the prospective client (including consent to any measures taken to protect their confidential information) CS & CF 6.5(b). For consent to be "informed", the existing/former client must have an understanding of any possible prejudice that may arise if they consent to you also acting for the prospective client.

"Adverse interest" is not defined by the SRA, but the 2007 SRA Code of Conduct indicated that an adverse interest may arise "where one party is, or is likely to become, the opposing party on a matter, whether in negotiations or some form of dispute resolution".

Where adverse interests do exist, the types of measures that might satisfy CS & CF 6.5(a) include: adopting systems that can effectively identify potential confidentiality issues; staffing separate, distinct teams on work involving clients with adverse interests; using separate servers to prevent teams from accessing the confidential information of clients with adverse interests; encrypting/password protecting confidential information; ensuring those working for clients with adverse interests know not to cross the information barrier in place; and ensuring staff are properly trained in these exercises.

Conflicts of Interest

Conflicts of interest is an incredibly important topic and one that comes up frequently in exams. This section covers conflicts that arise between a firm or solicitor and one of their clients ("own interest conflicts") and conflicts that arise or could arise as a result of a firm or solicitor representing two or more clients ("client conflicts"). Most of the references below apply to both the Code for Solicitors and the Code for Firms, as the rules are the same in each.

In general, where an own interest conflict or a client conflict arises or could arise, then you must refuse to take on a new client (or cease acting for one or more of your existing clients) unless and until there ceases to be a conflict. Note however that there are limited exceptions in relation to client conflicts, which are explored in more detail below.

The SRA has provided further guidance around conflicts in a publication called "Ethics Guidance – Unregulated organisations – conflict and confidentiality" ("SRA Guidance") which also applies to organisations that are authorised by the SRA, as well as solicitors, RELs and RFLs who work for organisations that are not authorised by the SRA.

Failure to avoid conflicts could result in firms/solicitors failing to uphold Principle 3 (act independently), Principle 4 (act in clients' best interests) and Principle 5 (deliver a proper standard of service). Accordingly, there are various actions firms must take in order to avoid conflicts.

Steps to identify conflicts

When deciding whether to take on a new client, you must consider whether the proposed work could conflict with your own interests or the interests of any existing clients. Accordingly (and In accordance with CF 2.1), firms must have effective systems and controls in place to enable them to identify/assess potential own interest conflicts (covered in CS & CF 6.1) and client conflicts (covered in CS & CF 6.2). These systems and controls must be appropriate to the size and complexity of the firm and the nature of the work undertaken.

Checking for conflicts typically involves carrying out searches against a prospective client's name and company number (and those of any parent companies or subsidiaries) and the names of the counterparties involved (if any). Searches might also cover a broad range of other information, including the names of directors and details of other parties involved (e.g. the target company in an acquisition context).

Own interest conflicts

You are prohibited from acting for a client where there is an own interest conflict, or a significant risk of such a conflict arising CS & CF 6.1.

> **Own interest conflict:** a conflict of interest that arises where a solicitor's duty to act in the best interests of a client in relation to a particular matter conflicts (or there is a significant risk that it will conflict) with that solicitor's own interests in relation to that matter or a related matter.

Client conflict

You are also generally prohibited from acting for a client where there is a client conflict, or a significant risk of one arising CS & CF 6.2.

> **Client conflict:** a conflict of interest that arises where a solicitor owes separate duties to act in the best interests of two or more clients in relation to the same (or a related) matter, and the interests of those clients conflict (or there is a significant risk that they could conflict). For example, a solicitor would be unable to represent opposing parties in a contentious matter.

It is clear from the SRA's definition that solicitors must act in the best interests of *every* client (i.e. they can't prioritise one over the other), and a conflict would arise where the circumstances *compromise* (or *could* compromise) the solicitor's ability to do so. For example, if circumstances arose in which recommending a particular course of action to Client A could prejudice Client B, a client conflict would exist.

Exceptions

There are two exceptions that enable law firms to act for multiple clients (with appropriate safeguards in place) where a client conflict would otherwise prevent them from doing so. Note that these exceptions *do not apply* to own interest conflicts.

1. Substantially Common Interest CS & CF 6.2(a)

> **Substantially common interest:** where there is a clear common purpose between the clients and a strong consensus on how this is to be achieved SRA Glossary.

Where there is a substantially common interest (as defined above), you may continue to act for both clients if:

(a) **The clients all give informed written consent to you acting** CS & CF 6.2(i). SRA Guidance indicates that solicitors must ensure clients have sufficient knowledge and understanding of the situation to comprehend what they are consenting to;

(b) **Where appropriate, you put in place effective safeguards to protect the clients' confidential information** CS & CF 6.2(ii). SRA Guidance indicates that a solicitor should not act if there might be situations where they cannot share relevant information with all of the clients, either due to one client prohibiting such disclosure, or because it would prejudice one or more of the clients' best interests; and

(c) **You are satisfied it is reasonable for you to act for the clients** CS & CF 6.2(iii). SRA Guidance indicates that when determining what is reasonable, solicitors should consider, for example, the parties' respective knowledge and bargaining power, the extent to which substantive negotiations between the parties might be necessary, and the extent to which acting for both parties gives rise to any genuine benefits for the parties involved (e.g. lower costs, quicker time frames, greater convenience etc.).

SRA Guidance provides examples of where this exception *might* apply, including where parties instruct a solicitor to advise them on entering into a lease as joint tenants, or setting up a business as partners. It is unlikely that the above criteria would be fulfilled if: you are unable to act even handedly between the parties; the parties have different interests in the outcome (e.g. in a buyer/seller scenario, the buyer would want a low price, whereas the seller would want a high price); or there is an imbalance of bargaining power between the parties.

2. Clients Competing for the Same Objective CS & CF 6.2(b)

> **Competing for the same objective:** this is a situation where two or more clients are competing for an "objective" which, if attained by one client, will make that objective unattainable to the other client(s). "Objective" includes acquiring assets, entering into contracts or taking advantage of business opportunities by way of an auction/tender process, via a private bid process, or through some form of insolvency process (e.g. a liquidation) SRA Glossary.

Where multiple clients are "competing for the same objective", you may continue to act for those clients if:

(a) **The clients all give informed written consent to you acting** CS & CF 6.2(i);

(b) **Where appropriate, you put in place effective safeguards to protect the clients' confidential information** CS & CF 6.2(ii); and

(c) **You are satisfied it is reasonable for you to act for the clients** CS & CF 6.2(iii).

Professional Conduct & Regulation

This exception *might* apply where multiple creditors are seeking to recover debts during an insolvency process, multiple bidders are seeking to acquire a business during an M&A auction process, or multiple businesses are tendering for the same contract. It will not apply where clients are on opposing sides of litigation (e.g. claimant and defendant) or on opposite sides of a transaction (e.g. buyer and seller). Note that this exception is more restrictive than the Substantially Common Interest exception, as it only applies where clients are sophisticated users of legal services.

When answering a question to which this exception relates, remember that the clients must be *competing* against each other (not "working together towards") for *the same* (not "a similar") objective. For example, in the context of the purchase of a property, the exception wouldn't apply to the borrower acquiring the property and the lender providing the mortgage, as the borrower is looking to borrow and the lender is looking to lend (i.e. their "objectives" are different), and neither is competing against the other.

Beth, a solicitor at Adams Night, has been approached by Sean, Tony and Kai, who are seeking assistance with the dissolution of a partnership named Code Red (they are the only partners). Following a significant drop in profits over the past few years (the reasons for which is a matter of contention between the partners), the partners have agreed to liquidate the partnership and distribute the assets equally between themselves (as provided for in the Partnership Agreement). Can Beth act for all three partners in relation to this matter?

1. Explain the issue/potential issue

Acting for all three partners may give rise to a client conflict.

2. Explain why this is an issue

A "client conflict" arises where a solicitor owes separate duties to act in the best interests of two or more clients in relation to the same or related matters and those duties conflict or there is a significant risk that they might conflict.

CS 6.2 prohibits Beth from acting where there is a client conflict (or a significant risk of a client conflict arising), unless the "substantially common interest" exception (CS 6.2(a)) or the "clients competing for the same objective" exception (CS 6.2(b)) apply. In addition, where a client conflict exists, it may be difficult to uphold Principle 3 (remain independent) and Principle 7 (act in the best interests of each client).

3. Apply these principles to the facts of the case

CS 6.2 might prohibit Beth from acting for multiple parties if the parties' interests in the outcome conflict. The partners are in disagreement as to why the business experienced a loss in profitability over the past few years, which gives rise to the risk that each will later argue that they are entitled to a larger share of the partnership's assets (if they end up blaming each other for the company's failure).

4. Consider how you could resolve the (potential) issue

CS 6.2(b) is not relevant as the clients are not *competing* for the same objective. However, CS 6.2(a) – the substantially common interest exception – may be relevant here if there is a clear common purpose and a strong consensus as to how this is to be achieved. All the partners want the same outcome – the dissolution of the partnership – and there appears to be a consensus, as all the partners appear to have agreed to the equal distribution of assets. It could be argued that any risk of a client conflict is peripheral to the common purpose put forward by Sean, Tony and Kai.

However, Beth should be sure to explain the relevant issues and risks to Sean, Tony and Kai (and ensure they understand them) and secure their written consent. She must also be satisfied that it is reasonable to act for all three. This may be a reasonable conclusion for Beth to reach, as using only one law firm is likely to speed up the process, simplify things for the clients and keep costs down.

It would be unlikely that Beth would be able to continue acting for more than one of the clients if, at a later stage, the relationship between those clients breaks down and as a consequence their interests directly conflict, or the parties require a lawyer to negotiate on matters of substance on their behalves. However, at this stage, on the facts, these circumstances do not seem to apply and Beth should therefore be able to act for Sean, Tony and Kai in light of CS 6.2(a).

Cooperation & Accountability

Cooperating with the SRA, regulators and the Legal Ombudsman

CS 7 & CF 3 set out standards of cooperation and accountability that must be met by those authorised by the SRA, including requirements to cooperate with the SRA, regulators and ombudsmen in connection with the provision of legal services. In order to meet these standards, you should, among other obligations:

- Keep up to date with the law and regulation governing the way you work CS 7.1 & CF 3.1;

- Ensure you are able to justify your decisions and actions in order to demonstrate compliance with your obligations under the SRA's regulatory arrangements CS 7.2;

- Cooperate with the SRA, other regulators, ombudsmen, and those bodies responsible for overseeing and supervising the delivery of (or investigating concerns in relation to) legal services CS 7.3 & CF 3.2;

- Act promptly to take any remedial action requested by the SRA CS 7.10 & CF 3.4; and

- Be honest and open with clients if things go wrong. If something goes wrong, you should where possible put right any loss or harm and explain fully and promptly what has happened and the likely consequences. If the SRA requests you to investigate whether there may be a claim against you, you should provide the SRA with a report setting out the outcome of such investigation and (where applicable) notify those that may have such a claim CS 7.11 & CF 3.5.

Professional Conduct & Regulation

Provision of information

There are also various provisions within the SRA Standards relating to the provision of information. These include the following:

- The SRA should be provided with full and accurate explanations, information and documents, whenever requested CS 7.4 & CF 3.3;

- Information should be available to the SRA for inspection as required CS 7.4 & CF 3.3;

- Those authorised by the SRA should not attempt to prevent others from providing information to the SRA (or an equivalent body) CS 7.5 & CF 3.11;

- The SRA must be kept up to date with any criminal charges, insolvency events and material changes to the information it holds on record CS 7.6;

- Firms must keep the SRA up to date with any indicators of serious financial difficulties, insolvency events, or decisions to cease operating as a legal business, as well as any changes to information that has been recorded in the SRA register CF 3.6. Firms must also report any material changes to information previously provided to the SRA and any false, misleading, inaccurate or incomplete information CF 3.8.

- Those authorised by the SRA must promptly report to the SRA any facts or matters that they reasonably believe are capable of amounting to a serious breach of the SRA's regulatory arrangements by any person or entity regulated by the SRA (including themselves/their entity) CS 7.7 & CF 3.9. If instructed to do so, firms authorised by the SRA must investigate whether such breaches have occurred CF 3.9, whilst individuals must promptly inform the SRA of anything that they reasonably believe should be brought to the SRA's attention so that the SRA may investigate or exercise its regulatory powers accordingly CS 7.8.

- Authorised firms must provide the SRA with an information report in the prescribed form on an annual basis or within such timeframe as is specified by the SRA CF 3.7.

The Solicitors' Disciplinary Tribunal

Clients cannot complain directly to the Solicitors' Disciplinary Tribunal; cases must be referred to it. Once referred, the Solicitors' Disciplinary Tribunal has the power to strike off or suspend solicitors from practice, reprimand solicitors, fine solicitors (with the funds going to HM Treasury) or award costs against a party to the proceedings. It cannot award compensation however. Note that the SRA, as well as those that are the subject of complaints, can appeal Solicitors' Disciplinary Tribunal decisions to the High Court.

Advertising & Publicity

Publicity

The SRA Standards also govern the ways in which firms may market themselves. To broadly summarise, firms are expected to avoid inaccurate and/or misleading publicity so as to preserve the trust placed by the public in solicitors, law firms and the provision of legal services CS 8.8 & CF 7.1(c). Publicity relating to a firm's fees (and its policy on interest payments) must also be clear and accurate CS 8.7 & CF 7.1(c).

Publicity includes all marketing materials and promotional activity, including the firm's name, description, website, adverts, stationery (e.g. email signatures and letterheads), marketing materials (e.g. brochures), promotional press releases, media communications and direct approaches to prospective/existing clients and other individuals. This applies to written, electronic and in-person publicity, but not press releases prepared on clients' behalves CS 8.8 & CF 7.1(c).

Approaching prospective clients

Solicitors and their firms are generally free to publicise their services, but cannot make unsolicited approaches to members of the public (other than current and former clients) either in person or by telephone for the purpose of doing so CS 8.9 & CF 7.1(c). Making unsolicited approaches of members of the public *by email or post* is not prohibited, but approaching people in the street, at hospitals, at the scene of an accident or at a port of entry into the UK would likely constitute non-compliance.

SRA Transparency Rules

The SRA Transparency Rules ("SRA TRs") also govern the information that solicitors must make available to clients and prospective clients, including information relating to costs and certain regulatory information.

Costs information SRA TRs Rule 1

Authorised firms who offer any of the services set out in SRA TRs Rules 1.3 & 1.4 are obligated to publish certain costs information on their websites.

- In the context of individuals, these services include residential conveyancing, the administration of estates, certain immigration-related work, certain advice to employees in connection with unfair and wrongful dismissal, and representation at the Magistrates Court in relation to certain road traffic offences (and connected advice) SRA TRs Rule 1.3.

- In the context of businesses, these services include certain advice to employers in connection with unfair and wrongful dismissal, assistance with debt recovery up to the value of £100,000 and certain advice in connection with licensing applications for commercial premises SRA TRs Rule 1.4.

The specific information that must be provided includes: the total cost (or, where not practicable, the average fees or typical fee range); how costs are calculated (e.g. by reference to fixed fees or hourly rates); the experience and qualifications of those carrying out the work and their supervisors; an explanation of any likely disbursements, including the cost (or, where not practicable, the average cost or typical cost range); whether fees or disbursements will attract VAT and if so, what this will cost; details of what is included as part of any fixed price or fee estimate (and explicit notification of services that might be expected to be included but are not), as well as information on the key stages of the matter (and the likely timescales for each); and, if the firm offers conditional fee or damages-based agreements, the circumstances in which clients might incur costs SRA TRs Rule 1.5. The information provided must be clear, accessible and set out in a prominent place on the website SRA TRs Rule 1.6.

Regulatory information SRA TRs Rule 4

On their websites, authorised firms must prominently display their SRA numbers and the SRA's digital badge SRA TRs Rule 4.1. Firms' letterheads and emails must also display their SRA authorisation number and include the words "authorised and regulated by the Solicitors Regulation Authority" SRA TRs Rule 4.2.

Solicitors who do not practice through an SRA-regulated firm must - where they are not required to meet the minimum terms and conditions required by the SRA Indemnity Insurance Rules - inform all their prospective clients of this fact (before being engaged by those prospective clients) and specify which alternative insurance arrangements are in place. Where applicable, such solicitors must also explicitly inform clients that they will not be eligible to apply to the SRA Compensation Fund for a grant SRA TRs Rule 4.3.

Managing Your Business

Compliance and business systems

CF 2 sets out various requirements relating to governance, internal systems and regulatory controls with which authorised firms must comply. These include the requirement to:

- Have in place effective governance structures, arrangements, systems and controls to ensure: that the firm and its managers and employees comply with regulatory and legislative requirements; that its managers, employees and interest holders avoid causing or substantially contributing to breaches of the SRA's regulatory arrangements; and that its compliance officers are able to discharge their duties under CF 9.1 and CF 9.2 CF 2.1;

- Maintain records to demonstrate compliance with any obligations arising out of the SRA's regulatory arrangements CF 2.2;

- Remain accountable for SRA compliance where work is carried out through others (including managers, employees and contractors) CF 2.3;

- Actively monitor the firm's financial stability and the viability of its business CF 2.4; and

- Identify, monitor and manage all material risks to the business, including those that may arise from any connected practices CF 2.5.

Firms may be required to demonstrate compliance with the SRA Standards, including the compliance of individuals working for the firm.

Reserved legal activities

The SRA Glossary states that "reserved legal activities" has the meaning given in Legal Services Act 2007 s. 12. This section sets out six specific legal services activities than may only be carried on by those who are authorised or exempt. These reserved legal activities include:

- Exercising a right of audience;
- The conduct of litigation;
- Reserved instrument activities;
- Probate services;
- Notarial services; and
- The administration of oaths.

Compliance Officers for Legal Practice & Compliance Officers for Finance and Administration

Firms are expected to appoint a Compliance Officer for Legal Practice ("**COLP**") and a Compliance Officer for Finance and Administration ("**COFA**"). These roles must be designated to a manager/employee of the firm (or a related authorised body) of sufficient seniority and responsibility to perform the role, and the appointments must be approved by the SRA SRA Authorisation of Firms Rules ("**AFR**") Rule 8.1. A law firm authorised by the SRA must have *at least* one manager or employee - or must procure the services of an individual - who is a lawyer (and has practised as such for a minimum of three years) and supervises the work undertaken by the law firm AFR rule 9.4.

The same person *can* be both the firm's COLP and COFA, although COLPs (*unlike* COFAs) *must* be legally qualified *and* authorised to carry on reserved legal activities by an approved regulator AFR rule 8.2(d). Moreover, COLPs and COFAs cannot be individuals who are disqualified under the Legal Services Act 2007 s. 99 AFR Rule 8.2 (c).

Note that although the COLP is responsible for the firm's compliance (including compliance with the SRA Standards), responsibility for managing the firm - and thus responsibility for breaches of the Standards - ultimately rests with the *owners* of the firm.

Professional Conduct & Regulation

Money Laundering

Money laundering typically involves a party trying to turn the proceeds of crime into money that appears to have come from a legitimate source. Money laundering is an important topic on the LPC. Firms are responsible for checking that clients are not money laundering and can face serious sanctions if they (even inadvertently) facilitate client money laundering. The Proceeds of Crime Act 2002 and Money Laundering Regulations 2017 are the main sources of law for this topic.

Assessing risk

On the LPC, you may have to identify attributes and activities arising out of the facts of a particular question that indicate there is a high risk that money laundering has occurred/is occurring. If such attributes/activities are evident, this means you may be required to take certain action, for instance reporting the client to the firm's Money Laundering Reporting Officer.

High-risk attributes

- **Nationality/Residence:** the client is from and/or resides in a country that has been classified as high risk, for instance: North Korea, Iran, Ecuador, Yemen, Algeria and Myanmar.
- **Occupation:** does the client regularly work in high-risk jurisdictions, or have they recently attended (for instance) an offshore investment conference in a tax haven?

High-risk activities

- **Payment:** payment in cash could suggest the money comes from the proceeds of crime, especially where part of the payment (e.g. a deposit) has not gone through the firm's client account and/or has been paid by someone other than the buyer. Overpayments into the firm's bank account could indicate money laundering. If there is a significant discount or premium on the purchase price, this could also indicate the underlying motive for the transaction is to launder money. There is also a greater risk of money laundering where the transaction is high value and/or offshore funds are used (especially if the client is unwilling to provide evidence of the source of the funds).
- **Family:** transactions/arrangements between family members indicate a higher risk that money laundering is involved.
- **Solicitor(s) instructed:** if the client instructs a more junior member of staff than would typically be expected for the type of transaction, or a member of staff in an area outside their normal area of expertise, this could indicate an intention to launder money. The same applies if the client is based elsewhere, but instructs you anyway (despite there being solicitors in more convenient/logical locations).
- **Nature of the transaction:** high-risk activities also include: unusual or large "one-off" transactions (especially high-value transactions carried out by individuals); transactions that the client wants completed in an abnormally quick timeframe; and transactions for which one side has not instructed a solicitor. Transactions involving property held for less than six months, or involving back-to-back sales could also indicate that money laundering is occurring.

Offences Under the Proceeds of Crime Act 2002

If the firm facilitates money laundering, it may be liable under the Proceeds of Crime Act 2002 ("POCA 02").

Direct involvement offences

The main "direct" or "first tier" offences under POCA 02 are set out below. For these purposes, property is "criminal property" if it constitutes a person's benefit from criminal conduct and the alleged offender knows *or suspects* this is the case POCA 02 s. 340(3).

(a) Transferring or concealing criminal property POCA 02 s. 327.

(b) Involvement in an arrangement that facilitates the acquisition, retention or use of criminal property POCA 02 s. 328.

(c) Acquiring, using or possessing criminal property without paying adequate consideration or making an adequate disclosure POCA 02 s. 329.

Solicitors may be held liable for the above offences if their actions *contribute* to/*facilitate* the commission of those offences. Therefore, a solicitor who becomes involved in mortgage fraud is at risk of committing an offence under POCA 02 ss. 327-329, as they may inadvertently (for instance) transfer or facilitate the use of funds fraudulently obtained by their client (such funds being "criminal property"). Note that they could also be liable for fraud under the Fraud Act 2006.

Defence

However, the statutory provision dealing with each of those offences specifies that a solicitor will commit no offence if:

(a) That solicitor makes an authorised disclosure under POCA 02 s. 338 (or had a reasonable excuse for not doing so) POCA 02 s. 327(2), s. 328(2), s. 329(2); or

(b) That solicitor knows/reasonably believes that the relevant criminal conduct occurred in a country outside the UK and was not, at the time it occurred, unlawful under the criminal law that was then applicable in that country POCA 02 s. 327(2A), s. 328(3), s. 329(2A). For example, dealing in the UK with client money that was generated from the legitimate sale of cannabis in a licensed coffee shop in Amsterdam would not constitute an offence.

Authorised Disclosure

POCA 02 s. 338 explains what is meant by "authorised disclosure" for the purposes of defence (a) mentioned above. Solicitors who know or suspect that they are dealing with the proceeds of crime (in light of the high risk attributes/activities mentioned above) must, in the course of their employment, disclose this fact to the firm's nominated officer (e.g. its Money Laundering Reporting Officer). The disclosure must be made either:

(a) Before the alleged offender does the prohibited act POCA 02 s. 338(2); or

(b) While the act is taking place, so long as the disclosure is made by the alleged offender, on their own initiative, as soon as is practicable after they first know/suspect that the property constitutes criminal property POCA 02 s. 338(2A); or

(c) After the act has occurred, provided there was good reason for the delay in disclosure (e.g. if the alleged offender was threatened with physical harm unless they immediately deposited funds that they suspected to be the proceeds of crime) and the disclosure was made, on the solicitor's own initiative, as soon as was practicable POCA 02 s. 338(3).

Note, in this context "alleged offender" is referring to the solicitor who *would be* committing a direct involvement offence if they failed to make an authorised disclosure. In addition, POCA 02 s. 338(4) clarifies that making an authorised disclosure will not constitute a breach of any duty of confidentiality towards a client.

Penalties

Under POCA 02 s. 334(1), if found guilty of one of the aforementioned direct involvement offences, the offender is liable to:

- **Summary conviction:** imprisonment for up to 6 months and/or a fine not exceeding the statutory maximum.

- **Indictment:** imprisonment for a term not exceeding 14 years and/or a fine.

"Regulated sector" offences

POCA 02 imposes further reporting obligations upon people that undertake work in the "regulated" sector. Failure to meet these obligations can give rise to liability for a number of "second tier" offences. For instance, liability may arise simply for failing to report a suspicion that someone is attempting to launder money, regardless of whether you are actually involved in the acquisition, transfer, concealment or retention of criminal property.

> 📖 **"Regulated Sector":** POCA 02 Schedule 9 clarifies that work in the "regulated sector" includes the participation in financial or real property transactions concerning: (i) the buying and selling of real property or business entities; and (ii) the managing of client money, securities or other assets.

Questions on this topic during the LPC are likely to involve work being undertaken in the "regulated sector", so when answering such questions, you may have to consider both the direct offences dealt with above, and the rules set out below.

Your reporting obligations

Under POCA 02 s. 330, you will be deemed to have committed an offence if:

(a) You know, suspect, or have *reasonable grounds* for knowing or suspecting that someone is engaged in money laundering POCA 02 s. 330(2); and

(b) The relevant information came to you in the course of your business (and that business operates in the regulated sector) POCA 02 s. 330(3); and

(c) You fail to make the required disclosure to the firm's money laundering reporting/nominated officer POCA 02 s. 330(4) as soon as is practicable after receiving the information (reporting to a different manager, e.g. the managing partner, is not enough). Disclosures must include (if known): (a) the identity of the person suspected of money laundering; (b) the whereabouts of the laundered property; and (c) details of the information that arose suspicion POCA 02 s. 330(5).

Clear evidence is not required for this obligation to arise – merely suspicion - and "suspicion" is judged against the objective standard: would a *reasonable* person have been suspicious? Note that no offence is committed if the circumstances in POCA 02 s. 330(6)+(7) exist.

Professional Conduct & Regulation

Reporting obligations of the firm's Money Laundering Reporting/Nominated Officer

Once you have made a disclosure to the firm's Money Laundering Reporting Officer (MLRO)/Nominated Officer, the obligation shifts to that officer to take further action and failure to do so could constitute an offence on their part. Note that if the MLRO is unaware of the offence/suspicion, they cannot be liable for an offence.

The MLRO must decide whether the information reported to them must be reported to a person authorised to receive such a report by the National Crime Agency POCA 02 s. 331(4). A Suspicious Activity Report must be made if:

(a) The MLRO knows, suspects, or has *reasonable grounds* for knowing or suspecting that someone is engaged in money laundering POCA 02 s. 331(2); and

(b) They received the relevant information in consequence of a disclosure made under POCA s. 330 POCA 02 s. 331(3); and

(c) They know the identity of the suspected money launderer and/or the whereabouts of any laundered property, or reasonably believe that their information can identify (or assist in the identification of) either POCA 02 s. 331(3A).

Disclosures must include (if known): (a) the identity of the person suspected of money laundering; (b) the whereabouts of the laundered property; and (c) details of the information that arose suspicion POCA 02 s. 331(5). Once the MLRO has filed a Suspicious Activity Report, no more work should be done for the client in question for at least 7 working days POCA 02 s. 336(7), unless consent is given to the MLRO under POCA 02 s. 336(2) for the firm to continue undertaking work for the client in question before the expiry of this period.

Tipping Off

POCA 02 s. 333A prohibits a person from making a disclosure that could impede an investigation relating to money laundering, for instance, telling a client that they are being investigated for money laundering. If you have to terminate your retainer with the client, you *cannot* explain that this is in light of a money laundering investigation that they are facing/might face. Committing the "tipping off" offence can lead to imprisonment for up to three months and/or a fine (on summary conviction) and imprisonment for up to two years and/or a fine (on conviction on indictment) POCA 02 s. 333A(4).

Penalties

Under POCA 02 s. 334(2), if found guilty of one of the aforementioned regulated sector offences, the offender is liable to:

- **Summary conviction:** imprisonment for up to 6 months and/or a fine not exceeding the statutory maximum.
- **Indictment:** imprisonment for a term not exceeding 5 years and/or a fine.

Rolando, a wealthy man from Yemen, has just returned from a business convention in Algeria. Rolando has never instructed the firm before. You are a trainee and Rolando has asked that you (and you alone) act for him on the purchase of his brother's luxury apartment in Kensington, London. He wants to complete the transaction within the next week.

1. Explain the issue/potential issue

On the facts, Rolando exhibits some high-risk attributes, as he comes from Yemen and seems to have dealings involving Algeria. In addition, Rolando's intended purchase of a luxury property from one of his family members in an abnormally short timeframe encapsulates a number of high-risk activities, as does the fact that he is requesting that a trainee alone manages the transaction. The facts therefore indicate that there is a risk that money laundering is occurring.

2. Why is it an issue on the facts?

First tier offences

Under the Proceeds of Crime Act 2002 ("POCA 02"), it is an offence to transfer (s. 327), facilitate the acquisition or use of (s. 328), or possess or use (s. 329) criminal property. Property is "criminal property" if it constitutes a person's benefit from criminal conduct and the alleged offender knows *or suspects* this is the case POCA 02 s. 340(3). Based on the aforementioned high-risk attributes and activities relating to Rolando's instructions and actions, there are reasonable grounds for suspicion that the proceeds Rolando intends to use for the proposed transaction could constitute his benefit from criminal conduct. There is therefore a risk that by acting on the purchase, you could be transferring and/or facilitating the use of the proceeds of crime.

Second tier offences

POCA 02 also sets out offences that apply to work in the regulated sector. The work requested by Rolando is in the "regulated sector" as POCA Schedule 9 defines work in the regulated sector as including the buying and selling of real property. As mentioned, there are reasonable grounds for suspecting that Rolando is engaged in money laundering, and as this information came to you in the course of your business, there is a risk that you will commit an offence under POCA s. 330 if you undertake Rolando's instructions.

3. Which action should you take?

You should make an authorised disclosure to the firm's Money Laundering Reporting Officer, explaining your suspicion, identifying Rolando and providing any information relevant to your suspicions. This will give you a defence against any relevant first tier offences under POCA 02 s. 338 and second tier offences under POCA 02 s. 330(4).

Client Due Diligence (CDD)

The Money Laundering Regulations 2017 ("MLRs 17") may apply to particular work undertaken by solicitors. Where they apply, the firm must undertake "client due diligence", the level of which will depend on the circumstances.

Do the Money Laundering Regulations 2017 apply?

The MLRs 17 apply to work undertaken by "independent legal professionals" Regulation 8(2)(d) (and by the other "relevant persons" listed in Regulation 8(1), including banks and auditors). "Independent legal professionals" is defined by Regulation 3(1)(d) as including firms and sole practitioners who are, by way of business, providing legal services to others as part of financial or real property transactions concerning:

- The buying and selling of real property/business entities.
- The managing of bank accounts or client money/assets.
- The formation, operation or management of companies and trusts.

For the purposes of the LPC, the MLRs 17 are likely to apply to any transactional work mentioned in an exam question on this topic, but are unlikely to apply to, for instance, litigation (as litigation is unlikely to require the above services). Note that in practice, most firms routinely carry out standard client due diligence on new clients anyway.

Must customer due diligence (CDD) steps be undertaken?

If the MLRs 17 apply, this does not in itself mean that CDD steps must be taken. Customer due diligence measures need only be applied where the relevant person (i.e. the independent legal professional):

(a) Establishes a "business relationship" MLRs 17 Reg 27(1)(a), for example at the commencement of a professional relationship with a client that has an expected element of duration;

(b) Carries out an "occasional transaction" for the client/customer MLRs 17 Reg 27(1)(b) that amounts to a transfer of funds exceeding €1,000 (Euros). "Occasional transaction" is defined in Reg 3(1) as a transaction that is carried out other than as part of a business *relationship* (i.e. a high value one-off transaction);

(c) Suspects that the client is money laundering or financing terrorism MLRs 17 Reg 27(1)(c) (consider the high risk attributes and activities mentioned in the Proceeds of Crime Act 2002 section above); or

(d) Doubts the authenticity or adequacy of documents, data or information obtained for the purposes of client identification/verification MLRs 17 Reg 27(1)(d).

What level of customer due diligence must you undertake?

If the MLRs 17 apply and CDD steps must be taken, the circumstances will dictate the *level* of CDD that must be undertaken. CDD can be simplified, standard or enhanced and there may be an additional obligation to conduct on-going monitoring.

Standard CDD Regulation 28

Standard CDD requires you to identify the customer and verify their identity on the basis of documents, data or information (e.g. birth certificates, passports, certificates of incorporation etc.) obtained from a reliable and independent source (e.g. Companies House) Reg 28(2). You must also obtain information on the purpose and intended nature of the business relationship Reg 28(2)(c).

Where the client is an entity that has beneficial owners, sufficient measures (such as those mentioned above) must be taken to verify the identity of those beneficial owners Reg 28(4).

- Note that "beneficial owners" has a different meaning to that attributed to it in trusts law; for the purposes of the MLRs 17, the "beneficial owners" are essentially those that own and/or control the client Reg 5(1).

- For instance, if the client is a private limited company, the "beneficial owners" will include shareholders holding/controlling 25% or more of that company's voting rights Reg 5(1)(b) and its directors Reg 5(1)(c).

Firms must also undertake on-going monitoring of their client relationships as part of standard CDD. For instance, if an existing client of the firm ends up with new shareholders that own 25% or more of its voting rights, the firm will need to undertake new CDD on those new shareholders. Similarly, firms must monitor whether clients start exhibiting high-risk attributes or undertaking high-risk activities.

Simplified CDD Regulation 37

The MLRs 17 acknowledge that certain types of clients/institution will already have passed through stringent due diligence checks. Accordingly, CDD may be undertaken where the prospective client falls into one of the categories set out in Reg 37, most notably:

- Credit or financial institutions that are subject to the requirements of the money laundering directive;

- Credit or financial institutions in non-EEA states that impose requirements equivalent to those imposed by the money laundering directive, provided those institutions are supervised for compliance;

- Companies with securities listed on a regulated market (e.g. the London Stock Exchange). This is based on the fact that such companies will already have been subject to due diligence measures as part of listing process; and

- UK public authorities and certain non-UK public authorities that are trusted with public functions.

The Law Society's Anti-Money Laundering Practice Note paragraph 4.8 (which may form part of your course materials) provides further guidance on simplified due diligence and the types of clients to which it applies.

Reg 37(1)(a) states that simplified CDD can only replace standard CDD where you have carried out a risk assessment under Reg 18(1). If simplified CDD has been used, an ongoing monitoring of the relationship must be carried out for events that may trigger the need to apply standard (or enhanced) CDD.

Enhanced CDD and on-going monitoring Regulation 33

Under Reg 33(1), greater enquiries must be made where:

- There is a high risk of money laundering or terrorist financing;

- A business relationship is established with a person based in a high-risk country;

- The transaction is complex and unusually large, or there is an unusual pattern of transactions and the transaction/transactions has/have no apparent economic or legal purpose; or

- The client is a politically exposed person (e.g. a politician) or a family member or associate of such person.

Enhanced CDD involves obtaining further identification documents, ensuring such documents are verified, and establishing the sources of funds and general purpose behind the relevant transaction.

The Law Society's Anti-Money Laundering Practice Note 4.9 provides further guidance, recommending (for instance) that steps be taken to check that passports are genuine and the purpose of the retainer is legitimate. It also recommends that enhanced ongoing monitoring be carried out.

On-going monitoring Regulation 28(11) and 33(1)

Independent legal professionals must also undertake on-going monitoring of their business relationships with clients. They should check that circumstances do not change to the extent that the risk of money laundering increases. Transactions should be scrutinized to this effect, with particular attention paid to any suspicious changes in ownership/business structure/sources of funds.

When should CDD be carried out?

CDD should usually take place before a business relationship is established or a relevant transaction is carried out Reg 30(2). However, it can take place *during* the establishment of a business relationship, if this is necessary to avoid interrupting the normal conduct of business and there is little risk of money laundering or terrorist financing occurring Reg 30(3). It must however take place *as soon as practicable* after contact with the client is first established.

Financial Services and Markets Act 2000

Firms require authorisation from the Financial Conduct Authority ("FCA") before undertaking certain types of work. This serves to protect customers from advisors that are not qualified to provide advice in certain contexts. We have set out the general rules and definitions below, followed by a flow chart to help you answer exam questions.

The general prohibition

There is a general prohibition against carrying on a "regulated activity", unless you are authorised to do so or are an exempt person Financial Services and Markets Act 2000 ("FSMA 00") s. 19(1).

- **"Regulated activity":** means a specified activity that is carried on by way of business (i.e. in the course of business as a solicitor) and relates to a specified investment FSMA 00 s. 22. Examples of what constitute specified activities and investments are provided in the Financial Services and Markets Act 2000 (Regulated Activities) Order 2001 ("FSMA(RA)O 01") (see below).

- **"Specified activity":** FSMA(RA)O 01 Part II sets out examples of specified activities for the purpose of FSMA 00. For the purposes of the LPC, the most relevant examples include: **arranging deals in investments/securities** (for instance helping a client to buy or sell securities) FSMA(RA)O 01 Article 25; and **advising on investments** FSMA(RA)O 01 Art 53. Art 53 applies if you are giving advice on the merits of a particular investment (e.g. whether the shares of Company X should be purchased), as this involves an element of opinion and a recommendation as to a course of action. However, giving generic advice may be ok, for instance explaining the differences between shares and bonds or providing an overview of how equity investments are doing in general.

- **"Specified investment":** FSMA(RA)O 01 Part III sets out examples of "specified" investments for the purposes of FSMA 00. The most relevant include: **rights under insurance contracts** Art 75, **shares** Art 76, **bonds** Art 77, **rights under a pension scheme** Art 82, and **rights under regulated mortgage contracts** Art 88.

Exclusions

If the activity in question is "excluded" (see below), then it will not constitute a "regulated activity" and authorisation will therefore not be required.

Specific exclusions

Many of the "specified" activities have corresponding exclusions. These exclusions are set out in the article that follows the article detailing the relevant "specified activity". For instance:

- FSMA(RA)O 01 Art 25 lists "arranging deals in investments" as a specified activity, whilst the relevant exclusions relating to this activity are set out in Art 26.

- Where the party is **dealing with/through authorised persons**, has **not advised the client on the merits** of entering into the transaction, and **accounts to the client for any payment/commission** received, Art 22 provides an exclusion for Art 21. The same applies to *arranging* deals with/through authorised persons, for which Art 29 provides the exclusion. These exclusions do not apply to contracts of insurance however Art 22(2)(a).

General exclusions

There are also general exclusions that can enable parties that are carrying out regulated activities to continue their business without first securing FCA authorisation. Notable examples include:

- Where the party is dealing in investments as principal whilst **acting as trustee or personal representative** Art 66.

- Where the activity in question can reasonably be regarded as a **necessary/integral part** of other services provided, and the relevant party's profession/business does not otherwise consist of regulated activities Art 67.

- Where the relevant party is **dealing with the acquisition/disposal of shares in a body corporate** on behalf of another party, and either: (a) those shares consist of 50% or more of the voting shares in the body corporate; or (b) those shares, together with any already held by the person acquiring them, consist of 50% or more of the voting shares in the body corporate Art 70.

Insurance Mediation Activities

Note that the exclusions contained in Art 66 and Art 67 do *not* apply to insurance mediation activities Art 4(4A). "Insurance mediation activities" include: introducing, proposing or carrying out other work preparatory to the conclusion of contracts of insurance, or concluding such contracts.

Remember this when applying exclusions in your exam if the question involves insurance work (e.g. if the relevant "specified" investment is an insurance contract). To ascertain whether an exclusion applies to an insurance mediation activity, look for the phrase "This article is subject to Article 4(4A)" at the end of that particular exclusion. If that phrase is present and the activity in question falls under the Art 4(4A) definition of insurance mediation activities, then the firm will not be able to rely on that exclusion.

Exemption

If you are carrying on a regulated activity that is not excluded, FSMA 00 s. 327 may still exempt you from the requirement to secure FCA authority. The exemption applies where the following criteria are fulfilled:

- The person carrying out the regulated activity must be a *member of a profession* (e.g. a solicitors) FSMA 00 s. 327(2)(a);

- The person must not receive payment/commission for undertaking the work, unless the client consents or any payment/commission is passed onto the client FSMA 00 s. 327(3);

- The activity must be *incidental* to (i.e. a small part of) the overall piece of work being undertaken for the client FSMA 00 s. 327(4). For instance, if you are helping a client to purchase a property, helping that client to secure buildings insurance in respect of that property would only be a small part of the overall work being completed. You could not however benefit from this exemption if you were undertaking a regulated activity in isolation for a client; and

- The person must comply with the relevant professional body's rules FSMA 00 s. 332(3), for instance the SRA Financial Services (Scope) Rules 2001 (the "Scope Rules") and the SRA Financial Services (Conduct of Business) Rules 2001.

The Scope Rules and Conduct of Business Rules

If the circumstances set out in FSMA 00 s. 327 exist, then you must assess whether the Scope Rules still prevent the exemption from applying. The most important rules for the LPC are rules 3, 4 and 5.

Scope Rule 3

- This sets out certain sorts of activities that law firms are prohibited from carrying out regardless of the circumstances. These include market making in investments and effecting and carrying out contracts of insurance as principle.

Scope Rule 4

- This that the regulated activity in question must be **incidental** to (i.e. a small part of) the overall work being done by the firm, and that you must **account to the client for any related payment/commission** received from third parties. These requirements will invariably be met if you have fulfilled the FSMA 00 s. 327 requirements.

- Scope Rule 4 also states that the activity must **arise out of, or be complementary to**, the professional services being provided to the client. This means that the regulated activity must have arisen as a natural consequence of the non-regulated work being carried out. For instance, if you have helped to distribute the proceeds bequeathed in a will to a client, subsequently advising that client on how to invest the funds they have received would *not* arise out of/complement the work done in relation to the will. It is a separate matter altogether and would therefore not satisfy Scope Rule 4. In contrast, the above buildings insurance example would probably satisfy Scope Rule 4.

- Note that the "complementary" requirement may be harder to fulfil than the "incidental" requirement, as "complementary" requires that the regulated activity forms a *necessary/natural* part of the overall work, whereas "incidental" only requires that the regulated activity is a small part of the overall work being undertaken (regardless of whether the regulated activity is actually *necessary*).

Scope Rule 5

- This sets out specific restrictions that apply to certain types of work, regardless of whether the requirements in FSMA 00 s. 327 and the other Scope Rules have been met. Examples include work involving: personal pension schemes, regulated mortgage contracts and insurance mediation.

The SRA Financial Services (Conduct of Business) Rules 2001 set out certain information that solicitors must provide to their clients and various procedures that must be followed where regulated work is being undertaken. For instance, clients must be told that you are supervised by the SRA rather than the FCA.

Conclusion

If you can comply with both FSMA s. 327 *and* the Scope Rules, you do not need authorisation to undertake the relevant activity. You must however comply with the SRA Conduct of Business Rules (and remain in compliance with the Scope Rules) and ensure you are authorised by the SRA to carry out the activity in question. If you are undertaking a regulated activity for which there is no applicable exclusion or exemption and you are not authorised by the FCA, you should either: secure authorisation (if possible) from the Financial Conduct Authority or the Prudential Regulation Authority (PRA), and comply with the relevant FCA/PRA handbook; or refuse to undertake the work.

Penalties

Under FSMA 00 s. 23(1), if a person undertakes regulated activities without authorisation and no exemption or exclusion applies, they could be liable to:

- **Summary conviction:** imprisonment for up to 6 months and/or a fine not exceeding the statutory maximum.

- **Indictment:** imprisonment for a term not exceeding 2 years and/or a fine.

Applying FSMA 00

The General Prohibition
FSMA 00 s. 19(1)

State the general prohibition on undertaking a regulated activity if you are not authorised or exempt. Briefly set out the FSMA s. 23(1) penalties that apply if you undertake regulated work in violation of the general prohibition.

Specified Investments
FSMA(RA)O 01 Part III

Are you dealing with a specified investment, e.g. shares or bonds? If no, then no authorisation is required. If yes, move onto the below step.

Specified Activities
FSMA(RA)O 01 Part II

Is the activity relating to the specified investment a specified activity, e.g. arranging/advising on investments? If no, then no authorisation is required. If yes, move onto the below step.

Exclusions
FSMA(RA)O 01

Assess whether any of the specific or general exclusions apply. If an exclusion applies, the work can be undertaken without FCA/PRA authorisation. If no exclusion applies, move on to consider whether an exemption applies.

Exemption
FSMA 00 s. 327

Are you a member of a profession carrying out regulated work that is incidental and complementary to the overall work being done? Will you account to the client for any commission received? If yes, next assess whether the Scope Rules can be complied with. If no, you must secure FCA/PRA authorisation.

Scope Rules / Conduct of Business Rules

Assess whether you would be complying with the Scope Rules if you continued to undertake the regulated activity in question without securing FCA/PRA authorisation. If yes, no authorisation is required, but note that you must be authorised by the SRA and comply with its Conduct of Business Rules. If no, secure FCA/PRA authorisation or refuse to undertake the regulated activity.

Professional Conduct & Regulation

Mr Hidalgo has won £500,000 damages following litigation. He has asked you - his solicitor - to advise him on whether to invest the winnings in shares and if so, which companies to invest in. Is FCA/PRA authorisation required?

General prohibition

FSMA 00 s. 19 sets out a general prohibition against undertaking regulated activities, unless you are exempt or authorised to do so. Regulated activity means a specified activity that is carried on by way of business and relates to a specified investment (FSMA 00 s. 22). We must first consider whether Mr Hidalgo is asking you to undertake a regulated activity.

Specified investment? Specified activity?

FSMA(RA)O 01 Art 76 lists shares as specified investments, whilst FSMA(RA)O 01 Art 53 lists advising on investments as a specified activity. We can therefore conclude that the work Mr Hidalgo is asking you to undertake is a regulated activity. We must next consider whether there are any exclusions that apply.

Exclusions?

The specific exclusions relating to advising on investments (set out in FSMA(RA)O Art 54 and Art 54A) do not appear to apply on the facts.

None of the general exclusions appear to apply on the facts. You would not be dealing with investments through an authorised person (Art 22); you are not acting as a trustee or personal representative (Art 66); advising Mr Hidalgo on how to invest his funds cannot reasonably be regarded as a necessary/integral part of the services provided in relation to the litigation (Art 67); and you are not advising on the purchase/sale of a body corporate (Art 70). As no exclusion applies, FSMA s. 327 should next be considered.

Exemption?

As a solicitor, you are a member of a designated body and you could agree to account to Mr Hidalgo for any commission you receive as a result of undertaking the regulated activity. This means that FSMA 00 s.327(2)(a) + s. 327(3) can be satisfied. However, as mentioned, the work requested does not appear to be incidental to the overall work that you are undertaking for Mr Hidalgo, meaning that FSMA 00 s. 327(3) does not apply. It is worthy to note that this also means that you would be unable to comply with Scope Rule 4. For these reasons, no exemption is available.

As Mr Hidalgo is asking you to undertake a regulated activity and there is no applicable exclusion or exemption, you must either refuse to undertake the work or obtain FCA authorisation (which will involve you having to comply with the FCA Rule Book).

You are acting for Ms. Crimmens on her purchase of a new property. Having conducted investigations into the property, you believe she should take out restrictive covenant insurance on the property. Ms. Crimmens has asked you to research into different policies and advise her as to which policy she should take out.

General prohibition

FSMA 00 s. 19 sets out a general prohibition against undertaking regulated activities, unless you are exempt or authorised to do so. Regulated activity means a specified activity that is carried on by way of business and relates to a specified investment (FSMA 00 s. 22).

Specified investment? Specified activity?

An insurance policy is a specified investment under FSMA(RA)O 01 Art 75. Advising on the merits of contractually based investments (e.g. an insurance contract) falls within the definition of specified activities set out in FSMA(RA)O 01 Art 53. We can therefore conclude that the work Ms. Crimmens is asking you to undertake is a regulated activity.

Exclusions?

The specific exclusions relating to advising on investments do not appear to apply on the facts.

None of the general exclusions appear to apply on the facts. You would not be: dealing with investments through an authorised person (Art 22); acting as a trustee or personal representative (Art 66); or advising on the purchase/sale of a body corporate (Art 70). Advising Ms. Crimmens on which restrictive covenant insurance to take out could probably be reasonably regarded as a necessary part of the overall work being done in relation to her property purchase (for the purposes of the Art 67 exclusion). However, the Art 67 exclusion does not apply to insurance mediation activities in light of Art 67(3)/Art 4(4A). As no exclusion applies, FSMA s. 327 should next be considered.

Exemption?

As a solicitor, you are a member of a designated body; you could agree to account to Ms. Crimmens for any commission you receive as a result of undertaking the regulated activity; and advising on restrictive covenant insurance policies could probably be regarded as "incidental" to (i.e. a small part of) the overall work being carried out in relation to the property purchase. This means that the FSMA 00 s. 327 requirements are probably satisfied. We must however also consider whether you could take on the work in compliance with the Scope Rules.

The Scope Rules/Conduct of Business Rules

Scope Rule 3 does not prohibit advising on insurance contracts. Advising on insurance contracts in this context appears to be incidental to, and arise out of, the work relating to the property purchase, suggesting Scope Rule 4 does not pose any issue (so long as you account to the client for any payment/commission received as a result of undertaking the regulated activity). Scope Rule 5.6 states that firms can only undertake insurance mediation activities if they are registered in the Financial Services Register and have an appointed Insurance Mediation Officer (who is made known to the FCA).

On the facts, it appears that you can advise Ms. Crimmens on restrictive covenant insurance policies if: you account to the client for any related payment/commission received; you comply with the requirements in Scope Rule 5.6 and with the SRA Conduct of Business Rules; and you are authorised by the SRA.

Also available from City Career Series

Join our LinkedIn community

This group was set up to enable candidates pursuing a career in commercial law to access and share tips, insights and resources relating to commercial law applications, interviews and internships.

We regularly share our own knowledge and experience, as well as tips around employability and commercial awareness, key legal and commercial definitions, links to other great resources and opportunities, early previews of new books and exclusive discounts.

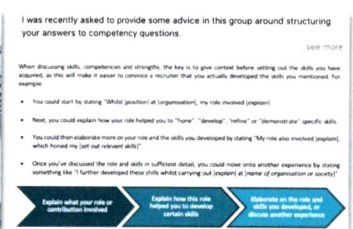

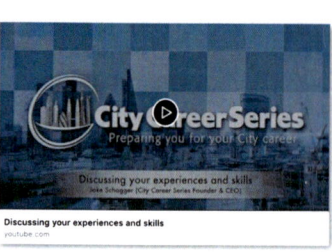

Join the exclusive City Career Series Commercial Law Applicants group on LinkedIn via:

www.linkedin.com/groups/8944518

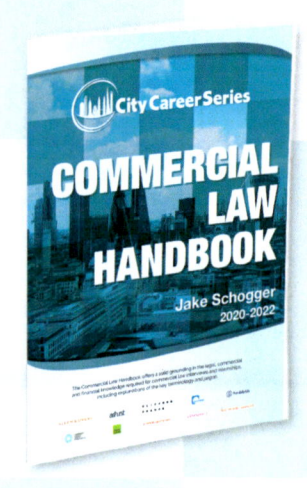

Commercial Law Handbook

The Commercial Law Handbook offers a solid grounding in the legal, commercial and financial knowledge required for commercial law interviews and internships, including explanations of the key terminology and jargon. This includes detailed advice and insights covering:

- Commercial awareness and case study interviews, assessment centres, and how to gain insights into the legal profession.
- What "commercial awareness" means, why it is relevant, how it might be assessed and how to build it.
- How to structure your responses when discussing current affairs and tackling case study questions.
- The role of commercial lawyers, trainee solicitors more specifically, and the main commercial law practice areas.
- Core commercial law principles, including explanations of how contracts are formed, how contractual terms can be used to allocate risk and how security can operate to protect lenders and facilitate corporate borrowing.
- Strategic challenges and commercial considerations relating to starting, running and growing a business.
- Different methods of financing and selling businesses, including the benefits and drawbacks of loans, bonds and IPOs.
- The M&A process, complete with an overview of the key parties that are typically involved and the various issues that can arise.
- Basic economics concepts and financial accounting principles, plus an introduction to Microsoft Excel.
- Key transactional documents and contractual clauses commonly used by commercial lawyers.
- How to convert internships into full-time jobs.

Application, Interview & Internship Handbook

The Application, Interview & Internship Handbook offers a comprehensive range of tips, insights and guidance designed to help you successfully negotiate the recruitment process for a wide range of City careers. This includes detailed advice on:

- Boosting your employability, including how to accumulate key experiences that can facilitate your personal development.
- Networking confidently and effectively, including an explanation of why networking is important.
- Identifying your priorities and distinguishing between different graduate opportunities.
- Successfully approaching CVs, cover letters and LinkedIn profiles.
- Structuring application answers and preparing effectively for assessment centres.
- Tackling the most commonly asked competency, strengths-based and ethical questions, including illustrative examples of how to draw skills and strengths from your experiences.
- Articulating your career and firm motivations and carrying out targeted research to support your answers.
- Building your commercial awareness, including your knowledge and understanding of topical current affairs and industries.
- Approaching psychometric, situational judgement and e-tray tests.
- Converting internships into graduate job offers.

CityCareerSeries.com/Store   amazon.co.uk

Professional Skills

Professional Skills

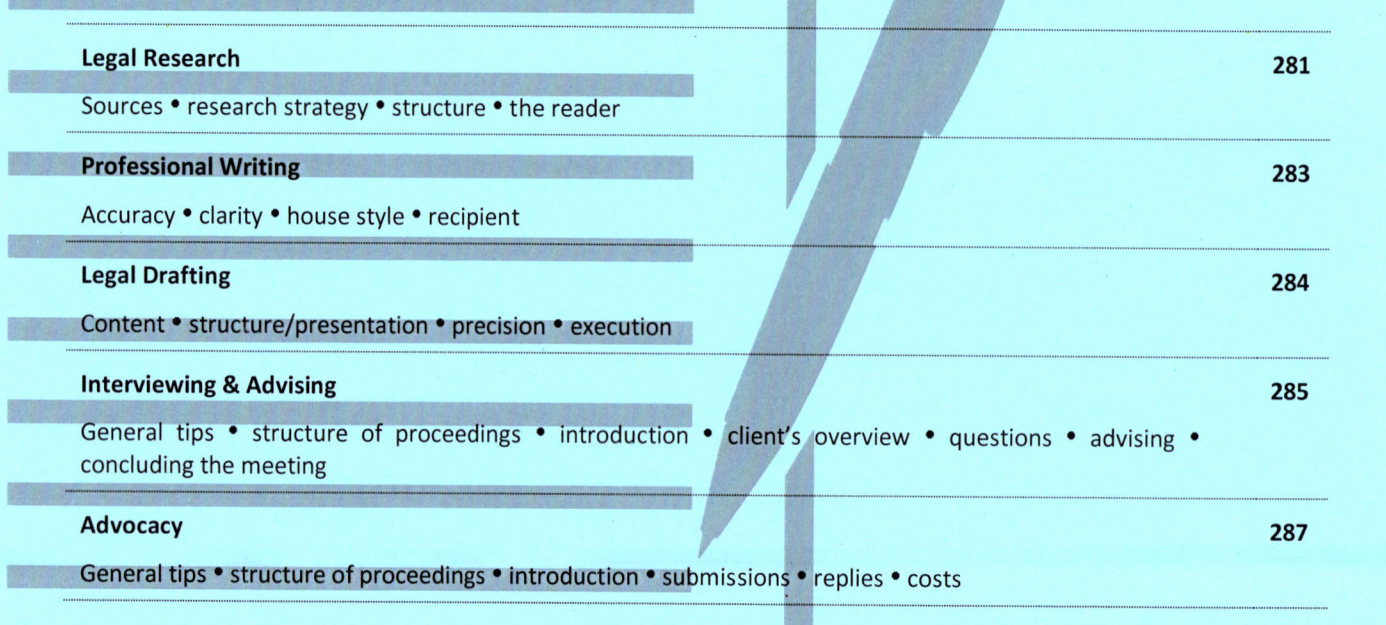

Legal Research — 281
Sources • research strategy • structure • the reader

Professional Writing — 283
Accuracy • clarity • house style • recipient

Legal Drafting — 284
Content • structure/presentation • precision • execution

Interviewing & Advising — 285
General tips • structure of proceedings • introduction • client's overview • questions • advising • concluding the meeting

Advocacy — 287
General tips • structure of proceedings • introduction • submissions • replies • costs

Legal Research

The legal research module aims to help you to research effectively using a range of reliable sources in order to reach (where possible) a set of reasonable conclusions and practical solutions/recommendations. You are typically assessed on the basis of a written assessment (as opposed to an exam).

Sources

The sources that are most typically used in practice include:

- **Primary sources:** primary legislation (Acts of Parliament), secondary legislation (Statutory Instruments and Codes of Practice), regulations and case law (transcripts, as opposed to third party summaries or commentary),

- **Secondary sources:** sources that provide commentary on or relay information from primary sources, for instance journals, articles, practitioner texts (e.g. Chitty on Contracts), encyclopaedias (e.g. Halsbury's Laws of England) and legal dictionaries.

- **Databases:** you can access both primary and secondary sources through databases such as WestLaw, Lexis Nexis and Practical Law (PLC).

The sources you use must be reliable in the sense that they are:

- **Accurate:** sources such as WestLaw, Lexis Nexis, Practical Law, The Takeover Code, and Halsbury's Laws of England offer content that is written by professionals with a strong understanding of their respective fields and/or is based on primary source materials (such as case transcripts). These sources also tend to link to useful commentary on particular subjects. The same cannot be said for sources such as Wikipedia and blogs that appear following a basic Google search.

- **Up-to-date:** cases may be overruled or successfully appealed, and statutes are repeatedly amended and repealed. It is best to access cases and statutes through WestLaw or Lexis Nexis, as these clearly indicate whether the relevant case or statute remains "good law" (i.e. valid). Conversely, Legislation.gov.uk is not always up-to-date, and hard copy books may have been published before certain changes to the law took place, so these sources should not be used unless you check the validity of the information provided.

- **Relevant:** ensure your sources are relevant. For cases, check the level of the court when assessing the extent to which that law will be applied by other courts. Also check that regulations apply in the jurisdictions that are relevant to your client.

When working on your assessment, be sure to use the sources that you have been recommended, as you may be marked down for using sources that could not be relied upon in practice.

Research Strategy

Different people approach research in different ways. Consider starting with secondary sources, which tend to give a greater overview of a topic and thus will give you a better understanding of the context of the issues you have been asked to research into. You can use these secondary sources to identify particular primary sources that can be used to help you subsequently hone in on particular issues.

Make sure you stick to the question(s) that you have been set. It can be easy to go off on a tangent, but this could adversely impact your grade on the LPC and will waste the time of others in practice. If a new question arises that could be relevant to the case, this is always something you could mention at the end and ask whether the intended recipient would like you to undertake further research into that question.

Structure

A good structure for a research task could be the following:

Introduction: use a salutation if appropriate (e.g. Dear...) and briefly summarise the instructions you were given. This can help to show the recipient that you have understood their instructions.

Summary: concisely summarise the *results* of your research. This is important as clients are unlikely to read a long research note and supervisors may only have time to take away the key points from your work.

Facts: outlining the material facts clearly and succinctly can help to give your research document context, although this will not always be appropriate (especially in practice).

Issues: identifying and summarising the key legal issues that arise out of your client's situation can help to clarify the relevance and structure of your research document, whilst also helping you to ensure that you stick to these issues when carrying out and writing up your research. For instance, which risks does your client's situation give rise to? What are the potential obstacles/costs that your client faces? If you are asked to research particular issues in practice, setting out the issues in your research document may be unnecessary.

Law and application: once you have set the scene, you must apply the law to the facts/issues. This is the section that really demonstrates your research. Identify and cite/paraphrase the relevant (reliable!) sources of law and set out how your findings may affect your client in the context of their situation. This may include explaining the potential effects of any legal ambiguities.

Advice: on the LPC, you are typically required to give some advice based on the outcomes from your research. The advice will depend on the facts/issues in question, but where possible, set out the relevant practical steps that the client should take and identify any further information that you may require from the client. In practice this may not always be necessary, especially when you are undertaking your training contract. However, your supervisor may choose to discuss the issues with you, so consider how you would advise the client if asked to do so.

Sign off: a good sign off can involve offering to carry out any further/follow-on research that the recipient may require.

Sources: on the LPC you will be expected to cite your sources, including the date you accessed these sources. Different LPC providers will expect you to do this in different ways, so be sure to refer to any examples that you are given. For instance, some LPC providers expect you to provide a "research trail", including examples of the key words you used and processes you followed to reach certain conclusions.

Headings can help to clarify the structure and are usually recommended on the LPC and in practice.

The Reader

Consider the task you have been set and structure your research accordingly. You may be required to reference cases and statutes (perhaps using footnotes to do so) if carrying out research for another solicitor. If carrying out research for a client however, it is more likely that they will want a set of concise summary points without any legal jargon or references. Adhere to "house style" where possible/appropriate. Setting out your research in a familiar way can make it easier to digest for supervisors (and may give you marks on the LPC). Look at examples of documents created in house style to check whether you have applied it correctly.

Professional Writing

We have published an entire handbook on professional writing (our Business Writing Handbook) and any real detail on this topic is outside the scope of this handbook. Details of the Business Writing Handbook are provided on the inside cover at the start of this handbook. Below are some basic points to consider however.

Accuracy

It goes without saying, but spelling, grammar and punctuation are key. You cannot fully rely on the Microsoft Word spell checker, so always proof read multiple times (preferably having had a few hours away from the relevant document). Always check that parties' names and addresses are spelt correctly.

Clarity

Avoid particularly long sentences and paragraphs, as these can confuse the reader and create ambiguities. Avoid legal jargon and unnecessary (or unnecessarily long) words. Clients and supervisors want to read documents in plain English, not long, pretentious transcripts that are three times longer than is actually necessary.

House style

"House style" refers to a system of formatting and structuring documents employed by a firm to ensure that the firm's output looks consistent and professional to recipients (both internally and externally). Most City firms will have their *own* house style (as will LPC providers) and most place great importance on their employees adhering to this.

Numbers and dates are usually expressed as figures (although some firms want you to write out numbers in words up to a certain number). Using headings, bullet points and sub-clauses can help to improve your structure, although overuse of these could break up the document too much.

Recipient

Your tone, style, presentation and level of detail should depend on your intended recipient. For instance, if writing for a client, you would usually be expected to avoid legal jargon and legal references, and produce a note that is concise and easily digestible. In contrast, you may be expected to provide references and greater detail if writing a research note on a technical area of law for another solicitor.

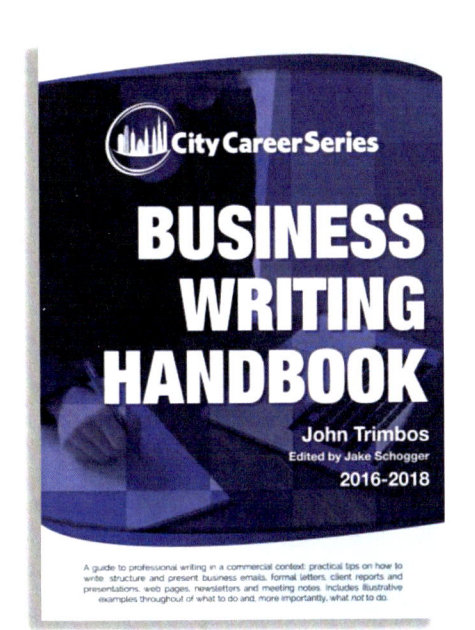

The **Business Writing Handbook** is a guide to writing professionally in a commercial context. It covers accuracy (including commonly misspelt words), brevity, clarity, style, proof reading and editing, and other fundamental writing concepts. It also provides practical tips on how to write, structure and present: business emails, formal letters, client reports and presentations, web pages, newsletters and meeting notes. It includes illustrative examples throughout of what to do and, more importantly, what not to do.

Purchasers of the LPC Handbook in 2021/2022 can access a 20% discount on the Business Writing Handbook if purchased from www.CityCareerSeries.com/Store. Use the **discount code LPCHANDBOOK2022** at the checkout.

Legal Drafting

In the context of the LPC, "legal drafting" usually refers to the drafting of contractual clauses and court documents. This is a different skill to professional writing. Whilst professional writing typically applies to correspondence and the exchange of information, legal drafting relates to incorporating/reflecting a client's instructions/intentions/commercial agreements/legal arguments into legal documents.

Some LPC providers assess drafting in a separate exam, whilst others assess drafting as part of the *Business Law*, *Property Law* and *Civil Litigation* modules. We have included drafting examples throughout the handbook (summarised below) rather than setting out drafting examples in a separate chapter, as we felt that this provided context that assists your understanding.

- **Business Law:** there is an entire chapter dedicated to drafting in the BLP module in this handbook. It includes contractual protections, boilerplate clauses, execution clauses and much more.
- **Property Law:** the Property Law module in this handbook includes advice on how to draft a contract for sale, a purchase deed (**TR1**), a registration form (**AP1**) and leasehold repair clauses.
- **Civil Litigation:** the Property Law module in this handbook includes advice on how to draft a Particulars of Claim, Defence and Witness statement.

Key Considerations

Always remember: **What? Who? When? Where? What** must be done? **Who** is responsible for taking this action? **When** must it be done by? **Where** should the relevant obligation(s) take place? When drafting clauses, consider the following:

Content

Many City firms have a database of precedents (templates or examples of certain types of contracts) that can be used as a basis for your drafting. "Boilerplate" clauses (market standard clauses) must usually be included in a contract, although you must amend/adapt these to suit your client's needs and reflect the commercial agreement reached by the parties (see the *"Boilerplate" clauses* section of the *Drafting* chapter of the *Business Law* module in this handbook).

Structure/presentation

Many City firms have a house style for contractual clauses. Adhere to house style and (where possible) reference precedent documents when drafting a contract. On the LPC, you are more likely to be required to draft, amend and/or comment on particular clauses from a contract however. Breaking up clauses into numbered lists can help to improve structure (and thus clarity). Remember to include "and" or "or" at the end of the penultimate entry in a list. The difference is important: "and" suggests *all* the elements of the list are required, where "or" suggests only one element is required.

Precision

If parties enter into a binding agreement on the basis of wording that does not actually reflect their intentions, the consequences could be incredibly costly. It is essential to be as precise as possible and leave little or no room for ambiguity as to the meaning of phrases/clauses. For instance, certain words may have different meanings in the context of contractual clauses (e.g. meanings attributed to certain phrases by the courts). If in doubt, check case law and legal commentary where necessary to assess whether a different meaning has been attributed to a particular phrase that you intend on using. Certain clauses may also be invalid in some contexts, for instance clauses that attempt to exclude liability for fraud or impose too harsh a penalty on another party.

Execution

The way in which a document must be "executed" (made binding) will depend on the type of document you are drafting. It is important to get the execution section right; the agreement may not otherwise bind the parties. You must consider who is executing the document (e.g. an individual, a company or a power of attorney etc.) and the type of document being executed (e.g. a simple contract or a deed). Execution clauses have been dealt with in much more detail in the *Execution Clauses* section of the *Drafting* chapter of the *Business Law* module in this handbook.

Professional Skills

Interviewing & Advising

You will usually undertake a couple of interviewing and advising mock assessments before your real assessment on the LPC. Use these to build up your confidence, as interviewing an actor in front of an assessor and a video camera on the day can be quite nerve-wracking. Below are some general tips to help you prepare. Be sure to check the specific course requirements of your LPC provider however, as there may be stock phrases that you are expected to use and a particular structure that you are required to follow. Make sure you dress professionally for the interview and treat the "client" with the same etiquette you would be expected to show with a real client. There may well be marks available for this. Speak slowly and try to come across as calm and confident. Adapt your tone to suit your client's mood. If your client starts crying for instance (it has happened!), be sympathetic. Avoid patronising the client however.

Interview Structure

1. **Introduction:** first you will greet the client, introduce yourself, state the cost of the interview and explain the interview structure.
2. **Client overview:** in this section, the client will explain to you why they have come to see a solicitor.
3. **Questions:** you will next have the opportunity to ask the client questions to clarify points and/or draw out any missing information.
4. **Advising:** next you will give the client some preliminary advice based on what you have been told and the relevant applicable law.
5. **Conclusion:** finally, you will conclude the meeting by explaining the firm's fee structure, detailing other elements of client care and setting out an action plan for the future.

Introduction

- Introduce yourself, shake the interviewer's hand, perhaps offer them something to drink and invite them to take a seat (adapt this accordingly depending on the position/actions of your interviewee). Briefly set out the structure of the interview. For instance, explain that you will: take their contact details, ask them to take you through the background of the problem and the issues that have arisen, ask questions and request additional information if necessary, try to provide some preliminary advice, discuss the fee structure and elements of client care, then explain which further action both you and the interviewee should take. State the price of the interview (or if it is free, explain this) and finally, request and note down their contact details.

Client's overview

- Ask the client for a *brief overview* of why they are here, then summarise this back to them to ensure your understanding is correct.
- Next, ask the client to take you through the history of the problem in more detail. At this stage, you should engage with the client to show that you are listening (perhaps by nodding, retaining eye contact, making "um hum" noises etc.).
- Note down what the client tells you. Doing this effectively takes some practice, as the "client" may speak quite quickly, so use any mock assessments to hone your ability to take notes quickly. Listen out for key facts, for instance specific dates, prices, documents and third parties that are involved, as these may form the basis of your questioning. It may help if you split your note paper into two columns: one to record what the client is saying and one to record any questions that come to mind whist the client is speaking. This means you can avoid repeatedly interrupting the client at this stage to ask questions.
- At the end, summarise back to the client their key concerns and clarify whether there is anything else that they wish to add. You could say: "just to clarify, your main concerns are [a] [b] and [c]".

Questions

Do not rush into questioning the client. You could buy yourself time whilst you formulate/clarify the questions you want to ask, for instance by saying: "thank you very much for that. I am going to ask some questions in a moment, but before I do that, I'm going to take a minute to review my notes". Try not to break for longer than a minute however.

Your ability to question the client in an interview is key, so make sure you pay attention and make notes of missing information whilst the client is providing their overview. Try to use the same terminology as the client and avoid using legal jargon. Be descriptive where appropriate, rather than assuming that your client has an understanding of technical documents etc. Ask open questions when necessary to draw out the relevant facts and do not be afraid to ask follow on questions if the client does not directly/fully answer your questions.

Which information should you ask for?

Use your legal/technical notes to help you understand which information you need to provide some preliminary advice (and thus which information is still missing). Typical information that you may need to ask about includes:

- **Contact details:** of witnesses, suppliers, relevant employees and other third parties etc.
- **Documents:** including contracts, conveyances, terms and conditions, letters, trust deeds, receipts, adverts etc.
- **Dates:** for instance, was there an agreed completion date? When was the client dismissed from employment?

- **Quantification:** for instance, how much did the client pay? How much did they lose? How much would it have cost to source a product/service from an alternative supplier? Did the figures the client gave you include VAT?

- **Other details:** for instance, is the land in the dispute registered? Did your client take any mitigating action? Was the other side aware of the potential loses?

- **Objectives:** Also ask your client about their particular objectives. For instance, are they interested in preserving a relationship with the other side? This can affect the advice you give them in respect of potential remedies.

Advising

In this section, you need to formulate a good structure for the giving of advice. You could deal with each of your client's main concerns in turn, for instance:

1. Repeat the client's first main concern back to them.
2. Explain the law in relation to that concern, in the context of the client's position.
3. Outline the client's options.
4. Repeat this process in relation to the client's other main concerns.

The "bottom line" and other options for dispute resolution

Explain the "bottom line" to the client. This is effectively the worst-case scenario, which is typically litigation (or the dissolution of a partnership if the dispute involves a partnership). Next, explain the client's other options. These could include:

- Taking no action and waiting to see what happens.
- Entering into informal negotiations, for instance writing a letter to the other party in an attempt to reach a compromise.
- Methods of alternative dispute resolution, for instance mediation or arbitration.

Advantages and disadvantages

Set out the advantages and disadvantages of each option that is available for attempting to resolve the dispute, referencing the client's bargaining position, objectives and financial constraints.

- If the client wants to progress quickly, wants to avoid spending too much money, wants to retain a relationship with the other party or wants the issues at hand to remain confidential, then litigation is unlikely to be suitable. A negotiated settlement may be a better option as the process can be cheaper, quicker, more flexible, more conducive to preserving a working relationship between the parties (as it is less contentious than court proceedings), and confidential. Explain however that the effectiveness of informal negotiations depends somewhat on the bargaining power and attitudes of the parties.

- However, if the client wants a guaranteed and final/binding solution and/or wants to ensure that the other party cannot simply walk away or ignore their claims, litigation may be a more suitable option, especially if funding is not a real issue for the client. In addition, you could explain that the mere threat of litigation could encourage the other party to settle.

- Consider whether the client is worth suing. For instance, if the client has been declared bankrupt, they will probably lack the assets to satisfy any settlement reached.

Remember however that it is the *client's* decision. Do not tell them which decision to make, just set out the various implications of the different options that you present them with. The advantages and disadvantages of different methods of dispute resolution are set out in the *Alternative Dispute Resolution* chapter of the *Civil Litigation* module in this handbook.

Concluding the meeting

Supervision, fees and disbursements

- Clearly set out your position and hourly rate, explain who will be supervising you on the matter and their hourly rate, clarify whether these rates are inclusive of VAT, state who will be doing a majority of the work, and (if relevant) tell the client that you will look into whether state funding may be available. Explain to the client that they will also have to cover disbursements (e.g. court fees).

Client care

- Explain to the client how to proceed if they have any issues or complaints with the service you or your firm provides (for instance, tell them not to hesitate to speak to you or your supervisor about it in the first instance). Also tell your client that you will provide details of the firm's in-house complaints procedure in a client care letter that you will send after the interview.

Action plan

- Reiterate the plan going forward, as discussed with your client in the advising section of the interview. Restate the information/documents that you require them to send you and explain the next steps that you are going to take. For instance, do you now plan on sending a letter to the other side? Also explain the time frame for the relevant actions: when will you be sending the client care letter? By which date should they send you missing documents?

Conclude by reminding the client that you will set out all the above in a client care letter that will be sent to them after the interview. Finally, ask whether there is anything else you can help them with and if not, stand up, shake their hand and show them out of the room.

Professional Skills

Advocacy

The LPC Advocacy module typically involves you having to argue a case in front of some sort of adjudicator (e.g. a judge or master). You will take the role of claimant, applicant, defendant or respondent, with a colleague taking the opposing role. However, the format of the advocacy assessment can vary between LPC providers/courses, so make sure that you check whether the below is relevant before using it to help you study.

General Tips

Timing

- You will be given set timings for each stage of the proceedings and can be marked down if your speeches overrun. Time your speeches beforehand and leave some leeway in case you are asked more questions than you had expected on the day.

Documents

- You may have to prepare documents in advance, including a chronology of the events that led to the dispute. Check your LPC provider to determine the format for this. Check whether the judge has copies of any documents that they are supposed to have in advance and hand them your chronology.

Etiquette

- Familiarise yourself with the relevant terminology. For instance, refer to the judge using the correct term, which will be dependent on their rank/the "court" you are attending. You may have to refer to the adjudicator as "master" or "my lord", and should refer to other advocates as "my friend" if they are a solicitor, or "my learned friend" if they are a barrister.
- You will also probably be expected to use stock phrases for some parts of your speeches, so learn these in advance (see our suggestions later in this chapter, but also check whether your LPC provider has specific requirements).
- Make sure you dress professionally, as you would if you were going to court. It gives a stronger impression and there may well be marks available for this.

Performance

- Try not to be too reliant on your notes, as you may be assessed on how well you present (including, for instance, your level of eye contact).
- Speak slowly and clearly so that the judge has time to absorb (and if relevant, note down) what you are saying. If the judge is taking notes, give them a chance to finish before proceeding to the next point. This will reflect well on your advocacy skills. It may be useful to ask the judge if you can make your next submission before proceeding to do so.
- Remember, advocacy involves a level of performance. Think about how you can emphasise key points, perhaps by pausing after key statements.

Answering questions

- Know the case well, as you will pick up marks for answering questions accurately and confidently. Try to anticipate which questions you may be asked in advance by considering how you can justify/explain the weaker elements of your case.

Structure of Proceedings

In the main proceedings (e.g. a trial), the claimant will typically speak first. For an interim application, the applicant will typically speak first. For an appeal, the appellant will typically speak first. You should be told whether you will be speaking first in your assessment. If you are unsure, it is important that you check, as the structure of your speech will depend somewhat on whether you are speaking first or second (see below).

1. The party that speaks first will have to introduce themselves and the opposing counsel to the judge, and should then offer to give an overview of the background of the case. They will then have the opportunity to make their submissions, before briefly concluding.
2. The opposing party will then have the opportunity to make their submissions (incorporating references to the other party's submissions where appropriate), before briefly concluding.
3. The party that spoke first will then have the opportunity to reply to the other party's submissions.
4. Once the judge has made their decision(s), the parties will have the opportunity to make submissions and address the judge as to costs.

On the next page is an example structure for an interim application in civil proceedings.

Introduction

The person who speaks first should commence proceedings by introducing themselves, their firm, their client, the opposing advocate and the opposing advocate's client, for instance:

"Good morning Master, I am [name given in factual scenario] from [firm name], representing the Defendant, [company name]. My friend [name given in factual scenario] represents the claimant, [company name]."

Objectives

- The speaker should then state what they are seeking from the court, for instance:

"This is the defendant's application under [relevant CPR Rule/provision] for [subject of the application]."

Case facts

- Next, the speaker should offer to summarise the facts for the court. It is likely that this offer will be accepted in an assessment, so if you are speaking first, make sure you are able to succinctly summarise the case facts in advance (and if you are speaking second, you should be familiar with the facts anyway in case you are asked questions on them later).

- The opposing advocate will not have to reintroduce the other side during their opening speech, but should reintroduce themselves and their client, and state what they are seeking from the court.

Submissions

Explain why the facts you are highlighting support your application. Spell out *why* you are justified in seeking whatever it is you are seeking from the court. Reference your chronology when necessary throughout your speech to help guide the adjudicator. If relevant, tie the overriding objective (that cases should be dealt with justly and at proportionate cost CPR Part 1) into your submission and explain how it will be furthered if the judge finds in your favour. Conclude by summarising your submissions, then close by saying something such as: *"if you have no more questions, that concludes my submissions"*.

Replies

If you are the first party to speak, take notes while the opposing side is speaking so that you can structure a good set of replies to their submissions. If you are the second party to speak, take notes whilst the first speaker is speaking and be ready to adapt your prepared submissions to reference (and discredit/oppose) some of the points they make.

Costs

If you win the case

- If the adjudicator finds in your favour in relation to the main part of the case, then first draw their attention to the general rule under CPR 44.2(2)(a), that the unsuccessful party pays the costs of the successful party. You could then build on your argument, perhaps (if relevant) saying something like the following:

"Can I also draw your attention to CPR Part 44 Rule 2(2)(a). In deciding which order for costs to make, regard may be had to all the circumstances in this matter and the conduct of the parties. I would further ask you to consider CPR Part 1 Rule 3 that the parties are required to help the court further the overriding objective."

- Go on to then explain why the other party's conduct means that costs should be granted in your favour (e.g. that their application was vexatious and therefore a waste of time). To conclude, you could say something to the effect of:

"As you have found in our favour in this case, I ask that you award costs in any event."

> 📖 **Costs in any event:** the successful party in the interim application will recover their costs, regardless of which party is successful at the end of the trial.

If you lose the case

- If the judge finds in favour of the other party, you could say something to the effect of:

"Whilst I appreciate the consequences of the order you have made, I ask that you exercise your full discretion as to costs, which you are entitled to do under CPR Part 44 Rule 2(2)(b). In particular recognise the conduct of the parties here."

- Set out why the other party's conduct would justify derogation from the general rule that the unsuccessful party pays the costs of the successful party. You could also emphasise that your client has acted within the spirit of the pre-action protocols. If you have won one (or some) of the points in the case, or if the judge has agreed with a point you made in your submissions, you could say:

"You have agreed in part with the defendant's conduct in this case to date. Although you ordered (a), you also ordered (b)."

- To conclude, you might want to ask that your client be awarded costs in any event, especially if the judge has commented favourably on your conduct and the arguments you advanced. However, it is unlikely that this request will be granted; at best, the unsuccessful party can hope for costs in the case.

> 📖 **Costs in the case:** the costs of the interim hearing will be dealt with when costs are awarded at the end of the trial.